ANTIQUES
PRICE GUIDE **2009**

Miller's Antiques Price Guide 2009
By Judith Miller

First published in Great Britain in 2008
by Miller's, a division of Mitchell Beazley,
imprints of Octopus Publishing Group Ltd,
2-4 Heron Quays, London E14 4JP
Miller's is a registered trademark of
Octopus Publishing Group Ltd

An Hachette Livre Company
www.octopusbooks.co.uk

ISBN 978 1 84533 313 3

A CIP record for this book is available from the British Library

Set in Frutiger

Colour reproduction by Fine Arts, China
Printed and bound in China by C&C Offset Printing Co., Ltd.

Publishing Manager Julie Brooke
Editors Sara Sturgess, Stephen Wells
Editorial Assistant Katy Armstrong
Digital Asset Co-ordinator John Parton
Design and DTP Tim and Ali Scrivens, TJ Graphics;
additional design by Jeremy Tilston, The Oak Studio
Photographers Graham Rae, Elizabeth Field,
John McKenzie, Dave Pincott
Indexer Hilary Bird
Production Manager Peter Hunt
Jacket Design Tim Foster, Juliette Norsworthy

ANTIQUES
PRICE GUIDE **2009**

Judith Miller

MILLER'S

CONTENTS

LIST OF CONSULTANTS

CERAMICS

John Axford
Woolley & Wallis
51-61 Castle Street
Salisbury Wiltshire SP1 3SU

Judith Miller

FURNITURE

Lee Young
Lyon & Turnbull
33 Broughton Place
Edinburgh EH1 3RR

BAROMETERS

Leighton Gillibrand
Dreweatts
St. John's Place
Apsley Road Clifton
Bristol BS8 2ST

GLASS

Jeanette Hayhurst
Jeanette Hayhurst Fine
Glass
32a Kensington Church
Street, London W8 4HA

DECORATIVE ARTS

Michael Jeffrey
Woolley & Wallis
51-61 Castle Street
Salisbury Wiltshire SP1 3SU

ORIENTAL

John Axford
Woolley & Wallis
51-61 Castle Street
Salisbury Wiltshire SP1 3SU

CLOCKS

Robert Wren
Derek Roberts Antique
Clocks
25 Shipbourne Road
Tonbridge
Kent TN10 3DN

METALWARE

Trevor Kyle
Lyon & Turnbull
33 Broughton Place
Edinburgh EH1 3RR

JEWELLERY

Emma McMillan
Lyon & Turnbull
33 Broughton Place
Edinburgh EH1 3RR

HOW TO USE THIS BOOK

Running head Indicates the sub-category of the main heading.

The introduction Gives key facts about the factory, maker or style, along with stylistic identification points, value tips and advice on fakes.

Caption The description of the item illustrated, including when relevant, the period, the maker or factory, medium, the year it was made, dimensions and condition. Many captions have **footnotes** which explain terminology or give identification or valuation information.

The price guide These price ranges give a ball park figure of what you should pay for a similar item. The great joy of antiques is that there is not a recommended retail price. The price ranges in this book are based on actual prices, either what a dealer will take or the full auction price.

Page tab This appears on every page and identifies the main category heading as identified in the Contents List on pages 4-5.

A closer look Does exactly that. This is where we show identifying aspects of a factory or maker, point out rare colours or shapes, and explain why a particular piece is so desirable.

The object The antiques are shown in fulll colour. This is a vital aid to identification and valuation. With many objects, a slight colour variation can signify a large price differential.

Source code Every item has been specially photographed at an auction house, a dealer, an antiques market or a private collection. These are credited by code at the end of the caption, and can be checked against the Key to Illustrations on pages 683-684.

INTRODUCTION

It has been a very exciting year for me returning home to Miller's in time for our 30th Anniversary edition. Miller's is still the only global name in antiques and collectables and we are publishing now in more countries and being translated into even more languages. This mirrors the world of Antiques itself. When we published the first Miller's Antiques Price Guide in 1978 (with black and white slightly fuzzy images) the antiques world was more national if not regional. The Internet has changed all that. It has provided a global market place and has seen prices for say a Lalique 'Poissons' vase sell for similar sums in Sydney, Edinburgh, Chicago and Hong Kong. Knowing what you are looking at has never been more relevant. Being able to spot the genuine article from the fake; the high quality handcrafted from the mass produced; the rare from the common has become the vital tools of the antiques and collectables hunter. Our buying patterns and tastes may have changed but our need for authoritative price guides is a constant.

We are surrounded by the prophets of doom and gloom. The end of the antiques world has been predicted many times over the thirty years I have been producing Price Guides. This year is no different. Yes, some dealers' shops have closed but the dealers tend to reappear at antiques fairs or centres. Good specialist dealers and auction houses adapt and make the most of new opportunities. Many are taking advantage of the Internet boom and trading online where they can reach a global marketplace. Many people have prophesised the end of antique shops and the bricks and mortar auction. They see a world of cyber bidding and buying. While I absolutely accept that this has become an important part of our business, I believe there will always be the place for the thrill of finding a new treasure trove in an antiques shop you have just discovered and the silent joy when a much desired object is 'knocked down' to you, at auction, for less than your limit.

Another exciting development in October 2008 is the launch of our Millers website – millersantiquesguide.com. This has been in the planning stage for well over a year and we aim to provide a site for everyone who loves the world of antiques and collectables. It will attract the committed expert and the inquiring novice. You can search tens of thousands of antiques and collectables from around the world – with full captions and price ranges. We include easy-to-understand extra information, including top tips and special features to look for. You also have access to fully illustrated articles from myself and the Miller's team of experts, including many names from the Antiques Roadshow, both in the UK and US. As a global brand, Miller's team of experts travels the world to bring you the best of antiques and collectables. What's selling where? Where are the hidden treasures? Spot trends as they happen. If you are travelling to Budapest, Buenos Aires or Buffalo find out where to shop. The best dealers and auctioneers can be tracked down through our dealer and auctioneer locator linked to Google maps. We will keep you up-to-date with all the antiques news. You will be able to view videos that will help you get more out of antiques as we walk you through all aspects of buying, selling, identifying and valuing. This is an incredibly exciting development for Miller's in its 30th year. We may be involved in treasures from the past but we also embrace the technology of the future.

A red enamel and gilt metal singing bird box, ivory cover carved with a bird. RGA

A Daum etched and enamelled glass thistle vase, in autumnal palette. DRA

A rare Chinese Kangxi period blue and white bowl, decorated with prunus WW

Judith Miller.

THE PORCELAIN MARKET

The economy may be in turmoil but the antiques market, although a little lacklustre, has remained reasonably steady while the ceramic year has been very much the curate's egg: good in parts. Anything rare, early and of excellent quality has sold strongly but middle range ceramics have not fared as well and any damage has severely affected the value of these wares.

Berlin plaques must have an impressed KPM mark. As always, attractive, romantic, scantily dressed young women fetch a premium, but well-painted groups of figures are also selling well.

The market for English blue and white is still strong for well painted early examples with collectors paying top dollar for anything dated. Rare shapes such as egg cups are particularly in demand. Later transfer printed wares are not doing as well, particularly if they feature common patterns.

Early Chelsea still demands a premium and the market can accept damage. Dry-edge Derby figures remain rare and desirable, but later figures are less easy to sell unless they are of exceptional quality. Late 18th/early 19thC pieces with fine quality painting and gilding, like the botanical painting of Quaker Pegg, have risen in value steadily.

Although often summarily dismissed there are many fine pieces of Dresden, often painted by Hausmaler, to be found. Prices for Meissen remain very strong, particularly for pieces from 1720-50 and the work of J. G. Höroldt, C. F. Höroldt and J.J. Kandler. Some Samson work is now being collected in its own right – particularly desirable are the imitation Kakiemon ware and Chinese copies with elaborate gilt-bronze mounts. The market for good quality 18thC Sèvres remains very buoyant, as there is global demand for the high quality painting and gilding.

BERLIN

A late 19thC Berlin porcelain plaque, depicting 'Psyche in Moonlight', nude with a diaphanous cloth across her lap, mounted in a green plush and gilt frame.

5.75in (14.5cm) high

£1,500-2,000   **FRE**

A late 19thC KPM porcelain plaque, painted with a young maiden', impressed 'KPM' and sceptre.

The KPM mark denotes the Berlin porcelain factory.

7.75in (19.5cm) high

£2,800-3,200   **FRE**

A late 19thC KPM oval porcelain plaque, painted with a young beauty wearing a diaphanous dress, impressed 'KPM' and sceptre mark, framed and signed 'Wagner'.

6.75in (17cm) high

£1,800-2,200   **FRE**

MILLER'S COMPARES

An early 20thC Berlin porcelain roundel, depicting Lady Devonshire within a cobalt border, gilt details, signed 'Ullmer', in a giltwood frame.

Plaque 11.5in (29cm) diam

£400-500   **FRE**

A late 19thC KPM porcelain oval plaque, depicting a profile portrait of a young brunette beauty.

Plaque 8.5in (21.5cm) wide

£5,000-6,000   **FRE**

A late 19thC Berlin porcelain plaque, of a young maiden illuminated by a chamberstick, painted with 'Good Night'.

7in (28cm) high

£1,500-2,000   **FRE**

A 19thC Berlin porcelain plaque, depicting a young woman wearing a white head-covering and garland of leaves, her hands clasped to her chin, impressed mark '311C' and bearing paper label, framed.

Plaque 5in (12.5cm) wide

£1,500-2,500   **FRE**

The most desirable Berlin plaques on the market today usually feature a beautiful girl, such as the one shown above right. The further off the shoulder her clothes, the more suggestively they drape, and the more flesh that can be seen, the greater the value is likely to be. Collectors look for exceptional painting, with even skin tone and painstakingly detailed face, hair and breasts. Folds in clothing and other fabric should be realistic. The plaque shown here on the right has all of these, plus the artist has painted a crown of beautifully rendered flowers in her hair.

The stiff formality of plaques bearing historical portraits inspired by the English painter Thomas Gainsborough, such as the one on the left, are no longer as desirable. Equally unpopular in today's market are plaques painted with religious scenes.

A late 19thC Berlin painted porcelain plaque, painted with 'Springtime' after Jules Frederic Ballavoine, inscribed verso, framed.

7.5in (19cm) high

£350-450 FRE

A KPM porcelain plaque, 'Gypsy with a Birch Tree', attributed to Wallther, the figure leaning against a tree, a tambourine at her feet, impressed sceptre and 'KPM' marks, numbered '308/C'.

8in (20.5cm) high

£3,500-4,500 FRE

A late 19th/early 20thC KPM porcelain plaque, depicting a winged nymph by a pool, gazing at her reflection, impressed 'KPM' and sceptre marks, framed.

8.75in (22cm) high

£2,000-2,500 FRE

A late 19thC Berlin porcelain plaque, signed indistinctly, depicting Marie Antoinette, picking roses from a garden, framed.

9in (22.75cm) high

£1,500-2,000 FRE

A late 19thC Berlin porcelain plaque, depicting Queen Louise walking down the steps of a palace, after Richter, framed.

9.5in (24cm) high

£2,000-2,500 FRE

A Berlin porcelain plaque, 'Le Coupe Enchantee', after Georges Achille-Fould, depicting a young beauty seated on the edge of a table and raising a glass of wine, stamped 'Made in Germany', framed.

Plaque 5.5in (14cm) wide

£400-600 FRE

A 19thC KPM porcelain plaque, depicting a young beauty in Renaissance costume holding a basket of fruit, impressed 'KPM' and sceptre marks, framed.

Plaque 7.5in (19cm) wide

£3,500-4,000 FRE

A KPM artist signed hand painted porcelain plaque, depicting an Odalisque, verso impressed 'KPM' beneath the sceptre and signed lower right 'S. Miriam', the rectangular plaque in a vintage carved and moulded gilt-wood frame.

c1900

The plaque 15.75in (40cm) high

£10,000-15,000 JACK

A late 19thC KPM porcelain plaque, finely painted with the 'Fruit sellers' after Murillo, with a giltwood & gesso frame, impressed 'KPM' and sceptre mark.

12in (30.5cm) high

£8,000-10,000 FRE

A late 19thC KPM porcelain plaque, depicting a mother holding her young child, impressed 'KPM' and sceptre mark, framed.

9.75in (25cm) high

£3,000-3,500 FRE

PORCELAIN

A late 19thC large Berlin porcelain plaque, finely painted with a Tyrolean tavern scene, after Franz von Defregger, signed 'Defregger', dated and framed.

1877   *14.5in (37cm) high*

£4,200-4,600   **FRE**

A late 19thC Berlin porcelain plaque, painted with a tavern scene, framed.

9.5in (24cm) wide

£1,800-2,200   **FRE**

A late 19thC pair of KPM porcelain plaques, painted with bust length portraits of a young Gypsy boy and his companion, impressed 'KPM' and sceptre.

9.75in (25cm) high

£3,500-4,000   **FRE**

After Gerrit Dou, 'The Prayer of the Spinner', a KPM porcelain plaque, depicting an old woman praying over her meal, in a Dutch interior, in a giltwood frame.

11in (28cm) high

£5,000-7,000   **FRE**

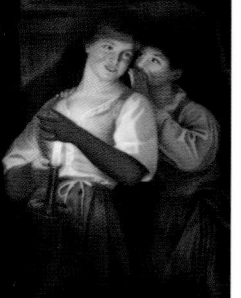

A late 19thC KPM porcelain plaque, depicting two young women whispering by candlelight, in the manner of Godfried Schalcken, impressed 'KPM' and sceptre marks.

7in (18cm) high

£1,000-1,500   **FRE**

A 19thC KPM porcelain plaque, painted with 'Meleager and Atlanta' after Peter Paul Rubens, in a giltwood & gesso frame, impressed 'KPM' & sceptre mark.

12in (30.5cm) wide

£6,000-8,000   **FRE**

A late 19th/early 20thC KPM porcelain plaque, 'Repenting Magdalena', depicting Magdalena with her eyes cast upward, printed sceptre and KPM marks, partial paper label, framed.

7.5in (19cm) wide

£2,000-3,000   **FRE**

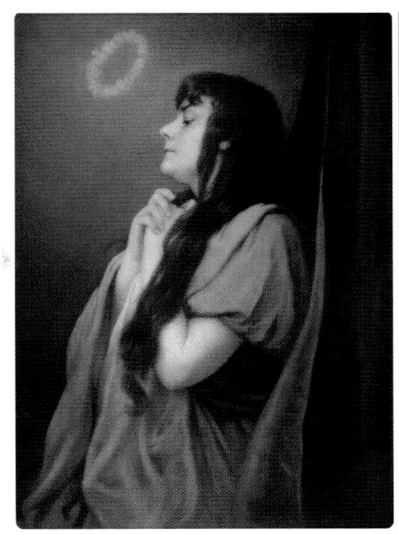

A KPM porcelain plaque, 'Jesus and John the Baptist', depicted as children, with Jesus reclining asleep in John's lap, a grazing sheep to the right, impressed 'KPM' and sceptre marks, in a giltwood frame.

Plaque 8in (20cm) wide

£3,500-4,000   **FRE**

After Gabriel Cornelius Ritter Von Max, 'The Vision', a KPM porcelain plaque, painted with a profile portrait of a young woman with long brown hair, her eyes downcast and hands clasped at her breast, a floral wreath appearing above her, impressed 'KPM' and factory marks, framed.

Plaque 9.5in (24cm) high

£2,500-3,500   **FRE**

A late 19thC 'Berlin'-style porcelain plaque, finely painted with a bust-length portrait of an elderly gentleman, after Balthazar Denner, impressed spurious 'KPM' and sceptre mark.

9.5in (24cm) high

£900-1,200   **FRE**

A late 19thC Berlin porcelain cabinet plate, decorated with a portrait of 'Blanche', within a gilt and cobalt border, signed 'Herner', pseudo blue beehive mark.

9.75in (24.5cm) diam

£200-300   **FRE**

A late 19thC KPM Art Nouveau porcelain vase, with a painted reserve depicting a bust length portrait of a young beauty inscribed 'Orientalin', enriched with gilt, blue sceptre mark.

19.25in (49cm) high

£4,000-4,500   **FRE**

A 19thC KPM porcelain and gilt bronze mounted bijouterie box, painted throughout, with crown finial, lined interior, and angel's mask motifs, raised on Rococo scroll feet, underglaze blue sceptre mark.

10.5in (26.5cm) wide

£2,800-3,200   **FRE**

A pair of Berlin brûles parfum and covers, painted with scenes of courting couples and flowers, blue sceptre marks.

c1880   *7in (17.5cm) high*

£250-300   **WW**

PORCELAIN

ESSENTIAL REFERENCE: BOW

Founded in mid-18thC at Stratford Langthorne, Essex. Bow was one of the first two porcelain factories in England.

Blue and white wares are divided into three periods:

- Early period 1749–54, thickly potted, glaze often blue/green.
- Middle period 1755–65, darker blue, thinly potted, relatively heavy.
- Late period 1765–76, marked deterioration in quality.
- Early polychrome wares decorated in 'famille rose' colours.
- In 1775 the factory was acquired by W. Dewsbury. All Bow moulds and tools moved to the Derby porcelain factory.

A rare early Bow white glazed teapot and cover, the globular body with applied flowering prunus, unmarked, damages and restoration.

c1750-55   7.5in (19cm) high

£500-800   **WW**

A rare Bow white glazed piggin, with applied prunus decoration, damages, the handle restored.

c1752-55   3in (8cm) high

£500-600   **WW**

A small Bow 'Jumping Boy' pattern blue and white plate, the border with Chinese emblems and flowers on hatched bands, a small restored chip at 12 o'clock.

c1760   6.5in (16.5cm) diam

£600-800   **WW**

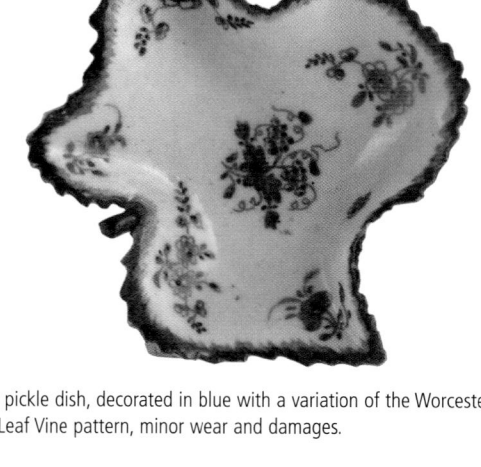

A Bow pickle dish, decorated in blue with a variation of the Worcester Pickle Leaf Vine pattern, minor wear and damages.

c1765   3.75in (9.5cm) high

£150-250   **WW**

A small Bow blue and white mug, painted with pine trees and rockwork flanked by huts, beneath a hatched border.

c1765   3.5in (9cm) high

£1,000-1,200   **WW**

A Bow figure of Ceres, emblematic of Earth, holding a cornucopia, a lion resting at her feet, minor damages.

c1758   (7.5in) 19cm high

£800-1,200   **WW**

A Bow figure of a dancer or gallant, in expansive pose before a tree stump on a moulded base, unmarked, damages and restoration.

c1756-58   7.25in (18.5cm) high

£500-700   **WW**

A Bow model of a flower girl, after Boucher, with blooms in her apron and a basket of grapes on her arm, barefoot on a shallow moulded base, incised 'AF' repairer's mark.

c1758   6in (15cm) high

£500-700   **WW**

A Bow figure of Spring, personified as a maiden, picking flowers from an encrusted vase, raised on a moulded circular base, some damage.

c1760-65   9.5in (24cm) high

£500-700   **WW**

A Bow figure of a sportsman, holding a gun in his left hand, a dog seated beside him, applied flowers to the base, unmarked, restored.

c1756-60   5in (13cm) high

£700-1,000   **WW**

CLOSER LOOK: BOW CANDLESTICKS

After c1755 Bow figures were well coloured and in characteristic colours which were dominated by: milky, deep sky-blue; rich egg-yolk yellow; and deep purplish puce.

Elaborate and overpowering treestump supports with floral bocage are typical of Bow figures after c1760.

Figures were slip-moulded which made a heavier body and necessitated careful construction so they did not collapse in the kiln.

After c1760 bases were modelled in the Rococo style and raised on high scroll feet.

A pair of Bow peacock candlesticks, each bird before flowering bocage, on a scrollwork base, red anchor and dagger mark, and blue cross mark to one, 'G' mark to the other, damages and restoration.

c1760   11in (28cm) high

    WW

£4,000-5,000

A pair of Bow frill vases and covers, with applied mask handles, painted with butterflies and insects amidst large applied flowers, the shoulders and necks pierced, the finials moulded as a bird tucking its head under one wing, damages and restoration.

c1760-70   11.75in (30cm) high

£700-1,000   **WW**

A pair of Bow vases, with orange blossoms, with applied mask handles, red anchor and dagger marks, damages and restoration.

c1770   7.25in (18.5cm) high

£1,000-1,500   **WW**

One of a rare pair of Bow eggcups, painted with stylised flowers in polychrome enamels, unmarked, one with a small rim chip.

c1750-55   2.75in (7cm) high

£3,500-4,500 PAIR   **WW**

A Bow octagonal plate, painted in polychrome enamels with peony, bamboo and insects above blue rockwork, unmarked, minor wear and damages, paper label for the E & J Handley Collection.

c1753   9.25in (23.5cm) diam

£500-700   **WW**

A Bow octagonal plate, painted in polychrome enamels with peony and an insect, unmarked, some damages, paper label for the E & J Handley Collection.

c1755   9in (23cm) diam

£400-500   **WW**

A rare Bow reticulated oval basket and cover, applied with blue and puce flowers, the handle modelled as a bird with its head tucked under one wing, standing on a branch, impressed 'T' mark, some restoration to the bird finial.

c1760-65   6.25in (16cm) high

£3,500-4,500   **WW**

PORCELAIN

A Caughley caddy spoon, printed in blue with a pagoda on an island and two small sailing boats.

c1780   *4in (10.5cm) high*

£600-800   **WW**

A Caughley strainer, printed in blue, with the 'Fisherman' or 'Pleasure Boat' pattern, the centre pierced with a cross-shaped pattern of holes, unmarked.

c1780-1790   *3.75in (9.5cm) high*

£150-200   **WW**

A Caughley teapot stand, printed with the 'Fisherman' or 'Pleasure Boat' pattern, unmarked, a tiny rim flake.

c1780   *6in (15cm) high*

£100-120   **WW**

A Caughley heart shaped dish, painted in blue with the 'Weir' pattern within a Greek key and panelled diaper border between gilt bands.

c1790   *10.75in (27cm) wide*

£300-350   **NEA**

A late 18thC Caughley sauceboat, cover and ladle, painted in blue and gold with flower sprigs and border patterns, 'S' mark to the base, minor faults and the cover a poor fit.

6.75in (17cm) high

£250-300   **WW**

ESSENTIAL REFERENCE: CHELSEA

The factory's early history is very vague but it may have acquired the knowledge of porcelain manufacture in 1742.

Triangle Period 1745–49:
- Wares scarce and costly.
- Mainly undecorated.
- Body comparatively thick, slightly chalky with 'glassy' glaze.

Raised Anchor Period 1749–52:
- Paste now improved.
- Mostly restrained decoration, either Kakiemon or sparse floral work.
- Most collectable ware of this and the Red Anchor period was fable decorated.
- Creamy, waxy appearance of glaze virtually indistinguishable from Red Anchor glaze.

Red Anchor Period 1752–56:
- Significant Meissen influence.
- Glaze now slightly opaque and paste smoother.
- Figures unsurpassed by any other English factory.
- Chelsea 'toys' are rare and expensive.

Gold Anchor Period 1757–69:
- Rococo influence, rich gilding and characteristic mazarine blue.
- Decoration quite florid in style, especially in comparison to earlier painting.
- Influenced by Sèvres.
- Thick glaze can craze.

A Chelsea model of a child, seated on a flared plinth, holding a globe, marked around the equator with the hours of the day, red anchor mark to the back of the base, restoration to the extremities.

c1755-60   *5in (12.5cm) high*

£1,800-2,200   **WW**

A rare Chelsea model of Cupid in disguise as a moneylender, wearing a black cloak and hat, standing on a gilt-decorated base, unmarked, restored.

c1755-60   *4.5in (11.5cm) high*

£600-900   **WW**

A Chelsea fable group, 'The Cock and the Jewell', with a cockerel and hens before flowering bocage, a jewelled necklace at their feet, raised and titled on a scrollwork base, unmarked, damages and restoration.

c1760   *8.75in (22cm) high*

£2,500-3,000   **WW**

A Chelsea model of a recumbent sheep, red anchor mark to the front of the base, restoration to the base and faint body cracks.

c1755   *4in (10cm) high*

£2,200-2,800   **WW**

A pair of Chelsea sweetmeat figures, modelled as bun-sellers, each beside a deep square-section basket, raised on scrollwork bases with applied flowers, gold anchor marks, some damage and restoration to both.

c1760-1765   *9.5in (24cm) high*

£1,000-1,500   **WW**

A Chelsea sweetmeat figure, modelled as a dandy in a long pink coat, lifting the lid on an oval basket, a dog seated beneath, raised on a scrollwork base, gold anchor mark, damages and restoration.

c1760-65   *7.75in (19.5cm) high*

£500-700   **WW**

CLOSER LOOK: CHELSEA GOLD ANCHOR MODEL

Figures made at Chelsea during the gold anchor period were often inspired by prints, the subjects of which the modellers embellished. Groups were often swamped by floral bocage.

The figures portrayed tend to have disproportionately small heads.

The bases were high, pierced and scrolled, heightened with gilding and applied flowers. Unlike most other Rococo bases, Chelsea bases were usually symmetrical.

Models tended to be extensively covered in high-quality gilding.

A rare Chelsea model of Hercules slaying the Lernaean Hydra, assisted by his nephew, Iolaus, who seals the neck stumps with a red hot brand, the bocage hung with the golden apples of the Hesperides, raised on a scrolled base, gold anchor mark, damages and restoration.

c1760-65   *13.75in (35cm) high*

£25,000-30,000   **WW**

A pair of Chelsea figures of sportsmen, one holding a gun, the other holding a dead game bird with a spaniel at his feet, both on floral scrolled bases, gold anchor marks, damages and restoration.

c1765   *8.25in (21cm) high*

£4,000-5,000   **WW**

A Chelsea fable candlestick, 'The Fox and the Goat', the goat's head protruding from the well shaft, the fox perched on the edge dispensing his wisdom to "Never trust the advice of a man in difficulties", gold anchor mark, some restoration.

c1765-1770   *10.5in (27cm) high*

£500-700   **WW**

A pair of Chelsea figures of Summer and Winter, personified as a young girl with a lap full of flowers, and as a man wrapped against the cold and smoking a pipe, on scrollwork bases, gold anchor mark to one, damage and restoration.

c1765   *5.25in (13.5cm) high*

£1,800-2,200   **WW**

A Chelsea plate, painted in the 'Warren Hastings' pattern, with panels of animals from 'Aesop's fables' to the moulded border, red anchor mark, restored.

c1753   *9.5in (24cm) high*

£1,000-1,500   **WW**

A Chelsea plate with ogee edge, painted in the Kakiemon palette with the 'Flying Fox' and 'Rooting Squirrel' pattern, unmarked.

c1753   *8.75in (22.5cm) high*

£1,000-1,500   **WW**

A Chelsea Rococo moulded plate, painted with panels of flowers within purple scrolling borders, red anchor mark, small rim chip.

c1755   *8.25in (21cm) high*

£400-600   **WW**

A 19thC Chelsea scent bottle with floral stopper, formed as a theatrical with a sword standing before a flower encrusted pillar, the base bearing the title 'Fidelle en Amitie'.

3.25in (8cm) high

£1,000-1,500   **WW**

A Chelsea rectangular octagonal dish, with moulded rim, painted with flowers, butterflies and insects, unmarked, some wear to the enamels.

c1755   *12.5in (32cm) high*

£650-750   **WW**

A Rococo-moulded Chelsea plate, the border painted with four pairs of colourful birds, the well with flower sprays and sprigs, a red anchor mark, faint rim cracks.

c1755   *9in (23cm) high*

£300-500   **WW**

A pair of Chelsea moulded plates, painted with flowers in polychrome enamels, red anchor marks, one heavily restored.

c1755   *8.5in (21.5cm) high*

£220-280   **WW**

A Chelsea dish, modelled as a large pink peony, the stalk forming the handle, some restoration.

c1755-60   *8.25in (21cm) diam*

£2,000-3,000   **WW**

A Chelsea silver-shaped botanical dish, painted with a floral specimen in polychrome enamels, red anchor mark, cracked and riveted.

c1755-60   *8in (20.5cm) diam*

£400-600   **WW**

A Chelsea plate, the well painted with flowers in polychrome enamels, the moulded rim with yellow birds in pairs, gold anchor mark.

c1760-65   *8.5in (21.5cm) high*

£500-700   **WW**

A Chelsea plate, painted with pomegranates amidst scattered insects, the rim with panels of exotic birds on a dark blue ground, gold anchor mark, some restoration to the rim.

c1765   *8.25in (21cm) high*

£700-900   **WW**

A Chelsea dish, with reticulated border, painted with flower sprays, gold anchor mark, some wear and minor damages.

c1765-69   8in (20.5cm) high

£350-400   WW

A pair of Chelsea cinquefoil lobed plates, painted with butterflies and gilt flowers, the rims with turquoise panels within gilt scrolls, gold anchor marks, probably refired, peppering and specking to the glaze.

c1765   9.25in (23.5cm) diam

£400-600   WW

A good pair of Chelsea tea bowls and saucers, finely painted with sprays of flowers in polychrome enamels, brown line rims, red anchor marks.

c1755

£2,500-3,000   WW

A Chelsea two-handled cup and saucer, the pine-cone moulding painted with gilt arrowheads on a puce ground beneath a gilded border of insects and flowers, gold anchor marks, some wear to the gilding.

c1765   6in (15cm) high

£1,800-2,200   WW

A pair of Chelsea Rococo moulded tripod stands, hung with bunches of grapes, the acanthus leaf scrolls picked out in puce, green and gilt, one with an anchor mark in puce.

c1752-58   5in (12.5cm) high

£1,200-1,500   WW

A pair of Chelsea strawberry-moulded sauceboats, the interiors with botanical specimens, flowers and insects, the handles formed as stalks, red anchor marks, both damaged and repaired.

c1754-56   6.75in (17cm) high

£1,400-1,800   WW

A Chelsea basket, painted with fruit and insects, with pierced and moulded rim, gold anchor mark, minor chips to the foot rim and wear to the enamel.

c1765   8.25in (21cm) high

£700-900   WW

A rare Chelsea white glazed bowl, with applied prunus decoration, unmarked, broken and repaired.

c1749-52   8in (20cm) high

£1,000-1,500   WW

A rare Chelsea wine cooler, painted with polychrome flower sprays, the sides moulded with bullrushes emerging from a shell motif, red anchor mark, restored.

c1755   10.25in (26cm) high

£800-1,200   WW

A set of six Coalport plates, the wells painted with flowers, the rims moulded with grapevines and gilded with scrolling motifs, one with a printed 'Society of Arts' mark.

c1820   *8in (20.5cm) diam.*

£600-900   **WW**

An early 19thC Coalport plate, painted in the manner of William Billingsley with panels of flowers on a scale blue ground, unmarked.

8.5in (21.5cm) high

£100-200   **WW**

A moulded Coalport plate, brightly painted with flowers and with gilt details to the border.

c1820   *9.25in (23.5cm) diam*

£100-200   **WW**

An early 20thC Coalport plate, the centre painted with a still life of fruit, signed 'Howard', within a raised gilt and pale yellow border.

10.5in (27cm) high

£300-400   **WW**

A pair of Coalport plates, naturalistically painted with birds and butterflies, on a pale green ground, one with a printed mark, some wear to the gilding.

c1870   *9.5in (24cm) diam*

£200-300   **WW**

A pair of Coalport two-handled vases, each ovoid body painted with birds amongst trees and flowers beneath a fluted waisted neck enriched with gilding, set with scroll and leaf moulded handles, raised on a circular foot, with gilt ampersand marks.

c1860   *12in (33cm) high*

£3,500-4,000   **SOTH**

An early 19thC Coalport campana vase, with gilt loop handles, each side painted with figures and buildings in a rural setting, the white ground gilded with garlands and foliate scrolls, tiny faults.

9.75in (24.5cm) high

£250-350   **WW**

A pair of Coalport ovoid vases and covers, painted by John Randall, with colourful exotic birds amidst fruit and flowers, moulded with gilt rope swags, unmarked, some restoration.

c1870   13.5in (34cm) high

£900-1,200   **WW**

A pair of late 19thC Coalport vases and covers, with colourful birds to one side, flowers and fruit to the other, on a blue-scale ground, printed factory marks and pattern numbers in gilt, restoration to both.

15.5in (39.5cm) high

£500-700   **WW**

A Coalport part tea service, comprising a teapot and cover, sugar bowl and cover, six cups and eight saucers, decorated with colourful flowers on pale yellow bands, enriched with gilding, pattern number 996, some damages.

c1825

£300-400   **WW**

A Coalport letter rack, moulded with leaves and painted with a basket of flowers, unmarked, damages and restoration.

c1825   7.75in (19.5cm) high

£320-380   **WW**

A mid-19thC large Coalport parian ware centrepiece, designed as a central support modelled as three symbolic angels, each holding their own attribute, their wings supporting a turquoise glazed and ivy gilded bowl with foliate and scroll pierced rim, all raised on a tri-partite plinth base, with conforming turquoise and gilt decoration, unmarked.

20.75in (53cm) high

£1,000-1,500   **HALL**

A limited edition Coalport model, 'The Pheasant', printed marks, no. 107 of 750, with a wood stand and reference sheet.

c1979   11in (30cm) high

£100-200   **WW**

DAVENPORT

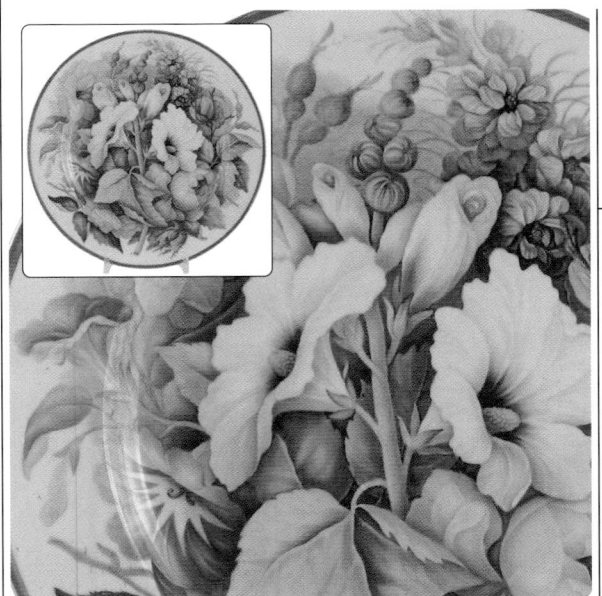

A fine Davenport porcelain plate, lavishly painted with roses, hollyhocks, phlox and Morning Glory, the border gilded, impressed factory mark.

c1820   9.25in (23.5cm) diam.

£1,000-1,200   **WW**

A 19thC Davenport mug, printed with the Royal coat of arms for Queen Victoria and the legend 'Imperial Measure', printed mark, minor damages.

5in (12.5cm) high

£100-150   **WW**

A Davenport spiral moulded vase, painted with a figure with four sheep before a house, the reverse with a panel of flowers on a cerise ground, with a richly gilded neck, handles and foot, unmarked.

c1835   8in (20.5cm) high

£150-200   **WW**

An unusual Davenport pink lustreware tea service, comprising teapot and cover, sugar bowl and cover, milk jug and cover, butter dish and cover, ten teacups and ten saucers, printed in black with a variant of the 'Swiss Pastime' pattern, black printed marks, minor faults.

c1835

£400-600   **WW**

PORCELAIN

ESSENTIAL REFERENCE: DERBY

The first porcelain factory in Derby was possibly started by André Planché and was operating experimentally by 1750.

Early period 1750-56
- Early soft paste is fine-grained and greyish and almost has the appearance of hard paste porcelain. Greyish white glaze.
- Figures are known as 'dry-edge' because the glaze was wiped off the edge of the bases to prevent them sticking in the kiln.

Later period 1756-69
- In 1756, William Dewsbury, John Heath and André Planché started what became the first Derby Porcelain Factory.
- Restrained decoration, with much of the body left plain, in the Meissen style.
- Excellent body, sometimes with faintly bluish appearance.

Chelsea-Derby 1770-84
- In 1770, Dewsbury bought the Chelsea factory and ran it until 1784 in conjunction with Derby.
- Chelsea-Derby figures made at Derby.
- Unglazed white biscuit figures. Move away from the academic Meissen style towards the more fashionable French taste.
- 1770s: body of silky appearance and bluish-white tone.
- 1780s: body very smooth with white glaze. Painting on such pieces is superb, especially the landscapes of Jockey Hill and Zachariah Boreman.
- 1780s and 1790s: noted for exceptional botanical painting by 'Quaker' Pegg and John Brewer.
- Around 1800 the body degenerated, becoming somewhat thicker, and glaze tended to crackle and allow discolouration.
- Products made at both factories bore the same mark – an anchor and the letter D.

Crown Derby 1784-1811
- Factory adopted a crowned D as its mark.
- Earlier styles continued to be made. Other products included Neoclassical tablewares, sometimes painted with naturalistic flowers, by William Billingsley and others. Statuettes produced after models by Jean-Jacques Spängler and Pierre Stephan.

Bloor Derby 1811-45
- Period of steady decline in which factory lost all individuality.

Royal Crown Derby
- Established in 1876. The factory remains active today.

A rare Derby dry-edge figure of a long-haired Cupid, seated on a cushion and holding a garland of flowers, unmarked, damaged, paper label for 'Frances L. Dickson collection' with handwritten note connecting it to the Glaisher Collection.

c1750   3.5in (9cm) high

£2,000-2,500   **WW**

A Derby figure of a dancing shepherdess, holding her skirt in her right hand with flowers in her left, a sheep recumbent at her feet, the base applied with flowers, some restoration.

c1754   6.5in (16.5cm) high

£350-400   **WW**

A Derby model of Neptune, standing before a dolphin on a tall base of shells and seaweed, gold anchor mark, some damages.

c1758-65   9.75in (25cm) high

£700-1,000   **WW**

A Derby model of lovers, the young gardener seated and holding a spade, his companion standing with a basket of flowers on her hip, some good restoration.

c1760-65   6in (15cm) high

£1,000-1,500   **WW**

A pair of Derby sweetmeat figures, each beside a rectangular box before tall flowering bocage, raised on a moulded circular base, damages and restoration.

c1765   8.75in (22cm) high

£700-1,000   **WW**

A large Derby model of Athena, resting her shield in her left hand, her right hand raised above her head, standing on a moulded circular base, damage and restoration.

c1765   13in (33.5cm) high

£300-400   **WW**

A Derby group of Spring and Winter, as a young girl with a basket of flowers and a sportsman with a gun and satchel, incised '68', losses and restoration.

c1760-70   9.25in (23.5cm) high

£650-750   **WW**

A large Derby model of Athena, her shield in her left hand, resting upon a stack of books atop of which sits an owl, some damage and restoration.

c1765   15.25in (38.5cm) high

£400-500   **WW**

A Derby model of a musician, playing a tambourine and blowing on a pipe, leant on a blossom encrusted tree stump, restored.

c1765   10.5in (27cm) high

£250-350   **WW**

A pair of Derby shepherds, the girl gathering flowers in her apron, with a sheep at her feet, the young man holding a pipe with a dog at his side, both on scroll bases, both figures restored.

c1765   7.5in (19cm) high

£500-600   **WW**

A Derby model of Neptune, his mantle billowing in the wind, standing beside a dolphin on a shell and scrollwork base, one arm broken and repaired.

c1765-69   8.25in (21cm) high

£350-450   **WW**

A pair of Derby figures of Spring and Summer, personified as children, Spring with a floral crown and a basket of flowers on his lap, Summer with a diadem of corn, holding a cornsheaf, both on scrollwork bases, some restoration to one figure.

c1765-70   5.5in (14cm) high

£450-550   **WW**

A Derby model of the Four Seasons, personified as four figures around an obelisk, holding flowers, fruit and corn, damages and restoration.

c1760-1770   9.5in (24.5cm) high

£600-900   **WW**

A pair of 18thC Derby figures of the Dresden shepherds, the woman collecting flowers in her apron wearing a white jacket and pink flower sprigged skirt, with a tree trunk and lamb at her feet, the man with a fruit basket, wearing a green and yellow cloak, a white polychrome flower sprigged coat and red gilt flower sprigged breeches, with a dog and a tree trunk by his feet, on Rococo bases.

9.75in (25cm) high

£1,000-1,200   **L&T**

A pair of Derby figures of musicians, he with a flageolet and tambourine, she with a triangle, both stood before flowering bocage on scrollwork bases, some restoration to both.

c1770   8.5in (21.5cm) high

£300-500   **WW**

A Derby candlestick, with two playful lambs beneath flowering bocage, raised on a scrollwork and shell base, some restoration.

c1765-1770   *8.75in (22.5cm) high*

£250-350   **WW**

A Derby candlestick figure, modelled as a young lady carrying flowers in her apron, and standing before a leafy flowering tree, some restoration.

c1770   *10.5in (26.5cm) high*

£400-500   **WW**

A Derby model of two goldfinches, feeding a nest of three chicks on floral bocage, raised on a scrollwork base, unmarked, restored.

c1765-70   *8in (20cm) high*

£400-500   **WW**

A Derby oval dish, painted with a large apple surrounded by various insects and butterflies, unmarked, wear to the enamels.

c1755-60   *9in (23cm) diam*

£450-550   **WW**

A Derby dish, moulded with leaves and grapes, picked out in polychrome enamels, the well painted with two birds, unmarked, minor faults.

c1758   *10.5in (27cm) diam*

£800-1,000   **WW**

A Derby plate, moulded with three geranium leaves to the centre, the rim with a geometric flower-studded design, painted with flower sprays in polychrome enamels, unmarked, chip to the foot rim, the enamels worn.

c1758-1760   7.25in (18.5cm) diam

£450-550   WW

A Derby leaf moulded dish, painted with flower sprays, each leaf edged in green enamel, the stalk forming a handle, unmarked, minor damages.

c1760-65   6.5in (16.5cm) diam

£500-700   WW

A late 18thC Derby plate, with a spiral fluted border and painted with a rose, a puce factory mark above pattern number 65, small restored rim chip.

9in (23cm) diam

£100-200   WW

A Derby Animal service plate, painted to the centre by John Brewer, with two donkeys in a landscape, crown and crossed baton mark, dots and 'D' in purple and pattern 268.

c1795-1800   8.75in (22.5cm) diam

£400-500   NEA

A Derby Rococo moulded flower vase, each side painted with an exotic bird before a flowering tree, unmarked, damages and restoration.

c1765   8.75in (22.5cm) high

£400-500   WW

A Derby Rococo vase, painted with birds and flowers, with applied flower heads, unmarked, small chips.

c1765   9in (23cm) high

£500-800   WW

CLOSER LOOK: DERBY CAMPANA VASE

William Pegg's painting is considered to be on a par with the best botanical still life painters of his day. His flowers have a three-dimensional quality and intensity.

Other artists of the time tended to paint in the centre or at random. Pegg painted across the entire surface.

Unlike most of his contemporaries, Pegg painted largely from nature rather than copying from botanical magazines of the period.

Named, signed pieces by Pegg are rare and desirable.

One of a pair of Derby third quarter 18thC painted 'frill' covered vases, the pierced domed cover with bird finial over an inverted baluster-form body painted with insects, with pierced trellis motif at the shoulder and encrusted with masks and floral garlands, on a spreading foot, unmarked.

11.5in (29cm) high

£350-450 PAIR   FRE

A Derby two-handled vase of elongated campana form, painted in the manner of Quaker Pegg, with a broad band of summer flowers including a passion flower, tulip and roses, against a black background, set with scroll and leaf moulded loop handles, raised on a socle foot and square base, red painted factory mark and number 24.

William 'Quaker' Pegg was the leading flower painter of his day. Born in 1775 he worked at the Derby factory for two short periods, the first from 1796 to 1801, and the second from 1813 to 1820. In 1800 he joined The Society of Friends and went on to develop a religious mania that resulted in him rejecting his own work as religious idolatry.

c1815   12.5in (32cm) high

£8,000-10,000   SOTH

PORCELAIN

A pair of Derby cos lettuce sauceboats, painted and applied with flowers, unmarked.

c1756   *7.75in (20cm) high*

£500-800   **WW**

A Derby cylindrical butter-tub and cover, painted with birds and flowers, a moulded strawberry knop to the cover, raised on three claw feet, unmarked, damage and restoration, the handles missing.

c1760   *4.5in (11.5cm) high*

£400-600   **WW**

A Derby silver-shaped cream jug, decorated in blue with a Chinese pagoda, unmarked, minor damages.

c1770   *4.75in (12cm) high*

£250-300   **WW**

One of a set of four Derby cornucopia wall pockets, modelled en rocaille and painted in coloured enamels with panels of exotic birds, one damaged with old repairs.

c1765   *Tallest 9.75in (24.5cm) high*

£6,000-8,000 THE SET   **DN**

A pair of early 19thC Derby models of a young man and woman, after Meissen, both seated, on pierced and gilded bases, incised model number marks, some restoration, the object in the man's hand replaced.

6.75in (17cm) high

£350-450   **WW**

A pair of Derby models, one of a man fitting a lady's shoe, the other of a gentleman having his shoe shone, each on pierced circular bases, imprinted and incised marks, some restoration.

c1820   *7in (18cm) high*

£200-300   **WW**

An early 19thC Derby bone china figure of Napoleon, standing beside a plinth inscribed with his birthday and date of death, raised on a square base, crowned 'D' mark in iron red, restored.

7.75in (20cm) high

£200-300   **WW**

A pair of Derby Mansion House dwarfs, based on a drawing by Jacques Callot, the first example holding a staff and wearing a hat bearing an advertisement form 'Mr. Curious' dog & monkey act', inscribed 'No. 227', the other example wearing a hat advertising a 'poultry sale', inscribed 'No. 227', both with crowned 'D' marks.

c1820   *the tallest 6.75in (17cm) high*

£600-800   **FRE**

A pair of early 19thC Derby two-handled vases, painted with flowers and gilt foliate motifs on a white ground, crowned 'D' and crossed batons marks in iron red, some restoration.

9in (23cm) high

£700-1,000 WW

A garniture of three Derby campana vases, painted with panels of flowers on a dark blue ground, highlighted with foliate bands of gilding, the handles of each vase formed as a snake, printed 'Bloor Derby' marks, some damages and restoration.

c1825 *8.25in (21cm) high*

£300-400 WW

A Derby bute-shaped teacup and saucer, painted with landscape panels in the manner of Jockey Hill, on a yellow ground, titled 'On the Coast of Sussex' and 'Near Rochester', some wear to the enamels.

c1800

£250-350 WW

A pair of early 19thC Derby cups and saucers, painted with rural scenes of Britain on a lavish blue and gilt ground, crowned crossed batons mark and each piece titled in iron red, some wear to the gilding

£200-250 WW

An early 19thC Derby porter mug, painted with a panel of flowers on a green ground, beneath a gilt scrolling foliate border, partial red printed mark to the base, rim crack.

6.75in (17cm) high

£150-200 WW

An early 19thC Derby porter mug, painted in the manner of Robert Brewer with Chatsworth Hall, on dark blue ground, crowned crossed batons and 'D' mark in iron red, titled to the base, restored.

7in (17.5cm) high

£150-250 WW

An early 19thC Derby botanical plate, painted in pattern number '141' with Caparis Spinosa, the caper shrub, titled to the base, painted crowned crossed batons mark in blue.

8.75in (22cm) diam.

£200-300 WW

A Derby bourdalou, painted with sprigged decoration in blue, green and gilt, unmarked. some wear.

c1800 *9.75in (24.5cm) high*

£400-600 WW

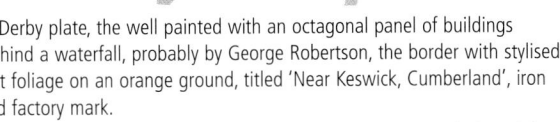

A Derby plate, the well painted with an octagonal panel of buildings behind a waterfall, probably by George Robertson, the border with stylised gilt foliage on an orange ground, titled 'Near Keswick, Cumberland', iron red factory mark.

c1812 *8.75in (22cm) diam.*

£200-300 WW

A Derby oval sauce tureen and cover, painted with a variation of the 'Kylin' pattern, a blue seal mark, a chip beneath the foot rim.

7.75in (19.5cm) high

£300-500   **WW**

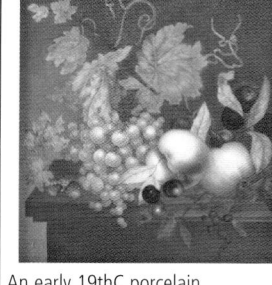

An early 19thC porcelain rectangular plaque, probably painted by Thomas Steele on a Derby blank, with a still-life of fruit spilling over a tabletop, in a gilt and black frame, restored.

12.5in (32cm) high

£400-500   **WW**

A Derby oval coffee pot, each side painted with a panel of flowers in the manner of William Billingsley, on a pale tangerine ground decorated with gilt foliage, unmarked, wear to the gilding.

c1800   *10in (25.5cm) high*

£300-500   **WW**

A Bloor Derby porcelain figure, 'The Tailor's Wife', on a naturalistic base, with gilt scrolled decoration, incised 'N62'.

c1820   *9.25in (23.5cm) high*

£650-750   **SWO**

A pair of first half 19thC Bloor Derby figures of Shakespeare and Milton, standing leaning on pedestals, each holding a scroll containing lines from 'The Tempest' and 'Paradise Lost', printed iron red marks.

10.25in (26cm) high

£600-1,000   **WW**

A large early 19thC Bloor Derby two-handled vase and cover, painted with flowers in the manner of William 'Quaker' Pegg, the handles rising from rams' heads, crowned 'D' mark in iron red, damaged and riveted.

14.5in (37cm) high

£800-1,200   **WW**

A Bloor Derby rectangular bowl, painted with a panel of birds in the manner of Richard Dodson within a blue gilt border, on an oval base, printed mark in iron red, damages.

c1830   *11.5in (29cm) wide*

£200-250   **WW**

A Royal Crown Derby ovoid jug, richly decorated in raised enamels, turquoise jewelling and gilding on a dark blue ground, printed and incised marks, date code for 1893.

7.25in (18.5cm)

£150-250   **WW**

A Royal Crown Derby urnular vase, painted and signed by W. E. J. Dean, with a castle in a river landscape, within a gilt shaped oval frame reserved on a cobalt blue ground, the rim moulded with egg-and-dart edged in gilt, gilt scroll acanthus moulded handles, painted marks in red, date code for 1920.

5in (13cm) high

£500-600   **NEA**

A Royal Crown Derby figure of Olga, wearing a long red fur-lined coat and pulling at the lead of a large dog, printed mark in iron red with date code for 1933.

6.5in (16.5cm) high

£150-250   **WW**

DRESDEN

A pair of late 19th/early 20thC Dresden vases and covers, of ovoid form, decorated with alternating panels of painted flowers reserved on a gilt ground and figural landscape scenes, the borders with scrolling gilt and stylised flower-heads on a white ground, blue painted mark.

21.75in (55cm) high

£900-1,200   **L&T**

A large pair of early 20thC Dresden centrepieces, each with a pierced basket on a tall column around which three figures stand, cross and 'T' marks, minor faults.

19.75in (50cm) high

£500-800   **WW**

A pair of late 19thC Dresden gilt-metal mounted vases and covers, each of ovoid form, the cover with rose-head finial and pierced panels, the body with twin scroll handles, both with painted landscape panels raised on four gilt-metal scroll feet.

16.5in (42cm) high

£2,400-2,800   **L&T**

A late 19thC Dresden porcelain cabinet plate, signed 'Klem', blue underglaze Dresden Richard Klem mark, frame.

9.5in (24cm) diam

£350-450   **FRE**

A pair of 20thC Dresden urn-shaped vases, painted with mythological and classical scenes on a gilt blue ground, crowned 'D' marks.

105in (26.5cm) high

£400-500   **WW**

A Frankenthal coffee cup, painted with two soldiers with spears in a landscape above Rococo scrolls, the base with impressed marks and an underglaze blue lion rampant, the gilt rim rubbed.

c1760

£300-400   **WW**

A Frankenthal teacup and saucer, painted with scenes of allegorical figures and flowers, bordered in purple and gilt, painted underglaze crowned 'CT' marks in blue and incised marks.

c1770   *5.5in (14cm) high*

£700-1,000   **WW**

An 18thC Frankenthal porcelain vase, with four women holding baskets of flowers.

14in (35.5cm) high

£1,000-1,500   POOK

A Frankenthal figure of a young woman, probably modelled by J. F. Lück, wearing a neckerchief and hat, and peddling a basket of fruit, painted and incised marks.

c1760   *5.5in (13.5cm) high*

£2,200-2,400   **WW**

FÜRSTENBURG

A Fürstenburg figure of a girl playing the lute, modelled by C.C. Schubert, restored, 'F' in underglaze blue.

c1775   *7in (18cm) high*

£400-500   **SOTA**

A late 18thC Fürstenburg figure allegorical for Winter, after the model by Desoches from 1773.

7.5in (19cm) high

£400-500   **SOTA**

A late 18thC Fürstenburg figure of a Putto in disguise, modelled wearing a bonnet and fan, fan, sleeves, arm and wings restored.

5.5in (14cm) high

£300-400   **SOTA**

A set of ten 18thC Fürstenburg porcelain cameo plates, each centrally painted with a portrait bust medallion depicting and inscribed with Greek scholars, underglaze blue marks.

9.5in (24cm) diam

£2,000-3,000 THE SET   **L&T**

PORCELAIN

ESSENTIAL REFERENCE: MEISSEN

Founded in Germany c1710, Meissen was the first porcelain factory in Europe.

- First wares: director, J. F. Böttger's fine, extremely hard red stoneware, with engraved designs. Stoneware superseded by white hard paste, discovered by Böttger and Tschirnhaus c1709.
- 1720–50: enamelling on Meissen unsurpassed. Löwenfink: bold, flamboyant chinoiserie or Japonnaise subjects, often derived from the engravings of Petruschenk, particularly on Augustus Rex wares. J. G. Höroldt: elaborate miniature chinoiserie figure subjects. C. F. Höroldt: European and Levantine quay scenes.
- Crossed swords factory mark used from 1723.
- In late 1720s, a glassier, harder looking paste introduced.
- Best figures are from the late 1730s and early 1740s, especially the great Commedia dell'Arte figures/groups. Finest Meissen figures by J. J. Kändler (chief modeller from 1733).
- Other modellers include Paul Reinicke and J. F. Eberlein.
- Extensive range of dinner services, tea and coffee services, candlesticks and other useful/decorative wears. Kändler designed the factory's most famous service, known as the 'Swan' service.
- The naturalistic flower subjects of the 1740s gradually became less realistic and moved towards the *manier Blumen* of the 1750s/60s.
- 1763: complete reorganisation of factory as Rococo fell out of fashion. Less-ornate Louis XVI style tablewares produced.
- The early 19thC saw the mass production of popular styles including the Biedermeier and early Neoclassical styles.
- Mid-19thC onwards: mass production of revived Rococo style, using 18thC moulds.
- 1920s and 1930s: Art Deco figures modelled by Paul Scheurich and Max Esser.
- Factory still active.

A Meissen figure of Vulcan, modelled as a bearded blacksmith, forging an arrowhead on his anvil, crossed swords mark to the back of the base, damages and restoration.
c1740-50   4.5in (11.5cm) high
£500-800   WW

A mid-18thC Meissen figural group of a young couple, crossed swords mark, minor losses to the hands.

4.25in (10.5cm) high
£900-1,200   WW

CLOSER LOOK: MEISSEN FIGURE

Johann Joachim Kandler arrived at Meissen in 1731 and dramatically improved the quality of the factory's figures. From 1740 until his death in 1775 his figures were the most admired part of Meissen's output.

The figures were modelled separately and then assembled. Some figures show so much movement they appear lifelike.

The modelling of faces is usually severe but with subtle colouring. Hair is usually finely executed with black or dark brown brush strokes. The bright enamel colours are typical of 18thC Meissen.

Early bases were mounds with applied flowers, but by the 1740s these became heavier and decorated with Rococo scrolls.

A mid-18thC Meissen white glazed figure of Cupid, a bow and quiver of arrows on his back, raised on a square base with applied flowers, crossed swords mark, damages and losses.
5in (12.5cm) high
£170-220   WW

A Meissen model of a pastry seller, holding a basket overflowing with cakes and buns, a cross swords mark to the back of the base, minor damage.
c1755   7.75in (19.5cm) high
£2,500-3,000   WW

A mid-18thC Meissen porcelain figure, 'Caliope', modelled by J. J. Kandler (1706-1775), the figure seated under a tree and writing music, a putto playing the lute to her right, books and pipes to her feet, incised 'Caliope' at the rear of the base and applied with flowering branches, traces of cross swords in blue.
9.5in (24cm) high
£3,500-5,000   FRE

A Meissen figure of an Native American squaw, wearing a skirt and cloak of colourful feathers, holding a bow and arrow, with a quiver of arrows by her side, faint mark to the base, losses and restoration.

c1760   *6in (15.5cm) high*

£900-1,000   **WW**

A mid-18thC and 19thC Meissen figure of Cupid, in disguise as a wig-maker, and a Berlin-style figure of Cupid disguised as a girl, both marked in underglaze blue, damages and restoration.

3.5in (9cm) high

£350-450   **WW**

A late 18thC Meissen scent bottle, modelled as a man holding a dog, which looks over his shoulder, the dog's head forming the stopper, blue crossed swords mark, the dog's tail restored.

3.25in (8.5cm) high

£500-700   **WW**

A late 18th/early 19thC Meissen figure of a lady hunter, holding a gun with a small dog at her feet, crossed swords mark with a star beneath the hilts, restoration to the barrel of the gun.

5.5in (13.5cm) high

£400-600   **WW**

An 18thC Meissen model of a sheep, standing four square on a leaf-encrusted base, unmarked, damages.

2.5in (6.5cm) high

£300-500   **WW**

A mid-18thC Meissen lamb, lying on a moulded base, its head turned to dexter and a pink ribbon tied in a bow around its neck, faint mark to the base.

2.75in (7cm) high

£400-600   **WW**

A Meissen Böttger porcelain saucer, decorated with applied sprigs of leaves and flowers, unmarked, some good restoration.

c1715-20   *5.25in (13.5cm) diam*

£600-800   **WW**

A rare Meissen Hausmaler plate, painted in the manner of Franz Ferdinand Mayer with figures and a donkey in a landscape scene, the rim with flower sprays, acanthus leaf scrolls and a bird on a branch, the reverse with a crossed swords mark, and incised marks to the foot rim, a small restored rim chip and a little wear to the gilding.

Hausmaler is German for 'home painter' and refers to an artist who decorated porcelain in his own studio, independently of factory supervision. The decoration of Hausmaler pieces varies in quality but can be of a very high standard, as in this case.

c1745   *8.75in (22.5cm) diam*

£3,000-4,000   **WW**

A Meissen saucer, painted with figures on horseback in a rural landscape scene on a gilt ground, crossed swords mark and gilt 'D', some wear to the gilding.

c1740   5in (13cm) diam

£400-600   **WW**

A Meissen saucer, the centre painted with a harbour scene, and with four figures, within an elaborate gilt-edged panel, the reverse with crossed swords marks and a dot between the hilts '43' impressed and 'VII' in gilt.

c1760   5.25in (13.5cm) diam

£200-250   **WW**

An 18thC Meissen plate with moulded osier border, painted with flower sprays, crossed swords mark.

Osier is a moulded pattern that simulates basket weave.

9.5in (24cm) diam

£180-220   **WW**

A mid-18thC moulded Meissen dish, painted with flower sprays in polychrome enamels, gilt decoration to the rim, crossed swords mark in blue.

11.5in (29.5cm) diam

£250-350   **WW**

A small 18th/19thC Meissen dish, painted probably outside the factory, with the 'Rock and Bird' pattern, crossed swords mark with a star above the hilts, a small rim crack.

6in (15cm) diam

£120-150   **WW**

A rare Meissen teabowl, painted with two panels of ships at sea in ornate gilt cartouches, divided by sprays of indianische Blumen, the base marked in gilt 'VII'.

c1735-40   3in (8cm) diam

£1,200-1,500   **WW**

An early Meissen bowl, probably decorated in the Augsburg workshop of Seuter, painted with Goldchinesen in various pursuits within exotic landscapes, above scrolling foliate designs, unmarked, a restored rim chip and haircrack, wear to the interior gilding.

c1720-1725   6.75in (17cm) high

£1,300-1,400   **WW**

A pair of 18thC Meissen Kakiemon cups, crossed swords mark in blue.

c1735

£1,000-1,500   **JN**

A Meissen bowl, painted with figures in a landscape, crossed swords mark, broken and repaired.

c1740   4.25in (11cm) diam

£200-250   **WW**

An early Meissen teapot and cover, painted in blue with a bird and flowering prunus above rockwork, crossed swords mark with 'W' between the hilts, incised 'X' near the foot rim, a small restored rim chip to the cover.

c1735 7in (17.5cm) high

£1,800-2,200 WW

A Meissen coffee pot and cover, with a clip handle, painted with Deutsche Blumen, crossed swords and incised marks, some damage and metal repair to the spout.

c1750 9in (23cm) high

£250-350 WW

An unusual 18thC Meissen porcelain and ormolu casket and cover, the burgundy ground with floral painted panels, surmounted by a lemon, supported on a finely cast ormulu swept case.

8.5in (21.5cm) high

£400-600 JN

A Meissen figure of a lady, seated by a table with a bible in her hand and spinning a wheel on a table beside her, crossed swords and incised marks to base.

c1860 6.25in (16cm) high

£700-900 SWO

A 19thC Meissen porcelain allegorical figure group, modelled as three scantily clad putti, each engaged in a different activity representing Sculpture, underglaze blue crossed swords mark.

8.25in (21cm) high

£800-1,000 FRE

A 19thC Meissen porcelain figure group, modelled as pair of boys in 19thC dress assisting a young girl as she walks on a pair of stilts, underglaze blue crossed swords mark.

8.75in (22cm) high

£700-1,000 FRE

A 19thC Meissen group of five children, playing the lute, piccolo and harp and one conducting, set on a naturalistic base with gilt decoration, cross swords mark in blue, incised 'B24'.

6.75in (17cm) high

£300-400 JN

A pair of Meissen groups, a Classical young lady standing beside a pedestal with a cupid and dog at her side and a Classical young lady standing beside a tree trunk, two cupids and a dog at her feet, cross sword mark in blue.

11in (28cm) high

£1,200-1,500 JN

A Meissen model of a flower girl, standing holding a basket of flowers under one arm, after a model by Acier and Schönheit, crossed swords mark and incised 'C68', minor damages.

c1880 7.75in (19.5cm) high

£450-550 WW

A Meissen model of a young girl, as the personification of Touch, seated by a table on which stands a parrot in a cage, from a model called 'Sentiment' by Johann Schönheit, crossed swords mark and incised 'E4'.

c1880 5.75in (14.5cm) high

£700-1,000 WW

A Meissen model of a young girl, as the personification of Sight, seated at her dressing table and looking at her reflection in a mirror, from an earlier model by Johann Schönheit, crossed swords mark and 'E3' incised.

c1880   *5.75in (14.5cm) high*

£700-1,000   **WW**

A 19thC Meissen model of 'Les Amies', with a young lady consoling her friend, before a plinth with an urn and Cupid's instruments of love, the oval base with billing doves and a discarded love letter, incised and faint crossed swords marks, minor damage.

9.5in (24cm) high

£800-1,000   **WW**

A large late 19thC Meissen allegorical figure group, emblematic of Geography, comprising a maiden standing before a globe, a tablet in her hand and attended by four putti with various devices, behind her a seated putto, beneath a palm tree, blue crossed swords and incised marks.

16in (40cm) high

£6,000-8,000   **FRE**

A 19thC Meissen porcelain figure group, 'Parcae', after a model by J. J. Kandler, modelled as Chronus assisting the three fates Atropos, Clotho and Lachesis as they spin, measure and cut the thread of Life, and accompanied by a putto, on a stepped shaped base, blue crossed swords marks, incised 'N33' and impressed '137' and '57'.

15in (38cm) high

£4,000-6,000   **FRE**

A 19thC Meissen figure of a young boy, smartly dressed in a pink tunic and breeches holding a flower wreath on a gilt scrolled base, unmarked.

5in (12.5cm) high

£300-400   **JN**

A 19thC Meissen Putti standing by an urn, holding a wreath and flowers, a quire of arrows by his side, the base inscribed 'Je les Courrone', crossed swords mark in blue, incised 'J3, 25, 14'.

5in (12.5cm) high

£400-600   **JN**

A pair of late 19thC Meissen figural condiments, modelled as a man and female in traditional costume, each holding a flower encrusted covered ewer, blue crossed swords marks.

Highest 7.25in (18.5cm) high

£1,200-1,800   **FRE**

A 19thC Meissen figural group of Ceres, the goddess of agriculture, gathering sheaves of corn with three putti, one with a basket of apples on his head, crossed swords mark, incised and painted numbers, damages.

7.75in (19.5cm) high

£600-800   **WW**

A pair of 19thC Meissen figural Season groups, after the models by J.J. Kändler, depicting Summer and Autumn, each modelled with Classical figures seated on billowing Rococo clouds, supporting a plaque painted with figures on horseback, raised on shaped bases applied with flowers and grapes, crossed swords marks, some losses and restoration.

13in (33cm) high

£3,000-5,000   **WW**

A pair of 19thC Meissen porcelain sweetmeat dishes, each reclining figure in 19thC costume supporting a floral encrusted bowl, raised on a scrolled base, gilt details, underglazed blue crossed swords mark.

12in (30.5cm) long

£1,500-2,000   **FRE**

A late 19th/early 20thC Meissen porcelain figure, modelled as a shepherdess holding a lamb on her hip, underglaze blue crossed swords mark, incised and impressed marks.

11.5in (29cm) high

£300-500   **FRE**

A late 19th/early 20thC Meissen porcelain figure, modelled as a woman feeding birds, her apron filled with crumbs, underglaze blue crossed swords mark, incised 'L 73'.

10.5in (26.5cm) high

£500-600   **FRE**

An early 20thC Meissen porcelain group, modelled by Professor Paul Scheurich, depicting a lady and her attendant, seated cross-legged holding a gilded apple behind her back, whilst the eastern attendant pleads with her, clinging to the folds of her skirt, blue cross sword mark, incised signature 'SCHEURICH 19'.

11in (28cm) high

£1,800-2,200   **L&T**

A 20thC Meissen model of five putti, personifying the five Senses, painted in polychrome enamels on a rockwork base, crossed swords and other incised marks, some damages and restoration.

6in (15.5cm) high

£500-700   **WW**

A pair of early 20thC Meissen porcelain figures, depicting a gentleman suitor and his companion, blue underglaze crossed swords marks.

18.5in (47cm) high

£4,000-6,000   **FRE**

A 20thC Meissen model of Harlequin, posing before a tree stump on a flower encrusted base, crossed swords mark, minor chip to one of the flowers.

7.75in (20cm) high

£400-600   **WW**

A Meissen blanc de chine figure, of Diana the Huntress, impressed and blue cross sword marks 'Weifs', incised 'A 1046'.

11.75in (30cm) high

£700-900   **L&T**

A mid-19thC Meissen figure of a badger, after a model by J. J. Kandler, the snarling crouching figure naturalistically painted, raised on an oval base, blue crossed swords mark.

7.75in (20cm) high

£700-1,000

L&T

A 19thC Meissen porcelain figure of an elephant, standing on a naturalistic base, blue crossed swords mark.

12.25in (31cm) high

£1,500-2,000

L&T

A 19thC pair of Meissen model pugs with a puppy, painted in shades of brown, wearing blue collars with gilt bells, the female with crossed swords mark in blue and incised '1169'.

9.5in (24cm) high

£3,000-4,000

SOTA

A 19thC Meissen figure of a pug with a puppy, sitting with one paw raised, the puppy sitting beneath her stomach, naturalistically painted, blue crossed swords mark.

8.75in (22cm) high

£1,000-1,500

L&T

A pair of late 19thC Meissen magpies, each with long tail extending upwards, perched on a naturalistically modelled tree trunk, blue painted crossed swords mark.

20.75in (53cm) high

£2,500-3,000

L&T

A late 19th/early 20thC Meissen porcelain figure, of a Danish hound, the seated dog naturalistically painted in brown and white, blue crossed swords mark.

6.75in (17cm) high

£500-800

L&T

A 19thC Meissen model of a magpie, perched on a rocky base, cancelled crossed swords mark, good restoration to the beak.

20.75in (53cm) high

£500-700

WW

A pair of late 19thC Meissen porcelain candlesticks, formed as seated pan and a mermaid each with a cupid resting on their laps, raised on naturalistic Rococo bases, blue crossed sword mark.

13.25in (33.5cm) high

£1,000-1,500   **FRE**

A pair of 19thC Meissen four light candelabra, each with central sconce and three arms, with moulded floral and leaf decoration, one supported by a man and girl, the other by a lady and boy, on a Rococo plinth.

18in (46cm) high

£1,500-2,000   **L&T**

A 19thC Meissen style blanc de chine comport base converted to a lamp, with central column support surrounded by four putti representing the four seasons, on a circular base with floral swags, and four square feet.

19.75in (50cm) high

£1,500-2,000   **L&T**

One of a pair of late 19th/early 20thC Meissen figural candelabra, each having one central and three scrolling candle arms, encrusted with flowers and with acanthus drip pans, the stem mounted with figures emblematic of Spring and Summer, on a square base with outscrolling corners, blue underglaze crossed swords mark, incised '128'.

19.5in (49.5cm) high

£1,500-2,000 PAIR   **FRE**

A 19thC Meissen mirror, of cartouche easel form, the frame surmounted by a pair of winged cherubs and encrusted with flowers, with four small cartouche-shaped panels painted with songbirds.

23.5in (60cm) high

£2,000-3,000   L&T

A pair of late 19thC Meissen urns and covers, blue painted crossed swords mark.

11.5in (29cm) high

£2,500-3,000   L&T

An early 20thC Meissen leaf-shaped dish, painted in blue with the Onion pattern, with an applied twig handle.

10in (25cm) diam

£40-60   WW

Two 19thC ornithological plates, one Meissen with cancelled crossed swords mark, the other Sèvres-style with interlaced 'L's', damages and restoration.

9.75in (24.5cm) diam

£80-100   WW

An early 20thC Meissen porcelain cup and saucer, of quatreform, painted with flowers and insects, the exterior applied with forget-me-knots, blue crossed swords mark.

Cup 3in (7.5cm) high

£200-300   FRE

An early 20thC Meissen three piece coffee service, of Classical form, the segmented bodies decorated with alternating panels of floral garlands and scrolls against a white ground with gilt enhancements, the coffee pot with a female mask spout.

Coffee pot 10.25in (26cm) high

£300-500   FRE

An early 20thC Meissen porcelain dessert service, painted with flowers on a white ground with gilt highlights, comprising a coffee pot, covered sugar bowl, creamer, 12 cake plates, and two cups and saucers, blue crossed swords mark.

Coffee pot 8in (20.5cm) high

£700-1,000   FRE

A Meissen 'Pink Dragon' porcelain coffee service, comprising a coffee pot, cream jug, covered sugar bowl, two cups, two saucers and two side plates, blue underglazed crossed swords mark.

Coffee pot 6in (15cm) high

£400-600   FRE

MINTON

The Minton factory was founded at Stoke-on-Trent, Staffordshire, in 1793, by Thomas Minton. The factory initially produced earthenware. From c1798 to c1810 Minton produced soft paste porcelain wares. They tended to be thinly potted with a slightly greyish glaze, sometimes with black flecks in it. The majority of wares were decorated with Neoclassical designs. After 1821 Minton made hard paste porcelain. It is rarely flawed and usually covered with a thin, glassy, smooth glaze. Wares tend to be copies of Sèvres or Meissen.

In 1849 Joseph-François Léon Arnoux became artistic director and decoration became richer, with vibrant ground colours – particularly turquoise – and excellent gilding. The factory became famous for its majolica wares. In 1873: 'Minton' mark became 'Mintons'. The factory remains active today.

A Minton bone china flatback model of a German peasant couple, standing on a green base inscribed 'Berne'.

c1825   5.75in (14.5cm) high

£200-300   WW

A Minton coloured parian model of Red Riding Hood, impressed mark and date code, the basket's handle restored.

1864   6.25in (16cm) high

£80-120   WW

A late 19thC Minton parianware group of Ariadne and the panther, probably by John Bell, holding a draping cloth, on a rectangular plinth, impressed mark, date code, damages.

1864 12in (30cm) wide

£600-900   L&T

A Minton porcelain 'Wellington' vase, painted with brightly coloured flowers, against a powder blue gilt enhanced ground, raised on a socle foot and pedestal base.

11.75in (30cm) high

£1,200-1,800   L&T

A Minton vase, painted with a woodpecker on a turquoise cloisonné glaze, printed and impressed marks with date code, the neck reduced and restored.

7in (18cm) high

£150-250   WW

A Minton bone china ormolu-mounted reticulated vase and cover, signed by Antonin Boullemier, on a dark blue ground, impressed marks and dated, cover restored.

1873   11.25in (28.5cm) high

£700-1,000   WW

A Minton pâte-sur-pâte vase, depicting two doves, flowers and arrows, applied gilt ring handles, impressed marks, date code.

1876   9.75in (24.5cm) high

£500-700   WW

A Minton plate, with a reticulated border of flowers and lattice work, the well painted with a musician entertaining two young ladies before a waterfall scene, signed by Anton Boullemier, within a pink and gilt border, impressed and printed marks, date code.

1890   10.5in (26.5cm) diam

£900-1,200   WW

A pair of late 19th/early 20thC Minton plates, the borders decorated with three pâte-sur-pâte panels of young girls and cherubs, signed 'AB' and 'A Birks' for Albion Birks, restored.

10.5in (27cm)

£300-500   WW

PORCELAIN

A Rockingham figure of a beggar boy, wearing a green tunic edged in gilt, on a naturalistically encrusted circular base, incised 'N36'.

1826-42   *5in (12.5cm) high*

£800-1,000   NEA

A Rockingham spill vase, the panel painted by Thomas Searle, within matt and burnished rectangular gilt border, gilt rims, painted Griffen mark in orange.

c1830   *4.25in (11cm) high*

£350-450   NEA

A rare Rockingham hexagonal scent bottle, applied with naturalistically moulded flowers and foliage, painted with gilt foliage within a gilt rim, flower finial.

c1830-42   *5in (13cm) high*

£500-600   NEA

A Rockingham pot pourri basket, painted with a river landscape, encrusted with flowers and foliage, on acanthus feet, printed griffen mark in puce and 'C3' in gilt.

c1830-42   *4.25in (11cm) diam*

£800-1,000   NEA

SAMSON

Opened in Paris in 1845, Edmé Samson's factory made copies of Chinese, German and English porcelain, French faience, Dutch Delft, and some Strasbourg wares.

It was known for its excellent copies of Meissen and Chinese porcelain. However, its fakes of English soft paste porcelain are easier to detect, as Continental hard paste was used.

All wares originally had 'S' within mark, but this has proved easy to remove. Production ended in 1969 and the factory's moulds were sold in 1979.

A pair of late 19thC Samson models of lovers, after Derby, painted marks, minor damages.

12.5in (31.5cm) high

£250-350   WW

A large late 19thC Samson model, 'The Music Lesson', after Chelsea, gold anchor mark and gilt Samson mark, some restoration.

13in (33cm) high

£300-500   WW

A 19thC Samson model of a Kakiemon elephant, based on a 1680 Japanese model, raised trunk, red and cobalt blue saddle, well-modelled details.

11in (28cm) high

£700-1,000   FRE

A late 19thC Samson assembled garniture, in the Worcester manner, comprising three vases and covers, each of hexagonal form, the dark blue ground with gilt scroll framed panels painted with flowers and exotic birds, faux Worcester fret mark.

Largest: 16in (41cm) high

£1,200-1,800   L&T

A pair of late 19thC Samson Worcester-style jugs, painted with birds and gilded foliage, the spouts moulded as bearded faces, unmarked, one handle restored.

8.25in (21cm) high

£200-300   WW

A large 19thC Samson gilt-bronze mounted porcelain brule-parfum, in the Chinese taste with an acorn knop and scrolling handles, above a foliate pierced rim, raised on a fluted wreath cast socle and shaped square base, decorated with carp on a mottled cobalt ground, gilt details.

30in (76cm) diam

£10,000-15,000   **FRE**

A late 19thC Samson hexagonal-section bottle vase, decorated in the Chantilly style with flowers, leaves and insects, hunting horn mark.

7.25in (18.5cm) high

£100-150   **WW**

A 19thC Samson tea urn and cover, in the Japanese style, raised on three gilt painted boys with pewter nozzle.

14in (35.5cm) high

£300-500   **FRE**

A set of twelve 19thC Samson porcelain plates, in the Chinese export style, each decorated with floral sprays centred by a pseudo armorial crest.

9.5in (24cm) high

£700-1,000   **FRE**

SÈVRES

With the decline in popularity of Meissen in the mid-18thC, the Vincennes/Sèvres factory in France (est. 1740) became arguably the most important porcelain factory in Europe.

- First director, Claude-Humbert Gérin, made a soft paste porcelain much whiter than that of other French factories.
- In 1745 Louis XV granted the factory a 20-year exclusive privilege to produce porcelain.
- Early wares heavy in form and painted with small flower sprays with gilt trellis and scrollwork borders.
- 1748: goldsmith Jean Claude Chambellan Duplessis hired to create new Rococo forms. Lighter, more elegant shapes.
- From 1753, other factories forbidden to use Vincennes subjects, colours, and gilding by the king.
- The factory moved to Sèvres, near Paris in 1756.
- Hard paste porcelain used from 1768. Coloured and patterned grounds with little of the body left showing.
- Late 1770s: Sèvres produced strictly geometric shapes based on antique vases and urns. Subdued sepia/greys instead of bright Rococo colours and decorated with Classical motifs.
- Early 1780s: 'jewelled' (drops of enamel) decoration introduced.
- Following the Revolution, porcelain sold to be decorated in Paris and London.
- Rich 'Empire' style developed early 19thC.
- Art Nouveau style adopted in late 1890s. Art Deco in 1920s.
- Currently, produces simplified versions of 18thC wares.

A large Sèvres bisque statue, entitled 'Après le Bain', with a metal band around the foot, engraved 'Sèvres 1845'.

1845   *26.75in (68cm) high*

£5,000-8,000   **L&T**

One of a pair of late 19thC Sèvres porcelain, bisque and gilt bronze mounted candelabra, blue marks.

14.75in (37.5cm) high

£1,500-2,000   **FRE**

A pair of 19thC Sèvres style porcelain figures of Cupid & Psyche, enriched with gilt, formed as Cupid seated on rockwork, and Psyche seated on a draped rock concealing Cupid's bow, on moulded bases, pseudo Sèvres mark.

11in (28cm) high

£800-1,200   **FRE**

A pair of 18thC Sèvres ormolu vases, mounted in the 19thC, each body decorated with reserves of figures in 18thC costume within a gilt border, all on a bleu celeste ground, gilt details throughout.

27in (68.5cm) high

£10,000-15,000 **FRE**

A 19thC Sèvres vase, with domed lid and berry finial over a painted body with a scene depicting Napoleon on horseback, on a gilt enhanced ground, raised on a socle base.

37.5in (95cm) high

£3,000-4,000 **FRE**

CLOSER LOOK: SÈVRES COVERED VASE

The vase was made in the late 19thC – possibly to commemorate the 1892 quadricentennial of Columbus' discovery of the Americas.

The shape of the vase, and features such as the finial on the cover and the mask scroll supports on the base, recall the Neoclassical style of 150 years before. However, if this vase had been made in the 18thC the gilt mounts would have been more restrained and more of the porcelain left undecorated.

The faces of Columbus and the cherubs have been skillfully painted, with exceptional detailing. This is also evident in the details shown in the fabrics.

The vase is decorated with high quality raised gilding.

A late 19thC Sèvres commemorative porcelain and gilt bronze covered vase, the ovoid sides painted with Columbus discovering the New World, the reverse depicting a winged cherub holding aloft an American flag, raised by three mask scroll supports, ending on a tri-form base and claw feet.

22.5in (57cm) high

£2,000-3,000 **FRE**

A late 19thC large Sèvres-style porcelain Art Nouveau vase, with gilt bronze finial, sides painted with a bust-length portrait of a young beauty and a gilt-enriched ground, on a socle base.

26in (66cm) high

£2,000-3,000 **FRE**

A pair of late 19thC Sèvres-style vases and covers, the body with painted with rural scenes framed by shaped moulding with twin masks, underglaze blue painted mark.

10.5in (27cm) high

£1,200-1,800 **L&T**

A pair of late 19thC Sèvres jewelled 'Hollandaise' vases and underdishes, with a 'jewelled' frame and depicting a Classical figure, the other flowers, trophies and a dove.

7.5in (19cm) high

£2,000-3,000 **L&T**

A pair of early 20thC Sèvres-style apple-green gilt metal mounted covered vases, with scroll handles, painted with scenes of lovers, raised on socle bases, and signed 'M. Gravey'.

30.5in (77.5cm) high

£1,500-2,000 **FRE**

A pair of late 19thC Sèvres-style porcelain and ormolu candelabra, the ovoid sides painted with romantic scenes of lovers and floral bouquets, against gilt-enhanced turquoise ground, flanked by twin goat-form handles and surmounted by ornate foliate scrolling branches, raised on triform sphinx cast feet.

A pair of Sèvres French silver-mounted porcelain vases, each of baluster form with a beaded rim and gilt snowflake decoration on a cobalt ground, raised on a circular foot, dated.

1922-23   *19in (38cm) high*

£2,500-3,000   **FRE**

21.75in (55cm) high

£2,000-3,000   **L&T**

A 19thC Sèvres biscuit porcelain model of Cupid, standing on one foot upon a lavender cylindrical plinth, mounted with a gilt metal candle-holder in the form of roses, incised 'L's' mark, damages.

14.75in (37.5cm) high

£150-250   **WW**

A Sèvres porcelain covered sugar bowl, with a berried finial, decorated with reserves of foliate sprays on a gilt enriched bleu celeste ground, decorators mark for Claude Antoine Tardy, gilders mark for Jean Chauvaux.

c1780   *4.25in (11cm) high*

£1,500-2,000   **FRE**

A Sèvres ecuelle, cover and stand, decorated with a band of alternating large and smaller panels enclosing flowers and chinoiserie garden scenes united by floral festoons enclosed by a double band of pearls within gilt bands, all against a lime green ground, crowned interlacing L's and date letters 'FF' in gold, painter's mark of a flower in gold.

c1783

£5,000-7,000   **SOTH**

A Sèvres écuelle, cover and stand, with gilt side handles, painted with colourful bands of scrolling foliage between apple-green bands, interlaced 'L's' marks in gilt enclosing 'LL' and blue enamel marks, some restoration and wear.

1789   *8in (20.5cm) diam*

£400-600   **WW**

An 18thC Sèvres porcelain ecuelle and cover, with later decoration, the domed cover and sides with naturalistic entwined scroll handles, painted with oval reserves depicting figural port scenes, against a blue ground enriched with gilt, painted interlaced green 'L' mark.

6.25in (16cm) high

£1,500-2,500   **L&T**

A Sèvres écuelle, cover and stand, painted with a garland of flowers below a gilt honeycomb border, minor wear to the gilding, restoration to the knop, various printed marks.

1847   *9in (23cm) diam*

£350-450   **WW**

A 19thC Sèvres-style wine cooler, painted on one side with Classical figures in a coach being drawn by lions, the other side with flowers, on a dark blue ground within gilt borders, cancelled interlaced 'L's' mark, some wear and scratching to the enamels.

6.75in (17cm) high

£350-450   **WW**

PORCELAIN

A Sèvres cup (Gobelet Enfancé), painted each side with a harbour scene by Morin, against a blue ground with gilded dots (mouches d'or). Interlaced 'L's, date letter 'O' and painter's mark 'M' in blue.

c1767   3.5in (8.8cm) high

£800-1,200   SOTH

A Sèvres cup and saucer (goblet litron of the first size), the cup decorated with an exotic gilt-framed scene of a Turk seated smoking on a terrace, two servants by his side, the saucer painted with a panel of a group of travellers in an Egyptian landscape, both against a beau bleu ground, an elaborate diaper scrollwork cartouche running around the edge of the rims. Interlacing 'L's and date letters 'bb' in blue, painter's mark 'LG' possibly for Etienne-Henry Le Guay.

c1779

£5,500-6,500   SOTH

A Sèvres cup and saucer (goblet litron of the first size), decorated with a beau bleu ground, a gilt laurel wreath medallion enclosing a basket with flowers and fruit against a pale yellow ground, wide bands of elaborate gilt foliage scrollwork just beneath the gilt serrated rims 'Sevres RF' and painters mark 'LG' in blue enamel to the base, incised 'Louis'.

Louise-Antoine le Grand (1776-1817) was employed by the Sèvres factory as a gilder and painter.
c1793-94

£2,500-3,000   SOTH

CLOSER LOOK: SÈVRES CUP AND SAUCER

Charles Nicolas Dodin was considered to be one of the best miniature artists at Sèvres and was top of the artists' hierarchy.

His work made its way into the best French and other European collections, including those of Louis XV and his mistresses, Madame de Pompadour and Madame du Barry, as well as Louis XVI and Catherine the Great of Russia.

For much of his career Dodin painted mythological and allegorical figures and genre scenes based on works of the great masters of the 17thC and 18thC. He used engravings, and sometimes the original works, to guide him.

A Sèvres cup and saucer, the cup finely decorated by Charles-Nicolas Dodin with a scene of children playing instruments, dressed in revival costumes accompanying a girl playing the harpsichord. The saucer decorated with a similar terrace scene of a young painter behind his canvas looking at his young model, his pupil sitting on a pillow by his side, a large column just visible behind heavy green velvet drapery, the bleu nouveau ground decorated with finely tooled elaborate gift festoons and strapwork alternated by classical vases. Blue interlaced L's mark enclosing date letter 'ff', painter's mark 'k' for Dodin, gilder's mark for Le Guay, incised 36 to cup and 37 to saucer.

Charles-Nicolas Dodin worked 1754-1803. The scenes are taken from two of the overdoors painted by Carle Vanloo for Madame de Pompadour's Salon de Compagnie at the Château de Bellevue and engraved by Fessard.
c1783

£30,000-35,000   SOTH

A 19thC Sèvres-style porcelain covered cup and trembleuse stand, the domed lid with a berry finial, the tapered cylindrical sides with twin scroll handles, painted with an oval reserve depicting a bust length portrait of a lady, within a turquoise jewelled border and against a pink gilt enriched ground, the conforming stand painted with trophy motifs, interlaced S-mark, signed 'Moriot'.

£350-450   FRE

A small 19thC Sèvres-style teapot and cover, each side painted with figures on a blue ground, enriched with gilding and jewelling, interlaced 'L's' to the base, some restoration.

5in (13cm) high

£250-350   WW

A Sèvres small oval teapot and cover, theiere 'Calabre', painted with two oval panels of trophies, one with emblems of Love, the other with maritime associations including a compass and an anchor, reserved on a pale-pink ground with blue and gilt oeil de perdrix ground, the cover with floriform finial, smudged and indistinct remnants of marks, minor wear.

c1775   4.25in (11cm) high

£1,500-2,000   DN

A Sèvres Louis Philippe porcelain cabaret set, comprising a teapot, creamer and sugar, two cups and saucers and tray, each painted with reserves depicted romantic scenes and musical trophies against gilt enhanced cobalt blue grounds, red and blue printed marks.

c1846   *Teapot 5in (12.5cm) high*

£700-1,000   **FRE**

A 19thC Sèvres pink-ground and silver-overlay cabaret service, comprising a teapot, covered cream jug, covered sugar bowl, cup and saucer and tray, all with reserves decorated with pastoral scenes and silver filigree, interlaced blue 'L's and date mark 'C', decorator's marks for Chabry.

Teapot 6.5in (16.5cm) high

£2,000-3,000   **FRE**

A 19thC Sèvres-style porcelain tea service, comprising a teapot, covered sugar bowl and a cream jug, each decorated with foliate sprays and bleu celeste collars, gilt details.

Teapot 7.5in (19cm) high

£1,500-2,000   **FRE**

A Sèvres shaped oval stand, painted with a central shaped oval panel with four gilt shell-shaped C-scrolls, within an elaborate border of puce shell-shaped panels and laurel wreaths suspending puce swags within a blue and gilt cailloute ground, blue interlaced 'L's mark, dated letter 'I' and a decorator's mark of a heart device for 'A. Fontelliau', paper label for 'Klaber and Klaber', small area of restored gilding to rim.

1761   *7in (17.5cm) long*

£1,500-2,500   **DN**

A pair of Sèvres dark-blue-ground shaped oval dishes, each painted with four panels of flowers, within foliate gilt C-scroll borders, one with interlaced 'L's mark and date code script 'G' decorator's mark, one cracked.

1769   *10.5in (27cm) long*

£4,000-5,000   **DN**

An 18thC Sèvres porcelain oval platter, painted with a Louis XIV battle scene, entitled 'PRISE DE COURTAI' with reserves depicting bust length portraits of Louis XIV and courtiers, signed 'Leber', interlaced blue 'L's mark.

17in (43cm) high

£1,800-2,200   **L&T**

A pair of Sèvres porcelain plates, each painted with morning glory sprays within yellow borders painted with blue and puce berried foliate garlands, interlaced 'L's marks, painters mark 'GM'.

9.5in (24cm) diam

£500-800   **L&T**

A set of four Sèvres plates, blue interlaced 'L's marks and painter's mark for Laroche.

c1790   *9.5in (24cm) diam*

£1,500-2,000   **L&T**

A set of six late 19thC Sèvres portrait plates, each painted with a different three-quarter portrait of a noted French beauty, within turquoise and gilt scrolling bands, signed 'Pinel', printed factory and Chateau des Tuileries marks".

9.5in (24cm) diam

£400-600   **FRE**

PORCELAIN

An 18thC Sèvres porcelain ewer and saucer, each moulded in high relief with bullrushes and branches, painted with shaped reserves of exotic birds and shell motif, against gilt-enhanced cobalt blue 'L's' marks, saucer bears paper label 'Coleccion SANTARELLI, Buenos Ayres'.

Ewer 5.5in (14cm) high

£3,000-3,500　　　　　　　　　　　　　　　　　　**L&T**

A late 19th/early 20thC Sèvres gilt-bronze mounted porcelain clock garniture, comprising a clock and pair of ewers, the clock with porcelain dial painted with Roman numerals above two figures in 18thC costume and surmounted by an urn finial with lion mask handles hung with garlands and centred by a portrait medallion, the ewers with griffin handles decorated with recumbent females, raised on a circular base, the case stamped '8 Pe Mourey 74'.

Clock 20in (51cm) high

£1,500-2,000　　　　　　　　　　　　　　　　　　**FRE**

SPODE

An early 19thC Spode ice pail, cover and liner, with gilt scroll handles, decorated in the Imari palette with flowers and bold foliage, painted Spode mark and pattern number '1599' with an additional liner.

12.25in (31cm) high

£1,500-2,000　　　　　　　　　　　　　　**L&T**

A pair of Spode bone china ovoid vases, each painted with a panel of a young lady on a gilded blue ground, each base inscribed in French with a semi-erotic verse, painted factory marks, each with some good restoration.

c1825　　　　　　　6in (15.5cm) high

£1,000-1,400　　　　　　　　　　　　**WW**

A garniture of three early 19thC Spode flanged top beakers, decorated with pattern '3994' with purple convolvulus flowers and gilded leaves on a white ground, painted marks in iron red, minor damages.

£400-600　　　　　　　　　　　　　　**WW**

A Spode bone china basket, the sides moulded as scallop shells, painted in polychrome enamels, the interior highlighted with shades of pink, unmarked.

c1810　　　　　6in (15cm) high

£500-800　　　　　　　　**WW**

An early 19thC Spode comport, painted with a scene of York Minster within a moulded gilt border of foliage, stylised flowers and shells, painted 'Spode' mark, minor cracks.

13.5in (34cm) diam.

£300-400　　　　　　　　**WW**

An early 19thC Spode box and cover, richly decorated in pattern no. 1166, with polychrome flowers on a blue and gilt scale ground, painted pattern mark, minor wear to the gilding.

2.75in (7cm) high

£450-550　　　　　　　　**WW**

A pair of early 19thC Spode cups and saucers, richly painted with flowers, the cups with an elaborate gilded rim, painted mark.

5.75in (14.5cm) high

£350-450　　　　　　　　**WW**

ESSENTIAL REFERENCE: TUCKER

The Tucker porcelain factory was established in 1825 by William Ellis Tucker in Philadelphia, Pennsylvania. First US porcelain factory of note.

- Early wares painted with scenes in sepia and dark brown.
- In 1823 the firm became 'Tucker & Hulme' and then 'Tucker Hemphill' in 1831.
- 1833-36: the factory run by Joseph Hemphill with Tucker's brother, Thomas, as manager.
- During Hemphill period, wares became much richer. Patterns derived from Sèvres. Heavy gilding with brightly painted flower decorations.
- Factory closed in 1838.

A rare Philadelphia Tucker porcelain vaseform pitcher with polychrome floral sprays.

9.25in (23cm) high

£1,800-2,200   NA

A mid-19thC Tucker Philadelphia pitcher, with scalloped rim, hand-painted with sprays of flowers, unmarked, chip to spout, a few flakes to glaze.

8.5in (21.5cm) wide

£600-900   DRA

VIENNA

Porcelain factory founded in 1719 in Vienna, Austria, by Claudius Innocentius Du Paquier, with the assistance of staff from Meissen.

- Body: distinctive smoky tone, sometimes greenish. Similar to Meissen wares in form but with denser decoration: chinoiseries, fleurs des inde, naturalistic flowers (from 1725, before they appeared at Meissen) and extensive use of trellis work or 'Gitterwerk'. Known for Baroque style.
- 1744: Du Paquier relinquished factory to the state. Factory adopted the Austrian shield as a mark.
- c1750: new patterns introduced on Rococo tablewares.

- Plain bases used from mid-1760s.
- 1784: ailing factory unsuccessfully offered for sale. But under the direction of Konrad von Sorgenthal, the factory was transformed into a prosperous concern.
- Simple geometric forms and wares decorated in strong colours and raised gilding. Joseph Leithner introduced a dark-blue glaze in the 1790's, known as 'Leithner blue'.
- Factory closed in 1864.
- Late 19thC: other factories in Vienna and the surrounding area producing similar wares with the style now known as 'Vienna'.

CLOSER LOOK: VIENNA VASE

A late 19thC Vienna porcelain covered urn, the amphora-shaped body with pierced handles and a fluted neck, the body decorated with an oval reserve of a young beauty holding a floral bouquet, within a gilt border on an iridescent oxblood ground, gilt details throughout.

21in (53.5cm) high

£5,000-7,000   FRE

The flared neck is embellished with twin scroll handles in the sinuous, Rococo Revival style. 18thC Rococo handles would be less ornate than these 19thC examples.

Borders of solid colour alternating with a gilded pattern are typical of Vienna.

The gilding on late 19thC Vienna wares copied the heavy, three-dimensional style that had been introduced in the late 18thC.

Sensitive painting of complex scenes – such as this interior featuring scenes from the life of Napoleon Bonaparte – were deftly handled by the factory's artists and appealed to the fascination with history that was popular at the time.

A late 19thC Vienna porcelain vase, painted with Napoleonic interior scenes, against a gilt enriched cobalt blue ground, blue beehive mark.

£8,000-10,000   FRE

29in (73.5cm) high

PORCELAIN

A late 19thC Vienna porcelain cabinet vase, 'Reflection', decorated with a portrait on an iridescent sang du boeuf ground with gilt highlights, painted and blue underglazed marks, signed 'Wagner'.

7in (18cm) high

£600-900   **FRE**

A large Royal Vienna covered vase, painted with three Classical beauties, with raised gilt floral decoration, the gilt metal mounted cover with a pinecone finial, blue beehive mark.

c1890   *33.5in (85cm) high*

£5,000-7,000   **FRE**

A set of twelve late 19thC Vienna porcelain plates, each painted with a young draped beauty within riverside and garden landscapes, entitled verso, blue beehive mark.

9in (23cm) diam

£7,000-9,000   **FRE**

A late 19thC framed oval Vienna porcelain plaque, finely painted with a biblical scene depicting Samson & Delilah, within a baroque gilt enhanced border.

16.25in (41cm) wide

£2,500-3,000   **FRE**

A late 19thC Vienna porcelain cabinet plate, depicting a Gypsy woman, within a gilt enriched celadon lustre border, blue beehive mark, illegible inscription to the reverse.

9.5in (24cm) diam

£300-400   **FRE**

A late 19th/early 20thC Vienna porcelain cabinet plate, depicting the figure of Echo, within a cobalt and gilt enhanced border, underglaze blue beehive mark, framed.

9.5in (24cm) diam

£450-550   **FRE**

A late 19thC Vienna cabinet plate, depicting Napoleon's withdrawal from Russia, signed 'Wagner', within a red and gilt enhanced border, underglaze blue beehive mark, framed.

9.5in (24cm) diam

£1,500-2,000   **FRE**

A rare cased set of six mid-18thC Vienna custard cups and covers, each painted in polychrome with forget-me-not sprigs beneath leaf trails, shield marks.

3.25in (8.5cm) high

£800-1,200   **WW**

A Vienna coffee can and cover, painted with a battle scene between the Romans and the Sabines, painted shield mark, the knop broken and repaired.

c1804   *3.5in (9cm) high*

£700-900   **WW**

A 19thC Vienna-style coffee can and saucer, painted with a man sitting cross-legged beside a woman with an arrow through her heart, raised gilding to the coloured panel ground.

£450-550   **WW**

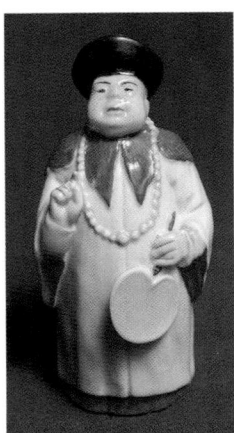

ESSENTIAL REFERENCE: WORCESTER

Porcelain factory founded in 1751. Took over the stock and secrets of Lund's Bristol porcelain factory the following year.

- First porcelain of soft paste, including soaprock (steatite).
- 1751-56: useful wares, especially tea wares, and vases. Chinoiserie motifs in underglaze blue/enamel colours.
- c1751-53: blue and white and 'famille verte' polychrome wares produced.
- c1752-54: incised cross or line mark used.
- cl755-60: polychrome decoration crisp and clean. Almost all patterns based on Chinese prototypes.
- Transfer printed wares appear c1757. At first overglaze in black, by 1760 also underglaze in blue.
- 1760-76: most blue and white pieces marked with a crescent.
- 1760s: much rich enamel painting apparently executed outside the factory.
- Post 1760s saw a tendency to imitate Sèvres.
- The factory was bought by Thomas Flight in 1783 for sons, Joseph and John. Formula for paste modified.
- 1793-1807: named 'Flight & Barr'.
- 1807-14: named 'Barr, Flight & Barr'
- 1814-40: named 'Flight, Barr & Barr'.
- 1840: amalgamated with factory started by R. Chamberlain with production moving to their workshops.
- 1852: renamed 'Kerr & Binns'.
- 1862: renamed 'Royal Worcester'. Period of elaborate, richly gilded/painted and jewelled decoration.
- 1870s-80s: Japanese influence.
- 19th/early 20thC: many wares decorated with rich bunches of flowers or fruit on a cream or light ground.
- Factory still active.

A Worcester feather moulded coffeepot and cover, painted in blue with two birds above leafy tendrils, 'C' mark, rim crack.

c1765   *9in (23cm) high*

£300-400   **WW**

A Worcester mustard pot and cover, printed in blue with flowers and butterflies, printed crescent mark, small chips to the knop.

c1770

£150-250   **WW**

A Worcester teapot and cover, printed in blue with flower sprays and butterflies, crescent mark, a small crack to the tip of the spout.

c1770   *7.5in (19cm) high*

£150-250   **WW**

A large Worcester blue and white teapot and cover, decorated with the 'Mansfield' pattern, blue crescent mark, knop riveted.

c1770   *8.25in (21cm) high*

£250-300   **WW**

An 18thC Worcester covered jug, with strap handle, blue painted with floral sprays and butterflies.

11.5in (29cm) high

£400-600   **DAH**

A Worcester tankard, printed with Liberty seated among trophies of war, a portrait of George II, and a warship, 'RH Worcester' mark and anchor rebus for Richard Holdship.

c1755-60   *6.25in (16cm) high*

£1,200-1,400   **WW**

A fine Worcester cylindrical mug, printed in black from a design by Robert Hancock with the arms of the Grand Lodge and the motto 'Amor Honor Et Justitia Sit Lux Et Lux Fuit' amidst Masonic emblems, with three figures to the left, paper labels for the Zorensky Collection and the Sir Jeremy Lever Collection, a 2cm haircrack to the rim.

c1760-62   *4.75in (12cm) high*

£1,000-1,500   **WW**

A Worcester 'King of Prussia' mug, printed in black by Robert Hancock with a half-length portrait of Frederick the Great above the date '1757' gesturing towards trophies of war and battle honours, 'RH' monogram for Hancock and anchor for Richard Holdship.

1757 was a year into the Seven Years War (1756-63) which saw Prussia, Hanover and Great Britain allied against the might of Austria, France and much of the Holy Roman Empire. The names inscribed on the flags are Frederick's victories or those of his marshals against France and Austria. The outcome of this truly global war was to see two relatively small powers emerge with significant gains, Prussia supplanting the Holy Roman Empire in importance in the German region and Britain supplanting France as the major European colonial power (France would loose most of her North American possessions).

3.25in (8.5cm) high

£500-700   **DN**

A Worcester blue and white sauceboat, painted with the 'Little Fisherman' pattern, open crescent mark.

c1765   *6in (15.5cm) high*

£350-450   **WW**

A Worcester two-handled sauceboat, painted in blue with a Chinese landscape to the interior, the exterior with four chinoiserie cartouches, workman's mark, minor wear and damages.

c1760   *6.5in (16.5cm) high*

£250-350   **WW**

A Worcester strap-fluted sauceboat, painted in blue with flowers and leaf sprigs, open crescent mark.

c1770-80   *5.5in (14cm) high*

£150-250   **WW**

A Worcester blue and white fluted jug, painted in blue with the Mansfield pattern, painted crescent mark.

c1760   *3.75in (9.5cm) high*

£500-700   **WW**

A Worcester shell moulded pickle dish, painted in blue with the 'Two-Peony Rock Bird' pattern, workman's mark to the base, two rim chips.

c1754-58   *3.5in (9cm) high*

£200-300   **WW**

A Worcester shell moulded pickle dish, painted in blue with the 'Two-Peony Rock Bird' pattern, workman's mark to the base.

c1754-58   *4.25in (11cm) high*

£400-500   **WW**

A Worcester leaf moulded pickle dish, painted in blue with the 'Two-Peony Rock Bird' pattern, workman's mark, minor damages and restoration.

c1754-58   *4.5in (11cm) high*

£200-300   **WW**

A Worcester leaf moulded pickle dish, painted in blue with the 'Two-Peony Rock Bird' pattern, workman's mark, a small chip to one point.

c1755-60   *4in (10cm) high*

£450-550   **WW**

A Worcester pickle dish, painted in blue with the 'Pickle Leaf Daisy' pattern, the exterior moulded, workman's mark in blue.

c1760-65   *5.5in (14cm) high*

£600-800   **WW**

A Worcester pickle dish, painted in blue with the 'Pickle Leaf Vine' pattern, crescent mark, minor glaze chips to the rim.

c1760-70   *3.25in (8.5cm) high*

£100-200   **WW**

A Worcester 'Blind Earl' sweetmeat dish, painted in blue with leaves and insects, open crescent mark.

The design originated at the Chelsea porcelain factory and was also produced at Worcester from the 1750s. In the 19thC the pattern was named after the Earl of Coventry, who lost his sight in a riding accident. He ordered a service in this pattern so that he could feel the raised decoration.

c1765   *6in (15cm) high*

£900-1,200   **WW**

A small Worcester basket with reticulated sides, printed in blue with the 'Pine Cone' pattern, crescent mark.

c1770-80   *4.5in (11.5cm) high*
£400-500   **WW**

A Worcester chestnut basket and cover, with applied twig and flower handles, the lobed body printed with quatrefoil flower heads, crescent mark, damages and restoration.

c1770-75   *8in (20.5cm) high*
£300-400   **WW**

A Worcester basket with pierced rim, printed in blue with 'The Pine Cone' pattern, open crescent mark.

c1775-85   *8.5in (21.5cm) high*
£250-350   **WW**

A Worcester moulded salad bowl, printed in blue with various flower sprays and a hatched border, open crescent mark.

c1775-85   *9.75in (24.5cm) high*
£400-600   **WW**

A Worcester blue and white bowl, painted in the 'Floral Queen' pattern.

c1770   *6in (15.5cm) high*
£250-350   **WW**

A Worcester moulded leaf dish, printed in black with three butterflies within a painted pale green border, unmarked, the handle broken and repaired.

c1757   *7in (17.5cm) high*
£400-500   **WW**

A Worcester octagonal plate, painted in the Kakiemon palette with the 'Quail' pattern, unmarked, rim chip and crack.

c1760   *9.25in (23.5cm) high*
£100-200   **WW**

A pair of Worcester basket stands with pierced floral rims, painted with flower sprays, the handles formed as twigs with applied flower heads, unmarked, damages and restoration.

c1765   *10in (25.5cm) high*
£600-800   **WW**

A Worcester 'Blind Earl' sweetmeat dish, painted in the Japanese style with flowers within a border of iron red, black and gilt starbursts, paper label for the Zorensky Collection.

c1765-70   *6in (15cm) high*
£800-1,200   **WW**

A Worcester plate, painted with the 'Sir Joshua Reynolds' pattern within a gilt-decorated blue border, an upper case 'W' mark, paper label for the M. H. Stieglitz Collection.

c1770   *7.5in (19cm) high*
£350-400   **WW**

A Worcester double leaf moulded dish, painted with chrysanthemum and prunus in the Imari palette, paper label for the Zorensky Collection, restored cracks.

c1770   *10.25in (26cm) high*

£150-250   **WW**

A late18thC Worcester 'Blind Earl' sweetmeat dish, painted in the 'Rich Queen's' pattern, square seal mark in blue, some restoration.

6.25in (16cm) high

£350-450   **WW**

A Worcester Imari palette dish, of kidney form in the 'Pavilion' pattern, the central reserve depicting a pavilion, prunus tree and clouds, the border with alternating foliate and dragon panels, with gilt highlights.

10in (25.5cm) long

£300-400   **FRE**

An early Worcester sauceboat, silver shape, moulded with Rococo scrollwork, the scroll handle with pronounced thumb-rest, painted in coloured enamel with oriental figures and flowers, the interior with flowers and foliage, on footed base, cracked.

c1753   *7.5in (19cm) wide*

£300-350   **NEA**

A small Worcester jug, richly painted in the Imari palette with the 'Queen Charlotte' pattern, seal mark to the base.

c1770   *3.25in (8cm) high*

£500-700   **WW**

A Worcester teapot and cover, painted in polychrome enamels, with four Chinese figures and a cat, applied flower finial, unmarked.

c1770   *7in (18cm) high*

£500-800   **WW**

A Worcester feather-moulded baluster cream jug, with scroll handle, painted in the famille rose palette, with flowering shrub, a crane, and an insect, workman's mark.

c1760   *3.5in (9cm) high*

£1,800-2,200   **DN**

A Worcester blue scale porcelain teapot, with floral reserves on a blue scale ground, gilt details, underglazed blue half moon mark.

c1770   *5.5in (14cm) high*

£400-600   **FRE**

A pair of 18thC Worcester pierced circular baskets, the blue scale ground painted with garlands, blue square seal mark, one repaired.

7.5in diam

£1,500-2,500

JN

A Worcester blue-ground guglet and fluted basin, the guglet of octagonal pear shape, painted with two large gilt-edged panels of exotic birds, the neck reserved with two smaller panels of birds in flight.

c1768-70   basin 11in (28cm) wide

£8,000-10,000

SOTH

A Worcester two-tiered scallop shell sweetmeat dish, painted with flowers and encrusted with polychrome shells, unmarked, restored.

c1765-70   7.5in (19cm) high

£600-900

WW

A pair of Worcester blue-scale ground hexagonal vases and covers, painted with Kakiemon style panels of birds and flowers within elaborate gilt frames against a blue-scale ground, fretted square mark in underglaze-blue.

c1770   11.75in (30cm) high

£11,000-13,000

SOTH

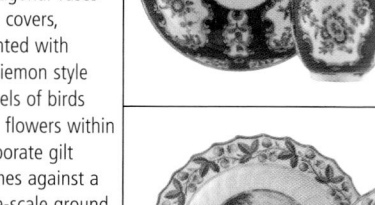

A Worcester scale blue coffee cup and saucer, painted with panels of flowers, square seal marks.

c1770

£150-250

WW

A Worcester bowl, decorated with a bleu céleste ground within a gilt border, crossed swords mark with '9' between the blades, some wear to the enamel.

c1775-85   6.25in (16cm) high

£250-350

WW

Left: A Flight & Barr circular scalloped topographical fruit plate, with a gilt rim, the border decorated in sepia with strawberry plants, the well also decorated in sepia with a view of 'West Wycombe Park, the seat of Sir John Dashwood King, Bart', with fishermen by a river in the foreground, painted mark 'Flight & Barr, Wor.r Manufacturers to their Majesties' and place name.

c1795   9in (23cm) diam

£200-300

L&T

Centre: A Flight & Barr scalloped oval single handled topographical fruit dish, with a gilt rim, the border decorated in sepia with strawberry plants, the well also decorated in sepia with a view of 'Cowes Castle, Isle of Wight', painted mark 'Flight & Barr, Wor.r Manufacturers to their Majesties' and place name.

c1795   8in (20cm) wide

£350-400

L&T

A Barr Worcester tea service, comprising a teapot, cover and stand, a sugar bowl, milk jug, cake plate, slop bowl, six tea cups, five coffee cans and six saucers, richly decorated in gilt leaves and floral swags on a dark blue ground, incised marks.

c1798

£1,200-1,800

WW

Right: A Flight & Barr circular scalloped topographical fruit plate, with a gilt rim, the border decorated in sepia with strawberry plants, the well also decorated in sepia with a view of 'Friar's Carse, Dumfries-shire, the seat of Robert Riddell, Esq', with fishermen by a river in the foreground, painted mark 'Flight & Barr, Wor.r Manufacturers to their Majesties' and place name.

c1795   9in (23cm) diam

£300-400

L&T

CLOSER LOOK: BARR, FLIGHT AND BARR VASE

Barr, Flight and Barr's Neoclassical decoration was increasingly exuberant and sophisticated.

The marbled ground painted around the neck of the vase is typical of Worcester at this time.

This vase is in the fashionable Neoclassical urn shape and features dolphin and shell handles. These are less restrained than many examples of the period and have been extravagantly gilded.

The flowers are almost lifelike. Worcester was renowned for its high quality painting during the early 19thC.

An early 19thC Flight Barr and Barr Worcester plaque, painted with flowers on a dark green ground, probably by Samuel Astles, in a gilt and velvet frame, impressed marks.

11in (28cm) high

£900-1,200   **WW**

A Barr, Flight & Barr two-handled vase, shield-shaped body painted with a panel of flowers against a blue ground within a gilt frame, reserved on a black and white marbled ground, the shoulders set within gilt dolphin and shell moulded handles, raised on a gilt square base and four paw feet, puce script mark.

c1810   *14.25in (36cm)*

£4,500-6,500   **SOTH**

An early 19thC Flight Barr and Barr muffin dish and cover, printed in black with farming figures and harvest scenes on a pale yellow ground, impressed crowned 'FBB' mark, some wear to the gilding.

8.25in (21cm) high

£350-400   **WW**

A Flight Barr and Barr Worcester soup tureen, cover and stand, painted with a band of leaves and flowers in purple and gilt, impressed mark to the stand, some wear to the gilding and a small restored chip.

c1825

£250-350   **WW**

A pair of 19thC Worcester porcelain 'Dr. Syntax' plates, titled 'Dr. Syntax reading his town (?)' and 'Dr. Syntax loses his wig', each scene within a gilt-enriched cobalt border decorated with floral sprays.

8.5in (21.5cm) diam

£700-900   **FRE**

A pair of Royal Worcester candlestick figures, modelled as a young man and woman carrying baskets on their shoulders, details highlighted in pink, green, blue and gilding, green printed marks, date code.

1864   *11in (28cm) high*

£350-450   **WW**

A pair of Royal Worcester figural casters, moulded as a boy and a girl in Victorian dress, printed marks.

c1880   *7in (18cm) high*

£400-600   **WW**

PORCELAIN

A pair of Blush Worcester porcelain figural vases by James Hadley, depicting a girl and boy playing a whistle and drinking from a jug, each flanking an ovoid urn, on rockwork circular bases.

c1890 *7.25in (18.5cm)*

£1,000-1,200 **HT**

A Royal Worcester miniature Toby jug, standing wearing a red coat and holding a goblet, printed mark and date code.

1931 *3.5in (9cm) high*

£70-100 **WW**

A pair of Royal Worcester figures, 'Joy' and 'Sorrow', by James Hadley, printed marks, date code, slight scratches and crazed.

1932 *9.5in (24cm) high*

£800-1,000 **A&G**

A Royal Worcester model of a sheep, standing on a green base with head turned to dexter, modelled by B Bargas, printed mark and model number '3155'.

c1936 *5in (13cm) high*

£600-900 **WW**

A Royal Worcester figure of Wellington, from the Famous Military Commanders series, modelled by Bernard Winskill, limited edition number 324 of 750, raised on wooden display stand, with certificate and original packing.

17in (43cm) high

£1,200-1,400 **HALL**

A Royal Worcester figure of Napoleon Bonaparte, after David, from the Famous Military Commanders series, modelled by Bernard Winskill, limited edition number 179 of 750, raised on wooden display stand, with original certificate and packing.

15.75in (40cm) high

£800-1,200 **HALL**

A Royal Worcester vase, decorated with chrysanthemums on a blush ground, printed mark with date code, some wear to the enamels and gilding.

1890 *11.25in (28.5cm) high*

£150-200 **WW**

An unusual pair of Royal Worcester vases, each supported on the backs of three black swans on trefoil bases, the purple glaze fading to white at the shoulders, restored rim chip to one vase, printed factory mark and date code.

1863 *8.5in (21.5cm) high*

£400-600 **WW**

A pair of Royal Worcester porcelain vases, of waisted form painted by Jas. Stinton with pheasants, signed, with gilded rim and foot.

1922 *7.5in (19in) high*

£1,000-1,500 **HT**

A late 19thC Royal Worcester part dinner service, comprising a meat plate, ten dinner plates and soup plate, decorated in blue, red and gilt with stylised flowers and foliage and decorative bands, printed and impressed marks.

Meat plate 17.25in (44cm) wide

£120-180 ROS

A Royal Worcester low comport, painted by J. Ruston, the gold-painted body with a jewelled border and edged vignettes, painted with satyrs and nymphs being attacked by a grotesque monster.

12in (30.5cm) diam

£400-500 SWO

A pair of Royal Worcester vases by Harry Davies, each pedestal ovoid vase enamelled with castles and ruins against a mountainous and woodland landscape with figures to the foreground, each within gilt reserve and against cobalt ground, the shoulders applied with gilt highlighted and scroll moulded handles below a flared neck, all raised on canted square plinth base, green printed mark and model number '1969', date code.

1909 *20in (50.5cm) high*

£6,000-9,000 HALL

A Royal Worcester plate, decorated with a girl standing in the front door of a thatched cottage, signed 'C. Creese', titled 'Harrington' to the reverse, printed mark and date code.

1930 *8.75in (22.5cm) high*

£100-150 WW

A Chamberlain's Worcester shaped rectangular tray, painted with a titled view 'Osterley Park', within a surround of applied brightly coloured shells and seaweed, moulded gilt scroll and foliate rim, red-painted script mark and title.

c1840 *13.25in (33.5cm) wide*

£800-1,000 SOTH

A pair of Chamberlain's Worcester plates, the centres painted with flowers, the pink borders with gilt coral trails, printed marks.

c1845 *9.5in (24cm) diam*

£250-350 WW

An early 19thC Chamberlain's Worcester plate, the well decorated with chrysanthemums in overglaze blue enamel, the border with flowers in the Kakiemon palette, printed mark.

9in (23cm) diam

£70-100 WW

A Chamberlain's Worcester model of a milkmaid, wearing a plumed hat and with a milk churn hanging from one arm, painted mark, restored, one churn missing.

c1830 *7in (17.5cm) high*

£50-150 WW

A 19thC Chamberlain's Worcester cup and saucer, well painted with colourful flowers encircled by gold foliage on a blue ground, printed marks.

£350-450 WW

An early 19thC pair of Chamberlain's Worcester plates, a matching cup and saucer, and a waste bowl, all decorated in the Imari style with pattern number 276.

8.5in (21.5cm) diam

£250-350 WW

A Chamberlain's Worcester double-walled reticulated sugar bowl, the handles painted as bamboo, painted mark.

c1850 *5.5in (14cm) high*

£300-500 WW

PORCELAIN

BELLEEK

Founded in 1857 in the village of Belleek, Ireland, by John Caldwell Bloomfield, David McBirney and Robert Armstrong, Belleek Pottery initially produced earthenware fired with peat. These early wares included floor tiles and hospital ware.

- In 1863, a number of Stoke-on-Trent craftsmen joined the firm and it began to successfully produce Parian porcelain.
- By 1865, Belleek had established a growing market throughout Ireland and the UK and was exporting pieces to the US, Canada and Australia.
- The factory produced a wide variety of wares, including porcelain vases, flower-pots and centrepieces, often decorated with flowers, or marine motifs. The factory also produced a range of approximately 30 figures and busts. Belleek's most extensive range was tea ware. More than 36 patterns have been used, including 'Shamrock', 'Tridacna', and 'Neptune'. They are typically off-white, green or pink coloured.
- The openwork baskets, with applied flowers, for which Belleek is famous, were designed and developed by William Henshall, one of craftsmen from Stoke-on-Trent. The earliest baskets to be introduced were the 'Henshell', 'Convolvulus', 'Twig', 'Sydenham' and 'Shamrock' designs. The finest is thought to be 'Rathmore'.
- Covered baskets were particularly difficult to produce as both pieces were made at the same time and were prone to failure.
- The history of the factory has been divided into nine periods, and the marks change accordingly.
- The factory is still in operation today.

A late 19thC Belleek oval lidded basket, the cover applied with thistles, shamrock and roses, impressed 'Belleek Co. Fermanagh' mark, the basket handles missing, other minor damages.

12.25in (31cm) high

£550-750   **WW**

A Belleek porcelain reticulated fruit basket, having a basket weave centre bowl with an interlaced border applied with various flowers and branch-form handles, impressed 'BELLEEK' and 'IRELAND'.

9.5in (24cm) diam

£500-700   **FRE**

A Belleek porcelain reticulated covered basket, of oval form with a latticework body and interlaced loop border applied with roses, thistles and shamrocks and with twin branch-form handles, the cover similarly decorated, impressed 'BELLEEK' and ''IRELAND'.

12in (30.5cm) wide

£800-1,000   **FRE**

A pair of 19thC Bing & Grondhal bisque figures, depicting Jason and his golden fleece and Venus holding an apple, impressed marks.

13.75in (35cm) high

£1,200-1,800   **L&T**

A set of twelve late 19thC Bodley and Son porcelain plates, by J. Birkeek, and retailed by Bailey, Banks & Biddle, Philadelphia, each painted with different game bird, printed mark.

9in (23cm) diam

£1,000-1,500   **FRE**

A Champion's Bristol teapot, with an associated pottery cover, painted blue 'X' mark

c1770-1780   *8.25in (21cm) high*

£250-350   **WW**

A set of twelve 19thC Capodimonte porcelain plates, decorated with different armorial crests within a gilt border, the rims moulded with continuous Classical landscapes depicting figures in various pursuits, blue underglazed mark.

10in (25.5cm) diam

£1,200-1,800   **FRE**

A late 18thC Chantilly plate, painted in blue with a floral design, the rim lobed and moulded, unmarked.

9.5in (24cm) diam

£50-80   **WW**

A Copeland Parian bust of Princess Alexandra, raised on a socle, sculpted by F. M. Miller for the Crystal Palace Art Union, impressed marks including the date.

1863   *11in (30cm) high*

£180-220   **WW**

A Copeland Parian bust of Spring, sculpted by L. A. Malempré, impressed marks including publication date.

1870   *12.25in (31cm) high*

£200-300   **WW**

A late 19thC Copeland china trough and stand of elongated rectangular form, with scrolling rim, the sides painted with holly, printed Copeland mark and registration mark.

Trough 25in (63cm) wide

£700-1,000   **L&T**

A pair of 19thC Copenhagen bisque porcelain figures in the form of Classical figures, raised on square bases, blue wave mark.

13in (33cm) high

£1,500-2,000   **L&T**

A late 18thC Copenhagen tureen and cover, of oval form, the cover with pear-form finial, the borders with moulded basket work, painted with flower sprays and further flower sprigs.

12.5in (31.5cm) high

£800-1,200   **L&T**

CLOSER LOOK: GIRL IN A SWING ÉTUI

'Girl in a Swing' is the name attributed to a London porcelain factory, established by Charles Gouyn, which operated from 1749-59 from his Bennet Street home.

Gouyn was a china retailer and jeweller who specialised in making novelties such as scent bottles, small figures, étuis and bonbonnières.

The name was derived from some figures attributed to his factory, which are now in London's Victoria & Albert Museum and the Boston Museum of Fine Arts.

An H & R Daniel botanical dessert service, comprising a tazza, two sauce tureens, stands and covers, four dishes, four small stands, twelve plates, each piece painted with a different flower, damages and restoration.

c1835

£400-600   **WW**

A Doccia plate, painted with scattered floral sprays in the manner of Chinese famille rose.

c1760   *10.5in (27cm) diam*

£150-200   **WW**

A late 18thC Doccia model of a young woman, wearing a purple shawl and a dark blue skirt, holding a spotted yellow bundle, restoration to her right arm.

5.5in (14cm) high

£900-1,200   **WW**

A rare Girl in a Swing étui, the cylindrical body delicately painted with flower sprays, the lid formed as the head of a young lady, wearing a mask and a white headscarf, her eyes set with single cut diamonds.

c1755   5in (12.5cm) high

£5,000-6,000   **WW**

PORCELAIN

A Höchst figure of a little barrel maker, large haircrack through his body, crowned wheel mark in underglaze blue, raised hand restored.

c1765   4in (10cm) high

£300-400   **SOTA**

A Höchst figure of a boy leaning forward with outstretched arm, holding a bird, standing on a naturalistic base, wheel mark in underglaze blue, incised N and 18.

                    25in (10.5cm) high

£600-800   **GORL**

A Höchst figure of a girl, holding a grapevine, on a rockwork base, wheel mark in iron red, minor damages.

c1760   6.25in (16cm) high

£400-600   **WW**

A late 19thC Hutschrenreuther porcelain plaque, 'Marguerite', the standing figure with daisies in her hair, numbered '311', signed 'Wagner'.

                    7.25in (18.5cm) high

£1,500-2,000   **FRE**

A blue and white coffee cup, probably Isleworth, painted with a mountainous Chinese landscape, minor chips and firing faults.

c1760-70   3in (8cm) high

£500-700   **WW**

A pair of English pâte-sur-pâte vases, probably by George Jones, of flattened ovoid form, the sides painted and hand-tooled in white slip with a nymph and a cherub fishing beside a pond, with gilt loop handles and marked in gilt '5639 13'.

c1880   6in (15cm) high

£2,000-3,000   **FRE**

A late 18thC Kloster-Veilsdorf figure of a bacchante, draped with an applied grapevine and with flowers garlanded in her hair, restored.

                    7.5in (19cm) high

£350-400   **WW**

An Isaac Broome parian bust of Ulysses S. Grant, signed 'BROOME Sculp'1876 LENOX Pottery 1914'.

                    9.75in (24.5cm) high

£1,000-2,000   **DRA**

A Limoges porcelain plaque, 'Gypsy', painted with a dark-haired beauty adorned in gold jewellery, wearing a head scarf.

£600-800   **FRE**

A Limoges chocolate set, comprising: a tray, a chocolate pot and cover, a sugar bowl and cover, a milk jug and three cups with covers, moulded with foliate scrolls and painted with sprays of flowers within gilt borders, printed marks.

c1900

£200-300   **WW**

A Christian's Liverpool teapot and cover, painted with flowers in polychrome enamels, the shoulders with gilding over a blue ground, the knop formed as a flower, minor damages.

c1770-75   8.75in (22cm) high

£300-500   **WW**

A late 18thC Liverpool porcelain teapot and cover, painted with flower garlands in polychrome enamels.

8.25in (21cm) high

£350-400   **WW**

A pair of Longton Hall figures of an abbess and her novice, seated reading from religious texts, unmarked, restoration to both.

c1755-60   5in (12.5cm) high

£1,200-1,400   **WW**

A Lowestoft blue and white teabowl, printed with the 'Good Cross Chapel' pattern, rim crack.

c1780-90   3in (7.5cm) high

£500-700   **WW**

ESSENTIAL REFERENCE: LUDWIGSBURG

Ludwigsburg was one of the many porcelain factories to emulate Meissen wares.

- The factory was founded in Württemberg, Germany, in 1758 by Duke Karl Eugen, starting in a barracks but later moving to a small castle.
- Its first director was Joseph Jakob Ringler, who remained there until 1802.
- Ringler had stolen the secret formula from his previous employer, the Vienna factory, and went on to sell it to Höchst, Strasbourg and Nymphenburg.
- Ringler brought with him Gottlieb Friedrich Riedel, who had been director of painting at Frankenthal.
- Riedel's influence led to the creation of some of Ludwigsburg's finest wares, the Rococo figures.
- Some of the best Rococo pieces were modelled by Johann Christian Wilhelm Beyer.
- Ludwigsburg has a smoky grey-brown tinge to the body of a piece.
- On areas of a figure that have been left white, this greyish glaze gives it the appearance of marble.
- The figures are crisply modelled but tend to lack the movement of Meissen, appearing rather stiff with bland faces.
- Wares were decorated in subtle pastel shades which complimented the smoky tone of the Ludwigsburg glaze.
- The key colours are greyish pinks, blues and greens with yellow, iron-red, black and gilding.
- Ludwigsburg bases vary widely from simple, mottled green-brown grass or rockwork mounds and slabs, to rich Rococo forms, with gilded highlights.
- Despite the input of Neoclassical sculptor Johann Heinrich von Dannecker in the 1790s, and a brief revival at the turn of the century, the factory went into decline and closed in 1824.

A late 18thC Ludwigsburg figure of a female folk dancer, holding a percussion instrument in each hand, raised on a small scrolled base, painted and incised marks, minor damages.

6in (15.5cm) high

£500-700   **WW**

A Ludwigsburg group of a fortune teller, modelled by Johann Valentin Sonnenschein, interlacing 'C' in underglaze blue, restored.

c1775   8.25in (21cm) high

£400-600   **SOTA**

PORCELAIN

A pair of late 18thC Ludwigsburg figures of putti musicians, one playing a violin, the second a triangle, raised on plinths, crowned double 'C' monogram marks, minor damages.

5.5in (14cm) high

£250-350   **WW**

A Lynton bough pot and cover, of bombé form, the central panel painted and signed by Stefen Nowacki, with a scene of a Dutch man o' war and other ships, the reverse with shells, seaweed and coral, the turqouise ground with a raised gilt lattice, gilt rim, detachable pierced cover with circular gilt flower holders, printed marks in gilt.

10.5in (27cm) wide

£1,000-1,500   **NEA**

A 20thC Lynton bower pot and cover, painted by Stefan Nowacki with a scene of ships at sail in a stormy sea before a cliff-top fort in the distance, within a richly gilded panel on a blue-scale ground, the cover pierced with seven holes, printed factory mark.

7.25in (21.5cm) high

£400-600   **WW**

A pair of Mennecy cups and trembleuse saucers, painted with sprays of pink roses and other blooms, the cup handles formed as stalks issuing from leaves and berries, incised 'D.V' marks, minor wear.

c1760

£1,700-2,000   **WW**

An early 19thC New Hall part tea service, comprising teapot and cover, sugar bowl, cover and stand, milk jug, cake plate, slop bowl, five teacups, three coffee cups and six saucers, decorated with oak leaves and acorns in gilt and dark blue, pattern number 524, some damages.

£250-350   **WW**

A pair of 19thC Niderviller urns and covers, each cover surmounted by acorn finial with bisque fern leaf decoration, the body with applied bisque floral garlands and with female mask handles on a pink and gilt ground, with opposed armorials, one depicting Romulus and Remus suckling, with the initials 'SPQR', above reeded support and faux marble plinth, applied mark to foot.

14in (36cm) high

£1,000-1,500   **L&T**

A mid-18thC moulded Nymphenberg plate, the centre painted with a landscape scene in a Rococo vignette, bordered by leafy swags, impressed mark.

10in (25.5cm) diam

£600-900   **WW**

A late 19thC Paris porcelain and gilt-metal-mounted vase centrepiece.

17in (43cm) wide

£1,000-1,200   **DN**

An early 19thC Pinxton coffee can, painted with a scene of a double-arched bridge over a river, a very faint hairline crack near the base.

3.25in (8cm) high

£300-400   **WW**

A Rockingham tea service, comprising teapot and cover, sugar bowl and cover, milk jug, bowl, fourteen plates, twenty one cups and nine saucers, pattern number 1461, with a different botanical painting on each piece, printed marks, some damages.

c1840

£1,300-1,500   **WW**

A mid-19thC Staffordshire porcelain vase, encrusted all over with apple blossom, some damages.

7in (18cm) high

£100-150   **WW**

A Swansea moulded teacup and saucer, with a wishbone handle, painted with pink roses and gilt sprigs, unmarked.

c1820

£300-400   **WW**

A Tournai teapot (théière globulaires) and cover, from the Duc D'Orléans service, decorated with a blue band set with gilt floral festoons flanking two large geometric medallions enclosing ornithological and two small round medallions enclosing butterflies, the cover with an acorn finial and similar decoration, the base with the names of the birds in black script. '10(...)' in underglaze blue and incised 'B' to the pot, '12' in underglaze-blue to the cover.

In 1787 the Tournai factory received an order for a service for Philippe-Joseph, Duc d'Orléans (1747-93). It is not known whether the entire service was delivered to the Palais-Royale in Chantilly. but it is certain that not all pieces were delivered in 1791. This extensive service comprised a total of 1593 pieces, of which 594 were sold to the Prince of Wales. In total there were three different shapes of teapots made for the service, the théière de forme calabre, théière litron and théière globulaire, all of which were produced in two sizes. This teapot of the largest size, another teapot of this size is kept in the Royal Collection in Windsor. Not even the Royal Manufactory at Sèvres ever produced a service of this extraordinary size. By way of comparison, the Sèvres service for Louis XV (1753-55) consisted of 493 pieces, and the service made for Catherine the Great of Russia (1776-79) comprised 706 pieces.

c1787   *4.75in (12cm) high*

£13,000-15,000   **SOTH**

ESSENTIAL REFERENCE: UNION PORCELAIN WORKS

The Union Porcelain Works was a large American factory that produced porcelain heavily influenced by German porcelain.

- The company was founded in Brooklyn, New York, in 1861, by Thomas Carll Smith (1815-1901).
- Much of the company's wares were produced from a hard paste porcelain.
- Produced inexpensive robust wares, such as door plates and knobs. It also produced commemorative vases, such as the 'Centenary' range, and tableware, including oyster plates.
- Karl Müller was art director from the early 1870s and introduced a characteristically bizarre style, his designs featuring mandarin-head finials, polar bear handles and rabbit-form feet.
- The factory closed in the 1920s.

A moulded and polychromed porcelain ice pitcher, designed by Karl L. H. Müller, the 'Uncle Sam' pitcher, moulded with walrus spout and polar bear handle on ovoid body, moulded with relief figures of King Gambrinus, the Norse God of beer, offering a drink to Brother Jonathan, a character from Royall Tyler's comedy, 'The Contrast', who came to symbolise America and Uncle Sam, the obverse with a fight scene between Bill Nye and Chinese Gambler AH Sin, popular characters of the time, signed 'Union Porcelain Works Greenpoint, N.Y.'.

9.75in (25cm) high

£4,000-6,000   **FRE**

A rare Union Porcelain Works Century vase, designed by Karl Mueller, with buffalo handles decorated in pâte-sur-pâte with busts of George Washington and several vignettes of historical moments, signed with UPW medallion, small chip to bison horn, light wear to gilt at rim.

The large, original example was made for The Philadelphia Centennial Exposition of 1876. This is one of the 14 smaller versions produced after it.

12.75in (32cm) high

£11,000-13,000   **DRA**

PORCELAIN

A porcelain figure of two putti and a goat, possibly Vauxhall, the goat munching on grapes, raised on a scrollwork base with applied flowers, unmarked, damages and restoration.

c1758-60   *6in (15cm) high*

£1,300-1,500   **WW**

A 19thC painted ceramic tile, by Joseph Zasche (Austrian, 1821-1881), with a scene after Albert Jules Edouard's ':a Music sur la Terrasse', framed.

Tile 10in (25.4cm) high

£250-300   **FRE**

A 19thC English loving cup, with turquoise ground, decorated with gilt scrollwork reserved with a rectangular panel depicting a fanciful bird, the reverse with a river landscape.

c1875   *24cm wide*

£300-400   **NEA**

An English painted porcelain plaque, depicting a man wearing a fur coat and holding a spear climbing rocks, possibly John the Baptist, dated and signed 'Slocomb'.

1881   *11.25in (28.5cm) high*

£350-400   **FRE**

A 19thC bisque figure of Cupid, stringing his gilt-brass bow, seated on a draped pedestal with quiver below, on an elliptical serpentine marble base with neoclassical gilt-metal braces, on turned feet.

14in (36cm) high

£1,800-2,200   **L&T**

A pair of 19thC bone china botanical plates, and a matching tazza, lavishly painted with colourful flowers, together with five dishes with similar decoration, the tazza cracked.

10.5in (27cm) diam. max

£200-300   **WW**

An English porcelain cylindrical inkwell, the top painted with a band of flowers, the side with three figures in a landscape, unmarked.

c1825   *4in (10cm) high*

£300-400   **WW**

A bone china plaque painted with the Aintree legend 'Red Rum', standing beneath a tree before a winding river, signed 'Leighton Maybury', painted mark and dated, framed.

1977   *14.5in (37cm) high*

£500-800   **WW**

An English bone china commemorative cup and saucer, printed with a border of safari animals and titled 'Souvenir of the British Empire Exhibition, Wembley, 1925'.

£60-90   **WW**

A mid-19thC English bone china plaque, painted with a Swiss alpine view, verso with iron-red inscription 'Viege or Visp with Monte Rose painted by R. Abbot', mounted in giltwood and gesso frame.

Plaque 6.5in (16.5cm)

£700-900   **DN**

A 19thC bone china jug, painted with bands of flowers on a gilt ground, with the initials 'AB' to one side and 'CB' to the other within oval panels, unmarked, some wear to the gilding.

7in (18cm) high

£500-700   **WW**

A blanc de chine porcelain figure, modelled after the Barberini Faun, seated on a tree stump, applied with fruiting vines, raised on a Rococo scroll base.

13.75in (35cm) high

£1,400-1,600   **L&T**

Four plates, by Joseph Crawhall II, each hand-painted with exotic birds, with two examples bearing thumbnail head and shoulder self-portraits on reverse, all signed, three also dated 'Oct 1885', 'Oct 1885' and 'Nov 1885'.

1885

£1,500-2,000   **A&G**

A late 19thC French painted ceramic tile, by Laure Levy (French, 1866-1954), with scene depicting a coastal chateau and figures in a small rowing boat, signed 'Laure Levy', framed.

8.25in (21cm) high

£200-300   **FRE**

A pair of 20thC Continental porcelain yellow-ground vases and covers, in the Worcester style, painted with panels of parakeets and flowers, unmarked, minor wear to the gilding.

14.25in (36cm) high

£200-300   **WW**

A pair of 18th/19thC French Kakiemon style vases on brass mounts, of octagonal bottle form, scroll leaf-painted neck, the ovoid body painted with floral sprays and blue and red butterflies, brass mount to base.

8in (20.5cm) high

£900-1,200   **FRE**

A French polychromed and gilt porcelain deep dish, oblong shape decorated with crossed anchors and French and American flags above 'The Steamer Chateau Yquem' within a scrolled gilt reserve.

c1900   *15in (38cm) wide*

£400-600   **FRE**

A pair of early 20thC Chelsea style porcelain figures, modelled as a seated gentleman and a lady, he with a dog at his feet, she with a sheep, gold anchor mark.

7.5in (19cm) high

£400-600   **FRE**

A Louis XV style blue porcelain and gilt-metal-mounted urn, the upper half with floral garlands and opposing ribbon tied oval portrait medallions, the leafy scroll side supports with female portrait heads and lower hairy paw feet, the fluted spreading foot on a shaped plinth base.

24in (61cm) high

£400-500   **L&T**

An 18thC Continental porcelain moulded cylindrical étui, painted in purple with scenes of young ladies and gentlemen before trees and Classical plinths, a restored chip.

4.5in (11.5cm) high

£700-1,000   **WW**

PORCELAIN

A 19th/20thC Continental porcelain tea service, comprising a tray, teapot and cover, sugar bowl, milk jug, four cups and four saucers, decorated with panels of birds and flowers on a yellow and gilt ground, printed overglaze marks.

£50-150 WW

A pair of 19thC Continental sweetmeat figures, modelled as musicians, painted with birds, insects and flowers, elaborate 'F' mark to the base, some restoration.

7.25in (18.5cm) high

£200-300 WW

A 19thC miniature porcelain basket of seashells, either side pierced with a hole, unmarked.

2in (5cm) high

£300-400 WW

A pair of 19thC German porcelain figures, modelled as a shepherd and shepherdess, on naturalistic base, underglazed blue pseudo 'Augustus Rex' marks.

9in (3.5cm) high

£600-900 FRE

A late 19thC German porcelain plaque, depicting an interior stable scene of two horses fighting while a stable hand intercedes, an officer standing by, framed.

Plaque 15in (38cm) wide

£3,000-5,000 FRE

A German porcelain plaque, 'The Prodigal Son in the Tavern', after Rembrandt Van Rijn, depicting a Dutch interior with a cavalier and his mistress, spurious impressed cross swords mark, framed.

Rembrandt's painting showed himself and his wife Saskia.

6.75in (17cm) high

£1,500-2,000 FRE

A large Italian ceramic model of a cockerel.

26.5in (67cm) high

£1,200-1,500 L&T

An Italian porcelain model of a dancing man, wearing a green jacket, standing on one leg and holding a posy of flowers, raised on a circular base, two fingers chipped.

c1780-90 *7in (17.5cm) high*

£2,000-2,500 WW

THE POTTERY MARKET

The pottery market has seen a move away from a market where age alone would guarantee strong prices. Any piece that has come on the market that is early, an unusual shape, and particularly well painted has sold well. Dated pieces retain their popularity.

In delftware, patriotic and topographical scenes have grown in popularity, whereas simply painted chinoiserie pieces have been quite sluggish. Unusual subject matter and shape, such as the wig stand on page 69, have been at a premium.

Naïve pottery, with good provenance, has been a strong seller. The Shelley collection in the US saw strong prices for redware,

particularly for a piece that ticks all the boxes, like the lidded jar on page 72.

Creamware is a perpetual favourite. The market is fuelled by interior decorators who like plain creamware in interesting shapes. Commemorative ware has to have a good subject to attract much interest. The same can be said for transfer-printed ware.

Interesting and unusual subject matter will add value and interest. Collectors are extremely discerning and search out the rare and exceptional pieces.

DELFT

An English delft sweetmeat or pickle tray, London or Liverpool, painted in blue with floral sprays within a diaper band border.

c1760

£1,000-1,200　　DN

A pair of Lambeth delft blue and white plates, painted with shepherd and shepherdess in romantic landscape with ruin.

9in (22cm)

£650-750　　DN

A small delftware plate, probably Lambeth, painted with stylised tulips on a pale blue ground, some crazing to the glaze.

c1720-30　　9in (23cm) diam

£200-300　　WW

A delftware dish, painted with a tulip design within a geometric border, possibly Bristol or Brislington, minor good restoration.

c1740　　13in (33cm) diam

£1,500-2,000　　WW

A large blue and white delftware dish, possibly Bristol, minor damages.

c1720　　14in (36cm) diam

£250-350　　WW

A delftware charger, painted in blue with a castle surrounded by boats, on a powdered manganese ground, possibly Wincanton or Bristol.

c1740-1750　　11.5in (29.5cm) high

£400-600　　WW

A mid-18thC delftware charger, painted with a stylised border of flowers and pineapples, some restoration to the rim.

13.5in (34cm) high

£300-500　　WW

A delftware Adam and Eve charger, painted in polychrome with the doomed couple flanking a tree around which a serpent coils, a few small rim chips and glaze lacking from the rim.

From the 1630s to the 1730s, blue-dash chargers, made of tin-glazed earthenware with abstract, floral, religious, patriotic or topographical motifs, were produced by London and Bristol potters. They were decorated in a broad, rough style, in blue, green, tawny-yellow, and rich purplish-brown. The image of Adam and Eve was particularly popular. The fruit which Eve is handing to Adam is typically orange in colour, so it is possible that these dishes are intended as a satire on the ascension of William and Mary of Orange.

c1740   13in (33.5cm) high

£3,500-4,500   WW

A late 17thC oval Delftware three-footed bowl, with rope-twist handles, the interior painted with a figure, the sides with rockwork, plantain and foliage, perhaps Brislington, a few small glaze chips.

8.25in (21cm) high

£1,000-2,000   WW

A large 18thC delft bowl, painted in blue with figures in a village setting, the interior with trees, some restoration to the foot rim.

10.5in (26.5cm) high

£500-700   WW

An 18thC polychrome delftware dish, painted with a pattern of stylised flowers and a banded hedge, minor chips to the glaze at the rim.

13.5in (34cm) diam

£300-500   WW

An 18thC delftware plate with a scalloped rim, painted in blue with a fence, peonies and fronds of foliage, the border with panels of lattice and flowers, minor rim flakes.

8.75in (22cm) diam

£150-250   WW

A mid-18thC delftware dish, painted in polychrome enamels with a pattern of star flowers and leaf fronds within a stylised floral border, minor wear to the enamels.

13.5in (34cm) diam

£1,000-1,500   WW

An English delft blue and white shallow bowl, possibly Bristol, painted with a bird in flight above sponge-decorated trees, blue dash border,

c1700.   9in (22cm) diam

£1,000-1,200   DN

An early 18thC London delft blue and white powder bowl, well painted with a stylised fish within a lappet border, some rim and footrim chips.

9in (23cm) diam

£800-1,200   DN

A mid-18thC delftware bowl, painted in polychrome enamels with a landscape scene, minor cracks and glaze chips.

6.75in (17cm) high

£400-600 WW

An 18thC delftware bowl, painted in polychrome enamels with flowers and insects above a palisade, the interior painted in blue with concentric bands and a floral spray, some damages.

10.5in (27cm) high

£250-350 WW

An 18thC English delft polychrome bowl, decorated with scrolling foliage to the rim, the well decorated with chinoiserie scene with a fence, bold flowers and foliage and an exotic bird in flight.

13.75in (35cm) diam.

£600-800 L&T

A mid-18thC delftware small rectangular flower brick, painted in blue with peony and other flowers above a palisade, the top pierced with nineteen symmetrically arranged holes, '2' mark, damages.

5.5in (14cm) high

£250-350 WW

An English delft flower brick, probably London, painted in blue in panels of Oriental flowering shrubs with birds in flight, rim chips and wear to leading edges.

c1760 *5.75in (14.5cm) long*

£600-800 DN

A London delft blue and white urn, moulded with two masks and painted with churches within a landscape of sponge decorated trees,

c1760. *6in (15cm) high*

£800-1,000 DN

CLOSER LOOK: DELFT WIG STAND

A wig stand was an important accessory at a time when wigs were fashionable.

Delftware was inspired by Chinese ceramics and so Oriental decoration is typical

The blue washed areas are 'trekked' or outlined in black, which characterises a good deal of the delftware in the late 17th/18thC.

Typically, the ceramic is covered with a glaze with many 'pin holes' which were caused when air bubbles in the glaze exploded during firing.

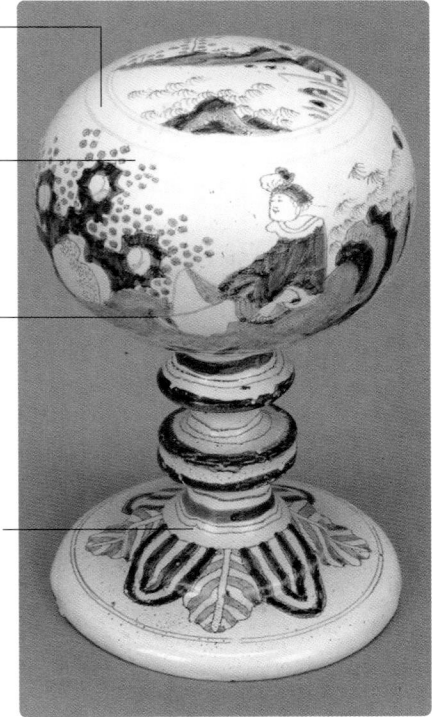

A delft wig stand with top section supported on a double-knopped stem and stepped conical foot, painted in shades of manganese and ochre in the Transitional style.

c1700 *7in (17cm) high*

£5,000-6,000 DN

An 18thC Dutch Delft model of a blue and white seated dog, wearing a collar and holding an object in its mouth, damages.

6.5in (16.5cm) high

£600-800 WW

An early 18thC delftware gallipot or cylindrical drug jar, decorated with concentric manganese bands, probably London, broken and restored.

6.25in (16cm) high

£400-600 WW

A pair of 19thC Dutch Delft tea canisters, with metal mounts and covers, decorated with panels of figures in seascapes on a scrolling foliate ground, minor damages.

5in (12.5cm) high

£150-250 WW

A Dutch Delft octagonal-section baluster vase, De Metalen Pot, painted in shades of iron-red, green and blue with a lappet shoulder of panels of single flowers above a field of floral sprays, iron-red mark.

c1700

£250-350 DN

A late 17th/early 18thC German faïence charger, possibly Frankfurt, decorated after a Wan-Li original, some glaze flakes.

15.75in (40cm) diam.

£300-400   **SOTA**

An 18thC Frankfurt faïence dish, decorated after Wan-Li examples, some minor chips and flakes.

15in (38.5cm) diam.

£500-600   **SOTA**

An Eloury-Porquier Quimper platter, painted with a cornucopia pattern including a bird and butterflies, with rope twist handles, painted monogram mark, one handle restored.

c1850   *20.75in (53cm) high*

£150-250   **WW**

An Italian 18thC faïence plate, probably Savona, the octagonal well decorated in blue with rabbits and a bird, within a shaped foliate border, damages and restoration.

10in (25.5cm) diam

£3,000-4,000   **WW**

A faïence jug, probably Spanish, painted in blue with geometric and foliate bands, the neck bearing the inscription, 'Soy de Manuela Cerrian de Miguel' and the date, the neck and spout damaged.

1852   *9.75in (24.5cm) high*

£50-150   **WW**

A German faïence tankard, with a pewter cover, the lid with an inscription, and engraved with the initials 'F.G.M.W.' and the date, impressed marks to the lid, damages.

1754   *10.25in (26cm) high*

£250-350   **WW**

An 18thC French faïence waisted tambour decorated jardinière, with twin rope-twist handles and decorated with blue line and foliate bands, on a heavily carved ebonised stand.

19.75in (50cm) wide

£800-1,200   **L&T**

A late 18thC Continental faïence model of a cat, seated on a rectangular base, its right forepaw resting on a mouse, probably Brussels.

5.5in (14cm) high

£2,200-2,500   **WW**

An Italian maiolica tile, moulded in relief with a sunburst panel inscribed 'IHS', painted in a ochre glaze and reserved on a blue ground.

9in (23cm)

£500-600 **DN**

A 19thC Cantigalli twin-handled vase, each side painted with a Roman profile portrait surrounded by musical and Classical motifs, the handles formed as snakes above a grotesque mask, cockerel mark to the base, one handle restored.

12.5in (32cm) high

£400-600 **WW**

A Naples maiolica albarello, painted in blue with a townscape and inscribed in manganese and date.

1775 *10.5in (27cm) high*

£500-700 **DN**

A late 18thC Naples maiolica albarello, typically painted in blue with a panel of a townscape, footrim chip.

7.75in (20cm) high

£250-350 **DN**

REDWARE

Redware is the term used to describe the everyday porous red-brown pottery produced largely in the US from the 17thC.

- Early redware was fairly crude in shape and typically covered in lead glaze in browns, yellows, orange or copper green to make it watertight.
- Decoration is bold and lively. The finish is distinctly rustic. Simple slip-decoration was popular from the late 17thC.
- Some wares were made at small potteries, like that of Andrew Duché, and by part-time potters.
- Although redware became less common during the 19thC when mass-produced functional ware became readily available, it continues to be made today.

An early 19thC redware toddy plate, probably Hartford, Connecticut, with free-form mottled yellow slip with green splotches, from the Shelley Collection.

4.75in (12in) diam

£1,500-2,000 **POOK**

A 19thC North Carolina or Pennsylvania redware pie plate, with yellow, green, and brown slip dot and circle flower decoration on an orange-glazed ground.

8.25in (21cm) diam

£1,000-1,500 **POOK**

A 19thC Pennsylvania redware pie plate, probably Dryville, with green and brown four-line slip decoration, from the Shelley Collection.

7.75in (19.5cm) diam

£3,000-4,000 **POOK**

A 19thC Pennsylvania redware pie plate, impressed 'W. Smith Womelsdorf', from the Shelley Collection.

7.75in (20cm) diam

£3,000-4,000 **POOK**

An American redware plate, by Simon Singer (1822-94) Haycock Township, Bucks County, Pennsylvania, inscribed 'M. Singer Applebackville, Bucks Co. Penna', from the Shelley Collection.

12.5in (32cm) diam

£1,500-2,000 **POOK**

A Chester County, Pennsylvania vibrant redware flowerpot and undertray, possibly by Vickers Pottery, from the Shelley Collection.

c1820   *6.75in (17cm) high*

£2,500-3,000   **POOK**

An early 19thC Pennsylvania redware flower pot and undertray, with vibrant yellow and black slip decoration on an orange glaze, from the Shelley Collection.

£500-600   **POOK**

A Chester County, Pennsylvania earthenware jar, attributed to Vickers Pottery, with scraffito leaf decoration, inscribed 'H.g', and dated, from the Shelley Collection.

1808   *8in (20.5cm) high*

£5,000-6,000   **POOK**

A 19thC American redware flower pot, attributed to Absalom Bixler, Earl Township, Lancaster County, Pennsylvania, with relief bird figure, from the Shelley Collection.

6in (15cm) high

£15,000-20,000   **POOK**

A mid-19thC Pennsylvania moulded redware jar, Mechanicsburg, Lancaster County, the front and back with recessed panels with relief figures of George Washington, inscribed 'Washington', the sides with relief figures of hunter and deer, inscribed 'Swope Pottery' for Henry Swope, with overall manganese splash decoration on an orange glaze ground, the base impressed 'GALL', from the Shelley Collection.

9.25in (23.5cm) high

£2,500-3,500   **POOK**

An American redware canister, North Carolina, of coiled form with bands of yellow and green slip on an orange-glazed ground, from the Shelley Collection.

c1800   *6.5in (16.5cm) high*

£6,000-7,000   **POOK**

An American glazed redware lidded jar, Montgomery County, Pennsylvania, all on an orange ground, from the Shelley Collection.

c1780-1840   *10.5in (26.5cm) high*

£10,000-15,000   **POOK**

A late 18th/early 19thC Bristol County, Massachusetts, green-glazed redware covered jar, ovoid form with green copper oxide glaze, the cover with reduced band, minor wear to cover edge.

10.5in (26.5cm) high

£15,000-20,000   **SK**

An English redware canister, with brown squiggle line decoration, initialled 'R.O.', dated.

1764   *4.75in (12.5) high*

£1,500-2,000   **POOK**

An Astbury-type redware mustard pot and cover, sprigged with pipe clay ornaments, restoration to the cover.

c1740   *3.5in (9cm) high*

£250-350   **WW**

A 19thC redware globular pot-pourri vase and cover, decorated with flowers, butterflies and insects, minor damages.

10.5in (26.5cm) high

£100-200   **WW**

An American redware pitcher, probably Chester County, Pennsylvania, with overall black manganese glazing and relief initials 'JF', with relief birds and stars, from the Shelley Collection.

c1800-10   10.5in (26.5cm) high

£3,000-4,000   **POOK**

An American moulded redware pitcher, Virginia, attributed to Solomon Bell, with relief hunting scene, retaining orange glaze with green and brown slip decoration, from the Shelley Collection.

8in (20cm) high

£2,000-3,000   **POOK**

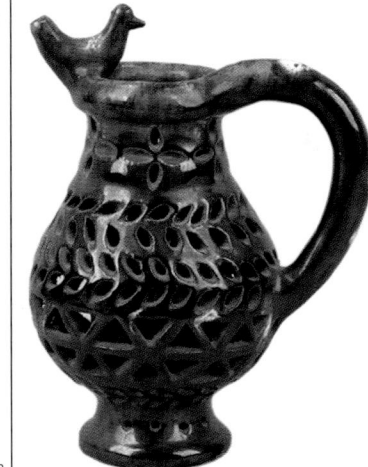

A 19thC American redware puzzle jug, possibly Pennsylvania, with bird spout and overall dark brown manganese glaze and white dots.

From the Shelley Collection.

6in (15cm) high

£4,000-5,000   **POOK**

A Staffordshire redware teapot and cover, in octagonal shape and moulded in relief with Oriental subjects.

c1755   4in (10cm) high

£600-800   **DN**

A Staffordshire redware teapot, of Elers type, cylindrical form with short spout, sprigged with stylised flowers, carved wood replacement cover.

c1700   4in (10cm) high

£1,500-1,800   **DN**

An American redware standish, Montgomery County, Pennsylvania, with dog finial, inscribed 'William Hamalman Medinger 1855', from the Shelley Collection.

William was the father of Jacob Mendiger.

7.75in (19.5cm) high

£2,500-3,500   **POOK**

An American redware ring vase, Montgomery or Bucks County, Pennsylvania, dated, from the Shelley Collection.

1815   8.75in (22cm) high

£3,000-4,000   **POOK**

An American pierced redware footed covered dish, by David Haring (1801-71), Nockamixon Township, Bucks County, Pennsylvania, with rope-twist handles, retaining an overall green glaze, from the Shelley Collection.

6in (15cm) high

£12,000-15,000   **POOK**

A 19thC redware bird-on-stump whistle.

8in (20.5cm) high

£150-350   **POOK**

CLOSER LOOK: REDWARE WALL POCKET

Daniel Peter Shenfelder (1830-1904) started his pottery c1869. Clay for his stoneware was shipped from Delaware, while red clay was dug on his own property. The pottery also made bricks.

In redware Shenfelder made fancy pie plates, vases, sponge cake dishes and large plates with flower designs on them. The applied decoration was carried out by his daughter Mary.

This is a very rare piece by Shenfelder and probably his finest exisiting work .

Shenfelder used this stamped mark on his work.

A 19thC American redware wall pocket, Reading, Pennsylvania, with mask decoration and yellow glaze with green and brown splash, impressed 'D.P. Shenfelder, Reading, PA', from the Shelley Collection.

10.75in (27.5cm) high

£22,000-28,000   **POOK**

POTTERY

An English large 18th/19thC brown-glazed slipware charger, with honey-coloured zigzag, scroll and waved line design, below a toothed rim.

17.75in (45cm) wide

£2,000-3,000 HALL

An American slipware plate, Southwestern Pennsylvania, the centre with three black, green and yellow tulips arising from a yellow heart surrounded by bands of wavy yellow and green slip decoration, all on an orange-glazed background, dated.

1816 *12in (30.5cm) diam*

£50,000-60,000 POOK

A Continental Moravian slip-decorated plate, with yellow and manganese petal decoration, dated, from the Shelley Collection.

1824 *11.5in (29cm) diam*

£2,000-3,000 POOK

ESSENTIAL REFERENCE: SLIPWARE CHARGER

The decoration of a leaping stag with a tree and flowering vine is well executed and exceptionally sophisticated for 18thC earthenware.

The pottery was covered with a layer of slip (liquid clay) glaze and the outline of the design incised into it. This technique is known as sgraffito.

The design was then embellished with further coloured slips to enhance the finished charger.

Dated ceramics such as this one tend to command a premium.

A late 18thC American earthenware charger, attributed to Isaac Stout, Bucks County Pennsylvania, with sgraffito decoration, the centre with a leaping stag, flanked by tree and flowering vine and fence in orange, green, yellow and brown slip, dated. From the Shelley Collection.

1790 *14in (35.5cm) diam*

£50,000-60,000 POOK

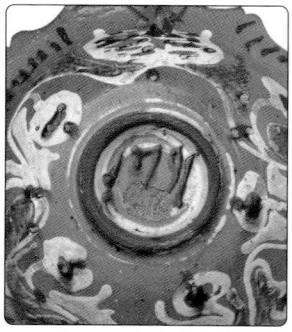

An earthenware barber's bowl, with profuse yellow, green, cream and brown slip flowers, vines and line decoration, dated 1791. From the Shelley Collection.

1791 *6.5in (16.5cm) diam*

£500-1,000 POOK

A 19thC English earthenware bird whistle, in the form of a brown-glazed parrot with yellow slip decoration and round base.

5in (13cm) high

£200-300 POOK

A 19thC Devon slipware bottle vase, decorated with three stencilled fern fronds.

8.5in (21.5cm) high

£100-200 WW

An English 19thC slipware model of a cradle, decorated in a buff glaze with a pattern of swirls and geometric motifs in dark brown, the base unglazed, damages.

11.5in (29.5cm) high

£500-700 WW

ESSENTIAL REFERENCE: AGATEWARE

Agatewate is made from coloured clays which are combined to suggest the veining of a hard stone like agate. It was made in ancient Roman times and was popular in18thC England.

- Initially, the clays were mixed randomly, resulting in broad veining. Thomas Whieldon greatly improved agateware in the 1740s by using white clays stained with metallic oxides. The resulting clay was prone to blurring and so it was shaped in two-part moulds, polished after firing, and glazed.
- A typical golden-yellow glaze is on early ware, but after about 1750 it is transparent or blue grey.
- Josiah Wedgwood used the process to make onyx or pebbled vases closely imitating natural agate.

A mid-18thC agateware compressed circular teapot and cover, minor faults.

5.25in (13.5cm) high

£400-500   WW

A mid-18thC solid agateware sugar bowl and cover, with a cylindrical body and flattened knop, some good restoration to the cover.

4.5in (11.5cm) high

£150-250   WW

Two similar Staffordshire agateware balls.

c1750   2in (5cm) diam

£600-800   DN

CREAMWARE

Creamware was developed c1740 by the potteries of Staffordshire. An improved type was made in 1765 by Josiah Wedgwood, who called it 'Queen's ware' in honour of Queen Charlotte.

- The clay was mixed with flint to produce a ware that was durable, relatively cheap, light weight and as thin as porcelain.
- Creamware was versatile and could be finely moulded before being printed or painted, under and over the glaze.
- By the late 18thC, creamware had become the standard household pottery, driving many tin-glazed earthenware factories out of business.

A late 18thC Liverpool creamware commemorative mug, of cylindrical form, decorated with 'America Declared Independent July 4 1776',

5in (12.5cm) high

£2,500-3,500   FRE

A Liverpool creamware cylindrical mug, transfer-printed with 'An East View of Liverpool Light House & Signals on Bidston Hill'.

1796   4.75in (12cm) high

£1,000-1,500   WW

A Liverpool creamware commemorative mug, decorated with ribbon border inscribed with the names of sixteen states and the verse 'Oh Liberty thou Goddess Heavenly bright. Profuse of Bliss and pregnant with delight Eternal pleasures in they presence reign and smiling plenty leads thy wanton train',

6.25in (16cm) high

£1,000-1,500   FRE

A late 18th/early 19thC transfer-printed creamware commemorative mug, the cylindrical form decorated with the Ropemaker's arms and inscription 'Behold our support'.

6in (15cm) high

£500-800   FRE

An early 19thC pink lustre and magenta transfer-printed creamware mug, decorated on each side with an eagle and shield, 'E Pluribus Unum' and 'May Success Attend Our Agriculture Trade'.

4in (10cm) high

£900-1,100　　FRE

A Liverpool printed Pilchard Fishery creamware commemorative jug, decorated with a vignette of a brig under a press of sail and titled 'SUCCESS TO THE PILCHARD FISHERY', verso with an oval panel of a woman with cornucopia titled 'PEACE AND PLENTY', beneath the spout inscribed to 'MICHAEL & JANE TONKIN'.

c1790　　　　　　*5.75in (14.5cm) high*

£1,200-1,800　　DN

An early 19thC Liverpool pitcher, with Hope on one side, a ship flying the American flag on the other, and spread-winged eagle and shield with a Jefferson quotation.

9in (23cm) high

£400-600　　FRE

A gilt hand-decorated creamware presentation pitcher, each side decorated with a three-masted ship flying the American flag, a figure of a man with a hammer burying a barrel, the inscription 'John Dockity' under spout enclosed by floral vine, band at top and trellis border at foot.

8.25in (21cm) high

£1,000-1,500　　FRE

An early 19thC Liverpool creamware marriage pitcher, decorated on one side with 'The Arms of Deering', the reverse with 'The Arms of Carver' and below the spout, with the initials 'ED'.

11in (28cm) high

£800-1,200　　FRE

CLOSER LOOK: CREAMWARE TEAPOT

It is decorated on both sides with an iron red floral wreath, inscribed 'No Stamp Act' on one side and 'American Liberty Restored' on the other.

The fact that the teapot was made in England for the American market to celebrate the repeal of the act illustrates how important trade with the American colonies was to British industry.

This piece documents a significant moment in American history. This is only the fourth known example. The other three are in the Smithsonian, Colonial Williamsburg, and the Peabody-Essex Museum in the US.

The teapot has a crabstock spout and handle.

A pre-Revolutionary War English creamware teapot and cover, of ovoid form, from the Shelley Collection

The 1765 Stamp Act was a tax imposed on the American colonies by the British Government. It required the colonists to pay a tax on every piece of printed paper they used. Once in effect, the tax met with great resistance as the colonists insisted that they could be taxed only with their consent and it was repealed in the following year.

1765-1766　　　　　　*5in (12.5cm) high*

£80,000-100,000　　POOK

POTTERY

A Staffordshire creamware teapot and cover modelled as a cauliflower, bullet-shaped with auricular handle,

c1765. *6in (15cm) high*

£1,000-1,500 DN

A probably mid-18thC Astbury/Whieldon type creamware figure of a musician, some good restoration.

5in (12.5cm) high

£500-600 WW

A black transfer-printed and polychromed punch bowl, probably Herculaneum, the interior decorated with oak leaf border and rare ship-building scene heightened in polychrome above 'John Johnson', the exterior decorated with the Great Seal of the United States, Washington Map of the United States, King Neptune, and 'His Excellency General George Washington, Marshall of France...'.

11in (28cm) diam

£2,000-3,000 FRE

PEARLWARE

A Staffordshire pearlware commemorative plaque, for Queen Caroline, moulded in relief with bust profile of George IV's infamous wife, painted in shades of blue, green and ochre, reserved on pink lustre ground.

Caroline of Brunswick married George IV whilst he was the Prince of Wales. George had already married a Catholic, Maria Fitzherbert, but he needed a wife who was Protestant and of royal blood if he wanted to ascend the throne. The marriage was unhappy. Caroline was forbidden to see their only daughter, Charlotte, and from 1814 she travelled in Europe, leading a bohemian and decadent life. After the death of George III in 1820, Caroline returned to England. Despite great popular support, George IV was determined that she would never be crowned Queen and had her barred from his coronation. Caroline fell seriously ill on the day of the coronation and died three weeks later, convinced she had been poisoned.

c1820 *6in (15cm) diam*

£400-600 DN

A late 18thC pearlware oval straining dish, with decorative piercing and a green underglaze border.

13in (33.5cm) diam

£200-300 WW

A large late 18thC pearlware meat dish, painted in blue with a Chinese figure holding a parasol before a pagoda, moulded feathered rim, unmarked, minor damages.

20.5in (52cm) diam

£150-250 WW

A mid-19thC Swansea pearlware plate, painted in red, blue and green with a vase of flowers in the well and a garlanded border, with lustre details, impressed 'Dillwyn Swansea' mark.

8.5in (22cm) diam.

£300-500 WW

An 18thC unusual pearlware candle niche, painted in blue with a young man wearing a necklace.

c1750   *9.75in (25cm) high*
£600-800   **WW**

An early 19thC brown-glazed pearlware jug, printed in yellow with a portrait of Lord Nelson on a ground of flowers and scrolls, a small chip to the spout.

                           6in (15cm) high
£250-350   **WW**

A large early 19thC pearlware punch pot, printed in blue with figures in a Chinese riverscape, unmarked, the damaged spout with a metal replacement.

                          15.75in (40cm) high
£200-300   **WW**

A pearlware mug, printed in blue with panels of buildings on a floral ground, minor damages.

c1825   *5.5in (14cm) high*
£100-150   **WW**

A pearlware harvest jug, painted with a mock heraldic shield, between two figures above the motto 'Farmers Arms', an inscription under the spout, damages.

1808   *8.75in (22.5cm) high*
£150-200   **WW**

A matched pair of Staffordshire pearlware figural groups, the oblong moulded base with sponged decoration.

                          6.5in (16cm) long
£2,500-3,500   **NA**

A 19thC Staffordshire pearlware spill vase, modelled as a tree stump with three recumbent sheep at the base amidst applied flowers and grass, minor damages.

                        8.75in (22.5cm) high
£150-200   **WW**

PRATTWARE

A dated Staffordshire Prattware model of a longcase clock, painted in shades of blue, green and ochre, restored.

1794   *9in (23cm) high*
£400-600   **DN**

A Staffordshire Prattware model of a longcase clock, painted in shades of blue, green and ochre.

c1800   *8in (20cm) high*
£300-400   **DN**

A Prattware caster, painted with a repeated floral motif, the pierced top with radiating ochre stripes, damages.

c1800   *5in (12.5cm) high*
£50-150   **WW**

An early 19thC small Prattware flask, each side moulded with figures and decorated in blue, green, yellow and ochre.

                          2.5in (6.5cm) high
£250-350   **WW**

MOCHAWARE

Mochaware is a type of slip-glazed earthenware made to resemble mocha stone (moss agate). It was popular in the UK, France and the US from the late 18thC to the late 19thC.

- Early pieces feature seaweed-like slip decoration which resembles mocha stone.
- The surface consists of layers of slip, usually a base coat topped with one of the more distinctive motifs arranged within glaze bands of contrasting colour. There may be as many as twenty six of these decorative bands on a large piece such as a jug.
- Mochaware motifs include seaweed, earthworm, cat's eye, and marble or tortoiseshell.

A 19thC rare Mochaware covered bowl, with blue, black and green bands and seaweed decoration on a brown ground.

11in (28cm) diameter

£6,000-7,000   POOK

An early 19thC Mochaware basin, with looping earthworm decoration, base chips.

10.75in (27.5cm) diam.

£4,000-5,000   SK

An early 19thC Mochaware covered chamber pot, with looping earthworm decoration.

8.5in (21.5cm) high

£1,500-2,000   SK

A Mochaware cylindrical mug, decorated in brown, cream and caramel-coloured combed slip between green bands.

c1800   6in (15cm) high

£2,500-3,000   WW

A large mid-19thC Mochaware jug, a replacement metal handle and other damages.

12.5in (32cm) high

£400-600   WW

STAFFORDSHIRE

The Staffordshire ceramics trade developed round five main towns — Stoke-on-Trent, Burslem, Hanley, Tunstall, and Longton which were home to over 1,000 factories by the end of the 19thC, including Wedgwood, Spode and Ridgeway.

- The rich natural resources of clay and coal made Staffordshire an ideal location. White clay was also brought in from Dorset, Devon and Cornwall.
- Designers and potters moved between factories, so many similar shapes and patterns emerged.
- During the 19thC, the Staffordshire companies became increasingly well known for their pottery figures, which were copies of high-quality porcelain. These pieces were often inspired by Derby and Chelsea and depicted rustic, allegorical or biblical scenes.
- The ceramics industry has declined in recent times, but several companies still flourish in the Staffordshire area.

A 19thC pearlware Toby jug, wearing a long red coat and resting a foaming jug of ale on his knee, unmarked.

9.5in (24cm) high

£150-200   WW

An early 19thC Staffordshire pearlware Toby jug, restoration to the hat and feet.

9.75in (25cm) high

£500-600   WW

A Staffordshire Toby jug, with black tricorn hat and pink jacket, holding a foaming jug of ale, on canted square brown-line base .

c1825   9.5in (24cm) high

£120-180   DN

A Staffordshire Toby jug and cover, with black tricorn hat and jacket holding a foaming jug of ale and a pipe, on canted square red-line base.

c1840   10.25in (26cm) high

£120-180   DN

A Staffordshire Toby jug, black tricorn hat and brown jacket, seated with a foaming jug of ale, canted square base.

c1830   *9.5in (24cm) high*

£150-250   **DN**

A Staffordshire pearlware Toby jug, typically modelled seated holding a foaming mug of ale, flaking and old repairs.

c1820   *9.5in (24cm) high*

£200-300   **DN**

A pearlware Toby jug, possibly Yorkshire, typically modelled seated with foaming jug of ale, painted and sponged with coloured enamels.

c1835   *10in (25cm) high*

£150-250   **DN**

A Victorian Staffordshire earthenware foot bath, with twin cast foliate handles and grey glaze with green diagonals.

£150-200   **BIG**

A Staffordshire Gaudy Welsh presentation pitcher, of baluster form, inscribed 'Mary Brayshaw Died Febry 3 1837 aged 62 years'.

8in (20.5cm) high

£400-600   **FRE**

Two 19thC Staffordshire figures of the Queen of Prussia and Queen Victoria.

Tallest 16.5in (42cm) high

£150-200   **POOK**

A pair of 19thC Staffordshire figures of the Duke and Duchess of Edinburgh.

17.25in (44cm) high

£200-300   **POOK**

A rare Staffordshire pottery two-handled leech jar and cover, bearing the gilt inscription 'Leeches' on a dark blue banner, with pierced lid.

11.75in (30cm) high

£2,000-3,000   **WW**

A pair of 19thC Staffordshire models of King Charles spaniels, damages.

7.5in (19cm) high

£50-150   **WW**

A mid-19thC Staffordshire part dessert service, comprising seven plates and three dishes. painted with views of 19thC American life, including views of Native American Indians at Lake Winnipesaukee, the White House and figures above the Hudson River, all within gilded pale blue borders and titled to the reverse.

£1,000-1,500   **WW**

POTTERY

An early 19thC Staffordshire silver resist lustre ovoid jug, with angular handle, decorated with spots and ears of wheat beneath scaling.

c1810   *4.25in (11cm) high*

£100-150   **NEA**

A 19thC pottery lustreware model of a lion, resting on a marbled base, some restoration.

10.25in (26cm) high

£100-200   **WW**

A black transfer-printed and pink lustre box, rectangular form, the lid decorated with a naval battle scene of the Constitution and the Java, interior with Sunderland splotches.

6in (15cm) wide

£200-300   **FRE**

TRANSFER-PRINTED WARE

Transfer printing was a cheaper and quicker alternative to hand painting. It was used from the late 18thC to mass produce ceramics.

- Blue and white chinoiserie designs, like the extremely popular 'Willow' pattern, were often applied to table wares.
- The decoration on early pieces can exhibit huge variances in shade. Some very rare examples were filled in by hand using coloured enamels.
- Production had vastly increased by c1815, and by c1835 it was possible to print smoother designs in several colours.
- Transfer-printed ware may be distinguished from hand painting by the cross-hatching created by the engraving on the copper plate. Sometimes the edges of the printed design are not a perfect match.
- Transfer printing is still used to decorate ceramics today.

A historical blue transferware platter, Bennett Pottery, Baltimore, Maryland, oblong form decorated with 'Pickett's Charge Gettysburg' enclosed by an oak leaf and acorn border with portrait medallions of General Robert E. Lee, General William. S. Hancock, General Jas Longstreet and General G.G. Mead.

13in (33cm) wide

£500-1,000   **FRE**

An historical blue and white transfer decorated A A Staffordshire pottery platter, by James and Ralph Clews, Cobridge, England, depicting the 'Landing of Gen. LaFayette at Castle Garden New York 16 August 1824,' with printed title, and impressed maker's mark on the reverse.

1820's   *19in (48cm)*

£1,000-1,500   **SK**

A large Copeland and Garrett New Stone dish, printed in blue with the 'Grasshopper' pattern, printed and impressed marks, some wear and scratching.

c1840   *19.75in (50cm) diam.*

£200-300   **WW**

A Herculaneum Pottery blue and white charger, printed with 'View in the Fort, Madura' from the Indian series.

c1820   *13in (33cm) diam*

£250-350   **DN**

A pair of 19thC Hicks, Meigh and Johnson blue printed venison dishes, each with scalloped, gadrooned border, the well decorated with figures beside a tree on a riverine landscape with a pagoda behind.

c1822-35   *21.5in (55cm) wide*

£800-1,200   **L&T.**

A blue transferware well and tree platter, Jones & Son, 1826-1828, decorated with 'Death of General Wolfe' from the 'British History' series.

20in (51cm) wide

£1,000-2,000   **FRE**

A John & William Rigdway, Hanley historical blue transferware platter, decorated with 'Deaf & Dumb Asylum, Hartford Connecticut', from Ridgway's 'Beauties of America' series, within a rose and leaf medallion border.

1814-30   14.75in (37.5cm) wide
£500-1,000   **FRE**

A large Rogers pearlware dish, printed in blue with a figure tending an elephant, impressed marks.

c1820   20.75in (53cm) high
£200-300   **WW**

A 19thC blue and white meat dish, possibly Spode, depicting one Eastern scene with square buildings, overhanging trees and figures in the foreground.

19in (48cm) wide
£450-550   **JN**

A Ralph Stevenson, Cobridge, historical blue transferware platter, decorated with 'New York, Esplanade and Castle Garden', within a leaf and vine border, signed on ship's sail.

18.5in (47cm) wide
£1,500-2,500   **FRE**

A Canadian F. T. Thomas of Quebec transfer-printed plate, showing a scene of the 'St Louis Gate Porte St Louis' and with transfer-printed border of beavers amidst foliage.

9.75in (24.5cm) diam
£100-150   **TCF**

A Canadian F. T. Thomas, Quebec 'View Looking North From The Citadel' transfer-printed octagonal platter, from the 'Scottish Quebec Views' series.

c1874   13.75in (35cm) wide
£800-1,200   **TAC**

An Enoch Wood and Sons, Burslem, historical blue transferware platter, decorated with 'Christianburg Danish Settlement on the Gold Coast of Africa', within a shell border with irregular centre.

1819-46   20.5in (52cm) wide
£1,200-1,800   **FRE**

An Enoch Wood & Sons, Burslem, historical blue transferware platter, decorated with 'Castle Battery New York', within a shell border with circular centre.

1815-1846   20.5in (52cm) wide
£1,000-2,000   **FRE**

An early 19thC historical blue transferware platter, unknown maker, decorated with 'Sandusky', within a rose and scroll border, mismarked 'Detroit'.

16.25in (41cm) wide
£2,500-3,500   **FRE**

A mid 19thC Ridgway 'Corey Hill' pattern tableware set, blue underglaze with chinoiserie decoration with flowers, buildings and scrolls embellished with red, green and pink enamel, some pieces highlighted with gilt, several backstamped with pattern name and/or make, including dinner plates, salad or luncheon plates, soup plates, dessert plates, cups, saucers, small shallow scallop-rimmed bowls, small shallow bowls, small plates, small serving bowls, butter pats, round serving bowls with handles, a round footed bowl, a covered butter dish with drainer, an oval footed serving bowl, an oval footed sauce dish with undertray, oval platters, a teapot, a covered sugar bowl, a cream jug, a chocolate pot, covered jar and a small jug, 162 pieces total, minor chips.

£1,000-2,000   **SK**

POTTERY

A James and Ralph Clews, Cobridge, historical blue transferware pitcher, decorated with 'Landing of Gen. Lafayette at Castle Garden New York, 16 August, 1824', within floral borders.

1829-36   *9in (23cm) high*
£1,500-2,000   **FRE**

A John & William Ridgway, dark-blue soup tureen and cover, with 'Cambridge College, Massachusetts', from the 'Beauties of America Series: Almshouse, Boston'.

15.5in (39cm) wide
£1,500-2,500   **NA**

A 19thC Ridgways 'India Temple' pattern hexagonal soup tureen, cover and two hexagonal stands, with printed mark.

c1814-30
£800-1,200   **L&T**

A graduated pair of 19thC blue printed ceramic footed twin-handled soup tureens and covers, decorated with figures in landscape settings, unmarked.

14.25in (36cm) and 13.5in (34cm) wide
£700-1,000   **L&T**

A Bathwell & Goodfellow medium-blue footbath, the interior depicting a pastoral view, printed overall with Italianate architectural and harbour views, unmarked.

19.75in (49cm) long
£1,000-2,000   **NA**

A James and Ralph Clews, Cobridge, historical blue transferware water pitcher, of ovoid form, decorated with 'Landing of Lafayette at Castle Gardens, New York, 16 August, 1824', within floral borders.

1829-36   *9.75in (25cm) high*
£300-500   **FRE**

A James and Ralph Clews, Cobridge, rare historical purple transferware flask, decorated with 'Hudson, Hudson River' from 'Picturesque Views' series.

1829-36   *9.5in (24cm) high*
£1,500-2,500   **FRE**

A Canadian F.T. Thomas of Quebec transfer-printed teapot, with scene of Lorette Falls, Chutes de Lorette, cracked.

Note the desirable beaver motif, hidden in the branches near the rim.

8in (20cm) high
£500-1,000   **TCF**

A Ralph Stevenson & Williams, dark-blue Staffordshire pierced centre bowl, printed title in underglaze-blue 'Vine Border: Battle of Bunker Hill'.

10in (25cm) long
£2,000-3,000   **NA**

A 19thC Mason's Ironstone part dinner service printed and painted with stylised chrysanthemum and foliage in the Imari palette, comprising a large twin-handled soup tureen and cover, a rectangular vegetable tureen and cover, a rectangular vegetable dish, two square vegetable tureens and covers, two twin-handled sauce tureens, covers and stands, five graduated ashets, a square-form dish, twenty-seven dinner plates, eighteen soup plates, fourteen dessert bowls, fifteen side plates and six cheese plates, impressed mark 'Mason's patent ironstone china'.

£4,000-6,000   L&T

A Turner's patent ironstone part dinner service, comprising three tureens and covers, four dishes, two sauce tureens and three stands, twelve ashets, fourteen bowls, eight side plates, a gravy boat, and two tureen covers.

Large tureen14in (35cm) wide

£2,000-3,000   L&T

A Turner's stone china plate, painted with pine and flowers in the Imari palette, painted mark 'Turner's Patent'

8.25in (21cm) diam.

£40-60   WW

A 19thC ironstone rectangular Imari pattern asket, decorated in the typical palette.

21in (53cm) wide

£500-700   L&T

An early 19thC Mason's ironstone 'Japan' pattern vase and cover, impressed mark 'Mason's patent ironstone china'.

16in (40.5cm) high

£1,500-2,500   L&T

An early 19thC ironstone 'Japan' pattern fruit cooler and liner, with twin dragon's head handles.

8.75in (22cm) high

£1,000-1,500   L&T

A matched pair of early 19thC ironstone 'Japan' pattern sauce tureens and covers, each of ribbed form, with flower-head finial and twin shell-form handles, above a pierced gilt leaf decorated oval foot, one impressed with 'Mason's patent ironstone china'.

7.75in (20cm) high

£800-1,200   L&T

A set of early 19thC ironstone 'Japan' pattern cider jugs, each with a serpent handle, two Mason's Patent Ironstone with blue printed mark.

Largest: 5.5in (14cm) high

£1,500-2,500   L&T

A matched set of three 19thC Mason's ironstone red-printed tureens, covers and two stands of serpentine octagonal form, two covers, both stands and two bodies decorated with a chinoiserie landscape scene, the other cover and body decorated with an English figural landscape with building, together with one ladle.

14in (35cm) wide

£350-450 SET   L&T

POTTERY

A Palissy style circular charger, by Mafra of Caldas De Rainha, with applied lizards, a tortoise, a snake and worms on a bed of extruded clay, impressed mark.

c1880   *10.5in (26cm) diam*

£400-500   SWO

A late 19thC Portuguese Palissy style dish, decorated with a pair of lizards fighting on a mossy base, with two stag beetles, impressed factory marks, some restoration.

7in (18cm) diam

£70-100   WW

A mid-19thC English phrenological head, as an inkwell, stamped 'By F. Bridges, Phrenologist'.

5.5in (14cm) high

£250-350   WW

A shouldered Decalcomania vase, of tapering cylindrical form, with narrow neck, decorated with opposed gothic panels and figures of angels and saints on a cream painted ground.

Decalcomania is a decorative technique by which engravings or prints are transferred onto pottery or other materials. It was invented in England by the Frenchman Simon Francois Ravenet in the 1750s. The term Decalcomania was coined in the 1870s.

12.25in (31cm) high

£350-550   L&T

STONEWARE

Stoneware is made by mixing clay with a stone flux and firing the mixture at high temperature to fuse the ingredients. The first European stoneware was made towards the end of the Middle Ages in Germany.

- It was more durable and watertight than earthenware. This made it particularly suitable for making steins, the lidded drinking vessels popular in Germany.
- Stoneware was often given a decorative salt glaze. Unglazed stoneware includes Wedgwood's Basalt and Jasper wares.
- White stoneware was very popular, as it emulated the properties of Oriental porcelain.
- Stoneware was eventually superseded in popularity by pale, opaque earthenwares like creamware.

An American 19thC six-gallon stoneware water jug, impressed 'M. Woodruff Cortland', with vibrant goony bird decoration, from the Shelley Collection.

This humourous bird is an unusual and desirable form of decoration.

18in (45.5cm) high

£25,000-30,000   POOK

A dated stoneware English Bellarmine jug, typically moulded with a mask to the neck and with three raised oval panels, one with Tudor rose surmounted with a crown, the central example with a coat of arms and the third with 'ER' cypher for Queen Elizabeth I surmounted with a crown.

1576   *7in (18cm) high*

£4,000-5,000   DN

A dated stoneware English Bellarmine jug, typically moulded with a mask to the neck and with three raised oval panels, one with a Tudor rose surmounted with a crown, the central example with royal coat of arms and the third with a portcullis.

1576   *8in (20cm) high*

£4,000-5,000   DN

A 17thC Spanish salt-glazed wine jug, with applied bacchic mask motifs flanked by four rams, and further applied relief decoration.

24in (61cm) high

£3,000-4,000   FRE

CLOSER LOOK: STONEWARE JUG

The decoration featuring a woman with a parasol and exaggerated hoop skirt is very unusual. Birds and flowers are more usual subjects for stoneware jugs.

Bold decoration in a deep blue such as this is highly sought after by collectors.

Stoneware jugs and crocks were essential household items in the 18th and 19thC. They were used for storage.

The shape of stoneware vessels changed in the mid-19thC. Ovoid vessels tend to date from the first half of the century, while cylindrical containers date to the second half.

An American 19thC stoneware jug, with cobalt decoration, inscribed indistinctly 'gal that wo_ the water', from the Shelley Collection.

8.25in (21cm) high

£25,000-30,000   POOK

An American mid-19thC cobalt blue decorated stoneware crock, embellished with a stylised flower blossom, and Albany slip-glazed interior, marked 'ALBANY, N.Y.'.

11.75in (30cm) high

£200-300   SK

An American mid- to late 19thC stoneware jug with parrot, with applied handle, marked 'WHITES UTICA,' impressed maker's mark, chips.

11in (28cm) high

£200-300   SK

An American mid- to late 19thC blue stoneware jug, ornamented with a bird perched on a branch, marked 'HENRY LUTHER Amsterdam NY,' with lip chips.

13.75in (35cm) high

£200-300   SK

A New York City cobalt blue floral stamp-decorated stoneware jug, attributed to Clarkson Crolius, minor imperfections.

c1800   14.5in (37cm) high

£1,000-2,000   SK

A large late 19thC English stoneware jug, with twin handles, decorated with moulded hunting scene.

19in (48cm) high

£700-1,000   L&T

A Raeren stoneware and pewter-mounted bauerntanzrug, the brown-glazed body moulded with a frieze of dancing couples under arcs, the neck with ribbed decoration.

1598   10.25in (26cm) high

£2,500-3,500   SOTA

A late 16thC large Siegburg pewter-mounted schnelle, moulded in relief with three identical panels depicting Christ, Mary Magdalene and Saint Anne, signed 'HH' for Hans Hilgers.

14.75in (37cm) high

£3,500-4,500   SOTA

A 17thC German salt-glazed stoneware Bellarmine jug, decorated all over with a mottled 'tiger ware' glaze, handle restored.

9in (23cm) high

£200-250   DN

POTTERY

ESSENTIAL REFERENCE: BELLARMINE

Bellarmine jugs (also known as greybeard jugs) were one of the most common forms of German stoneware. They were made from the mid-16thC to the late 18thC and exported throughout Europe. They were also made in England.

- They were originally made in Flanders to ridicule Cardinal Robert Bellarmine (1542-1621), who was a great opponent of the Reformed Church there. It is believed that it was common for Protestants wishing to insult the Cardinal to smash the jugs, after drinking.
- These corpulent, typically salt-glazed, jugs had a rude likeness of the cardinal and his large, square, ecclesiastical beard at the neck.
- They vary greatly in height and were mainly used in taverns as decanters between the cask and the table, with the smaller pieces used as drinking mugs.
- At one time the jugs were also frequently used as 'witch bottles'. This entailed filling the jug with certain articles, sealing it and burying it. This was done in order to deflect a witch's curse.

A 17thC German stoneware jug of Bellarmine type, with loop handle and typically moulded with a mask to the neck above an oval cartouche of a lion rampant, manufacturing faults.

10.5in (27cm) high

£500-600   DN

A 17thC German brown salt-glazed stoneware Bellarmine jug, typically moulded with a mask above an oval boss with a stylised flowerhead, decorated all over with a tiger glaze.

9in (23cm) high

£400-600   DN

A 17thC German salt-glazed stoneware Bellarmine jug, typically moulded with a mask and decorated with a grey-green glaze, some footrim chips.

7.25in (18.5cm) high

£300-400   DN

An American late 18th/early 19thC incised and cobalt blue-decorated stoneware flask, ovoid flattened form with cobalt-filled incised monogram 'HAH', flower blossom and scrolled foliate motifs, neck repair.

7in (18cm) high

£4,000-6,000   SK

An American dated blue-decorated stoneware hip flask, possibly New York, the front inscribed with the initials 'P.F.K', within a stylised pot of flowers, flanked by trailing vines, the back with the same initials above a large sunflower.

1853   *5.5in (14cm) high*

£9,000-11,000   POOK

A late 19thC American stoneware ring bottle, probably New York, with overall blue glazing, inscribed with suns and stars on one side and a stylised basket and trailing vine on the other.

7.75in (20cm) high

£3,500-4,500   POOK

A Bennington, Vermont stoneware three-gallon crock, with cobalt butterfly and rose amidst scrolls, by J. Norton & Co.

c1840   *12.75in (32cm) high*

£500-1,000   NA

A Galesville, New York stoneware six-gallon churn, with cobalt pea fowl and plant, of swelled cylindrical form, marked 'W.A. LEWIS'.

c1860   *18.75in (47cm) high*

£5,000-8,000   NA

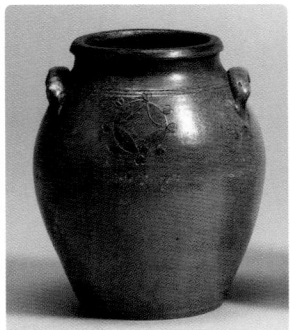

An early 19thC incised cobalt blue-decorated stoneware jar, possibly by David Morgan, New York City, with applied lug handles, and minor chips.

9in (23cm) high

£1,000-1,500   **SK**

A late 18th/early 19thC incised floral-decorated stoneware jar, probably from New York City or northern New Jersey, repaired handles.

9.5in (24cm) high

£1,000-1,500   **SK**

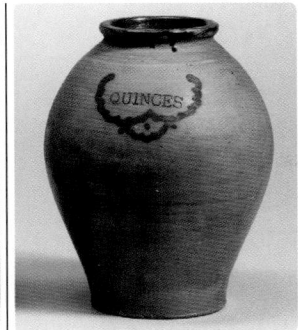

A 'Quinces' cobalt blue stoneware jar, by Clarkson Crolius Sr., New York City, with impressed maker's mark and minor rim and base chips.

1797-1815   *10in (25.4cm) high*

£2,000-2,500   **SK**

A Harrisburg, Pennsylvania stoneware crock, stamped 'Wilson's & Young', with cobalt floral decoration.

c1855   *11in (28cm) high*

£2,500-3,500   **POOK**

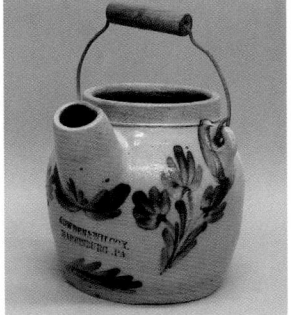

An American stoneware batter jug, with wire and wood handle, decorated with cobalt blue leafage, impressed 'Cowden & Wilcox / Harrisburg PA'.

7.5in (19cm) high

£2,500-3,000   **ALD**

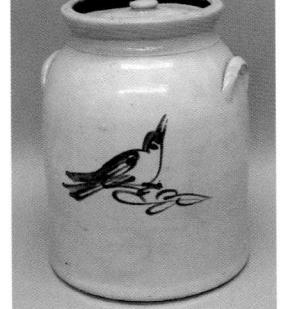

An American stoneware crock, decorated with a Fulper bird in colbalt blue, with twin moulded handles, cover with chipped edge.

12.75in (32.5cm) high

£150-250   **ALD**

A large 18thC salt-glazed stoneware mug, decorated with 'The Punch Party', metal mount to the rim, unmarked, damages.

7in (17.5cm) high

£300-500   **WW**

A London salt-glazed stoneware mug, possibly Vauxhall or Mortlake, inscribed 'Geo Pearce 1735', later silver mounts hallmarked for London 1921, faint crack in base.

9in (23cm) high

£3,000-4,000   **DN**

A Staffordshire salt-glazed stoneware teapot and cover, painted in coloured enamels with sprays of flowers reserved on a dark red/brown ground, with naturalistically modelled twig spout and handle.

c1760   *4in (10cm) high*

£600-800   **DN**

A set of three mid-19thC Doulton stoneware barrels, decorated with bands of moulded vine leaves and the Royal coat of arms, named 'brandy', 'rum' and 'gin', one with tap, impressed mark 'Doulton and Watts, London'.

£900-1,200   **L&T**

A mid- to late 19thC cobalt-decorated stoneware three-part water cooler, Philadelphia or Baltimore, flattened lid on bulbous filter segment and straight-sided base decorated with crossed floral fronds and banding, some chips.

13in (33cm) high   *4in (10cm) high*

£3,000-5,000   **FRE**

A pair of 19thC blue stoneware candlesticks, the columns and flared bases painted with flowers, unmarked.

8in (20.5cm) high

£200-300 PAIR   **WW**

POTTERY

CLOSER LOOK: STONEWARE STAG

This stoneware folk art figure of a stag is highly unusual and virtually in mint condition, making it desirable to collectors.

The figure was hand moulded and has a very expressive face with a carved, open mouth and full set of teeth.

The stag rests on a shallow platform with its legs stretched forwards. It has a paddle-form tail.

The tan glaze is decorated with cobalt spots.

An exceptional stoneware figure of a recumbent stag, probably western Pennsylvania, with blue dot highlights, expressive open mouth, resting on a free form platform.

c1875   14.5in (37cm) long

£50,000-60,000   **POOK**

A 17th/18thC stoneware globular money box, the buff body partly glazed, with a knopped finial, some restoration.

3in (7.5cm) high

£200-300   **WW**

A 19thC white stoneware pot-pourri basket and cover, painted with a border of flowers, impressed '3' and painted pattern number.

5.5in (14cm) high

£200-300   **WW**

WEDGWOOD

A 19thC Wedgwood black basalt plaque, moulded with a maiden playing a lyre with Cupid holding a wreath, 'Wedgwood' impressed.

6.75in (17cm) high

£200-300   **WW**

A mid-19thC Wedgwood basalt hedgehog crocus pot and underplate, modelled with openwork body, raised on a quatreform base, impressed 'Wedgwood'.

These hedgehog-shaped pots were designed to hold crocus bulbs and were used indoors.

10in (25.5cm) wide

£500-1,000   **FRE**

A pair of Wedgwood black basalt inkwells modelled as sphinx couchant, on rectangular plinth bases with urns between their fore-paws, the urns with liners, impressed marks, one liner a replacement, some minor damage and repair.

c1800   6in (15cm) long

£1,000-1,500   **DN**

A 19thC Wedgwood bronzed basalt vase, of pedestal ovoid form, the plain body with two applied gilded handles and raised on circular pedestal base, impressed 'Wedgwood' and incised '943'.

12.25in (31cm) high

£500-700　　　　　　　HALL

A 19thC Wedgwood hedgehog crocus pot, the creamware body glazed throughout in green lustre, with naturalistic finish, impressed mark, lacking stand.

8.25in (21cm) long

£200-300　　　　　　　HALL

A 19thC Wedgwood blue jasper ware cheese bell and stand, with a frieze of cherubs playing musical instruments, the stand with further oak leaf and acorn band, impressed mark.

11in (27.5cm) diam

£350-450　　　　　　　L&T

A 19thC Wedgwood blue jasper ware cheese bell and stand, with a continuous frieze of Classical female figures, above a band of acorns and oak leaves, the stand with similar band, impressed mark.

12.75in (32cm) diam

£500-700　　　　　　　L&T

A pair of late 19thC Wedgwood green jasper ware bottle vases and stoppers, each with four Classical figures, impressed mark and backstamp for Humphrey Taylor & Co., one stopper restored.

10.5in (26.5cm) high

£350-450　　　　　　　WW

A pair of 19thC Wedgwood black jasper ware covered urns, the ovoid sides decorated in applied white relief with a band of Classical maidens, raised on socle bases, impressed marks.

8.75in (22cm) high

£350-550　　　　　　　L&T

An Adams blue-jasper oval two-handled sugar box and cover, sprigged in white relief with Classical subjects, the cover surmounted with a swan finial, impressed mark, cracked.

c1800　　*6.75in (17cm) wide*

£200-300　　　　　　　DN

A 19thC blue jasper ware cheese bell and stand, with rope-twist finial above bands of acorns and oak leaves and a continuous hunting scene.

11.5in (29cm) diam

£400-600　　　　　　　L&T

A late 19thC German black jasper ware inkwell, the globular well decorated in applied white relief with signs of the zodiac, the dished stand sprigged in white with a band of oak leaf and figural oval reserves.

5in (13cm) high

£300-500　　　　　　　L&T

TERRACOTTA

A large early 19thC terracotta chinoiserie vase, on circular foot and square painted softwood faux marble plinth.

102cm high

£3,500-4,500　　　　　　　L&T

A late 19thC terracotta model of a pug, the well-moulded cast glazed brown, the face applied with two glass eyes.

11in (28cm) high

£200-300　　　　　　　FRE

ORIENTAL

CHINESE REIGN PERIODS AND MARKS

Imperial reign marks were adopted during the Ming dynasty, and some of the most common are illustrated here. Certain emperors forbade the use of their own reign mark, lest they should suffer the disrespect of a broken vessel bearing their name being thrown away. This is where the convention of using earlier reign marks comes from – a custom that was enthusiastically adopted by potters as a way of showing their respect for their predecessors.

It is worth remembering that a great deal of Imperial porcelain is marked misleadingly and pieces bearing the reign mark for the period in which they were made are therefore especially sought after.

Early periods and dates

Xia Dynasty	c2000 - 1500BC	Three Kingdoms	221 - 280	The Five Dynasties	907 - 960
Shang Dynasty	1500 - 1028BC	Jin Dynasty	265 - 420	Song Dynasty	960 - 1279
Zhou Dynasty	1028 - 221BC	Northern & Southern Dynasties	420 - 581	Jin Dynasty	1115 - 1234
Qin Dynasty	221 - 206BC	Sui Dynasty	581 - 618	Yuan Dynasty	1260 - 1368
Han Dynasty	206BC - AD220	Tang Dynasty	618 - 906		

Ming Dynasty Reigns

Hongwu	1368 - 1398	Jingtai	1450 - 1457
Jianwen	1399 - 1402	Tianshun	1457 - 1464
Yongle	1403 - 1424	Chenghua	1465 - 1487
Hongxi	1425 - 1425	Hongzhi	1488 - 1505
Xuande	1426 - 1435	Zhengde	1506 - 1521
Zhengtong	1436 - 1449		

Ming Dynasty Marks

Jiajing	Longquing	Wanli	Tianqi	Chongzhen
1522 – 1566	1567 – 1572	1573 – 1619	1621 – 1627	1628 – 1644

Qing Dynasty Marks

Shunzhi	Kangxi	Yongzheng	Qianlong	Jiaqing	Daoguang
1644 – 1661	1662 – 1722	1723 – 1735	1736 – 1795	1796 – 1820	1821 – 1850

Republic Period

Xianfeng	Tongzhi	Guangxu	Xuantong	Hongxian (Yuan Shikai)
1851 – 1861	1862 – 1874	1875 – 1908	1909 – 1911	1915 – 1916

THE ORIENTAL MARKET

The trend in the Oriental market is still very much on the up with Chinese and other Far Eastern buyers continuing to drive the market. Consequently the areas that are doing particularly well are ceramics and works of art that were originally made for the home market. Chinese export wares such as armorial porcelains, which are traditionally popular with European and American buyers but are not to the Chinese taste, continue to lose ground unless they are exceptional.

Early ceramics have always been desirable, and they are even more so now. The market for transitional blue and white wares from c1640-50 as well as Kangxi porcelains (1662-1722) even those made for export if in Chinese shapes such as yen yen vases.

Pieces from the 19th and 20th centuries, which traditionally were not as sought after as earlier wares, are achieving good prices if they are of good quality, have the correct reign mark, and were made for the home market. The trend can also be seen in contemporary Chinese art where a market exists that was not there ten years ago.

The glut of period and reproduction pottery burial figures has resulted in the only real area of Chinese art collection to experience a decline in demand and subsequent price.

Qing dynasty jade, scholar's objects, domestic Chinese furniture and cloisonné have all been in strong demand. A weaker domestic Japanese market and declining Western collecting base has contributed to a flat Japanese market. The very best examples of Satsuma, cloisonné, and Buddhist art has all continued to do well, mostly bought by Western collectors. Japanese porcelain has struggled recently to achieve prices comparable to ten or fifteen years ago.

Like the Japanese market South East Asian material has experienced less demand within the middle market (£1,5000-5,000) than the Chinese market, the very best examples of Korean ceramics and Khmer stone figures have been in high demand but overall it is a hit and miss period for Japanese and South East Asian works of art.

John Axford, Woolley & Wallis, Salisbury

A Chinese Yangshou culture pottery Neolithic jar, decorated with geometric designs and four loop handles.

c2000 BC   10.25in (26cm) high

£400-500   **WW**

A Chinese pottery Han Dynasty vase, moulded round the shoulder with animals and masks beneath a degraded green glaze, old wear and damage.

11in (28cm) high

£200-300   **WW**

A pair of Chinese Han Dynasty grey pottery burial figures of female attendants, signs of red and black pigment, on a contemporary wood stand.

Tallest 11.75in (30cm) high

£1,500-2,500   **FRE**

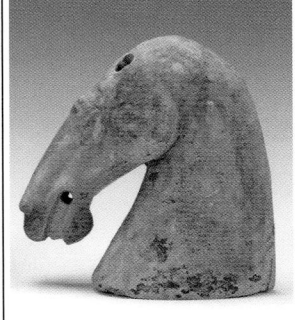

A Chinese Han Dynasty pottery horse head, of typical Han form, potted with a curved neck, strong jaw and open strong mouth, two holes potted to the top of the head, signs of sediment.

2.25in (5.5cm) high

£150-250   **FRE**

A Chinese Tang Dynasty sancai pottery model of a horse, modelled as a long-legged pony, brown body, buff face and green saddle, all four legs attached to a rectangular pottery base.

£2,500-3,500   **FRE**

A Chinese late Song Dynasty yingqing model of a boat, of squat proportions and light celadon glaze, with openwork superstructure and hull decorated with moulded lotus joined by scrolling leaves.

3in (7.5cm) long

£200-400   **FRE**

A Chinese Song Dynasty water dropper, in the form of a recumbent ox, with moulded body, open mouth and horns, blue underglazed highlights to celadon-white ground, raised on four bracket feet.

3in (7.5cm) wide

£500-800   **FRE**

A Chinese Song Dynasty Jizhou bottle jar, of ovoid form, potted with a short fluted neck, the body splashed with brown-buff colour spots over a brown to black glaze, underside glazed black.

9in (23cm) high

£600-800   **FRE**

A large Indo-Chinese Song Dynasty celadon-glazed bowl, incised exterior border to deep sides showing elongated leaves, the interior incised lotus flower medallion to centre and foliate leaf border to sides, some crazing to underglaze, slight wear to interior and rim.

11in (28cm) diam

£700-1,000   **FRE**

A 12thC Chinese tortoiseshell-glazed bowl, of deep U-shape form, brown glaze with light yellow suffusion, raised on circular unglazed foot.

4.5in (11.5cm) diam

£250-450   **FRE**

A large Chinese Yuan Dynasty tea-dust type glazed stoneware wine jar, of compressed ovoid form, small rim mouth and short neck, all over a circular base.

20in (51cm) high

£1,000-1,500   **FRE**

A Chinese Yuan Dynasty tea-dust type glazed stoneware wine jar, of ovoid form, the short neck supports an everted rim, the glaze runs from light brown at the broad shoulder to dark green to a circular foot.

32in (81cm) high

£800-1,200   **FRE**

A Chinese late Song or Yuan period 'hare's fur' glaze bowl, rounded sides raising from a small straight potted unglazed foot, overall black glaze with brown russet rim and 'hare's fur' markings to the interior.

£400-600   **FRE**

A Chinese Ming period Cizhou painted slip pottery figure of Quanyin, modelled wearing a robe-like headdress and partially open robe, knees crossed, over a graduating base.

13in (33cm) high

£300-500   **FRE**

A large Chinese Ming period Cizhou urn, of baluster form, white slip over a stoneware body, exposed lugs to shoulder, painted sparely with iron-brown bands to the neck and shoulder and abstract work to the body.

30in (76cm) high

£700-1,000   **FRE**

A large Chinese late Ming Dynasty green-glazed vase, the globular vase surmounted by a long slender neck, with a fine crackled green glaze thinning at the neck.

14.5in (47cm) high

£750-1,000   **FRE**

A Chinese Wanli period blue and white ovoid vase, the body painted with the 'Three Friends of Winter': pine, prunus and bamboo formed as trees forming four shou characters, the base with a four-character Xuande mark, but Wanli.

7in (18cm) high

£3,500-4,500   WW

A Chinese Wanli period Kraak porcelain double gourd vase, decorated around the lower body with flower sprays and symbols in pomegranate-shaped panels, the upper bulb with panels of flowers and foliage.

10.75in (27cm) high

£2,000-2,500   WW

A Chinese Wanli period blue and white double gourd vase, painted with sparrows in flight, amidst the 'Three Friends of Winter', unmarked, the neck reduced.

c1600   *11.5in (29cm) high*

£800-1,200   WW

A large Chinese Wanli period blue and white ovoid vase, decorated with four panels containing lotus and chrysanthemum, and with smaller floral panels to the shoulder, cracked and repaired around the rim.

14.25in (36cm) high

£2,000-2,500   WW

A Chinese Wanli period Kraaksporselein pear-shaped bottle vase, decorated in underglaze blue with precious objects and fruiting branches.

12.5in (32cm) high

£400-600   DN

A Chinese blue and white Transitional vase, painted with bamboo, peony and four birds squabbling in mid air, beneath finely incised bands.

c1640   *7.75in (19.5cm) high*

£1,500-2,000   WW

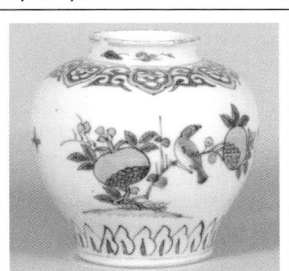

A Chinese Transitional porcelain small jar, decorated in underglaze blue with birds in pomegranate branches, rui border.

4.75in (12cm) high

£500-800   DN

A Chinese blue-painted bottle vase, Kangxi period, with long neck above globular body, decorated with a continuous landscape scene depicting scholars, literati and sages enjoying the beauties of the surrounding lake, pavilions, bridges, boats and mountains.

17.5in (44.5cm) high

£13,000-18,000   L&T

CLOSER LOOK: KANGXI BLUE AND WHITE VASE

Porcelain from this era was more refined than previously.

The quality of the painting is exceptional, with plenty of well-executed details in the expressions on the faces and the clothing.

The glaze tended to be glassy and very thin.

Landscape scenes painted in the Kangxi era often suggest a craggy remoteness. They tend to wrap around the piece rather than be limited to panels.

A large Chinese Kangxi period blue and white baluster vase, the flared neck with a band of key fret above a continuous scene of nine figures, including a fisherman casting in a mountain lake, a jui fungus mark.

17in (43cm) high

£26,000+   WW

A 17thC Chinese blue and white ovoid vase and cover, painted with alternate roundels of dragon and phoenix divided by lotus, the shoulder with prunus flowers on cracked ice, chips around the rim of the cover.

11.5in (29cm) high

£1,000-1,500   **WW**

A Chinese Kangxi period blue and white gourd vase, painted with scrolling foliage and lotus flowers, six-character Chenhua mark.

9.25in (23.5cm) high

£2,000-2,500   **WW**

A Chinese blue-painted 'Red Cliff' vase, with flared neck and square tapered body, the neck decorated with bamboo, two sides decorated with the two 'Odes to the Red Cliff' by the Song poet Su Dongpo (1037 - 1096), two sides with finely painted landscapes, unglazed foot rim with glazed recess bearing six-character Kangxi mark and period.

This is one of a number of 'Red Cliff' vases made in the 1690s and painted with identical scenes, possibly taken from woodblock prints, which appear to be from the same kiln in Jingdezhen. The Red Cliffs of the poem were purported to be the site of the Battle of the Red Cliffs in AD208.

c1690   *21.5in (55cm) high*

£25,000-30,000   **L&T**

A Chinese blue-painted square tapering vase, Kangxi mark and period, the flared neck decorated with bamboo, each side of the body with a panel of different plants: magnolias, chrysanthemums, prunus and lotus, all with birds in the branches, two opposed sides with poems, unglazed foot with glazed recessed square bearing six-character mark.

This is one of a group of similar vases made in the 1690s, which appear to be the productions of a small number of non-imperial kilns in Jingdezhen.

c1690   *21.5in (54.5cm) high*

£28,000-32,000   **L&T**

A Chinese Kangxi period blue and white bell-shaped candlestick, decorated with the wa wa playing on a fenced terrace, a flower spray round the narrow neck, beneath four auspicious symbols, small frits, six-character Chenghua mark but Kangxi.

5.5in (14cm) high

£800-1,200   **WW**

A Chinese Kangxi period blue and white vase, painted with six figures, plantain and rockwork, small chips around the foot rim, together with a wood cover.

8.5in (21.5cm) high

£1,000-1,500   **WW**

A Chinese Kangxi period blue and white brush stand, cylindrical form with an open mouth, painted to show a rocky village landscape.

5.75in (14.5cm) high

£1,000-1,200   **FRE**

A Chinese Kangxi period blue and white baluster vase, painted with two scaly four-clawed dragons, in pursuit of pearls of wisdom above breaking waves, the base with an artemesia leaf, together with a wood cover and stand.

11.25in (28.5cm) high

£3,000-3,500   **WW**

A small Chinese Kangxi period blue and white pear-shaped vase, decorated with three panels of peony and chrysanthemum.

6in (15.5cm) high

£300-400   **WW**

A Chinese Kangxi period blue and white double gourd vase, decorated with scrolling lotus, the base with an artemesia leaf, old restoration to the neck.

10.5in (26.5cm) high

£400-500   **WW**

A pair of Chinese Kangxi period bottle vases, with onion necks and decorated in underglaze blue with archaistic lappets.

11.75in (30cm) high

£1,800-2,200   DN

A Chinese Kangxi period blue and white ewer and cover, decorated with two Europeans sitting naked on rockwork amidst flowers and foliage, one holding a scythe, frits and firing cracks.

7in (18cm) high

£1,000-2,000   WW

A Chinese Kangxi period blue and white triple gourd vase, of graduating triple-gourd form, painted with violet blue to show a leaf border to slender neck, cranes, Fu lions and Buddhistic symbols, neck may have been ground down.

9in (23cm) high

£350-450   FRE

A Chinese Qianlong period blue and white Ming-style vase, painted with a frieze of archaic foliage between upright and pendant stiff leaves, the neck applied with a pair of cylindrical handles joined by a key fret band, Qianlong six-character seal mark.

7.75in (19.5cm) high

£8,000-10,000   WW

An 18thC Chinese blue and white guglet with a hua shih glaze, decorated with panels of figures, flowers and butterflies.

9.5in (24cm) high

£450-650   WW

An 18thC Chinese blue and white ovoid vase, decorated with four dragons amidst clouds above a band of breaking waves.

8.25in (21cm) high

£1,200-1,500

WW

A small Chinese blue and white vase, painted with two panels of figures, the base with a six-character Kangxi seal mark but later.

7in (18cm) high

£550-650

WW

A large pair of 19thC Chinese blue and white vases, with wood bases.

23.5in (60cm) high

£30,000-35,000

SOTP

A Chinese blue and white vase, painted with birds and lion dogs, amidst rocks and waves, the neck reduced.

10.75in (27.5cm) high

£300-400

WW

A 19thC Chinese Export baluster vase, decorated in underglaze blue with two pairs of Dutch fishermen, four-character Kangxi mark.

7.5in (19cm) high

£250-350

DN

A Chinese 19thC blue and white beaker vase, potted with a trumpet mouth and splayed foot, painted in rich violet blue tones to show a Lao Tzu with attendant amongst rock work and trees to the mouth and neck, four immortals to the bulbous body and two figures among a mountainous forest to the foot.

18in (45.5cm) high

£800-1,200

FRE

A pair of 19thC Chinese blue-painted flasks, each having shoulders decorated with stylised scrolling foliage, the sides with dragons amongst clouds, some damage.

11.5in (29.5cm) high

£1,800-2,200   **L&T**

A 19thC Chinese blue and white double gourd vase, decorated with prunus on a blue ground, four-character Kangxi mark.

12.25in (31cm) high

£150-250   **WW**

A 19thC Chinese Transitional-style blue and white sleeve vase, painted with two ducks and a woodcock amidst lotus, the shoulder and foot with incised bands, the rim with a firing fault and small chip.

10.75in (27cm) high

£120-180   **WW**

A 19thC Chinese blue and white small rouleau vase, decorated with warriors and panels of calligraphy, a four-character Kangxi mark.

10.5in (26.5cm) high

£400-600   **WW**

A 19thC Chinese blue and white Transitional-style sleeve vase, painted with aquatic birds amidst lotus, between anhua bands.

14.75in (27cm) high

£550-750   **WW**

A 19thC Chinese blue and white yen yen vase, painted with figures fishing from a boat and in discussion, in a rocky landscape, unmarked.

16.75in (42.5cm) high

£700-1,000   **WW**

(Centre) A pair of 19thC Chinese Export Canton candlesticks, worked in the typical Canton palette, blossoming trees, rockworks and pagodas.

12in (30.5cm) high

£200-300   **FRE**

(Outside) A pair of 19thC Chinese Export Canton vases, the neck panelled by a leaf border, the body worked in Canton palette, the base with floral sprays.

12in (30.5cm) high

£900-1,100   **FRE**

A pair of large 19thC Chinese blue-painted vases and covers, decorated with dragons chasing birds of wisdom amongst the clouds, some damage.

24.5in (62cm) high

£1,800-2,200   **L&T**

A 19thC Chinese rouleau vase with painted decoration on a blue ground, depicting vases and boxes on stands and tables with flowers.

18in (46cm) high

£1,500-2,000   **L&T**

A 19thC Chinese blue and white tulip vase, decorated with scrolling chrysanthemum, damage to the neck.

9.75in (24.5cm) high

£300-400   **WW**

A 19thC Chinese blue and white vase, with a tall central neck with five apertures to the lobed body.

9.75in (24.5cm) high

£400-500   **WW**

A 19thC Chinese bottle vase, decorated in iron red and blue with a landscape scene and figures crossing a bridge beneath willow with mountains in the background.

14.5in (37cm) high

£1,000-1,500   **WW**

A pair of Chinese blue and white ovoid vases, decorated with birds perched on rockwork from which peonies grow.

c1900

6.75in (17cm) high

£400-500   **WW**

A pair of Chinese Export covered vases, the domed lids with f-lion finials, the baluster sides decorated with figures and pagoda within a continuous landscape.

12.5in (32cm) diam

£1,000-1,500   **L&T**

A 19thC Chinese blue and white moon flask, slender neck painted with a leaf border, the flat oval body applied with qilong to the shoulder in reverse, the body is painted with two oval panels depicting warring horsemen panelled by a foliate scrolling diaper.

10in (25.5cm) high

£700-1,000   **FRE**

A Chinese probably Tianqi period dish, with everted rim and decorated in underglaze blue with a figure of a sage beneath the moon.

8.75in (22cm) diam

£800-1,000   DN

A pair of 17thC Chinese blue and white dishes, painted with deer, bats and shrubs, contained in silk-lined case.

6.25in (16cm) high

£1,000-1,200   A&G

A Kangxi circular blue and white dish, decorated with fruit and leaves, bearing label of Jeffrey Waters, London, small chips to rim.

6.25in (16cm) diam

£1,200-1,400   A&G

A Kangxi period Chinese blue-painted charger, boldly decorated with a dragon and foliage to the well, blue-painted character mark.

13.25in (34cm) diam

£2,000-2,500   L&T

A 17th/18thC Chinese Swatow charger, of deep dished form with bronzed metal rim, blue-painted with a trellis work border interspersed with panels painted with stylised flowers, the well painted with an exotic bird amongst a profusion of flowers and foliage.

18in (45.5cm) diam

£700-900   L&T

A pair of Chinese blue and white dishes, with foliate rims and painted with flowering tree peonies issuing from rockwork, the backs with three flowering branches, with six-character Kangxi marks, one with a hair crack, both with rim chips.

14in (36cm) high

£1,800-2,200   WW

A pair of Chinese Kangxi period blue and white porcelain bowls, the lobed sides decorated with figure on a junk within a stylised foliate and geometric panelled border.

10.5in (26.5cm)

£1,500-2,000   L&T

A Chinese Kangxi period blue and white moulded dish, painted with four birds, a butterfly and flowers.

9in (23cm) high

£150-250   WW

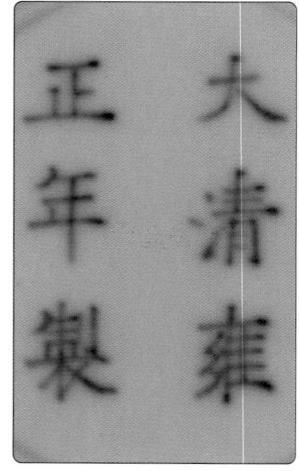

A Chinese Yongzheng period blue and white dish, the interior painted with a continuous scrolling lotus in a circular cartouche, the exterior with a similar lotus scroll, six-character mark of Yongzheng, one repaired crack.

8in (20.5cm) high

£1,200-1,500   WW

A large Chinese Qianlong period blue and white saucer dish, decorated with scrolling lotus flowers and leaves, unmarked.

c1780   *14.5in (37cm) high*

£4,000-6,000   WW

A Chinese Qianlong period Ming-style small saucer dish, decorated on the interior with a tied bouquet of lotus flowers and leaves, the rim and exterior with a continuous flower scroll, small rim crack and chips. Qianlong six-character mark.

4.5in (11.5cm) high

£800-1,000   WW

A Chinese Qianlong period blue and white rectangular dish, decorated with a pagoda landscape, light damage.

11.5in (29cm) high

£100-150   WW

An unusual 18thC Chinese blue and white Ming-style dish, painted with a band of asters, other flowers and foliage, unmarked.

6.25in (16cm) high

£300-400   WW

A Qianlong period Chinese Export shaped rectangular meat dish, decorated in blue with a river landscape.

13.5in (34.5cm) wide

£250-350   DN

A Chinese Qianlong period export canted rectangular meat dish, decorated in underglaze blue with a river landscape.

18in (46cm) wide

£250-350   DN

A pair of 18thC Chinese Export blue and white vegetable dishes, each decorated in underglaze blue with riverside landscape views with figures and pagoda.

14.75in (37.5cm) wide

£800-1,200   L&T

A pair of 18thC Chinese blue and white porcelain chargers, each decorated in underglaze blue with courtiers by pagoda, within a geometric border with foliate reserves.

14.5in (37cm) diam

£4,000-5,000   L&T

A pair of 18thC Chinese Export chargers, for the Near Eastern market, decorated in underglaze blue with foliate wreath within a border of finger citron and peaches.

14in (35.5cm) diam

£500-800   DN

A Qianlong period Chinese Export shaped oval dish, decorated in underglaze blue with figures by a pavilion in a river landscape.

15.25in (39cm) wide

£250-350   DN

A large 18thC Chinese blue and white dish, the centre painted with two squirrels on a grape vine beneath bamboo within a border carved with stylised scroll work, a faint rim crack.

15.5in (38.5cm) high

£250-350   WW

A Chinese Kangxi blue dragon circular dish.

1821-1850   *10in (25.5cm) diam*

£200-300   JN

ORIENTAL

A Chinese Wanli period Kraaksporselein barbed bowl, decorated in underglaze blue with a grasshopper and butterfly with a peony, panelled borders.

6in (15cm) high

£350-550 **DN**

A Chinese Kangxi period blue and white bowl, painted inside and out with a procession of four dragons, each with a lotus, six-character Chenghua mark, but Kangxi, a small rim chip.

8.25in (21cm) high

£600-800 **WW**

A Chinese Kangxi period blue and white bowl, blue double rings to base, of compressed globular form, gently flared rim, painted with a diaper to rim, lingzhi head band, enclosing a body of Indian lotus flowers and shou characters, blue ring to a short circular foot.

3in (7.5cm) wide

£600-1,000 **FRE**

A large Chinese Kangxi period foliate-rimmed blue and white bowl, modelled around a deep U-shaped body, the interior is incised to show sixteen lotus petals, the interior rim is panelled with a blue border of floral sprays, the interior medallion shows a very finely painted peony enclosed by double blue rings, the exterior is equally well painted to show petal-shaped panels of peony and lotus flowers, over a short circular foot, Kangxi Lingzhi mark in blue double circles.

10in (25.5cm) diam

£2,500-3,500 **FRE**

CLOSER LOOK: KANGXI BLUE AND WHITE BOWL

The false gadroon border around the rim of the bowl is repeated around the foot.

Flowers and plants were a popular decorative theme for Kangxi potters. Here, bamboo and flowering prunus are entwined around the sides of the bowl.

The mark inside the bowl dates from 1426-35, although the bowl was made over 200 years later. Potters used earlier marks to pay tribute to their ancestors.

The base is decorated with a floral medallion.

A rare Chinese Kangxi period blue and white bowl, decorated with bamboo and flowering prunus above a band of false gadroons, the rim with a key fret border, Xuande six-character mark to the interior.

5in (13cm) high

£10,000-15,000 **WW**

A Chinese Qianlong period bowl with a flared rim, painted in blue and underglaze copper red with three lion dogs chasing brocade balls, the base with a six-character Qianlong seal mark.

7.75in (19.5cm) high

£500-600 **WW**

A second half 18thC Chinese armorial large bowl, painted in blue with a crest of Larken within a Fitzhugh band and borders, small chips to the rim.

11.75in (30cm) high

£600-800 **WW**

A 19thC Chinese square-section bowl, the interior painted in blue with the eight Daoist Immortals encircling a dragon, the exterior with a raspberry glaze, six-character Xuande mark.

10.5in (26.5cm) high

£400-600 **WW**

A 19thC Chinese blue and white oval basket, the centre painted with a scene of boats on a river, pierced sides and blue-banded decoration to the rim.

10.5in (27cm) wide

£100-150 **ROS**

A pair of 19thC Chinese square-section flaring bowls, the exteriors decorated with a continuous lotus scroll in underglaze blue with gilt outlines, the interior and foot glazed in turquoise, each with a six-character seal mark.

5in (12.5cm) high

£600-800 WW

A large modern Chinese bowl, painted in the Yuan style, with lotus, breaking waves and precious objects.

16.25in (41cm) high

£100-200 WW

A late 18thC Chinese Export tureen, cover and stand, of typical farming hamlet scene, good leaf-shaped finial to slightly domed cover, rectangular base applied with animal head handles, over a shaped rectangular stand.

Stand 14.25in (36cm) wide

£800-1,000 FRE

A late 18thC Chinese Export blue and white tureen, of rectangular form, the domed cover is surmounted by a gilded berry finial, the base is applied with two moulded interlaced handles to the shoulder also partially gilded, painted in a blue canton palette.

12in (30.5cm) wide

£500-700 FRE

A late 18thC Chinese Export blue and white tureen and cover, of oval form, domed cover surmounted by a scrolled leaf, butterfly and ruyi clouds to cover, the base applied with two large shell-shaped handles, typical palette painted to body.

14in (35.5cm) wide

£800-1,200 FRE

A Chinese Kangxi period blue and white porcelain teapot, of fluted conical form with domed cover and rigid handle, spout replaced.

7.25in (18.5cm) high

£350-450 L&T

A Chinese Kangxi period wine pot in the form of a pomegranate, decorated in underglaze blue with pomegranates and flowering branches.

4.75in (12cm) high

£1,000-1,200 DN

A 19thC Chinese blue and white Cadogan teapot, formed as a peach, and painted with birds perched amidst flowers and foliage.

8.25in (21cm) high

£200-300 WW

A Chinese Kangxi period blue and white brushpot, painted with a fisherman on a riverbank watching a swooping bird catch his fish while his rod lies at his feet, all in a continuous mountain river landscape, a hair crack.

6.5in (16.5cm) high

£3,000-4,000 WW

A large 19thC Chinese Kangxi style blue and white brush pot, decorated with male figures in a landscape scene, the reverse painted with a feather.

10in (25.5cm) diam

£800-1,200 L&T

A Chinese blue and white cylindrical brushpot, decorated with scrolling leaves and lotus flowers, a four-character Xuande mark.

c1900 *5.5in (14cm) high*

£300-500 WW

A 17thC Chinese Export ware small wine cup decorated in underglaze blue with a dragon.

1.5in (4cm) high

£150-250 DN

A Chinese Kangxi period blue and white wine cup, with 19thC silver metal mounts.

4.25in (10.5cm) high

£250-350 WW

A Chinese blue and white Kangxi stem cup, with three young boys in a garden, bears label 'Glasgow art galleries and museums', slight crack.

3.75in (9.5cm) high

£1,000-1,500 JN

A Chinese chamber pot, from the Nanking Cargo, painted in blue with a trailing vine, 'Christie's Nanking Cargo' label.

c1750 *6in (15.5cm) high*

£250-350 WW

A Chinese blue and white barrel-shaped mug, painted with peony and prunus issuing from rockwork, small rim chip.

c1780 *15.25in (13.5cm) high*

£70-100 WW

An 18thC pair of Chinese blue and white silver shaped sauce boats, each painted with birds, rockwork, and flowers beneath pine trees, one handle damaged.

10in (25cm) high

£150-250 WW

A large 18thC Chinese blue underglazed porcelain tile, of tall rectangular form, well-painted scrolling cloud diaper over two court officials writing at a table.

17in (43cm) high

£500-700 FRE

A pair of probably 19thC Chinese garden seats decorated with flowers and precious objects in white slip on a pale blue ground.

19in (48cm) high

£3,000-3,500 DN

A pair of 19thC Chinese Export tea bowls and two saucers, the bowls with European white metal handles, one of the saucers has the seal stating 'Duveen, Liverpool'.

£100-200 DN

A 19thC Chinese blue and white beehive-shaped waterpot, Kangxi mark.

3.75in (9.5cm) high

£100-200 WW

CLOSER LOOK: IMPERIAL 'DRAGON' STEM CUP

When the bowl is exposed to the light a double dragon which has been superimposed into the porcelain is revealed.

The bowl has been incised with a dragon chasing a pearl which became a prominent decorative symbol in 15thC China. A dragon can symbolise success, wealth, power, bravery and nobility. If it loses the pearl it becomes helpless and incapable of action.

Monochrome wares were made for the four altars used for imperial ceremony and sacrifice. Brilliant yellow ceramics were used at the Altar of Earth. Because they were destined for the Imperial family they are of the highest quality.

The chenghua reign mark refers to the period from 1465-87.

A rare Chinese Imperial 'Dragon' stem cup, deep U-shaped form, incised to show a dragon chasing a pearl, with double dragon superimposed into the porcelain revealed when exposed to light, the bowl is supported above a circular base, Chenghua blue six-character mark.

Deaccessioned from the Shanghai Museum between 1993-96.

5.5in (14cm) high

£1,500-2,500   **FRE**

A 16thC Zhengde single yellow-glazed circular shallow dish, hairline crack.

1.75in (4cm) high

£3,000-3,500   **A&G**

A Chinese Kangxi period Imperial Lemon-yellow saucer dish, finely potted with shallow curved sides rising from a short circular foot, covered in a bright imperial lemon-yellow glaze, Kangxi blue six-character mark to base.

7in (18cm) diam

£1,500-2,500   **FRE**

A Yongzheng circular shallow dish, painted with green foliated medallions on yellow ground, two repaired small chips to rim.

5.75in (15cm) diam

£2,000-2,500   **A&G**

An 18thC Chinese Imperial Yellow dragon incised bowl, the exterior incised finely to show two elongated dragons chasing the flaming pearl of happiness among clouds, the interior and exterior are glazed in a rich lemon yellow, unglazed base, Chenghua blue six-character mark.

5.25in (13cm) diam

£2,000-3,000   **FRE**

A Chinese Guangxu period yellow-glazed bowl with everted rim, incised on the exterior with dragons chasing flaming pearls above rockwork and breaking waves, six-character mark of Guangxu.

6.75in (17cm) high

£600-800   **WW**

ORIENTAL

A Chinese Kangxi period blanc de Chine standing figure of Guanyin, with traces of original red pigment.

15.25in (39cm) high

£100-200   **WW**

An early 18thC Chinese blanc de Chine figure of Guanyin, seated on rockwork holding a child in her arms, some damage.

7in (17.5cm) high

£300-400   **WW**

A Qianlong blue blanc de Chine group, of a woman with a child on her shoulders and a young girl at her side carrying a mask, standing on a plain unglazed base.

c1750   *7in (18cm) high*

£300-400   **JN**

A 20thC Chinese blanc de Chine figure of Guanyin, standing holding a flask, and raised on a lotus throne, some good restoration.

19.75in (50cm) high

£80-120   **WW**

A first half 17thC Chinese blanc de Chine model of a Buddhistic lion dog, seated with his left paw on a brocade ball, some restoration.

20.75in (53cm) high

c1700

£1,000-1,500   **WW**

A rare Chinese Kangxi blanc de Chine model of a European figure, seated on the back of a standing kylin, its head turned to dexter, minor good restoration.

c1700   *5in (13cm) high*

£1,000-1,500   **WW**

A pair of 19thC Chinese Export porcelain blanc de chine figures of parrots, perched on tree stumps, with rock-form bases.

17.5in (44cm) high

£1,000-1,500   **NA**

A 17thC Chinese blanc de Chine tripod censer, decorated with the eight trigrams and raised on animal mask feet.

9.5in (24cm) high

£500-700   **WW**

A Chinese blanc de Chine rhinoceros horn libation cup, applied with moulded kylin and prunus.

c1700   *5.75in (14.5cm) diam*

£500-700   **WW**

A 17th/18thC Chinese qingbai moulded silver rimmed lotus-form bowl, of deep U-shape with a moulded foliate rim mounted in a silver band, moulded lotus petals worked to the body, raised on a small circular foot.

6in (15cm) diam

£250-350   **FRE**

An 18thC Chinese white-glazed incised dish, modelled after earlier examples, the porcelain dish of slightly rounded form with plain cavetto, the centre incised to show a floral blossom issuing broad leaves, raised on an unglazed white porcelain foot.

11in (28cm) diam

£800-1,200   **FRE**

A Chinese Ming Dynasty white slip-glazed porcelain vase, of slender pear-shaped form, slightly flared mouth, waisted slender neck leading to a globular body, raised on a circular foot, glaze of light blue at rim to white with crackle underglaze.

16.5in (42cm) high

£1,500-2,500   **FRE**

A Chinese cylindrical brushpot, moulded in high relief, with two geese beneath lotus upon which a kingfisher is perched, four-character moulded Qianlong seal mark, a few small chips to the moulding.

5in (12.5cm) high

£250-350   **WW**

ORIENTAL

A large probably 18thC Chinese flambé vase, heavily potted with a small rim mouth of mushroom glaze above a shouldered ovoid body finely glazed raspberry, blue and purple to the exterior and interior, raspberry glaze to base.

8in (20.5cm) high

£500-1,000   FRE

A small 18thC Chinese bottle vase, decorated with a copper red glaze with considerable green flecking.

8.25in (21cm) high

£100-200   WW

An early 19thC Chinese red flambé-glazed inverted pear-shaped vase, with elephant heads to the shoulders.

11in (28cm) high

£1,200-1,500   WW

A 19thC Chinese red flambé-glazed bottle vase, together with a hardwood stand.

15.25in (39cm) high including stand

£1,100-1,400   WW

A probably 19thC Chinese Oxblood vase, short potted neck glazed light celadon, ovoid raspberry body over a tapered unglazed foot, the underside glazed light celadon with a splash of raspberry.

3.5in (9cm) high

£250-350   FRE

A 19thC Chinese copper red bottle vase, the colour thinning from the neck to a mushroom tone.

11.75in (30cm) high

£150-250   WW

A 19thC Chinese flared shallow bowl, decorated with an all-over flambé red glaze, draining from the rim.

10.5in (27cm) diam

£100-200   WW

An 18thC Chinese Langyao bottle vase, long slender neck leads to short globular body above a long cylindrical foot, the glaze runs from light whitish celadon from the mouth to rich raspberry to the body and exterior of the foot, the base is glazed white.

9.25in (23.5cm) high

£1,800-2,500   FRE

An early 18thC Chinese Langyao miniature vase, heavily potted with a short slender neck, open white glazed mouth, wide shoulder, raspberry red glaze thinning at the rim and shoulder, the base white with double blue ring, minor chipping to base.

An 18thC Chinese Langyao water pot, sloping ovoid sides, small-rimmed mouth, the glaze thins from light mushroom to raspberry to the base, the base is glazed.

3.5in (9cm) diam

£400-600   FRE

4.25in (11cm) high

£200-300   FRE

An 18th/19thC Chinese Langyao brush vase, circular cylindrical form, glaze runs from raspberry around the rim to light celadon to the body and interior, glazed base, chips to interior of mouth.

4.75in (12cm) diam

£250-350   FRE

A Chinese 19thC Langyao peach bloom vase, potted with a slender neck above a compressed globular body, light raspberry glaze running from the rim, mottled green spots to the body, recessed unglazed marked base, knife cut marks to base, Qianlong blue archaic mark.

7in (18cm) high

£250-350   FRE

ORIENTAL

A Chinese possibly Kangxi period peach bloom amphora, of typical form, open mouth with slender neck above a shouldered body and recessed base above a wood stand, Kangxi blue six-character mark, repair to neck.

A 19thC Chinese peachbloom-glazed brush washer, the base with a six-character Kangxi mark.

4.75in (12cm) high

£100-200   WW

5.5in (14cm) high

£350-500   FRE

A pair of early 19thC Chinese coral-red bowls.

5.5in (14cm) diam

£3,500-5,000   SOTP

A 20thC Chinese coral-glazed eggshell porcelain ovoid vase with a flared neck, a fine gold line rim, the base with a four-character gilt 'shen de tang zhi' mark: hall for the cultivation of virtue.

10.25in (26cm) high

£600-800   WW

A 17thC Chinese porcelain blue glazed vase, of globular shape with a tall neck, having 18thC ormolu scrolled mounts.

17in (44cm) high

£2,500-3,000 SWO

A 17thC Chinese bowl with a slightly everted rim covered in a deep blue monochrome glaze, six-character Xuande mark.

7.5in (19cm) high

£800-1,200 DN

A Chinese Qianlong period blue ground teabowl and saucer, decorated in gilt with lotus and dragons, some wear, small chips and probably associated, each with a Qianlong seal mark.

4.5in (11.5cm) high

£200-300 WW

A Chinese Qianlong period blue monochrome dish, of slightly rounded form, brown fired rim, strong blue underglaze raised on a thin circular foot, Qianlong seal mark.

10.5in (26.5cm) diam

£1,000-1,500 FRE

An 18thC Chinese powder blue monochrome vase, of tapering shouldered form, good even powder-blue glaze over white porcelain circular base unglazed.

12in (30.5cm) high

£250-350 FRE

An 18thC Chinese flambé brush wash, rich raspberry ground glaze highlighted with blue and purple, good unglazed wide mouth, interior glazed raspberry, the base glazed a dark brown, minor scratching to the interior.

5in (12.5cm) diam

£300-500 FRE

An 18th/19thC Chinese blue ground saucer dish, moulded and carved as a lotus flower, cracked and riveted.

12.75in (32.5cm) high

£50-150 WW

A Chinese lobed blue ground bowl, decorated in gilt with a stork, jui fungus, and mandarin ducks swimming amidst lotus, gilt seal mark for Xianfeng.

5.5in (14cm) high

£100-200 WW

A 19thC Chinese powder blue ovoid vase, decorated in gilt with panels of figures, on a scrolling ground, some wear to the gilding.

10in (25cm) high

£150-250 WW

ORIENTAL

A 19thC Chinese rectangular-section baluster vase, lightly moulded with long life characters and bifid dragons, with a pale blue glaze, Qianlong six-character seal mark but later, drilled hole to the base.

11in (28cm) high

£100-200   **WW**

A 19thC Chinese ovoid vase, decorated with a gilt dragon phoenix amidst cloud scrolls above breaking waves on a blue ground, some wear to the gilding.

3in (7.5cm) high

£100-200   **WW**

A pair of 18thC Chinese turquoise glazed ormolu-mounted porcelain vases and covers, each of swollen form with a berried finial, the collar cast with scrolls and foliage, raised on a leaf-cast scrolling base, the mounts struck with export stamps.

16.5in (42cm) high

£6,000-8,000   **FRE**

A large 18th/19thC Chinese turquoise glazed brush pot, finely incised body showing a Roman key border above a flower medallion, bat, ruyi cloud and foliate scroll body over a border of scrolling sea, Qianlong incised seal mark.

7.5in (19cm) high

£300-500   **FRE**

A 19thC Chinese rectangular section Ge-yao ware vase, the neck with animal masks handles.

10.25in (26cm) high

£500-700   **WW**

A Chinese 19thC clair de lune glazed vase, the compressed circular body with a tall cylindrical neck around which is coiled a bifid dragon, Qianlong six-character seal mark.

4.75in (12cm) high

£100-200   **WW**

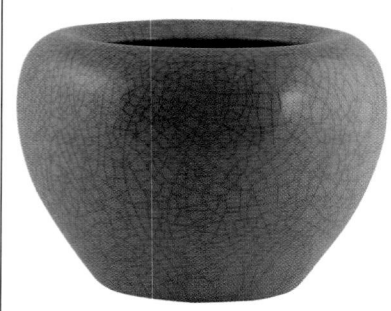

A 19thC Chinese crackle glaze bowl, with inturned rim.

9in (23cm) high

£600-800   **WW**

A 19thC Chinese lavender-glazed bowl, the rim applied with a dragon and a bat, six-character Yongzheng mark, but later, a wood stand.

10.5in (27cm) high

£100-200   **WW**

A 19thC Chinese baluster vase and lid, decorated overall in a faintly crackled green vase.

15.75in (40cm) high

£800-1,200   **WW**

A 19thC Chinese green glazed bottle vase, moulded as a lotus flower, from which rise reeds and prunus flowers, six-character Qianlong mark moulded to the base.

16.75in (42.5cm) high

£400-600   **WW**

A small Chinese early Ming dynasty celadon tripod censer, the slightly flared cylindrical body crisply moulded with the eight trigrams.

3.25in (8cm) high

£600-700   **WW**

A pair of 18thC Chinese Export celadon glazed and painted models of doves, well-modelled incised eyes, feather and branch to base, signs of brown paint to beak and branch.

7in (18cm) high

£600-800   **FRE**

A Chinese celadon cong, moulded with the eight trigrams on each face, six-character mark of Yongzheng but later.

7in (18cm) high

£350-450   **WW**

A late 19thC Chinese celadon glazed moonflask, each side decorated with the Yin Yang symbol encircled by the eight trigrams, together with a wood stand.

c1900   *7.5in (19cm) high*

£500-600   **WW**

A 19th/20thC Chinese celadon glaze archaic style incised vase, trumpet neck incised to show leaves, the pear-shaped body is incised to show dragons amongst scrolling leaves and lotus flower, circular graduating base.

13in (33cm) high

£150-250   **FRE**

A rare probably 19thC Chinese porcelain Ding, simulation bronze, of archaic form, each side decorated with taotie masks, and raised on splayed feet, the body splashed with turquoise and heightened with gilding, the base with a moulded six-character Qianlong mark, all on an elaborate and reticulated hard wood stand, the cover set with a jade knop, minor repairs.

17.5in (44.5cm) high overall

£6,000-8,000   **WW**

A Chinese Ming Dynasty gold-splash censer, the thin rimmed mouth leads to a rounded tapered body terminating in a circular impress marked foot, the body splashed irregularly with gold, Jianwen four-character mark.

4.5in (11.5cm) diam

£500-800   **FRE**

A 19thC Chinese brown-glazed bottle vase, with a moulded writhing dragon around the neck.

13in (33cm) high

£500-700   **WW**

A 19thC Chinese flambé glazed shallow bowl, the unctuous glaze flecked with turquoise.

10.5in (27cm) high

£200-300   **WW**

A 19thC Chinese ovoid vase with tall flaring neck and lion mask handles, decorated with a dark brown glaze, incised four-character Qianlong mark.

14.25in (36cm) high

£300-400   **WW**

A Chinese Ming Dynasty black and brown glazed wine jar, the rust brown slip under a black glaze, revealing brown at the small neck and small handles to the shoulder, tapering ovoid body over a circular base.

22in (56cm) high

£300-500   **FRE**

A Chinese Ming period tea-dust type and black glazed stoneware wine jar, small rounded rim over a short broad tea-dust glazed shoulder, leading to black body.

24in (61cm) high

£500-800   **FRE**

A large Chinese Ming Dynasty black glaze stoneware wine jar, rounded rim over a short neck issuing from an ovoid wide shouldered body, applied with neifu 'inner palace' characters, body tapering to a circular foot.

24in (61cm) high

£2,000-3,000   **FRE**

A 19thC Chinese robin's egg glaze vase, of shouldered ovoid form, ribbed potted neck, purple glaze to the shoulder leading to light blue, unglazed white base marked with double blue circles, imperfection of glaze to shoulder.

7.5in (19cm) high

£400-600 **FRE**

A 19thC Chinese ge-type glazed brush pot, of waisted moulded tall 'rocky' form, crackle glaze to celadon underglazed, unglazed stoneware base rim.

4in (10cm) high

£250-350 **FRE**

One of a pair of 19thC Chinese Fukien bowls, each moulded in the form of a flower with overlapping petals, and a central bloom to the interior.

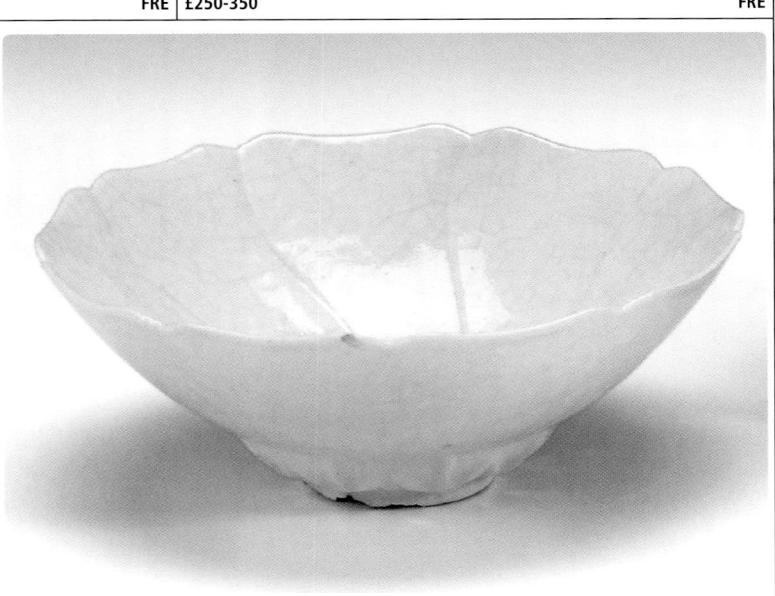

5in (12.5cm) diam

£180-220 PAIR **FRE**

A 19thC Chinese crackle glazed compressed circular brush washer.

7in (18cm) high

£80-120 **WW**

ORIENTAL

ESSENTIAL REFERENCE: FAMILLE VERTE

Literally meaning 'green family', Famille Verte was adopted during the Kangxi period (1662-1722).

● It evolved from the five colour Wucai style.

● The predominant colours are bright apple green and iron red, combined with blue, yellow and aubergine. With the exception of cobalt blue and copper red, these enamels were painted over the glaze.

● Flowers combined with black speckled diapers are common in small patterns. Larger designs include landscapes and gardens, figures, the Eight Precious Things, and the Eight Buddhist Emblems. Some designs may include the coats of arms of wealthy northern European families as many large dinner services were commissioned.

● Famille Verte was produced well into the 20thC, but the most desirable pieces are from the Kangxi period.

A Chinese Kangxi period porcelain famille verte baluster vase, converted to a lamp with good gilt-bronze mounts, well-painted with Buddhistic symbols to a green scrolling border to the shoulder, the body painted with a continuous figural scene.

Porcelain 10in (25.5cm) high

£700-1,000   FRE

A pair of Chinese Kangxi period famille verte bottle vases, decorated with phoenix amongst peony.

7.75in (19.5cm) high

£600-800   DN

A 19thC Chinese famille verte baluster vase, painted with six panels containing flowers, four-character mark.

14.5in (37cm) high

£300-400   WW

A pair of 19thC Chinese famille verte rouleau vases, painted with the eight horses of Mu Wang.

10.25in (26cm) high

£800-1,200   WW

A 19thC Chinese porcelain famille verte vase, of tapering rectangular form, leaf border to neck, scrolling leaf border to four panels depicting mountain landscapes, good cast bronze base mount stamped 'R860'.

Porcelain 19in (48cm) high

£400-600   FRE

A pair of late 19thC Chinese Canton famille verte vases, decorated with panels of figures and birds in branches, one with a small rim chip.

10in (25cm) high

£250-350   WW

A large late 19thC Chinese famille verte covered jar, of baluster form, the cover of domed form, surmounted with a gold finial, the green ground enamelled with butterflies and floral sprays.

25in (63.5cm) high

£700-1,000   FRE

A pair of Chinese Kangxi period famille verte ewers and covers, decorated with bands of flowers and foliage around the bodies.

8.75in (22.5cm) high

£1,400-1,600   WW

A 19thC Chinese famille verte ewer, the cylindrical body divided by three horizontal shallow ribs, and decorated with fabulous animals, in yellow and aubergine on a green swirling ground, damage to the spout.

14.25in (36.5cm) high

£450-550   WW

A Chinese Kangxi period famille verte moulded dish, decorated with a phoenix in flight above a lion dog, the border with panels of birds, beasts, flowers, trees and rockwork, lingzhi mark, a faint rim crack.

9.5in (24cm) high

£1,200-1,500   WW

A Chinese Kangxi period famille verte saucer dish, painted with flowers inside cartouches, and a central stylised flower, the centre with a drilled hole.

10.5in (26.5cm) high

£150-250   WW

A pair of Guangxu famille verte enamelled chargers, well-enamelled Roman key border green ground rim enamelled with lotus leaves and shou symbols, the yellow ground interior is enamelled to show an iron red and black dragon among white blossoms.

c1900   *16in (40.5cm) diam*

£600-900   FRE

A Chinese Kangxi period famille verte bowl, decorated with panels of flowers and foliage, the interior decorated with lotus, leaves and flowers, rim chips.

11.5in (29.5cm) high

£800-1,000   WW

A matched pair of 19thC Chinese famille verte fish bowls, enamelled with floral sprays and animals to a scrolling green lead ground, one enamelled with fish and reeds to the interior.

15in (38cm) high

£600-1,000   FRE

A pair of 19thC Chinese famille verte Buddhistic lion dogs, on their backs playing with brocade balls, and raised on reticulated bases, both with some repairs.

5in (13cm) high

£350-450   WW

A Chinese Kangxi period famille verte libation cup, enamelled on the biscuit with lion mask and Wang characters, applied dragon handles.

3.75in (9.5cm) high

£800-1,000   DN

FAMILLE ROSE

A small Chinese Yongzheng period famille rose vase, loosely painted with colourful flowers, the neck reduced.

6.5in (16.5cm) high

£180-220   WW

A Chinese Yongzheng period famille rose vase, painted with figures and foliage, and with a flying bat, cracked to the neck.

10in (25.5cm) high

£450-650   WW

An unusually large Chinese Qianlong period famille rose moonflask

19.25in (49cm) high

£150,000-200,000   SOTP

A rare Chinese Qianlong period yellow famille rose wall vase, Qianlong mark.

8in (20cm) high

£40,000-50,000   **SOTP**

A small Chinese Qianlong period famille rose double vase, painted with flowering branches issuing from verdant rockwork, the reverse with further flowers and foliage.

5in (13cm) high

£2,500-3,500   **WW**

A pair of large late 18th/early19thC Chinese famille rose vases, each with well-balanced long flared slender neck, above shouldered globular body, painted in mirror image from mouth to base to show four blackbirds amongst peony, floral sprays, gnarled tree trunks and flying butterflies, over drilled wood bases, possibly Qianlong blue seal mark drilled through.

22.5in (57cm) high

£8,000-12,000   **FRE**

A small pair of 19thC Chinese famille rose vases, each painted with two black ducks beneath rockwork and peony, each with calligraphy to the reverse, each marked with 'Ju ren tang zhi' (Hall where Benevolence Resides).

5.5in (13.5cm) high

£1,000-1,200   **WW**

A 19thC Chinese famille rose ovoid vase with tall flaring neck, decorated with three maiden immortals riding in a log boat amidst breaking waves, the neck painted with Shoulao and an attendant, Qianlong six-character mark.

12.25in (31cm) high

£1,100-1,300   **WW**

A pair of 19thC Chinese famille rose gourd-shaped vases, painted with panels containing bats, flowers and lanterns, one with a rim crack.

15.75in (40cm) high

£2,500-3,000   **WW**

A 19thC Chinese famille rose moon flask, one side painted with figures hunting, the reverse with pheasants on rockwork, all on a coral ground scrolling foliage, flowers and shou characters, the base with a four-character mark, small rim fault.

14.25in (36cm) high

£1,000-1,200   **WW**

A 19thC Chinese famille rose landscape floor vase, of baluster form, applied with four Qilong to the shoulder, and four Fu lions and lug handles, well-painted to the interior of the flared scalloped mouth, neck and body showing a procession and landscape.

23.5in (59.5cm) high

£2,500-3,500   **FRE**

A pair of 19thC Rose Medallion baluster floor bases, well-painted and applied with gilded qilong to the shoulder and Fu dog handles, scalloped flared mouth, the body painted with a procession of approximately forty-five figures painted in four reverse panels on a ground of green scrolling leaves and butterflies.

35in (89cm) high

£8,000-10,000   **FRE**

A 19thC Chinese Canton famille rose baluster vase, decorated with panels of figures and flowers.

14in (35.5cm) high

£300-400   **WW**

A pair of 19thC Chinese famille rose moon flasks, painted with battle scenes and phoenix, on a pink and leaf scroll ground, one with damage to the neck.

10.25in (26cm) high

£250-350   **WW**

A 19thC Chinese famille rose pear-shaped vase, decorated with long life symbols and continuous lotus scroll on a pink ground, the foot encircled by a band of false gadroons, the neck with a jui scroll.

6.75in (17cm) high

£300-400   **WW**

A Chinese Republic period famille rose bottle vase, of globular form, a long slender neck leads to a body finely painted to show five boys playing in a garden, above a well-carved wood stand, Qianlong iron red four-character mark.

6.5in (16.5cm) high

£800-1,200   **FRE**

A Chinese Republic period famille rose brush pot, of cylindrical form, painted orange and black to the body to show lady attendants in discussion.

7in (18cm) high

£300-500   **FRE**

A large Chinese Republic period famille rose brush pot, of cylindrical form, painted with a detailed continuous landscape and a black inscription and red seal mark.

7.5in (19cm) high

£350-450   **FRE**

A pair of 19th/20thC Chinese famille rose covered jars, converted to lamps, painted green, blue and orange to show court attendants in a summer garden, drilled and wired over a timber stand.

20in (51cm) high

£500-700   **FRE**

A 20thC Chinese famille rose bottle vase, decorated with butterflies and flowers, the base with a six-character Xuantong mark but later.

16in (40.5cm) high

£500-700   **WW**

A pair of 20thC Chinese mille fleurs ovoid vases with cylindrical necks, each decorated overall with densely packed flower-heads and foliage, one neck damaged, six-character Qianlong marks.

13.5in (34cm) high

£900-1,200   **WW**

A pair of massive first half 20thC Chinese famille rose bottle vases, each painted with three panels containing vases and baskets with flower set against a mille fleurs ground, the bases with four-character Qianlong marks in iron red, together with stands, one with damage to the neck.

23in (58.5cm) high

£3,000-4,000   **WW**

A Chinese Export Yongzheng period famille rose plate, painted in bright and brilliant enamels to show an official in a riverscape followed by an attendant.

8.5in (21.5cm) diam

£500-700   **FRE**

A pair of Chinese Yongzheng period famille rose saucers, delicately painted with two small children playing with a lady seated on a daybed, one damaged.

4.5in (11.5cm) diam

£300-400   **WW**

A Chinese Qianlong period famille rose plate, decorated with a pagoda landscape.

8.75in (22.5cm) diam

£100-150   **WW**

A pair of Chinese Qianlong period octagonal famille rose plates, decorated with flowers, storks and butterflies.

8.75in (22.5cm) diam

£150-250   **WW**

An 18thC Chinese famille rose chamfered rectangular dish, decorated with a boy riding a buffalo amidst landscape.

13in (33cm) high

£300-400   **WW**

A Chinese Qianlong period famille rose and bianco-sopra-bianco oval moulded dish, decorated with a central panel depicting an elephant and rider, flanked by flowers and rockwork.

8.75in (22.5cm) high

£900-1,200   **WW**

An 18thC Chinese famille rose dish, painted with two colourful birds on a flowering branch.

12.5in (32cm) diam

£600-800   **WW**

A mid-19thC Chinese Canton famille rose tazza, decorated with six figures in a garden.

9.5in (24.5cm) high

£60-100   **WW**

A 19thC Chinese Canton famille rose dish, painted with twelve figures in a garden and on a veranda.

14.75in (37.5cm) diam

£700-900   **WW**

A 20thC Chinese famille rose peach dish, decorated with a peach tree bearing six ripe fruit, Yongzheng seal mark.

7.75in (19.5cm) diam

£250-350   **WW**

A Chinese late Jiaqing period famille rose medallion bowl, decorated with four circular cartouches of figures and landscapes, on a sgraffito blue ground, the interior in underglazed blue with a central circular cartouche of two figures with an oxen in a landscape, Jiaqing six-character seal mark, some repair.

5.75in (14.5cm) high

£2,000-2,500   **WW**

CLOSER LOOK: FAMILLE ROSE LOTUS BOWL

The porcelain has been moulded and decorated to resemble a lotus flower. The delicate famille rose decoration is highlighted with gilding.

This shape is echoed in the carved wood base.

In China the lotus flower is a symbol of purity as it is a beautiful flower that rises from muddy waters. It is also one of the eight Bhuddist symbols of good fortune.

The Jaiqing period lasted from 1796-1820. The mark is usually painted in this seal mark style, rather than in conventional script.

A Chinese Jiaqing period famille rose lotus moulded shallow bowl, the interior glazed in turquoise, the petal moulded exterior painted in pink and white, the recessed foot with a six-character Jiaqing mark in iron red, together with a carved wood stand.

7in (18cm) high

£3,500-4,500   **WW**

A large Quianlong famille rose hunting bowl, the exterior with two shaped panels depicting a hunting scene with dogs and European riding horses. The interior with a European hunting man holding his gun and two dogs.

11.25in (28.5cm) diam

£2,000-2,500   **SOTA**

A Chinese famille rose Mandarin palette bowl, decorated with panels of figures at leisure before watery landscapes, on a coral ground, a rim crack.

c1780   *11.5in (29cm) high*

£350-450   **WW**

An important Chinese Export porcelain punchbowl, with an enamelled exterior of the Hongs at Canton with western figures and ornate inner borders, the flags depicted are those of Denmark, France, Sweden, Britain and Holland.

c1780-85   *14.5in (37cm) diam*

£30,000-50,000   **NA**

A Chinese famille rose medallion bowl, well-painted with panels of birds, butterflies and flowers, on a complex yellow diaper ground, six-character Qianlong mark.

8.75in (22cm) high

£450-550   **WW**

A Chinese Qianlong period famille rose porcelain bowl, the sides decorated in polychrome with reserves depicting figures in scenic views.

10.25in (26cm) diam

£800-1,000   **L&T**

A rare pair of Chinese Daoguang period famille rose phoenix bowls, each finely decorated with four mythical birds amidst flowers and foliage, bordered by fine gilt bands, each with a four-character 'shen de tang zhi' mark: hall for the cultivation of virtue, one with minor damage.

5.75in (14.5cm) high

£2,500-3,500   **WW**

A Chinese famille rose bowl, decorated on the exterior with flower heads on a geometric ground, the interior with cockerels beneath a tree, Daoguang six-character mark but later, restored.

7.25in (18.5cm) high

£150-250   **WW**

A pair of Chinese Daoguang period famille rose bowls and covers, decorated with colourful medallions, each piece with a six-character Daoguang mark.

3.5in (9cm) high

£1,200-1,800 PAIR   **WW**

A Chinese Daoguang period famille rose landscape bowl, the deep bowl with a shaped and gilded rim, leading to a continuous landscape scene with a black inscription, Daoguang iron red seal mark to base.

6.75in (17cm) diam

£450-550   **FRE**

A 19thC Chinese rose medallion gilt-bronze-mounted porcelain punch bowl, with a beaded and pierced rim, the bowl decorated with alternating reserves of figures and floral studies, raised on a pierced stepped base, the handles cast with garlands.

15.5in (39.5cm) diam

£1,500-2,500   **FRE**

A large 19thC Chinese blue ground jardinière, decorated with four famille rose panels of figures in landscapes, lion mask handles beneath the rim.

16in (41cm) high

£1,500-2,000   **WW**

A Chinese famille rose bowl, painted with a mille fleurs design on a gilt ground, four-character Qianlong mark, but later.

5.5in (14cm) high

£250-350   **WW**

A 19thC Chinese famille rose phoenix bowl and cover, decorated with five mythological birds, amidst colourful foliage and flowers, the base and cover with an iron red jui fungus.

4.5in (11cm) high

£250-350   **WW**

A large famille rose bowl, decorated with panels of exotic birds, flowers, rockwork and bamboo on a pink ground, a star crack to the base.

c1900

15.75 (40cm) high

£70-100   **WW**

A 20thC Chinese famille rose mille fleurs U-shaped bowl, four-character Qianlong mark.

2.75in (7cm) high

£150-250   **WW**

An 18thC Chinese famille rose teapot and cover, painted with birds amidst rockwork and flowers.

7in (18cm) high

£800-1,000   **WW**

A Chinese Qianlong period famille rose teapot and cover, decorated in pseudo tobacco leaf style.

8.25in (21cm) high

£900-1,200   **WW**

A 20thC Chinese famille rose teapot and cover, finely painted with ten figures in a garden, the base with a six-character Guangxu mark.

6.75in (17cm) high

£400-600   **WW**

A Chinese Yongzheng period famille rose small teabowl and saucer, painted with colourful deer, and a monkey in a peach tree.

£250-350   **WW**

A Chinese Tongzhi period, Canton famille rose teabowl and saucer, each piece decorated with panels of figures and calligraphy.

5in (12.5cm) high

£250-350   **WW**

A pair of Chinese Guangxu period famille rose flared U-shaped cups, each finely painted with a dragon and phoenix amidst clouds and above bands of breaking waves, the rims with square scrolls, each with a six-character Guangxu mark.

2.75in (7cm) high

£300-500   **WW**

A 19th/20thC Chinese famille rose cup and saucer, glazed in a puce ground, the U-shaped cup is enamelled to the interior to show a pink peony, the exterior of both is finely painted to show a village landscape.

£250-350   **FRE**

One of a pair of 18thC Chinese Export covered baluster vases, painted with a panel of green enamelled frogs, grasshoppers and red lotus flowers, over wood stand.

11in (28cm) high

£600-800 PAIR   **FRE**

An 18thC Chinese famille rose group depicting the twin Genii of Harmony and Mirth, both seated on a rock, one with an open green robe, holding a sceptre, the other in a yellow robe, holding a lotus flower, with a bat painted on the plinth.

8.5in (21.5cm) high

£800-1,200   **L&T**

A 19thC Chinese famille rose model of a standing phoenix, on a pierced rockwork base, some restoration.

12in (30.5cm) high

£100-200   **WW**

A large 20thC Chinese famille rose model of Buddhai Ho Shang, seated wearing floral robes and raised on a hardwood throne, the base with an impressed mark.

10.5in (27cm) high

£700-1,000   **WW**

A 20thC Chinese famille rose model of a scholar seated on a tiger, holding a sceptre in his right hand and with a short sword to his back.

12.5in (32cm) high

£100-150   **WW**

An 18thC Chinese famille rose cylindrical box and cover, probably for silk, the exterior finely decorated with lotus, bats and peaches, and with formal flowers to the top, the interior turquoise-glazed with a central projection and a flange pierced with nine holes.

1.75in (4.5cm) high

£5,000-7,000   **WW**

A Chinese cylindrical Mandarin palette mug, decorated with a panel of figures, a minor fault to the rim.

c1780   *5in (13cm) high*

£200-300   **WW**

An 18thC Chinese famille rose circular tureen and cover, the knop painted with an iron red chrysanthemum head, the handles in the form of shells, the cover and body painted with peacocks, peonies, rockwork and gilt bamboo.

10.25in (26cm) wide

£1,200-1,800   **L&T**

An 18thC Chinese Export desk set, well-painted in puce, famille rose and black enamel to the rear, the cover to the ink trough is painted with floral sprays and song birds, the inkwells painted to all four sides, black, puce and two famille rose scenes, one well-repaired.

8.5in (21.5cm) wide

£1,300-1,600   FRE

A 19thC Chinese famille rose tazza, decorated with scrolling lotus on a lime green ground.

4.75in (12cm) high

£500-700   WW

A set of four Chinese Republic period famille rose porcelain plaques, well-painted landscape, four columns of black script and red seal mark, rosewood frame.

48in (122cm) high

£500-700   FRE

A pair of early 20thC Canton garden seats, each profusely decorated with flowers on a green ground and with opposed rectangular panels painted with ladies in domestic settings, surrounded by bossed borders.

18.75in (47.5cm) high

£1,700-2,000   L&T

A pair of 20thC Canton garden seats, decorated with scrolling foliate borders, raised bosses and alternating panels of good luck symbols on a pink ground and exotic birds in a rocky landscape.

19.25in (49cm) high

£1,000-1,500   L&T

FAMILLE NOIRE

An unusual Chinese Kangxi period (1662-1722) famille noire octagonal vase, black ground decorated with green scroll work and petal medallions panelling twenty-eight allegorical scenes, Kangxi blue six-character mark to impressed base.

Literally meaning the 'black family', famille noire has black ground of brownish pigment from cobalt and manganese overlaid by a thin greenish enamel.

The decoration on 17th/18thC wares was of higher quality and more detailed than 19thC famille noire.

19.75in (50cm) high

£1,000-1,500   FRE

A Chinese early Kangxi period famille noire vase, heavy construction, wide rim over a short neck leading to a slightly shouldered cylindrical body, decorated with green lotus flowers issuing leaf scrolls.

10in (25.5cm) high

£800-1,000   FRE

A pair of mid-19thC Chinese Kangxi style famille noire vases, each of tapered square form decorated with cherry blossoms.

19.5in (39.5cm) high

£2,000-3,000   FRE

A 19thC Chinese famille noire cylindrical vase, decorated with flowering prunus.

11.5in (29cm) high

£200-300   WW

A pair of Chinese Yongzheng period armorial plates, well-painted with the arms of Lord Ross of Halkhead and the motto 'Think On'.

1732

9in (22.5cm) high

£1,500-2,000

WW

A pair of Chinese Armorial en grisaille decorated bowls, the rim decorated with flower sprigs to each side and crests to top and bottom, the well with gilt border and decorated with a copy of a European print 'The Rescue of Andromeda' showing Perseus driving his sword into the sea monster.

c1745

9.25in (23.5cm) diam

£1,500-2,000

L&T

A Chinese famille rose armorial plate, decorated in the centre with the arms of Gale.

c1745

9in (23cm) high

£500-700

WW

A pair of Chinese famille rose armorial plates, painted with the arms of Willey, the rim with three flower sprays, some damage and restoration.

c1745

9in (23cm) high

£50-150

WW

A Chinese Qianlong period porcelain saucer dish, the white ground with grisaille decoration and centred by a coat of arms for the Saunders family, enriched with gilt.

9in (22.5cm) diam

£200-300

L&T

A pair of Chinese Qianlong period en grisaille small armorial pudding bowls, each painted with a shield-shaped coat of arms.

6.25in (16cm) high

£250-350

WW

A late 18thC Chinese armorial sauce tureen and cover, decorated with oval crests of a hand holding a cross and encircled by the motto 'Deo Juvante', some wear.

7.75in (19.5cm) high

£450-550

WW

A pair of early 19thC Chinese armorial oval trencher salts, decorated with gilt crests within a gilt and black lattice border, some wear to the gilding.

4in (10.5cm) high

£250-350

WW

An 18thC Chinese Imari part dinner service, with a geometric border interspersed with oval flower panels, the well with boldly painted chrysanthemums, comprising a serving plate and twenty dinner plates.

Serving plate 12.25in (31cm) diam

£2,000-3,000   L&T

An 18thC Chinese Imari charger, painted with gilt sprays of chrysanthemums, peony, and a butterfly in cobalt blue, orange and gilt.

16in (40.5cm) diam

£350-450   FRE

An 18thC Chinese Imari chamber pot.

6.5in (16.5in) diam

£400-600   SOTA

An 18thC Chinese Imari covered tankard, gilt-metal rimmed cover and thumb piece, painted with orange and gilt pomegranate and cobalt blue foliate sprays to a moulded tapering cylindrical body, missing partial fruit finial.

11in (28cm) high

£600-1,000   FRE

A rare late 18thC probably Chinese sectional armorial Imari ewer, of classic Georgian style, moulded shell-form cup and base, leaf moulded handle, the cup painted with a crest, iron red, cobalt blue and gilt scrolls and floral garlands throughout.

11in (28cm) high

£400-600   FRE

A set of three 19thC Chinese Imari porcelain dishes, decorated in underglaze blue and iron red with scrolling foliage and trellis panels, centred by flowering urns.

8.25in (21.5cm) diam

£550-650   L&T

CHINESE POLYCHROME

A Chinese Transitional Wucai sleeve vase, painted with eight figures, pine and a vertical band of jagged rocks, the neck with two boys holding fly whisk, the neck damaged.

Wucai literally means 'five colours' and refers to porcelain painted with overglaze enamel colours: red, yellow, black and occasionally turquoise.

c1640-50   *16in (40.5cm) high*

£300-400   WW

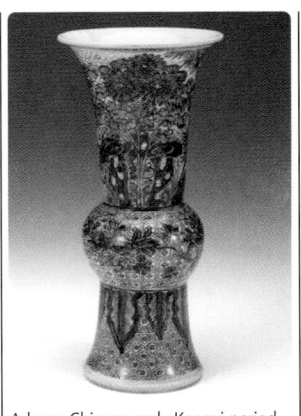

A large Chinese early Kangxi period Wucai beaker vase, the flared mouth leads to a tapering neck painted to show blue rock work and red and blue chrysanthemums over a scale-like red ground, the bulbous centre shows yellow and red pomegranates over square patterned ground, the outswept base is painted to show a broad leaf border on a cross hatched and flower red ground, repainted interior.

15.5in (39.5cm) high

£1,000-2,000   FRE

CLOSER LOOK: QIANLONG BOTTLE VASE

By the Qianlong period Chinese porcelain was very fine and white and so decoration was often used sparingly to display this.

Much decoration from the Qianlong period is in this painterly style and features rocky landscapes with pavilions similar to this one.

En grisaille decoration refers to painting in different tones of grey and black.

Potters at this time created neat, smooth ceramics with rounded footrims.

A Chinese Qianlong period pear-shaped bottle vase, with a long slender neck, well-decorated en grisaille with pavilions in a rocky landscape.

16.5in (42cm) high

£26,000-30,000   WW

A 17thC Chinese Wucai jar, decorated in underglaze blue and coloured enamels with boys amongst scrolling foliage, the shoulders with peony and chrysanthemum, cracks.

9.5in (24cm) high

£450-550   **DN**

CLOSER LOOK: QILIN BOTTLE VASE

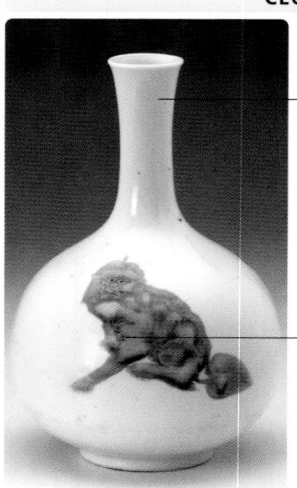

The bottle vase shape originated in China, possibly in the late Tang dynasty (618-907).

The vase is painted with three qilin. The qilin is a hybrid: it is usually portrayed with hooves like a horse, a tail like an ox, a deer's body with scales in five colours and backward antlers.

Despite its appearance it was a peaceful, benevolent creature.

As a hybrid the qilin had the potential to metamorphose and the three depictions on the vase may reflect this.

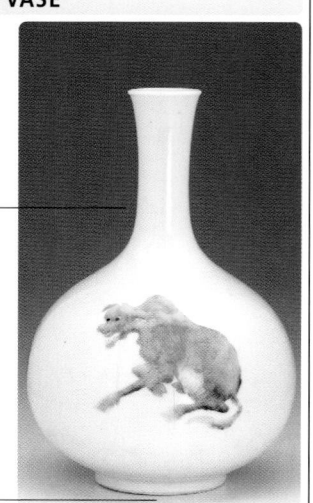

An 18thC Chinese copper-red and blue underglazed bottle vase, everted rim over a slightly waisted slender neck issuing from a compressed bulbous body, freely painted with three copper-red qilin with blue eyes.

10in (25.5cm) high

£3,500-4,500   **FRE**

A Chinese Kangxi period Gu shaped vase, decorated with moulded panels of ladies and flowers.

11.5in (29cm) high

£900-1,100   **DN**

A small Chinese pear-shaped vase, decorated with a green spotted peachbloom glaze, the base with a six-character Kangxi mark and paper label for 'B and V Lake Collection'.

2.5in (6cm) high

£200-300   **WW**

One of a pair of 18thC Chinese Export covered baluster vases, the covers are surmounted by orange acorn finials painted with lotus leaves and a blue diaper to rim, the bases are painted with a scrolling blue and pink border to the neck and base, flanking a panel of green enamelled frogs, grasshoppers and red lotus flowers, over wood stand.

11in (28cm) high

£600-800 PAIR   **FRE**

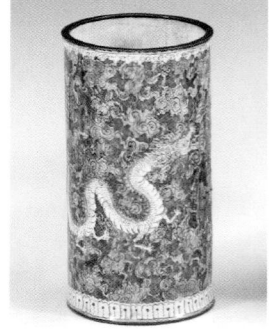

A pair of Chinese Export underglaze blue and clobbered rectangular section vases and covers with dog of fo finials.

c1800   *11.5in (29cm high) high*

£800-1,200   **DN**

A 19thC Chinese Canton enamel brush pot, of long cylindrical form, enamelled to show a blue and red scrolling ground and a finely painted yellow dragon chasing a pearl in reverse, Qianlong six-character mark.

4.25cm (11cm) high

£500-700   **FRE**

A pair of 19thC Chinese vases, decorated in polychrome, with figures in a garden.

5.5in (14cm) high

£700-1,000   **WW**

A large 19thC Chinese baluster vase and cover, moulded in relief with the po ku or a hundred antiques, all on a yellow ground, damage to the neck.

25.25in (64cm) high

£800-1,200   **WW**

A large 19thC Chinese pink sgraffito ground vase, decorated with figures and stylised butterflies, faint body crack.

24.5in (62cm) high

£700-900   **WW**

A large 19thC Chinese baluster vase, decorated in iron red, with lion dogs at play amidst brocade balls, the reverse with four columns of calligraphy.

24in (61cm) high

£150-250 **WW**

A probably late 19thC Chinese Yenyen vase, decorated in coloured enamels with shou and phoenix medallions on a yellow ground, six-character Kangxi mark.

18.5in (47cm) high

£1,200-1,800 **DN**

A Chinese ovoid vase and cover, painted with lotus on a yellow ground.

c1900 *8.75in (22cm) high*

£50-150 **WW**

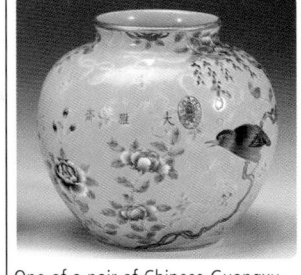

One of a pair of Chinese Guangxu period Dayazhai vases, of globular form, gilt rim leading to a typically painted scene of songbirds among flowing wisteria and blossoms, minor wear to body, three-character mark and Dayazhai seal to shoulder, Yong Qing Chang Chun iron red character mark.

9in (23cm) high

£700-1,000 PAIR **FRE**

A Chinese Republic period vase, the neck with dragon handles, the body painted with two panels containing a young man and woman in a landscape, and panels with Tang dynasty poems, all on an iron red and blue ground, with a Qianlong mark, but Republican period.

13in (33cm) high

£1,000-2,000 **WW**

A Chinese Republic period puce enamel vase, gilt-rimmed straight neck, with a blue lotus flower diaper neck above a finely painted body showing scholar and consort resting, black inscription to body, iron red four-character mark.

The Chinese Republic period (1911-49) saw much political turmoil and ended with the founding of The People's Republic of China.

9in (23cm) high

£150-250 **FRE**

An 18th/19thC Chinese moulded twin-fish vase, each carp with well defined scales and open mouth, base drilled.

10.25in (26cm) high

£400-600 **WW**

A Chinese, Tianqi/Chongzhen period, hexagonal Wucai small dish, decorated with the 'Three Friends', pine, prunus and bamboo.

c1630 *5in (13cm) high*

£1,000-1,500 **WW**

A Chinese, Chongzhen period, porcelain Wucai hexagonal small dish, decorated with insects on pomegranate.

c1630 *5.5in (14cm) high*

£400-600 **WW**

A Chinese late Ming period Wucai charger, deep-edged circular charger, orange line border enclosing yellow, green and orange enamelled foliate scrolls, together with a timber stand.

10.5in (26.5cm) high

£150-250 **FRE**

A rare Chinese Kangxi period Kakiemon style plate, of slightly rounded form, brown rim, the interior enamelled yellow, blue, green and iron red to show songbirds and pine trees, blue leaf inside double blue rings.

8.5in (21.5cm) diam

£300-600 **FRE**

A small Chinese porcelain canted square stand, Yongzheng mark and period, decorated with dragons on a yellow ground, bears 'Sydney L Moss Ltd' label.

4.25in (10.5cm) wide

£800-1,200   L&T

A Chinese Qianlong period magic square calligraphic saucer dish, painted in iron red and black, with Arabic script.

6in (15cm) high

£700-1,000   WW

An 18thC Chinese Export charger, slightly raised rim painted with blue scrolling diaper interrupted by orange and gilt panels and foliate sprays, the interior is painted with a central medallion of vases, rock work and floral sprays.

15in (38cm) diam

£400-500   FRE

An unusual 19thC Chinese Kakiemon plate, of moulded petal form, slightly U-shaped, painted to the interior to show three tigers, green enamelled figure and a bamboo grove.

9.5in (24cm) diam

£400-500   FRE

An unusual 19thC Chinese Kakiemon plate, of moulded petal form, slightly U-shaped, painted to the interior to show three tigers, green enamelled figure and a bamboo grove.

9.5in (24cm) diam

£400-500   FRE

A pair of 19th/20thC Chinese Canton plates, decorated with figures in various pursuits in mountainous landscapes, one with a faint hairline.

8.5in (21.5cm) high

£700-900   WW

A pair of 20thC Chinese cultural revolution propaganda chargers, with Mao and Lin Biao, both of slightly rounded form, ivory crackle glaze, transfer painted with script.

11in (28cm) diam

£500-700   FRE

A Chinese Wanli period Wucai bowl, the exterior brightly painted with four figures divided by lanterns, the rim with stylised flowers, the interior with an underglaze blue five-clawed dragon, a six-character Wanli mark, cracked and riveted.

6.5in (16.5cm) high

£1,200-1,800   WW

A Chinese Wanli period Wucai lower section of a covered box, decorated on the exterior with four dragons contesting flaming pearls, Wanli six-character mark, some damage.

8.25in (21cm) high

£1,500-2,000   WW

A rare pair of Chinese polychrome crane bowls, each decorated with a wide band, the birds standing and in flight amidst rockwork and jui beneath pine, each with a six-character Qianlong mark.

5.5in (14cm) high

£2,000-3,000   WW

A large Chinese Daoguang period yellow-glazed dragon bowl, Daoguang mark.

7.25in (18.5cm) diam

£8,000-10,000   SOTP

A Chinese Kangxi period brinjal bowl, decorated with splashes of yellow, green and aubergine, repairs.

7.5in (19 cm) high

£80-120 **WW**

A large 19thC Chinese Canton bowl, painted with panels containing figures on a ground of flowers and foliage, some faults.

15.5in (39.5cm) high

£200-300 **WW**

A Chinese Guangxu period bowl, decorated in iron red and enamels with dragons above waves, six-character Guangxu mark in blue.

6in (15cm) diam

£350-550 **DN**

A Chinese Guangxu period enamelled fish bowl, well-enamelled roman key band to rim, enamelled with a ruyi border above a body of blue and green lotus leaves and white egrets, enamelled to the interior to show iron red fish.

16in (40.5cm) high

£1,000-1,500 **FRE**

A 20thC Chinese eggshell porcelain bowl, the exterior decorated with peacocks amidst rockwork and peony, the interior with a blue scaly dragon, six-character Qianlong mark, boxed.

9.75in (24.5cm) high

£650-850 **WW**

A Chinese Kangxi period biscuit porcelain model of Li Po, the drunken poet, decorated in green, aubergine and yellow.

7.5in (19cm) high

£600-800 **WW**

A Qianlong polychrome-coloured figure of a man, in brightly coloured robes.

c1770 *7.5in (19cm) high*

£400-500 **JN**

A late 19thC enamelled porcelain model of Kannon seated over a beast, well-modelled figure seated open-legged, draped in a gold, green and red enamel robe, handles supported by a gold sword, the beast enamelled green with a purple scrolling tail.

10in (25.5cm) high

£500-1,000 **FRE**

A flambé glazed stoneware model of a warrior, wearing a long red cloak.

c1900 *15in (38cm) high*

£600-800 **WW**

A pair of Chinese Kangxi period, enamel on biscuit seated lion dogs, each decorated in aubergine, yellow and green.

11.5in (29cm) high

£3,000-4,000 **WW**

A pair of Chinese Kangxi period biscuit figures of Buddhist lion dogs, seated on rectangular stands, each decorated in yellow, green and aubergine, extremities restored.

7.5in (19cm) high

£350-550 **WW**

A pair of 18thC Chinese Export porcelain models of Indian elephants, each with its head lowered and standing four square, decorated with pale tangerine-coloured skins and black beady eyes.

6.75in (17cm) high

£4,000-6,000 **WW**

A rare early 19thC Chinese Export porcelain lantern cover of naïve cat form, body of incised white and black spotted glaze, pierced eyes, ears, mouth, underside and quatrefoil medallion to rear, boxed.

9in (23cm) long

£2,500-3,000 **FRE**

An early 20thC Chinese Export model of a pug dog, modelled seated, decorated with an orange coat, wearing an iron red collar with a gilt bell, black pupils and claws.

11in (28cm) high

£300-500 **FRE**

A Chinese Export Qianlong period tobacco leaf mug, finely painted in the typical palette of gilt, orange, cobalt blue, pinkish yellow and green leaves, with small floral sprays over a white ground, bamboo moulded handle.

5.5in (14cm) high

£1,700-2,000   **FRE**

One of a pair of large late 18thC Chinese Export mugs, hand painted figural scene to the blue panelled front, multi-colour and blue floral sprays to the rear, applied with a handle also painted with a blue floral swag.

5.5in (14cm) high

£500-1,000 PAIR   **FRE**

An unusual 18thC Chinese fan-shaped tea canister and cover, the lid inscribed 'Hexsan', the side painted with a small figure in a boat beneath a massive rock and pine trees, a small chip to the lid and some wear.

4in (10cm) high

£300-400   **WW**

An 18thC Chinese three-colour model of a basket of peaches, the fruit graduated, leading from a circular scalloped basket from five, four, three, and lastly a single fruit, all applied with leaves.

5.75in (14.5cm) high

£250-500   **FRE**

A Chinese Export Qianlong period tureen and stand, of shaped rectangular form, slightly domed cover surmounted by orange flower model and animal heads to shoulder, painted to the cover, body and stand with floral swags.

10in (25.5cm) high

£1,500-2,000   **FRE**

A small 18thC Chinese Export sacred bird and butterfly tureen, of oval form, gilt finial surmounting a domed cover over a base applied to with two gilt handles, decorated with orange painted floral swags and birds, with gilt bands.

8in (20.5cm) wide

£500-800   **FRE**

A 19thC Chinese rectangular cricket cage, one face painted with figures and a spotted horse, four further faces reticulated, the stopper lacking,

8in (20.5cm) high

£350-450   **WW**

A pair of 20thC Chinese small oval jardinières, standing on four legs, decorated with shaped cartouches depicting maidens in interiors and landscapes.

10.25in (26cm) high

£500-600   **WW**

ESSENTIAL REFERENCE: KAKIEMON

Kakiemon is a style of decoration named after the potter Sakaida Kakiemon (1596-1666), who is credited with its introduction.

- The wares are very smooth, milk-white porcelain with a flawless glaze over which decorations are overpainted in orange-red, green and lilac-blue, sometimes with yellow, turquoise and gold.
- Kakiemon patterns are mainly flowers and figure motifs. The elements are asymmetrically and sparsely painted, enhancing the prominent white ground.
- The quality of this ware set a standard for European porcelain in the early 18thC.

A Japanese Kakiemon porcelain winepot or teapot, with arched handle, fixed with chrysanthemum flower pinions, above globular body, the cover decorated in polychrome enamels with a garden scene, the body with plant scrolls, with gilt highlights.

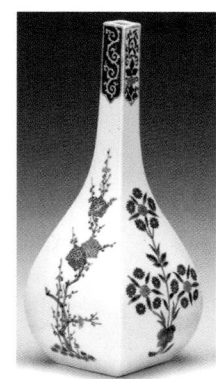

c1680   5in (13cm) high

£1,200-1,800   **L&T**

A late 17thC Japanese Kakiemon tokkuri, flared open mouth, short neck, square rectangular body, painted with a blue leaf band to neck, green scrolls amongst orange flowers to shoulder, the four panels of the body are painted differently, probably depicting the seasons, with yellow and orange flowers to purple tress branches and green, blue and yellow rock work, some repair.

11in (28cm) high

£3,000-5,000   **FRE**

A Japanese Kakiemon teabowl, delicately painted with a Bijin, with an attendant holding a fan between two birds, the reverse with bamboo and a peony spray.

c1700   3in (7.5cm) high

£700-1,000   **WW**

A large 18thC Japanese Kakiemon basin, moulded deep U-shape, brown rim leading to a band of green scrolling leaves surrounding yellow and iron red fruit and flowers, the central medallion painted to show ho-o birds over rock work and blossoming trees, floral sprays to the exterior.

13.5in (34cm) diam

£1,200-1,800   **FRE**

A late 18th/19thC Japanese Kakiemon bottle vase, of square pear bottle form, painted iron red scroll to long straight neck, iron red scroll to long straight neck, four different floral sprays to body, square recessed base.

11.75in (30cm) high

£700-1,000   **FRE**

JAPANESE IMARI

Imari porcelain is the European name for the porcelain made for export at Arita on Kyushu, and shipped from the port of Imari from the late 17thC.

- Imari porcelain is richly decorated in dark underglaze blue and red enamels and gold or silver, combined with turquoise, green, aubergine and yellow enamel in the form of flowers, figures, ships, etc.
- Production of Imari porcelain was given a boost when instability in China disrupted the Dutch East India Company's supply of porcelain, forcing the Dutch to turn to Japanese producers.

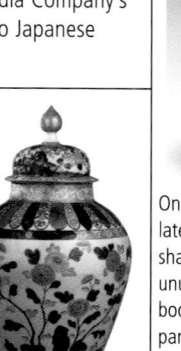

A pair of 17thC Japanese Imari jars with covers.

c1680   22in (56cm) high

£8,000-10,000   **SOTP**

One of a pair of late 17thC and later Imari bottle vases, of pear shape, painted red scrolling neck, unusual green leaf panel neck, the body painted with four cobalt-blue panelled cherry blossom scenes.

9in (23cm) high

£1,200-1,800 PAIR   **FRE**

A large Japanese Imari baluster vase and cover, typically decorated with panels of landscapes and flowers, on a blue ground with gilt and iron red chrysanthemums, some extensive restoration.

c1700   27in (69cm) high

£450-550   **WW**

A large early 18thC Japanese Imari baluster vase and cover, typically decorated with panels containing shi shi and cranes amidst bamboo, together with a carved wood stand, minor damage.

24in (61cm) high

£600-1,000   WW

An early 19thC Imari covered tea caddy, of tall rectangular form, cylindrical cover painted to show gilt, cobalt blue and iron red chrysanthemum and peony.

7.5in (19cm) high

£250-450   FRE

A late 19thC Japanese Imari vase, the shoulder underglazed and enamelled to depict bamboo leaves and ducks amongst peony, surrounded by a ground of small vignette of landscapes.

32in (81cm) high

£1,800-2,200   FRE

An unusual late 19thC Imari kendi, of garlic mouth form, trumpet neck, ovoid body with wide short spout, decorated in cobalt blue, orange, gilt and green to show ladies in the pursuit of leisure.

9.5in (24cm) high

£300-500   FRE

A 19thC Japanese Imari double gourd vase, of bulbous double form, well painted in cobalt blue, gilt and orange, showing ho-o, dragons and floral sprays.

13in (33cm) high

£500-1,000   FRE

A pair of large 19thC Japanese Imari vases and covers, each of baluster form, with shi-shi finials, finely decorated with bands of flowers and foliage with further pots of flowers, red painted signature.

24.75in (63cm) high

£2,500-3,500   L&T

A 19thC Japanese Imari ginger jar and cover, decorated in the typical palette with exotic birds and foliage, the domed lid surmounted by a fu-lion finial.

15in (38cm) high

£300-500   L&T

A large late 19thC Japanese 'turtle back' Imari bottle vase, of compressed ovoid form issuing from a long slender neck, the body is moulded with graduating hexagonal panels, each painted cobalt blue, gilt and orange, showing songbirds, floral sprays and landscapes.

28in (71cm) high

£1,500-2,000   FRE

A late 19thC Japanese Imari bottle vase, well painted, of tall rectangular form, small domed neck, painted with floral panels in reverse, signed.

8in (20.5cm) high

£500-700   FRE

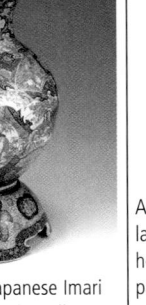

A large late 19thC Japanese Imari vase on stand, extremely well painted and gilded, typical palette of cobalt blue, gilt and orange depicting fans and medallions of ho-o birds and figures to a detailed blue and orange scrolling diaper and ground.

32in (81cm) high

£5,000-7,000   FRE

A large 19thC sectional Imari lantern, of cylindrical pillar form, hexagonal base, cylinder column painted to show coiling gilt dragons on a white porcelain ground, the pierced domed and hexagonal cover well painted in the typical Imari palette.

46in (117cm) high

£7,000-10,000   FRE

ORIENTAL

A pair of 19thC Japanese Imari censers, of compressed globular form, the cover surmounted by blue applied dragon, the pierced body painted orange, cobalt and light blue to show cloud scrolls, the body applied with two dragons in reverse to the shoulder, the base painted with a gilt fan motif.

17.5in (43cm) high

£3,500-5,000   **FRE**

A Japanese Fukugawa Imari ovoid vase, decorated with three panels, containing iris, peony and a pair of mandarin ducks, some glaze cracks, three-character mark, together with a wood stand.

c1900   *10in (25cm) high*

£100-200   **WW**

A Japanese Arita Imari dish, decorated with a central basket of flowers and with panels of prunus and chrysanthemum to the border.

c1700   *11.25in (28.5cm) high*

£500-700   **WW**

An unusual early 18thC Japanese Imari saucer, painted with figures leading a buffalo, and seated with a large flask inscribed 'FW'.

5in (13cm) high

£500-700   **WW**

A pair of late 19thC Japanese Imari chargers, of slightly rounded form, gilt scrolls over a black ground to the rim, four seasonal landscapes to the interior over a ground of grey and red.

16in (40.5cm) diam

£800-1,200   **FRE**

A pair of 19thC Japanese Imari chargers, decorated to the border with stylised flower heads and phoenix, and to the well with bold flowers and foliage with a central flower head.

14.5in (37cm) high

£700-900   **L&T**

A late 19thC Japanese Imari charger, of slightly rounded form, painted with two village scenes in reverse among of ground of scrolling blue and gilt leaves, blue foliate sprays to underside, seven spur marks to base.

16in (40.5cm) diam

£400-600   **FRE**

A late 19thC Japanese Imari charger, of slightly rounded form, depicting grey and green enamelled horses on a white ground, red scroll and grassy hill to the foreground.

16in (40.5cm) diam

£400-600   **FRE**

A late 19thC Japanese Imari bowl, of deep U-shape form, orange geometric diaper to interior broken by four vignettes of green enamelled floral sprigs and roundrels of ho-o birds, the central medallion painted to show a gold and orange peony.

8in (20.5cm) high

£500-700   **FRE**

A large 19thC Japanese Imari bowl, of deep U-shape form, shaped gilt rim, enamelled green, iron red and blue to the interior showing six panels painted in reverse to the sides and a central medallion of ho-o and flowers, blue underglazed floral sprays to underside, six blue character marks.

£500-800   **FRE**

A rare late 17th/18thC Japanese Imari model of bijin, brightly painted with black hair, iron red robe with green and blue leaved thistles and gilt chrysanthemum.

4in (10cm) high

£4,000-5,000   **FRE**

A late 18th/early 19thC Japanese Imari model of a boy, blue and orange robe, the urn painted with orange and iron red scrolls and winged ho-o bird-like figures.

8.25in (21cm) high

£2,000-3,000   **FRE**

ESSENTIAL REFERENCE: SATSUMA

Satuma wares are named after a feudal province at the southern tip of the Japanese island of Kyushu.

- Due to its close proximity to the Korean peninsula, the Satsuma province benefited from an influx of Korean master potters following the Japanese invasion of Korea in 1597.
- The first wares were simple tea ceremony vessels decorated with crackled yellow glaze on a cream ground.
- The Satsuma potters had began to learn enamelling, gilding and other decorative techniques from Arita and Kyoto by the end of the 18thC.
- The best Satsuma pieces were produced from the mid-19thC. These are essentially paintings in miniature and took several months to make.
- Satsuma patterns include figures, flowers and Japanese fauna. Many Satsuma designs use perspective to create complex multi-layered scenes.
- Quality varies from the oldest, carefully decorated pieces and the later, gaudy items made for the export trade.

CLOSER LOOK: SATSUMA VASE

The high quality, complex gilding covers the neck of the vase and the bird-form handles. It was applied on top of the glaze and so stands proud of the surface.

The repeated motifs were usually painted freehand.

Scenes of people going about their daily business, or showing processions and ceremonies, were popular themes for decoration.

The mark states that the vase was made in Kyoto – one of the main areas of Satsuma production.

A 19thC Meiji Kyoto Satsuma earthenware vase, possibly Shoho Takara Honzan, with shogun crest, possibly depicting the tale of Genji, of baluster form, heavily gilded body, the slightly bulbous mouth leads to a pair of applied bird-form handles, the neck painted with a patchwork of gold, red, blue and brown leading to a body finely painted to show a phoenix in flight above a detailed landscape and figures to one side and a winter landscape and figures in reverse, roman key border to base, gold seal mark signed Kyoto.

38in (96.5cm) high

£10,000-12,000   FRE

A late 19thC Japanese Satsuma vase, well-painted, figural and landscape scenes to gilt and blue gourd panels, signed 'Ryozan'.

5.5in (14cm) high

£800-1,000   FRE

A large Meiji Satsuma earthenware vase, by Hosai, finely enamelled tapering shoulder-form vase, rim mouth above a short neck, the shoulder enamelled with blue, orange and gold chrysanthemums, the body is enamelled with floral sprays above a cobalt blue crosshatched border and scrolling base, blue enamel Shimazu family crest, enamelled 'Dai Nippon Ijuin Satsuma Yaki'.

Meiji pieces date from 1868-1912.

19in (38cm) high

£2,500-3,500   FRE

A 19thC Satsuma oblong dish, decorated with warriors in a battle scene within a fan-painted panel, two corners slightly chipped and craze.

£1,500-2,000   A&G

A Japanese Meiji period Satsuma dish, painted with four ladies and a child in a pentagonal panel, four-character seal mark.

7in (18cm)

£700-900   WW

A rare late 19thC Japanese Satsuma earthenware Fu lion model, well potted to show open painted mouth and eyes, gilt and cobalt blue collar, and bow around his midsection, gilt signature to base.

11.75in (30cm) high

£2,000-3,000   FRE

A rare late 19thC Japanese Satsuma earthenware model of a buffalo and boy, modelled as a dark-haired boy ascending a recumbent buffalo, decorated with a gilt rope, saddle and tunic finely enamelled with cobalt blue, red and gold, well potted.

6.5in (16.5cm) high

£3,000-4,000   FRE

A late 19thC Japanese Satsuma koro, cover and stand, with a pierced lid and carrying handles, the bodies painted with warriors.

6in (15cm) high

£300-500   JN

ORIENTAL

A pair of 19thC Satsuma square tapered vases, painted with panels of male and female figures, with ebonised wood stands.

4.75in (12cm) high

£200-300　　　　　　　　**A&G**

A late 19thC Satsuma earthenware model of an official, the figure seated in a horseshoe-style chair, dressed in an open robe, fan in hand, the robe and fan very finely painted with scroll work and feathers, gold detail to the face, wood grain to the chair.

11in (28cm) high

£1,500-2,500　　　　　　**FRE**

A large early 20thC Japanese Satsuma floor vase, of baluster form, enamelled gold, green and white to show figures to a winter landscape, gold diaper and birds in low relief to neck.

43in (109cm) high

£1,200-1,800　　　　　　**FRE**

An early 20thC Japanese Satsuma earthenware tea caddy, by Bizan in the style of Yabu Meizan, of tall rectangular form, associated silver cover, depicting four panels: 'Girl's Day Festival', 'Lake Biwa' and wisteria all surrounded by bordering flowers.

5in (12.5cm) high

£1,800-2,200　　　　　　**FRE**

OTHER JAPANESE CERAMICS

One of a pair of late 19thC Japanese Seto vases, of baluster form, flared mouth issuing from a neck applied with two moulded handles, the body is raised on a circular base, very finely painted blue on a white ground to show flowers and scrolls to the rim and base and fine songbirds and blossoms to the body.

18in (45.5cm) high

£500-700 PAIR　　　　　　**FRE**

A massive pair of 19thC Japanese blue and white jardinières, the bodies painted with pheasants amidst flowers and foliage, the necks with cranes and cloud scrolls.

20.5in (52cm) wide

£500-800　　　　　　　　**WW**

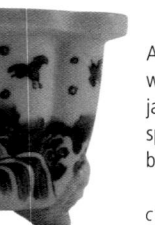

A Japanese blue and white quatre-lobed jardinière, painted with sparrows in flight above breaking waves.

c1900　　7.5in (19cm) high

£80-120　　　　　　　　**WW**

An early 20thC Japanese reticulated vase, with a central solid cylinder, painted in blue with irises, six-character mark, together with a wood stand.

c1900　　10.5in (26.5cm) high

£2,500-3,500　　　　　　**WW**

An Edo period Arita model of a Karashishi.

c1700　　9in (23cm) high

£3,500-4,500　　　　　　**SOTP**

A Japanese Edo period Arita-style dog model, probably Kutani, well-potted puppy with cheerful expression, gilt and red-painted eyes and mouth, painted with light orange and black markings.

4.5in (11.5cm) high

£500-600　　　　　　　　**FRE**

A pair of early 18thC Arita models of puppies, both modelled as seated cheerful puppies, legs and head over their chests, painted with gilt and red collars, eyes and mouths, black spots to face, body and ears, repaired.

7.5in (19cm) high

£4,000-5,000 FRE

CLOSER LOOK: ARITA COCKEREL AND COPY

Potters working in and around the town of Arita made models such as the one on the right for export to Europe from the late 18thC.

The French factory Samson made copies of Oriental and European porcelains. They may have been commissioned to make a copy of the original Japanese model.

The red, green, gold and black glazes are typical of decoration on Arita porcelain.

The enamelled bamboo sprigs echo the bamboo moulding of the base.

An 18th/19thC Japanese Edo period Arita model of a cockerel and a matched Samson model, modelled seated open-mouthed over a bamboo moulded oval base, well-painted iron red face and tail feathers, gilt beak and tail feathers, feathers to the body painted black and red, green enamelled bamboo sprigs to base.

14in (35.5cm) high

£3,000-4,000 FRE

A pair of 17thC and later Japanese dog models, one Arita and a matched model, the Arita dog modelled on all fours, tail coiled, head slightly down-turned, painted with green, iron red and black spots, iron red collar and mouth, together with an earthenware seated model decorated in a similar fashion.

Arita dog 8.5in (21.5cm) high

£14,000-16,000 FRE

A 19thC Japanese blue and white Arita lacquered vase, with a flared blue and white neck and circular base, and a central body lacquered black and red to show a deer amongst pine trees.

15in (38cm) high

£700-1,000 FRE

A large 19thC Japanese earthenware Seto ware vase, attributed to Seto, of tapering shouldered form, short neck painted light sky-blue leading to a cream ground, body incised and applied to show a white dragon emerging from a dark blue sea.

24in (61cm) high

£2,000-3,000 FRE

A late 19thC Japanese studio earthenware vase, by Kozan, of baluster form, gosu blue hydrangea, chrysanthemum and gilt butterflies on a cream ground, signed 'Kozan, Makuzu'.

£2,000-3,000 FRE

ESSENTIAL REFERENCE: NABESHIMA

Nabeshima porcelain was made from the late 17thC in Okawachi, north of Arita, on Kyushu, Japan.

- The porcelain was named after the ruling clan who patronised its production.
- The majority of the production was flatware.
- The body is virtually flawless and potted very thinly.
- The most common themes are seasonal flowers or wintry trees, sometimes combined with underlying or juxtaposed patterns derived from waves, trelliswork or basketry. The intricacy of this decoration suggests the use of a stencil or some kind of transfer-printing technique.
- Nabeshima designs are often outlined in underglaze blue with enamel infilling of iron red, turquoise, yellow, pale manganese, and black detailing. The glaze is of a soft, pale, grey-blue tone.

A 17th/18thC Japanese blue and white Nabeshima footed dish, of slightly rounded form, underglazed blue depicting chrysanthemums and leaves, 'comb tooth' pattern to foot.

7.75in (19.5cm) diam

£500-700 FRE

ORIENTAL

A 18th/19thC Japanese Nabeshima dish, of circular form depicting gifts underglazed in blue and a profusion of hydrangea in red, yellow and green enamels.

6.5in (16.5cm) diam

£1,000-1,500   FRE

A 19thC Japanese Nabeshima 'bamboo' dish, of slightly rounded form, slight peak to interior of dish, blue underglazed ground, enamelled green, white and gold to depict snow-capped bamboo grove and gilt spring, spur marks to base.

7.25in (18.5cm) diam

£400-600   FRE

A rare late 19thC Japanese Nabeshima celadon and blue underglazed dish, centre moulded with the sixteen-petal kiku, blue underglazed dragons and scrolls.

12in (30.5cm) diam

£400-600   FRE

A Japanese porcelain vase, designed by Makuzu Kozan, painted with lilies on a shaded green ground, the base with a six-character mark.

8.25in (21cm) high

£1,500-2,000   WW

A late 19thC Japanese studio porcelain vase, by Kozan, of baluster form, depicting iris and white reeds on a celadon ground, signed 'Makuzu Kozan'.

8in (20.5cm) high

£600-800   FRE

A pair of late Meiji/early Taisho period Kutani vases by Watano, each of baluster form, decorated with a continuous mountainous landscape between bands of foliate decoration.

18.5in (47cm) high

£2,500-3,500   FRE

PERSIAN & MIDDLE EASTERN CERAMICS

A probably 12thC Persian conical bowl, decorated with geometric patterns in green and brown, damaged and restored.

6.5in (16.5cm) high

£250-350   WW

A probably 12thC Persian pottery bowl, decorated with a stylised floral pattern in green and brown.

9.25in (23.5cm) high

£250-300   WW

A probably 12thC Middle Eastern pottery bowl, decorated with four yellow panels, surrounded by black swirling motifs, sections broken and re-glued.

8.5in (21.5cm) high

£200-250   WW

An 18thC Persian blue-painted kendi, the neck and shoulders decorated with bands of stylised flowers and foliage, the sides with panels of birds and animals within landscapes, black painted mark.

8.5in (21.5cm) high

£9,000-12,000   L&T

An unusual 20thC sawatow Islamic influenced white enamelled blue glazed charger, the large slightly rounded charger painted with a floral diaper edge, floral springs in reverse to the cavetto, and a central medallion of three radiating blossoms issuing broad leaves, raised on a circular foot with unglazed sand infused base.

17in (43cm) diam

£700-1,000   FRE

A 16th/17thC Chinese cloisonné gu beaker, decorated with scrolling lotus on a turquoise ground, six-character Jingtai mark, some surface wear.

12.25in (31cm) high

£2,500-3,500   **WW**

ESSENTIAL REFERENCE: CLOISONNÉ CARP

Models of carp leaping were popular during the Qianlong period, (1736-1795) often in the form of porcelain tureens and jadeite vases.

The demand for quality gilt-bronze and cloisonné items has increased greatly in the last 5 years.

The pair were modelled to inspire the auspicious symbolism of a fish leaping at the dragons gate - a successful person standing out from others.

The quality of the pair is total, from well-carved 'sea scroll' wood base to heavy gilt-bronze mounts, thick multi-layer enamel, and well-reticulated fins.

They were likely produced from an Imperial workshop. They are in excellent condition - only minor stress has occurred to the fins, not a bad toll for 200 years

A pair of rare Chinese Qianlong/Jiaqing period cloisonné carp, mirror modelled, of free-flowing naturalistic form with mouth open, fins and tail shaped in the manner of jumping, decorated with red head, blue and black eyes, pink, white and red scales, positioned above a scrolling gilt-metal sea, over a carved wood base.

12in (30.5cm) high

£30,000-40,000   **FRE**

A large Chinese Qianlong period cloisonné enamel tripod censer and cover, with a compressed globular body rising from three tall gilt lion-mask-headed legs, set at the shoulder with two large rectangular handles, profusely decorated around the exterior with leafy lotus strapwork between gilt lappets and keyfret bands, the domed cover surmounted by a pierced gilt dragon finial.

18.75in (47.5cm) high

£15,000-20,000   **WW**

A pair of late 18thC Chinese cloisonné ovoid vases, decorated with prunus, lotus and chrysanthemum.

9.5in (24cm) high

£2,000-3,000   **DN**

A19thC Chinese cloisonné gu shaped vase, decorated with taotie masks and stylised decoration on a blue ground.

11in (28cm) high

£350-550   **DN**

A pair of 19thC Chinese cloisonné bottle vases, each decorated with flowers, foliage and rockwork, on a geometric white ground, the necks with a continuous lotus scroll.

11in (28cm) high

£1,000-1,200   **WW**

A late 18th/early 19thC Chinese cloisonné and bronze tripod censer, possibly re-gilded, the cover pierced, domed and surmounted by a squirrel above a fruit vine, over a compressed globular base mounted with animal heads and vine to the shoulder, raised on three long gilded legs, medallion to underside of body, Ming four-character mark.

8in (20.5cm) high

£350-450   **FRE**

An 18th/19thC Chinese cloisonné tripod censer, finely enamelled compressed globular form, raised on three short legs and with two arch-form handles, enamelled to show twelve Indian lotuses joined by scrolling leaves, together with a later carved wood and jade-mounted cover, Ming four-character mark.

5in (12.5cm) high

£1,700-2,000   **FRE**

An 18th/19thC Chinese cloisonné bowl, decorated with two phoenix amidst a continuous flower and leaf scroll above a band of stiff leaves, Jingtai mark.

8.75in (22.5cm) high

£250-350   **WW**

A 19thC Chinese cloisonné censer, with gilt-metal mounts to the rim and with lion dog handles, all raised on three elephant head feet, the base with a four-character Jingtai mark.

6.25in (16cm) high

£2,500-3,500   **WW**

A 19thC Chinese oval quatrefoil-section cloisonné bowl, decorated with a continuous lotus scroll in black on a yellow ground.

10in (25cm) high

£350-450   **WW**

A 19th/20thC Chinese cloisonné censer, with a gilt rim, each side decorated with a panel of Arabic script, raised on three feet.

5.5in (14cm) high

£500-600   **WW**

One of a pair of late 19thC Chinese cloisonné jardinières, of shaped rectangular form, Indian lotus joined by scrolling leaves, gilt Roman key edge above wood stands.

6in (15cm) high

£300-400 PAIR   **FRE**

A pair of Chinese cloisonné shallow dishes each decorated with Pekinese, birds and trees.

c1800   *5.5in (14cm) diam*

£180-220   **DN**

CLOSER LOOK: CHINESE CLOISONNÉ PLAQUES

The cloisonné technique dates back to 1400BC. To create the design thin strips of metal were soldered onto the surface of the plaques to form individual cells. These were filled with powdered enamel and then fired in a kiln.

The plaques were made in the 18thC and have survived exceptionally well. Any damage to the enamel would be costly to repair and so their good condition adds to their value.

The artist who decorated the plaques was exceptionally skilled as he has created an intricately detailed and naturalistic pattern using the enamels.

The paper label on the back of the plaques suggests they were made for the very lucrative French market.

A pair of Chinese Qianlong period cloisonné circular plaques, each depicting exotic birds, blossom and bold flowerheads, against a blue ground.

Bears French paper label 'Fabrique d'Emaux Cloisonne de Teuo-Tcheng. La seule et veritable fabrique d'emaux cloisonnes de Teuo-Tcheng se trouve a Peking en dehors de la porte Tsien-men vers le milieu de la rue Yan-mei-tchou-sie-kiai (cote nord)'.

15.5in (39.5cm) diam

£12,000-15,000   **L&T**

A pair of late 19thC Chinese cloisonné altar sticks in the form of elephants, modelled standing over rectangular double lotus-form plinth bases with yellow and blue alternating enamelled bands, the elephants mounted with candle holders.

24in (61cm) high

£1,500-2,000 **FRE**

A pair of Chinese, Qianlong/Jiaqing period, cloisonné candlesticks, each with butterflies on a blue ground, the base with endless knots on a blue ground.

3.75in (9.5cm) high

£500-700 **DN**

A 18thC Chinese cloisonné belt hook, decorated with stylised flowers on a turquoise ground, the terminal formed as dragon's head.

4in (10.5cm) high

£1,200-1,800 **WW**

A second half 19thC Chinese carved hardwood box and cover set with cloisonné panels decorated with dragons.

7.5in (19cm) high

£220-280 **DN**

A 19th/20thC Chinese cloisonné peach-form covered box, cover featuring enamelled yellow ground panel depicting five Fu bats surrounded by a blue lotus flower and scroll body, the interior enamelled to show bats and cloud scrolls.

7in (18cm) high

£300-500 **FRE**

JAPANESE CLOISONNÉ

A 19thC Japanese cloisonné palace vase, attributed to Ando, of baluster form, depicting doves, songbirds, wisteria, peonies to a ground off brown pyrites.

The Ando company was established by Ando Jubei in 1880. The Ando trademark, referred to as the 'flower' or 'Maltese Cross' or 'sand dollar', is typically formed in wire in the centre of the base.

54in (137cm) high

£5,000-7,000 **FRE**

A rare early 20thC Japanese cloisonné enamel nagari-gusuri vase, by Ando, of baluster form, depicting leaves and grapes in low relief over a transmutation mottle brown ground, Ando mark to base.

6in (15cm) high

£800-1,200 **FRE**

An unusual early 20thC Japanese cloisonné vase, by Ando, of baluster form, depicting flying doves, on a graduated blue to soft orange ground, silver mounts, mark of Ando Jubei.

14in (35.5cm) high

£1,300-1,500 **FRE**

One of a pair of late 19thC Japanese cloisonné vases, attributed to Hattori, of baluster form, depicting a blue iris on a taupe ground with good diaper pattern to border, shakudo mounts.

15in (38cm) high

£1,200-1,400 **PAIR** **FRE**

A small early 20thC Japanese cloisonné vase, by Ando, of baluster form, depicting koi fish swimming on a light green ground, silver mounts, Ando mark to base.

2.75in (7cm) high

£1,500-2,500 **FRE**

An early 20thC Japanese cloisonné moriage vase, attributed to Hattori, depicting white flowers and reeds in low relief on a celadon ground.

6in (15cm) high

£600-800 FRE

An early 20thC Japanese cloisonné enamel basse-taille vase, by Kawaguchi, of baluster form, depiction Kannon aside a green coiled dragon in low relief, the silver base incised with splashing waves, marked with S inside double triangle to base, minor damage.

7in (18cm) high

£600-800 FRE

A late 19thC Japanese cloisonné basse-taille vase, by Kumeno, of pear-shaped form, elongated neck depicting a profusion of flowers on a purple to clear enamelled ground incorporating a gin bari technique, the silver base incised with a profusion of waves, signed 'Kumeno Teitaro'.

15.5in (39.5cm) high

£800-1,200 FRE

One of a pair of late 19thC Japanese cloisonné vases, in the style of Namikawa, attributed to Shibata, of baluster form, depicting gifts of the takaramono and various formed cartouches depicting Japanese birds and flowers all on a black ground, border work characteristic of the early Namikawa workshop.

7in (18cm) high

£1,000-1,500 PAIR FRE

An extremely rare late 19thC Japanese cloisonné and enamelled solid gold vase, by Namikawa Sosuke, the elongated baluster-form vase depicted alternating herringbone design incised into a solid gold body encased in a red to clear enamel solid gold mounts, impressed seal mark to solid gold base.

7.5in (19cm) high

£20,000-30,000 FRE

A late 19thC Japanese cloisonné vase, by Hattori Tadasaburo, of baluster form, depicting furling lotus leaves and blossoming lotus on a light blue ground, signed with an impressed mark Hattori on leaf.

12.5in (32cm) high

£2,000-3,000 FRE

A late 19thC Japanese Ota Tamashiro cloisonné vase, fashioned in the Namikawa style, ovoid form depicting prunus and songbirds over a midnight blue ground, the shoulder with geometric diapering, signed 'Ota'.

3.5in (9cm) high

£1,500-2,500 FRE

A late 19thC Japanese cloisonné enamelled basse-taille vase, by Kumeno Teitaro, of compressed ovoid form, on a rare indigo ground depicting daisies and spider mums, incised alternating decorations to silver body.

3in (7.5cm) high

£3,000-4,000 FRE

An early 20thC Japanese cloisonné basse-taille vase, by Kumeno Teitaro, compressed ovoid form with a long slender neck, the shoulder depicting flying cranes and speckled gold stone, the body depicting splashing waves incised in silver, impressed mark to base.

4.5in (11.5cm) high

£1,000-1,500 FRE

A Japanese cloisonné vase, by Namikawa Yasuyuki, of ovoid form with elongated neck depicting a sprig of blossoming flowers and butterflies all in gold wire with shakodo mounts on a blue ground, signed silver tablet, 'Kyoto Namikawa'.

3.75in (9.5cm) high

£2,000-3,000 FRE

A Japanese Namikawa Yasuyuki cloisonné vase, of ovoid form with stout neck and geometric pattern, signed 'Kyoto Namikawa'.

3.25in (8cm) high

£8,000-12,000 FRE

A late 19thC large Japanese cloisonné gin bari vase, of baluster form, depicting a multitude of flowers and birds on a blue ground, damage.

24.5in (62cm) high

£3,000-4,000 FRE

A pair of late 19thC Japanese cloisonné vases, of baluster form with flared mouth, well-enamelled silver wired floral garden amongst a bamboo fence to dark blue ground, diaper neck and foot, gilt-metal mounts and wood stands.

17in (43cm) high

£2,000-3,000 FRE

A late 19thC Japanese cloisonné censer, in the style of Namikawa, on a yellow speckle ground, with dragons, butterflies and phoenixes associated cover with banded butterflies.

3.5in (9cm) high

£600-800 FRE

A large late 19thC Japanese cloisonné covered urn, attributed to Namikawa Workshop, of compressed octagonal form applied with two handles, eight faceted panels, body and cover depicting various mythological creatures on speckled ground incorporating arabesque shield designs to outer body and well-detailed geometric diapering and pattern banding by a profusion of detailed flower heads.

17in (43cm) diam

£7,000-10,000 FRE

ESSENTIAL REFERENCE: JAPANESE CLOISONNÉ KORO

A pair of rare late 19thC Japanese cloisonné enamelled censers, by Hattori Tadasaburo, depicting solid gold dragons amongst silver waves, silver covers.

Hattori Tadasaburo was one of the great artists in the golden era of Japanese enamels. He was active in the late 19th/early 20thC.

4in (10cm) diam

£3,000-4,000 FRE

Namikawa Yasuyuki (1845-1927) was one of the greatest artists of his era. A former Samurai, he began his artistic career c1868 and founded his own studio.

He helped to develop a semi-transparent mirror black enamel that became the hallmark of most of his work.

His attention to detail enabled him to create intricate wirework designs. His early pieces are traditional in subject matter, featuring stylised botanical and formal geometric motifs. In general, his later work is more pictorial and shows nature scenes or views from around Kyoto, where he worked.

In 1896 he became Imperial Craftsman to the court of the Emperor Meiji, guaranteeing a domestic market for his work and increasing its value. He retired in 1915 and his company closed soon afterwards.

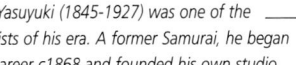

A late 19thC Japanese cloisonné koro, by Namikawa Yasuyuki, depicting white crane and pine on a soft green landscape over a light blue ground, silver pierced cover, signed 'Kyoto Namikawa' on a raised silver tablet.

3.5in (9cm) high

£10,000-15,000 FRE

A late 19thC Japanese cloisonné jar and cover, in the style of Honda Yasuburo, of ovoid form, depicting arabesque shields with alternating mythological creatures, cover banded with ju-i beads, gilt kiku finial and mounts.

5in (12.5cm) high

£2,000-3,000 FRE

A late 19thC Japanese cloisonné Namikawa style koro, with detailed design in fine gilt wire depicting various roundels with a kiku finial and slightly domed cover, the shoulder with draped tapestry designs.

4in (10cm) high

£1,500-2,500 FRE

A late 19thC Japanese cloisonné koro, in the style of Namikawa, depicting various roundrels of alternating creatures amongst stylised waves on a black ground with gilt wire intricately detailed and gilt kiku finial.

4.5in (11.5cm) high

£1,200-1,800 FRE

A late 19thC Japanese cloisonné Kyoto school ewer, in the style of Namikawa, depicting fine gilt wire and roundrels with a stylised geometric pattern, possibly lacking cover.

7in (18cm) high

£500-600   FRE

A late 19thC Japanese cloisonné teapot, in the style of Namikawa Yasuyuki, depicting arabesque shield design with alternating kirin and ho-o, the shield banded by Mikado family crest.

Handle up 7in (18cm) high

£2,000-3,000   FRE

A Japanese cloisonné sake pot, in the style of Namikawa Yasuyuki, of short ovoid form, with complex geometric borders and designs, the base with a profusion of waves and kiku.

7in (18cm) diam

£2,500-3,500   FRE

A late 19thC Japanese cloisonné creamer, in the style of Namikawa, depicting stylised waves and kiku with complex geometric roundrels.

6in (15cm) long

£1,500-2,000   FRE

A Japanese Meiji period cloisonné rectangular box and domed cover, decorated with a flowering prunus on a silver foil ground, slight wear.

8.25in (21cm) high

£120-180   WW

A 20thC Japanese cloisonné small box and cover, finely decorated with quail and flowers reserved on a pale blue ground, gilt interior engraved with houses.

3.5in (9cm) high

£250-350   DN

A rare pair of late 19thC Japanese cloisonné kogos, male and female in the style of Honda Yasuburo, depicting various butterflies and moths, the borders with various family mons, the base with rare speckle ground.

3.5in (9cm) diam

£2,500-3,000   FRE

A Japanese Meiji period cloisonné square tray, decorated with a cockerel, a chick pecking at the grass at its feet, the rim decorated with dragonflies on a floral and foliate scroll, the reverse with a circular cartouche of fruit and nuts on a blue ground, two-character inscription, possibly Hosen, and red seal.

10.75in (27.5cm) high

£1,200-1,800   WW

A late 19thC Japanese cloisonné rectangular tray, decorated with a mallard drake in flight, signed 'Namikawa Sosuke', some surface cracks.

6in (15cm) wide

£3,000-4,000   DN

A rare late 19thC Japanese cloisonné two-fold table screen, in the style of Namikawa Kyoto school, depicting ho-o and dragons with bordering kiku design and well-designed coiled gilt wire, base depicting solid silver filigree stylised waves and kiku, verso with a solid gilt finish depicting cranes and Mount Fuji, mounted with alternative silver hinges and wood frame.

8.5in (21.5cm) high

£2,500-3,500   FRE

A rare 19thC Japanese plique-a-jour lantern cover, attributed to Ando Workshop, of oval form, depicting a landscape with temples, a waterfall and a profusion of foliage.

5in (12.5cm) high

£3,000-4,000   FRE

A pair of 19th/20thC Chinese hexagonal-section enamel vases, painted with birds, butterflies, deer and buffaloes.

15in (38cm) high

£600-1,000 **WW**

A pair of late 19thC Chinese bronze and champleve enamel ovoid vases with bands and pendant lappets of enamel.

12.5in (32cm) high

£200-300 **DN**

A Chinese bronze and champleve enamel koro and cover with kylin finial.

c1900 *15in (38cm) high*

£70-100 **DN**

A Canton enamel wine pot and cover, of Near Eastern form and decorated with two heart-shaped panels, Shoulao and other figures.

16in (41cm) high

£550-650 **DN**

A fine Canton enamel fishbowl of circular shape, the centre decorated with flowers and fruit on a turquoise background, the deep, rounded sides and everted rim decorated with fruit and flowers against a vibrant blue background, the exterior with three writhing stylised dragons on a turquoise background, some restoration.

c1800 *16.5in (42cm) diam.*

£2,500-3,500 **SOTA**

A Chinese Canton enamel square-section vase, each face painted with a songbird amidst flowers and foliage, all on a blue scrolling lotus ground.

8.75in (22cm) high

£600-1,000 **WW**

A 20thC Chinese Canton enamel supper set, comprising eight fan-shaped dishes and a circular central dish, decorated with figures and a rocky landscape, cased.

17in (43cm) high

£300-400 **WW**

A Chinese Ming period bronze foliate-form vase, of ribbed foliate baluster form, layered foliate baluster form, layered foliate short neck, applied with two dragons in reverse, raised on a circular foot.

11in (28cm) high

£1,500-2,000 **FRE**

A 17thC Chinese bronze gu-shaped vase, of archaic form.

13.5in (34cm) high

£200-300 **WW**

A Chinese bronze vase, the body with shield-shaped panels, the waisted neck with fabulous animal handles, six-character Qianlong mark.

13.5in (34cm) high

£1,800-2,200 **WW**

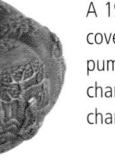

A 19thC Chinese bronze vase and cover, formed as a compressed pumpkin, cast with figures and shou characters, the base with a six-character Xuande mark.

5.75in (14.5cm) high

£1,000-1,500 **WW**

A 17thC Chinese Ming Dynasty bronze meiping, wide rim over a short waisted neck leading to broad shoulder rounding to tapering body over a hexagonal base raised on lingzhi scrolling feet joined by low shaped apron.

12in (30.5cm) high

£1,500-2,000   FRE

A Chinese late Ming Dynasty bronze archaic Ku-form vase, square flared mouth over square pillar body incised with archaic style coiled dragons on Greek key ground.

6in (15cm) high

£200-300   FRE

A late 17thC Chinese bronze yen yen vase, cast with a wide flared foliate mouth, tapering to a neck banded with a diaper and lingzhi heads leading to a shouldered body cast with ruyi head in high relief, raised on an openwork circular base, with ruyi and beaded scrolling apron.

17in (43cm) high

£600-800   FRE

A 19thC Chinese bronze pear-form vase, the slightly flared mouth issues from a waisted slender neck leading to an ovoid body raised on a circular foot, signed 'Sen'.

7.5in (19cm) high

£250-350   FRE

An 18th/19thC Chinese bronze archaic style vessel, heavily cast bronze vessel with two free-hanging handles to the shoulder over a circular base, signs of corrosive patination.

13in (33cm) high

£150-250   FRE

A 17thC Chinese bronze censer, the body cast with taotie masks, the foot with geometric motifs, the handles formed as animal heads, six-character Xuande mark.

7.75in (19.5cm) high

£400-500   WW

A 19th/20thC Chinese bronze incense burner and cover, with an animal knop and side handles, the body decorated with the eight trigrams.

10.75in (27cm) high

£120-180   WW

A 17thC Chinese bronze incense burner, in the form of a kylin, standing four square, traces of gilding, slight damage.

8.25in (21cm) high

£200-300   WW

A 17thC Chinese bronze censer, formed as a pumpkin, the handles as rats, all decorated with gold highlights and raised on three tall feet, some damage.

5.25in (13.5cm) high

£1,000-1,500   WW

A 17thC Chinese bronze tripod censer, with curved handles and taotie masks cast to the body, the wood cover with a carved soapstone knop, raised on an elaborate lotus stand.

11.25in (28.5cm) high

£1,000-1,500   WW

A 17thC Chinese bronze censer, the body cast with taotie masks, the rim with fabulous animals, the handles cast as animal heads.

2.25in (5.5cm) high

£300-500   WW

A Chinese Ming dynasty bronze lozenge-shaped koro and cover, with kylin finial and scroll handles, the sides with archaistic decoration.

14.5in (37cm) high

£650-750   **DN**

A 17th/18thC Chinese well-cast gold-splash bronze tripod censer, of compressed globular form cast with hoop handles to rim, with irregular gold splashes, raised on three triangular feet, good patina, Xuande six-character mark.

4.5in (11.5cm) wide

£350-550   **FRE**

An 18th/19thC Chinese '100 character' bronze censer, of ovoid form, the pierced cover surmounted by a Fu dog, the body applied with qilong handles with the body decorated with bats to one side and four columns of twenty-five characters to the other, raised on three dragon feet mask feet, signs of water patination to interior and feet.

10.5in (26.5cm) high

£500-700   **FRE**

A Chinese bronze censer, cover and stand, finely modelled and pierced with dragons and clouds, the sides with ring handles and beasts leaping over waves, six-character Xuande mark, but possibly 18thC.

7.5in (19cm) high

£4,500-5,500   **DN**

A late Western Zhou period Chinese bronze ritual food vessel (gui), of circular convex form, the two large handles with animal head ornaments projecting from the sides, raised on a tall foot-rim and square base, all decorated with vertical ribbing and simplified border decoration of animal heads and rosettes, with a later inscription to the interior.

10.25in (26cm) high

£20,000-25,000   **L&T**

A Chinese Zhou period bronze ritual vessel (Pou), the body with three vertical flanges, each section with taotie masks on a leiwen ground.

7in (18cm) high

£800-1,200   **WW**

A Chinese, Western Han Dynasty, bronze Xian, or steamer, with taotie mask and ring handles, in three sections.

13.75in (35cm) high

£400-600   **DN**

A pair of Chinese Qianlong period bronze incense burners of compressed globular form, shallow beaded rim, applied with two lion masks supporting free-hanging ring handles, raised on a small fluted foot, Qianlong six-character mark.

7in (18cm) diam

£1,800-2,200   **FRE**

An 18th/19thC Chinese gold-splash bronze brush wash, of cylindrical form with everted rim, heavily gold-splashed wall, raised on a flared circular foot.

9in (23cm) wide

£400-500

FRE

A 19thC Chinese bronze and mixed metal jardinière, of octagonal form, rim inlaid with silver Roman key diaper, applied with two lion mask handles in reverse, with six panels applied with copper five-claw dragon flanked by eight mixed metal Buddhist symbols over a conforming base.

10in (25.5cm) diam

£200-300

FRE

A Chinese late Ming dynasty gilt-bronze figure of Guanyin, seated in lalitasana mudra, a figure of Buddha in his crown.

9in (23cm) high

£3,500-4,500

WW

A Chinese Qianlong period gilt-bronze figure of Buddha, seated in lalitasana mudra, on a tall rectangular stand, nine-character Qianlong mark, nimbus missing.

7.7in (19.5cm) high

£1,000-1,500

WW

A rare 16th/17thC Ming dynasty gilt-bronze figure of Wen Ch'ang, the god of literature, seated wearing elaborate robes with cloud scroll borders, a scholarly headdress and holding a sceptre, raised on a hardwood stand.

9.25in (23.5cm) high

£12,000-15,000

WW

An 18thC or later Tibeto-Chinese gilt-bronze figure of Vajrabhairava in Yabyum, with his shakti, the bull-headed and multi-armed god trampling on prone figures on a lotus throne, some repair.

6in (15cm) high

£600-800

WW

An 18thC Chinese bronze model of a billy goat, standing four square on an associated rectangular stand, traces of gilding.

4.75in (12cm) high

£200-300

WW

A rare pair of 18thC Chinese Qianlong period gilt-bronze Buddhist lions, the mythical beasts standing four square, each with a tightly curled mane and bushy eyebrows, the prominent back bones with well-cast coats falling to either side and with extravagant flowing tails, their mouths agape baring their teeth and protruding tongues, both richly gilded with original pigment remaining.

9.25in (23.5cm) high

£20,000-25,000

WW

An 18thC Tibeto-Chinese gilt-bronze figure of Tsong Ka Pa, seated in lalitasana mudra, his robe incised and with lotus blossoms at each shoulder.

9.6in (24cm) high

£2,500-3,500   WW

A Chinese early Qing period bronze rabbit-form incense burner, the long-eared rabbit cast on all fours, downcast face, hollowed open section to the centre of the back, fine patina.

6.5in (16.5cm) high

£350-450   FRE

A Chinese early Qing period bronze rabbit-form incense burner, the long-eared rabbit cast on all fours, downcast face, hollowed open section to the centre of the back.

6.5in (16.5cm) high

£350-450   FRE

A Chinese late Ming period bronze brush rest, modelled as a smiling boy reclining over an elbow.

3in (7.5cm)

£500-800   FRE

A rare Chinese Ming Dynasty gold lacquered bronze statue of the infant Buddha, standing on a single lotus base, typically modelled with left arm bent pointing upwards, right downwards, simple tunic modelled to show a four-claw dragon.

6.25in (16cm) high

£1,500-2,000   FRE

A Chinese late Ming/early Qing period bronze Fu lion, heavily cast model, open mouth, scrolling fur to head, body and tail, the head opens, hinged at the rear, paw supported above a pierced ball, over a carved wood stand.

Lion 11in (28cm) high

£1,000-1,500   FRE

A Chinese pair of bronze oil lanterns, each of pagoda form, with hexagonal body above turned and pierced column and foot.

20.5in (52cm) high

£800-1,200   L&T

A Chinese bronze belt hook, inset with turquoise, silver and gold, probably Warring States period, cracks.

6.25in (16.5cm) high

£200-300   WW

A Chinese Han-style bronze belt buckle, inlaid with silver geometric designs.

5in (13cm) high

£300-400   WW

A Chinese Ming Dynasty bronze mirror of circular form, fluted recessed rim around a central pierced knob, good patina to underside.

8.5in (21.5cm) diam

£80-120   FRE

A 19thC Japanese model of a hawk, with hawthorn blossom decoration, the hawk perched on a bronze rustic bow.

20in (51cm) high

£2,500-3,500   A&G

A late 19thC Japanese bronze female figure, wearing long robes and a headdress, on oblong base.

11.5in (29cm) high

£150-200   A&G

A large 19thC Japanese bronze censer, decorated with panels of water birds, amidst lotus, reeds and breaking waves, the handles as the rice god Daikoku beneath a giant bag of rice, the reticulated lid with sages beneath a pine tree, a six-character inscription to the base.

17in (43cm) high

£1,000-2,000   WW

A Japanese Meiji period bronze jardinière, decorated with two quail, heightened in gold and silver, beneath foliage and flowers, the base inset with a later signed panel.

10.25in (26cm) high

£600-800   WW

A Japanese Meiji period bronze figure of a hawk, raised on a later painted wooden base.

6in (15cm) high

£1,000-2,000   FRE

A Japanese Meiji period bronze and mixed metal plaque, depicting a hawk atop a branch looking to the night sky.

22.75in (58cm) wide

£8,000-10,000   FRE

A Japanese Meiji period bronze group, of two tigers attacking an elephant, rootwood base with presentation plaque inscribed, 'Presented to Dr W.C. Davey by the Senior Staff of the Dunlop Rubber Company, Kobe, Japan, April 8th, 1936'.

15.75in (40cm) wide

£1,500-2,000   DN

A Japanese bronze bowl, cast with a band of birds and flowers.

c1900   12.25in (31cm) high

£150-200   DN

A 19thC Japanese bronze vase, cast in relief with carp and crayfish amongst crashing waves.

12.25in (31cm) high

£100-150   DN

A Japanese Meiji period bronze vase, of naturalistic form, with leaf, twig and berry decoration, and a hardwood base.

8.5in (21.5cm) high

£120-150   ROS

A large 18th/19thC Japanese bronze temple bell, of dome form, cast to show four seasonal scenes to the body, dragon head hook bracket, beaded panelling to the top and pierced to the base, cast with chrysanthemum to prong.

32in (81cm) high

£2,500-3,500   FRE

A late 19thC Japanese bronze koro, by Suzuki Masayoshi, signed 'Dai Nippon Suzuki Masayoshi Zo', missing figure to base, possibly a bird.

51in (129.5cm) high

£700-1,000   FRE

A pair of early 20thC Japanese bronze and gilt figures, decorated with gilt headdress and robes, above an inlaid wood stand.

7in (17cm) high

£3,500-4,500   FRE

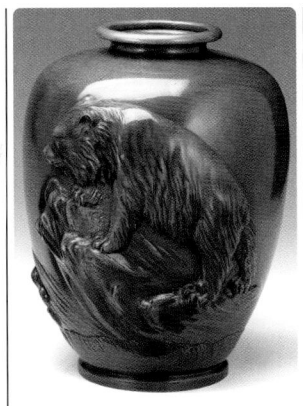

A late 19thC Japanese bronze vase, of pear shape, applied with a tiger over rock work, mark to base.

14.5in (37cm) high

£400-500   FRE

A late 19thC Japanese bronze vase, of ovoid form, rimmed mouth above a short neck worked to show a large bear over rock work raised on a circular base.

15in (38cm) high

£700-1,000   FRE

A late 19thC Japanese bronze, mixed metal and silver-covered tripod burner of Koro, the pierced silver cover worked with thirteen applied flowers, covering a bronze ovoid body worked to show three doves in a grass bed, mark to base.

5.5in (14cm) high

£2,000-3,000   FRE

A 19th/20thC Japanese bronze presentation vase, of elongated pear-shaped form, flared trumpet mouth, applied with a single gilt-metal chrysanthemum.

11in (28cm) high

£500-600   FRE

An early 20thC Japanese bronze elephant, modelled with trunk down, large long tusks and ears, marked.

8in (20.5cm) high

£200-300   FRE

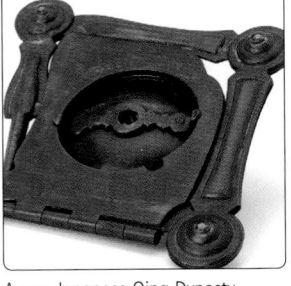

A Japanese bronze vase, finely cast with a band of irises and leaves, signed 'Shomei' or 'Masaaki'.

c1900   *10in (25cm) high*

£700-900   DN

A Chinese early Ming dynasty copper revolving bracelet, the main band with dragons and pearls, perspex stand.

2.75in (7cm) diam

£400-600   DN

An early 19thC Japanese copper lacuna lacquered vase, of meiping form, broad shoulder below a short neck and flared mouth, the body shows gold, silver and tin tone, recessed circular foot.

11in (28cm) high

£1,000-1,500   FRE

A rare Japanese Qing Dynasty copper travelling folding pricket, of compressed triangular form, expanding to reveal tri-bracket rotating openwork platform base, three arm vertical pricket stand, and circular support, impressed mark.

13in (33cm) high

£1,000-1,500   FRE

ORIENTAL

A Chinese Export silver box, the rectangular hinged top decorated with immortals atop cloud banks looking down on attendants astride fish and turtles and surrounded by a sea serpent, the front and sides decorated with a continuous village scene, marks rubbed.

c1860   7.75in (20cm) wide
£1,200-1,800   FRE

A Japanese Meiji period silver and mixed metal vase, of baluster form, decorated with a continuous river scene, 'Spink & Sons' label to the underside.

10in (25.5cm) high
£700-1,000   FRE

A late 19thC Japanese silver and enamel vase, well-enamelled slender neck vase, over a triform base, enamelled to show flowers and birds.

7in (18cm) high
£2,500-3,500   FRE

A 19th/20thC Japanese silver and enamel censer, of ovoid form, the surmounted domed cover worked to show berries and leaves, the body well-enamelled in various colours to show highlighted flowers.

5.5in (14cm) high
£800-1,200   FRE

A 19th/20thC Japanese silver presentation covered censer, of typical form, pierced foliate cover, moulded tripod base, applied with a single gilt-metal chrysanthemum, pressed mark.

6in (15cm) high
£1,000-1,500   FRE

A late 19thC Japanese silver cigar box, of rectangular form, worked to show in high relief carp, lotus flowers and reeds over a hammered ground, impressed mark to base.

9.5in (24cm) long
£1,200-1,400   FRE

A late 19thC Japanese silver miniature chest, hoop handle surmounting a tall rectangular chest, pressed with blossom flowers, two latched doors revealing four wood drawers with silver handles.

6in (15cm) high
£700-1,000   FRE

A late 19thC Japanese silver miniature chest, with a hoop handle surmounting a tall rectangular chest, pressed to show songbirds and blossoms, with two latched doors revealing three black lacquered drawers.

5.5in (14cm) high
£700-1,000   FRE

An Edo period shakudo tsuba, signed 'Otsuki Korin', and two fushi Kasirae.

The tsuba 3in (8in) high
£3,500-4,500   SOTP

A Japanese Edo period iron shakudo tsuba, of oval form, carved in low relief to show a dragon to either side, signed.

3in (7.5cm) diam
£250-350   FRE

A Japanese Meiji period mixed metal Samurai warrior, wearing a uniform inlaid with gilt-metal stylised flower heads and circles, wearing a katana and carrying a spear, standing on a naturalistic base.

9.5in (24.5cm) high
£4,500-5,500   L&T

A Japanese Meiji period pair of mixed metal vases, each with flared neck and globular body decorated with birds in flight above a riverine reeded landscape, signed.

6.25in (16cm) high

£3,000-5,000   **L&T**

A 20thC Himilayan mixed metal vajra, inlaid with lapis lazuli, coral and turquoise.

8.25in (21cm) high

£250-350   **WW**

A pair of late 19thC Japanese mixed metal vases, of cylindrical form, lion masks to the shoulder in reverse, worked to show a songbird amongst a blossoming tree.

12in (30.5cm) high

£700-1,000   **FRE**

One of a pair of late 19thC Japanese mixed metal vases, of trumpet form, well inlaid with silver gilt-bronze to two archaic-form handles and the rim, the body applied with gilt-bronze, silver and copper to show floral sprays and well-cast song birds.

12in (30.5cm) high

£1,000-2,000 PAIR   **FRE**

One of a pair of 19th/20thC Japanese mixed metal vases, of sectional form, gilt-metal ground, two white enamel panels applied with mixed metal to show floral sprigs and birds.

6in (15cm) high

£300-500 PAIR   **FRE**

A Japanese silver-coloured metal novelty box and cover, formed as an artillery shell with a reeded copper base band, engraved with prunus blossom and with a gilt interior, stamped mark, 8.25oz (260g).

6.25in (16cm) high

£150-200   **DN**

A 17th or 18thC Indian white metal circular vase, with a everted rim chased with foliate decoration, the sides with scrolling foliate borders and a band of repoussé figures, on four bun feet.

4in (10.5cm) high

£450-550   **L&T**

A Japanese komai tea caddy, of hexagonal form, the cover and shoulders decorated with geometric designs, the sides with alternate panels of vines and landscape scenes, signed.

5in (13cm) high

£2,500-3,000   **L&T**

An unusual 19thC Japanese metal inro, inset with eight emblems, and signed on a pad.

2.25in (5.5cm) high

£300-400   **WW**

A Chinese hand mirror, with a white jade handle, the back set with a spinach jade bi, with semi-precious stones, with a Charlotte Horstmann invoice from the 1950s.

11.75in (30cm) high

£700-800   **WW**

A rare 19thC Thai rose gold and gilded sectional offering bowl, of overall ovoid form, comprising of four sections, a small domed cover revealing a second open-work handled flat domed cover enclosing an openwork rim and footed bowl fitting a Y-shaped bowl.

7in (18cm) high

£1,500-2,000   **FRE**

A 19thC Thai gilt-metal figure of Sakyamuni, standing, hand raised in abhaya mudra, face in expression of joyful meditation, over a graduated plinth.

29.5in (75cm) high

£500-700   **FRE**

A Chinese silver-coloured metal three-piece tea service by Luen Wo, of baluster form chased with dragons amidst clouds, with lobed rims and dragon handles, on five-tow feet, engraved with a monogram, stamped marks, 42.25oz (1412g) gross.

Luen Wo was a prolific maker located at 42 Nanking Road, Shanghai at the end of the 19thC and beginning of the 20thC.

The tea pot 9.25in (23.5cm) long

£2,500-3,500   **DN**

ORIENTAL

A 17thC Chinese jade carving of a recumbent horse, the stone with brown inclusions.

3.5in (9cm) high

£350-550   **WW**

A probably 19thC Chinese white jade carving of two love birds, on a lotus leaf and clasping a jui fungus.

3in (7.5cm) high

£5,000-6,000   **WW**

A pair of Chinese green jade carved models of horses, each in movement wearing reins and a long decorative saddlecloth, on fitted hardwood stands.

4in (10cm) wide

£800-900   **L&T**

A 19th/20thC Chinese jade carving of a recumbent kylin, the stone flecked with brown.

2.75in (7cm) high

£600-800   **WW**

A Chinese celadon-coloured jade carving of a mythical beast, baring its teeth and raised on a wood stand.

5.5in (14cm) high

£200-300   **WW**

A Chinese jade carving of a fabulous animal.

3.25in (8cm) high

£60-100   **WW**

A Chinese probably Ming dynasty calcified jade carving of a recumbent horse, with a monkey clambering on its back.

3in (7.5cm) high

£3,000-5,000   **WW**

A Chinese jade carving of two fish, embracing a pearl.

4in (10cm) high

£150-250   **WW**

A Chinese late Qing Dynasty white jade bird grouping, of long rectangular form, carved to show six birds joined by a swag of grain, detail-carved feathers and base, over a wood stand.

9in (23cm) long

£700-1,000   **FRE**

A Chinese pale celadon jade carving of a drum, surrounded by three boys.

3in (8cm) high

£450-550   **WW**

A 19thC Chinese celadon and russet jade figure of Quanyin, well-carved, worked to show a flowing headdress, left hand holding a vase, draped in flowing robe, over a double lotus throne.

14in (35.5cm) high

£2,000-3,000   **FRE**

A Chinese pale green jade carving in the form of a flowerhead, the central spirally carved stamen formed as an incense holder, with subsidiary bowl-form flowerhead, surrounded by carved leaves.

3.5in (9cm) wide

£10,000-15,000   **L&T**

An 18thC Chinese jade vase, made for the Mughal market, the spherical body crisply carved with stylised flowers and foliage between bands of stiff leaves, the cylindrical neck carved with a lotus pattern, the interior set with a darker green reticulated jade panel, the two handles formed as buds.

4in (10cm) high

£7,000-10,000　　WW

A Chinese late Qing Dynasty white and brown russet jade vase, of shouldered rectangular form, tapering flared mouth above four well-carved panels depicting scholars amongst mountainous forests, tall rectangular base.

14in (35.5cm) high

£1,000-1,500　　FRE

An 18thC or later Chinese white jade pouring vessel, finely carved with a bifid dragon to the rim, and a lion mask beneath the spout, each side with a phoenix roundel, together with a hardwood stand.

4.75in (12cm) high

£2,500-3,000　　WW

A small Chinese jade twin-handled koro and cover, the cover decorated with a lion dog, above three elephant head and ring handles, the body with twin dolphin head and ring handles, with carved lion head decoration above three paw feet.

3.75in (9.5cm) high

£1,000-1,200　　L&T

A 17thC Chinese jade fish gong, the green stone with hardstone eyes, wood stand.

17.75in (45cm) long

£1,800-2,200　　DN

A pair of Chinese circular jade screens, each applied with various hard stones depicting exotic birds amongst flowers and rockwork, with a pierced decorative hardwood stand.

12.25in (31cm) diam

£6,000-7,000　　L&T

A 19thC Chinese pale green jade carved and pierced shaped contemplation screen, with central character mark and relief carved geometric decoration, on pierced stand.

9.5in (24cm) wide

£2,500-3,500　　L&T

A 19thC Chinese jadeite pendant, carved with a peach, two Buddhist hand citron and a bat.

2.75in (7cm) high

£200-300　　WW

A 19thC Chinese white jade pendant, carved on one side with boys riding a hobby horse the other with a lady at a loom.

2.25in (5.5cm) high

£1,500-2,000　　WW

A pair of Chinese white jade bangles.

3in (8cm) diam

£550-650 **WW**

A pair of oblong green onyx bookends, with painted bronze double-budgerigar mounts on foliated boughs.

5.25in (13cm) high

£350-450 **A&G**

A 19thC Chinese 24k gold and jade dress ring, the delicately modelled ring set with a fine spinach green round cabochon stone to a hand-worked bezel showing coiled dragons, inscription to verso.

Stone 0.25in (0.5cm) diam

£450-550 **FRE**

A 19thC Chinese jade belt buckle, carved with two moths.

3.5in (9cm) high

£350-550 **WW**

A Chinese Qing Dynasty golden zitan and celadon jade-mounted scroll weight, of long rectangular form, fitted with a well-carved celadon jade handle in the form of joined scrolling mythical beasts.

8.75in (22cm) long

£1,200-1,800 **FRE**

A 19thC and later Chinese zitan seal box, the box of rectangular form, the cover waisted at the sides, the base fitted with three panelled bays over bracket feet, enclosing three celadon jade seals with the characters for happiness, prosperity and longevity in three different scripts.

4.5in (11.5cm) long

£400-600 **FRE**

HARDSTONE / SOAPSTONE

A Chinese late Ming Dynasty gilded black limestone Quanyin, the single carved section worked to show a seated Quanyin, down cast head covered in a long free-flowing robe, left knee raised supporting the left arm grasping a rolled scroll, hollowed base, signs of a red lacquer.

8.5in (21.5cm) high

£250-350 **FRE**

A 17th/18thC Chinese soapstone carving of Guanyin seated, wearing robes finely incised and decorated in gilt with roundels and borders, her hair, face and other details picked out in black and red.

7.5in (19cm) high

£3,000-4,000 **WW**

A 19thC Chinese yellow soapstone carving of a seated figure, wearing robes and holding a tablet, one foot restored.

5in (12.5cm) high

£350-450 **WW**

A 19thC Chinese white Shoushan stone figure of Quanyin, finely carved to show a downcast head, her left hand holding a sceptre with one knee bent, good detail to the face and robe.

9in (23cm) high

£700-900 **FRE**

A 19thC Chinese moss agate cup, the body carved with small studs.

1.5in (4cm) high

£150-250 **WW**

A 20thC Chinese hardstone censer and cover, with a lion dog knop and handles, a wood stand.

5in (13cm) high

£400-500 **WW**

A Chinese hardstone small bowl, the moss green stone with white flecks.

4in (10cm) high

£200-300 WW

A Chinese soapstone seal, carved with two mythical beasts.

2.25in (5.5cm) high

£350-450 WW

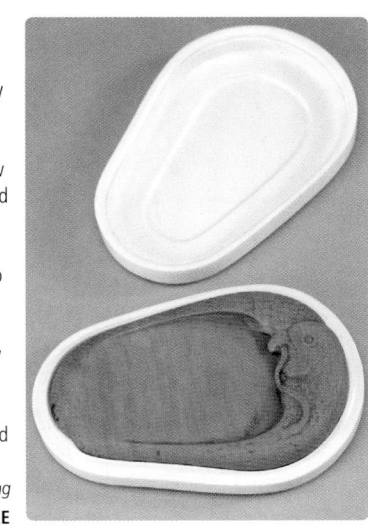

An important Chinese early Qing Dynasty Songhua ink stone, of overall tapering oval form, delicately hollow trough framed by a detailed low relief carved parrot grasping a corded tassel from its beak continuing to the rounded edge and underside grasped by two detailed clawed feet below a finely incised artist's seal and four-character mark, together with a later carved ivory cover and base.

4in (10cm) long

£10,000-15,000 FRE

SCHOLAR'S ROCK

A Chinese Song Dynasty or later jade stone scholar's rock, yushi, of boulder fragment form, the rock enhanced to resemble a bamboo grove under the lee of a great mountain, creamy white and black inclusions, original inscription to front reading 'bamboo grove seen from afar', yuedao, and a further collector's inscription for the 'Guo' family, raised on a fitted shaped and beaded hongmu stand.

5.5in (14cm) high

£3,000-4,000 FRE

A large Chinese late Ming/early Qing period shangdong Scholar's rock, the well-balanced rock shows various perforated and hollowed surfaces, with an intricate pattern of interconnecting arm-like protrusions, raised on a wood base.

16.5in (42cm) high

£4,500-5,500 FRE

A Chinese lingbi upright scholar's rock, single section of rich dark black slate of tall upright high balanced form, resembling a towering mountain, raised on a fitted and carved wood base.

8in (20.5cm) high

£3,500-4,500 FRE

A small Chinese grey lingbi scholar's rock, of pierced mountainous form, some white inclusions, over a shaped wood stand.

3in (7.5cm) high

£600-800 FRE

A small Chinese lingbi scholar's rock, of wide mountainous form, naturally formed with several protrusions and hollowed valleys, raised on a fitted wooden base.

3.75in (9.5cm) high

£600-800 FRE

An exceptional Chinese Qianlong period burl wood scroll pot, of slightly waisted cylindrical form, the fine textured protruding and knotted burl wood body ranges in colour from grey to dark brown, over a huanghuali solid section base with eleven rows of inscribed script and two artist's seals with red pigment, calligraphic inscription to base.

10in (25.5cm) high

£15,000-20,000   **FRE**

A 18thC Chinese huangyangmu/boxwood libation cup, of oval form, incised rim over a body finely carved in high relief to show an openwork base issuing a peach branch and leaves forming a handle, the exterior finely carved to show a continuous scene of gentlemen in pursuit of leisure with attendants.

3in (7.5cm) high

£1,200-1,800   **FRE**

A late 18thC Chinese huanghuali snuff box, of square 'face' form, the slightly domed oval cover reveals a hollowed interior, the base worked to show recessed branch-like inclusions, raised over four branch-like legs.

2.5in (6.5cm) wide

£200-300   **FRE**

A Chinese Qing Dynasty huangyangmu/boxwood circular 'upside-down' dice box with four dice, of circular form worked with a thin beaded cover, opening to reveal a base recessed with 12 hollows, enclosing four ivory dice.

2.5in (6.5cm) diam

£200-300   **FRE**

A 19thC Chinese huanghuali Qin-form box, the box of instrument form inlaid with mother-of-pearl and brass.

10in (25.5cm) long

£600-800   **FRE**

A 17thC Chinese Kangxi period huanghuali seal chest, of tall rectangular form, the top panel inlaid with ivory to show stylised dragons to the corners within a framed border, the two matched doors and side panels decorated with matching inlaid bands, revealing three long huanghuali drawers, raised one a beaded and finely scrolling shaped base, original brass hardware.

14in (35.5cm) wide

£4,000-5,000   **FRE**

A Chinese Qing Dynasty Imperial huanghuali artemisia leaf-form box, of two well-matched parts, the finely figured huanghuali ribbed cover carved in medium relief to show stem and veins, over a deep base.

7.5in (19cm) long

£2,500-3,500   **FRE**

A 17thC Chinese Yinxiang period huanghuali and brass-bound seal box, of tall square form, the flat domed lid opens to reveal a fitted brass-bound tray, terminating in a scrolling shaped apron and bracket footed base.

6in (15cm) wide

£600-800   **FRE**

A 19thC Chinese Muzhen period tanxiang or sandalwood pillow, with two incised characters within an intaglio medallion carved in imitation of a rubbing reading 'prolong the years' with inscription:

'Ye Xiangzhi, zi: Zidong said that, while plowing the land of Xianyang, [he came across] an ancient roof tile piece with the words 'prolong the years' written in reverse and that could barely be seen', the underside inscribed with two inscriptions, the first reads 'The Han Emperor Huangdi bestows this rhapsody, the great wing rises, the clouds fly and scatter. After distinguishing oneself across the country, I return to my home town, comforted by knowing that brave soldiers are protecting the four corners', the second inscription reads 'Bowing to the Stone Tower, someone copied the Han dynasty Stele of Dafeng Rhapsody'.

11in (28cm) long

£8,000-10,000   **FRE**

An unusual Chinese late Ming period huanghuali saddle, of typical U-shape form, rectangular Greek key incised sides, two iron-bound arches, one carved to show a Fu lion.

14in (35.5cm) long

£1,800-2,200   **FRE**

A Chinese Qing Dynasty huanghuali kite spindle, the rounded handle issues from a cylindrical brass pin-mounted rotating spindle.

9in (23cm) long

£1,500-2,000 FRE

A 17th/18thC ivory and brass huanghuali cased scale, the incised tapered ivory arm strung with a free-hanging tray and weight, both finely incised with three-claw dragons, together with an associated set of brass weights.

12in (30.5cm) long

£800-1,200 FRE

An 18thC assembled Chinese huanghuali and white metal plated tea service, comprising five small U-shaped cups of solid hollowed huanghuali lined with white metal plated copper moulded inserts, together with a large matched zitan and white metal cup and saucer.

2in (5cm) high

£250-350 FRE

An unusual Chinese Qing Dynasty eagle feather and huangyangmu fan, the wing form grouping of sixteen feathers supported by a triple lotus-form head and rounded handle.

19in (48cm) long

£150-250 FRE

A Chinese Ming Dynasty lacquered huanghuali Buddha sakyamuni figure, finely carved in relief, serene face with slightly closed eyes, red pigment to lips, free-flowing red lacquered robe, slightly exposing the chest.

7in (18cm) high

£400-600 FRE

A Chinese early Qing Dynasty huanghuali panel, of square form with bevelled edge, well-carved to show a central medallion of a stag raised on a scrolling sea below ruyi clouds, and the symbol for longevity worked in reverse.

16in (40.5cm) wide

£800-1,200 FRE

An 18thC Chinese huangyangmu/boxwood ruyi sceptre, of long lingzhi form, the openwork head carved to imitate a drying and aging lingzhi, issuing from multi-stem handle carved to show recesses and small lingzhi heads, the base bound in cord thread, boxed.

10in (25.5cm) long

£3,000-4,000 FRE

A 17thC or earlier Chinese huanghuali folding mirror stand, jingjia, with stylised official's hats and scroll protruding top rail, over a lattice bracket stand, fitted to the base with a shaped supporting cross bar platform, held by a hinged lattice frame, over joined straight plank base.

14.75in (37.5cm) high

£4,000-5,000 FRE

A Chinese early Qing Dynasty 'golden thread' zitan brush pot, of five-plank construction, rounded joined edge, raised on four bracket feet, recessed base, fine 'golden thread' throughout.

4.75in (12cm) high

£1,800-2,200 **FRE**

A possibly 18thC Chinese Zitan wood flower vase, of lotus petal section.

16in (41cm) high

£600-800 **DN**

A small 18thC Chinese zitan peach blossom or foliate-form brush pot, of hexafoil form, seven-plank construction, scalloped beaded rim, the underside incised to show a flower petal.

4.25in (10.5cm) high

£1,500-2,000 **FRE**

An 18thC Chinese zitan and embedded pebble brush pot, of single section form, well-hollowed interior revealing a gold thread grain, the exterior wall very finely embellished to resemble a tree trunk and abstractly a 'ghost face'; with delicately hollowed trunk recesses and weathered surfaces partially engulfing a mottled green pebble, raised on three small bracket feet.

6in (15cm) high

£10,000-15,000 **FRE**

A Chinese Qing Dynasty 'golden thread' zitan brush pot, of inverted waisted section form, constructed of five shaped panels.

4in (10cm) high

£1,800-2,200 **FRE**

A 19th/20thC Chinese Zitan brush pot, of thin cylindrical form, well-carved to show sages among a mountainous landscape, gnarled panel in reverse.

8in (20.5cm) high

£450-550 **FRE**

An 18thC Chinese zitan brush pot, of tree trunk form, one side naturally formed with gnarled irregular swirling veined surfaces, interrupted with apertures, verso inscribed with the phase 'Zuoren youem yidian shuzin' or 'A man requires a measure of a merciful heart', followed by a seal, the polished rim leading to a cliff-like naturally irregular interior.

6.25in (16cm) high

£5,000-7,000 **FRE**

A rare 18thC burl-zitan ink stone cover and hongmu base, four-character inscription to stone, the naturalistic-shaped porous stone inscribed with four-character seals to the base, covered by a single section of hollowed burl zitan with fine golden thread and black tight grain figuring, over a shaped hongmu base, raised on four bracket feet.

6.25in (16cm) wide

£1,500-2,000 **FRE**

A Chinese mid-Qing Dynasty zitan square corner box, of rectangular form with highly figured grain, the cover with rounded edge and beaded rim, over a match base.

4in (10cm) wide

£300-500 **FRE**

A rare Chinese Qing Dynasty zitan watch stand, section construction and banjo form, carved in medium relief in a European rococo style, circular beaded recess worked to the centre.

5.5in (14cm) long

£350-550 **FRE**

A 14th/15thC Tibetan purple zitan lacquered Buddha figure, finely carved figured seated in dhyanasana with hands in abhaya and varada mudras, face with delicate features, open flowing robe, over a double lotus throne, with relic intact to base.

7in (18cm) high

£4,000-6,000   **FRE**

An 18thC Chinese huamu burl brush pot and nanmu stand and cover, the single section partially reticulated burl wood pot finely hollowed, the exterior reveals a cameo-like skinned body of yellow hues, terminating in matched nanmu shaped cover and openwork base.

7.5in (19cm) high

£4,500-5,500   **FRE**

A pair of Chinese late Qing Dynasty hongmu lanterns, of square form, with insert panels fitted to a humpback jointed frame.

20in (51cm) high

£500-800   **FRE**

A 19thC Chinese hongmu framed mirror, of tall rectangular form with a band of stylised lotus flowers issuing leaves joining Fu bats framing a recessed Greek Key band framing a period mirror, iron free-hanging hook.

16in (40.5cm) high

£500-800   **FRE**

A pair of 18th/19thC Chinese hongmu metamorphic or folding book stands, folding to reveal a rectangular book platform, supported by a hinged adjustable stand.

21in (53.5cm) wide

£500-700   **FRE**

A 19thC Chinese hongmu brush pot, hollowed from a single trunk, resembling the Chinese symbol of eternity of two raised square tiers and two recessed squares, issuing from a single large square, raised on four small bracket feet.

3in (7.5cm) high

£1,500-2,000   **FRE**

A Chinese Qing Dynasty hongmu tray, of simulated bamboo rectangular form, the gallery edge worked to show bamboo stems joined at the corners, single plank base.

20in (51cm) long

£550-750   **FRE**

An unusual 19thC hongmu bone or ivory inlaid picnic box, of four tier sectional form, each inlaid with three bands of bone or ivory oval panels, the twin hinged handles carved in low relief to show tight scrolls locked in place by two grasshopper-form pins surmounted to the cover, the shaped base carved with scroll work.

16in (40.6cm) wide

£500-800   **FRE**

A Chinese late Ming/early Qing period wood carved figure of Quanyin, carved with down-turned dressed head, flowing robe, holding a child in her arms, standing over a lotus throne, signs of colour pigment.

14.5in (37cm) high

£600-800   **FRE**

A 17thC or later Chinese hardwood carving of Guanyin, seated with one knee raised, resting on pierced rockwork, paper label for 'Spink & Son', some old repairs.

10.25in (26cm) high

£1,200-1,800   **WW**

A large late 19thC softwood model of a buffalo, of long recumbent form, inlaid bone eyes and inset horns.

15in (38cm) long

£200-300   **FRE**

ORIENTAL

A late 18th/early 19thC Japanese burl wood basket, carved from a single section of burl wood, the hoop handle of three branch form, the rounded tray reveals an oval openwork hollow, the underside reveals a fine gnarled and knotted surface, overall finely enhanced.

13in (33cm) high

£1,800-2,200   FRE

A small 19thC Japanese burl wood lingzhi-form tray, finely figured stand enhanced to show an aged five head lingzhi, delicately worked continuation to underside, tomobako reads 'camphor wood free-form carved tea tray', signed Shiro or Haku Dou Saku.

6in (15cm) high

£200-300   FRE

An early 19thC Japanese okimono of a wasps' nest, hollowed and enhanced wood nest, enclosing three free-moving ivory grubs, and five sedentary ivory grubs, enclosed in a tomobako box.

3.5in (9cm) high

£1,200-1,800   FRE

A 19thC Japanese boxwood okimono of a boar, modelled seated with legs carved in fine detail verso, raised front legs, head held high looking forward, inlaid with ivory eyes and tusks, finely carved hair and detail throughout, enclosed in a 19thC black lacquer box.

2.5in (6.5cm) high

£1,500-2,500   FRE

A 19thC Japanese wood netsuke, carved as a warty toad crouched on a sandal.

2.25in (6cm) high

£350-450   WW

A 19thC Japanese root wood hibachi, extensively hollowed from a single waisted oval trunk section, thick incised edge, gnarled and polished tight grain exterior, two-plank pine base, missing copper insert.

25in (63.5cm) wide

£600-800   FRE

A 19thC Japanese wooden inro, decorated with lotus branches, flowers and leaves, a two-character mark to one end.

3.5in (8.5cm) high

£500-700   WW

A Japanese ivory and boxwood figure of a man with a broom, incomplete.

c1900   *9in (23cm) high*

£350-550   DN

A 19thC Japanese Komai kidney-shaped box and cover, decorated in gold and silver with pavilions in a landscape.

2.5in (6cm) high

£400-600   WW

A 19thC Japanese Noh mask, possibly Otobide, carved wood, gilt pigment on gesso, gilt-metal eyes, storage box.

9in (23cm) high

£150-250 FRE

A 19thC Japanese Noh mask, possibly Shaka Buddha, carved wood polychrome over gesso, gilt-metal eyes, inscribed to the interior.

11in (28cm) high

£120-180 FRE

A 19thC Japanese Noh mask, Buaku, carved wood, polychrome over gesso, gilt horns, one gilt-metal eye, one missing.

9in (23cm) high

£150-250 FRE

A 19th/20thC Japanese Noh mask, Choreibeshimi, carved wood polychrome over gesso, insert gilt-metal eyes.

9in (23cm) high

£200-300 FRE

A late 19th/early 20thC Japanese Noh mask, Ko-omote, carved wood polychrome over gesso, storage case.

9in (23cm) high

£150-250 FRE

A 19th/20thC Japanese Noh mask, carved wood painted and gilt highlights, applied hair, with storage bag.

9in (23cm) high

£400-600 FRE

A 20thC Japanese Noh mask, Fukai, carved wood polychrome over gesso with storage bag.

9in (23cm) high

£200-300 FRE

A 20thC Japanese Noh mask, Ko-omote, carved wood and polychrome, inscribed to the interior, minor losses, with storage bag.

9in (23cm) high

£200-300 FRE

A 19thC Burmese gilt and black lacquered wood Buddha figure, seated in padmasana with the right hand in bhumispara mudra.

5.5in (14cm) high

£120-180 FRE

A rare Burmese Qing Dynasty polychrome wood articulated tattoo model, of male adult form, articulated torso and limbs, white polychrome body painted red and black depicting significant tattooed areas.

9in (23cm) high

£350-550 FRE

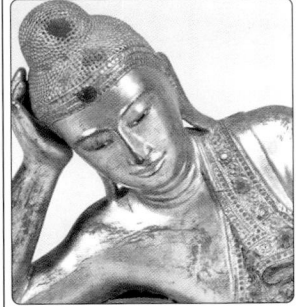

A Thai carved wood and gilt reclining Buddhistic figure.

40.25in (102cm) long

£400-500 DN

ORIENTAL

A 17thC Chinese Bitong period bamboo brush pot, of slender cylindrical form, gently flared mouth carved in medium to high relief to show a continuous mountainous landscape with a figure over a mule or donkey ascending followed by an attendant, the verso carved to show plum blossoms in high relief.

4.25in (11cm) high

£800-1,200   FRE

A 19thC Chinese bamboo brushpot, decorated with figures on a veranda beneath foliage, the reverse with four columns of calligraphy.

5.25in (13.5cm) high

£150-250   WW

A late 19th/early 20thC bamboo brushpot, carved with two travellers in a landscape.

6in (15cm) high

£150-200   DN

An 18th/19thC Chinese bamboo model of a snake, of twisting coiled form, detail enhanced body and well-polished gold brown patina, Japanese torobako box reading 'natural bamboo root snake okimono'.

3in (7.5cm) high

£700-1,000   FRE

An 18thC Chinese shaped bamboo brushpot, carved in shallow relief in liu ching technique with figures crossing a bridge in a landscape.

5in (13cm) high

£250-350   DN

A late 19thC Chinese bamboo brushpot carved with figures and attendants in a landscape.

6.25in (16cm) high

£200-250   DN

An 18thC Chinese rhizome bamboo seal, the tapering cylindrical body with rhizome growths issuing from a cylindrical growth issuing from a cylindrical stem supported by three smaller stems, incised with two characters to base, red pigment to seal.

2in (5cm) high

£2,000-3,000   FRE

A pair of Chinese carved bamboo cylindrical incense boxes, pierced and carved with immortals in a bamboo grove.

12.5in (32cm) high

£300-400   DN

A 17th/18thC Chinese bamboo root brush pot, of gnarled bamboo root form, the interior lacquered black.

3.75in (9.5cm) high

£500-1,000   FRE

A small Chinese Qing Dynasty bamboo skin brush pot, of tall square form, of five-plank construction, raised on four low relief carved bracket feet.

3.75in (9.5cm) high

£150-200   FRE

An 18thC Chinese shaped bamboo brushpot, carved in shallow relief in liu ching technique with figures crossing a bridge in a landscape.

5in (13cm) high

£250-350   DN

A large 19thC Chinese bamboo brush pot, finely carved pot in medium relief, carved to show a continuous garden scene with scholars amongst pine trees and a scrolling sea.

7in (17.5cm) high

£200-400   FRE

A bamboo and shell seal, of square form, carved in high relief and openwork to show a scholar among a pine tree grove, signed for early Qing Dynasty to side, shell or horn incised seal plate, associated silver inlaid lacquer box.

£250-350   FRE

A Chinese Qing Dynasty double form gourd and stand, of fine golden brown patina, over a circular bracket footed wood stand.

9.5in (24cm) high

£100-200   FRE

A Chinese Qing Dynasty elongated gourd, long brown stem issues from an elongated double gourd form body, good golden brown patina, with modern wood stand.

18in (46cm) high

£300-400   FRE

A Chinese Qing Dynasty triple gourd and stand, the graduated triple gourd raised on an open work scroll form stand.

13in (33cm) high

£400-600   FRE

A Chinese Qing Dynasty partially lacquered knotted gourd and stand, the knotted neck issuing from a broad compressed double gourd body, over a fine circular base supporting four free-moving spheres.

16in (40.5cm) high

£400-600   FRE

A pair of Chinese Qing Dynasty natural double form gourds on sectional gourd stands, the bound stem coil in mirror image issuing from golden brown double gourds over pierced stands of gourd centres.

10in (25.5cm) high

£500-800   FRE

A 19thC bamboo bound form natural gourd bottle, enhanced by binding to resemble bamboo stem fitted with wood stopper and yellow jadeite ring, raised on a root wood stand.

11in (28cm) long

£250-350   FRE

A 19thC Japanese natural gourd, of waisted double form, fine white metal stopper, cloth bound enclosing an ivory ring or hyowa netsuke, fine golden brown to dark brown patina, encased in tomobako.

10in (25.5cm) high

£300-500   FRE

A 19thC Japanese double hyowa netsuke and spout natural gourd, fine slight double gourd form, fitted with wood stopper, brass fitted nozzle or spout, cloth supporting an ivory and tortoiseshell hyowa netsuke, silk case and tomobako.

8.5in (21.5cm) high

£400-600   FRE

HORN

A rhinoceros horn libation cup, carved in the form of a lotus flower with waves around the base, with two small snails to the interior, some damage.

4.25in (11cm) wide

£16,000-20,000   L&T

A Chinese rhinoceros horn libation cup, carved with a guei dragon and archaistic patterns.

3.25in (8.5cm) high

£200-300   DN

An early 19thC Chinese carved rhinoceros horn seal, finely carved with a phoenix on a ground of scrolling lotus.

3in (7.5cm) high

£150-250   DN

A late 16th/early 17thC Chinese carved red lacquer incense box and cover, decorated with lychees amidst foliage, on a diaper moulded ground, cracks and chips.

3in (7.5cm) high

£4,000-5,000   WW

A Chinese export lacquer games box, with folding chess/backgammon board and a drawer containing an export ivory red and white chess set, complete but damaged.

£600-800   DN

A Chinese Qianlong period Imperial lacquer edict case, of rectangular form, carved in high relief, the front panel shows a two-character medallion 'Jade Temple'.

18in (45.5cm) wide

£2,500-3,000   FRE

A 17thC or later Chinese red lacquer cup, with a loop handle and three feet, decorated with fruiting lychee, beneath a key fret band, a metal lining, damages.

3in (8cm) high

£500-600   WW

A Chinese gilt-metal-mounted red lacquer wall vase, carved with five bats around a shou character, fixed wood stand.

c1800   *7in (18cm) high*

£2,000-2,500   WW

CLOSER LOOK: LACQUER DISH

Lacquer has been used since c400BC. Layers of sap from the Rhus vernicifera tree create a hard surface that can be carved in relief.

It was a speciality of craftsmen in the Court workshops of Peking from the 16thC.

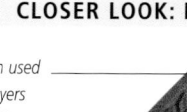

The dish is carved in deep relief with four figures and a pagoda, beneath a pine tree. The borders are decorated with flowers and foliage. The dish has survived in remarkable condition.

The six-character mark relates to the Jiajing period which lasted from 1522-66.

A Japanese Meiji period gold lacquer hexagonal box and cover, containing three lozenge-shaped boxes and covers, decorated with a mountainous landscape, and with stylised motifs.

5in (12.5cm) high

£500-800   WW

A 19thC Japanese lacquer square box and cover, decorated with a phoenix on a black ground, gilt leaf-scroll borders.

11.25in (28.5cm) wide

£250-350   DN

A rare Chinese Jiajing period red lacquer octagonal dish, moulded and carved, cracks and losses.

6.75in (17cm) high

£5,000-6,000   WW

ESSENTIAL REFERENCE: INRO

An inro is a small rectangular box made up of sections, used to hold herbs or tobacco.

- Inros are usually decorated with lacquer.
- In the absence of pockets in traditional Japanese costume, inros hang from the obi (sash) of the kimono using a netsuke (toggle).
- In use in Japan from the mid-16thC, inros are still made today.

A 19thC Japanese gold lacquer inro, decorated on each side with lakes and mountains.

3.5in (9cm) high

£700-900   WW

A pair of 19thC Japanese inro, including a five-case inro with orange-brown lacquer to a brown lacquer body showing a seated figure fitted with an agate omjime and frog form toggle, together with a well-lacquered butterfly six-case inro with stained ivory omjime and a very well carved nut kagamibuta, signed 'Masatama'.

£600-800   FRE

A pair of Chinese Jiaqing period blue Beijing glass shallow bowls, each incised on the base with a four-character Jiaqing mark.

6.5in (16.5cm) high

£2,500-3,500   **WW**

A large late 18th/early19thC Chinese Beijing sapphire-blue glass vase, the ovoid body with a tall flared neck and chamfered rim, unmarked.

14.5in (36.5cm) high

£4,000-5,000   **WW**

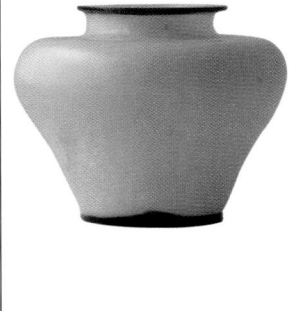

A 19thC or earlier Chinese Beijing glass compressed baluster vase, the white metal body with a claret red foot rim and mouth.

5in (12.5cm) high

£400-600   **WW**

A Chinese yellow Beijing glass compressed circular vase.

4.5in (11cm) high

£150-250   **WW**

A 19thC Chinese Beijing amethyst glass bowl, raised on a small foot, a rim bruise.

4.25in (11cm) diam

£70-100   **WW**

A Chinese Beijing glass bowl, the white metal overlaid in green with shibumpkin swimming amidst lotus flowers and leaves, wheelcut Qianlong four-character mark but later, with wood stand.

6.75in (17cm) high

£250-350   **WW**

A 20thC Chinese Beijing amber-coloured glass bottle vase, the base with a four-character Qianlong mark.

14.5in (37.5cm) high

£200-400   **WW**

SNUFF BOTTLES

A 19thC Chinese lavender-coloured jadeite bottle, with flecks of apple green.

2.25in (6cm) high

£850-950   **WW**

A Chinese jade snuff bottle, carved with a pavilion and figures in a watery landscape.

2.75in (7cm) high

£1,000-1,500   **WW**

A 19thC Chinese jade snuff bottle, carved with a horse beneath a willow tree.

3in (8cm) high

£600-800   **WW**

A rare Chinese celadon jade rectangular snuff bottle, carved with birds and bamboo.

2.5in (6.5cm) high

£3,000-4,000   **WW**

ORIENTAL

A Chinese Qianlong period pale celadon jade snuff bottle, formed as a fabulous fish amidst pomegranate leaves, other leaves and scrolls.

3.5in (9cm) high

£3,500-4,500   **WW**

An early 19thC Chinese celadon jade pebble-form snuff bottle, of tall pebble form, well-hollowed, square jadeite stopper.

3in (7.5cm) high

£500-700   **FRE**

A 19thC Chinese famille rose double-necked moulded snuff bottle, decorated with a multitude of small figures.

2.75in (7cm) high

£350-450   **WW**

A Chinese possibly Guangxu period porcelain snuff bottle, of flattened double gourd form, decorated with bats on a yellow ground and a lapis lazuli stopper, four-character mark of Guangxu.

2.5in (6.5cm) high

£500-700   **WW**

A Chinese porcelain snuff bottle, decorated with the eight horses of Mu Wang.

3.5in (9cm) high

£300-500   **WW**

A Chinese probably Yongzheng period turquoise-glazed porcelain snuff bottle, cylindrical form, orange glass and ivory stopper, Yongzheng seal mark to base.

3in (7.5cm) high

£300-500   **FRE**

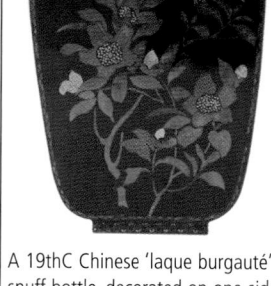

A 19thC Chinese ivory snuff bottle, carved as a quail, the eyes inlaid in horn.

1.75in (4.5cm) high

£800-1,000   **WW**

A Chinese ivory snuff bottle, one side finely engraved with a recumbent figure beside a water buffalo, the reverse with sixteen lines of minute calligraphy.

2.25in (6cm) high

£650-750   **WW**

A pair of 19thC ivory snuff bottles, of squat ribbed vegetable form, turned domed cover, raised on pierced wood stands.

3.5in (9cm) high

£700-1,000   **FRE**

A 19thC Chinese 'laque burgauté' snuff bottle, decorated on one side with figures on a pavilion, the other with a bird perched on a branch, Qianlong four-character mark.

3.25in (8cm) high

£1,300-1,500   **WW**

An early 19thC Chinese cinnabar lacquer on porcelain snuff bottle, of cylindrical form, lacquer on porcelain carved to show a continuous garden scene, matched red glass stopper.

3in (7.5cm) high

£250-350   **FRE**

A 17thC Chinese jichimu yoke-back chair, the protruding top rail supported by a recessed panelled and scrolling openwork back rest, shaped applied apron below pad hand rests, all above a beaded apron continuing to the straight rounded legs, joined by a flat rectangular footrest and partially rounded stretchers.

44in (105.5cm) high

£1,000-1,500   FRE

A pair of large 17thC Chinese yumu and lacquer Official's Hat chairs, the shaped back rail supported by an S-shaped plain back rest, the heavily constructed rectangular framed and cane seat over a shaped apron continuing down the leg, rectangular foot rest and rounded stretchers joining slightly rounded and beaded legs.

48in (122cm) high

£2,500-3,500   FRE

A pair of Chinese early Qing Dynasty lacquered jumu and iron-mounted yoke-back chairs, the S-shaped arms supported by straight iron and shaped jumu posts, a single plank seat over a straight apron continuing to the legs, rounded foot rest and stretchers.

47in (119cm) high

£1,000-1,500   FRE

A 17th/18thC Chinese yumu partially lacquered low-back Southern Official's back chair, with a well-carved and beaded ruyi scroll shaped apron to three sides and below three rounded stretchers a slightly higher rounded back stretcher.

40in (101.5cm) high

£400-600   FRE

A late 18thC Chinese black-lacquered yumu horseshoe-back chair, the back is supported by a pierced Shou character, the panel worked to show Buddhistic symbols, shaped apron, all over a foot rest and straight low stretchers joining rounded legs.

41in (104cm) high

£800-1,000   FRE

A pair of 18thC Chinese yumu yoke-back chairs, the protruding top rail, supported by a solid S-shaped back rest, sinuously rounded scrolling arms and side posts, rectangular framed seat with woven cane rest, S-shaped apron leading to a foot rest and four low joined rounded legs.

46in (117cm) high

£800-1,200   FRE

An 18thC Chinese root wood armchair, the square-form back and shaped armrests comprised of an open lattice work of gnarled joined root-like protrusions finely enhanced to show a tight light brown figured grain, flat yumu insert seat all over an openwork apron and four strong straight gnarled legs.

35in (89cm) high

£4,000-5,000   FRE

A pair of 18thC Chinese bamboo horseshoe chairs, of split cane beaded horseshoe back, supported by an open lattice work back rest, the arms supported by three straight posts, lacquered square seat, all raised on stretcher straight legs.

36in (91.5cm) high

£300-400   FRE

A pair of 19thC Chinese yumu low back Southern Official's hat chairs, the slightly concave back rail supported by a plan S-shaped back rest, shaped arms supported by plain posts, rectangular insert seat, shaped apron continuing down the legs, straight plain footrest and double cross stretchers to the side, signs of lacquer.

38in (96.5cm) high

£500-700 PAIR   FRE

An unusual 19thC Chinese jichimu wingback armchair, of Western influence, the high straight caned back rest framed by two D-form wings and supported by seven palmate head back rails, the straight arm rest supported by a single low stretcher, the square-framed caned seat raised over two cabriole carved front legs and outswept rear legs.

44in (112cm) high

£3,000-4,000   FRE

A rare Chinese late Ming Dynasty tielimu and iron-mounted folding stool, jiaowu, of simple X-form design, woven cotton seat panelled by two square-form seat sections, the apron of both carved in high relief to show scrolling leaves within a beaded edge, the two rounded legs are joined by concealed iron pins and mounts, the joining foot rest fitted to the lower section of both legs, raised on flat rectangular feet.

15in (38cm) high

£2,000-3,000   **FRE**

A pair of large Chinese Ming Dynasty hongmu caned waisted square stools, caned square insert framed top, waisted fluted and straight apron, rounded high hump-back stretchers joining straight slightly rounded legs terminating in high hoof-shaped feet.

24.5in (62cm) wide

£3,000-5,000   **FRE**

A pair of Chinese Ming Dynasty yumu square waisted stools, of single plank and panel construction, swan-neck shaped plain apron issuing from cabriole legs joined by high hump-back and shaped stretchers, terminating in hoof foliate carved feet.

22.5in (57m) wide

£900-1,100   **FRE**

A 17th/18thC Chinese folding huanghuali stool, Jiaodeng, of eight piece construction, woven cotton seat set to two rounded legs, joined with brass foliate mounts concealing brass pins, the top and bottom horizontal section forming the seat frame and stretched feet, highly figured warm toned patina.

18in (45.5cm) high

£5,000-7,000   **FRE**

An unusual Chinese Qing Dynasty softwood horse-shoe back and storage stool, the single section horse-shoe back rest surmounted a softwood hollowed single section trunk, fitted with a hinged demi-lune seat opening to reveal a storage space, iron banding to cylindrical body, all over a circular base raised on bracket feet.

24in (61cm) high

£400-600   **FRE**

A Chinese early Qing Dynasty root wood stool, of naturalistic form, oval rounded body highlighted by a highly figured open grain, somewhat resembling a brain or coiled animal model.

14in (35.5cm) high

£3,000-4,000   **FRE**

An unusual Chinese early Qing Dynasty root wood and softwood stool, the base of interconnected root wood pierced to show three openwork medallions, softwood insert seat, applied with three iron free-hanging handles.

15in (39cm) high

£800-1,200   **FRE**

A 17th/18thC Chinese root wood stool, the seat incised to show a lotus leaf, gnarled naturalistic apron and four tree trunk-form legs.

14in (35.5cm) high

£1,000-1,500   **FRE**

A Chinese early Qing Dynasty root wood stool, of naturalistic form, light brown highly figured grain, trunk-form legs, friction polished seat.

14in (35.5cm) high

£800-1,200   **FRE**

A large 17th/18thC root wood stool, of tripod form, flat friction polished seat, over a tree trunk form body and tree tapering gnarled legs.

21in (53.5cm) high

£800-1,200　　　　　　　　　　**FRE**

A rare pair of Chinese mid-Qing Dynasty root wood stools, of circular form, fitted with insert lacquered seat surface, partially enveloped by gnarled root wood descending to an openwork and protruding interlacing lattice apron above four gnarled and delicately enhanced naturalistically formed legs.

20in (50cm) high

£6,500-7,500　　　　　　　　　　**FRE**

An 18thC Chinese root wood stool, fine gold patina, tight figured grain and of cylindrical form, recessed seat.

20in (51cm) high

£2,500-3,500　　　　　　　　　**FRE**

An 18thC Chinese root wood stool, fine golden brown patina, gnarled body under a flat seat surface.

20in (51cm) high

£700-1,000　　　　　　　　　**FRE**

A 17th/18thC Chinese yumu bench, of rectangular form, the heavy single plank top, fine beaded and moulded edge, raised on rounded rectangular legs with beaded apron continuing to plain spandrels, resting on floor rails, well-figured grain.

57in (145cm) wide

£1,500-2,000　　　　　　　　　**FRE**

A Chinese early Qing Dynasty jumu recessed leg bench, of plank top form with flared ends, recessed straight legs flanked by joined phoenix head carved spandrels and shaped apron band, continuing to leg interior, well-figured surface.

46in (117cm) wide

£350-450　　　　　　　　　**FRE**

An 18th/19thC Chinese brown lacquered and caned day bed, the framed caned rectangular top over recessed side structured straight legs, moulded brackets and shaped apron.

76in (193cm) wide

£300-500　　　　　　　　　**FRE**

A 20thC Senufo hardwood bed, worked from a single section, braced head rest, rail to edge, with four inset tapering legs.

78in (198cm) long

£400-600　　　　　　　　　**FRE**

A 17thC Chinese nanmu black lacquered triangular table, of unusual 'turtle black' parquetry framed top, over a thin waist bulging wide curvilinear apron carved in high relief to show a beaded edge interrupted by shell-like medallions, raised on board cabriole legs terminating in low hoof feet.

72in (183cm) wide

£500-700 **FRE**

CLOSER LOOK: MING SIDE TABLE

The table has a large well-figured single plank top. A lesser table would have two or three thin planks set to the framed edge.

The table has thick single section rounded high-hump back stretchers rather than joined split joinery.

There are signs of dry lacquer to underside, this was often used during the late Ming early Qing period to guard against rot and insect attack. Later 19/20thC examples have a painted black lacquer imitating the correct late Ming lacquer.

There is good wear to feet and edge indicating correct wear consistent with age and use.

A Chinese late Ming Dynasty huanghuali side table, of single plank ice plate framed top, double rounded edge, all over a straight rounded high hump-back stretcher supporting eight oval moulded open medallions, raised on well-rounded cylindrical legs, well-figured grain throughout.

£30,000-40,000 **FRE**

A 17thC Chinese burl hualimu and tielimu square table, the partially lacquered thick single plank top shows age hollows and surface scarring, over a small waist, the apron carved in medium relief to show scrolling dragons framing a single character, the straight beaded legs joined by high humpback stretchers, terminating in hoof feet.

26in (66cm) wide

£7,000-10,000 **FRE**

A 17th/18thC Chinese huangulai flush-sided side table, the well-figured single rectangular-plank ice-plate framed top shows mortise and tenon joints to edge, over a plain beaded apron, above a high hump-back stretcher joining four straight square legs, terminating in high hoof feet.

33in (84cm) high

£20,000-25,000 **FRE**

A Chinese early Qing Dynasty jumu lacquered recessed-leg table, the thick single plank top terminating in shaped everted flanges, over a thin straight apron, the recessed legs panelled by scroll bracket-like spandrels, straight legs joined by two straight cross stretchers at both ends, minor traces of lacquer.

57in (145cm) wide

£500-700 **FRE**

A rare 17th/18thC tielimu folding wine table, the detached two-plank framed 'ice plate' edge top with hinged apron fits into two straight leg trestles, joined at the end by two rounded rectangular stretchers, good period wear to surface.

42in (106.5cm) wide

£400-600 **FRE**

A Chinese early Qing Dynasty softwood sectional square flush-sided table, comprising two triangular sectional tables, flush side legs joined by straight low stretchers, the longest edge carved in low relief to show coiled lotus leaves issuing from a lotus medallion, and Greek key frieze, terminating in hoof and square feet.

54in (137cm) wide

£500-600 **FRE**

CLOSER LOOK: ROOT WOOD TABLE

Root wood tables were designed to remove the scholar from his work and the straight lines of his study or office, and place him amid the undulating, swaying and uncontrolled flow of nature.

It is rare for tree roots to grow in this way to produce four practical legs.

It is rare to find an 18thC table – most date from the 19thC. It would have been costly when new.

The softwood table top is finely inserted and fitted with fine bamboo tenons.

A rare 18thC Qing Dynasty hetaomu and root wood side table, the rectangular highly figured Hetaomu insert single plank top joined by visible and raised bamboo mitred plugs, all above a fine and delicate bulging apron of open and gnarled root-work, raised on naturalistically enhanced cabriole legs and hoof feet.

52in (132cm) wide

£15,000-20,000 **FRE**

A large Chinese early Qing Dynasty yumu partially lacquered recessed leg altar table, of plank rectangular top applied with two shaped flanges, over beaded rounded straight legs and scrolling spandrels, joined at the ends by openwork panels depicting rock work.

100in (254cm) wide

£1,500-2,000 **FRE**

A large 18thC Chinese tielimu recessed legged painting table, the solid single plank top mounted with two everted flanges, all over a straight bracket apron, raised on straight round legs, joined at the end by two rounded short stretchers.

85in (216cm) wide

£800-1,200 **FRE**

An 18thC Chinese yumu and conglomerate liver stone insert side table, Tiaozhuo, the rectangular stone insert top resembling gold on red lacquer framed by highly figured yumu planks with ice-plate edge, short pierced key fretted waist, bead straight apron continuing down the slight cabriole leg, terminating in square scroll feel, sign of lacquer.

43in (109cm) wide

£1,800-2,200 **FRE**

An 18th/19thC Chinese hongmu and nanmu-burl wood waisted centre table, the square insert burl-wood top framed by four well-figured hongmu planks of 'ice-plate' edge, waisted and beaded apron joined by a high straight stretcher with three vertical struts, joining four straight and beaded legs terminating in hoof feet.

37in (94cm) wide

£1,200-1,800 **FRE**

A Chinese mid to late Qing Dynasty huanghuali recessed leg side table, of rectangular insert single plank and frame top, surmounted by two fluted triangular flanges, over straight beaded and joined legs, matched apron, legs joined by high pierced apron and solid feet to the side.

37in (94cm) wide

£10,000-15,000 **FRE**

A Chinese Qing Dynasty black lacquered wine table, the rectangular lacquered top rest over a thin waist and beaded apron carved to show stylised Fu bats and scrolls terminating at openwork and carved scrolling corners mounts, straight legs, interrupted by a scrolling hoof, continuing as a recessed straight leg terminating in a second scrolling hoof, signs of gilt lacquer.

60in (152.5cm) wide

£1,200-1,500 **FRE**

A 19thC Chinese rosewood altar table, the narrow rectangular top of mitred design above a frieze of open lotus scrolls, baluster and roundels, centred by a scroll work medallion, the ends similarly decorated, on square section legs with underscrolled feet carved with lotus fronds and united by upswept stretchers.

77.25in (196cm) wide

£2,500-3,000 **L&T**

A Chinese late Qing Dynasty black lacquer and bamboo square table, the well-lacquered black top rest over an open lattice work apron, raised on four straight low stretcher legs.

34in (81cm) high

£300-500 **FRE**

A Chinese Qing Dynasty hetaomu and lacquered bamboo side table, the double plank hetaomu top rests over an open lattice work of woven split bamboo lacquered brown, raised on six straight legs, joined by a rectangular foot base.

44in (112cm) wide

£300-400 **FRE**

A late 19thC Chinese huang huali centre table, formed of two D-shaped sections, with a relief carved and marquetry frieze and pierced corner brackets above shaped legs and scroll feet.

46in (116.5cm) diam

£650-750 **DN**

A mid-19thC Chinese hardwood side table, with a rectangular marble top above a carved frieze, on scroll carved cabriole supports raised on a platform.

62.25in (158cm) wide

£15,000-20,000 **SOTH**

ORIENTAL

A rare Chinese late Ming Dynasty huanghuali and partially lacquered stand, in a waisted kang table form, carved in low relief to show interlaced Indian lotus leaves and qilin to the centre and lion or dragon masks to the knee of cabriole legs, terminating in claw feet.

15.5in (39.5cm) long

£1,500-2,000 · · · · · · · · · · · · · · · · FRE

A 17thC Chinese huanghuali kang table, the rectangular single plank 'ice-plate' framed top rests over a thin waist and beaded slightly bulging apron, raised on straight cabriole legs terminating in scrolling hoof feet.

75in (190.5cm) wide

£6,000-8,000 · · · · · · · · · · · · · · · · FRE

A 17thC Chinese huanghuali kang-form table stand, the fine double plank insert and 'ice-plate' framed fluted and beaded edge over a plain waist, finely carved and beaded curvilinear apron continuing to cabriole legs, terminating in low hoof feet.

18in (46cm) wide

£10,000-15,000 · · · · · · · · · · · · · · FRE

A 17thC Chinese huanghuali waisted kang table, of double insert plank framed top, fluted and beaded edge, the beaded scrolling apron carved in low relief to show interlacing scrolls issuing from the apron edge to show a delicate ruyi, straight knee cabriole legs, terminating in scrolling hoofs.

35in (89cm) wide

£5,000-10,000 · · · · · · · · · · · · · · · FRE

An 18thC Chinese hongmu table stand, of kang form and two-plank insert and 'ice plate' edge construction with apron and high hump-back stretcher and scrolling legs carved to simulate bamboo shoots, good patina.

27ins (68.5cm)

£2,000-3,000 · · · · · · · · · · · · · · · · FRE

An 18th/19thC Chinese carved cinnabar lacquer table stand, of kang table form, the rectangular surface incised with cross-hatched motif over a Greek key edge and waisted diaper band, the wide shaped and beaded apron encloses a detailed ground carved in high relief showing Indian lotus flowers issuing scrolling leaves, continuing to cabriole legs terminating in hoof feet.

19.5in (49.5cm) wide

£2,200-2,800 · · · · · · · · · · · · · · · · FRE

A 19thC Chinese bamboo, coconut and hongmu 'turtleback' stand, in the form of a recess legged altar or side table, the hongmu framed rectangular top of parquetry coconut shell, the apron and straight legs of bamboo veneer.

20in (51cm) wide

£1,200-1,800 · · · · · · · · · · · · · · · · FRE

A 19thC Chinese tielimu waisted kang table, of single insert plank and panel top, fluted everted rim, the scroll-shaped apron beaded to the edge continuing to the cabriole legs, terminating in single scroll lingzhi feet.

36in (91.5cm) wide

£400-700 · · · · · · · · · · · · · · · · · · · FRE

A Chinese Qing Dynasty tielimu and burl wood square waisted table, of single burl wood insert plank construction, framed by four tielimu planks, the scrolling shaped apron carved in low relief to show ruyi scroll and foliate scroll to the cabriole leg, beaded apron edge continuing to a straight leg terminating in a scrolling hoof.

30in (76cm) wide

£300-400 · · · · · · · · · · · · · · · · · · · FRE

A pair of 19thC Chinese black lacquered softwood waisted tables.

An early 20thC Chinese hongmu kang table, of Western influence, the single insert plank and panel top over a triple rounded moulded edge, unusual twisted and joined 'rope twist' high stretcher joining simulated bamboo straight legs.

20in (51cm) wide

£600-1,000 · · · · · · · · · · · · · · · · · · FRE

59in (150cm) wide

£1,500-2,000 · · · · · · · · · · · · · · · · FRE

A 17thC Chinese single section 'tiger fur' stand, of rectangular form with slight undulating surface over a scrolling 'thorn' openwork apron raised on four slightly outswept bracket feet, fine 'tiger fur' figured surface.

14in (35.5cm) long

£1,000-1,500   FRE

A 17th/18thC Chinese yumu Fu Guai or shrine, insert with a detailed etched bronze basin, worked to show scholar on mule with attendants to the central medallion and diaper band to edge, a bulging apron carved in Ming style to show ruyi scrolls issuing from the edge, cabriole legs, scroll pad feet, raised on a circular sectional base, joined by fine butterfly.

22in (56cm) high

£500-800   FRE

An 18thC Chinese hongmu stand, the single section of rectangular form, terminating in two well-rounded ribbon scroll ends, well-figured patina.

17in (43cm) long

£500-800   FRE

An 18thC huamu burl scrolling ribbon-form stand, worked from a single section of highly figured burl wood, the long rectangular surface with rounded edge and gradually rounded ends to well-scrolled feet, rich brown patina.

23in (58.5cm) long

£4,000-5,000   FRE

A Chinese Qing Dynasty hongmu stone-inset stand, the orange-veined white stone inset to rounded hongmu frame above flush-side corner legs recessing at the knee, raised on scrolling feet.

14in (35.5cm) long

£300-400   FRE

A 19thC Chinese hongmu stand, of recessed oval form, the base finely embellished to simulate a gnarled root wood of intertwined and protruding figure-like growths, together with a fitted box.

5.5in (14cm) long

£250-350   FRE

An 18thC Chinese huangyangmu/boxwood reticulated stand, highly figured rounded edged surface with minor period inclusions, the base of finely embellished gnarled and protruding stylised roots reticulated resembling a near floating surface, dark coffee brown patina.

13in (33cm) high

£4,000-5,000   FRE

An 18th/19thC Chinese huangyangmu/ boxwood tea ceremony stand, of short circular naturalistic form, enhanced to show a light brown hue figured surface punctuated with several hollows and recesses.

6.5in (16.5cm) wide

£700-1,000   FRE

An 18th/19thC Chinese hongmu reticulated stand, of tall cylindrical form, carved from a single section finely enhanced to show a flat surface to the top, over a base of interlaced joined root-like protrusions, enhanced to show small wood hollows, and branch-like growths, fine rich brown to black patina.

9in (23cm) high

£800-1,000   FRE

A 19thC Chinese boxwood scholar's stand, the flat polished burl figured surface shows minor natural inclusions and undulation, raised on an interlacing network of root-form base.

8in (20.5cm) wide

£800-1,000   **FRE**

An unusual 18thC Chinese huangyangmu/boxwood stand, carved from a single section of well-figured huangyangmu simulating a root wood stand, carved and worked to show six protruding legs and various scrolling gnarled and recessed surfaces.

18in (45.5cm) wide

£6,000-8,000   **FRE**

A 17thC Chinese tielimu coffer, Liansanchu, the single plank rectangular framed top flanked by two everted flanges, all over a bank of three drawers, above a frieze of double-plank boards divided by a single vertical strut, raised on straight rounded and beaded legs, joined by a simple shaped apron.

66in (167.5cm) wide

£4,000-5,000   **FRE**

A Chinese early Qing Dynasty yumu and lacquered coffer, the long single plank top terminates in two everted flanges, over a bank of three short drawers, flanked by two carved spandrels, all above a two-door cabinet framed by two plain panels, raised on straight legs.

74in (188cm) wide

£500-700   **FRE**

A small Chinese late Ming Dynasty square corner black lacquered cabinet, the two heavily lacquered rounded framed doors open to reveal two long drawers flanking a pair of short drawers, pebble texture to lacquer.

23in (58.5cm) wide

£300-500   **FRE**

A Chinese late Ming/early Qing Dynasty tapered jumu cabinet, Yuanjiaogui, of slender proportions, protruding top frame with rounded corners supported on splayed posts enclosing two matched doors, all above a plain panel bisected by a single vertical strut, plain apron, the interior fitted with a shelf and a pair of drawers, baitong fittings, highly figured grain.

37.5in (95.5cm) wide

£4,000-6,000   **FRE**

A large Chinese Qing Dynasty hongmu square corner cabinet, of tall rectangular form, well-matched framed and panel sides and doors, opening to reveal a shelf over a bank of two short drawers, the base shelf rest over a plain beaded apron, raised on straight legs.

48in (122cm) wide

£5,000-6,000   **FRE**

A pair of 19thC Chinese hardwood sectional cabinets, each with pierced rectangular frame surmounted by an iron handle above four removable sections.

27.25in (69cm) high

£600-800   **DN**

A late 19thC Japanese cabinet, with open shelves surmounted by an ornate tiered temple roof design pediment, with fretwork panels depicting scrolls, serpents and sun motifs, with pierced gallery below and open shelves under, flanked by carved serpent-entwined uprights, the side panels decorated with inlaid leaf and flower pattern motifs, raised on carved legs.

50in (127cm) wide

£2,000-3,000   **A&G**

A late 19thC Japanese carved giltwood and black lacquer shrine, the tall rectangular cabinet encloses three sliding door shrines, surrounded by well-carved giltwood dragons and scrolls above three well-lacquered drawers, raised on a base of three short and two long wood-veneered drawers.

36in (91.5cm) wide

£350-450   **FRE**

An early 20thC Japanese gold on red lacquer chest, well-lacquered gold and silver over a red ground showing fans and circles enclosing stalks and songbirds, two doors reveal eight pull and sliding drawers, over a four-legged stand decorated in gilt scrolls.

20.5in (52cm) high

£1,000-1,500   **FRE**

A late 18th/early 19thC Chinese black lacquer and gilt-decorated cabinet on stand, the shaped and moulded pediment above two doors opening to an arrangement of drawers centred by a recessed pagoda section incorporating pierced fretwork panels, the stand with a pierced frieze, on hipped square section legs, claw-and-ball feet, damage, repair.

34.5in (88cm) wide

£2,500-3,000　　　　　　　　　**DN**

A 19thC Chinese Export lacquer secretary desk, in two parts, the upper section with shaped pediment and carved cartouche above two doors opening to fitted compartments, the lower section opens to reveal more compartments with drawer below on cabriole legs ending in paw feet.

65in (165cm) high

£1,500-2,000　　　　　　　　　**FRE**

A Chinese late Qing Dynasty agate chalcedony table screen and stand, the bevelled rectangular insert screen mottled with brown inclusions to a translucent ground, resembling a mist-filled mountainous landscape, supported by a carved and openwork zitan stand.

5.5in (14cm) high

£800-1,200　　　　　　　　　**FRE**

An 18thC Chinese nanmu table screen, openwork tall rectangular panel showing a bamboo tree ascending from rock-work, fitting within a bracket stand.

32in (81cm) high

£1,000-1,500　　　　　　　　　**FRE**

A late 18thC Chinese fossil stone table screen, the rectangular panelled fish bone pattern fossil stone panel fitted into a finely carved and reticulated hardwood base, pierced rectangular central insert panel and shaped side spandrels, the apron carved with a central character medallion, Fu bats and bird-like figures, the rectangular feet are carved in low relief to show fu bats.

24in (61cm) high

£7,000-10,000　　　　　　　　　**FRE**

A Chinese Qianlong period root wood reticulated and huanghuali table screen, fitted over a huanghuali base with double lotus supporting arms issuing from a plain frieze framed by four dragon coiled spandrels, raised on scrolling bracket feet.

27in (68.5cm) high

£15,000-20,000　　　　**FRE**

A pair of 20thC Chinese ivory table screens, of typical rectangular form, applied in high relief to show immortals amongst clouds, fine ink work to reverse with inscription.

19in (40cm) high

£1,500-2,000 PAIR　　　　　　　　**FRE**

CLOSER LOOK: CHINESE SCREEN

The screen features the Eight Immortals or Pa Hsein. They are one of the most popular subjects for decoration in China. The term 'Eight Immortals' is used to represent happiness and the number eight has become lucky thanks to its association with the immortals.

The carved sections of minerals and semi-precious stones used to decorate the screen stand proud of the lacquer ground to give a three-dimensional affect. It is evidence that the screen was a luxury item when it was made.

The screen is in good condition which adds to its desirability.

The combination of auspicious symbols and materials would have had a great resonanace for the screen's makers.

A 19thC Chinese spinach and celadon jade, rose quartz, lapis and coral four-panel screen, Hongmu framed red lacquer ground inlaid with brass, applied with various colour jade, quartz, lapis, coral and other minerals to show immortals and female figures among rock work and floral sprays, glazed later, metal hanging hooks surmounting panels.

79in (200.5cm) high

£10,000-15,000 **FRE**

A 19thC Chinese eight-panel screen, set with forty two blue and white porcelain panels, depicting figures in various pursuits in rocky landscapes, some damages and repairs.

57in (145cm) wide

£4,500-5,500 **WW**

A Chinese wallpaper-on-wood panelled screen, comprising twelve panels, decorated with ducks and carp in a pond surrounded by blossoming trees and flying birds, the lower section undecorated.

128.75in (327cm) wide

£2,000-3,000 **L&T**

A 19thC eight-panel coromandel black lacquer screen, one side with figures in the pursuit of leisure, lotus flowers and egrets on the other.

84in (213.5cm) high

£2,000-3,000 **FRE**

FURNITURE

THE FURNITURE MARKET

The market for antique furniture continues to improve thanks to a number of factors. Quality furniture is being seen as a suitable alternative to investing in shares, property or gold for the many people who are tired of or disillusioned with these traditional investments. Meanwhile, television programmes about antiques, and books such as *Miller's Antiques Price Guide*, have educated buyers about the importance of looking for quality as well as original condition and fine patina. Consequently, today's buyers are far more discerning about what they buy than many of their predecessors were twenty years ago.

English furniture from the Georgian to Regency eras (dating from c1760 to c1820) is in demand, probably because, in general, it was well made by skilled craftsmen. Pieces that have been well cared for over the years offer the quality and condition today's buyers are looking for.

Values for earlier furniture, while not at the height they were eighteen years ago, are slowly picking up and these pieces can work well in today's more minimal interiors. Oak in particular has seen a resurgence – fuelled in part by interior designers using it to great effect in minimal loft interiors.

Meanwhile, furniture from the mid to late 19th century continues to struggle. This is no doubt in part because the overblown excesses of the historical revival styles fashionable then do not suit early 21st century homes. Also, they may not be seen as offering such good value for money as earlier pieces made by hand rather than machine.

One current trend has seen people buying five or six pieces of good antique furniture and using them around the house mixed with contemporary pieces that complement them. The result is that people are more selective than they used to be and so better pieces are doing well, while other pieces continue to flounder.

Pairs of pieces of furniture, such as side tables, chairs and card tables have always sold well and when valuing them they were always worth more than just double the price of a single example as they are relatively unusual, very useable and easy to place around the home. However, over the past year buyers have been paying an even bigger premium for pairs – over three times the price of a single piece.

In general, this is an excellent time to buy, particularly good quality middle range furniture. When the market picks up, prices seem set to rise.

Lee Young, Lyon & Turnbull, Edinburgh

An early 19thC ash and fruitwood comb-back Windsor armchair, with two-piece horseshoe-shaped arms and D-shaped seat on turned legs.

£400-600   WW

A painted ash, oak and pine Windsor armchair, repair.

c1800

£1,000-1,200   DN

A set of six early 19thC ash and elm Windsor armchairs, the spindle-filled hoop backs with pierced splats above saddle seats, on ring-turned and splayed tapering legs.

£5,000-6,000 SET   L&T

A harlequin set of four early 19thC Windsor low-back armchairs, in ash, fruitwood and elm, three with crinoline stretchers.

£1,200-1,500   WW

An early 19thC fruitwood wheel-back Windsor armchair, with an elm seat, old worm.

£400-600   WW

A pair of mid-19thC ash, beech and elm high wheel-back Windsor armchairs, each arched back with central pierced vase splat above the crescent arm rail, above the dished solid seat on baluster-turned tapering legs, and an H-shaped stretcher, damage, lacking part.

£500-700   DN

A Victorian yew wood Windsor chair, raised on turned legs united by a crinoline stretcher.

£1,000-1,200 L&T

A Victorian yew wood Windsor chair, of typical form, united by a crinoline stretcher.

£1,100-1,300 L&T

A Victorian yew wood Windsor chair, raised on turned legs united by a crinoline stretcher.

£1,000-1,200 L&T

A late 17thC turned maple great chair, the ball-and-ring-turned finials over a three-slat back, and rattan seat supported by turned legs joined by double box stretcher.

£800-1,200 POOK

A mid-18thC oak child's high chair, damage, repair.

c1750

£800-1,000 DN

An early 19thC George III primitive ash armchair, the back with chamfered uprights and scalloped central rail, solid seat with splayed feet.

48in (122cm) high

£10,000-15,000 SOTH

A mid-19thC ash, oak and elm child's high chair, the square back with triple-spindle splat above a pair of turned arms with baluster terminals, centred by a woven seat on turned and square-section legs with peripheral stretchers.

14.5in (37cm) wide

£600-800 DN

A harlequin set of four ash and fruitwood spindle-back side chairs, with rush seats.

£250-300 SET WW

FURNITURE

A Queen Anne walnut chair, the cartouche-shaped back and seat covered with 18thC textile.

c1710

£1,500-2,000   **DN**

An early 18thC walnut chair, later banding.

c1720

£300-500   **DN**

A pair of George I walnut side chairs, the burr-veneered vase-shape splat backs with bell-shape needlework drop-in seats on shell-carved cabriole legs to pad feet, old restoration.

£2,500-3,500   **WW**

A pair of George II walnut and beech side chairs, each with vasiform-shaped and banded splat and leaf-carved top rail above a drop-in seat, raised on shell-carved cabriole legs ending in pad feet.

c1730   20in (51cm) wide

£1,500-2,000   **FRE**

A George II walnut chair, on shell-carved legs and carved claw-and-ball feet.

c1735

£300-400   **DN**

A George II walnut chair, repair, later elements.

c1740

£300-500   **DN**

An early 20thC George I style set of fifteen dining chairs, and a matched pair of armchairs.

£6,000-8,000 SET   **DN**

A pair of late 19th/early 20thC George II style mahogany hall chairs.

£500-700   **DN**

A pair of George III mahogany side chairs, the shaped top rail above a carved splat, the stuffed-over serpentine front seat above moulded and chamfered front legs with pierced brackets, the legs united by a stretcher, old restorations and replacements.

£2,000-2,500   **WW**

A George III mahogany chair, the shaped top rail above a Gothic arch pierced splint and drop-in seat, raised on cabriole legs with trefoil feet.

£600-900   **L&T**

CLOSER LOOK: A SET OF GEORGE III DINING CHAIRS

The shield-shaped backs, with pierced splats decorated with a vase of flowers, were probably inspired by George Hepplewhite's The Cabinet-Maker and Upholsterer's Guide (1788).

Sets of chairs became popular from the mid 18thC onwards.

Square tapered legs are typical of Hepplewhite's designs.

The shield-shaped backrests feature a splat painted with a flower-filled urn, surrounded by foliate trails.

A set of eight George III satinwood and painted dining chairs, comprising two armchairs and six sidechairs.
c1790

50in (19.75cm) wide

£20,000-30,000

FRE

A set of six George III mahogany and hide upholstered dining chairs, on shell-carved cabriole front legs and outswept rear legs, on pad feet.

£3,500-4,500 SET   **L&T**

A set of sixteen George III mahogany dining chairs, to include an armchair.
c1790

£7,000-10,000 SET   **DN**

A set of eight George III mahogany dining chairs, each with an X-shaped splat, stuffed-over leather seat and square tapering legs, including two elbow chairs, faults and repairs.
c1790

£1,500-2,000 SET   **DN**

A set of six George III mahogany dining chairs, the arched top rail on pierced and waisted splat with fluted base, drop-in seat in blue tapestry covering, raised on square tapering legs joined by stretchers.

£2,200-2,500   **HT**

A set of seven George III mahogany chairs, including an elbow chair, with arched top rail over pierced and waisted splat with heart to base, drop-in seats and floral needlework covering, on square tapering legs joined by stretchers.

£400-600 SET   **HT**

A set of seven late George III mahogany dining chairs, to include an armchair, each moulded rectangular back with triple vertical bar splats, above a bow-fronted seat on moulded square-section tapering legs, repair.
c1810

£1,200-1,800 SET   **DN**

A set of seven George III mahogany dining chairs, to include one armchair.
c1810

£800-1,200 SET   **DN**

A set of eight early 20thC George II style mahogany dining chairs, the broad backs carved with rosettes and leaves, centred by pierced vase-shaped splats, on square-section legs and H-stretchers.

25.25in (64cm) wide

£1,700-2,000 SET   **DN**

A set of eight 19thC mahogany hoop-back dining chairs, the husk carved top rails above pierced splats centred by leaf-carved rosettes, above serpentine floral woolwork drop-in seats on moulded square tapering legs, including two carvers with bold acanthus carved outscrolling arms.

£4,000-6,000 SET   **L&T**

A set of eight 19thC mahogany Gothic Chippendale dining chairs, the yolk-shaped top rails above relief-carved splats decorated with ogee tracery, on moulded square-section legs, the two armchairs with outscrolling leaf-carved terminals.

£8,000-12,000 SET   **L&T**

A set of twelve late 19thC mahogany dining chairs, in the Sheraton manner, the rectangular backs with leaf-carved crestings and triple spar splats above close-nailed hide stuff-over seats, on moulded tapering legs with spade feet, including two carvers.

£6,000-8,000 SET   **L&T**

A set of eight late 19thC Chippendale Revival dining chairs, the yolk-shaped top rails carved with leaf scrolls above Gothic pierced splats and drop-in bow-front seats, on square-section legs united by stretchers, including two carvers.

£1,500-2,000 SET   **L&T**

A set of twelve late 19thC mahogany hoop-back dining chairs, in the Hepplewhite taste, with pierced wheatsheaf splats above drop-in seats on square tapering legs united by stretchers, the pair of carvers of a later date.

£5,000-6,000 SET   **L&T**

A set of twelve Chippendale style mahogany dining chairs, the serpentine top rails above pierced splats decorated with quatrefoils and drop-in seats, on cabriole legs ending in claw-and-ball feet.

£2,000-3,000 SET   **L&T**

A set of ten George III style mahogany dining chairs, comprising two armchairs and eight side chairs, the carved and pierced backrest above a drop-in seat raised on straight legs.

38in (96.5cm) high

£2,000-3,000 SET   **FRE**

A set of six early 19thC Regency mahogany side chairs, each with inlaid and reeded tablet crest rail and reeded support enclosed by reeded stiles with rosette ears, trapezoidal green horse-hair-covered seats, reeded seat rail and legs ending in spade feet, rear legs canted.

£5,000-6,000   **FRE**

FURNITURE

A set of eight mahogany dining chairs to include a pair of armchairs, each moulded rectangular-shaped back and reeded bar splat above a rectangular seat, on turned tapering legs at the front.

c1815

£1,200-1,800   DN

CLOSER LOOK: WILLIAM TROTTER CHAIRS

William Trotter is the most famous of the Scottish Furniture Makers and worked from 9 Princess Street, Edinburgh, from 1810 until 1833.

The scroll top rails and bar backs are typical late Regency features as are the deeply scrolled reeded arms.

The use of prominent gadrooned carving and the distinctive reeded sabre legs and well-carved 'hairy paw' feet are a signature of Trotter's cabinet-work.

A set of eight Scottish George IV mahogany dining chairs, including two armchairs, by William Trotter.

£7,000-9,000   L&T

A set of four Regency simulated rosewood and brass marquetry dining chairs, each with rectangular back with pierced-bar splat, on sabre legs, damage, repair.

c1820

£600-800   DN

A set of eight Regency mahogany dining chairs, to include a pair of armchairs, each with moulded rectangular back with rope-twist-turned spar splat, above a square seat, on square-section moulded sabre legs, damage and repair.

c1820

£1,200-1,500   DN

A pair of Regency mahogany crossbanded dining chairs, by William Huxley, each with a rope-twist top rail, over a honeysuckle and S-scroll pierced back, above a replaced rattan woven seat on sabre front legs, stamped 'W. Hux', repairs and renewals.

£300-500   HALL

A matched set of ten mahogany dining chairs.

Six c1820, four 20thC

£2,000-3,000   DN

A set of five late Georgian mahogany dining chairs, including an elbow chair, the deep curved top rail with crossbanding, leaf-carved horizontal splat, drop-in seat, on turned and reeded front legs, splayed back legs.

£400-600   HT

A set of eight William IV mahogany dining chairs, the open arched backs with broad overscrolled top rails on reeded uprights with lotus-scroll capitals, on boldly turned and reeded front baluster legs with tapering feet.

£3,000-5,000   L&T

A set of six William IV rosewood dining chairs.

c1835

£1,500-1,800   DN

A set of six William IV mahogany side chairs, the moulded top rail centred with a stylised shell with two applied florets above a conforming horizontal splat, the drop-in seats later covered in tan leatherette on ring-turned and ribbed legs.

£1,000-1,500   WW

A set of eight William IV sabicu dining chairs, possibly Anglo-Indian, the volute-carved bar backs above scroll-and-rosette-carved middle rails and drop-in seats, on lappet-carved and reeded tapering legs, including two carvers.

Sabicu wood or sabicu has a rich mahogany colour. It is fairly heavy, hard and durable, and was selected for the stairs of the Great Exhibition of London in 1851.

£5,500-6,500 SET   **L&T**

A set of ten late 19thC Regency-style mahogany dining chairs, with foliate carved splats, overupholstered seats and fluted legs

£2,500-3,500 SET   **POOK**

ESSENTIAL REFERENCE: THONET

Michael Thonet (1796-1871) is well known for his revolutionary bentwood chairs.

- Thonet perfected his steam-bending process in 1842. Once softened with steam or boiling water, the wood could be moulded into almost any shape with the aid of a press. Beech was particularly suitable. This technique meant that furniture could be constructed from far fewer component parts and did away with dovetails or joints as the pieces could be held together with simple screws and nuts.
- In 1853, Thonet set up his own furniture company, Gebrüder Thonet, with his five sons. Within 20 years, it had offices in London and New York and, by the end of the 19thC, Gebrüder Thonet was operating more than 50 factories. The company had soon gained a reputation for innovation and contemporary design, which it maintained throughout the 20thC.
- From as early as the 1850s, Thonet produced furniture that could be packed flat for shipping and then assembled at its destination. The incredibly successful 'Number 14' chair was designed in 1859 and 50 million were sold by 1930. The No. 14 epitomised Thonet's brand of functional furniture for the masses rather than furniture as a signifier of wealth.
- The firm is still active today.

A set of six Austrian Thonet bentwood dining chairs, with scrolling backs, upholstered seats and conforming legs and under stretcher, each stamped 'Thonet'.

£400-600 SET   **DUK**

A set of eight mid-/late 19thC French mahogany dining chairs, with ormolu-mounted crest and seat rail on square tapering legs.

£2,000-2,500 SET   **POOK**

A set of nineteen Victorian oak dining chairs, in the 'Gothic' style, the baluster-turned padded backs and overstuffed seats, raised on turned tapered legs carved with flower-head motifs and ending in ceramic casters.

Some chairs are signed below the seat rails by an upholsterer for 'J. & T. Scott of Edinburgh'.

£9,000-12,000 SET   **L&T**

A set of four Victorian mahogany balloon-back dining chairs, with leaf-carved back above serpentine overstuffed seats upon turned front supports.

£50-70 SET   **ROS**

A set of six Victorian mahogany dining chairs.

c1870

£550-750 SET   **DN**

A set of eight 19thC Portuguese Rococo style dining chairs, comprising two armchairs and six sidechairs, each with shield-shaped backrest with a shell-carved toprail above a padded seat, raised on cabriole legs, carved at the knees with acanthus leaves and centred by a shell, ending in claw-and-ball-feet.

Armchair 49.25in (117.5cm) high

£2,500-3,500 SET   **FRE**

A set of eight late 19thC Victorian oak and leather upholstered dining chairs, including two armchairs.

£1,200-1,500 SET   **DN**

FURNITURE

A 16th/17thC Spanish walnut chair.

£800-1,200   DN

A pair of 18thC early Queen Anne walnut side chairs, arched, carved and pierced crest rail with scrolls, moulded back, shaped apron, on turned legs with Spanish feet and turned stretchers.

£1,000-2,000   FRE

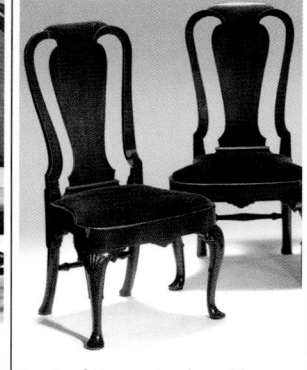

A pair of George I walnut side chairs, each with a shaped vasiform backrest and drop-in-seat, raised on shell-carved cabriole legs ending in pad feet.

c1715   40in (101.5cm) high

£600-800   FRE

A pair of George II mahogany side chairs, each with a solid splat and drop-in seat, on cabriole legs, damage, repair.

c1730

£150-250   DN

A pair of mahogany and marquetry chairs, inlaid, each cartouche-shaped back with central bar splat inlaid with a twin-handled bar, above a shaped drop-in seat, and cabriole legs carved with scroll terminals, on pad feet, damage, repair.

c1740 and later

£600-800   DN

A pair of French mahogany side chairs, with wide curved top rails and lattice splats, on sabre legs.

c1800

£450-550   DN

A Regency painted and parcel-gilt side chair, the lyre-shaped back above an overstuffed seat covered in buttoned grey fabric, raised on lappet-carved and fluted turned tapered legs.

£1,200-1,500   L&T

A set of six 19thC Victorian carved rosewood salon chairs, the caned oval backs centred by mask motifs, the caned serpentine seats with foliate tapestry loose cushions, raised on cabriole legs.

Armchairs 42in (106.5cm) high

£1,000-2,000   FRE

One of a set of three Victorian black lacquer bedroom chairs, parcel gilt and incorporating mother-of-pearl.

c1870

£100-150 SET   DN

A pair of Regency style simulated rosewood and parcel-gilt low chairs, of recent manufacture, the scrolling rectangular back with pierced bar splats, above the dished seat and arched legs.

£350-450   DN

A pair of late 19thC Italian Rococo style painted and parcel-gilt side chairs, each with a padded back and seat, the shell-carved front seatrail raised on leaf-carved cabriole legs.

38.5in (98cm) high

£300-500   FRE

A pair of 19thC Louis XV style carved beech chairs.

£250-350   **DN**

A pair of Charles II walnut hall chairs, the arched and carved top over the caned backrest and seat, raised on scrolling legs united by a pierced and carved stretcher.

50in (127cm) high

£1,400-1,800   **FRE**

A pair of Moravian walnut chairs, each with heart cutout backs, plank seats and splayed legs, together with similar oak example.

c1750

£500-700   **POOK**

A George IV mahogany hall chair, in the manner of Gillows, the heavily carved shell back to a tapering seat on ribbed tapering legs.

£450-550   **WW**

A pair of William IV mahogany hall chairs.

c1835

£700-900   **DN**

HALL CHAIRS

Introduced in Britain from the 17thC, hall chairs were designed to be placed in the entrance hall where they would be used by tradesmen and tenants waiting to be called into one of the main rooms.

- Hall chairs are rarely upholstered and usually lack arms.
- They are of sturdy construction.
- Hall chairs were also symbols of social status and were therefore increasingly made of mahogany, with solid backs and dished or shaped seats. Designs were bold and simple and were frequently embellished with the painted crest or coat of arms of the family who commissioned them.
- Thomas Chippendale, George Hepplewhite and Thomas Sheraton all included designs for hall chairs in their design books.

CLOSER LOOK: PAIR OF HALL CHAIRS

Derived from the Graeco-Roman vocabulary of architecture and ornament, C-shaped scrolls were a popular Neoclassical motif, and thus often appeared in Regency designs. Here, a pair of out-facing C-scrolls 'support' a larger, reeded scroll that terminates in stylised flowerheads.

Characteristically, the back legs of these chairs are in plain sabre form, while the front legs are turned and embellished with tapered reeding – a form of convex moulding particularly fashionable in the early 19thC.

Originating in Europe during the 12thC, heraldic decoration provided a visual means of representing the position and status of an individual, a family, or an organisation in society. Polychrome-painted and set in recessed roundels, the crests of these chairs are no longer attributable but, in the form of a hand holding aloft a scroll, probably indicate the owner's involvement in politics or the law.

A pair of Regency or George IV carved mahogany hall chairs, in the manner of Gillows.

c1820

£2,200-2,600   **DN**

FURNITURE

A set of three mid-Victorian carved and painted hall chairs, each heart-shaped back centred by an armorial shield depicting a dragon, the solid seat on turned tapering legs, damage.

c1860

£700-1,000   DN

A 19thC Black Forest carved walnut hall chair, the Gothic pierced and waisted back with a central bas-relief-carved owl perched upon an oak branch, with naturalistic glass bead eyes, the plank seat on leaf-carved cross-frame legs ending in incised scroll feet and joined by a moulded stretcher.

£1,000-1,500   L&T

A pair of late 19thC stained pine Gothic hall chairs, faults.

£300-400   DN

An early 19thC mahogany hall bench, the rectangular back with concave corners and a moulded edge centred with an inset painted armorial, with conforming arms and a channelled boarded tapering seat on square tapering legs.

53.75in (136.5cm) wide

£3,000-4,000   WW

A late 19thC mahogany and marquetry hall settle, with hinged seat.

48.75in (124cm) wide

£500-700   DN

An oak hall or window seat, in the manner of Schoolbred & Co., with turned terminals above the solid seat, on turned legs.

41.75in (106cm) wide

£400-600   DN

STOOLS

A James I oak joined stool, the single plank top above a channelled and ogee-arched frieze, on slender baluster-turned legs joined by stretchers.

22.5in (57cm) high

£600-1,000   L&T

A mid-17thC oak joint stool, the rectangular top with moulded edge above a moulded frieze on baluster-turned tapering legs and peripheral stretchers.

c1660

£1,800-2,200   DN

A late 17thC Charles II walnut joined stool, moulded top above a 'panelled' frieze and scroll apron, four baluster-turned legs with peripheral stretchers.

23.25in (59cm) high

£6,000-8,000   SOTH

An oak stool or side table, the rectangular top above a fluted and castellated frieze, above baluster-turned legs with peripheral stretchers and turned feet, the top probably later associated, damage, repair.

c1680   *30.75in (78cm) wide*

£1,300-1,600   **DN**

A George II elm stool, possibly a milking stool.

c1750   *7.75in (20cm) high*

£150-250   **DN**

A late 17thC style oak joined stool, with a moulded edge rectangular top to a shaped and moulded frieze, the block and turned legs with peripheral stretchers.

15.25in (38.5cm) wide

£450-550   **WW**

A 19th/20thC oak longstool, in mid-17thC style, the rectangular seat above a shaped frieze on baluster-turned and carved legs, joined by peripheral stretchers, damage.

48.5in (123cm) wide

£550-750   **DN**

A 19th/20thC Charles II style joined oak stool.

£150-250   **DN**

A late 18thC George III white painted hall stool, pierced saddle-shaped seat with a fluted frieze, on conforming square tapering legs, surmounted by scroll carving, painted decoration refreshed.

This stool was almost certainly made by Robert Child (d.1782) for Osterley Park House, Middlesex. This painted stool with its fluted frieze and legs capped by scroll pilasters is designed in the 'Roman' manner introduced and popularised by the court architect of King George III, Sir William Chambers and Robert Adam in the 1760s.

21.25in (54cm) wide

£16,000-20,000   **SOTH**

A George III mahogany framed stool, the rectangular seat above four carved cabriole legs on pad feet, damage, repair.

c1760   *22.5in (57cm) wide*

£400-600   **DN**

A Louis XVI painted stool, the padded seat covered in ivory damask, over a bellflower-carved frieze raised on turned tapered leaf-carved legs.

£1,300-1,500   **L&T**

An unusual late 18thC Chinese Export stool, the rectangular framed caned seat of slight concave form, above four delicate cabriole legs terminating in pad feet.

18.5in (47cm) wide

£500-700   **FRE**

A black painted and parcel-gilt stool in George III style, the needlework seat depicting floral garlands.

49.25in (125cm) wide

£400-600   **DN**

FURNITURE

ESSENTIAL REFERENCE: GILLOWS

Gillows of Lancaster (est. c1730) designed and made a vast quantity of furniture for the nobility, the gentry, and the newly emerging middle classes.

- Most 18thC Gillows furniture was made in the Neoclassical style, without decoration. Such pieces followed the designs of George Hepplewhite and Thomas Sheraton.
- After c1770, the furniture had an austerity reflecting that of contemporary architecture.
- Writing, library and dressing furniture often had hidden compartments and ingenious arrangements of small drawers.
- Gillows has always produced high quality furniture for the domestic and export markets and the firm is still active today.

A pair of Regency cross-framed stools, attributed to Gillows of Lancaster, the button-upholstered silk seats above scrolling X-frame legs with roundel patera terminals and central bosses, on ball feet united by pole stretchers, one stool of very slightly larger dimensions.

Largest: 21.75in (55cm) wide

£4,000-5,000   **L&T**

A large George IV rosewood upholstered stool, the drop-in seat above a moulded rounded frieze on reeded turned and tapered legs.

30.25in (77cm) wide

£1,500-2,000   **L&T**

An early Victorian rosewood footstool.

c1840

£150-250   **DN**

A Victorian period carved giltwood stool, the rectangular overstuffed seat covered in brightly coloured geometric needlework, above a panelled frieze and raised on spiral turned tapered legs.

32.75in (83cm) wide

£600-800   **L&T**

A pair of Victorian period rosewood stools, with blue suede upholstered drop-in seats, raised on C-scroll X-form supports and joined by turned stretchers.

18in (46cm) wide

£3,000-4,000   **L&T**

A Southern European painted and upholstered stool, the rectangular top covered in close-nailed embossed leather, on carved blue-and-gilt-painted cabriole legs and scrolled feet, joined by an X-stretcher.

23in (58cm) wide

£800-1,000   **L&T**

A mid-19thC mahogany adjustable piano stool.

£200-250   **DN**

A pair of Victorian period rosewood and upholstered stools, with blue suede upholstery, the circular drop-in seats within parcel-gilt-moulded surrounds on triple scroll supports and moulded cabriole legs with pad feet, undersides bear makers labels, 'W Constantine & Co., Leeds'.

19.75in (50cm) diam

£3,500-4,500   **L&T**

A mid-Victorian rectangular stool, the floral needlework-covered seat with braiding above a cream and gilt gesso base decorated with shells, scrolls and foliage, having a serpentine frieze and cabriole legs.

37in (94cm) wide

£800-1,000   **WW**

CLOSER LOOK: SHELL-SHAPED STOOL

The 19thC saw a growing interest in fanciful furniture such as this stool, as well as the increasing use of mechanisms such as the one used here to raise and lower the seat.

The stool has been decorated with good, strong, deep carving.

The wood has an attractive colour and shows excellent patination.

The carved paw feet have highly defined claws – proof that it is a quality piece.

A matching pair of Victorian giltwood rectangular stools, upholstered in a coloured striped material to cabochon frieze and cabriole legs with leaf carving.

24in (61cm) wide

£1,500-2,000   WW

A 19thC French carved walnut adjustable stool, in the form of an open shell, raised on a central lobed column containing a threaded mechanism, and three cabriole legs with carved paw feet.

c1860

23.75in (60cm) high

£2,500-3,500   RGA

A pair of 19thC Louis XV style giltwood banquettes, each with a tapestry-upholstered seat and foliate-carved, voluted armrests, leaf-carved rails, raised cabriole legs ending in scrolled toes.

78in (198cm) wide

£6,000-8,000   FRE

A rare 17thC oak child's box chair, of hexagonal design, the raised plank back with pierced strapwork cresting and pierced corner frets around a painted hexafoil medallion, the uprights slotted to receive a tray table, the interior formerly with a plank seat above a foot warming pan below, the front door on butterfly hinges with clasp and staple catch, clasp missing.

This intriguing and practical design allows a child little movement and affords safety. The tray has a simple self-securing action. This example shows Scots and Scandinavian influences.

34.5in (88cm) high

£5,000-6,000   L&T

A 20thC George III style carved mahogany framed window seat, the shaped seat flanked by scrollover arms, above a fluted and patera-carved frieze on square-section cabriole legs and tapering feet.

39.5in (100cm) wide

£500-700   DN

A Regency mahogany high chair, the shaped back with scrolling top rail, caned back and seat with restraining bar, on turned and octagonal legs on turned X-form stretcher, the legs with an adjustable foot rest, on a conforming base.

37in (94cm) high

£600-800   DUK

A Regency mahogany metamorphic library steps armchair, the bar back above a lion mask carved leaf-carved middle rail and downswept underscrolled arms with roundel bosses on ball supports, on front sabre legs with moulded tapering feet and splayed rear legs, a threaded screw releasing four internally hinged treads, the whole decorated with ebony lines.

£3,500-4,500   L&T

FURNITURE

A William IV mahogany-framed invalids' chair, by J. Ward, Leicester Square, London, in the form of a split cane upholstered library bergère, the over-scrolled back and padded scrolling arms above a button-upholstered seat with sliding foot rest on turned supports between a pair of brass mounted ten-spoke wheels with circular handrails and thumbscrew brakes, with a small rudder wheel to the rear, each wheel hub engraved with the maker's name.

30.25in (77cm) wide

£2,000-3,000   **L&T**

A mid-19thC mahogany and brass-mounted folding campaign chair, bearing makers label/plaque.
c1860

£600-800   **DN**

OPEN ARMCHAIRS

A carved oak panel-back armchair, Anglo-French, the twin-panelled rectangular back carved with Romayne portraits of a lady and gentleman above flowering urns, the solid seat flanked by rectangular arms, on stile legs and peripheral stretchers, repair, later elements to legs.
c1530   22.5in (57.5cm) wide

£4,500-5,500   **DN**

A James I Welsh dated oak panel-back armchair, the arched cresting rail with initials 'IH STP' and 'MC', the back panel incorporating three trident motifs, possibly stylised versions of the Prince of Wales feathers, the arms with projecting figural 'buttresses' and fluted supports, later stretchers, restorations.

One similar chair in the Burrell Collection, Glasgow, Scotland, another in Victor Chinnery's book 'Oak Furniture - The British Tradition', Woodbridge, 1979, and this chair would appear to be the only extant examples of chairs which feature figural supports at each arm. These devices create a sense of importance and would have emphasised the person seated. They have an almost architectural effect and seem reminiscent of the fitted ceremonial furniture seen in some of the great secular and ecclesiastical buildings of medieval England.
1624   52.25in (133cm) high

£12,000-18,000   **SOTH**

An early to mid-17thC Jacobean oak turner's chair, with exuberantly turned crest rail with typical baluster, ball, ring and sausage-turned back and arm rests, above a triangular seat supported by massive front legs joined by stretchers, retains an old, possibly original, dry painted surface.

£3,500-4,500   **POOK**

A Charles II walnut high back armchair, the rectangular back centred by a caned panel, the caned seat flanked by outswept arms, on S-scroll legs at the front and an H-stretcher, period elements.

£300-500   **DN**

A late 17thC Derbyshire oak low chair, the rectangular back with lobed and scroll-carved arched crest and bar splat, the solid seat above a drawer on block and turned legs and peripheral stretchers.
c1685

£1,200-1,800   **DN**

Left: A 17thC joined oak Caquetoire style armchair, the back with scroll-carved cresting above a fleur-de-lys emblem flanked by rosettes, the fielded panels with strapwork between stiff leaf uprights, the outswept arms on baluster supports above a solid triform seat with chip-carved rail, on baluster legs united by perimeter stretchers.

£2,000-2,500   **L&T**

40in (102cm) high

Right: A 17thC joined oak armchair, the fielded panel back with scroll-shaped cresting above outset arms and flank seat on square-section legs knopped at the ankle and block feet united by perimeter stretchers.

£1,000-1,400   **L&T**

A 17thC Dutch walnut Baroque armchair, with floral leather upholstery.

45in (114cm) high

£2,000-2,500 SOTA

A pair of 17thC style Northern European carved walnut high-back armchairs, with rectangular padded backrest and seat, the armrests with leaf-carved handholds, raised on turned and barley-twist supports, joined by stretchers, raised on bun feet.

25.25in (64cm) wide

£1,000-1,500 FRE

A pair of late 17th/early 18thC Italian walnut and parcel gilt armchairs, damage.

27.5in (70cm) wide Est

£2,000-2,500 DN

A walnut armchair, with later elements.

c1700 *24in (61cm) wide*

£500-600 DN

A matched pair of 19thC Moroccan walnut 'Savonarola' armchairs, each decorated with mosaic bone inlay in the Damascus taste, the shaped back rails with vignettes of ladies in the 17thC costume, composed of bone and cut metal, the slatted arms above solid seats, on downswept slatted cross-frame legs.

37.75in (96cm) high

£2,000-3,000 L&T

A George II probably Irish mahogany open armchair, the caddy-moulded back with a serpentine top rail above a bold acanthus-carved ribband splat and padded outscrolling arms with rosette and trailing acanthus leaf-carved terminals, the close-nailed stuffover seat on leaf-carved cabriole legs with acorn pendants, ending in claw-and-ball feet.

£3,500-4,000 L&T

A pair of George III style simulated bamboo cock-pen armchairs of recent manufacture, each rectangular back above a pair of conforming arms, the upholstered square seats on turned tapering legs and stretchers.

£350-450 DN

A pair of 20thC George III style carved mahogany elbow chairs, each shaped square back with pierced ladder splats, above a pair of serpentine shaped arms and dished square seats, on moulded square-section legs and H-shaped stretchers.

£600-800 DN

A mahogany elbow chair.

c1780 and later

£550-750 DN

A George III carved mahogany elbow chair, and a side chair of similar design after Sheraton, damage, repair.

c1790

£200-250 THE TWO DN

FURNITURE

A George III fruitwood corner armchair, the scroll arms above pierced vase-shaped splats with turned supports to a drop-in seat in square chamfered legs united by peripheral stretchers.

£400-600 WW

A George III mahogany library bergère armchair.

c1810

23.75in (60cm) wide

£1,200-1,500 DN

A George III oak and elm armchair.

c1810

£180-220 DN

An 18thC walnut Régence armchair, the padded armrest carved with leaves, the seat rail carved with a scallop, with embroidered upholstery, on cabriole legs.

42.25in (107.5cm) high

£2,000-3,000 SOTA

CLOSER LOOK: QUEEN ANNE CHAIR

The shaped spade back has an arched top. This chair is upholstered with contemporary gros point polychrome needlework.

The walnut of the tightly furled shepherd's crook arms, the legs and the stretchers is all of a beautiful patinated mellow colour.

The back legs have squared toes joined to the front legs by turned stretchers.

The rounded seat is raised upon turned legs with tobacco leaf-carved knees terminating in outswept pad feet to the front.

An English Queen Anne walnut open armchair with contemporary needlework.

c1710

24in (61cm) wide

£85,000+ PAR

A walnut armchair, some damage, repair.

c1720

27.5in (70cm) wide

£3,000-3,500 DN

An early 18thC probably Spanish carved walnut armchair, with shaped padded back, down-scrolled arms, rectangular padded seat on turned and block legs joined by stretchers, with light brown velvet upholstery.

£1,000-1,500 SOTA

A pair of mid-18thC Continental mahogany open armchairs, the foliate carved arms are outward scrolling, on fully carved cabriole legs terminating in scroll feet.

£2,500-3,500 POOK

A fine George II period mahogany open-arm chair, with deep carving to the front cabriole legs and arm supports.

c1755

37in (94cm) high

£50,000-55,000 BLY

A pair of George III mahogany framed 'Gainsborough' armchairs, the rectangular backs with serpentine crestings above out-scrolling padded arms with acanthus scroll-carved in-swept terminals and stuff-over seats, on square tapering sunken field moulded legs ending in block feet and united by chamfered H-stretchers, upholstered in close-nailed yellow damask.

31.5in (80cm) wide

£35,000-40,000 **L&T**

A pair of George III mahogany library armchairs, with an upholstered back and seat, raised on square legs united by straight stretchers one now raised on brass casters, the whole carved with blind fretwork.

c1775 *27in (68.5cm) wide*

£7,000-10,000 **FRE**

A 'French Chippendale' style carved mahogany framed fauteuil, the back of serpentine-arched cartouche-shaped outline above outscrolling padded arms with leaf and cabochon-carved terminals, the arm supports swept into the seat rails, the front apron with florets flanking rocaille, on cabriole rear and front legs embellished with foliage and ending in stiff acanthus scroll feet, the whole in close-nailed burgundy velvet upholstery.

£2,000-3,000 **L&T**

A George III giltwood and upholstered armchair, the oval back, padded open arms and seat covered in patterned cream silk, the leaf-carved downswept moulded arms above a bowed front rail and tapered fluted leg, re-gilded.

£1,500-2,000 **L&T**

An 18thC walnut fauteuil, in the French Hepplewhite taste, the rounded rectangular back above padded outscrolling arms and moulded serpentine seat rail, on moulded cabriole legs ending in tapered feet.

£3,000-5,000 **L&T**

A set of four 18thC 'French Hepplewhite' painted walnut fauteuils, the cartouche-shaped backs with floret crestings, the serpentine seats with floral-carved front rails, on moulded and shell-carved tapering cabriole legs on tapering feet, overpainted in ivory and green.

£4,000-6,000 SET **L&T**

A pair of French Louis XVI-style beech fauteuils, the oval backs lead to cushioned elbow rests, scrolling reeded arms, paterae-capped leg shoulders, over reeded column front legs, not upholstered.

c1800 *38in (96.5cm) high*

£1,000-2,000 **FRE**

A mid-18thC Irish style library armchair, the arm supports carved as scaly beasts with a concave seat rail, carved scrolling foliage on acanthus-capped cabriole legs with dolphin feet.

£1,500-2,000 **WW**

An Empire style gilt-bronze-mounted mahogany fauteuil de bureau, the curved backrest with a lyre-form splat above a leather-upholstered seat, raised on square tapered legs headed by female busts and ending in paw feet.

24.25in (62.25cm) wide

£1,500-2,000 **FRE**

A pair of Regency period simulated rosewood open armchairs, the overscrolled bar backs decorated with anthemia above volute scroll middle rails and reeded underscrolled arms, the split cane upholstered seats with buff leather squabs and reeded rails, on reeded sabre legs.

£1,600-2,000 **L&T**

A Regency mahogany Grecian style library chair, in the manner of Gillows of Lancaster, the arched wraparound back of 'cut-away' design, the cresting boldly carved with Neoclassical leaf scrolls above volute carved 'hips', with short turned and reeded legs.

£2,500-3,500 **L&T**

FURNITURE

A pair of Regency ebonised and giltwood armchairs, each with a turned bar back and three groups of vertical stretchers between downswept open arms on simulated bamboo tapering front legs, terminating in a splay foot.

£800-1,200   **HALL**

A Regency ebonised and painted armchair, faults.
c1820

£300-500   **DN**

A pair of George IV mahogany armchairs, each rectangular back with bar splat, flanked by a pair of downswept arms, on turned tapering legs at the front.
c1825

£800-1,000   **DN**

A 19thC Louis XV style carved oak armchair.

£500-700   **DN**

A pair of late 19thC Damascus hardwood, mother-of-pearl- and ivory mosaic-inlaid armchairs, the mihrab-arched bobbin work backs with carved crestings and finials above inlaid arms enclosed by bobbin work, on conforming aprons and turned feet.
23.75in (60cm) wide

£1,500-2,000   **L&T**

A simulated rosewood bobbin-turned armchair.
c1890

£600-800   **DN**

A pair of Italian Neoclassical style painted and parcel-gilt armchairs, each with a rectangular padded backrest and seat with foliate-carved toprail, the armrests carved with bell flower trails, raised on vasiform supports, the seat rails carved with further trails raised on leaf-carved round fluted legs.
23in (58.5cm) wide

£1,500-2,000   **FRE**

A 19thC Empire mahogany-framed bergère, the arms on swan neck-carved terminals, on turned and lappet carved legs ending in brass socket casters.

£2,000-3,000   **L&T**

An unusual carved Restoration mahogany armchair, Veuve Meunier, the rectangular padded backrest and seat with acanthus-carved armrests and scrolled handholds, raised on round lobed legs with leaf carved feet.
c1820   *26in (66cm) wide*

£1,000-1,500   **FRE**

An Empire mahogany armchair, by Jacob Freres, with reeded volute scroll-carved top rail, the downswept spreading arms with reeded lotus-carved shoulders and terminals, the similarly carved legs tapering to carved paw feet headed by anthemia and rosettes, the front seat rail stamped verso 'JACOB FRERES. R. MESLEE'.

£5,000-7,000 L&T

A William IV rosewood armchair, button-upholstered in pale green damask covering, arched back, padded open arms with scroll ends on shaped supports, overstuffed seat, leaf-carved turned legs with brass toes and casters.

£300-400 HT

A William IV mahogany library bergère armchair, faults.

c1835

£800-1,000 DN

An Anglo-Indian carved ebony armchair, the rectangular back with stylised shell-carved pediment, above reeded downswept arms, with foliate-carved terminals, above a profusely carved frieze, turned tapering and lappet-carved legs, damaged, repair.

c1840

£1,000-1,200 DN

A mid-19thC Anglo-Indian carved ebony easy chair, from Galle District, Ceylon, the caned scroll back with a foliate-carved crest rail, over scroll open arms, raised on shell-carved sabre legs ending in claw-and-ball feet.

£3,000-5,000 L&T

A rare Black Forest carved oak rocking chair, decorated to resemble tree root, covered in antique hide with brass studding.

c1860

£11,500-14,000 RGA

A 19thC mahogany 'Gainsborough' armchair, in the Chippendale taste, elaborately carved with leaf scrolls, on four cabriole legs bearing cabochon motifs, the front knees descending to tightly scrolled feet.

c1870

£6,500-8,500 RGA

A pair of unusual Renaissance style carved walnut armchairs, each with a padded back and seat, the leaf-carved armrests continuing to handholds modelled as heads of Native American chiefs, raised on leaf-carved, in-curved legs, joined by an H-stretcher and ending in paw feet.

26.75in (68cm) wide

£2,000-3,000 FRE

A 19thC polished steel R. W. Winfield & Co. patent rocking chair, Birmingham, England, the rectangular back above downswept arms forming the rocking base, with black hide slung seat and padded arms, the crossrails secured by bronze nuts.

25.75in (62cm) wide

£1,000-1,500 L&T

FURNITURE

A late 19thC oak framed Orkney chair, faults.

£800-1,200   DN

A pair of late 19th/early 20thC George III style black-painted and parcel gilt armchairs, damage, repair, some recent painting.

£700-900   DN

UPHOLSTERED ARMCHAIRS

A Charles II walnut or beech wing armchair, upholstered in red velvet with applied needlework fragments, raised on carved scrolling legs.
c1685   27in (68.5cm) wide

£4,000-6,000   FRE

A George II mahogany and upholstered wing armchair.

c1750

£3,000-4,000   DN

An American Queen Anne mahogany upholstered easy chair, signed 'N Bowen', Marblehead, Massachusetts, the serpentine crest above shaped sides and outward-scrolling arms with concave fronts tapering to the straight seat frame resting on frontal cabriole legs with conforming knee returns, joined to the raking chamfered rear legs by block, vase and ring-turned stretchers, very minor imperfections.

c1755   50in (127cm) high

£15,000-20,000   SK

A George III mahogany easy chair, the serpentine crest over scrolled arms supported by square moulded legs,
c1770

£2,000-3,000   POOK

A George III mahogany wing armchair, damage, repair.

c1780   32.25in (82cm) wide

£800-1,000   DN

A 19thC Louis XV style giltwood and painted 'bergère a oreillies', upholstered in 18thC Aubusson tapestry, the arched foliate-carved top rail above a padded back and loose cushion seat, the front seat rail carve to match, raised on leaf-carved cabriole legs ending in scrolling toes.

30in (76cm) wide

£1,500-2,000   FRE

A pair of George III style mahogany and upholstered wing armchairs, covered in stylised blue heraldic pattern fabric, raised on square tapered legs terminating brass cappings and casters.

£1,600-2,000   L&T

A late 19th/early 20thC Louis XV style carved giltwood and composition highback wing armchair, the frame decorated throughout with carved acanthus and scroll motifs, the rectangular wing back above a pair of downswept arms with scroll terminals, the seat on cabriole legs and scroll feet.

31.75in (81cm) wide

£700-1,000 DN

A Louis XVI style mahogany and gilt-bronze mounted swivel desk chair by Francois Linke, the arched back, padded scroll arms and loose cushion seat covered in yellow fabric, raised on turned fluted legs, headed by paterae and terminating in toupie feet, underside stamped 'F. Linke' in two places.

c1900 *24.5in (62.25cm) wide*

£3,000-4,000 FRE

A late 19th/early 20thC green buttoned leather-upholstered tub shaped armchair.

£500-700 DN

A late 19th/early 20thC George II style studded leather-covered tub armchair.

36.75in (119cm) high

£1,500-2,000 DN

An early 20thC George III style mahogany and red leather-upholstered wing armchair.

£1,500-2,000 DN

A walnut and upholstered armchair, stamped 'Howard & Sons', on baluster-turned tapering legs at the front, on later casters of recent manufacture, on rear leg stamped 'Howard & Sons Limited, Berners St'.

c1800 and later *31.5in (80cm) wide*

£3,000-3,500 DN

A Regency mahogany library bergère, upholstered in buttoned red leather, the seat frame resupported.

c1820

£12,000-15,000 SOTH

A Regency mahogany and leather-upholstered tub armchair, the rectangular back, out-scrolled arms and seat covered in close nailed button upholstered green leather, channelled arm ends and seat rail, with circular bosses on ring-turned tapering legs with brass caps and casters.

£3,500-4,500 L&T

A William IV mahogany framed and button-upholstered hide patent 'self-acting' library wing armchair, by George Minter of London, the back with adjustable 'rake' action, the seat with adjustable 'pitch' and an apron fitted with an integral sliding footrest, on a cantilever action, the legs stamped 'G. MINTER,55 GERRARD STREET SOHO VR PATENT 2007'.

George Minter is listed as a cabinet-maker, undertaker, bath chair and wheelchair maker working from various addresses in London from the 1820s to the 1850s.

44in (111cm) high

£3,500-4,500 L&T

FURNITURE

ESSENTIAL REFERENCE: BIEDERMEIER

- The main period of production was between c1805 and 1850.
- Biedermeier furniture was simple, Classical, and functional.
- Biedermeier was essentially a middle-class style, though it was also used in the private areas of noble houses. It placed emphasis on practicality and comfort. Furniture was, therefore, moderate in size, round in shape, comfortable and homely.
- It employed straight lines and lacked decorative carvings. Classical motifs were often used for decoration. However, the most important decorative feature was the grain of the wood, which was then emphasised with various pyramidal and fountain-like shapes. The most fashionable woods were mahogany and less costly local woods like walnut, cherry, pear, birch and ash.
- Upholstery was generally flat and square, made of silk or horsehair.
- By the mid-19thC, the style had begun to seem dowdy. It was at this time that it was given the name 'Biedermeier': a satirical term meaning 'the decent common man'. The style continued to decline in popularity until the beginning of the 20thC when it once again became much sought after and widely copied.

A pair of mid-19thC Biedermeier mahogany love seats, with straight crests, brass finials and animal paw feet on a plinth base.

38.5in (151.5cm) wide

£700-1,000   POOK

A Biedermeier satin birch wing armchair, upholstered in green and cream-striped floral tapestry covering, button-upholstered back, padded arms with scroll ends on shaped supports, overstuffed seats and splayed legs.

£450-550   HT

A late 19thC French mahogany-framed bergère, in the Empire taste, the arms with anthemion details on Egyptianesque caryatid supports tapering to sabre legs on carved paw feet.

£450-550   L&T

A pair of mid-20thC Victorian style Kelim upholstered armchairs, in the manner of Howard & Sons, raised on ebonised turned tapered legs ending in casters.

£1,500-2,000   L&T

A matched pair of late 20thC George III style mahogany-framed wing armchairs, each arched rectangular back above overscrolling arms, on moulded square-section legs and stretchers.

32.25in (82cm) wide

£550-650   DN

SETTLES, SETTEES AND SOFAS

An 18thC and later oak box seat settle, the carved top rail over four portrait-carved fielded panels above a lunette-carved back rail, between leaf-carved tapering uprights and open arms above a plank seat with sliding central well, over a long lunette-carved landscape panel to the front, between stile-end supports.

4.5in (126cm) wide

£2,500-3,000   HALL

A pair of 19thC William and Mary style stained walnut framed and upholstered settees, on ribbed inverted baluster legs with corrugated blocks united by pierced serpentine cross stretchers with leaf-carved boss finials, on bun feet.

55in (140cm) wide

£3,500-4,500   L&T

CLOSER LOOK: CHIPPENDALE SOFA

The design of this sofa is derived from an example in the third edition of Chippendale's 'The Gentleman and Cabinet-Maker's Director'.

The design of Chippendale's 'French' chairs, such as these, was ingeniously adapted to suit his clients by the subtle use of carved ornament, adapted to suit the decor of the room in which they were to be placed.

The various elements of the design and carving of this sofa, with its serpentine mahogany frame carved with Rococo motifs, bear particular similarities to a suite (including a pair of sofas) supplied by Thomas Chippendale to the Earl of Dumfries for Dumfries House in 1759.

The eight cabriole legs have acanthus-carved terminals and scroll toes.

A George III carved mahogany sofa, in the manner of Thomas Chippendale, with serpentine back, seat and scroll arms, legs damaged and repaired, lacking scroll toes to outer back legs, elements of frame later.

It is possible that this sofa was part of a commission given to Chippendale by Sir Robert Burdett for Ramsbury Manor in Wiltshire.

c1770   83.5in (212cm) wide

£40,000-50,000   **DN**

A George III Chippendale mahogany sofa, with an arched back, outward flaring arms, serpentine front seat rail, and square moulded legs joined by stretchers.

c1780   90in (228.5cm) wide

£5,000-6,000   **POOK**

A late 18thC Continental, possibly Italian, giltwood chaise longue, with a shell-carved curved back and footrest and loose cushion seat, raised on square tapered legs, carved with guilloche and carved at the knees with acanthus and shells.

86in (218.5cm) wide

£3,000-4,000   **FRE**

A George III carved giltwood sofa, with faults, wear and surface chipping.

c1780   73in (185cm) wide

£2,500-3,500   **DN**

A suite of Louis XVI giltwood seat furniture, comprising a pair of bergères and four 'fauteuils a la reine', raised on round tapered fluted, leaf-carved legs, the bergères stamped 'I. B. LELARGE'

c1780

£20,000-30,000   **FRE**

A Neoclassical Italian carved giltwood serpentine wallbench, raised on tapering, leaf-motif legs with scrolled acanthus heads and ball feet, the seat has a serpentine profile, with a frieze with florette-centred tablets within swags of husks,

c1785

£12,000-16,000   **PAR**

A George III mahogany camel-back settee, the padded back and out-scrolled padded arms raised on blind fretwork carved legs, ending in casters.

26in (66cm) wide

£2,000-3,000   **FRE**

A 19thC George III style mahogany camel-back settee.

36.5in (93cm) high

£3,000-4,000   **L&T**

A George III style upholstered and mahogany settee, the arched back, outscrolled arms and cushioned seat covered in rose check fabric, on shell and scroll-carved cabriole legs with pad feet.

77in (195cm) wide

£3,500-4,500   **L&T**

CLOSER LOOK: GERMAN EMPIRE SOFA

A rare German Empire sofa, based on designs by Karl Friedrich Schinkel, Berlin, solidly constructed and carved from beechwood and decorated with Neoclassical motifs.

Karl Friedrich Schinkel (1781-1841) was a prominent Prussian architect who worked predominantly in the Neoclassical style.

He was influenced by Greek rather than Imperial Roman architecture - possibly as a reaction to its link to the recent French occupiers.

Later, Schinkel embraced the Neo-Gothic style. The Bauakademie (English Building Academy) he built in Berlin, is considered a forerunner of modern architecture due to its use of red brick and the relatively streamlined facade of the building. By ignoring historical conventions, the building - which has since been demolished - was a forerunner of the clean-lined 'modernist' architecture that would become prominent in Germany early in the 20th century.

Schinkel also designed the Iron Cross medal of Prussia, and later Germany.

c1825

£15,000-20,000

The corners are formed by columns rising from lancette-shaped leaves and topped by spheres.

The seat a deux corps and backrest are upholstered and covered in golden coloured silk fabric worked in blue with a wreath of laurel incorporating an urn.

The sides are formed by winged and horned lions above circular medallions of laurel incorporating a lyre with eagle-headed finials.

The back is lightly curved and centred by a wreath of laurel incorporating musical instruments, the rectangular border formed by acanthus incorporating tambours.

53in (134cm) wide

SOTA

An early 19thC Regency brass-inlaid simulated rosewood window seat, with deeply reeded sabre legs and S-scroll-armed seat frame.

c1815

£10,000-14,000   **PAR**

A Regency mahogany framed 'Grecian' couch, the serpentine volute-carved top rail with gadrooned cresting and outscrolling acanthus carved arms, the moulded seat rail on turned and lappet-carved legs ending in brass socket casters.

88.5in (225cm) wide

£1,000-1,500   **L&T**

An early 19thC Empire mahogany and parcel gilt sofa.

92.5in (235cm) wide

£1,800-2,200   **DN**

One of a pair of Regency rosewood couches with a shaped show-wood back with scrolled and lobed crest, the outswept scrolling arms decorated with acanthus leaf carving, standing on moulded sabre legs ending in well-chased casters.

In the 18th and early 19thC the Classical designs borrowed from the ancient world were incorporated into all elements of buildings, furnishings and decoration. The obvious influences of ancient Rome and Greece can be seen in this sofa and the theme would undoubtedly have been carried through into the side chairs and open armchairs that would have been commissioned at the same time. Such seating furniture would have been placed in the formal drawing rooms of the period to show the owner's standing and their understanding of the Neoclassical taste. The size of such formal rooms would require suites of seating furniture to be positioned in symmetry to complete the ordered aesthetics of the Georgian period.

c1820.

34in (86cm) high

£35,000-40,000 PAIR   **RGA**

A George IV mahogany-framed sofa, the shaped rectangular back flanked by scroll arms, above the rectangular seat on sabre legs gilt-brass lion-paw caps and casters, damage.

c1825   80in (203cm) wide

£450-650
                                              DN

A pair of late Regency mahogany framed chaise longues, in the manner of Gillows of Lancaster, each with an arched and padded lotus scroll-carved three-quarter arm above a seat with carved acroteriae and squab cushion, on short gadrooned and reeded tapering legs with brass socket casters, upholstered in ivory silk damask with bolster cushions.

73.25in (186cm) wide

£4,500-6,500 PAIR   **L&T**

A William IV carved mahogany and upholstered sofa, with foliate-carved armrests.

c1830   82.25in (209cm) wide

£600-800   **DN**

A William IV mahogany settee, leaf-carved wavy top rail, above a padded back and loose cushion seat, the armrest upon turned supports, raised on bulbous lobed legs, ending in casters.

c1835   60in (152.5cm) wide

£1,200-1,800   **FRE**

A William IV rosewood sofa.

c1835   89.25in (227cm) wide

£3,000-3,500   **DN**

A William IV carved mahogany sofa, in the manner of Williams and Gibton.

88.5in (225cm) wide

£600-800   **DN**

A William IV, probably Anglo-Indian, carved rosewood day bed.

c1835

£1,000-1,500

77.5in (197cm) wide

DN

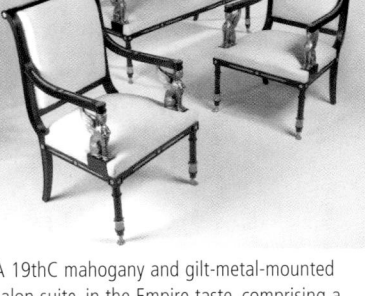

A 19thC mahogany and gilt-metal-mounted salon suite, in the Empire taste, comprising a pair of canapes, with downswept arms with rosette terminals, on winged sphinx caryatid supports, on turned legs with anthemion-cast mounts and gilt-metal feet, with four armchairs.

canapes 55in (140cm) wide

£8,000-10,000   **L&T**

A German polychrome-painted bench, inscribed 'Johann Deter', with overall incised tulip and foliate decoration.

35in (89cm) high

£2,500-3,500 POOK

A mid-19thC carved walnut settee, the button-upholstered double-ended back with central padded panel surmounted by a nesting bird, the open frame arms carved with vines and acanthus terminals, the concave stuffover seat with acanthus-carved scrolling legs, together with four side chairs en suite.

£1,200-1,500 SUITE L&T

A 19thC Italian painted wood and upholstered settee, the arched back, out-scrolled arms and serpentine seat covered in rose fabric, the channelled frame green and gilt painted, on cabriole legs with pointed feet.

66.25in (158cm) wide

£2,500-3,000 L&T

A Victorian rosewood sofa.

c1860 *61.5in (156cm) wide*

£900-1,100 DN

A Victorian mahogany-framed sofa, with green velvet-upholstered back and rolling arms upon turned supports.

£250-300 ROS

A small 19thC Continental giltwood settee, the shell-carved backrail above an upholstered back and seat and flanked by high scrolling armrests, over a carved and shaped frieze raised on four cabriole legs.

42in (107cm) wide

£1,200-1,500 FRE

A Victorian mahogany and button-upholstered chaise longue.

c1870 *69.25in (176cm) wide*

£500-700 DN

A late 19thC Biedermeier style birch-framed sofa, the square back flanked by a pair of pierced scroll arms inset with marquetry panels, on square tapering legs.

80in (203cm) wide

£500-700 DN

A pair of mid-19thC Louis XVI style giltwood settees, in the manner of Jean-Baptiste Sene, each with an Aubusson tapestry-upholstered back and seat, the horseshoe-shaped padded backrest continuing to leaf-carved hand holds with voluted supports, the bowed front seatrail raised on round, tapered, fluted legs, the whole carved with entrelac.

59in (150cm) high

£6,000-7,000   **FRE**

A 19thC Louis XVI style giltwood settee, the oval tapestry cushioned back and scrolling hand holds supported on short fluted tapering legs.

51in (129.5cm) wide

£1,200-1,500   **FRE**

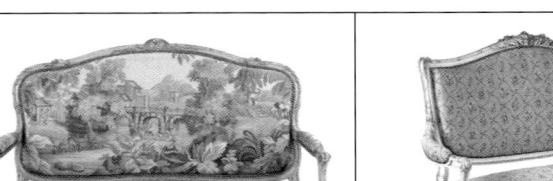

A late 19th/early 20thC French painted wood-framed settee, upholstered in Aubusson style tapestry with brass studs to a carved foliage scroll frame.

58.5in (148.5cm) wide

£3,000-4,000   **WW**

An early 20thC 'French 19thC style' cream painted and parcel-gilt sofa, the cartouche-shaped back carved with acanthus, above downswept arms with scroll terminals, the bowed seat on turned tapering and stop-fluted legs.

53.5in (136cm) wide

£800-1,000   **DN**

REFECTORY & GATELEG TABLES

A 17thC Spanish walnut refectory table, the plank top with cleated end rails above four spirally turned and splayed legs on turned feet united by scalloped and tablet-carved stretchers joined by a pair of wrought iron wrythen twist under braces.

51in (130cm) wide

£7,500-8,500   **L&T**

A Charles II oak refectory table, the cleated rectangular top above a moulded frieze, raised on gun barrel-turned legs, united by a perimeter stretcher, with restorations.

94.5in (240cm) wide

£2,500-3,500   **L&T**

An oak and walnut refectory table, the rectangular triple plank walnut top with cleated ends, above the carved frieze, on baluster-turned legs, block feet and peripheral stretchers, damage, repair.

c1680   *88.25in (224cm) wide*

£800-1,200   **DN**

FURNITURE

A 17thC oak 'credence' or folding table, the semi-circular folding top over an overlapping lunette and foliate-carved frieze, with central short frieze drawer between canted sides on heavy front corner ring-turned supports, with matching slender supports to the back corners and conforming single gate to the back, over a single plank shelf stretcher, above a shaped apron on heavy block feet.

The term 'credence table' is thought to come from the Italian credenza as these tables may have been used as serving boards. The best early oak tables feature fine quality carving and deep colour and should have been well preserved.

36.5in (92.5cm) wide

£8,000-12,000   **HALL**

A 17thC oak drop leaf refectory table in the Flemish taste, the flanked top with pull-out leaves at either end and above a channelled frieze with central fluted table, with gadrooned and under bulb-turned legs headed by tablets and fluted capitals on bun feet.

111in (282cm) wide (extended)

£1,800-2,200   **L&T**

A late 17thC oak refectory dining table, the rectangular top composed of four well-figured planks with cleated ends, the frieze with shaped corner frets enclosing a pair of frieze drawers with turned handles, on square-section legs with chamfered corners united by stretchers.

64.5in (164cm) wide

£1,600-1,800   **L&T**

A fruitwood and oak rectory table, the top 16th/early 17thC, the base of 20thC construction, the triple plank top with cleated ends, the base with X-frame trestle legs, damage, repair.

124.5in (316cm) wide

£3,000-5,000   **DN**

An early 18thC Italian walnut refectory table, some damage.

89in (226cm) long

£3,000-4,000   **DN**

A 19thC French walnut refectory table, the rounded rectangular plank top on associate moulded square legs and sloping bar feet joined by a bar stretcher.

89.5in (227cm) long

£1,700-2,000   **L&T**

An early 19thC American New England pine sawbuck table, with rectangular top over X-supports, retaining old red wash surface.

94in (239cm) long

£3,500-4,500   **POOK**

A late 19th/early 20thC oak draw-leaf refectory table, in 17thC style, the rectangular top above carved cup and cover legs headed by lion mask terminals, above an H-shaped stretcher and block feet.

83.5in (212cm) wide

£2,000-3,000   **DN**

A late 17thC oak gateleg oval table, with bobbin-turned legs and stretchers.

£350-450   DN

A late 17thC Charles II oak gateleg table, the oval top with drop leaves, raised on turned legs united by stretchers.

39in (99cm) wide

£250-450   FRE

An early 18thC oak gateleg table, the oval top above end frieze drawers with shaped aprons, on turned baluster and block legs united by peripheral stretchers.

54in (137cm) wide

£1,200-1,800   WW

PEDESTAL TABLES

A Regency mahogany and satinwood crossbanded breakfast table, the top with snap-over action above a plain spreading column on outswept reeded legs ending in plain brass caps and casters.

64in (163cm) wide

£1,000-1,500   L&T

A Regency mahogany and satinwood crossbanded rectangular breakfast table.

c1820   *63.75in (162cm) wide*

£650-750   DN

A Regency rosewood and satinwood banded breakfast table, damage, repair.

c1820   *28.75in (73cm) high*

£2,000-2,500   DN

A Regency rosewood circular breakfast table, the circular top with marquetry border and bead-moulded edge, above the turned stem and shaped plinth issuing four downswept legs, brass lappet cast caps and casters.

c1820   *50.5in (74cm) diam*

£6,000-8,000   DN

An American New York Federal mahogany breakfast table, with acanthus-carved standard, supported by carved legs, with animal paw feet.

c1825   *26.5in (67.5cm) wide*

£1,500-2,500   POOK

A Regency rosewood circular tip-up-top breakfast table, raised on an octagonal tapering column with triform base and paw feet.

54in (137cm) diam

£1,400-1,600   A&G

A Regency rosewood and brass-strung tilt-top breakfast table, the circular top with gadrooned edge and plain frieze on a stepped and beaded square-section pillar and concave platform base, raised on four sabre legs ending in brass paw caps and casters.

53in (134cm) diam

£2,200-2,800   L&T

FURNITURE

A late Regency mahogany breakfast table, the rectangular top with beaded edge above a square pilaster flanked by boldly carved and scrolled volutes on quadruped base with reeded scroll-cut sabre legs headed by roundels and ending in brass casters.

59.5in (151cm) wide

£1,800-2,200 **L&T**

CLOSER LOOK: GILLOWS TABLE

The quality of Gillows construction is evident in the 'invisible' wavy join to the decorative veneers and the bold execution of the edge and feet mouldings.

The burr-figured and quarter-veneered top has an egg and dart moulded edge and burr-veneered frieze with moulded lip.

The moulded detail on the central pillar is another typical Gillows detail, often encountered on the fold-over and sofa tables made by this firm.

The spreading hexagonal pillar features central gaitered banding with an ogee-moulded collar below, and sits on a triform platform base with rounded terminals and gadrooned bun feet with recessed casters.

A late Regency amboyna and rosewood circular tilt-top breakfast table, by Gillows of Lancaster, the base stamped 'GILLOWS' on the upper tenon.

50.5in (128cm) diam

£15,000-20,000 **L&T**

A George IV mahogany breakfast table, the top above a plain frieze and column stem issuing three outswept legs on carved lion paw feet and concealed casters, damage, repair.

c1825 *47.25in (120cm) diam*

£500-700 **DN**

A George IV rosewood circular breakfast table.

c1825 *44in (112cm) diam*

£800-1,200 **DN**

A George IV mahogany breakfast table, the rounded rectangular top with a reeded edge, raised on a turned column support and four downswept legs terminating in brass capped casters.

c1820 *56in (142cm) wide*

£1,000-1,500 **FRE**

A fine George IV circular rosewood tilt-top dining table of excellent figuring, in the manner of Gillows, set on a tapered column with lower carved collar to triform base.

c1825 *54in (137cm) wide*

£7,000-9,000 **RGA**

A mid-19thC, probably Scottish, mahogany breakfast table.

51in (130cm) diam

£7,000-10,000 **DN**

A William IV circular 'goncalo alves' breakfast table, the circular top above a plain frieze on a turned and lappet-carved stem, issuing three outswept legs, and on scroll-carved gilt casters, damage.

c1835 *54.75in (139cm) diam*

£2,500-3,500 **DN**

A William IV mahogany circular breakfast table, with faults.

c1835 *47.25in (120cm) diam*

£500-700 **DN**

A mid-19thC Victorian rosewood oval breakfast table, with moulded edge and hinged top, the lobed, baluster stem on four cabriole legs with scrolled feet and casters.

28.75in (73cm) high

£350-450 **DN**

A George III mahogany three-pedestal dining table, comprising a centre section and two D-shaped ends, raised on turned standards and ending in sabre legs, together with two leaf extensions.
c1800 *81in (206cm) wide open*

£3,500-4,500 **FRE**

A George III mahogany triple pedestal dining table, with tapered cylindrical pedestals supported by cabriole legs terminating in brass casters, with two leaves.

c1770 *191in (485cm) long*

£25,000-30,000 **POOK**

A 19thC Regency mahogany twin pedestal dining table, the top with reeded edge and two additional leaves, on baluster supports and downswept reeded tripod bases ending in brass claw caps and casters, with alterations and restorations.

118in (300cm) long

£8,000-10,000 **L&T**

A Regency period, probably Scottish, mahogany twin pedestal dining table, the rectangular top with moulded edge and single leaf, on fly arm supports above a pair of beehive-turned pillars each on a lappet-hipped and reeded downswept quadruped base ending in finely cast brass caps and casters.

67.75in (172cm) wide

£1,600-1,800 **L&T**

A George IV mahogany twin pedestal dining table, with two additional leaf insertions, the rectangular top with rounded corners, each pedestal formed of a turned and reeded stem, the plinth on four hipped and downswept legs, scroll feet and casters.
c1825 *29in (74cm) high*

£2,000-3,000 **DN**

A William IV, possibly Scottish, mahogany three-pedestal dining table, the centre pedestal with drop-down leaves and a single drawer at either end flanking D-shaped ends, each raised on acanthus-carved standards, in-curved rectangular platform and carved lion paw feet.
c1835 *97in (246cm) wide open*

£5,000-7,000 **FRE**

A mid-19thC William IV mahogany three-pedestal dining table, each pedestal with baluster-shaped stem, on three down-curved legs on brass casters, together with two additional leaves.

29.25in (74cm) long

£6,000-8,000 **SOTA**

FURNITURE

An 18thC and later mahogany twin pedestal dining table, each 'D' end centred by a rectangular central section, with two leaf insertions, adapted, parts associated, damage and repair.

29in (74cm) high

£1,000-1,500   **DN**

A 20thC George III style mahogany triple pedestal dining table, with two additional leaf insertions.

30.75in (78cm) high

£4,000-6,000   **DN**

A 20thC mahogany triple pedestal dining table.

115.5in (293cm) long

£600-800   **DN**

DROPLEAF TABLES

A George II mahogany dropleaf dining table, the rounded rectangular top above a plain frieze, raised on turned tapered legs ending in pad feet.

Extended 109.5in (278cm) wide

£1,300-1,500   **L&T**

An early 18thC mahogany dropleaf dining table, formerly part of a larger table.

c1730   *56.75in (144cm) long*

£600-800   **DN**

A George II mahogany dropleaf dining table, rectangular top incorporating twin hinged flaps, on shell terminals, carved cabriole legs and claw feet.

c1750   *28.25in (72cm) high*

£750-950   **DN**

An exceptionally large George III mahogany dropleaf dining table, the well-figured top of substantial gauge (3cm), above a plain frieze on turned gate-action legs ending in pad feet.

78.75in (200cm) wide

£30,000-40,000

L&T

A late 18th/early 19thC mahogany dropleaf dining table, the oval top incorporating two hinged leaves, on square-section legs, damage, and repair.

71in (180cm) wide

£750-950   **DN**

An early 19thC George III mahogany hunt or 'wake' table, surface marks and wear.

27.5in (70cm) high

£500-700   **DN**

A drawleaf dining table, by William Birch, High Wycombe, the square top inlaid with a chequer band, raised above square chamfered legs, linked by crossed stretchers centred by an inlaid rosette.

29.5in (75cm) high

£1,000-1,200   **L&T**

A 20thC Irish mahogany wake table, the narrow oval dropleaf top with rounded edge above eight moulded and chamfered square section legs with double gate action.

84.25in (214cm) wide

£2,500-3,500   **L&T**

EXTENDING TABLES

A George III mahogany D-end extending dining table, the later crossbanded top incorporating the rectangular central section with two hinged leaves, on square-section tapering leg, damage, repair.

c1800   *89in (226cm) wide*

£1,000-1,500   **DN**

A Regency mahogany triple section dining table in the manner of Gillows, crossbanded rectangular top with two additional leaves on slender turned and reeded tapering legs.

c1810   *161.5in (410cm) extended*

£25,000-30,000   **SOTH**

CLOSER LOOK: EXTENDING DINING TABLE

The brass-mounted scissor frame is stamped 'WILKINSON PATENT LONDON'. This ingenious form of extension allows the table to be reduced as a small foldover side table when not in use. Other leading firms of the period also experimented with this form of action, most notably Gillows of Lancaster.

The top consists of three well-figured full leaves and a narrow half leaf, all with a reeded edge.

The ring-turned tapering baluster legs end in brass socket casters.

A Regency period mahogany patent 'scissor-action' extending dining table, by Wilkinson & Wilkinson of London.

106.75in (271cm) wide

£15,000-18,000   **L&T**

A Regency mahogany extending dining table, with one leaf insertion, the moulded rounded rectangular top above a plain frieze, raised on reeded turned tapered legs terminating in brass cappings and casters.

88.5in (225cm) long

£2,500-3,000   **L&T**

A Regency extending mahogany dining table, in the manner of Gillows of Lancaster, the rounded rectangular top with reeded edge and two additional leaves on a sliding draw rail extension, the ebony-banded frieze above eight slender ring-turned tapering legs ending in brass socket casters.

99in (242cm) wide

£4,000-6,000   **L&T**

A late Regency mahogany extending dining table, the rounded rectangular top with three additional leaves above a plain frieze with lipped edge on lotus-turned tapering legs ending in brass socket casters.

117in (297cm) wide

£4,000-5,000 **L&T**

A late Regency mahogany extending dining table, with repair.

c1820 *107.75in (274cm) long*

£800-1,200 **DN**

A George IV mahogany D-end dining table, the frieze to each end decorated with ebonised stringing, raised on turned tapering legs, complete with two spare leaves.

108in (274cm) long

£2,000-2,500 **A&G**

A William IV mahogany extending dining table, moulded edge top including four additional leaves on reeded turned tapering legs, with two detachable central legs.

c1830 *149.5in (380cm) long extended*

£12,000-15,000 **SOTH**

A mahogany George IV extending dining table with two additional leaves.

104.25in (265cm) long

£4,000-6,000 **SOTA**

A Victorian plum pudding mahogany extending dining table, the rectangular top with moulded edge above the moulded frieze, on lappet-carved and octagonal baluster legs, brass caps and casters, with two additional leaf insertions.

c1840 *53.5in (136cm) wide unextended*

£3,000-4,000 **DN**

An early Victorian mahogany extending dining table, the oval top with one leaf.

c1840 *84.75in (215cm) long*

£1,300-1,800 **DN**

A Victorian mahogany extending dining table, with three additional leaves, faults, repair.

c1840 *59.5in (151cm) wide unextended*

£2,000-3,000 **DN**

A large Victorian oak extending dining table, with eight leaf insertions, the rounded rectangular top above a moulded and chamfered frieze, raised on turned and faceted baluster legs headed by carved flowerheads and terminating in rope-twist carved 'ankles', with brass-mounted cappings and ceramic casters.

85.5in (551cm) long

£4,500-5,500 **L&T**

A Victorian mahogany extending dining table, the rectangular top with rounded corners and moulded edge, above a plain frieze on baluster-turned and tapering legs, brass caps and ceramic casters, with two additional leaf insertions, damage, repair.
c1860   *50in (127cm) wide*
£2,500-3,000   **DN**

A Victorian mahogany extending dining table, by Joseph Fitter, Birmingham, the rectangular top opening with a crank to accommodate three additional leaves, raised on bulbous turned legs, ending in casters, the winding mechanism stamped 'Joseph Fitter, Birmingham'.
c1870   *137.5in (349cm) wide open*
£5,000-7,000   **FRE**

A Victorian mahogany extending 'Campaign' dining table, the rectangular top with a moulded edge with three additional leaves, on turned tapering legs with brass wheel casters.

Extended 125in (317.5cm) wide
£4,500-6,500   **DUK**

A 19thC mahogany extending dining table, the rectangular top with three additional leaves and a reeded edge above a plain frieze with reeded lip, on four square tapering legs ending in square feet, the sliding rails stamped 'W. MILLER / 11826 / ALEX - R MACKENZIE & CO. / GLASGOW'.
Extended 149in (378cm) wide
£3,000-4,000   **L&T**

A mid Victorian wind-out oak dining table, the rectangular top with moulded edge and rounded corners, opening to accommodate the four leaves, the top figured oak veneered over a plain frieze on four heavy leaf-carved and spiral-turned tapering supports terminating in salt-glazed casters.
58.25in (148cm) long closed
£3,000-4,000   **HALL**

An early 20thC mahogany extending dining table, with three additional leaf insertions.

£650-750   **DN**

PIER & CONSOLE TABLES

A mid-18thC Louis XV pair of carved and giltwood console tables, with white marble tops, overall carved and pierced with scallops.
38in (97cm) wide
£6,500-7,500   **SOTA**

A pair of Neoclassical satinwood and mahogany crossbanded demi-lune pier tables, the tops inlaid with halved fan paterae and swagged urns above faux fluted friezes, on square tapering legs with trailing husks and paterae capitals, each embellished with box and ebony lines.
57.5in (146cm) wide
£10,000-15,000   **L&T**

FURNITURE

ESSENTIAL REFERENCE: ROCOCO

By the 1730s, the heavy, symmetrical Baroque style was discarded in favour of the lighter, more colourful Rococo style. This style respected and imitated nature, and favoured asymmetry, which allowed a more realistic representation of the disorder of the natural world.

- Forms were embellished with delicate repeating rock and shell patterns (the term Rococo being derived from 'rocaille' meaning rockwork), light grotesques, chinoiseries and scrolls. The S-scroll, derived from the Classical volute, was extremely prominent, as were cartouches made up of multiple S- and C-scrolls. Furniture carved in this style was frequently smothered with gesso and gilding to create lavish works of art.

- The Rococo period was also strongly influenced by the Orient. The practise of japanning furniture (applying a shellac varnish to the surface in an imitation of Japanese lacquer) was widely used in Europe and America.

An unusual northern Italian Rococo walnut, olivewood and burlwood console table, probably Lombardy, the shaped quarter-veneered top with rounded fore corners inlaid with a cartouche above a single drawer, raised on cabriole legs with scrolling tops ending in stylised hoof feet, the dust board signed indistinctly 'Sagrind'.
c1750   *47.25in (120cm) wide*
£20,000-25,000   **FRE**

A pair of Irish George III style pine console tables, formerly with marble tops, the rectangular top over an egg and dart frieze carved with shells and scrolls, raised on cabriole legs ending in claw-and-ball feet.
                                    50.5in (128.5cm) wide
£3,000-4,000   **FRE**

A late Regency mahogany console table, the rectangular top with boldly gadrooned edge and ogee ripple-moulded frieze, on volute scroll legs ending in massive carved lion paw feet, united by a shaped shelf stretcher.
                                    42.25in (107cm) wide
£2,000-3,000   **L&T**

A set of two early 19thC and later walnut and carved mahogany console tables, of recent construction, each shaped walnut top above an acanthus-carved scrolling leg.
£300-500   **DN**

An Anglo Indian rosewood console table.

c1825   *55in (140cm) wide*
£2,000-2,500   **DN**

A William IV rosewood, giltwood and marble-mounted console table, faults.
c1835   *41in (104cm) wide*
£2,000-2,500   **DN**

FURNITURE

A pair of Neoclassical giltwood and gesso marble-top pier tables, of break-bowfront outline with concave sides, each with marble top inlaid with coloured anthemion stems and arabesques around a halved fan patera, each frieze with ribbon-tied giltwood festoons and four Wedgwood style green jasperware medallions flanking a central jasperware tablet decorated with Classical muses, on square tapering legs decorated with trailing bell flowers on guttae style block feet, both with marbleised green-painted decoration.

42.25in (107cm) wide

£10,000-15,000   **L&T**

A Rococo style giltwood console table and mirror, the shaped marble top over an ornate pierced scroll carved and foliate-carved frieze, raised on cabriole legs united by acanthus and foliate-carved stretchers, the mirror with a central bevelled rectangular plate within a gadrooned frame and floral etched margin plates, surmounted by a cartouche flanked by lions.

Console 56in (142cm) wide

£3,500-4,500   **FRE**

A pair of George III style mahogany satinwood and marquetry demi-lune console tables, of recent manufacture.

35.75in (116cm) wide

£800-1,200   **DN**

A large Louis XVI style giltwood console, the legs joined by an undulating stretcher rail, carved with flower-filled urns, adapted.

c1900

119in (302cm) wide

£15,000-20,000   **FRE**

A pair of late 19th/early 20thC George III style mahogany and paint-decorated console tables, the shaped top painted to show a lute and ribbon swags to the frieze over straight tapering legs.

34.5in (87.5cm) wide

£1,500-2,500   **FRE**

SIDE TABLES

A late 17thC Charles II walnut centre/side table, moulded top above a channelled frieze and scroll apron to all sides, with a single drawer, the square and bobbin-turned legs joined by conforming stretchers.

35in (89cm) wide

£15,000-20,000   **SOTH**

A Charles II oak side table, the rectangular top above a mitre-panelled drawer, on baluster-turned legs and an H-stretcher.

41.75in (106cm) wide

£550-750   **DN**

A William and Mary oak side table, with faults.

c1690   *32in (81cm) wide*

£2,000-3,000   **DN**

An early 18thC William and Mary walnut side table, the moulded top above a drawer with boxwood stringing, front apron with pierced fret brackets, square and bobbin-turned legs joined by conforming peripheral stretchers.

33in (84cm) wide

£12,000-15,000   **SOTH**

An 18thC and later George I walnut veneered side table, the rectangular top with quarter-matched veneers within feathered stringing and crossbanding, above a single frieze drawer above an arcaded frieze, on turned tapering legs with wavy X-form stretcher and ball feet.

30in (76cm) wide

£4,500-5,500   **DUK**

A mid-18thC occasional dropleaf side table, of small proportions, the re-entrant cornered top with caddy-moulded edge and rear dropleaf above plain frieze, on four scroll-carved slender cabriole legs ending in pad feet.

26in (66cm) wide

£5,000-7,000   **L&T**

A mid-18thC Dutch walnut and marquetry side table.

29in (74cm) wide

£2,000-3,000   DN

A George III mahogany side table, the rectangular top now with an additional rouge marble top above two frieze drawers, raised on canted square legs ending in block feet, the whole carved with blind fretwork and gothic tracery.

c1770   31in (79cm) high

£4,000-5,000   FRE

A George III satinwood, purpleheart and tulipwood-crossbanded demi-lune table, the top with a halved fan patera bounded by pole trophies united by ribbon-tied swags of ivy, on legs with inlaid simulated flutes, headed by tablet capitals with brass caps.

48in (122cm) wide

£4,000-6,000   L&T

A satinwood marquetry and kingwood-crossbanded side table, the top with central feather fan marquetry reserve, above a crossbanded frieze and on square-section tapering legs, damage, repair, adapted in part.

c1800 and later   43in (109cm) wide

£1,300-1,600   DN

A Regency walnut, rosewood-veneered satinwood-crossbanded and parcel-gilt side table, the narrow lobed top above an entablature frieze, centred by a sunken lozenge, on turned and reeded tapering legs united by an undulating shelf stretcher on toupie feet.

c1810   78in (198cm) wide

£100,000-150,000   L&T

A Regency mahogany side table, in manner of William Trotter of Edinburgh, the rectangular top above a frieze drawer and scroll-carved kneehole flanked by two short drawers with gadrooned handles, on volute scroll-carved cabriole front legs ending in scrolled feet and headed by sunken field capitals, the rear legs of turned tapering design.

46in (117cm) wide

£1,200-1,500   L&T

A mid-19thC American Rococo revival faux marble and rosewood side table, possibly Vermont, the shaped top above a conforming skirt with concealed drawer with flanking turned pendants on scroll-carved brackets and legs, the vase and ring-turned posts joined by a shaped central stretcher, original surface, minor imperfections.

37.5in (95.5cm) wide

£1,500-2,500   SK

A George III inverted bowfront serving table.

c1810   48.5in (123cm) wide

£1,800-2,200   DN

A William IV period mahogany serving table of impressive proportions, the top of break-bowfront outline with moulded frieze on eight turned tapering legs with bold acanthus leaf-carved capitals, on ring-turned feet.

113.5in (278cm) wide

£7,000-8,000   L&T

A 19thC Swiss Beromünster style Baroque walnut and marquetry side table, the rectangular top topped with étagère, inlaid with mahogany banding enclosing hunting scenes and centred by coat of arms, above two drawers, flanked by square baluster-shaped carved supports joined by marquetry-inlaid tier, on plinth base.

43.5in (110cm) wide

£2,500-3,500   SOTA

A 19thC Irish mahogany serving table, the rectangular top with moulded edge above plinth frieze on boldly carved volute-scroll front legs decorated with stiff leaf and foliate bosses, the rear legs of plain square section design.

82.75in (210cm) wide

£5,000-7,000   L&T

FURNITURE

A late 18thC satinwood and rosewood-banded writing table, possibly Channel Islands, the quadrant-beaded frieze with a drawer, on faceted tapering column terminating in petal-shaped lobes, the shaped base with bold leaf-carved paw feet.

c1795   29.25in (74.5cm) wide

£3,000-4,000   L&T

An American Philadelphia Federal mahogany writing table or desk, the rectangular top above apron with drawer to each end, on ring-turned and reeded legs, inverted pear-form feet, stamped 'T. Elwyn' on frame.

Thomas Elwyn came to Philadelphia in 1797, but moved to New Hampshire after marrying that same year. He did however maintain a house on Sansom Street in Philadelphia.

c1815   54in (137cm) long

£6,000-8,000   FRE

A Regency mahogany writing table, attributed to William Trotter of Edinburgh, the top inset with a black and gilt Greek Key tooled skiver and a sunken corrugated edge of vertical reeds, the frieze with sunken quadrant beading, enclosing a pair of drawers with foliate-cast pull handles and opposing simulated drawers, on baluster-turned legs headed by chamfered tablet capitals and ending in brass socket casters.

William Trotter is the most famous of the Scottish Furniture Makers and worked from 9 Princess Street, Edinburgh, from 1810 until 1833. During his lifetime Trotter worked for all the important Houses in Scotland, including Parliament House, Edinburgh in 1822 in readiness for the visit of King George III

60.25in (153cm) wide

£4,500-5,500   L&T

A Regency mahogany writing table.

c1820   30in (76cm) wide

£600-800   DN

A pair of George IV mahogany writing tables, attributed to Gillows, each with an opposing false drawer,

c1825   26.5in (67cm) wide

£3,000-3,500   DN

A William IV or early Victorian mahogany writing table, with two frieze drawers.

c1835   45.25in (115cm) wide

£650-750   DN

A Victorian Louis XV style burr walnut and kingwood-crossbanded writing desk, the serpentine-shaped top with an inset leather writing surface, over a shaped frieze with one drawer, raised on square cabriole legs decorated with gilt metal mounts.

32.5in (82.5cm) wide

£1,800-2,200   L&T

A 19thC Boulle marquetry writing table, in 'premiere partie' cut brass and scarlet tortoiseshell, the shaped aprons with Bacchus mask mounts, on cabriole legs headed by caryatids, the whole decorated with arabesques and foliate cast gilt-metal mounts.

55in (140cm) wide

£2,000-3,000   L&T

A mahogany, marquetry and gilt-metal-mounted writing table, stamped 'COLLINSON & LOCK', also stamped '....LONDON 3971' to the drawer.

Collinson & Lock was founded in 1870 by F. G. Collinson and C. J. Lock, former employees of the cabinet-makers and furnishers Jackson and Graham. With their experience of the revivalist styles the new firm became a leading 'Art Manufacturer', employing designers such as Edward Godwin, Henry Batley and Thomas Collcutt, many of whose designs were included in their first catalogue, 'Sketches for Artistic Furniture' (1871). Their furniture was exhibited in London (1871), Vienna (1873) and at the Philadelphia Exhibition (1876). The company was absorbed by Gillows in 1897, also exponents of revivalist furniture since the 1860s.

35.75in (91cm) wide

£3,000-4,000   DN

A late Victorian mahogany writing table, the rectangular top with moulded edge and gilt-tooled red leather inset, above two long drawers on turned tapering and fluted legs headed by stylised Corinthian capitals.

c1880   72.5in (184cm) wide

£1,200-1,500   DN

A Victorian walnut kingwood and floral marquetry writing table, in the French style, with gilt-metal mounts, the moulded edged serpentine oblong top with inset oval green leather writing surface, and marquetry floral sprays to each corner, frieze drawer with gilt foliate handles, raised on cabriole legs with splayed feet.

32in (81.5cm) wide

£700-900   **HT**

A George III style figured table, the shaped rounded rectangular top with an inset tooled green leather writing surface, above a frieze fitted with twelve drawers, raised on reeded tapering legs.

c1900   *78.25in (199cm) wide*

£5,000-7,000   **L&T**

An oak writing table, by James Shoolbred & Company, one drawer stamped by maker.

c1900   *36.25in (92cm) wide*

£450-550   **DN**

An Edwardian satinwood and painted writing desk, painted throughout with trailing flowers, the crossbanded rectangular top centred by a musical trophy over a frieze drawer, raised on carved square tapered legs.

42in (106.5cm) wide

£1,500-2,000   **FRE**

A mid-18thC Louis XV kingwood and rosewood bureau plat, the rounded rectangular top with an inset leather writing surface, over three real and two opposing dummy frieze drawers, with lateral slides, raised on cabriole legs, ending in hairy paw feet.

65.25in (165.5cm) wide

£2,000-3,000   **FRE**

A Louis XVI style gilt-bronze-mounted mahogany and plum pudding mahogany bureau plat, by Gervais-Maximilien Eugene Durand, the rectangular leather inset writing surface above one long drawer flanked by two short deep drawers, raised on square tapered fluted legs, the whole outlined in gilt-bronze, the underside stamped 'G. Durand'.

Gervais-Maximilien-Eugene Durand was born in Paris 1874 and he was the first of three generations of highly successful cabinet makers, exhibiting widely at the series of International Exhibitions. In 1890 his son, Frederic-Louis joined the firm which became known as Durand & Fils.

c1800

£2,000-3,000   **FRE**

A French satinwood bureau plat, the inverted moulded-edge breakfront top with an inset cloth to a raised galleried back with two pairs of leather-fronted drawers, the base with two frieze drawers, one with a brass label for 'P.A. Dunmas 24-26 Rue Notre Dame, Paris', on turned tapering fluted legs with gilt-brass sabots.

43.5in (110.5cm) wide

£1,000-1,500   **WW**

LIBRARY TABLES

A Regency mahogany kidney-shaped library table, in the manner of Gillows of Lancaster, the frieze with beaded edge on boldly beaded end standards filled with slender baluster uprights, on splay legs ending in finely cast brass foliate caps and casters.

37in (94cm) wide

£5,000-6,000   **L&T**

A Regency partridgewood and satinwood-banded library table, in the manner of Gillows, the rectangular top with rounded corners, above two drawers and a small pen drawer and two opposing false drawers, lyre-shaped trestle supports and two pole stretchers, each support issuing two downswept legs, lappet-cast gilt-metal caps and casters, damage, repair, legs possibly reduced in length.

c1820   *57.75in (147cm) wide*

£4,000-5,000   **DN**

A Regency mahogany partners' library table, the rounded rectangular top with matched flame veneers above a pair of frieze drawers to either side and a beaded edge, the large turned central pillar boldly carved with stiff lotus leaves and a gadrooned socle above a quadrapartite platform base, on gadrooned bun feet with recessed casters.

54.5in (138cm) wide

£2,000-3,000 **L&T**

A William IV rosewood library table, the rectangular top with moulded edge above a beaded frieze enclosing a pair of drawers, on baluster-shaped end standards and scroll-carved trestle base with bun feet.

55in (140cm) wide

£2,000-2,500 **L&T**

An Irish William IV rosewood library table, the rounded rectangular top above a two real and two opposing dummy frieze drawers, raised on twin end supports united by a turned cross stretcher, terminating in moulded scroll feet.

57.5in (146cm) wide

£2,500-3,000 **L&T**

A William IV Gothic style oak and leather-inset library table.

c1835   *65.75in (167cm) wide*

£2,500-3,500 **DN**

A George IV rosewood library table, the rectangular top with rounded corners above a pair of shallow frieze drawers, flanked by scroll brackets on ring-turned and ribbed baluster supports with leaf-and-dart-carved collars, the leaf scroll feet with sunken brass casters.

60in (152.5cm) wide

£1,500-2,000 **WW**

A 19thC partridgewood library table, the rounded rectangular top with gilt-tooled tan skiver and key fret-pierced gilt-metal three-quarter gallery above a pair of sunken field frieze drawers, on similarly moulded end standards on dual splay sabre legs ending in brass paw caps and casters.

40in (101cm) wide

£5,000-6,000 **L&T**

An early Victorian rosewood library table.

c1840,   *50.25in (128cm) wide*

£1,200-1,500 **DN**

An early Victorian rectangular mahogany library table, with moulded frieze, raised on scrolling end supports united by a single understretcher, on splay legs and carved bun feet.

54in (137cm) wide

£500-600 **A&G**

A 17thC and later Antwerp tortoiseshell and ebony table, the top adapted from a cabinet door inlaid in the centre with a star-shaped motif inlaid in bone, the surrounding strapwork enriched with inlay of tortoiseshell, a flat single drawer fitted below, supported on spirally fluted legs joined by a stretcher veneered en suite to the top.

53in (134cm) wide

£10,000-12,000 **SOTA**

An early 18thC Queen Anne walnut centre table, the boarded top with cleated ends, ogee arch frieze above square and baluster-turned legs joined by peripheral stretchers.

25.25in. (64cm) high

£5,000-8,000 **SOTH**

A 19thC Swiss Beromünster style Baroque mahogany, walnut, fruitwood and marquetry-inlaid table, the rectangular moulded table top inlaid with banding and hunting scenes, in the middle with text and dated, on square baluster-shaped legs joined by stretcher, with four extending leaves.

1712 *67in (170cm) wide without leaves*

£3,500-4,500 **SOTA**

An early 18thC American Queen Anne mahogany slab table, with oblong marble top with thumb-moulded edge, overhanging a base with scalloped skirt supported by cabriole legs with volute-carved knee blocks, terminating in trifid feet.

45.5in (115.5cm) wide

£15,000-20,000 **POOK**

A late 18thC Spanish walnut and bone-inlaid centre table, with faults.

58.25in (148cm) wide

£900-1,100 **DN**

A late 18thC George III mahogany rent table, the circular top over a frame with four drawers, above a turned standard supported by downward sloping moulded legs terminating in brass casters.

43in (109cm) wide

£1,500-2,500 **POOK**

A George III mahogany revolving oval drum table, the leather-inset oval top above a frieze with alternating drawers and hinged compartments, on a columnar standard supported on downswept tripod legs raised on casters.

c1800 *36in (91.5cm) wide*

£4,000-5,000 **FRE**

A Regency rosewood centre table, in the manner of Gillows of Lancaster, of small proportions, the rounded rectangular top with beaded edge above a beaded frieze with full width drawer, on reeded dual splay supports decorated with roundels and trestle base with four stiff leaf-carved sabre legs united by a waisted platform stretcher.

36.75in (93cm) wide

£3,000-4,000 **L&T**

A Regency mahogany drum library table, the moulded circular top with an inset leather writing surface, above four real and four simulated frieze drawers, on a ring-turned column support ending in three reeded downswept legs terminating in brass caps and casters.

50in (127cm) wide

£5,500-6,500 **L&T**

CLOSER LOOK: REGENCY CENTRE TABLE

Multi-functional furniture was popular in the Regency period because it was useful in varied social settings in the fluid arrangements of rooms.

This table has the usual tilt-top, which enabled the table to moved from room to room or put against the wall when not in use.

The use of calamander veneers reflects the contemporary taste for highly exotic timbers. The evolving fashion for Neoclassical design is here allied to the taste for a playful Gothick, a romantic version of ecclesiastical gothic in domestic settings.

The inlays are a reflection of the revival of interest in early Boulle-inspired brass inlaid French furniture, the Prince Regent being an avid collector of such items during the auctions following the French Revolution.

A Regency calamander and parcel-gilt centre table, with boulle inlays, the top veneered with figured veneers of calamander with a circular Boulle-inspired running brass border of S-scrolls, florettes and stylised anthemions within two inset brass lines. The frieze with a running brass Boulle-interlaced geometric pattern offset by tiny inlaid circles. The turned baluster base support with bandings of gilt gesso and a carved acanthus base above knulled carving on the platform, all inlaid with brass and supported by four giltwood leafy carved lion paw feet on casters.

c1815   *51in (129.5cm) wide*

£80,000-90,000   **PAR**

A late Regency mahogany drum library table, by James Winter & Son, London, with four cockbeaded frieze drawers with lion mask cast-brass pull handles, drawer stamped 'James Winter & Son 101 Wardour St. Soho. London'.

48in (122cm) wide

£4,000-6,000   **L&T**

A Regency mahogany drum library table.

c1820   *45.75in (116cm) diam*

£3,000-5,000   **DN**

A George IV pollard oak and parcel-gilt drum table, the circular top above a frieze of drawers and dummy drawers, raised on anthemion carved trefoil supports and a circular base with carved trefoil toes.

c1825   *52.5in (133.5cm) diam*

£3,000-4,000   **FRE**

A 19thC George I style giltwood centre table, the ornate foliate scroll-carved rectangular moulded top above a cavetto lattice and bellflower frieze, raised on acanthus-carved cabriole scroll legs.

46.75in (119cm) wide

£4,500-6,500   **L&T**

A William IV rosewood drum library table, the circular top with a gilt-tooled burgundy skiver above four frieze drawers with foliate cast-brass pull handles, on boldly turned and lappet-carved column and triform base with tapered bun feet and recessed casters.

53.75in (134cm) wide

£4,000-5,000   **L&T**

A 19thC Anglo-Ceylonese ebony and specimen wood centre table, the octagonal top with radiating veneers and a gadrooned edge, raised on turned supports, united by a galleried under-tier and ending in four cabriole legs with carved claw feet.

10.25in (26cm) wide

£2,000-3,000   **L&T**

A 19thC Italian specimen marble circular table top, on an ebonised baluster-turned stand.

25in (64cm) diam

£1,500-2,500   L&T

A Victorian mahogany extending dining table, by Joseph Fitter, Birmingham, the rectangular top opening with a crank to accommodate three additional leaves, raised on bulbous turned legs, ending in casters, the winding mechanism stamped 'Joseph Fitter, Birmingham'.

c1870   *137.5in (349cm) wide open*

£5,000-7,000   FRE

A Victorian walnut and marquetry centre table, the circular top profusely decorated with marquetry reserves of musical trophies, above a baluster-turned and lappet-carved stem issuing three scroll-carved downswept legs with acanthus-carved feet.

c1870   *32.75in (83cm) diam*

£2,500-3,500   DN

A late 19thC Roman 'Sites of the Grand Tour' micro-mosaic, sample marble and parcel giltwood occasional table, the top with a depiction of Saint Peter's Basilica and Piazza, with eight segments around with depictions of view of Rome, comprising the Pantheon, the Tomb of Caecilia Metella, the Senator's Palace, the Forum, The Flavian amphitheatre, the Temple of Vesta, the Castel Sant'Angelo and the Arch of Titus, surrounded by a border of various marbles and hardstones including lapis lazuli, Siena, portoro, brocatello and others, and interspersed with malachite and lapis lazuli borders, all in a marmo nero Belgio ground, the parcel giltwood and ebonised frieze below with three maiden's masks and three panther's masks, the fluted pedestal below with lobed and acanthus-carved capital and acanthus-carved and waisted socle, with three cavorting putti on the circular base with three projecting plinths, on acanthus-carved paw feet, restored.

26in (66.5cm) diam

£40,000-60,000   **DN**

A Louis XV style gilt-bronze centre table, the veined marble top raised on foliate-cast cabriole legs hung with garlands and joined by a shaped stretcher centred by a foliate-cast urn hung with garlands. This is almost certainly an exhibition piece.

c1875   69in (175.5cm) wide

£16,000-20,000   FRE

A 19thC satinwood, walnut and tulipwood-crossbanded centre table, in the Sheraton manner, the radially veneered top with smaller repeated radially veneered centre enclosing a penwork flowerhead, the outer border decorated with harewood and penwork arabesques, on slender tapering legs united by an upswept undertier on brass socket casters, the whole decorated in box and ebony lines.

30in (76cm) diam

£1,000-1,200   L&T

A 19thC French oval ormolu 'surtout de table', with later legs, the oval mirror within a fruiting vine gallery with shallow urns of fruit and arched supports with wreathed masks, on later carved giltwood and cream-painted square tapering legs.

37.5in (95cm) wide

£4,000-5,000   WW

ESSENTIAL REFERENCE: ELIZABETHAN REVIVAL

- The Elizabethan Revival style was first employed in the 1820s and encouraged by the novels of Sir Walter Scott.
- The style was largely achieved by applying late 16thC and 17thC ornament to existing forms. Strapwork and spiral turnings were particularly suited to the labour-saving machinery of the 19thC. Arabesques and caryatids were also popular.
- During this period, there was considerable destruction of 16th/17thC oak furniture, which was sawn up and used for its carved parts, which were then re-constructed to form contemporary furniture like sideboards.
- It was the height of fashion in the 1840s, being particularly used for dining room and hall furniture.
- By the late 1860s, the Elizabethan style began to merge into the Renaissance style, although it remained popular until the late 19thC.

A late 19thC Elizabethan revival carved oak and specimen wood marquetry centre table, in the manner of Richard Bridgens, the top with marquetry incorporating burr ash, pollard oak, yew, satinwood, rosewood, walnut and burr walnut, above a pierced scroll frieze and baluster legs.

55.5in (141cm) wide

£5,500-6,500   DN

FURNITURE

A late 19thC walnut, thuya, marquetry and gilt-metal-mounted centre table, the frieze drawer centred by a painted porcelain plaque.

46.5in (118cm) wide

£3,000-4,000   DN

A late 19thC mahogany drum table of George III style, the moulded circular top inset with tooled-leather writing surface, above six frieze drawers, alternating with dummy drawers, on panelled square section column and plinth base.

54.5in (138cm) diam

£3,500-5,500   L&T

A 20thC George III style mahogany and fiddle back mahogany drum table, the top above four small drawers, above an octagonal tapering stem with downswept legs, brass caps and casters.

30.25in (77cm) diam

£1,000-1,200   DN

A Neoclassical style giltwood painted and marble centre table, the circular marble-inlaid top sits above a plinth column applied with three giltwood swans raised on a triform base.

45in (114.5cm) diam

£1,200-1,800   FRE

A Neoclassical style giltwood painted and marble centre table, the circular inlaid-marble top supported by a gilded and ebonised column applied with three winged birds, above a triform base.

45in (114.5cm) diam

£1,200-1,800   FRE

A late 19th/early 20thC style French giltwood and composition centre table, with marble inset top, stylised shell and foliate-carved frieze above square section cabriole-shaped legs, damage.

39in (99cm) wide

£450-550   DN

£600-800   DN

A late 19th/early 20thC walnut and crossbanded hall table.

A late 19th/early 20thC Vienna style porcelain and giltwood centre table, the dished circular top decorated with a reserve of a flower girl on the steps, gilt details within a bleu celeste border, raised on three porcelain and gilt supports.

23in (58.5cm) diam

£4,000-6,000   FRE

A pair of Empire style mahogany marble-top gueridons, each with a circular black marble top above a plain frieze raised on in-curved trefoil column base carved with swans and raised on squat bun feet.

c1870   32in (81.5cm) diam

£2,000-3,000   FRE

A 19thC French marble-topped giltwood gueridon, of Louis XIV style, the moulded circular red/yellow marble top on central acanthus-carved column and four putto-carved columns joined by a curving X-stretcher, on paw feet.

32.5in (82cm) diam

£6,000-8,000   L&T

A late 19thC French transitional style gilt-bronze-mounted parquetry gueridon, the inset rectangular marble top over a cubic-veneered frieze with one drawer, raised on slightly splayed square legs united by an interlaced undertier and terminating in hairy hoof sabots.

11in (28cm) wide

£1,200-1,800   FRE

A Louis XVI style kingwood and crossbanded gueridon, with gilt-bronze mounts, the cubic-veneered circular top over a frieze with applied laurel leaf swag decoration, raised on square tapered legs.

c1900   19.5in (49.5cm) diam

£1,000-1,500   FRE

A pair of Louis XVI style mahogany, parquetry, and gilt-metal-mounted gueridons, the canted rectangular rouge marble tops with a three-quarter galleried edge, below is one frieze drawer, raised on slightly splayed square tapered legs, united by an undertier and terminating in hairy hoof sabots.

20.5in (52cm) wide

£1,800-2,200   FRE

A Louis XVI style gilt-bronze and malachite-veneered gueridon, in the manner of Adam Weisweiler, the circular top with a radiating design and a ribbon-tied rim above a frieze cast with entwined laurel garlands, the supports cast with female terms, joined by curved stretchers ending in leaf-cast feet, stamped 'Jansen', stamp partially effaced.

Adam Weisweiler was born in Neuwied in Germany in 1744. Records show that he was established in Paris in 1777. He became a maître-ébéniste (master cabinetmaker) in 1778. Weisweiler produced Neoclassical style furniture. He also frequently made furniture set with lacquer or pietre dure panels or Sèvres porcelain plaques, to obtain distinctive effects.

c1905   21.25in (54cm) diam

£8,000-10,000   FRE

FURNITURE

A late 19thC Louis XV style kingwood and marquetry bijouterie cabinet, the shaped rectangular top with an inset glazed panel, opening to reveal a velvet-lined interior, raised on square cabriole legs terminating in sabots.

39.5in (100.25cm) wide

£1,200-1,800   **FRE**

A late 19thC rosewood and marquetry bijouterie table.

21.75in (55cm) wide

£1,200-1,500   **DN**

A late 19thC walnut and floral marquetry vitrine table, with shell-centred leaf-carved aprons and shell and fruiting vine-carved cabriole legs ending in talon-and-ball feet.

29.25in (74cm) wide

£1,500-2,000   **L&T**

An Edwardian mahogany and satinwood crossbanded bijouterie table, the frieze decorated with ribbon-tied penwork swags, on lyre-shaped end standards with brass wires and applied roundels.

19.75in (50cm) wide

£1,500-2,000   **L&T**

A Regency nest of three rosewood occasional tables.

c1820   *17in (43.5cm) wide*

£500-700   **DN**

An Edwardian nest of four painted satinwood 'Quartetto' tables, the largest painted with ribbon-tied and swagged urns around a pair of cherubs cavorting in the clouds, the remaining tops decorated with festoons of flowers.

26.75in (68cm) high

£2,500-3,500   **L&T**

A mid-18thC mahogany 'handkerchief' table, the triangular top with conforming dropleaf above a plain frieze on turned legs ending in pad feet.

28in (71cm) high

£1,000-1,500   **L&T**

A Louis XVI ormolu-mounted mahogany 'vide poche', attributed to Jean-Henri Riesener, the rectangular top with hinged flat raised on columnar stiles continuing to fluted legs, raised on round tapered capped feet joined by an entwined shaped stretcher, the whole outlined with ormolu.

'Vide Poche' is the French term for a small table or dish in which the contents of pockets may be emptied.

c1775   *21.5in (54.5cm) wide*

£7,000-10,000   **FRE**

A late 18thC American Pennsylvania painted poplar table, the oblong battened lip top over a frame with a single drawer and turned legs terminating in pad feet, retaining its original red and yellow swirl decoration and brass hardware.

30in (76cm) high

£15,000-20,000   **POOK**

An early 19thC Swedish marble-top occasional table, in the Empire taste, the grey fossil marble top above a mahogany-veneered frieze on three painted and parcel-gilt inswept tapering legs headed by Egyptianesque carved bird head terminals and brass-strung amaranth tablet capitals, each leg with stiff leaf carving at its centre, united by a marble undertier.

29.5in (75cm) high

£2,000-3,000   **L&T**

A George IV mahogany side or centre table, with shaped top.

c1830   *43.75in (111cm) wide*

£700-900   **DN**

A French transitional walnut and tulipwood-inlaid petit table, the top of serpentine outline with moulded brass-bound edge, radially veneered and centred by a female sun mask, on cabriole legs, possibly reduced, united by a similarly veneered undershelf and ending in leaf-cast sabots with hoof feet.

17.75in (45cm) wide

£1,000-1,200   **L&T**

A 19thC scarlet japanned and gilt chinoiserie occasional table, the top with snap-over action, decorated with riverside pagodas and birds, on a slender spirally fluted baluster column and downswept tripod base painted with foliage, ending in giltwood ball feet.

30.25in (77cm) high

£600-800   **L&T**

A late 19thC French kingwood and tulipwood parquetry petit table, in the manner of Francois Linke, the top of serpentine outline with trellis bandings and raised brass-bound edge, the frieze with Rococo leaf-cast mounts, on cabriole legs with trailing leaf-cast putto mask figures ending in scroll-cast sabots.

29.5in (75cm) high

£2,000-3,000   **L&T**

A 19thC French rosewood, crossbanded and floral marquetry kidney-shaped occasional table, the top with heart motif pierced gallery and a festoon of wheat and flowers above a similarly inlaid frieze drawer and under-shelf, on cabriole legs, the whole with gilt-metal mounts ending in paw caster feet sabots.

27in (69cm) wide

£3,000-4,000   **L&T**

A 19thC Anglo-Indian Singhalese ebony and specimen wood occasional table, the octagonal top with radiating veneers and pewter line inlay, above a scroll-carved frieze, the acanthus-turned column support ending on a tripod base with claw-and-ball feet.

20.5in (52cm) wide

£1,500-2,000   **L&T**

A George IV style pollard oak coffee table, the rectangular cane top surmounted by a removable veneered centre section above a reeded frieze and raised on turned and reeded legs terminating in brass cappings and casters.

59.5in (151cm) wide

£2,500-3,000   **L&T**

A Louis XV style gilt-bronze-mounted marquetry two-tier side table, marquetry-inlaid graduating tiers raised on tapering legs ending in sabots.

38in (96.5cm) high

£7,000-10,000   **FRE**

A late 19th/early 20thC Middle Eastern hardwood camel carved occasional table, the kidney-shaped top with wide fruiting scrolling foliate-carved border, supported on the back of a naturalistically carved camel, standing on elongated octagonal plinth base.

30in (76cm)

£3,500-4,000   **L&T**

An Edwardian mahogany and marquetry occasional table, by James Shoolbred & Company.

c1910   *22in (56cm) wide*

£250-300   **DN**

FURNITURE

A late Georgian mahogany and satinwood-crossbanded sofa table, with two short drawers to the frieze, raised on splay legs terminating in brass capped feet and casters.

33.5in (85cm) wide

£1,200-1,500   A&G

An American Philadelphia Classical mahogany sofa table, rectangular top and conforming, round-cornered leaves with moulded edge on a moulded apron, raised on ring-turned and tapering reeded urn-form supports joined by scroll stretcher, arched leaf-carved and moulded legs ending in brass caps.

c1815   29.75in (75.5cm) wide

£3,000-4,000   FRE

A Scottish Regency mahogany and rosewood-crossbanded sofa table, with flame-figured top with quadrant beaded edge on a beaded platform base raised on hipped and moulded sabre legs ending in boldly cast foliate caps and casters.

41.75in (106cm) wide

£7,000-9,000   L&T

An unusually small Regency period mahogany sofa table, the top with a reeded edge above a frieze containing a drawer on one side, a dummy on the reverse, flanked by moulded tablets, raised on end supports and downswept legs decorated overall with reeded mouldings, in the manner of Gillows of Lancaster.

The reeded decoration to the end support as well as the legs is a feature found in recorded examples of the work of the Gillows workshop in Lancaster illustrated in the 'Gillow Archive', Westminster City Library, London.

c1815   28in (71cm) high

£10,000-15,000   RGA

A Regency rosewood and cut brass-inlaid table, on a pillar and platform base raised on sabre legs ending in paw caps and sabots, the whole decorated in brass arabesques and stringing.

28.5in (72cm) high

£2,000-2,500   L&T

A Regency rosewood and cut brass-inlaid sofa table, the end standards of waisted form, on dual splay sabre legs headed by gilt-metal rosettes and ending in lion paw caps and casters.

43.5in (110cm) wide

£4,000-5,000   L&T

A Regency mahogany sofa table, the rectangular top incorporating a pair of hinged flaps above two frieze drawers and two opposing false drawers, on square-section trestle supports, each issuing a pair of reeded downswept legs, brass caps and casters, repair.

c1820   37.5in (95cm) wide

£2,000-3,000   DN

A late Regency burr ash and oak sofa table, with central support and pedestal base.

c1825   65.5in (166cm) wide

£1,600-2,000   DN

A continental Biedermeier fruitwood sofa table, the moulded canted rectangular hinged twin-flap top above two frieze drawers, dummy drawers to the reverse, on faceted baluster column and shaped quadrapartite base with square tapering down scrolled legs with spreading feet.

56in (142cm) wide

£2,500-3,500   L&T

A Regency mahogany sofa table, faults.

c1820   28.25in (72cm) high

£600-800   DN

An American Federal cherry inlaid dropleaf table, probably southeastern New England, outlined in stringing, on conforming skirt centring a patera, refinished, minor imperfections.

c1790   20.25in (51.5cm) wide

£2,000-3,000   SK

A George III mahogany and crossbanded butterfly Pembroke table, damage.

c1790   27in (69cm) high

£650-750   DN

A late 18thC Chippendale walnut Pembroke table, rectangular top and shallow drop leaves, apron drawer with brass bail on square grooved and chamfered legs with X-stretcher.

Made from the 1750s, Pembroke tables were named after the first lady to order one. They had two side-flaps supported on hinged brackets which opened up to form the table top, and nearly all were fitted with casters. They were used for taking meals, playing cards, writing and needlework. They were largely replaced in the early 19thC by sofa tables.

47in (119.5cm) long

£1,500-2,000   FRE

An American Federal cherry-inlaid Pembroke table, from Rhode Island or Connecticut, inlaid with icicles and checkered stringing, and with faux and working inlaid drawers.

c1795

£3,500-4,500   SK

An American Federal mahogany-inlaid Pembroke table, probably from New York, edged and outlined in stringing, inlaid with ovals, and banded lower edge joining the square tapering legs, refinished, imperfections.

1795-1800

£2,000-3,000   SK

A Regency rosewood and satinwood-banded pedestal Pembroke table, damage.

c1820   28.75in (73cm) high

£1,500-2,000   DN

A George IV mahogany Pembroke worktable, with two drawers opposing false drawers.

c1825   16in (41cm) wide

£500-700   DN

A mahogany and marquetry Pembroke table, with frieze drawer at one end.

c1900   30in (76cm) wide

£400-600   DN

A George III mahogany folding card table, with faults.

c1780   35.75in (91cm) wide
£200-300   **DN**

A George III mahogany folding card table, with faults.

c1780   35.75in (91cm) wide
£200-300   **DN**

A George III mahogany folding card table, with faults.

c1780   35.75in (91cm) wide
£200-300   **DN**

A Dutch walnut and floral marquetry serpentine folding card table, damage, repair.

c1780   28.25in (72cm) wide
£2,300-2,500   **DN**

A George III mahogany and rosewood-crossbanded demi-lune foldover card table, the top decorated with an arched band of engraved marquetry leaf fronds above a boxwood-strung frieze, on square tapering legs with gaitered feet.

38.25in (97cm) wide
£5,000-6,000   **L&T**

A satinwood and tulipwood-crossbanded folding card table, the D-shaped top opening to a baize inset, above a plain frieze centred by a tablet panel with oval reserve, on square-section tapering legs, on later spade feet.

c1810   37in (94cm) wide
£2,000-3,000   **DN**

A George III mahogany and marquetry demi-lune card table, bears Leeds City Art Gallery paper label.

c1810   41.75in (106cm) wide
£800-1,200   **DN**

A Regency rosewood and satinwood-banded folding card table.

c1820   36in (91cm) wide
£500-700   **DN**

A Regency mahogany and brass-inlaid card table, the rectangular top with canted corners and inlay of scrolling brass work against an ebonised ground, the frieze with conforming brass inlay and ebony stringing, on ring-turned tapering legs with ball feet.

35.5in (90cm) wide
£800-1,200   **DUK**

A Regency rosewood and satinwood-banded card table, damage, with repair.

c1820   35.75in (91cm) wide
£900-1,200   **DN**

A Regency rosewood folding card table, damage, with repair.

c1820   36.25in (92cm) wide
£500-700   **DN**

A Regency mahogany and kingwood-crossbanded folding card table, the rectangular top with canted front corners above twin shaped trestle supports and a shaped stretcher, each trestle issuing a pair of down-swept legs, on gilt-brass lion paw caps and casters, damage.

c1820   35.75in (91cm) wide
£350-450   **DN**

A Regency pollard oak and ebony-strung card table, with faults.

c1820   35in (89cm) wide
£1,000-1,500   **DN**

A late Regency rosewood card table, probably by Gillows of Lancaster, the beaded swivel top with baize inset above a faceted spreading column decorated with two bold graduated bands of beading on a quadrapartite platform base raised on scroll-cut feet with gilt-metal shell caps and casters.

The Gillows sketch book illustrates several foldover tables with this distinctive treatment of the column i.e. both spreading and faceted with graduated rows of beaded or gadrooned moulding.

36.5in (93cm) wide

£3,000-4,000   L&T

A 19thC black boulle marquetry folding card table, of serpentine rectangular form, the top inlaid with brass, the frieze inlaid to all four sides, between cabriole legs on gilt sabots.

35in (89cm) wide

£3,000-4,000   DN

A George IV mahogany and satinwood-crossbanded folding card table, the D-shaped top above a plain frieze on turned and reeded tapering legs, repair.

c1825   36.25in (92cm) wide

£900-1,200   DN

A Victorian walnut folding card table, faults.

c1870   36.25in (92cm) wide

£500-700   DN

A Victorian burr walnut envelope card table, the moulded edged swivel top opening to reveal green baize lining, frieze drawer with turned wood handles, on turned tapering and fluted legs with brass toes and casters.

23in (58.5cm) wide

£700-900   HT

TEA TABLES

A George II mahogany tea table of dished rounded oblong form, plain frieze on club legs with pad feet.

27in (68.5cm) wide

£2,000-2,500   HT

A George III mahogany folding tea table.

c1790   34.25in (87cm) wide

£400-600   DN

A George II carved mahogany serpentine front tea table, with frieze drawer below the hinged top.

c1740   36.25in (92cm) wide

£1,000-1,500   DN

FURNITURE

A George III mahogany demi-lune folding tea table.
c1790   *35.75in (91cm) wide*
£700-1,000   **DN**

A Regency mahogany tea table, the D-shaped folding top above the strung frieze, on turned tapering legs.
c1820   *35.75in (91cm) wide*
£450-550   **DN**

A Victorian ebony and yew wood folding tea table, of oblong form, with marquetry and gilt-metal mounts, the swivel top with central cartouche depicting a vase of flowers on a scrolling foliate ground, opening to reveal interior with shaped baize lining, the mildly breakfront fascia with projecting corners, raised on fluted turned tapering legs with brass toes.
34in (86.5cm) wide
£1,200-1,800   **HT**

A probably Continental mahogany folding tea table, the rectangular top with waved edge above a conforming frieze on a pierced shaped stem and plinth base, with four scroll feet and later casters, damage.
c1870   *33.75in (86cm) wide*
£400-600   **DN**

GAMES TABLE

A George II mahogany fold-over games table, the top with projecting re-entrant corners enclosing guinea wells and baize inset above a frieze drawer in a cockbeaded surround, on lappet-carved tapering legs, with gate action, on pad feet.
35in (89cm) wide
£1,500-2,000   **L&T**

A Regency period rosewood and line-inlaid foldover games table, the rectangular top with canted corners and swivel action above a frieze with four canted corners, on four inswept scrolling legs, fluted and gilded on the angles, headed by giltwood ball capitals, ending in brass paw cappings and casters.
36.75in (93cm) wide
£1,500-2,000   **L&T**

A 19thC and later Regency style rosewood and satinwood-inlaid combined games and sofa table, the rectangular top incorporating a pair of hinged flaps, and centred by an inlaid chess board, the sliding section revealing the backgammon board, above a false drawer and a drawer, and two opposing false drawers, on square section trestle supports, each issuing a pair of downswept legs with brass caps and casters.
29in (74cm) wide
£1,500-2,500   **DN**

A Regency period mahogany and zebrawood-crossbanded foldover games table, the rounded rectangular top with broad crossbanded edge and subsidiary inner banded lines above conforming inlaid frieze, on four ring-turned part-ebonised pillar supports and four reeded tapering sabre legs ending in brass paw caps and casters.
34.75in (88cm) wide
£3,500-4,500   **L&T**

A 19thC walnut, purpleheart and bird's-eye maple-veneered fold-over games table, in the manner of Gillows of Lancaster, the top with arabesque inlaid corners enclosing a baize inset above an extending drawer with detachable side frieze mounts forming a centre standing table, the sunken frieze with central lozenge above turned and fluted tapering legs, the whole with banded and line-inlaid decoration.

35.75in (91cm) wide

£3,000-4,000   L&T

A 19thC Victorian burl walnut games table, by A. Blain, Liverpool, the shaped hinged triangular top opening to a baize inset surface marked at the corners with dishes, raised on cabriole legs with acorn and leaf-carved toes ending in casters, the slide out back with runners stamped.

48in (122cm) wide

£700-1,000   FRE

A 19thC Anglo-Indian games table, the octagonal top inlaid with an ivory and carved hardwood games surface, above a sectioned frieze with carved figural panels and four sandalwood-lined fitted drawers, on an octagonal carved column support raised on a carved four-point star base.

26in (66cm) high

£1,200-1,800   FRE

A Victorian burr walnut serpentine folding games table.

c1870   *35.75in (91cm) wide*

£1,000-1,500   DN

A Victorian japanned papier mâché gilt-painted pedestal games table, the circular top with mother-of-pearl chequer board centre on a slender baluster support and a circular platform on three short splay feet.

24.25in (61.5cm) diam

£350-450   HALL

A Louis XVI style gilt-bronze-mounted mahogany fold-over games table, by Gervais-Maximillien-Eugene Durand.

c1880   *33.25in (84cm) wide*

£3,500-4,500   FRE

A Napoleon III gilt-bronze-mounted burl walnut, marquetry and ebonised game table, the rectangular top with rounded fore corners inlaid with a flower-filled urn opening to a baize-lined playing surface, raised on round tapered stop-fluted legs.

c1890   *33in (84cm) wide*

£1,200-1,800   FRE

FURNITURE

A Louis XVI mahogany rafraichissoir, attributed to Jean-Joseph Gegenbach Dit Canabas, the rectangular top inset with grey marble and a pair of copper liners flanked by wells, above a plain rounded frieze with one drawer raised on slightly hipped abriole legs joined by two platform stretchers, ending in casters.

c1770   24in (61cm) high

£5,000-7,000   FRE

A George II oak lowboy, the rectangular top with cavetto-moulded edge above a full width caddy-moulded frieze drawer and a scroll-carved apron flanked by two conforming short drawers with brass open back plated drop handles, on tapering legs ending in pointed pad feet.

A Louis XV ormolu-mounted tulipwood and bois de bout poudreuse, the rectangular top with a hinged centre section with a mirror on the reverse, flanked by hinged side panels opening on velvet-lined wells above a slide-out writing surface and single drawer flanked by an arrangement of drawers and raised on slightly hipped cabriole legs ending in scrolling leaf-cast sabots, the whole inlaid with foliate sprays, the underside bearing spurious 'BVRB jme' stamp.

A George III mahogany kneehole dressing table.

30in (76cm) wide   *c1760   35.75in (90cm) wide*   *c1790*   *38.25in (97cm) wide*

£1,000-1,500   L&T   **£2,000-3,000   FRE**   **£300-500**   **DN**

A Louis XVI walnut, tulipwood, harewood and marquetry poudreuse, the central hinged flap on a ratchet support between a pair of similar hinged covers revealing a partially fitted interior, on bell flower-inlaid square tapering legs ending in fluted brass sabots.

A late George III bowfront mahogany dressing table, damage, repair.

c1790   31in (79cm) wide   *35.5in (90cm) wide*

£4,000-5,000   L&T   **£400-600**   **DN**

An Irish Regency mahogany dressing table, possibly Cork, the rounded rectangular top with a solid three-quarter gallery, above a central frieze drawer and arched reeded apron, flanked by two further short drawers to either side, raised on spiral reeded legs terminating in brass cappings and casters.

A Regency mahogany and ebony-strung gentleman's enclosed dressing table, the rectangular hinged top opening to a fitted interior, incorporating a raising mirror and later lidded compartments above an arrangement of four drawers and a commode drawer on turned tapering legs, gilt-brass caps and casters, damage, repair.

48in (122cm) wide   *c1820   22.75in (58cm) wide*

£5,000-6,000   L&T   **£600-800   DN**

FURNITURE

A 19thC Dutch mahogany and marquetry dressing table, lacks mirror supports, inlaid throughout with scrolling foliage, the oval mirror over a rectangular top and one frieze drawer, raised on twin scroll supports with carved paw feet.

39in (99cm) wide

£1,500-2,000 FRE

A Sheraton Revival satinwood and rosewood-crossbanded dressing table, the rounded rectangular swing mirror with re-entrant corners between slender uprights and two stage back drawers above a re-entrant cornered top enclosing a pair of frieze drawers on slender tapering legs inlaid with ebony lines on spade feet.

35.75in (91cm) wide

£2,000-3,000 L&T

A 20thC George III style satinwood gentleman's enclosed dressing table, the rectangular top incorporating two hinged flaps enclosing a fitted interior, with central ratchet-adjustable mirror flanked by lidded compartments, repair.

24.75in (63cm) wide

£500-700 DN

TRIPOD TABLES

A George III mahogany 'pie crust' occasional table, in the Chippendale manner, the top of serpentine outline with raised edge and a snap-over action above a turned and incised baluster column, on a cabriole tripod base ending in pointed pad feet.

28in (71cm) high

£3,000-4,000 L&T

A George III mahogany tripod table, the circular top with pie crust edge above the baluster-turned stem, on three downswept legs with stylised pad feet.

c1760 *29.5in (75cm) diam*

£2,000-3,000 DN

A George III mahogany supper table, the circular top pierced and carved with dish wells, each enclosed by leaf carving, raised on a leaf-carved standard and a tripod base, ending in claw-and-ball feet.

c1760 *32in (81cm) diam*

£3,500-4,500 FRE

A George II style mahogany tea table, the pie crust top over a birdcage and foliate-carved baluster standard with carved cabriole legs terminating in pad feet.

c1760 *29in (73.75cm) diam*

£700-1,000 POOK

A late 18thC George III brass-inlaid mahogany tilt-top tea table, the shaped rectangular top with a brass-inlaid balustered gallery, raised on a turned standard and tripod base, ending in slippered feet.

21.25in (54cm) wide

£5,000-7,000   **FRE**

A George III mahogany birdcage tripod table, the circular dished top and fluted column support raised on acanthus-carved cabriole legs ending in claw-and-ball feet.

31.5in (80cm) wide

£4,500-5,500   **L&T**

CLOSER LOOK: TRIPOD TABLE

The top is of an unusual undulating serpentine outline, which is a Chinese interpretation of a British pie crust edge, taken from an engraving.

A label underneath the top reads 'Lord Rofslyn'.

The spirally reeded baluster column and cabriole tripod base are engraved with rocaille decoration.

The feet are fitted with small recessed brass casters.

Brass mounts on the knees are a typical feature of Chinese Export furniture.

A rare George III padouk and brass-mounted 'Chinese Export' tilt-top occasional table.

25in (64cm) wide

£30,000-40,000   **L&T**

A George III mahogany tripod table, the circular tilt-top and vase-shaped turned column support raised on three cabriole legs ending in pointed pad feet.

29.5in (75cm) diam

£2,500-3,500   **L&T**

An unusual George III mahogany occasional table, the triangular top with three drop leaves on fly arm supports, above a fluted column with egg and dart-carved collar, on a shell and leaf-carved cabriole tripod base ending in claw feet, formerly with brass casters.

27.5in (70cm) wide

£3,500-4,500   **L&T**

A George III mahogany tripod table, the circular top and turned column support ending on three cabriole legs terminating in pad feet.

28.25in (71.5cm) high

£2,000-2,500   **L&T**

A late George III satinwood and kingwood-banded tripod table, the oval crossbanded top on a baluster-turned stem, above three downswept legs on spade feet, repair.

28.75in (73cm) high

£650-850   **DN**

A 19thC George III style carved mahogany supper table.

29.25in (72cm) high

£900-1,200   **DN**

An oak and pollard oak tripod table, with repair.

c1825 and later.   *33.75in (86cm) diam*

£700-1,000   **DN**

FURNITURE

A late George III satinwood and purpleheart-crossbanded oval work table, the hinged top above a cylindrical wool well, on slender tapering legs, requiring restoration.

21.75in (53cm) wide

£2,500-3,500   **L&T**

An American Federal mahogany work table, school of John and Thomas Seymour, Boston, the top with ovolo corners above two cockbeaded drawers, the ends with flame mahogany panels bordered with cockbeading, with pull-out bag frame to the right, all on quarter-engaged fluted vase and ring-turned reeded and tapering legs on turned feet and brass cap casters, replaced brasses, old finish.

c1805   30.5in (77.5cm) high

£12,000-15,000   **SK**

An American Federal inlaid mahogany sewing table, attributed to John and Thomas Seymour, Boston, Massachusetts, octagonal band inlaid top with single compartmented drawer, bag drawer below, on ring-turned and slender vasiform reeded posts, tall turned feet.

c1810   27.25in (69cm) high

£7,000-10,000   **FRE**

A George III style Edwardian satinwood and polychrome-painted work table, the octagonal hinged top above a foliate-painted frieze, on square-section tapering legs and an X-shaped stretcher.

c1910   16in (41cm) wide

£1,000-1,200   **DN**

A pair of Edwardian George III style mahogany and inlaid work tables.

c1910   16.25in (41cm) wide

£450-650 PAIR   **DN**

An American New England, Federal pine polychrome and gilt-decorated work table, the top painted with a landscape showing a group of buildings at a water's edge with an oval reserve, bordered by flowers and cornucopias, the sides and legs decorated with a variety of flowers, seashells and leafy wreaths, imperfections, paint wear.

c1810   28.75in (73cm) high

£5,000-6,000   **SK**

A Regency mahogany and ebony-strung work table, the hinged top on ratchet support and inlaid with a brass star to each corner, on lyre-shaped end standings applied with brass wires, on dual splay legs ending in Rococo cast caps and casters.

30in (76cm) high

£1,500-2,000   **L&T**

A Regency rosewood and boxwood-strung oval drum-shaped work table, the hinged lid enclosing a lined interior above two false drawers on a turned and parcel-gilt column and four sabre legs on ball feet.

c1820   32in (81cm) high

£1,500-2,500   **DN**

A Regency mahogany and sycamore-strung workbox on stand, with knopped legs and casters.

c1820   18.5in (47cm) wide

£700-1,000   **DN**

A Regency rosewood combined games and work table, the sliding and ratchet adjustable top opening to a backgammon board.

c1820   24.5in (62.5cm) wide

£1,500-2,000   **DN**

An early 19thC, possibly Irish, yew wood and specimen wood pedestal table, the rectangular top inlaid with a central radiating veneer design with fan spandrels, cross and feather banding, the frieze with a reel-moulded drawer, divided with a central pin cushion, on a ring-turned baluster stem to quatreform base on bun feet, one foot missing, minor veneer loss.

21in (53.5cm) wide

£1,500-2,000   **WW**

A William IV rosewood work table, the rectangular top with rounded corners above a fitted frieze drawer and upholstered needlework basket, on square tapering uprights with platform feet, with applied turned decoration and lobed feet.

24in (61cm) wide

£1,300-1,500 DUK

A mid-19thC mahogany Pembroke work table, the rectangular top incorporating twin hinged flaps, above two short and one long drawer, and three opposing false drawers, on turned tapering legs, brass caps and casters, damage.

19in (48cm) wide

£400-600 DN

A mid-19thC Anglo-Indian rosewood work table, with a fitted interior of compartments above a leaf and roundel-carved frieze with scrolled angle frets and wool well, on a foliate-carved and pierced trestle base with inscrolling feet.

32.25in (82cm) wide

£2,000-3,000 L&T

A 19thC American New England Sheraton tiger maple work stand, with three drawers and turned legs, the middle drawer inscribed on underside 'Clark Van Gorden Feb. 12 1856'.

17.25in (43.75cm) wide

£2,000-2,500 POOK

A Napoleon III gilt-bronze mounted tortoiseshell and brass boule marquetry ebonised and rosewood sewing table, the shaped rectangular top monogrammed 'NP', opening to a mirror on the reverse and an interior fitted with a sliding shelf above a slide out basket raised on cabriole legs, cast at the knees with chutes continuing to shell-cast sabots.

c1860

22.5in (57cm) high

£1,200-1,800 FRE

A Victorian rosewood combined games and work table, the rectangular top with central chess board above a drawer and sliding workbag on twin spiral-turned supports, and trestle feet with a stretcher and on four carved lion paw feet with concealed casters.

c1860

20.75in (53cm) wide

£400-600 DN

A Victorian figured walnut combined games and work table, the rectangular hinged top with bird's eye maple and walnut chessboard, opening to reveal a divided interior and workbag, above scroll terminals and a baluster-turned stem above cabriole-shaped downswept and cabochon-carved legs with scroll-carved feet, and brass casters, damage, repair.

19.75in (50cm) wide

£400-600 DN

A late 19thC Victorian rosewood and sycamore-strung work table, the hinged cover with mirror within, losses.

22.5in (57cm) wide

£300-500 DN

A French gilt-metal-mounted oval work table, the marble top with pierced three-quarter gallery, above a drawer and a solid undertier, cabriole shaped square-section legs with gilt-metal terminals and sabots.

23.5in (60cm) wide

£700-900 DN

An Edwardian satinwood octagonal work table, the hinged top opening to a removable tray incorporating open and lidded compartments, above pleated fabric covered sides, on square-section tapering legs, damage.

c1910

29.25in (74cm) high

£600-800 DN

An Edwardian mahogany oval worktable, the hinged rectangular top above a workbag, on square-section tapering legs and an X-shaped stretcher, on spade feet.

19.25in (49cm) wide

£450-650 DN

FURNITURE

A George III mahogany butler's tray, on later stand, the oval tray with hinged sides each with pierced handle apertures, damage, repairs.

c1790   Tray 26in (66cm) wide
£600-800   DN

A George III mahogany tray on stand.

c1800 and later   35.5in (90cm) high
£600-800   DN

A George IV mahogany and brass-bound butler's tray on stand, the hinged oval top with twin brass loop carrying handles, raised on a folding X-form stand.

39.54in (101cm) wide
£2,000-2,500   L&T

A George III style mahogany butler's tray on low stand.

£550-750   DN

A satinwood tricoteuse table in late 18thC style, the rectangular tray top with gallery incorporating a folding front section, on twin pierced and shaped trestle ends, with a galleried undertier, and each issuing a pair of downswept legs on casters.

c1910   22in (56cm) wide
£1,200-1,800   DN

A large English tôle tray.

c1800   25in (63.5cm) wide
£1,800-2,200   POOK

An early 19thC tôle oval tray, painted with Brook Watson being attacked by a shark in Havana harbour after John Singleton Copley 1778, the gilt-leaf-decorated gallery with pierced hand grips.

30in (76cm) wide
£1,200-1,500   WW

A late 18thC George III brass-bound mahogany tray of oval form with a scrolling handle at each end.

21.75in (55cm) long
£500-700   DN

An early 19thC Dutch mahogany and marquetry oval tray, decorated throughout with floral marquetry, with twin pierced handles to the gallery, damage, repair.

27.5in (70cm) wide
£100-150   DN

A William IV rosewood letter tray, with ring-turned handles.

11.25in (28.5cm) wide
£350-450   WW

A Victorian black lacquered and mother-of-pearl-inset papier-mâché tray, of cartouche form, the centre decorated with birds around an urn of flowers, with parcel-gilt foliate decoration to the raised edge.

c1880   17.75in (45cm) wide
£250-350   DN

A Victorian papier-mâché, gilt and mother-of-pearl-inlaid tray, of oval dished scalloped form, decorated with trees, foliage, boats, figures butterflies and pagodas.

30.25in (77cm) wide
£1,000-1,500   L&T

A Victorian black lacquer and polychrome-painted papier-mâché tray, decorated with pheasants and foliage.

30.75in (78cm) long
£1,500-2,000   DN

An Edwardian mahogany and marquetry oval tray.

c1910   26in (66cm) wide
£150-200   DN

A French walnut and iron-bound chest, in late Gothic style, the studded iron banding pierced with trefoils and terminating fleur-de-lys, on a plinth base, incorporating 15thC elements.

75.5in (192cm) wide

£5,000-6,000   SOTA

A Continental walnut and wrought iron-bound coffre fort, probably late 16th/early 17thC, of rectangular form with multiple iron straps attached by rivets secured by scrolled under-wires verso and an iron hasp and staple lock, the corners also reinforced with angle irons, the hinged top revealing a void, on short baluster-turned feet.

38in (97cm) wide

£2,500-3,500   L&T

A late 16th/early 17thC style panelled oak chest, the hinged lid above the twin-panelled front, centred by bog oak and holly parquetry lozenges, above shaped brackets and stile feet, repair.

30.25in (77cm) wide

£1,500-2,000   DN

A Charles II and later panelled oak chest, the hinged rectangular top above a triple-panelled front and frieze carved with lunette and foliate motifs, on later stile feet, repair, later elements.

44.5in (113cm) wide

£300-400   DN

A Charles II panelled oak chest, with damage, repair.

c1670   *48in (122cm) wide*

£250-350   DN

A Charles II oak mule chest.

c1680   *30.75in (129cm) wide*

£1,500-2,000   DN

A late 17th/early 18thC oak and elm boarded chest, the hinged rectangular top above later carved initials 'G M', on integral seat, damage, later elements to feet.

18in (46cm) wide

£350-450   DN

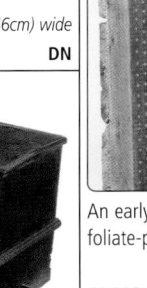

A mid-18thC Welsh oak coffer bach, the moulded edge top with later hinges, with a twin fielded panel front above a girdle moulding and two drawers, fitted later brass plate handles, on bracket feet.

26in (66cm) wide

£600-800   WW

An early 18thC and later North Italian carved cypress wood, coffer with foliate-panelled front, the cover interior with pen and ink decoration.

56.75in (144cm) wide

£1,500-2,000   DN

A George III oak mule chest, with damage.

c1780   *59in (150cm) wide*

£400-500   **DN**

A George III oak and mahogany crossbanded mule chest, the hinged top above six false drawers and three drawers, on ogee bracket feet.

65.75in (167cm) wide

£2,500-3,500   **DN**

A 19thC Italian hardwood and bone-inlaid cassone, the moulded rectangular hinged lid with central chequer-inlaid panel, above a moulded triple-panelled front, on moulded base with bracket feet.

49.25in (125cm) wide

£2,500-3,500   **L&T**

A 19thC camphorwood and brass-bound campaign chest, of impressive proportions, the hinged top with central plaque above doubled recessed handles and lock escutcheons flanked by brass drop carrying handles.

60in (137cm) wide

£2,500-3,500   **L&T**

A late 18thC Venetian cedar wood chest, decorated overall with pokerwork figural scenes and motifs in the Renaissance style, the centre of the hinged, rectangular cover with a monumental armorial on a cross-hatched ground, flanked by rectangular reserves depicting nobles and soldiers in landscapes, with conforming sides and front, with iron lock and key, restoration, later casters.

63.75in (162cm) wide

£800-1,200   **DN**

CHESTS-OF-DRAWERS

A late 17thC fruitwood small chest, with a moulded edge top and three graduated geometric panel front drawers fitted with face drop handles, split style mouldings on later bracket feet, old worm.

32.25in (82cm) wide

£2,000-3,000   **WW**

A Charles II oak chest-of-drawers, the rectangular top above two short and three long mitre panel drawers, on later turned feet, damage, repairs.

c1680   *39.75in (101cm) wide*

£800-1,200   **DN**

A Charles II panelled oak chest-of-drawers, the rectangular top with moulded edge above four long panel drawers, on plinth base, damage, lacking feet.

c1680   *41.25in (105cm) wide*

£800-1,200   **DN**

A Charles II panelled oak chest-of-drawers, the rectangular top with moulded edge above four long panel drawers, on plinth base, damage, lacking feet.

c1680   *41.25in (105cm) wide*

£800-1,200   **DN**

An English William & Mary oak and pine chest-of-drawers, with a moulded edge top overhanging a case with four drawers with applied mouldings forming geometric panels, resting on ball front feet.

36in (91.5cm) high

£1,500-2,000   **POOK**

A late 17thC stained oak chest, the rectangular top with moulded edge above four long geometrically panelled drawers with bifurcated scroll handles and pierced escutcheons, the sides of plain single panel form, on skirted base and bun feet.

38.5in (98cm) wide

£1,000-1,500   **L&T**

CLOSER LOOK: CHARLES II CHEST

Following the Restoration of Charles II in 1660, walnut became the most popular wood for English furniture.

The building boom that followed the Great Fire of London in 1666 led to specialisation within the furniture trade. Chests and other case furniture were made by cabinetmakers while chair making became a specialised task. While the nobility commissioned extravagant pieces of furniture, simpler well-crafted pieces were made for city merchants and the country gentry.

This chest has deep, crisp carving which is evidence that it was made by a skilled craftsman.

Decorative techniques such as marquetry also became common – probably as a reaction to the severity of design during Oliver Cromwell's rule.

A Charles II walnut, oak and bone marquetry chest-of-drawers.
c1680   *36.25in (92cm) wide*
£4,000-5,000   **DN**

A late 17thC Charles II yew wood chest-of-drawers, the moulded rectangular top over two short drawers and three graduated long drawers, raised on stile feet.
38in (96.5cm) wide
£2,500-3,500   **FRE**

A late 17thC William and Mary oak chest-of-drawers, the rectangular top above three graduated drawers, each with carved and fielded panels, raised on bracket feet.
32.75in (83cm) wide
£1,000-1,500   **FRE**

A walnut-veneered and oak-crossbanded chest in the George I manner, the quarter-veneered top with herringbone-banded and crossbanded edge, the graduated and lipped drawers with brass drop handles between caddy moulded uprights, on skirted base with bracket feet.
30in (76cm) wide
£1,000-2,000   **L&T**

A George II burr walnut and featherbanded chest-of-drawers, the quarter-veneered top with moulded edge above a brushing slide.
c1735   *228.5in (90cm) wide*
£13,000-18,000   **DN**

A George II mahogany dressing chest, the caddy-moulded top with a brushing side, cockbeaded drawers, with solid brass escutcheons and ring handles.
34in (86cm) wide
£2,500-3,500   **L&T**

An early 18thC and later oak and walnut chest-of-drawers, the rectangular top above two short and three long graduated drawers, on bracket feet, damage, repair.
39.75in (101cm) wide
£800-1,200   **DN**

A mid-18thC burr elm and chequer-banded chest, with quarter-veneered top, the cockbeaded drawers with Rococo cast brass handles and escutcheons, on bracket feet.
31in (79cm) wide
£10,000-12,000   **L&T**

A mid-18thC George II mahogany chest of four graduated drawers, with slide.
30.75in (78cm) wide
£1,000-1,500   **DN**

A Continental, probably South German, walnut serpentine-fronted chest-of-drawers.

c1750   45.75in (116cm) wide
£1,500-2,000   DN

An early George III oak chest-of-drawers.

c1760   36.25in (92cm) wide
£700-1,000   DN

An early George III elm chest-of-drawers.

c1760   37.75in (96cm) wide
£800-1,200   DN

A George III mahogany serpentine chest-of-drawers, the rectangular-shaped top above four long graduated drawers, on shaped bracket feet.

c1770   39.75in (101cm) wide
£1,800-2,200   DN

A George III oak chest-of-drawers, the rectangular top above two short and three long graduated drawers, on bracket feet, damage.

c1780   37.5in (95cm) wide
£700-1,000   DN

A George III oak chest-of-drawers.

c1780   37.75in (96cm) wide
£500-800   DN

A George III mahogany crossbanded chest-of-drawers.

c1780   36.5in (93cm) wide
£700-1,000   DN

A George III mahogany chest-of-drawers, with a brushing slide.

c1780   200.5in (79cm) wide
£1,200-1,800   DN

A Dutch walnut and floral marquetry chest-of-drawers, of serpentine outline, damage, repair.

c1780   34.25in (87cm) wide
£2,000-3,000   DN

A George III mahogany serpentine chest-of-drawers, with damage.
c1790   41.75in (106cm) wide
£5,000-6,000   DN

A George III mahogany serpentine chest, the top with moulded edge and projecting corners above two short over three long graduated and cockbeaded drawers with brass drop handles, on bracket feet.

44in (112cm) wide
£6,000-8,000   L&T

A small 18thC and later walnut dressing chest, with feather and crossbanding, the burr-veneered top with a slide, the drawers with replaced handles and escutcheons, on bracket feet

£2,500-3,500   WW

A George III oak and mahogany crossbanded chest-of-drawers, the rectangular top above two short and three long graduated drawers, on bracket feet.

c1810   44in (112cm) wide
£500-800   DN

A late George III mahogany serpentine chest, the boxwood-strung top with crossbanded edge, above four cockbeaded drawers with bone escutcheons and brass pull handles, on shaped apron and high splayed bracket feet.

37.5in (95cm) wide
£3,500-4,500   L&T

A George III mahogany chest-of-drawers, attributed to Gillows, the moulded top over a brushing slide and four long graduated drawers flanked by fluted quarter columns, raised on splayed bracket feet.

43in (109cm) wide
£2,000-3,000   L&T

A Regency mahogany and ebony-strung bowfront chest, the top with crossbanded frieze above four long graduated drawers and oval stamped brass handles emblematic of Nelson's battles, on splayed bracket feet.

36.25in (92cm) high
£2,000-3,000   L&T

An early 19thC mahogany and marble-topped chest, in the Empire taste, possibly Russian, the drawers with lion mask ring handles and anthemion cast escutcheons, with similar mounts to uprights, legs with front facing gilt-metal paw feet.

36.5in (92.5cm) wide
£3,000-4,000   L&T

A Regency mahogany bowfront chest-of-drawers, with repair.

c1820   42in (107cm) wide
£600-800   DN

A Regency mahogany bowfront chest-of-drawers.

c1820   *44in (112cm) wide*

£600-800   **DN**

A Regency mahogany bowfront chest-of-drawers.

c1820   *42in (107cm) wide*

£600-800   **DN**

A 19thC Dutch walnut marquetry serpentine chest, profusely inlaid with floral marquetry all over, the moulded shaped rectangular top above three shaped long drawers, with carved paterae escutcheons, on ogee bracket feet.

49.25in (125cm) wide

£2,500-3,500   **L&T**

A Victorian burr walnut chest-of-drawers, the moulded top over four long drawers, flanked by canted Doric-form fluted corners, raised on a plinth base.

25.25in (64cm) wide

£6,000-8,000   **L&T**

A Victorian mahogany and brass band campaign chest-of-drawers, the rectangular top above two short and three long graduated drawers, on turn feet, damage.

c1870   *39in (99cm) wide*

£600-800   **DN**

A late 19thC mahogany and crossbanded campaign chest, the sides with brass drop carrying handles.

40in (102cm) wide

£1,200-1,800   **L&T**

ESSENTIAL REFERENCE: CAMPAIGN FURNITURE

A Victorian hardwood campaign secrétaire chest-of-drawers, the upper central drawer with fall front opening to small drawers and pigeon holes.

Campaign – or 'knockdown' – furniture was designed to be luxurious yet easily portable. An essential part of any wealthy military officer's equipment it might be as simple as a folding chair or as extravagant as a half-tester bed.

The earliest pieces were probably made during the Napoleonic Wars (1800-15). The most popular piece was the Wellington chest, named after the famous Duke and featuring a hinged, lockable bar which secured the drawers.

Later in the 19thC the brass-bound chest-of-drawers became the staple piece of campaign furniture.

Campaign furniture might be screwed together and even flat packed for transportation. Sometimes even the crates could be used as furniture.

Features include inset handles, detachable feet and brass-bound corners.

c1860   *41.75in (106cm) wide*

£1,200-1,800   **DN**

A pair of early 20thC Louis XV style mahogany, rosewood and elm chests-of-drawers, on cabriole legs.

12.5in (32cm) wide

£1,000-1,500   **FRE**

An Edwardian painted satinwood tall chest-of-drawers, raised on turned legs.

42in (106.5cm) wide

£1,500-2,000   **FRE**

A mid 18thC German Baroque walnut commode, possibly Dresden, the waved front accommodating four long drawers, on bun feet.

44in (112cm) wide

£4,000-5,000   **SOTH**

A Swedish Rococo gilt-brass-mounted walnut and sycamore commode, the liver-veined marble top of serpentine outline above three short feather-banded drawers and two long drawers, raised on slightly splayed bracket feet.

c1750   *51in (129.5cm) wide*

£3,500-4,500   **FRE**

CLOSER LOOK: GEORGE III COMMODE

Henry Hill was a cabinet maker, auctioneer and agent for the Sun Insurance Company from about 1740 to 1777. Although he gained commissions from elsewhere, his clientele was mostly based in his native county of Wiltshire.

The well-fashioned serpentine front is a sign of quality craftsmanship.

The keeled front angles and distinctively shaped apron, as well as thick cockbeaded mouldings are characteristic of the work of Henry Hill of Marlborough.

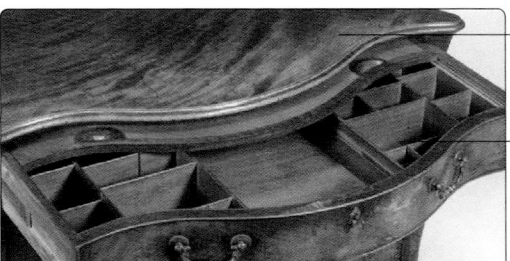

The well-figured mahogany top has excellent patination

The brushing slide reveals an arrangement of fitted compartments, which again indicates a piece of fine quality.

A George III mahogany serpentine-fronted commode attributed to Henry Hill of Marlborough, the top drawer opening to a baize-inset slide, moving to reveal an arrangement of compartments, lacking former ratchet adjustable mirror.

c1770   *41.75in (106cm) wide*

£35,000-40,000   **DN**

A kingwood, rosewood and amaranth marquetry commode, stamped 'F.RUBESTUCK', white marble top above breakfront housing three frieze drawers and a pair of long drawers inlaid with an arrangement of musical trophies flanked by panels depicting scientific trophies, the sides inlaid en suite, applied with mounts of gilt-bronze, raised on cabriole legs.

Francois Rübestuck (c1722-1785), in spite of a relatively short career, demonstrated great ability to interpret the styles of his day: the Louis XV period, the Transitional period, and the Louis XVI period. He is notable for a number of commodes and secrétaires veneered in Chinese or Japanese lacquer of the Louis XV period. His later work is notable for its marquetry panels, particularly those depicting musical trophies.

c1770   *58.25in (148cm) wide*

£35,000-40,000   **SOTA**

A Transitional tulipwood, stained fruitwood and amaranth marble top commode, the marble top of breakfront outline above two drawers with quarter-veneered reserves, the side panels veneered to match, raised on slightly hipped cabriole legs ending in sabots, stamped 'Stumpf, JME'.

c1770   *38in (96.5cm) wide*

£2,000-3,000   **FRE**

FURNITURE

A German small Neoclassical commode, veneered in fruitwood, tulipwood and ebonised wood forming a trellis at the top, cubicle parquetry to the sides.

c1780   30.25in (77cm) wide

£3,500-4,500   SOTA

A late 18thC Louis XVI rosewood and parquetry commode, possibly by Stumpf, the red-grey marble top above three short drawers and two long drawers, raised on square tapered legs, the whole inlaid with parquetry reserves, the sides veneered with diaper panels.

49.5in (126cm) high

£6,000-8,000   FRE

A George III mahogany commode, the shaped top of serpentine form over four long graduated drawers raised on splayed bracket feet.

c1780   42in (106.5cm) wide

£1,500-2,000   FRE

An 18thC Dutch burr walnut bombé commode, the serpentine-moulded top over three long graduated drawers, flanked by outset corners, raised on scroll feet.

32.75in (83cm) wide

£1,200-1,800   L&T

ESSENTIAL REFERENCE: MARQUETRY

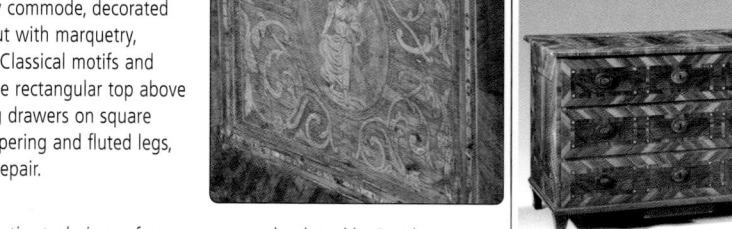

A late 18thC Italian walnut and marquetry commode, decorated throughout with marquetry, depicting Classical motifs and foliage, the rectangular top above three long drawers on square section tapering and fluted legs, damage, repair.

The decorative technique of marquetry was developed by Dutch cabinetmakers and introduced to Britain in the early 18thC.

It is a type of decorative veneer: small pieces of coloured woods and/or materials such as ivory, bone and mother-of-pearl were laid out in a pattern and then applied to the carcass of a piece of furniture.

There were several forms: floral marquetry was fashionable from c1660-90 and seaweed or arabesque from c1690.

Marquetry fell out of fashion in the early 18th century in England, but was revived in the 1760s and 1770s.

c1780   47.5in (121cm) wide

£7,000-10,000   DN

A late 18thC Transitional French provincial rosewood tulipwood and marquetry commode, with breche d'aleps marble top, each side panel decorated with a large urn, on cabriole legs ending in gilt-metal sabots.

37.5in (95cm) wide

£3,500-4,500   L&T

An 18thC Maltese walnut and boxwood-strung serpentine-front commode.

43.25in (110cm) wide

£6,000-8,000   DN

A late 18thC German Neoclassical walnut and rosewood-banded commode, the rectangular top over three long drawers, raised on squat square tapered legs.

48in (122cm) wide

£3,500-4,500   FRE

A George III mahogany serpentine-front commode, the moulded edge top above three long graduated drawers, with dummy fronts and satinwood edging and stringing, with gilt-brass swan neck handles, on bracket feet.

40in (101.5cm) wide

£3,500-4,500   WW

FURNITURE

An Italian olivewood and boxwood-strung serpentine-front commode.
c1800 35.5in (90cm) wide
£6,000-8,000 **DN**

An early 19thC Italian inlaid walnut commode, the later top with Carrera marble, the two drawers decorated with sunburst motifs, feather and geometric banding flanked by inlaid reeding, raised on square tapering legs.
52.5in (133cm) wide
£3,500-4,500 **A&G**

CLOSER LOOK: ITALIAN NEOCLASSICAL COMMODE

The marquetry decoration covers the top, front and sides of the commode and is bordered by bands of geometric motifs which are continued onto the legs and feet.

The commode is similar to the work of Giuseppe Maggiolini who was renowned for austere furniture decorated with pictorial marquetry.

Many different types and colours of timber were used to build up the pictures – here they are views of Classical buildings.

Most Maggiolini furniture is in the 18thC French style but decorated with marquetry rather than veneers.

A late 18thC northern Italian Neoclassical walnut, burl walnut and marquetry commode, from Lombardy, in the manner of Giuseppe Maggiolini, the rectangular top with scroll banding, above three graduating long drawers inlaid with architectural parquetry, side veneered to match, raised on square tapering legs.
54in (137cm) wide
£18,000-22,000 **FRE**

A 19thC American mahogany commode, the cockbeaded drawers with brass drop-handles between spiral-twist turned Ionic style pilasters, on boldly carved lion paw feet.
46.5in (118cm) wide
£1,000-1,500 **L&T**

A pair of French marble-topped stained wood commodes, of Louis XVI style, each with moulded veined red marble top above three drawers, carved with drapery swags, above stiff leaf frieze with central trophy tablet.
30in (76cm) wide
£3,500-4,500 **L&T**

A pair of 19thC continental mahogany convex commodes, line-inlaid overall, each with moulded convex rectangular top above three long graduated drawers, on square tapering legs.
46.5in (101cm) wide
£5,500-6,500 PAIR **L&T**

A pair of Italian Neoclassical style walnut commodes, the rectangular tops over two short drawers and two long drawers, flanked by half pilasters and raised on square tapered legs.
40in (101.5cm) wide
£1,500-2,000 **FRE**

A 19thC Victorian painted bombé commode, the shaped moulded top centred by a floral reserve flanked by ho-ho birds, over two long drawers with conforming decoration, raised on splayed square tapered legs.
40in (101.5cm) wide
£2,000-3,000 **FRE**

A continental carved walnut serpentine-fronted commode, in the early 18thC style, the two doors opening to the interior painted with heraldic devices to the reverse of the doors.
71.25in (181cm) wide
£1,500-2,000 **DN**

A William and Mary walnut oyster-veneered and marquetry cabinet-on-chest, the top and base associated, the moulded cornice above one frieze drawer and a fall-front inlaid with foliate reserves, centred by a flowering urn opening to reveal a fitted interior with drawers, pigeon holes and a mirrored door, the lower section with two short and two long drawers, with further marquetry-inlaid panels, raised on later squat bun feet.

45.75in (116cm) wide

£4,500-5,500 L&T

A second quarter 18thC George I walnut cabinet-on-chest, with ogee cornice above two break-arch panel inlaid quarter-veneered doors enclosing three reverse graduated long drawers, the base with three further drawers, on later bracket feet.

43.25in (110cm) wide

£3,000-4,000 DN

An 18thC German walnut and fruitwood-inlaid 'Aufsatzschrank', restorations to cornice, altered.

73.25in (186cm) high

£2,500-3,500 SOTA

A George II walnut and featherbanded chest-on-chest.

c1740　67.75in (172cm) high

£3,500-4,500 DN

A George II walnut and feather-banded chest-on-chest, the cavetto moulded cornice over three short and three long graduated drawers, flanked by reeded canted corners, the lower section with three further long graduated drawers, raised on bracket feet.

37.5in (95cm) wide

£8,000-10,000 L&T

A mid-18thC walnut and satinwood-banded chest-on-chest, the cavetto cornice above two short and six graduated drawers with brass drop handles headed by fluted angles and centred by a brushing slide, on high shaped bracket feet.

41.25in (105cm) wide

£8,000-10,000 L&T

A mid-18thC George II walnut and feather-banded chest-on-chest, raised on later bracket feet.

42.75in (108.5cm) wide

£6,000-8,000 FRE

A George III mahogany chest-on-chest, the lower section with a slide-out brush board above three long graduated drawers, raised on ogee bracket feet.
c1760   *42in (106.5cm) wide*
£2,500-3,500   **FRE**

A George III mahogany chest-on-chest, the satinwood-inlaid cornice with dentil moulding, the base with batchelor slide, with original brasses, on straight bracket feet.
c1770   *74in (188cm) high*
£3,500-4,500   **POOK**

A George III mahogany secrétaire chest-on-chest.
c1770   *45in (114.5cm) wide*
£2,500-3,500   **DN**

A George III mahogany chest-on-chest, the dentil moulded cornice above two short and three long drawers, the base with three long graduated drawers on bracket feet.
c1780   *42.5in (108cm) wide*
£3,500-4,500   **DN**

A George III Channel Islands mahogany chest-on-chest, the canted top half with a moulded and carved egg and dart cornice above parquetry and marquetry frieze, with two short and four long graduated drawers flanked by faux stop-fluted pilasters, the base with four long graduated drawers, all chestnut lined and fitted with later oval brass plate handles, on feathered bracket splay feet.
85.5in (217cm) high
£2,500-3,500   **WW**

A late 18thC mahogany chest-on-chest, the upper section with cove and dentil moulded cresting above two short and three long cockbeaded drawers, the lower section with three long cock-beaded drawers, on straight bracket feet.
87in (221cm) high
£2,000-3,000   **FRE**

A George III mahogany chest-on-chest, the cockbeaded drawers with brass drop handles, on shaped bracket feet.
54in (137cm) wide
£1,200-1,800   **L&T**

A George III oak chest-on-chest, with cavetto moulded cornice, two short over three long drawers with brass drop handles, the lower section with three long drawers, on bracket feet.
65.25in (165.5cm) high
£800-1,200   **HT**

A Georgian mahogany tallboy, with flared cornice, decorated with shark's tooth inlay, with inlaid bird's-eye maple panels, raised on bracket feet.
74in (188cm) high
£1,200-1,800   **A&G**

A George III mahogany secretary bookcase, the broken-arch bonnet over two mullioned doors, resting on a lower section with butler's desk and three drawers.
c1770
£6,000-8,000   **POOK**

A George III mahogany secretary desk, the lower section with a fall front enclosing a fitted interior with shell-carved prospect door, above four drawers supported by ogee bracket feet.
c1770   *81in (205.5cm) high*
£2,500-3,500   **POOK**

An early 19thC Regency rosewood veneer three-part secretary, with two brass mullion doors, flanked by gilded pilasters, above a lower section with butler's desk.
40in (101.5cm) wide
£2,500-3,000   **POOK**

A Regency mahogany secrétaire bookcase, the deep secrétaire drawer with fitted interior and a short deep drawer, adapted, the pair of panelled doors between lattice-inlaid uprights.
50.5in (128cm) wide
£1,500-2,000   **L&T**

A Regency mahogany secrétaire bookcase, with twin glazed doors above four drawers, losses.
c1815   *37in (94cm) wide*
£1,000-1,500   **DN**

A George II walnut bureau bookcase.
c1735   *39.5in (100cm) wide*
£18,000-22,000   **DN**

A Victorian mahogany bureau bookcase in 18thC style, with fitted interior, the drawers between cluster column corners on leaf-carved ogee bracket feet.
48.25in (122cm) wide
£2,000-3,000   **L&T**

An 18thC Georgian walnut and elm bureau cabinet in two parts, the associated lower section with a fall front opening to a fitted interior, raised on bracket feet.
37.75in (96cm) wide
£4,000-6,000   **FRE**

An 18thC Italian burl walnut and crossbanded bureau bookcase, the arched top over two panelled doors enclosing shelves, the lower section with a fall front opening to reveal a fitted interior, above two long drawers, raised on cabriole legs.

25.75in (65.5cm) wide

£2,000-3,000   **FRE**

A George III large breakfront mahogany bureau bookcase, the fall-flap below decorated with inlaid banding, opening to reveal a fitted interior of short drawers and a central cupboard, raised on a plinth base.

102in (259cm) wide

£2,500-3,500   **A&G**

CLOSER LOOK: 18THC BUREAU BOOKCASE

Coxed and Woster were active during the period 1700-1720 and one of relatively few London cabinet makers to label their work. The firm was particularly adept at making bureau cabinets and bookcases.

Their bookcases were often veneered with exotic burr woods with kingwood crossbandings and pewter stringing. Sometimes the cabinets were stained to simulate tortoiseshell.

The fitted fall front encloses drawers, pigeon holes and a sliding well.

The crossbanded frieze is fitted with two short side drawers above an arrangement of two short and two long graduated drawers divided by ovolo mouldings.

With Baroque style gilt-brass escutcheons, handles and hinges.

An early 18thC mulberry wood, kingwood-crossbanded and pewter line-inlaid bureau bookcase, in the manner of Coxed & Woster, the skirted apron rail on bun feet.

81in (206cm) high

£12,000-18,000   **L&T**

An early 19thC George III mahogany bureau bookcase.

41.75in (106cm) wide

£800-1,200   **DN**

An Edwardian inlaid mahogany bureau bookcase, decorated all over with satinwood crossbanding and boxwood stringing, with a fitted interior, four long graduated drawers under fitted brass handles, raised on bracket feet.

36in (91cm) wide

£600-800   **A&G**

An early 20thC Venetian painted and lacca povera bureau bookcase, decorated with rural coastal scenes, the arched pediment over two cupboard doors enclosing shelves and pigeon holes, the lower section with a fall front, opening to reveal a fitted interior, below are three long drawers, raised on bracket feet.

Lacca povera (poor man's lacquer) was developed in mid-18thC Venice as a relatively inexpensive substitute for fashionable lacquerwork. Engravings were cut out, coloured and pasted onto a surface before being coated with layers of varnish to mimic the high gloss effect of traditional lacquerwork.

26.75in (68cm) wide

£1,200-1,800   **FRE**

FURNITURE

A George II mahogany breakfront tambour bureau bookcase, the projecting base with centre section with sliding curved tambour front, opening to reveal a fitted interior with slide-out writing surface, with shaped apron, on splayed bracket feet.

84.25in (214cm) wide

£10,000-15,000   L&T

A George III mahogany breakfront secrétaire library bookcase, the central fitted fall front drawer enclosing drawers and pigeonholes.

c1780   104.25in (265cm) wide

£5,000-6,000   DN

A George III mahogany bookcase, the moulded cornice of breakfront outline over four astragal glazed doors enclosing adjustable shelves, the lower section with three long drawers flanked by two cupboard doors, raised on a plinth base.

c1780   100in (254cm) wide

£3,000-4,000   FRE

A George III mahogany breakfront bookcase, the key fret swan neck pediment with carved rosettes on a pierced trellis surmounted by an 'icicle'-carved plinth.

101.5in (258cm) wide

£10,000-12,000   L&T

CLOSER LOOK: GEORGE III BOOKCASE

During the reign of George III the Rococo curves of the early 18thC were gradually supplanted by rectilinear Neoclassical forms. However, curvaceous Rococo forms were often still in evidence – here as a concave breakfront beneath a sinuous scrolled acanthus pediment.

The Neoclassical vocabulary is also evident in the pair of fluted pilasters with Corinthian capitals incorporating rows of acanthus leaves and caulicoli.

The paterae centred in diamond mouldings on the blind base doors. In the form of a formalised flower, they were derived from oval or circular ceremonial Roman dishes.

An important George III mahogany concave breakfront bookcase, in the manner of Thomas Chippendale, possibly Irish, carved cornice crowning a pair of concave astragal glazed doors.

86.75in (220cm) wide

£35,000-45,000   L&T

A George III mahogany breakfront bookcase, the broken triangular pediment with dentil moulding above a fluted and roundel-carved frieze and four 13-pane astragal glazed doors enclosing a later silk-lined interior with glass shelves, the lower part with four panelled cupboard doors, on a plinth base.

105 in (267cm) wide

£25,000-30,000 **L&T**

A large mahogany breakfront bookcase of George III style, the moulded dentilled cornice above six astragal glazed doors, enclosing adjustable shelves, the projecting lower section with six cupboard doors, enclosing shelves, on plinth base.

166.25in (422cm) wide

£18,000-22,000 **L&T**

A 19thC Georgian mahogany library cabinet, with open swan-shaped pediment, above four glazed astragal panelled doors, the lower section with twelve drawers, on a plinth base, labelled 'Wylie & Lockhead Ltd. Glasgow'.

93.25in (237cm) high

£4,000-5,000 **SOTA**

A Regency mahogany breakfront library bookcase.

c1815   *96.75in (246cm) wide*

£12,000-15,000 **DN**

A Regency mahogany breakfront library bookcase, the projecting cornice with plain frieze above four lancet arched astragal glazed doors enclosing shelves, the under-cabinet with four panelled cupboard doors enclosing shelves, the whole divided by pilaster uprights with lotus leaf-carved capitals.

95.25in (242cm) wide

£5,000-6,000 **L&T**

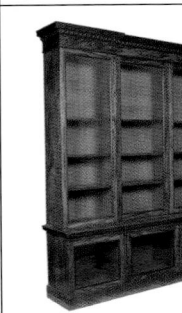

A Regency mahogany breakfront secrétaire bookcase, ebony line-inlaid overall, the projecting lower section with hinged secrétaire drawer, enclosing fitted interior, with shaped apron on bracket feet.

67.75in (172cm) wide

£7,000-9,000 **L&T**

A 19thC mahogany breakfront open bookcase with flared cornice above adjustable shelves, a pair of fielded panelled doors below, flanked by further open shelves, raised on a plinth base.

98in (249cm) wide

£2,500-3,500 **A&G**

A Victorian mahogany inverted breakfront library bookcase, the cornice enclosing 'secret' cupboards, the glazed doors enclosing adjustable shelves, a commemorative plaque dedicated to the memory of 'Dr Archibald W. Harrington 1878-1953'.

109.5in (278cm) wide

£10,000-12,000 **L&T**

FURNITURE

A George III mahogany library bookcase, with swan neck pediment and wirework doors, the base with kneehole section, losses.

c1800   68in (173cm) wide
£3,000-4,000   DN

A Regency mahogany bookcase, the moulded cornice above four astragal glazed doors, damage.

c1820   98in (249cm) wide
£2,500-3,500   DN

A William IV or early Victorian rosewood bookcase, minor losses.

c1840   62.25in (158cm) wide
£1,200-1,800   DN

A Victorian oak library bookcase, the scroll-carved pediment with acroteriae, the under-cabinet with a pair of doors decorated with armorial shields on a plinth base.

74.75in (190cm) wide
£2,000-3,000   L&T

A 19thC mahogany bookcase cabinet, the projecting cornice above a pair of brass lozenge trellis and mesh-fronted doors enclosing shelves, the undercabinet with two panelled doors, on a plinth base, adapted.

54.25in (138cm) high
£1,500-2,000   L&T

A pair of late Victorian mahogany and glazed library bookcases, one base section with two drawers and two doors, the other with two registers of four graduated drawers, with carved pierced lattice-work pediment.

c1890   49.5in (126cm) wide
£1,500-2,000 PAIR   DN

A Sheraton revival mahogany and satinwood crossbanded bookcase, with boxwood and ebony stringing, the base with two panelled doors enclosing shelves, flanked by pilasters on an inverted breakfront plinth.

60.5in (154cm) wide
£1,000-1,500   DN

A laurel wood bookcase, Ambrose Heal, Heal & Son, bears paper label inscribed 'Signed Edition Series/ designed by/ Ambrose Heal/ made by Heal & Son/ 1929,' and also bearing retailers label 'Heal & Son No. D 391/ Laurel Bookcase/ Not for Sale'.

36.25in (92cm) wide
£6,000-8,000   L&T

A walnut bookcase cabinet, Ambrose Heal, Heal & Son, rosewood banding, the double-domed top with astragal glazed doors enclosing adjustable shelves, above a pair of frieze drawers with ivorine pull handles and with a pair of cupboard doors below, the whole raised on convex-moulded trestle feet, bears ivorine makers label and paper label inscribed 'Signed Edition Series/ designed by/ Ambrose Heal/ made by Heal & Son/ 1929'.

39.5in (100cm) wide
£5,500-6,500   L&T

A late George III painted satinwood and tulipwood crossbanded low bookcase, the top with pierced brass gallery and border of trailing flowers, with reeded projecting corners and painted lozenge trellis sides.

c1790   64in (128cm) wide

£12,000-15,000   **L&T**

An early 19thC Regency simulated rosewood and parcel-gilt open bookcase, the grey marble top above a frieze with stellar motifs between a pair of stylised roses, on caryatid uprights flanking two reeded shelves.

40.5in (103cm) wide

£35,000-40,000   **SOTH**

A Regency rosewood low library bookcase, with a moulded frieze applied with Neoclassical bronze mounts, the open shelves flanked by gilt-wire trellis doors with pleated red silk linings and rosettes to each corner.

81.25in (206cm) wide

£3,000-4,000   **L&T**

A Regency mahogany double-sided waterfall bookcase, the arched top above four graduated open tiers, raised on twin end supports, ending in reeded downswept legs terminating in brass hairy paw caps and casters.

60.25in (153cm) wide

£3,500-4,500   **L&T**

A pair of early 19thC Anglo-Indian rosewood and gilt-metal-mounted bookcases, the shelves flanked by brass-mounted split baluster columns on skirted brass-bound bases and gilt-brass talon and ball feet.

c1835   40.25in (102cm) wide

£6,000-8,000   **L&T**

A Regency mahogany waterfall bookcase, with two open shelves above an arrangement of six small drawers and a further shelf between moulded uprights, on splay bracket feet.

36in (91.5cm) wide

£2,000-3,000   **DUK**

CLOSER LOOK: REGENCY SECRÉTAIRE

Heinrich Ludwig Goertz was born in Hanover but emigrated to England in 1800 where he was employed by the Royal Family for over quarter of a century.

The quality of this pair of cabinets and their high style design is reminiscent of furniture supplied to the Prince Regent (later George IV) at Carlton House in London and the Royal Pavilion in Brighton.

The three shelves are supported on finely-turned gilt-brass baluster uprights joined by cross-framed engine-turned braces centred by rosette bosses.

The fall fronts open to reveal a fitted interior with pigeon holes and drawers, a hide writing slope and pen trays, above cupboard doors fitted with gilt-brass trellis grilles backed by silk.

A rare pair of Regency rosewood and gilt-brass-mounted secrétaire bookstands, attributed to Heinrich Ludwig Goertz.

c1810   66.5in (169cm) high

£20,000-25,000   **L&T**

FURNITURE

A 17thC and later Flemish tortoiseshell, ebonised and ivory-inlaid cabinet-on-stand, the galleried top over an arrangement of drawers inlaid with hunting scenes, centred by a cupboard door, opening to reveal a parquetry-veneered temple style interior, the rectangular stand with three conforming drawers, raised on spiral turned supports joined by stretchers.

41in (104cm) wide

£5,000-6,000   **FRE**

A 19thC Spanish tortoiseshell, ivory, rosewood and ebonised cabinet-on-stand, in Baroque style, the top with pierced railing and gilt-bronze mounts, the central door with coat of arms and Classical figure, flanked on each side by two columns, between four drawers containing sixteen Classical scenes, the stand with three short drawers, each with two Classical scenes, on spiral legs, all-over applied with small rosettes and ivory-inlaid putti and masks, all sides with inlaid light wood banding, incorporating earlier elements.

51.25in (130cm) wide

£15,000-20,000   **SOTA**

A Dutch tortoiseshell, ebony and ebonised cabinet-on-stand.

c1700 and later   *34.75in (88cm) wide*

£8,000-10,000   **DN**

A Walnut and cross-banded chest-on-stand, on later turned bun feet, faults, repair.

c1700   *41in (104cm) wide*

£3,000-4,000   **DN**

An Indo-Portuguese Goan padouk and marquetry 'contador'.

The bird carving on the feet derives from 17thC Iberian furniture.

c1730   *46.5in (118cm) high*

£30,000-35,000   **DN**

A late George III mahogany cabinet-on-stand, the rectangular top above two doors opening to an arrangement of satinwood-veneered drawers, the stand with a plain frieze on square section tapering legs headed by patera terminals, on spade feet.
c1810

£1,500-2,000   DN

A Regency mahogany secrétaire, in the manner of Gillows of Lancaster, the deep secrétaire with ebony stringing and fitted interior, the drawers with foliate cast gilt-brass bandings and ebonised pull handles, with reeded tapering legs.
39in (110cm) wide

£3,000-4,000   L&T

An 18thC japanned cabinet-on-stand, the cabinet with two cupboard doors painted with Classical figures on a black ground, elaborate brass hinges and lock plate, enclosing an interior with various drawers, painted with Chinoiserie scenes of birds and figures in landscapes, the stand with shaped apron, on cabriole legs with pad feet.

Japanning - a process where items were coated with layers of coloured varnish to imitate genuine Chinese or Japanese lacquer - was first used in Europe in the mid-17th century. It was used on anything from small boxes to large pieces of furniture and was often combined with chinoiserie decoration.

38.75in (98cm) wide

£6,000-8,000   L&T

A 19thC German walnut, ivory and pewter-inlaid cabinet-on-stand, probably Braunschweig, with two doors depicting satyrs, a central maenad and Medusa head, above drawer, on stand with crossed stretchers.

48.75in (124cm) high

£2,500-3,500   SOTA

A 19thC Japanese black and gilt lacquer cabinet-on-stand, the two panelled cupboard doors decorated with figures and buildings in landscapes enclosing an architectural balconied interior, with galleried shelves, drawers and doors, on British stand with pierced fretwork frieze and triple cluster column legs, scrolled spandrels, on chamfered block feet.

36in (91cm) wide

£4,000-5,000   L&T

A Louis XV style gilt-bronze-mounted amaranth mahogany cartonnier, the upper section with six tooled leather-covered drawers above a writing slide, raised on cabriole legs terminating in gilt-bronze sabots, stamped twice to the underside 'L. Cueunieres, Ebeniste'.
c1880

31in (79cm) wide

£8,000-10,000   FRE

FURNITURE

An 18thC North Italian fruitwood and kingwood-veneered display cabinet, the lower section with extractable surface above two-door front, inlaid with lozenge-shaped marquetry.

82.25in (209cm) high

£5,000-6,000 SOTA

A late 18thC and later Dutch walnut and floral marquetry display cabinet, damage, repair, the marquetry later.

84.75in (215cm) wide

£5,500-6,500 DN

ESSENTIAL REFERENCE: REGENCY SECRÉTAIRE

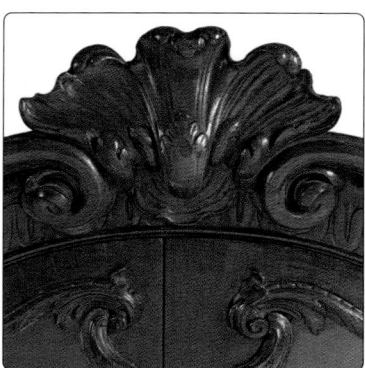

William (c1703-1763) and his son John (1729-1796) Linnell were important London carvers and cabinet-makers. Initially working in the Rococo style, John had adopted the Neoclassical style by c1765. He was among the craftsmen commissioned by Robert Adam to make furniture to his Neoclassical designs.

Both father and son were accomplished carvers and would have had similarly skilled workers among their 40 employees. This can be seen in the quality of the shell-carved cresting at the centre of the arched top.

The lower section has two ogee-moulded frieze drawers over two oval panel parquetry-banded doors, opening to reveal two further small drawers.

The cabinet is raised on shell and scroll bracket feet.

An important George III period mahogany, padouk and inlaid display cabinet, attributed to William and John Linnell, two glazed panel doors enclose adjustable shelves.

31.5in (80cm) wide

£70,000-100,000 L&T

A late 18th/early 19thC Dutch walnut and marquetry display cabinet-on-chest.

37in (94cm) wide

£3,500-4,500 DN

A mid-19thC and later pine cabinet, with repair.

52in (132cm) wide

£1,200-1,800 DN

A French Empire mahogany side cabinet, the marble top above a full length door, below an arched frieze between turned columns headed by engine turned capitals decorated with anthemia, on bun feet.

64in (163cm) high

£1,500-2,000 L&T

A pair of mahogany side cabinets in the George III manner, with brass diamond trellis doors.

£3,000-4,000 L&T

A pair of French Paul Sormani mahogany and kingwood vitrines, applied with gilt-bronze mounts, the painted panel door flanked by curve and bevelled edge glass doors, signed 'P SORMANI & FILS, 10 RUE CARLOS'
c1880   *59in (150cm) high*
£55,000-65,000   **SOTH**

A late 19thC Louis XV-style kingwood and Vernis Martin vitrine.

Vernis Martin was a japanning technique developed in France in the reign of Louis XIV (1643-1715). It is named after the brothers Martin, but it is used to describe similar work by other craftsmen. It was not as durable as the oriental lacquerwork but it had a brilliancy that made it highly fashionable.
52.75in (134cm) wide
£4,500-5,500   **L&T**

A late 19th/early 20thC Louis XV style gilt-bronze-mounted mahogany Vernis Martin vitrine, with a single glazed door headed by caryatids and decorated with amorous reserves, raised on downswept legs.
41.5in (105.5cm) wide
£3,500-4,500   **FRE**

A late 19th/early 20thC Venetian painted side cabinet, with an apron drawer raised on tapered Doric style supports, united by a wavy X-shaped stretcher.

34in (86.5cm) wide
£3,000-4,000   **FRE**

A late 19thC Louis XV style gilt-bronze-mounted rosewood Vernis Martin vitrine, with a single glazed door, the whole decorated with reserves.

30in (76cm) wide
£3,500-4,500   **FRE**

An Edwardian mahogany and inlaid display cabinet, of serpentine form, the projecting cornice with faux flutes and vine scrolls interspersed by roundels, the four panel doors decorated with ribbon-tied paterae, the whole highlighted with abalone shell inlay.
64.5in (164cm) wide
£8,000-10,000   **L&T**

A Georgian style mahogany bowfront standing corner cabinet, with astragal door enclosing shelves, a fielded panelled door below, raised on shell-carved dwarf cabriole legs with claw-and-ball feet.
29in (c73.5m) wide
£400-600   **A&G**

An Edwardian mahogany and marquetry-inlaid side cabinet, in the manner of Edwards & Roberts, the panelled cupboard doors inlaid with flowering cornucopia and angel mask motifs, raised on bellflower-carved square tapered legs.
72in (183cm) wide
£6,500-7,500   **L&T**

An Edwardian mahogany display cabinet, the rectangular top above a blind fret frieze, and two astragal glazed doors, above two drawers, on carved cabriole-shaped legs ad stylised claw-and-ball feet.
c1910   *48in (122cm) wide*
£600-800   **DN**

An Edwardian mahogany and marquetry standing corner cupboard, with dentil cornice and faux fluted frieze, the base with a pair of fielded panel satinwood-banded doors inlaid with musical trophies and foliage.

41in (104cm) wide

£4,500-5,500   **WW**

An Edwardian rosewood and marquetry display cabinet, retailed by Maple & Co, bearing ivorine retailer's plaque.

43in (109cm) wide

£3,500-4,500   **DN**

An early 20thC satinwood and polychrome-painted bowfront display cabinet, the door centred by a portrait of a female, damage.

28.25in (72cm) wide

£3,000-4,000   **DN**

SIDE CABINETS

One of a pair of early 18thC Italian walnut side cabinets, damage, repair.

76.5in (194cm) wide

£10,000-12,000 PAIR   **DN**

A late 18thC German pair of Louis XVI mahogany demi-lune side cabinets, the marble tops above a central drawer and two drawers hinged on either side, a large compartment below with corrugated door, the legs inlaid in brass and fluted, tapering at the bottom.

47.5in (121cm) wide

£10,000-15,000   **SOTA**

A pair of 18thC style black lacquer and gilt chinoiserie bowfront corner cupboards, the doors painted with birds, pagodas and scenes from domestic life, enclosing shaped shelves, with brass cock's heads hinges, on skirted cavetto moulded bases.

35.5in (90cm) high

£800-1,200   **L&T**

A second half 18thC and later Italian burr yew corner cupboard.

21.75in (55cm) wide

£500-800   **DN**

An early Regency satinwood and rosewood crossbanded side cabinet, the associated marble top above an inlaid frieze and a pair of silk-lined cabinet doors with roundel-applied corners, on short square tapering legs.

c1805   *40.5in (103cm) wide*

£28,000-32,000   **L&T**

A Regency rosewood mahogany-veneered and parcel-gilt breakfront side cabinet, with three sunken field frieze drawers above a cupboard door with circular frame moulding and lozenge frame moulding to the flanking doors, divided by reeded uprights headed by corrugated capitals, on short faceted legs with brass ball feet.

Many stylistic aspects of this cabinet suggest the hand of the London furniture maker John McLean. In particular, the use of reeded or corrugated decoration within a sunken 'tablet'.

48in (123cm) wide

£18,000-22,000   **L&T**

CLOSER LOOK: SECRÉTAIRE CABINETS

These cabinets were made to designs by Gillows which adds to their desirability. These show the style of moulding and marquetry the cabinetmakers were to use.

Gillows was renowned for making furniture in the Neoclassical style, using the grain of the wood as decoration rather than relying on carving, gilding or other methods.

The fall front opens to reveal a series of drawers.

A matched pair of George III satinwood and marquetry secrétaire cabinets, in the manner of Gillows, one with associated mahogany shelf section. c1790

32in (81cm) wide

£12,000-15,000　　　　　　　　　　　**DN**

A Regency mahogany side cabinet, the top decorated with boxwood lines above a pair of doors with curved gilt-brass trellis grilles lined with silk, enclosing a shelved interior.

36 in (91.5cm) wide

£1,200-1,800　　　　　**L&T**

A late 19thC pair of Regency style rosewood small side cabinets, with gilt mounts and French feet.

34in (86.5cm) high

£2,500-3,500 PAIR　　　　**POOK**

A Regency period Gonzalo Alves wood collector's cabinet, the rectangular top with gadrooned edge above a full-width drawer decorated with sunken field beaded quadrant moulding and lined with blue paper, the pair of panelled cupboard doors similarly decorated and enclosing a bank of shallow full width drawers, flanked by beaded uprights with leaf scroll capitals and halved paw feet, on a gadrooned plinth base.

47.25in (120cm) wide

£5,500-6,500　　　　　　　　　　　**L&T**

A Regency rosewood breakfront side cabinet.

c1820　　　　*72in (183cm) wide*

£4,500-5,500　　　　**DN**

A William IV mahogany inverted breakfront side cabinet, the four doors opening to shelved interiors.

86.25in (219cm) wide

£1,500-2,000　　　　**DN**

A French Empire mahogany secrétaire abbatant, the rectangular top with a projecting full width frieze drawer above a panelled fall enclosing a fitted interior and a pair of cupboard doors, each framed with brass mouldings between turned columns, on short square tapering legs headed by lyres and gilt-metal foliate capitals.

36in (91cm) wide

£800-1,200　　　　**L&T**

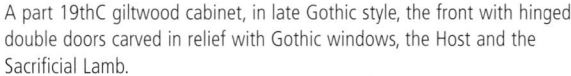

A part 19thC giltwood cabinet, in late Gothic style, the front with hinged double doors carved in relief with Gothic windows, the Host and the Sacrificial Lamb.

42.5in (108cm) high

£4,000-5,000　　　　　　　　　　　**SOTA**

A Victorian walnut pedestal cabinet, with inlaid floral marquetry to the frieze, the door decorated with tulipwood, flanked by applied gilt-metal foliate motifs and further inlaid marquetry foliate swags, raised on a cut-away plinth base.

42in (188cm) high

£700-1,000   **A&G**

A Victorian walnut and marble-mounted side cabinet, the cartouche-shaped mirror panel with acanthus scroll-carved frame.

c1870   *53.5in (152cm) wide*

£450-550   **DN**

A Napoleon III boulle and ebonised side cabinet, with gilt-bronze mounts, the rectangular top over one cupboard door with foliate brass inlay and central Classical-mounted motif, raised on a plinth base.

c1860   *32in (81cm) wide*

£2,500-3,500   **FRE**

A Victorian figured walnut and banded side cabinet, the rectangular top above two glass-panelled doors, flanked by split column terminals, on a plinth base and turned bun feet.

c1870   *40.25in (102cm) wide*

£500-700   **DN**

A 19thC Napoleon III gilt-bronze-mounted and hardstone-inset ebonised side cabinet, the top of breakfront outline above a cupboard door centred by a ribbon-tied floral bouquet, the flanking slender cupboard doors inset with foliate trails, raised on toupie feet, the whole outlined in gilt-bronze.

65in (165cm) wide

£3,500-4,500   **FRE**

CLOSER LOOK: REGENCY SIDE CABINET

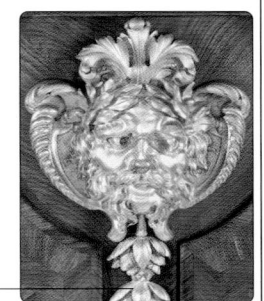

The corners of the front are decorated with gilt-bronze paterae-trailing husks.

Both the cupboard doors and the sides are inset with lacquer panels painted with figural landscapes.

The front of the cabinet is centred by a gilt-bronze satyr mask.

The serpentine apron is embellished with gilt-bronze ribbon-tied foliate mounts headed by chimera.

A Louis XVI style gilt-bronze-mounted kingwood and tulipwood lacquer meuble a hauteur d'appui, retailed by Ch. Deville & J. Maubert Sucrs, Paris, the rectangular verde antico marbled top over egg and dart moulding, opening to a shelved interior, on waisted bracket feet, many of the mounts stamped 'MB', the backboard with a partially effaced retailers brand 'Ch DEVLLE K. MAUBERT SUCR 281 Avenue de l'Opera et Rue Gaillon PARIS'.

c1880

£12,000-15,000

62in (157.5cm) wide

FRE

A matched pair of late 19th/early 20thC carved oak cabinets, in the Gothic taste, of slightly varying proportions.

57.5in (146cm) wide

£4,000-6,000 PAIR

DN

A pair of early 20thC George II style satinwood and marquetry demi-lune side cabinets, each with marquetry reserves throughout depicting musical trophies, bell flowers and paterae, each with a central covered door, above square section tapering legs, damage, repair.

33.75in (86cm) wide

£6,000-8,000

DN

A late 19th/early 20thC Anglo-Indian carved rosewood and satinwood cabinet, the rectangular top with moulded edge above a central door and flanking panels carved profusely with scrolling and meandering foliate motifs, on a plinth base.

47.25in (120cm) wide

£1,000-1,500

DN

A late 19th/early 20thC satinwood and marquetry cabinet.

43.25in (110cm) wide

£1,200-1,800

DN

FURNITURE

A Regency brass-inlaid rosewood chiffonier, the shelved back with a three-quarter pierced brass gallery, the lower section with two frieze drawers over grille doors, raised on splayed feet.

c1815   36.75in (93.25cm) wide
£2,500-3,500   FRE

A Regency mahogany chiffonier bookcase, the arched back above two shelves on S-scroll and brass vine supports, the glazed base with a pair of cabinet doors decorated with a brass foliate trellis, on plinth base with bun feet.

35in (89cm) wide
£1,000-1,500   L&T

A Regency rosewood and brass-mounted chiffonier.

c1820   42in (107cm) wide
£1,000-1,500   DN

A mid-19thC mahogany chiffonier, with shelf above two doors.

42.5in (108cm) wide
£500-700   DN

A late Regency chiffonier, attributed to a design by Thomas King, the pair of panelled doors, enclosing an adjustable shelf, between broad pilaster uprights decorated with elongated lotus stems and dual carved rosettes.

A similar example with pleated doors and ledge back is illustrated in Thomas King's Sketch Book (1835), the carving on the uprights is identical.

50in (127cm) wide
£1,800-2,200   L&T

A Victorian mahogany chiffonier, frieze drawer with brass lion mask handles.

36in (91.5cm) wide
£500-800   HT

A Victorian burr walnut breakfront credenza, with a central panelled and arabesque door, the whole with gilt-metal mounts.

73in (185cm) wide
£2,500-3,500   L&T

A Napoleon III kingwood, tulipwood marquetry and bronze-mounted side board, on scrolled feet, all-over inlaid with floral marquetry.

57.5in (146cm) wide
£6,000-8,000   SOTA

A Victorian figured walnut and marquetry breakfront side cabinet, the rectangular crossbanded top above a central door, flanked on each side by a glass-panelled door, divided by ebonised columns, on a plinth base, damage.

c1870   73.25in (186cm) wide
£4,000-5,000   DN

A Victorian burr-walnut and kingwood crossbanded side cabinet, faults.
c1870   *59.5in (151cm) wide*
£1,000-1,500   **DN**

A third quarter 19thC tortoiseshell, brass marquetry and ebonised side cabinet, with black marble top, faults.
£1,000-1,500   **DN**

A last quarter 19thC Victorian burr-walnut, inlaid and ebonised breakfront credenza.

64.5in (164cm) wide
£2,000-3,000   **DN**

A French kingwood credenza, by François Linke, applied with gilt-bronze mounts, of bowed breakfront form, the frieze drawer above a panel door inlaid with radiating veneers and flanked by open marble shelves with mirror backs, the inside backs of the locks stamped 'C LINKE SERRURERIE PARIS'.
c1890   *57.75in (147cm) wide*
£10,000-15,000   **SOTH**

BEDSIDE CABINETS

A George III mahogany night table or commode, with faults.
c1790   *19in (48cm) wide*
£600-800   **DN**

A George III mahogany washstand.
c1790   *13in (33cm) wide*
£250-350   **DN**

A George III mahogany tray-top commode, with damage.
c1790   *22.75in (58cm) wide*
£600-800   **DN**

A mahogany bedside cupboard, with damage.
c1790 and later   *19.25in (49cm) wide*
£250-350   **DN**

A George III mahogany bedside cupboard, the top with pierced carrying handles.

17.25in (44cm) wide
£2,500-3,500   **L&T**

A pair of George III style mahogany night commodes.

22in (56cm) wide
£2,000-2,500 PAIR   **L&T**

A pair of Regency mahogany bedside cupboards.

c1820
£5,500-6,500 PAIR   **DN**

A pair of early 19thC satinwood and ebony bedside tables, with bowfront chequered tambour doors, on slender square tapering legs.
32in (82cm) high
£2,000-3,000 PAIR   **L&T**

A matched pair of early 20thC beech and pine simulated bamboo bedside cabinets.
The largest 15.75in (40cm) wide
£800-1,200   **DN**

A late 19th/early 20thC mahogany and gilt-metal-mounted bedside cupboard.
17.75in (45cm) wide
£700-1,000   **DN**

A late 17thC oak buffet of narrow proportions, the pendant and strapwork-carved frieze inscribed with the initials 'MBM' and dated, above a Celtic style strapwork-carved cupboard door, a small guilloche-carved door and a larger strapwork-carved door with wrought iron loop handles, between channel-moulded uprights and panelled sides, on stem feet.

1696   *66.5in (169cm) high*
£3,000-5,000   **L&T**

A 17thC and later Charles II oak court cupboard, the rectangular moulded top above a carved frieze and two tiers separated by a drawer, raised on foliate-carved cup-and-cover and scroll-capped supports, on a moulded plinth base.

49.5in (125.5cm) wide
£700-1,000   **FRE**

A 19thC and later carved oak cupboard, in part constructed from old timbers, damage, repair.

51.25in (130cm) wide
£750-950   **DN**

A late 17thC Flemish oak and lignum vitae buffet, the top with crossbanded decoration, with carved lion mask capitals on columns, the cupboard doors enclosing a shelved and inlaid interior, on a skirted apron with cabochon frieze and projecting corners carved with cartouches, on boldly turned spherical feet.

72in (183cm) wide
£2,000-2,500   **L&T**

An Elizabethan oak court cupboard, the rectangular top with moulded edge and geometric inlaid frieze on gadrooned and carved melon-turned supports with ionic style capitals, the lower shelf enclosing a gadrooned full width drawer on similarly turned supports united by an inlaid undershelf, on stem feet, period and later parts.

47.25in (120cm) wide
£1,800-2,200   **L&T**

An early 17thC oak livery cupboard, the rectangular two-plank top over a dentil-moulded and lunette-carved frieze and a rectangular single panelled cupboard door with nulled moulded border, flanked to each side by matching canted panels, between two palmette-carved cup-and-cover supports over a lunette-carved long frieze drawer, above an open cupboard and two heavy front corner leaf-carved baluster supports, over a wavy scroll front rail on block front feet.

48.25in (122.5cm) wide
£3,000-5,000   **HALL**

An early 18thC 'cwpwrdd deuddarn', with a pair of fielded panel doors, the left with an interior locking bar, flanking a central panel above three frieze drawers and a pair of twin-panel doors, enclosing a shelf, brass work later, one panel door missing lock.

57in (145cm) wide
£800-1,200   **WW**

An cak dresser base.

c1660 and later *75.5in (192cm) wide*
£1,500-2,000 DN

An early 18thC oak dresser, the twin boarded top with a moulded edge and canted corners above three frieze drawers, fitted later brass handles and escutcheons, with a girdle moulding on turned baluster block legs with turned feet.

89.75in (228cm) wide
£3,500-4,500 WW

A Welsh oak dresser base, with a moulded edge top, an elaborate scalloped skirt and cabriole front legs terminating in slipper feet.

c1750 *75in (190.5cm) wide*
£3,000-5,000 POOK

A late 18thC George III oak dresser. *71in (180.5cm) wide*
£2,400-2,600 DN

A Georgian mahogany dresser, fitted with six short drawers with later embossed brass handles and inlaid lozenge-shaped bone escutcheons, with a pair of panelled doors, raised on bracket feet.

62in (157cm) wide
£1,500-2,000 A&G

An 18thC rectangular oak dresser, three short drawers fitted to the frieze, with brass drop handles, a pair of panelled doors below with heavy iron hinges, raised on later bun feet.

84in (213cm) wide
£1,000-1,200 A&G

A small 18thC oak dresser, the boarded top above an applied moulded frieze and two drawers, fitted replaced pierced brass plate handles and escutcheons above a shaped apron on square legs, old restoration.

20in (51cm) high
£800-1,200 WW

A late 18thC oak dresser, with a moulded edge top above four frieze drawers, fitted replaced brass plate handles with shaped aprons on ring-turned baluster supports to a stretchered pot board, restoration and replacements.

80in (203cm) wide
£1,000-1,200 WW

A George III fruitwood low dresser, with moulded edge top, two small central cockbeaded drawers with brass drop handles, flanked on either side by a large drawer, raised on club-front legs and pad feet.

68in (172.5cm) wide
£1,200-1,400 HT

FURNITURE

A George II oak dresser, blind fretwork frieze and scrolled corner frets between quadrant corners, the lower part of inverted breakfront form, on skirted base with ogee bracket feet.

91.25in (232cm) wide

£5,500-6,500   L&T

A mid-18thC French carved oak dresser, the plate rack with moulded cornice above three shelves with spindle-supported gallery sections, the rectangular top with a moulded edge above a pair of shaped panel doors, enclosing a shelved interior on square-section cabriole legs and carved scroll feet, damage, repair.

57.5in (146cm) wide

£1,500-2,000   DN

A mid-18thC George II oak high dresser, with plate rack, a pot board beneath the drawers.

58.25in (148cm) wide

£1,700-2,000   DN

An English one-piece pine pewter cupboard.

c1800   56.5in (143.5cm) wide

£400-600   POOK

An 18thC Welsh oak pewter cupboard, with two open shelves above a base with three drawers supported by square legs.

66.5in (169cm) wide

£800-1,200   POOK

A late 18thC French cherrywood, elm and marquetry dresser or 'vaisellier', with cornice and gallery to the plate rack, above drawers and doors.

90in (227cm) high

£1,700-2,000   DN

An early 19thC late George III oak high dresser, the plate rack with moulded cornice above three open shelves flanked by two cupboard doors, the base with rectangular top above an arrangement of seven drawers centred by two doors, on brackets, damage, later elements.

72in (183cm) wide

£3,000-4,000   DN

A late George III elm dresser, with plate rack.

c1810   72.5in (184cm) wide

£2,500-3,000   DN

A late 18thC George III mahogany sideboard, with bowfront top over two highly inlaid bottle drawers flanking a central drawer supported on square tapering line-inlaid legs on spade feet.

66in (167.5cm) wide

£2,500-3,500 POOK

A George III mahogany serpentine sideboard, the brass gallery flanked on each side by a deep drawer, on square-section tapering legs and spade feet, damage.

c1790 *67in (170cm) wide*

£600-800 DN

A George III mahogany bowfront sideboard, some damage.

c1790 *54.5in (138cm) wide*

£4,000-5,000 DN

A late 18thC George III mahogany sideboard, the serpentine front with central long drawer, flanked by two bottle drawers and two cupboard doors, supported by square tapering legs with paterae and entwined serpent inlays, terminating in spade feet.

90in (228.5cm) wide

£4,500-5,500 POOK

A late George III mahogany and tulipwood-crossbanded sideboard, of break-bowfront outline, the staged tambour back with corner swing doors above a tablet-centred frieze drawer, the top veneers with 'plum pudding' figuring and an end-facing pot cupboard.

46.75in (119cm) wide

£2,000-2,500 L&T

A late Georgian mahogany serpentine-front sideboard, decorated with boxwood edging, fitted with a single drawer to the frieze with a convex panel door, and a deep drawer, all fitted with lion mask ring handles, raised on square tapering legs with spade feet.

53.5in (136cm) wide

£500-700 A&G

A George III mahogany and banded bowfront sideboard, the rectangular shaped top above a central drawer with sliding writing surface and four further drawers, around the central arch on square section tapering legs, and spade feet, damage, possibly adapted.

c1810 *42in (107cm) wide*

£800-1,200 DN

An early 19thC late George III mahogany and sycamore-strung bowfront sideboard.

66in (168cm) wide

£1,800-2,200 DN

A Regency mahogany and boxwood-strung and inlaid twin pedestal sideboard, with inverted breakfront enclosing three frieze drawers and beaded doors enclosing shelves.

54.25in (138cm) wide

£2,500-3,000 L&T

A Regency mahogany sideboard, with a pair of concave-fronted drawers and deep cellaret drawer flanked by a deep drawer and an out-swinging cellaret drawer with lead lining, with lion mask handles.

83.5in (213cm) wide

£1,700-2,000 L&T

A Regency mahogany and boxwood-strung sideboard, of break bowfront form, the stage back with four tambour doors above a 'plum-pudding'-figured top with three inlaid frieze drawers flanked by a deep cellaret drawer, panelled as two, and a cupboard door, with brass oval-stamped handles, the arched recess with a pair of tambour doors, on partridgewood-veneered uprights and square tapering legs with leaf-carved capitals and gaitered feet.

79.5in (202cm) wide

£3,500-4,000 L&T

FURNITURE

A Regency mahogany twin pedestal sideboard, satinwood crossbanded and boxwood line-inlaid overall, the D-shaped reeded centre section with two moulded frieze drawers, flanked on each side by a pedestal with reeded rectangular caddy top above two moulded cupboard doors, the lower flanked by spirally reeded columns, on reeded short sabre legs.

100.5in (225cm) wide

£1,700-2,000 **L&T**

A small late Regency bowfront mahogany sideboard in the manner of Gillows, the shaped top above three frieze drawers around an arched apron, raised on reeded turned tapered legs.

41.5in (105cm) wide

£2,000-2,500 **L&T**

A Regency mahogany and marquetry serpentine-fronted sideboard, faults, repair.

c1820 *65in (165cm) wide*

£3,000-4,000 **DN**

A late Regency mahogany sideboard.

c1820 *65in (165cm) wide*

£1,000-1,500 **DN**

A George IV mahogany pedestal sideboard, faults.

c1825 *81in (206cm) wide*

£2,500-3,000 **DN**

An early 19thC mahogany pedestal sideboard, decorated all over with satinwood crossbanding, boxwood stringing and inlaid urn motifs, the small raised back with carved scrolling decoration, the centre section fitted with three small drawers to the frieze, flanked by the pedestals, each with a hinged cover and false drawer above an arched panelled door, recessed and flanked by turned pilasters enclosing a bottle drawer and shelves, raised on turned tapering feet.

94in (239cm) wide

£1,500-2,000 **A&G**

A William IV mahogany twin pedestal sideboard, of inverted breakfront type, with four moulded frieze drawers and a pair of panelled cupboard doors flanked by columnar uprights, the whole enhanced by flame-figured and plum pudding veneers.

90.25in (229cm) wide

£1,000-1,500 **L&T**

A George IV Scottish mahogany pedestal sideboard, the pedestals fitted with two drawers above a cupboard door, the left opens to slide-out shelves, the right opens to a cellaret, each carved with acanthus supports, raised on leaf-carved feet.

c1830 *80.75in (205cm) wide*

£2,000-2,500 **FRE**

A William IV mahogany pedestal sideboard.

c1835 *71.25in (181cm) wide*

£800-1,200 **DN**

A South West German or Alsace Renaissance oak, walnut and fruitwood-parquetry cabinet, built in three sections, the top frieze sculptured with winged putti, flowers and a central cartouche, the central part with two architectural doors decorated with acanthus leaves, winged putti and scallop shells, flanked and divided by turned columns, the lower corpus with one long drawer, flanked by two lion heads, each holding brass rings, sides panelled, on ball feet, dated.

1626   *82.75in (210cm) wide*

£10,000-15,000   **SOTA**

A late 17thC Dutch ebony, ebonised and rosewood Baroque cupboard or 'Kussenkast', the lower part with two larger doors above two drawers, all doors divided and flanked by pilasters, upper and lower part divided by lion-headed drawer, panelled sides, ball feet, damages.

97.75in (248cm) high

£6,500-7,500   **SOTA**

A 17thC Dutch oak and ebonised five-door Renaissance cupboard, the frieze with male and female masks, above three small panelled doors and two large geometrical panelled doors, panelled sides, overall with ebonised banding, altered.

78.75in (200cm) high

£3,000-4,000   **SOTA**

A 17thC Dutch oak and ebonised Renaissance cupboard, alterations.

73.25in (186cm) high

£3,500-4,500   **SOTA**

A 17thC South Netherlandish Renaissance carved oak cupboard, with doors depicting allegorical figures, all flanked and divided by fluted pillars, two drawers with lion-headed handles, on ball feet.

84.25in (214cm) high

£6,500-7,500   **SOTA**

A 17thC and later Dutch Renaissance oak and ebony cupboard, the interior with two pierced doors and one drawer, the lower frieze carved with acanthus leaves, alterations.

56.75in (114cm) wide

£3,000-4,000   **SOTA**

A 17thC Dutch Baroque oak, ebony and rosewood cupboard or 'Kussenkast', the protruding cornice above a pair of raised panelled doors, enclosing an interior with shelves and one drawer, flanked and divided by pilasters with Corinthian capital, a long drawer below, sides with panels and pilaster, on large ball feet, alterations.

80in (203cm) wide

£12,000-14,000   **SOTA**

A mid-18thC North German walnut, ivory and pewter parquetry and marquetry cabinet, Braunschweig Rococo, the corners with elegant floral inlay and rocaille carvings, on rocaille-carved curved feet.

84.25in (214cm)

£30,000-35,000   SOTA

A mid-18thC Dutch Rococo burr walnut display cupboard, pair of glazed doors, the lower section now also fitted with glazed doors, ball feet.

94.5in (240cm) high

£4,500-5,500   SOTA

A mid 18thC German walnut, fruitwood and mother-of-pearl marquetry Baroque cabinet, probably Frankfurt, the door with male figure of Justice, a griffin and a baldequin, on bun feet.

79in (201cm) high

£30,000-40,000   SOTA

A mid-18thC South-German Baroque walnut, fruitwood and marquetry cabinet, the lower part with hinged central sloping fall front, above central door, on six bun feet, alterations.

65in (162cm) wide

£5,000-7,000   SOTA

A late 18thC French pine standing cupboard, the upper section with two field panelled cupboard doors, the base with three drawers above two doors on stile legs, damage.

56in (142cm) wide

£800-1,200   DN

A late 18thC oak standing corner cupboard.

c1790   39.75in (101cm) wide

£1,200-1,500   DN

A 19thC South German walnut and burr walnut cupboard, possibly Freiburg, in Baroque style, the frieze with male masks alternating fruit above two sculptured doors, each with a male and female mask, opening to a later interior flanked by columns, sides panelled.

100in (254cm) wide

£4,500-5,500   SOTA

An early 19th century North Wales oak deuddarn, with panel doors, one revealing a fitted interior of two short drawers and two pigeonholes, over two short frieze drawers above two doors to the base, fitted with turned wooden handles with mother-of-pearl centres, raised on tall bracket feet.

44in (112cm) wide

£2,500-3,000   HALL

An early 19thC Welsh oak press, with a pair of arched fielded panel doors enclosing later shelves with a quadruple-panel front base above a pair of apron drawers on moulded stile feet, handles later, one drawer missing its base.

54.5in (138.5cm) high

£3,000-4,000   WW

A massive 19thC French provincial walnut buffet a deux corps, with two moulded panelled cupboard doors, flanked by concave doors, the projecting lower section with three cupboard doors, shaped apron, on scrolled feet.

93in (236cm) wide

£3,000-4,000   L&T

A pair of pitch pine press cupboards, each decorated all over with simulated bamboo mouldings, above two short drawers, on ring-turned feet.

53.75in (136cm) wide

£2,600-3,000   L&T

A Flemish oak cabinet, in late Gothic style, the front inserted with panels carved in relief with Gothic tracery, two doors in the centre, the sides with broad linen fold panels, one above the other, upper lock detached.

46.5in (118cm) high

£3,000-4,000   SOTA

A late 18thC Normandy carved oak armoire, with profusely carved cornice, panel doors and drawer.

84.75in (215cm) high

£1,600-2,000   DN

An early 19thC French oak armoire, the arched bonnet with foliate and cherub decoration.

88in (223.5cm) wide

£4,000-5,000   POOK

A French walnut and cherrywood armoire, the arched cavetto cornice above a pair of asymmetric panelled doors with pierced brass escutcheons inscribed 'E.P. 1834', enclosing a shelved and hanging interior.

92.5in (235cm) high

£1,200-1,800   L&T

A late 18thC Dutch mahogany armoire, the cornice of swan neck outline centred by acanthus scroll and laurel swag above a pair of well-figured arched panel doors enclosing shelves and five shallow drawers, the lower part of bombé form with three long cockbeaded drawers, on a shaped apron and boldly carved claw-and-ball feet headed by stiff acanthus, the whole with Neoclassical gilt metal handles.

97.25in (247cm) high

£3,000-5,000   L&T

CLOTHES PRESS

A George III oak press cupboard.

c1780   *60in (152cm) wide*

£700-900   DN

A George III oak press cupboard, damage, repair.

c1780   *78.75in (200cm) wide*

£800-1,200   DN

A late 18thC French carved oak press cupboard or 'deux corps', with a cornice and two doors above drawers and further doors.

88in (224cm) high

£1,600-2,000   DN

A late 18thC black lacquer and gilt-japanned clothes press, some repair.

c1780   *41in (104cm) wide*

£3,000-4,000   DN

FURNITURE

A George III mahogany linen press, with a dentil cornice above a pair of fielded and crossbanded panelled doors enclosing sliding shelves, two short and two long graduated drawers below fitted later moulded brass handles, raised on bracket feet.

50in (127cm) wide

£1,200-1,400   **A&G**

A Regency Channel Islands mahogany linen press, inlaid stringing, the detachable cornice above a pair of rosewood-banded doors enclosing two slides, the four drawers fitted with embossed shell brass plate handles.

51.25in (130cm) wide

£1,500-2,000   **WW**

A George IV mahogany linen press, with a pair of panelled cupboard doors opening to four sliding adjustable shelves, above two short drawers and two long drawers raised on bun feet, the top right drawers stamped 'Wilson 68 Great Great Queen St. London'.

c1820   *50.5in (128cm) wide*

£2,000-3,000   **FRE**

A Regency mahogany clothes press, the arched and moulded cornice above two doors, enclosing five sliding trays, above two further doors enclosing sliding trays on outswept bracket feet.

37in (94cm) wide

£2,500-3,000   **DN**

A mid-19thC Victorian mahogany linen press.

43.25in (110cm) wide

£300-400   **DN**

An early 19thC mahogany linen press, the moulded and beaded cornice over two panelled and crossbanded doors with brass trim and leaf-carved cusped corners now enclosing a hanging space, two short over two long drawers with pierced brass ring handles, beaded base and turned bun feet.

78.75in (200cm) high

£1,000-1,500   **HT**

A late 19thC North European mahogany clothes press.

55in (140cm) wide

£900-1,100   **DN**

A Regency mahogany break-front wardrobe, the detachable moulded cornice above a pair of rectangular panel doors, enclosing a later rail, previously with slides, the doors divided by a ribbed and turned girdle, on a plinth base.

94.75in (240.5cm) wide

£4,500-5,500　　　　　　　　　　　　　　　　**WW**

An early 19thC Scottish mahogany wardrobe, the moulded cornice above veneered frieze, over two cupboard doors with graduated moulded panels, enclosing hanging space, above three short drawers, shaped apron, on stile feet.

62.25in (158cm) wide

£1,200-1,400　　　　　　　　**L&T**

A Regency mahogany breakfront wardrobe.

c1820　　　　　*91.25in (232cm) wide*

£3,000-4,000　　　　　　　　　**DN**

A Victorian mahogany compactum.

c1860　　　　　*82.75in (210cm) wide*

£700-900　　　　　　　　　　**DN**

An early 20thC mahogany and satinwood wardrobe.

44in (112cm) wide

£250-350　　　　　　　　　　**DN**

A Victorian mahogany break-front wardrobe, in the French Rococo taste, the arched cornice with leaf-scroll cresting above a mirrored door flanked by a pair of arched and asymmetric panel doors with ribbon-tied torch and quiver trophies, on a shaped apron and short acanthus-carved cabriole legs, enclosing fitted and hanging interiors, a serpentine-front dressing chest, of two short over three long graduated drawers with Rococo-carved decoration and scrolling gilt-metal handles, on short leaf-carved cabriole legs, and a swing mirror kneehole dressing table, of similar design, en suite, possibly made by Whytock and Reid.

94.5in (240cm) wide

£4,500-5,500　　　　　　　　　　　　　　　　**L&T**

A Victorian satin walnut break-front wardrobe, with detachable cavetto moulded cornice above a central bevelled rectangular plate flanked by a pair of panel doors, enclosing slides and hanging rails, on a plinth base.

88in (223.5cm) wide

£400-500　　　　　　　　　　　　　　　　**WW**

An American Massachusetts mahogany block-front kneehole desk, the base resting on short claw-and-ball feet.

c1765   31.25in (79.5cm) wide
£1,500-2,500   **POOK**

A satinwood and mahogany-banded kneehole desk, the rectangular top with later leatherette inset, and with rear superstructure with pierced three-quarter gallery, above an arrangement of five drawers around the central kneehole, on square-section tapering legs, and later block feet, damage, the top later associated.

c1910 and later   49.5in (126cm) wide
£350-450   **DN**

A 20thC cream-painted and parcel-gilt kneehole desk, in 19thC Continental style, the rectangular top with green leather inset above an arrangement of seven drawers around the central kneehole, on squat cabriole legs and scroll feet, damage.

46in (117cm) wide
£550-650   **DN**

A Sheraton Revival satinwood-crossbanded and floral-painted kneehole desk, by Edwards & Roberts, the top of inverted break-front form with gilt-tooled tan leather skiver above a frieze drawer flanked by hipped tapering pedestals each with four short graduated drawers, on splay legs, the sides decorated with ribbon-tied lyre trophies.

41.75in (106cm) wide
£4,500-5,500   **L&T**

A George II feather-banded walnut kneehole desk, the quarter-veneered top above a compartmentalised long drawer.

30.25in (77cm) wide
£4,000-5,000   **FRE**

A George II yew wood kneehole secretaire desk, with boxwood and ebonised stringing, the walnut top crossbanded, all fitted replaced brass plate handles, on bracket feet.

32in (81cm) high
£2,500-3,500   **WW**

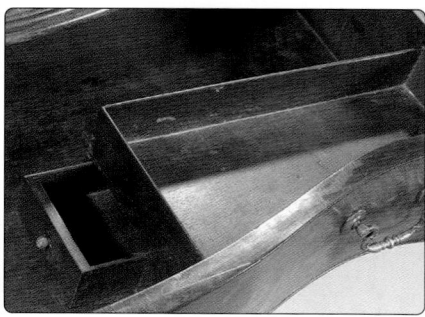

An early George III mahogany serpentine-fronted kneehole desk, with crossbanded and strung moulded top, the front and sides outswept to fluted angles.

47.75in (121cm) wide
£2,500-3,500   **DN**

A large mahogany partners' desk, in the manner of Thomas Chippendale, the rectangular top with gilt-tooled burgundy skiver above a fluted and swag-carved frieze with a pair of arched central drawers above substantial wreath-carved pedestals, each with twin lion mask and husk-carved pilaster uprights, ending in hairy paw feet, the sides similarly carved and decorated.

78.75in (200cm) wide
£5,000-6,000   **L&T**

A late 19thC George III style octagonal mahogany partners' desk, by H. Samuel, London, the shaped top with outset corners and a tooled green inset leather writing surface over a panelled frieze with four drawers, shell and seaweed-carved pedestals, each with three further long graduated drawers, flanked by panelled cupboard doors, raised on a carved plinth base, the top of the pedestal stamped 'H. Samuel, London', in several places.

53in (135cm) wide

£40,000-50,000   **L&T**

A George III mahogany partners' desk, the rectangular brown tooled leather insert top over three frieze drawers, flanked by two banks of three drawers.

54in (137cm) wide

£1,200-1,800   **FRE**

An early 19thC mahogany partners' desk, the top above three sunken field frieze drawers to either side with foliate-cast brass ring handles, each pedestal with three drawers opposed by panelled cupboard doors, on plinth bases.

59in (150cm) wide

£2,500-3,500   **L&T**

A 19thC patridgewood partners' desk, with tooled skiver and leaf-carved edge above three frieze drawers to either side and floret and ribbon-carved lip, each pedestal with three frieze drawers opposed by fielded panel cupboard doors edged with leaf-carved mouldings, on similarly carved plinth bases.

60in (152cm) wide

£3,000-5,000   **L&T**

A Victorian mahogany pedestal partners' desk, the rectangular top with leather inset above an arrangement of drawers around the central kneehole, the opposing side with three drawers above two doors, on plinth bases.

c1860   *60.5in (154cm) wide*

£2,800-3,200   **DN**

An early 20thC George II style mahogany double sided library desk, pedestals with six graduated drawers in two tiers, the opposing sides with a cupboard enclosing a shelf, on carved ogee bracket feet.

64in (163cm) wide

£12,000-18,000   **SOTH**

A Victorian partners' pedestal desk, one drawer bearing stencilled makers name 'J.J. BRYNE G. HENRY ST. DUBLIN'.

54.25in (138cm) wide

£2,500-3,000   **DN**

An Edwardian mahogany partners' desk, the tooled black hide top with gadrooned edge, the desk on short leaf-carved cabriole legs with claw-and-ball feet.

60.25in (153cm) wide

£1,500-2,500   **L&T**

A George III style yew partners' pedestal desk, of recent manufacture.

72in (183cm) wide

£800-1,200   **DN**

FURNITURE

An 18thC George III walnut feather-banded pedestal desk, the rectangular writing leather-inset surface above three drawers and two banks of three drawers.

53in (134.5cm) wide

£3,500-4,500   **FRE**

A late 19thC mahogany pedestal partners' desk, the rectangular top with moulded edge and gilt-tooled green leather inset, above three frieze drawer, and three further opposing each side with a pair of doors to the plinth, on plinth bases.

59.5in (81cm) wide

£2,500-3,500   **DN**

ESSENTIAL REFERENCE: GOTHIC REVIVAL

The Gothic Revival, or Neo-Gothic, was one of the most prominent 19thC revival styles, though in Britain and Germany it was more of a continuation, as the style had remained popular.
- The Gothic Revival was encouraged by designers like A. W .N. Pugin and W. Burges.
- The Gothic style became closely linked to the revival of Catholicism within the Anglican Church. Furniture designers took inspiration from the church architecture of the Middle Ages, employing pointed arches, latticework, quatrefoils and heraldic motifs in heavy woods like oak, which were darkened.

A 19thC Gothic Revival oak twin pedestal partners' desk, the rectangular top with inset skiver and moulded edge above opposing frieze drawers and panelled pedestals each with two bays of open shelves headed by leaf-carved corbels, each end with frieze drawers above wire mesh-panelled doors enclosing shelves, on moulded plinth bases, the drawers with Gothic style sunken field trefoil mouldings.

64.5in (164cm) wide

£8,000-12,000   **L&T**

A late Victorian walnut and burr walnut pedestal desk, repair.

c1880   *48in (122cm) wide*

£800-1,000   **DN**

A Victorian mahogany twin pedestal partners' desk.

c1880   *63.5in (161cm) wide*

£2,500-3,500   **DN**

A late 19thC Victorian mahogany and leather-inset pedestal desk.

48in (122cm) wide

£650-850   **DN**

An early 20thC mahogany 18thC style serpentine-front pedestal desk.

54.25in (138cm) wide

£800-1,200   **DN**

An early 20thC oak tambour-top pedestal desk.

60in (152.5cm) wide

£700-900   **DN**

A George III mahogany architect's desk, by Gillows, the rectangular moulded, hinged and ratcheted top above a secrétaire drawer, revealing a tooled leather writing slide, above five dummy drawers and two banks of two drawers, raised on a plinth base.

c1780   *49in (124.5cm) wide*

£6,000-8,000   **FRE**

A late 18thC George III mahogany architect's table, the rounded rectangular top over one frieze drawer, opening to reveal a leather inset writing surface and compartmentalised interior, flanked by slides, raised on chamfered square legs.

31.5in (80cm) wide

£1,000-1,500   **FRE**

A German amaranth and brass-inlaid architect's table, in the manner of David Roentgen, the carcass of oak, the rectangular top trimmed in brass, inset with hinged and spring-loaded panel covered in green leather, tooled in gold, the top adjustable in height and supported by rods of square cross-section, accommodated inside the front legs, fitted with single drawer covered with sliding writing surface and separate compartment for writing implements, the sides fitted with two retractable surfaces, also covered in green leather and tooled in gold, recessed panels of sides trimmed in brass, the tapering legs inlaid with plain brass panels, on toupie feet and casters, five brass panels detached, one missing, small section of lectern ledge extant.

1777   *36.5in (93cm) wide*

£15,000-20,000   **SOTA**

A 19thC walnut, crossbanded and gilt-metal-mounted writing desk, in the French Transitional taste, by Whytock & Reid of Edinburgh, to designs by Sir Robert Lorimer, on slender cabriole legs with leaf-cast sabots.

Lorimer adopted the continental 'high style' during a period in his career around 1910 although he was also deeply interested in vernacular styles and the Arts and Crafts movement.

44.75in (114cm) wide

£3,000-4,000   **L&T**

A découpage slope-top desk on stand, the sloping desk top hinged over a single drawer, over tapering column supporting a shelf.

33in (84cm) high

£400-600   **FRE**

An early 18thC, possibly Dutch, Northern European rosewood, marquetry and part ebonised writing desk, the rectangular top with a superstructure fitted with an arrangement of drawers, above a writing surface and two drawers raised on baluster-turned legs, joined by a shaped X-stretcher, the whole inlaid with elaborate foliate and floral marquetry incorporating birds.

62in (157.5cm) wide

£5,000-6,000   **FRE**

DAVENPORTS

The davenport is named after Captain Davenport who ordered the first recorded example of the small writing cabinet from Gillows of Lancaster in the 1790s.

- Most davenports were made from mahogany, rosewood or burr-walnut.
- The basic form consists of a small chest-of-drawers below a desk compartment. Most davenports have four drawers that open at the side of the base, with simulated drawer fronts on the opposite side. Some have cupboards concealing the drawers. The arrangement is always symmetrical.
- The first davenports had a top writing section which slid forward and was supported by an iron rod sliding into holes in the top and bottom. From c1840, the desk section was generally fixed in the writing position, supported by elaborately scrolled or turned supports. Earlier examples had brass handles, which tended to be replaced with turned wood in the Victorian period.
- Mechanical or 'harlequin' davenports often had concealed drawers or compartments in a rise which ran on a leather belt and weights.
- The davenport continued to be popular until the end of the 19thC, though these later examples are often over-ornamented and clumsy.

A Regency Andaman padouk and ebonised davenport, the Gothic pierced brass gallery above a leathered slope enclosing a fitted interior of short drawers, with a pen drawer to side, above a full-width slide to each side, the sliding kneehole with decorative carved and fluted corbels and four long graduated drawers flanked by simulated drawers, the locks stamped 'BRAMAH 184 Piccadilly', the simulated drawers also fitted with Bramah escutcheons and with conforming turned ebony pull handles, on short feet with casters, the whole highlighted with ebony-framed edges and cockbeadings, on short tapered bun feet.

22.25in (56cm) wide

£2,000-3,000 **L&T**

A George IV mahogany davenport, the leather inset slant front opening to an interior fitted with small drawers set on brass runners to slide and retract, the cupboard door to the side fitted with an arrangement of drawers, numbered '1' through '10', raised on bun feet and casters.

c1820 *17in (43cm) wide*

£1,200-1,800 **FRE**

A Regency mahogany davenport attributed to Gillows, the sliding top with a reeded edge with two real and two false drawers, the left ivory handle pulls to release the side ink drawer, fitted wood knob handles, the turned feet with sunken brass roller casters.

20.25in (51.5cm) wide

£3,000-4,000 **WW**

A mid-19thC large Anglo-Indian rosewood and satinwood Bombay Presidency davenport, the writing surface opening to reveal a fitted interior with drawers and pigeon holes, with two lateral cupboard doors each enclosing four drawers, raised on carved block feet terminating in casters.

30in (76cm) wide

£6,000-7,000 **L&T**

A George IV mahogany davenport, in the manner of Gillows, the top with pierced three-quarter brass gallery above the hinged fall, the pedestal with a slide above four long drawers and four opposing false drawers, on baluster-turned legs, brass caps and casters.

c1825 *17in (43cm)*

£1,500-2,500 **DN**

A 19thC partridgewood davenport, the slope enclosing a fitted interior of drawers, the front and back with projecting sunken field canted corners, one side with sliding pen drawer and shallow drawers above a panelled cupboard enclosing four long drawers with recessed brass handles with blind panelled opposing side.

20.5in (52cm) wide

£1,500-2,000 **L&T**

A late 17thC century oak bureau, the rectangular fall opening to a fitted interior incorporating an arrangement of small drawers, above two short and two long mitre-panelled drawers, on stile feet, damage, repair.

31.5in (105cm) wide

£3,500-4,500 DN

A George I walnut and feather-banded bureau, the fall front enclosing a stepped fitted interior with pigeon holes, drawers and a covered well, below are two short and two long-graduated drawers, raised on later bracket feet.

42in (107cm) wide

£1,500-2,500 L&T

A George I walnut bureau, the drop-front reveals an interior fitted with pigeonholes flanked by two small drawers above a tooled green leather writing surface, over three long drawers, raised on bracket feet.

c1730   41in (104cm) wide

£1,000-2,000 FRE

A George II walnut bureau, the herringbone-banded top above a sloping crossbanded fall enclosing a fitted interior above three long graduated drawers with pierced brass bat-wing handles on shaped bracket feet.

c1740   41.25in (105cm) wide

£1,500-2,500 DN

A George III mahogany bureau, the fall front enclosing a pagoda interior with blind fretwork, over a case with fretwork corners supported by an elaborately carved bracket base.

c1760   42in (106.5cm) wide

£2,500-3,500 POOK

A George III mahogany bureau, damage.

c1780   36.5in (93cm) wide

£400-600 DN

A late 18thC George III lacquered secrétaire bureau, with sloping hinged flap, enclosing a writing interior, above five drawers, on bracket feet, damages to lacquer work.

41.75in (106cm) high

£7,500-8,500 SOTA

A George III mahogany bureau, the fall front enclosing a fitted interior with star-inlaid prospect door, over a case with four drawers supported by flaring French feet.

c1790   42.5in (108cm) wide

£600-800 POOK

A late 18thC George III oak bureau, with fall front above four graduated drawers.

37.75in (96cm) wide

£350-450 DN

A late 18thC Italian Lombard walnut and crossbanded bureau, faults, repair.

44.5in (113cm) wide

£17,000-20,000 DN

FURNITURE

An 18thC Italian walnut, satinwood and marquetry bureau, with sloping fall inlaid with a basket of flowers within a parquetry border and enclosing a fitted interior of four drawers around a shaped arched open recess, two frieze drawers above two long drawers inlaid sans traverse with similar decoration, on square tapering legs.

48in. (122.5cm) wide

£8,000-10,000   SOTH

A late 18thC probably Dutch Continental mahogany bombé bureau, with fully fitted interior.

38in (99cm) wide

£600-800   DN

An early 19thC Dutch mahogany and marquetry cylinder bureau.

54in (137cm) high

£1,500-2,000   DN

An early 19thC and later walnut bureau, the rectangular fall opening to a fitted interior with a central door surrounded by an arrangement of five drawers and a well section, above a drawer, the stand with two short drawers on baluster-turned tapering legs, and an X-stretcher, on turned bun feet, damage, repair.

26.5in (67cm) wide

£900-1,100   DN

A late 19thC mahogany and ebony-mounted bureau cabinet, by Lamb of Manchester, the top of one drawer stamped 'LAMB MANCHESTER'.

29.25in (74.5cm) wide

£3,500-4,500   DN

A late 18thC German mahogany and brass-mounted cylinder bureau, bronze-galleried top above cylinder opening to reveal a writing interior and sliding surface.

48.75in (124cm) wide

£4,500-5,500   SOTA

A 19thC French Empire gilt-brass mahogany bureau à cylindre, with a fitted interior, with central clock with countwheel bell striking anchor escapement, signed 'Bechot'.

63.75in (162cm) high

£6,500-7,500   SOTA

A Regency mahogany and gilt-metal-mounted cylinder bureau, stamped 'W Priest 1-2 Tudor Street, Blackfriars', with pierced gallery and red marble-inset top, the fall enclosing a fitted interior, the sliding leather inset writing surface with central rachet-adjustable section, on turned tapering legs, brass caps and casters.

c1820   32.75in (83cm) wide

£1,500-2,000   DN

A George IV pedestal cylinder desk, the reeded top above a roll front with fitted interior and writing slide, on bracket feet, the whole inlaid with ebony lines, the top drawer stamped 'T. Willson 68 Great Queen Street, London'.

53in (135cm) wide

£3,500-4,500   **L&T**

A late 19thC Louis XVI style mahogany and gilt-bronze-mounted bureau à cylindre, the fall with fitted interior and a brushing slide with inset baize writing surface, raised on turned fluted legs terminating in toupie feet.

30in (76cm) wide

£1,200-1,800   **FRE**

An Edwardian satinwood cylinder bureau, crossbanded with ebony stringing and foliate marquetry, with fitted interior and writing slide, the drawers with brass ring handles, raised on square tapering legs with spade feet and casters.

36in (91.5cm) wide

£2,000-3,000   **HT**

A mahogany, partridge-wood and harewood-crossbanded Carlton House desk, by Gillows of Lancaster, the centre of the frieze drawers stamped GILLOWS, on turned and fluted tapering legs headed by stiff lotus leaf capitals.

54.75in (139cm) wide

£8,000-9,000   **L&T**

A late Victorian satinwood and marquetry Carlton House desk.

First named in a cost book of Gillows in 1796, Carlton House desks are named after the residence of the then Prince of Wales.

48.25in (122.5cm) wide

£4,500-6,000   **WW**

An Edwardian mahogany Carlton House desk, crossbanded with stringing, the frieze drawer over kneehole flanked on either side by two small drawers, brass drop handles, raised on square tapering legs and spade feet.

53.25in (135.5cm) wide

£800-1,200   **HT**

A 19thC burr walnut and arabesque inlaid bureau de dame, the fall enclosing a fitted interior of drawers and pigeon holes above a well, on cabriole legs, decorated with Rococo cast giltmetal mounts and sabots.

33.5in (85cm) wide

£1,500-2,000   **L&T**

A Louis XV style kingwood and amaranth bureau de dame, The slant front opening to an arrangement of drawers, the frieze drawer raised on cabriole legs cast with chutes, the gallery stamped 'ML BB'.

28.75in (73cm) wide

£1,500-2,500   **FRE**

A 19thC English kingwood, crossbanded and porcelain-mounted bonheur du jour, the serpentine top with a frieze drawer applied with porcelain panels, on cabriole legs united by cross stretchers with a porcelain medallion boss.

A bonheur du jour is a delicate lady's writing desk with a flat writing surface with tiered drawers and compartments at the back. It was introduced in the 18thC and became increasingly popular in the 19thC. This design, which is common in 19thC French furniture, is rare from an English workshop. The usual Sèvres porcelain panels have been substituted by delicately painted English examples.

54.75in (139cm) wide

£4,000-5,000   **L&T**

A late 19thC mahogany, satinwood-banded and chequer-strung English bonheur du jour, in the Louis XVI taste, the wide skiver draws forward to reveal a pen try and inkwell recess, on inlaid and reeded tapering legs headed by simulated flutes and ending in brass casters.

41.75in (106cm) wide

£4,500-5,500   **L&T**

An Edwardian satinwood, crossbanded and painted bonheur du jour, the raised top fitted with two short drawers and one long drawer, the lower section with a further frieze drawer, raised on slightly splayed slender square tapered legs.

21in (53.5cm) wide

£1,200-1,800   **FRE**

A late 1600s William & Mary painted mirror, the sarcophagus top retaining its original marbleised surface.

28.25in (72cm) high

£2,000-3,000 **POOK**

A William & Mary mirror, with walnut veneer frame enclosing an elaborate silk-on-silk needlework bezel with scalloped edge.

c1690 *29.75in(75.5cm) high*

£2,500-3,500 **POOK**

A Queen Anne burl walnut veneer looking glass, with arched crest and bolection-moulded frame enclosing two bevelled glass plates, the upper with cut floral decoration.

c1710 *39in (99cm) high*

£1,500-2,500 **POOK**

An American Queen Anne mahogany looking glass, with scalloped and pierced crest over a bolection-moulded frame with bevelled edge plate.

c1710 *30.75in (78cm) high*

£1,500-2,500 **POOK**

A pair of German giltwood console mirrors, possibly Dresden.

In the early 18th century King Friedrich August 'der Starke' I (1670-1733) of Saxony, chose Dresden to be his glamourous cultural metropolis. As part of this programme, in 1709 the 'Zwinger', an ensemble of beautiful buildings and gardens was started. The main artist was the sculptor Balthasar Permoser (1651-1732), whose style was to remain dominant in Saxony and Brandenburg for the coming decades. In 1945 it was completely destroyed and took 20 years to rebuild. These mirrors were undoubtedly made after Permoser's death. Apart from South German Rococo influences they also reflect features from the works of Johann August Nahl and of other leading designers.

£22,000-28,000 PAIR

78.75in (200cm) high

SOTA

A George II mahogany looking glass, with scrolled crest and stepped mirror plates with gilt liner, retaining an old dry surface and original glass.

c1730 *

£4,500-5,500 **POOK**

A mid-18thC George II walnut and parcel-gilt-framed wall mirror, scrolled broken pediment with eagle surmount, rectangular plate flanked by leaf and berry festoons, some regilding and with a later bevelled plate.

66in (167cm) high Est.

£6,000-8,000 **SOTH**

An unusual and small George II yew wood mirror, with a shaped cresting and apron with wrong iron candle arm, the mirror plate within an arched moulded frame.

8.25in (21cm) wide

£3,000-4,000 **L&T**

An American Queen Anne walnut veneer looking glass, the scalloped crest with parcel-gilt shell over a base with candlearm.

c1760 *26in (66cm) high*

£1,300-1,500 **POOK**

An early George III mahogany-framed wall mirror, the rectangular plate within a cartouche-shaped frame surmounted by a pierced central anthemion, damage.

c1760   *38.5in (98cm) high*

£350-450   **DN**

A Georgian burl veneer looking glass, with pierced and scalloped crest and gilt liner.

c1770   *42in (106.75cm) high*

£700-1,000   **POOK**

A Chippendale mahogany looking glass, with scalloped crest and base.

c1770

£400-600   **POOK**

A mid-18thC mahogany and parcel-gilt wall mirror, with broken-arch pediment, decorated with central gilt cartouche and dentil moulding, the original mirrored plate below flanked by applied carved foliate side supports.

26in (66cm) wide

£1,200-1,500   **A&G**

A Chippendale mahogany looking glass, the scrolled crest with parcel-gilt phoenix above a rectangular plate with gilt liner and scrolled base.

c1780   *26.75in (68cm) high*

£250-350   **POOK**

A late 18thC Chippendale mahogany and giltwood mirror, with swan's neck cresting centring a phoenix, surmounting a shaped frame, and giltwood liner enclosing mirror plate, regilded.

66in (167.5cm) long

£3,500-4,500   **FRE**

An 18thC Flemish carved giltwood wall mirror, the bevelled rectangular plate with eight further margin plates, the moulded frame surmounted by a scrolling foliate carved cresting.

45.75in (116cm) high

£3,500-4,500   **L&T**

A George III mahogany-framed wall mirror, the cornice decorated with scallop shell motif, flanked by bellflowers, with acanthus leaf brackets to each side and foliate carved scrolls below.

30in (76cm) wide

£400-600   **A&G**

A small pair of 18thC carved giltwood looking glasses, the rectangular plates within ornate openwork foliate and scroll-carved frames.

19.75in (50cm) high

£8,500-9,500   **L&T**

A George III period mahogany wall mirror, the later rectangular plate within an ornate openwork Rococo scroll-carved frame.

41.25in (105cm) high

£4,000-5,000   **L&T**

A pair of 19thC George III style carved giltwood mirrors, in the manner of Thomas Chippendale.

36in (91.5cm) wide

£25,000-30,000   **FRE**

CLOSER LOOK: GIRANDOLE MIRROR

As mirrors did not receive the same wear and tear as furniture such as tables and chests, the frames were often intricately carved and decorated with gesso and gilt.

The bead moulding and plume and bellflower swag are typical of the Neoclassical motifs fashionable from c1800. Here they are combined with a stand reminiscent of the earlier Rococo style.

Large plates of glass such as this were not made until the late 18thC.

The technique of Takamakie lacquer originated in Japan and this panel may have been made there.

A rare late 18th/early 19thC Chinese Export giltwood girandole mirror in the George III style, the oval plate within a fluted and bead-moulded frame, surmounted by a stylised plume and bellflower swag cresting, the openwork apron centred by a Takamakie lacquer panel and issuing two outscrolling candle branches.

18.75in (47cm) wide

£3,500-4,500   **L&T**

A pair of late George III giltwood and gesso pier mirrors, the corrugated ovolu frames with a leaf paterae to each corner surmounted by scrolled and festooned crestings.

35.75in (91cm) high

£4,000-5,000   **L&T**

A pair of George III style carved giltwood wall mirrors, the shaped rectangular bevelled plates within ornate open Rococo scroll frames, surmounted by ho-ho birds.

30.75in (78cm) wide

£800-1,200   **FRE**

An American giltwood convex mirror, with spread-winged eagle pediment and foliate drop, retaining an unidentified partial maker's label.

c1800   *40in (101.5cm) high*

£1,000-1,500   **POOK**

An early 19thC American massive giltwood convex mirror, the foliate crest with opposing eagle heads flanking a plinth with spread-winged eagle.

60in (152.5cm) high

£6,000-8,000   **POOK**

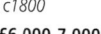

A giltwood convex mirror, with eagle crest and carved foliate drop.

c1800   *50in (127cm) high*

£6,000-7,000   **POOK**

A Regency giltwood convex wall mirror, the circular plate within a reeded ebonised slip and moulded frame with applied ball spacers, surmounted by an eagle cresting, over acanthus-carved apron from which issue two outscrolling branches.

40in (102cm) high

£3,000-5,000   **L&T**

A Regency giltwood and gesso convex wall mirror, the circular plate within a reeded ebonised slip and ball-moulded frame, surmounted by a flaming urn finial, the foliate-carved apron centred by a lion mask medallion.

53in (135cm) high

£3,500-4,500   **L&T**

A giltwood convex mirror, bearing the label of Thomas Fentham, the crest with recumbent stag, above a circular mirror plate with rope-twist surround and foliate drop.

c1800   *41.5in (105.5cm) high*

£3,500-4,500   **POOK**

A giltwood overmantel mirror, in Regency style, of recent manufacture, the sphere-mounted frieze above acanthus and lyre-mounted panels and three bevelled plates flanked by reeded split columns.

57in (145cm) wide

£700-900   **DN**

A Regency giltwood overmantel mirror, the rectangular plate surmounted by an eagle cresting and flanked by fluted columns headed by flaming torches.

46in (117cm) high

£3,000-4,000   **L&T**

A Regency carved giltwood and gesso overmantel mirror, the rectangular plate surmounted by a cavetto-moulded cornice, over a Greek key- and drapery-carved frieze, flanked by Doric pilasters headed by lion mask motifs.

53in (135cm) wide

£4,000-5,000   **L&T**

A Regency giltwood pier glass, the oblong plate below a frieze of classical charioteers flanked by foliate cluster columns headed by Egyptian caryatids, moulded cornice with applied orbs over stiff leaf banding flanked by lion masks, moulded base and ebonised plinth.

47.5in (120.5cm) high

£500-700   **HT**

An American Federal large giltwood mirror, moulded cornice with acorn drops, above a foliate-decorated frieze, with eglomise panel.

c1825   *59in (150cm) high*

£1,200-1,800   **POOK**

An American late Federal stencil-decorated mirror, with eglomise panel of a church.

c1825   *27in (68.5cm) high*

£1,500-2,500   **POOK**

An American Classical New England stencil-decorated mirror, the rectangular frame with gilt-stencilled floral designs and square corner blocks with rosettes, minor imperfections.

c1825   *27in (68.5cm) long*

£1,300-1,500   **SK**

A 19thC 'mid-18thC' style giltwood and gesso overmantel mirror, the cartouche-shape frame with ten subsidiary plates divided by acanthus-carved scrolls surmounted by an outstretched eagle above an icicle-carved frieze and scallop shell pendant.

59in (150cm) wide

£2,200-2,800   **L&T**

A Victorian gilt composition wall mirror, the profusely decorated and pierced pediment above a central plate flanked by two further plates, above a scroll and cabochon-decorated pendant frieze, damage.

c1870   *39.5in (100cm) wide*

£800-1,000   DN

A Victorian giltwood and gesso picture frame wall mirror, the rectangular bevelled plate within an ornate shaped openwork foliate, shell and S-scroll frame.

41.75in (106cm) wide

£3,000-5,000   L&T

A 19thC Flemish carved and stained pine mirror, in the Baroque taste, the frame with scrolling foliage and leafage around a medieval mask, flanked by male masks at the corners and spire finials.

57in (145cm) high

£2,500-3,500   L&T

A 19thC French giltwood cushion wall mirror, the bevelled octagonal mirror plate in moulded frame with further sloping mirror panels, with acanthus-carved angles and pierced cartouche cresting.

36.25in (92cm) wide

£2,500-3,500   L&T

One of a pair of 19thC French wall mirrors, each with rectangular mirror plate in moulded frame with harebell chain to the top, surmounted by stepped pediment with three urns.

18.25in (46cm) wide

£6,000-8,000 PAIR   L&T

A 19thC French giltwood wall mirror, the rectangular mirror plate in rope-twist frame, with Greek key tablet top and triple cartouche surmount, suspending floral swags.

34.75in (88cm) wide

£1,000-2,000   L&T

One of a pair of 19thC Rococo style carved and parcel-gilt walnut-framed wall mirrors, losses, repairs.

36.5in (93cm) high

£800-1,200 PAIR   DN

A 19thC gilt gesso Rococo design overmantel mirror, with three panels surmounted by a ho-ho bird, fruiting vines and scrolls.

61in (155cm) wide

£1,200-1,500   A&G

A pair of 19thC North Italian giltwood and gesso wall mirrors, each of cartouche-shaped form, boldly carved with flower heads and acanthus scrolls, the festooned crestings with pendant trefoil decorated friezes, the plates with oxidised silvering centred by engraved representations of medieval-style knights on Rococo plinths, holding a short sword and spear respectively.

23.25in (59cm) wide

£3,500-4,500   L&T

A 19thC French giltwood pier mirror, the rectangular plate with bas relief carved inner slip bordered by four subsidiary plates, the Baroque-style cresting with a festooned surmount, the scroll-carved frame entwined with carved flower-heads.

38.5in (98cm) wide

£2,500-3,500   **L&T**

A late 19thC Italian ebonised and giltwood wall mirror, the rectangular plate within margin plates decorated with marlins, scrolling masks, flowering urns and paterae to the corners, the stop-fluted outer frame with foliate scroll corners.

50in (127cm) wide

£1,200-1,800   **L&T**

A late 19thC Victorian carved oak-framed arch-topped wall mirror, probably adapted from a cheval mirror, later elements.

73.25in (186cm) high

£500-700   **DN**

A late 19thC French giltwood wall mirror, the rectangular mirror plate in mirrored, moulded and foliate-carved frame, with mirrored cartouche surmount centred by a carved basket of flowers.

21.75in (55cm) wide

£2,000-2,500   **L&T**

A Victorian mahogany-framed cheval mirror, with arched plate, inverted tapered supports with extending candle holders, scrolled feet joined by a stretcher.

£250-350   **GIL**

An Empire gilt-bronze-mounted mahogany and cheval glass, by Johannes Klinckerfus, the arched mirror plate within a mahogany frame set with gilt-bronze stars, supported by columns, joined by circular baluster-shaped supports, on down-scrolled feet, allover fitted with gilt-bronze mounts.

c1815-1820   *41.75in (106cm)*

£15,000-20,000   **SOTA**

A Regency mahogany and ebonised cheval mirror, the rectangular plate flanked by baluster-turned supports surmounted by urn finials, on plinth bases and four gilt-metal scroll feet, with casters, damage.

c1820   *36.25in (92cm) wide*

£1,200-1,800   **DN**

An Edwardian mahogany cheval mirror.

c1910

£1,200-1,500   **DN**

FURNITURE

A walnut dressing mirror, later gilt repair.

c1740   20in (51cm) wide
£350-550   DN

A George II walnut dressing mirror, faults.

c1750   23.75in (60cm) high
£350-450   DN

A mid-18thC George III mahogany and parcel-gilt dressing table mirror, with serpentine-fronted base.

          26.75in (68cm) high
£350-450   DN

A George III mahogany dressing table mirror, with bow-fronted base.

c1800   24in (61cm) wide
£250-350   DN

A George III mahogany bowfront dressing table mirror, faults.

c1810   21.75in (55.5cm) wide
£200-300   DN

An early 19thC George III mahogany and sycamore-strung dressing table mirror, the shield-shaped plate held in twin serpentine uprights, on a serpentine-fronted base with three drawers, on waisted bracket feet.

          25.25in (61.5cm) high
£700-900   DN

A George IV mahogany dressing table mirror, the adjustable oval plate held in twin serpentine uprights, the bowfront base with three drawers, on waisted bracket feet.

c1825   22.5in (57cm) high
£650-750   DN

A 19thC French brass toilet mirror, the circular looking glass supported by a demi-lune bracket, leading to two free-swing candle holders, the column decorated with a leaf and berry motif.

          15.5in (39.5cm) high
£400-600   FRE

An American Pennsylvania late Federal mahogany and tiger maple shaving mirror.

c1835   29.25in (75.25cm) wide
£2,000-2,500   POOK

SHELVES

An early George III set of oak hanging shelves.

c1760   38.5in (98cm) wide
£200-300   DN

A late 18thC American Pennsylvania mahogany hanging corner shelf, with elaborately scalloped sides and seven tiers.

          42.5in (108cm) high
£3,000-5,000   POOK

A George III mahogany wall-shelf, with three graduating tiers above two drawers, the whole carved and pierced with fretwork.

c1775
£1,200-1,500   FRE

FURNITURE

A pair of Regency chinoiserie-painted open wall shelves, of serpentine-sided outline, each with an arched cresting above three open shelves flanked by corner shelves, the whole bordered with giltwood foliage and pendant husks and decorated with scenes from Chinese courtly life, each on a pierced acanthus leaf apron centred by a carved cabochon.

31in (79cm) wide

£3,000-4,000 **L&T**

An early 19thC American yellow pine hanging corner shelf, with beaded edge shelves and scalloped base, retaining a blue surface.

39.5in (100.5cm) high

£2,000-3,000 **POOK**

An early 19thC American painted pine hanging shelf, with scalloped sides and plate racks above a lower section with pegs, retaining an old ochre surface.

41.75in (106cm) wide

£2,500-3,500 **POOK**

A mid-19thC American pine hanging shelf, with cut-out scrolled ends joining four shelves, and painted dark brown.

30in (76cm) wide

£900-1,200 **SK**

A pair of Victorian mahogany whatnots, the acanthus-carved arched backs above five serpentine graduated tiers, raised on baluster spiral-turned upright supports.

32.5in (82cm) wide

£2,500-3,500 **L&T**

A set of 19thC mahogany hanging wall shelves.

41.25in (105cm) high

£350-500 **DN**

A set of 19thC French walnut hanging shelves.

42.5in (108cm) wide

£350-450 **DN**

ÉTAGÈRE

A pair of Regency style black japanned and painted bronze étagères, the three rectangular tiers with chinoiserie decoration, raised on turned supports.

25in (63.5cm) wide

£1,500-2,000 **FRE**

A Continental rectangular mahogany étagère, with four tiers and a stepped top.

c1830 *31in (79cm) wide*

£650-750 **DN**

A William IV rosewood three-tier whatnot, the scroll supports with scroll terminals.

c1835 *44.5in (113cm) wide*

£800-1,200 **DN**

A 19thC French purpleheart and kingwood-banded étagère, of rectangular form with tray top and two open shelves, each quarter-veneered, the ends also matched-veneered, on chamfered uprights on angular cabriole legs, the whole with rocaille-cast gilt-metal mounts ending in sabots.

26.75in (68cm) wide

£2,500-3,000   **L&T**

A Victorian walnut four-tier whatnot.

c1870   *21.75in (55cm) wide*

£450-550   **DN**

A Victorian mahogany trolley, attributed to Howard & Sons, the two rectangular galleried tiers with pained spindles, raised on baluster-turned supports terminating in brass cappings and casters.

30in (76cm) wide

£2,500-3,500   **L&T**

A pair of Regency style rosewood and gilt-metal étagères, the two shaped rectangular tiers with spiral-reeded ball finials and turned supports, terminating in brass casters.

c1900   *15.25in (39cm) wide*

£3,000-4,000   **L&T**

A pair of brass and burr maple two-tier étagères, the rectangular tiers with inset glass panels, raised on turned supports with lobed finial and terminating in casters.

18in (49cm) wide

£2,000-2,500   **L&T**

DUMB WAITERS

A George III mahogany three-tier dumb waiter, with a spirally fluted baluster column ending in a cabriole tripod base with pad feet.

41.75in (106cm) high

£4,500-5,500   **L&T**

A George III mahogany dropleaf dumb waiter, of three graduated circular shelves with reeded edges on baluster column and downswept tripod base with brass box casters.

23.5in (60cm) diam

£2,200-2,800   **L&T**

A William IV mahogany two-tier dumb waiter.

c1835   *30in (76cm) wide*

£350-450   **DN**

FURNITURE

ESSENTIAL REFERENCE: BLACK FOREST WARES

Though named after Germany's Black Forest region, Black Forest carvings were first created in Switzerland in the early 19thC. By the 1850s their work was receiving acclaim at international exhibitions from London to Chicago to Paris

● In Europe, Black Forest wares became a symbol of wealth with many of the finest pieces becoming part of Royal collections or those of elite Victorian travellers. There was great demand in the US for pieces featuring native animals such as eagles.

● Examples featuring dogs are rarer than those featuring bears and required greater skill, so these tend to be more desirable. Signed pieces and those by certain families, like the Huggler family, command a premium.

A German Black Forest carved walnut hat/umbrella stand, with a spread-winged eagle above a shield-form mirror and mountain goat.

c1895   88in (223.5cm) high

£6,000-8,000   **POOK**

A 19thC century finely carved Black Forest dog hall stand, modelled as a long haired terrier seated on its hind legs begging, raised on a naturalistic shaped base with inset drip tray.

43in (103cm) high

£7,000-10,000   **L&T**

A George IV period mahogany hat and coat stand, the ring-turned twin section stem with lotus leaf-cast brass hooks and central stick supports, the whole ending in a cast iron square dished base.

70.75in (180cm) high

£3,000-4,000   **L&T**

A late Victorian bamboo hall stand, raised on four open step legs with two chrysanthemum and bat-carved trays, the stem with root and bar supports.

79.5in (202cm) high

£300-500   **WW**

A cold painted cast iron hall stand, the rectangular canted corner base on leaf-scroll feet with a central reeded stem with paw-scroll supports and an eight-ring stick division, above three tiers of open scroll hooks.

72in (183cm) high

£700-900   **WW**

A Victorian cast iron stick stand, painted black, the top with six circular apertures to a lift-out tray.

25in (63.5cm) high

£250-350   **WW**

A late 19th/early 20thC turned brass and iron corner stickstand, the base with lift-out tray, faint stamped registration number.

24.5in (62cm) high

£250-350   **WW**

A late 19th/early 20thC turned brass and cast iron semi-circular stick stand, with five divisions.

25.5in (65cm) high

£350-450   **WW**

An early 20thC turned brass and cast iron four-division stick stand, with lift-out tray.

24.5in (62cm) high

£200-300   **WW**

A carved mahogany and caned tapering cylindrical stick stand, with a lift-out zinc liner.

25.25in (65cm) high

£700-900   **WW**

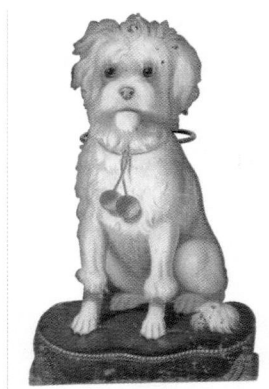

A late 19thC painted sheet iron dummy board stick stand, decorated with a terrier.

24in (61cm) high

£2,000-2,500   **DN**

A pair of George I carved giltwood torchères, the bead-moulded dished tops with an undulating frieze with acanthus-carved baluster-turned column supports, ending on three conforming cabriole scroll legs.

43.75in (111cm) high

£3,500-4,500   **L&T**

A George II mahogany kettle stand, with pie crust top, damage to top edge.

c1730   *18.5in (47cm) high*

£2,000-3,000   **DN**

A mid-18thC George II mahogany candle or kettle stand.

27.25in (69.5cm) high

£2,000-2,500   **DN**

CLOSER LOOK: GEORGE III CANDLESTANDS

The dished top with piecrust border is typical of candlestands made in the Chippendale style and highly desirable to collectors, especially when found on a period piece.

A pair of stands will be worth up to three times as much as a single example.

The stands were designed to hold little more than a candlestick. Any excess pressure may cause the pole to break – usually where it meets the top or the legs.

The deep carving and turning on the pole are signs of a quality piece.

The colour and patination of the wood also add to the desirability of the stands.

A pair of George III mahogany candlestands, some damage.

In a report on these stands, author R.W. Symonds notes that half of one of the lengths has been restored and states that this 'damage was caused through something falling on the top through the explosion of a German bomb at Ovenden House, Sundridge, Kent, the country residence of Lord Plender on the night of April 19th, 1941'.

c1760   *42.25in (107cm) high*

£20,000-25,000   **DN**

A Louis XVI painted torchère stand, with Sienna marble top, raised on three leaf-carved supports, ending in a triform base.

46in (117cm) high

£1,200-1,800   **L&T**

A pair of mahogany torchères.

c1780 and later   *71in (180cm) high*

£1,000-1,500   **DN**

FURNITURE

An unusual Regency cast iron gueridon, in the manner of Thomas Hope, the top inset with a central bronze medallion depicting Virgil reading to figures inscribed: 'VIRGILIVS APVD MECENATEM TVA MECANAS HAVD MOLLIA JVSSA', the fluted Ionic style column surmounted by a winged sphinx with a lizard with prey in its jaws above an anthemion-cast base of three inscrolling monopaediae with claw feet.

30in (76cm) high

£2,200-2,800   **L&T**

A pair of 19thC walnut and satinwood sculpture pedestals, with rouge marble tops.

43.75in (111cm) high

£2,000-3,000   **L&T**

A 19thC French giltwood torchère, the moulded circular top on hexagonal and acanthus-carved baluster column, on three S-scrolled legs.

12.75in (32cm) diam

£500-800   **L&T**

A pair of Neoclassical satinwood and painted pedestals, the crossbanded moulded square tops on a panelled square tapered column, painted with urns and trailing bellflowers, raised on moulded plinth bases.

47.5in (120.5cm) high

£1,500-2,500   **FRE**

A 19thC oak and walnut candlestand.

34.75in (88cm) high

£400-600   **DN**

A pair of 19thC French Empire style marble-topped mahogany demi-lune pedestals, each with black marble D-shaped top above bowfront column with gilt-metal winged Classical maiden mount, on moulded plinth with further mounts.

21.75in (55cm) wide

£2,200-2,800 PAIR   **L&T**

A pair of Empire style stained fruitwood pedestals, of square tapered form, applied with a gilt-metal mount.

66in (167.5cm) high

£1,500-2,500 PAIR   **FRE**

A 19thC Venetian giltwood and polychrome lacquer blackamoor torchère, the figure standing upon a gondola holding a fan and supporting an elaborately draped plinth 'revealed' at one corner to show a carved and moulded edge, on a faceted column applied with a swag and an octagonal plinth base raised on four large paw feet.

in (108cm) high

£2,500-3,500   **L&T**

A North Italian walnut, ebonised and painted wood blackamoor pedestal, the moulded circular top supported on the head of a carved kneeling figure, on moulded circular plinth base.

15.74in (40cm) diam

£1,200-1,500   **L&T**

An elaborately carved Italian walnut torchère stand, the circular moulded top resting on the head of a winged sphinx, standing on cartouche-shaped base with paw feet.

18.25in (46cm) diam

£1,000-1,500   **L&T**

A pair of Neoclassical style carved mahogany figural torchère stands, each with a marble top supported by Classical maidens, raised on claw feet.

40in (101.5cm) high

£1,500-2,500   **FRE**

A pair of late 19thC cast iron torchères by Antoine Durenne, both stamped 'A. Durenne' on base.

61.5in (156cm) high

£3,000-5,000   **POOK**

A pair of Empire style stained fruitwood pedestals, of square tapered form, applied with a gilt-metal mount.

66in (167.5cm) high

£1,500-2,500   **FRE**

A George III mahogany adjustable writing table, the ratchet-adjustable top above a false drawer, and two flanking drawers with divided interiors, the revolving height-adjustable stem on four downswept legs, pad feet and brass casters.

c1780   26.25in (67cm) wide

£2,000-2,500   **DN**

A pair of Regency mahogany reading stands, the tops with moulded book-rests on brass quadrant ratchet supports and brass thumbscrews to adjustable columns, on baluster columns with gadrooned triform bases with underscrolled feet decorated with roundels.

29.25in (74cm) high

£3,500-4,500   **L&T**

A Regency mahogany duet stand, shaped supports with two brass candle arms on tripod base.

44in (112cm) high

£800-1,200   **GORL**

A William IV mahogany folio stand, with trellis-framed wings on adjustable ratchet supports, on dual outsplaying legs ending in brass paw caps and casters.

24in (61cm) wide

£2,000-3,000   **L&T**

A William IV rosewood adjustable duet stand.

c1835

£3,000-4,000   **DN**

A mid-19thC walnut quintet music stand, with turned central finial, with five brass candle sconces, on a turned column, supported on a tripod base.

49.5in (126cm) high

£1,200-1,800   **DN**

A 19thC mahogany, simulated rosewood and brass-strung Campaign duet stand, the lattice-framed rests with hinged folding mechanism flanked by a pair of engine-turned gilt-brass sconces, on an adjustable turned and ringed column with acanthus-carved base, on downswept tripod base ending in brass box casters.

19.75in (50cm) wide

£4,500-5,500   **L&T**

A late 19th/early20thC carved mahogany artist's folio stand, the hinged panel carved with a central palette and brushes within a surround depicting flowering foliage and two birds within a paterae and scroll-carved border, above a frieze carved with an owl in flight, on anthemion-carved trestle supports, with a lion mask below, above a pair of downswept legs with scroll feet, the panel above signed 'L Fruillini, Firenze'.

£3,000-5,000　　　　DN

A George III mahogany and boxwood-strung oval urn table, the top with galleried edge and cup slide above an undulating frieze on slender splayed square tapering legs ending in spade feet.

14in (36cm) wide

£1,200-1,800　　L&T

A George III mahogany kettle stand, the galleried top above a slide.

c1780　　13in (33cm) wide

£1,500-2,500　　DN

A military washbasin, the silver-plated basin sits fitted into a brass inlay mahogany rectangular box.

c1820　　16in (40.5cm) wide

£500-700　　FRE

A 19thC Continental rosewood bird's eye maple and tulipwood billet doux, the rectangular fall front inset with a beaded needlework panel, opening to reveal an interior fitted for writing, raised on upright supports and downswept part-ebonised legs.

21in (53.5cm) wide

£400-600　　FRE

A William IV rosewood teapoy, the hinged top opening to a fitted interior with two bowl apertures and a lidded canister, on a baluster-shaped stem and lobed plinth with four scroll feet and concealed casters.

c1835　　30in (76cm)

£450-650　　DN

A Victorian figured walnut teapoy, the hinged oval top above the moulded and gadrooned frieze on the baluster-turned and reeded stem issuing three leaf-carved downswept legs and scroll-carved feet, damage.

c1860　　28.75in (73cm) high

£350-450　　DN

An American Queen Anne mahogany pole screen, possibly Philadelphia, the elaborate needlework panel depicting two figures in a pastoral setting, above a suppressed ball standard supported by cabriole legs terminating in pad feet.

61.5in (156cm) high

£2,000-3,000 **POOK**

A late 18thC George III mahogany pole screen, the elaborate rolled paper shield-form screen with central oval portrait, above a baluster standard supported by carved cabriole legs terminating in scroll feet.

54.5in (138.5cm) high

£1,500-2,500 **POOK**

A pair of rosewood and gilt-metal-mounted pole screens, in the manner of Gillow, each rectangular panel cornered by scroll terminals, the base with turned and reeded faceted stem, and issuing three outswept feet on reeded bun feet, damage, repair.

c1825 *55in (140cm) high*

£2,000-3,000 **DN**

A large Victorian walnut-framed Regimental cheval firescreen, for the Cameron Highlanders, the Rococo-carved frame with putto and thistle-pierced cresting above military trophies and stylised banners surmounted by wreaths, on scrolling trestle base, the wool-work panel with armorial bearing flanked by two highland riflemen, inscribed 'Arriverete Pro Rece Et Patria '92 – MAYA'.

43.25in (110cm) wide

£800-1,200 **L&T**

FURNITURE

A George III brass-bound mahogany cellaret on stand, the hinged lid opening to a plain interior well, with flanking loop handles, on later square tapered legs ending in brass cappings and casters.

c1780   17.5in (44.5cm) wide
£1,500-2,500   **FRE**

An American Norfolk, Virginia Federal mahogany cellaret, rectangular lift lid fitted with a brass plate inscribed 'Capt. E. Kennedy United States Navy', and opening to fitted well of fifteen compartments and back counter board, above three graduated cockbeaded drawers flanked by reeded panels, on ring-turned tapering legs with inset brass bails to sides, repairs to rear corners of top.

PROVENANCE: Captain Edmund P. Kennedy of Norfolk, Va., had command of the famous ship, The Hornet, in 1825, and sailed to the West Indies and Gulf of Mexico.
c1800   40.5in (103cm) high
£6,000-8,000   **FRE**

£2,000-3,000

CLOSER LOOK: GEORGE III CELLARET

This oval cellaret with its fluted lid relates to a number of well-known examples from collections that are attributed to Gillows.

This coopered shape is typical for cellarets. However, the fluted lid with finial and carved legs lift it above the norm.

The cellaret was made from well-figured mahogany and has an excellent patina – adding to its desirability.

Gillows is also known to have made a number of cellarets with reeded baluster legs.

A George III mahogany cellaret, in the manner of Gillows, some loss to top finial.

The term 'wine cooler' is commonly interchangeable with the term 'cellaret'. However, not all wine coolers are cellarets – a cellaret has a lockable lid, making it a 'little cellar', a wine cooler does not.
c1800   26.75in (68cm) wide
£12,000-18,000   **DN**

A George III mahogany and crossbanded octagonal cellaret, with later baize-lined interior on tapering square-section legs with brass casters, the whole decorated with boxwood lines.
18.5in (47cm) wide
£850-950   **L&T**

A George III mahogany and brass-bound wine cooler, of oval section, with twin carry handles and later ogee bracket feet.

31.25in (79cm) wide
£700-900   **L&T**

A George III mahogany cellaret.

c1810   20.5in (52cm) wide
£400-600   **DN**

A Regency mahogany sarcophagus cellaret, in the manner of Gillows, later carved overall with foliate decoration, the rounded rectangular shallow domed hinged lid above heavily gadrooned feet with wood casters.
32.75in (83cm) wide
L&T

A Regency mahogany table cellaret, with domed top and square-section tapering body, damage, later elements.
c1820   17.25in (44cm) high
£400-600   **DN**

A William IV mahogany cellaret, the interior stamped 'JAMES WINTER & SONS 101 WARDOUR ST. SOHO, LONDON'.

c1835   30in (76cm) wide
£1,500-2,000   **DN**

A late 18thC French carved walnut hutch, the arched pediment carved with twin heart motifs and foliage above the pierced and arched door, flanked by turned spindle columns to the front and sides, above a sheaf-carved frieze and scroll-carved feet, damage.

32.25in (82cm) wide

£700-900 DN

A 19thC Classical mahogany canterbury, crossing uprights with applied wreaths and scrolls, single beaded drawer, on turned legs and casters.

23in (58.5cm) wide

£900-1,200 FRE

A late Regency mahogany canterbury, damage, repairs.

c1820 *20.5in (52cm) high*

£1,000-1,500 DN

A late Regency mahogany canterbury.

c1820 *19.75in (50cm) wide*

£1,500-2,000 DN

A William IV rosewood canterbury, with four yoke-shaped divisions crested by foliate ornaments terminating in turned cross rails, the cockbeaded frieze drawer on short turned and lappet-carved legs with brass socket casters, stamped 'Johnson & Jeanes, 67 New Bond Street'.

26.75in (68cm) wide

£1,000-1,500 L&T

A William IV rosewood canterbury, in the manner of Gillow, the X-frame upper section with three divisions and centred by lyre terminals above a drawer on turned tapering and reeded legs, brass caps and casters, damage, lacking minor parts.

c1835 *21in (53cm) wide*

£1,200-1,500 DN

A late 19thC Victorian walnut canterbury, with shelf.

37.5in (95.5cm) high

£500-700 DN

A late Victorian brass and oak canterbury, revolving on an open triform stem, the ironwork stamped 'Hall BM'.

35.25in (89.5cm) high

£150-250 WW

A late Victorian oak and brass canterbury.

34in (87cm) high

£150-250 WW

FURNITURE

A Regency mahogany jardinière, in the manner of Gillows, of X-form with an inset tin liner, raised on outscrolling legs united by a shaped apron.

22.5in (57cm) wide

£1,500-2,000　　　　**L&T**

A Napoleon III gilt-metal-mounted amboyna jardinière.

c1870　　　　*15in (38cm) wide*

£550-650　　　　**DN**

A late 19thC satinwood oval jardinière, the sides decorated with four chinoiserie lacquer panels depicting figures in garden landscapes within ebonised, line-inlaid and floral-painted outer borders enclosing a metal liner on four splayed square-section legs with inswept feet.

27in (69cm) wide

£2,500-3,500　　　　**L&T**

A pair of late 19thC Continental brass jardinières, each with stylised lion masks to back and front.

11.25in (28.5cm) wide

£250-350　　　　**DN**

A 19thC 'Grotto' jardinière, the rectangular canted cornered top with a brass lift-out tray with applied floral decoration and shaped apron with fir cone-decorated frieze on a branch stem to shaped base with lug feet.

32.5in (85cm) high

£1,000-1,500　　　　**WW**

A late 19th/early 20thC Continental gilt-brass jardinière, cast with panthers' heads at the corners, with zinc liner.

15.75in (40cm) wide

£250-350　　　　**DN**

An early 20thC American bird cage model, of square form, painted timber and steel construction, caging fifteen bird models.

37in (94cm) high

£350-450　　　　**FRE**

A late 19th/early 20thC steel bird cage model, of arch form, steel and timber construction, caging twelve bird models.

31in (78.5cm) high

£250-300　　　　**FRE**

A George III mahogany library step ladder, the four graduated steps with shaped aprons.

65.75in (167cm) high

£2,500-3,500　　　　**L&T**

A late 18th/early 19thC set of mahogany library steps, the frame supporting three steps below an octagonal handle, damaged, lacking parts.

59in (150cm) high

£4,000-5,000　　　　**DN**

An Iberian walnut and brass wine rack, the rectangular base with one drawer, surmounted by a wirework frame, supporting nine bottles.

16.5in (42cm) wide

£1,500-2,000　　　　**L&T**

A late 18th/19thC oak child's cradle, the canopy with shaped frieze above panelled back and sides.

21.25in (54cm) wide

£350-450 **DN**

An early 19thC late Empire mahogany cradle, the supporting columns carved with acanthus leaves and resting on lion paws, the interior lined with mustard-coloured silk, retaining pillow and duvet.

53.25in (135cm) wide

£1,500-2,500 **SOTA**

A William IV mahogany and canework cradle.

c1825, *39.5in (100cm) wide*

£200-300 **DN**

An Empire mahogany and gilt-bronze-mounted bed, the columns at the front supporting Medusa mask roundels, with engine milled socle collars.

c1810 *78.75in (200cm) long*

£800-1,200 **DN**

A 19thC Anglo-Indian 'European Classical Revival' style ebonised rosewood four-poster bed.

£5,000-10,000 **GUIN**

A late 19thC Anglo Indian carved and stained hardwood four-poster bed, the openwork headboard with lion and unicorn cresting.

88.5in (225cm) long

£4,500-5,500 **DN**

A 19thC George III style mahogany four-poster bed.

79.5in (202cm) long

£5,000-6,000 **DN**

A late 19thC Louis XV style rosewood and marquetry bedstead, with gilt-brass mounts, the headboard with applied brass trade label for 'DRUCE & CO Upholsters & Cabinet Makers, Baker Street, London. W. From Second Hand Department'.

81in (205cm) long

£2,000-3,000 **WW**

FURNITURE

A 17thC and later South German marquetry miniature table cabinet, of various woods, the front doors inlaid with floral motif, opening to an arrangement of drawers around a central door, all with marquetry depicting townscapes, on a modern plinth base.

9.75in (24.5cm) high

£1,000-1,500 **FRE**

A rare American Queen Anne miniature painted pine and maple tall chest, in two parts, the top with a cove cornice above two small drawers over three long drawers, resting on a base with two small drawers, pronounced scalloped skirt, and cabriole legs terminating in crooked feet.

c1750 *48in (122cm) high*

£10,000-15,000 **POOK**

A late 18thC American miniature blanket chest, Lancaster County, Pennsylvania, the front with typical incised shell carving with trailing vines, above two shell-carved drawers, flanked by delicately chamfered and fluted corners supported by short ogee carved bracket feet, from the Shelley Collection.

15.5in (39.5cm) wide

£10,000-15,000 **POOK**

A late 18thC Louis XIV style amaranth and walnut miniature bureau mazarin, the rectangular parquetry-inlaid top above one small drawer and one deep drawer flanked by banks of three drawers, raised on square tapered legs joined by shaped stretchers ending in bun feet, stamped 'I Viez'.

12.5in (32cm) high

£600-800 **FRE**

A Regency rosewood and sycamore-strung miniature chest of drawers.

c1815 *14.5in (37cm) wide*

£700-1,000 **DN**

An American Clay Township, Lancaster County, Pennsylvania painted pine miniature blanket chest, by Joseph Long Lehn (1798-1892), with iron red ground, green, red, and yellow pinstriping and découpage floral sprays.

8.25in (21cm) wide

£600-800 **POOK**

A Victorian walnut miniature chest of drawers, the rectangular top above two short and three long drawers, on a plinth base.

c1880 *20.5in (52cm)*

£200-300 **DN**

An 19thC Louis XV/XVI style kingwood and parquetry miniature commode, the later ebonised wood top above three drawers on slightly hipped cabriole legs, fitted with gilt-bronze leafy mounts throughout.

10.75in (27.5cm) wide

£600-800 **FRE**

CLOSER LOOK: MAHOGANY TEA CHEST

This unusual chest was made with high quality fittings and has survived in near mint condition.

Each panel is decorated with inlaid quatrefoils. The rectangular body has canted corners and a hinged lid with a kingwood sloping edge.

The scroll handle is hallmarked with lion passant and makers initials 'J.S.'.

Inside is a pair of rectangular canisters, lead-lined with sliding faceted cover and turned ebonised lid with inset disc engraved with a crest, flanking a further canister with sliding domed cover.

An early George III mahogany tea chest, with silver-lined inlay and ebonised moulding, the front inset with pierced Gothic escutcheon.

10.25in (26cm) wide

£12,000-15,000   WW

A George II burr walnut bombé tea caddy, the hinged lid with a scroll handle, opening to reveal a compartmented interior with brass fittings, raised on squat bracket feet.

8in (20.5cm) wide

£2,500-3,000   L&T

A George III fruitwood 'apple' tea caddy, the hinged lid opening to reveal a lined interior.

4in (10cm) high

£1,700-2,000   L&T

A George III fruitwood 'apple' tea caddy with hinged lid.

4.5in (11cm) high

£1,100-1,300   L&T

An 18thC fruitwood 'pear' tea caddy, of typical form, the hinged lid with a curved stalk.

6.75in (17cm) high

£1,500-2,000   L&T

An 18thC fruitwood 'pear' tea caddy, of typical form, the hinged lid with a curved stalk finial.

7.5in (19cm) high

£4,000-5,000   L&T

A late 18thC George III mahogany tea caddy of oval section, with bone-inset diamond escutcheon, the interior with subsidiary cover.

6in (15cm) wide

£400-600   DN

A late 18thC George III mahogany and marquetry tea caddy, the hinged cover with fan patera in an oval reserve and cavetto edging, the interior previously with twin divisions, lacking interior divisions.

12in (30.5cm) wide

£120-180   DN

A late 18thC George III tortoiseshell-veneered tea caddy, of rectangular section, with ivory banding.

5in (12.5cm) wide

£2,000-3,000   DN

A George III tortoiseshell and ivory-strung decagonal tea caddy, the front inset with a vacant shield within a gold and mother-of-pearl dot border, with drape above a bright cut escutcheon, the hinged top with a gold loop handle and dot star, the inner lid with a turned ivory handle, with key.

5in (12.5cm) high

£5,500-6,500   WW

A late 18thC Georgian rolled paper tea caddy, of navette form with brass finial, inlaid with foliage on a scroll ground, opening to reveal a satinwood inner lid.

7.5in (19cm) wide

£700-1,000   HT

A late 18thC George III satinwood and crossbanded tea caddy, of oval section, the cover with brass swing handle, the interior with metal lining.

6.25in (16cm) wide

£650-850   DN

A George III harewood and marquetry-inlaid tea caddy, the square sides and domed lid inlaid with stylised trailing bell flowers and burr wood oval panels, opening to reveal a conforming covered interior.

5.75in (14.5cm) wide

£1,500-2,000   L&T

A late George III rosewood and brass bound tea caddy, the hinged lid enclosing a compartmented interior with brass fittings, raised on bracket feet.

8.75in (22cm) wide

£1,000-1,500   L&T

A George III walnut and parquetry tea caddy, the ogee moulded hinged lid, opening to reveal a compartmented interior with brass fittings, raised on later claw-and-ball feet.

8.5in (21.5cm) wide

£900-1,100   L&T

A George III mahogany and kingwood crossbanded tea caddy, of cubic form, the hinged lid opening to reveal a parquetry-inlaid interior with covered compartments.

5in (12.5cm) wide

£400-600   L&T

A George III ivory tea caddy, of canted rectangular form, with tortoiseshell inlay and silver mounts, the hinged lid enclosing a covered compartment.

4in (10cm) wide

£1,200-1,800   L&T

A late George III mahogany tea caddy, elaborately inlaid throughout with boxwood stringing, ivory flowerheads, roundels and mother-of-pearl, the hinged lid revealing a central cut glass bowl flanked by lidded compartments, the underside of lid radial-veneered, the whole raised on ball feet.

12.5in (31.5cm) wide

£1,500-2,500   L&T

A late George III or Regency burr yew wood and gilt-brass-mounted tea caddy, with twin subsidiary covers within.

c1810   8.25in (21cm) wide

£250-350   **DN**

A Regency rosewood and sycamore-strung tea caddy, of sarcophagus form, with repoussé brass and ring handles, the fitted interior with twin subsidiary caddies with hinged covers and a central cut glass bowl.

c1815   13in (33cm) wide

£100-150   **DN**

A Regency rosewood tea caddy, of sarcophagus form, the interior with twin subsidiary caddies and a glass bowl.

c1815   15in (38cm) wide

£280-320   **DN**

A Regency pen work tea caddy, of canted rectangular form, decorated with griffins, foliage chequer banding and geometric designs, the hinged lid enclosing a covered compartmented interior.

7in (18cm) wide

£900-1,200   **L&T**

A Regency mahogany and brass moulded tea caddy, of rectangular form with ebonised and brass moulding, sand winged brass escutcheon, the lid with an ivory ball finial, opening to a compartmented interior comprising three removable lidded mahogany tea containers.

c1815   10.5in (26.5cm) wide

£700-1,000   **FRE**

A Regency rosewood tea caddy, of sarcophagus form.

c1815   13.5in (34cm) wide

£300-400   **DN**

An early 19thC Regency tortoiseshell tea caddy, with retail label for 'F. L. Hausburg, Goldsmith & Jeweller, Old Post Office Building, Liverpool'.

7in (18cm) wide

£2,600-3,000   **FRE**

A Regency tortoiseshell and ivory tea caddy, of canted rectangular form, the hinged lid enclosing two conforming covered compartments.

7in (18cm) wide

£2,000-3,000   **L&T**

A Regency bowfront tortoiseshell tea caddy, the radiating fluted front with a domed hinged lid, opening to reveal two covered compartments, raised on four ball feet.

7in (17.5cm) wide

£1,800-2,200   **L&T**

A Regency tortoiseshell tea caddy, of serpentine form, the moulded hinged top opening to reveal two lidded wells raised on bun feet.

c1820   8in (20.5cm) wide

£1,200-1,800   **FRE**

A Regency blonde tortoiseshell tea caddy, of sarcophagus shape with ivory stringing, the hinged cover with a plated ball finial, to a twin-lidded interior with turned ivory handles, on ball feet.

8.25in (21cm) wide

£1,500-2,000   **WW**

An early 19thC Regency tortoiseshell tea caddy, the pagoda-form top of serpentine outline with brass name plate, over a conforming body with a brass escutcheon, opening to a compartmented interior, on ball feet.

7.5in (19cm) wide

£700-1,000   **FRE**

A late Regency tortoiseshell bowfront tea caddy, with silver stringing and a floral mother-of-pearl-inlaid front, the hinged pagoda lid with a plaque inscribed 'J & E Lister to F H & M Firth', the interior with a pair of lidded compartments with vegetable ivory handles, on turned feet.

7.5in (19cm) wide

£1,800-2,200 **WW**

An unusually large Regency gonzalo alves and crossbanded tea caddy, of sarcophagus form and with twin lion-mask-and-loop handles, the moulded top enclosing a typical fitted interior with an associated Bristol blue glass mixing bowl, raised on claw-and-ball feet.

17in (43cm) wide

£1,800-2,200 **L&T**

An early 19thC oak fruitwood and boxwood parquetry-decorated tea caddy, the hinged lid revealing star-inlaid liner, together with parquetry-decorated caddy spoon.

£300-400 **LOC**

A Regency chinoiserie-decorated tea caddy, the hinged lid opening to reveal a foliate penwork-decorated interior with two lidded wells, the swelled side with cornucopia loop handles, raised on brass feet.

8.75in (22cm) wide

£300-500 **FRE**

A large George IV tortoiseshell tea caddy, of bombé form, the carnet moulded hinged lid enclosing a twin-lidded interior with central cut glass bowl, with ivory paterae bun side handles and conforming feet.

13in (33cm) wide

£2,500-3,500 **L&T**

A George IV or William IV rosewood and mother-of-pearl-inlaid tea caddy, of sarcophagus form, twin subsidiary caddies within, damage.

c1830 *12.75in (32.5cm) wide*

£200-300 **DN**

An early 19thC yew wood tea caddy, with banding and stringing, the hinged lid to a pair of hinged lidded canisters flanking a later glass bowl.

12.25in (31cm) wide

£220-280 **WW**

An early 19thC burr yew wood tea caddy, with boxwood stringing, the interior previously divided.

7.5in (19cm) wide

£150-250 **WW**

A George IV tortoiseshell tea caddy, the hinged pagoda top with a vacant plaque, the interior with a single lidded compartment, the front with a pressed fan motif and with beaded mounts, on ball feet.

4.5in (11.5cm) wide

£1,500-2,500 **WW**

A George IV tortoiseshell tea caddy, with white metal stringing, the sides with pressed Gothic windows, the hinged pagoda lid with an ivory finial, the inner lid with ivory banding and finial, revealing a divided interior, on brass ball feet, with key.

7in (8cm) high

£6,000-8,000 **WW**

A Victorian dome-top burl walnut tea caddy, with parquetry banding, opening to reveal a twin compartment interior, the covers lacking.

c1840 *8in (20.5cm) wide*

£120-180 **FRE**

A mid-19thC cut brass and tortoiseshell tea caddy, the hinged cover to a pair of yew wood-lidded canisters.

9.5in (24cm) high

£400-600   **WW**

A Victorian papier mâché tea caddy, with simulated malachite borders and floral-decorated, the hinged lid to a pair of lidded compartments with mother-of-pearl floret handles.

9.25in (23.5cm) wide

£200-400   **WW**

A Victorian papier mâché tea caddy, by Jennens and Bettridge, of bombé form, with canted corners, polychrome-decorated and inlaid mother-of-pearl, the hinged lid with a pair of lidded compartments and mother-of-pearl handles, the underside stamped 'Jennens & Bettridge Makers to the Queen', '9' over '19' and painted '52'.

9.75in (25cm) wide

£500-800   **WW**

A 19thC Sorrento ware tea caddy, the walnut ground with multi-strung borders, the hinged lid centred with a marquetry panel of figures dancing, the inside with a floral panel and a pair of hinged lidded canisters with marquetry figure panels.

10.75in (27.5cm) wide

£350-450   **WW**

A late 19thC French lacquered brass inlay tea caddy, of rectangular form, the blue lacquer ground finely inlaid with brass foliate scroll work, the hinged lid encloses two covered caddies and weights.

8in (20.5cm) wide

£300-500   **FRE**

A 19thC French rosewood, cut pewter, brass and ivory tea caddy, of slight bombé form, the hinged lid to a pair of lidded compartments.

8.75in (22cm) wide

£300-500   **WW**

A Victorian satinwood and polychrome-decorated tea caddy, with crossbanding and stringing, the hinged lid to a pair of hinged canisters decorated with portrait miniatures of a lady and gentleman, flanking a bowl aperture.

11.5in (29cm) wide

£600-800   **WW**

A late 19thC Chinese lacquer tea caddy, of concave-sided octagonal form, decorated with figures and foliage, the hinged lid to a pair of lidded pewter canisters, on carved giltwood claw feet.

9in (23cm) wide

£350-450   **WW**

A 19thC continental papier mâché tea caddy, decorated with oriental scenes, the hinged lid to a divided interior.

8.75in (22cm) wide

£150-250   **WW**

An early 20thC Chinese hexagonal painted wood tea caddy, decorated figures in garden landscapes, the hinged lid with a lift-out pewter canister, on carved giltwood winged claw feet.

6in (15cm) high

£250-350   **WW**

A George V tortoiseshell and silver-mounted tea caddy, of octagonal form, the hinged cover velvet-lined with remains of foil to the interior, hallmarked Birmingham.

1910   *4.75in (12cm) wide*

£500-700   **WW**

An 18thC Indo-Portugese tortoiseshell and ivory work box, the panelled sides with foliate and scale decoration, opening to reveal a foliate scroll-inlaid compartmented interior with central well and inset mirror plate.

4in (10cm) high

£3,000-4,000   **L&T**

A mid-17thC Charles II elaborate needlework casket, with raised work flowers, insects, birds, fruit, trees and man and woman on an ivory satin ground.

12.5in (32cm) wide

£3,500-4,000   **POOK**

A late George III oyster laburnum box, the hinged lid with mirror inset to the underside, with fitted interior above two drawers, later adapted with divisions in the drawers as a collector's cabinet, one drawer containing shells.

19.25in (49cm) wide

£500-600   **DN**

An early 19thC Vizagapatam ivory workbox, decorated throughout with trailing foliage and anthemion and with oval side carrying handles, the hinged lid enclosing a lidded and compartmented interior above a drawer.

11.25in (28.5cm) wide

£1,000-1,500   **L&T**

A late Regency blonde tortoiseshell work box, with white metal stringing, the hinged lid with an inset plaque to a paper-lined vacant interior, on brass ball feet.

12in (30.5cm) wide

£1,500-2,000   **WW**

An early 19thC Indian Vizagapatam ivory box, of domed waisted form, with etched bands of interlaced leaves and flowerheads, ribbed lid, on outsplayed bracket feet.

11.5in (29cm) wide

£1,000-1,500   **L&T**

A fine early 19thC Indian Vizagapatam ivory work box, of sarcophagus form, the reeded lid and sides decorated with bands of fruiting vines, opening to reveal a fitted interior, raised on lobed bun feet.

13in (33cm) wide

£2,500-3,500   **L&T**

A William IV or early Victorian rosewood and mother-of-pearl-inset workbox, of sarcophagus form with bun feet with foliate panels to cover and front, the fitted interior with lift out tray.

c1835   *12in (30.5cm) wide*

£180-220   **DN**

A mid-19thC Victorian mahogany and parquetry work box, of sarcophagus form, the top with geometric inlay, above ogee sides, on bun feet, with a brass swing handle at each end, the velvet-lined fitted interior with lift out tray.

12.5in (20cm) wide

£450-550   **DN**

A mid-19thC rosewood combined musical and sewing box, in the form of a piano, the fitted interior with various implements, some associated.

11.5in (29cm) long

£500-700 **DN**

A 19thC Anglo-Indian workbox, possibly Vizagapatam, with inlaid rosewood exterior, the hinged lid opening to reveal a sandalwood interior over a long drawer to the base, with losses.

14in (35.5cm) wide

£500-600 **HALL**

A 19thC Anglo-Ceylonese bone-inlaid calamander and specimen wood box, Galle District, of shaped rectangular form, the hinged top opening to a bone-inlaid specimen wheel to the reverse and two tiers of compartmentalised trays fitted with specimen wood lids.

15in (38cm) wide

£700-1,000 **FRE**

A 19thC Anglo-Indian Vizagapatam ivory-inlaid hardwood dressing box, with chevron banding and inlaid throughout with scrolling foliage and stylised motifs, centred by a shaped reserve depicting two peacocks standing beneath a tree, the hinged lid opening to reveal a compartmented interior with covered wells, a removable tray and mirrored plate.

18in (46cm) wide

£2,000-3,000 **L&T**

A late 19thC Victorian walnut, marquetry and crossbanded workbox, with ogee moulded sides.

14in (35cm) wide

£250-350 **DN**

A late 19thC Ceylonese calamander and ivory-inlaid workbox, with scalloped sides, the interior inlaid with ivory engraved in red and black ink and silver wire-inlaid chevron-decorated borders. Rear elevating section with five drawers incorporating three-quarter-length portraits of a king and dignitaries and the front section with two compartmentalised removable trays, each compartment lid of the lower tray inlaid with a different specimen wood.

The scalloped interior is a design derived from 18thC bible boxes produced under Dutch colonial patronage in Matara, a town in the Galle district. Parallels can also be drawn with the ripple and scalloped mouldings featured on some 17th and 18thC furniture produced in the Netherlands. The central figure in this box seems to be wearing a stylised British naval uniform and one wonders if it could be a representation of William IV. The figures in profile could well represent Ceylonese noblemen.

17.75in (45cm) wide

An Anglo-Indian horn and ivory sewing box, Vizagapatam, with pierced and lac decoration, the sandalwood interior with divided and lidded compartments.

8.5in (21.5cm) wide

£200-300 **WW**

£4,000-5,000 **SOTH**

A Newport, Rhode Island, Federal maple and mahogany-inlaid lap desk, the top centring a rosewood star and oval within a rectangle of stringing, corner quarter fans and rosewood edging, on conformingly inlaid case, the facade centring a shield, the sides with small drawers fitted with brass bail pulls, on a later mahogany base, refinished.

c1810   20.75in (52.5cm) wide

£2,000-2,500   **SK**

A Regency mahogany and brass-bound miniature writing slope.

c1815   7in (18cm) wide

£250-300   **DN**

A George IV mahogany boxed writing slope, by T. Handford, with brass corners and sunken handles, the interior with two trade labels 'T. Handford Improved Writing Desk Manufactory No. 7 Strand, London', the other promoting a travelling trunk.

     22in (55.5cm) wide

£300-500   **WW**

A 19thC leather writing slope, gilt and silver-gilt mounts to all corners and rope-twist gilt-metal handles.

Made by F West, No 1 St James's Street, London, and manufacturer to Queen Victoria. Original interior of green leather and velvet with gold tooling, lined with green silk and fitted with a removable green-tooled leather blotter pad. The first removable tray contains gilt and silver-gilt tools and objects including a pen tray with spaces for ink bottle, vesta box and candle holder, scissors, ruler, rubber and dividers, as well as gold pen, pencil, seal, knife and spatula. On either side of the tray is a book: a journal to record notes and addresses, and a cash book, started by the owner in 1856, to record income and expenditure. Under the first tray is a second, to hold stationery. Below is a secret floor for secret correspondence. All the gilt-metal mounts, including the screws, are engraved. The original owner was Lady Jane Lissey Harriet Levett, who was given the box as a wedding present in 1856. She used the cashbook from 1856 until just before the birth of her third child in November 1863.

c1855   15in (38cm) wide

£7,000-9,000   **RGA**

A late19thC Victorian walnut and parquetry-banded combination workbox and writing slope, with fitted interior.

     11.75in (30cm) wide

£150-250   **DN**

A 19thC Indian Khatamkari stationery box, ivory-veneered within borders of geometric patterns, the hinged lid revealing a sandalwood interior of five graduated divisions, some losses.

     8.25in (21cm) wide

£150-250   **HALL**

A Victorian burr walnut stationery cabinet, having a pierced fret fitted interior, damages.

     14in (35.5cm) high

£150-250   **WW**

A late 17th/early 18thC ebonised and tortoiseshell table cabinet, probably Spanish, the hinged lid above a concave compartment and a pair of panelled doors, enclosing a cupboard door and seven drawers.

20.5in (52cm) wide

£1,500-2,500   **L&T**

An early 18thC Italian bone-inlaid ebony table cabinet, Naples, the drawers inlaid with circular motifs, the sides with bale handles and shaped inlaid designs, the back with similar inlay raised on bun feet.

30.5in (77.5cm) wide

£3,500-4,500   **FRE**

An early 18thC Indo-Portuguese tortoiseshell and ivory table cabinet, hinged front panel lacking, damage, repair.

18in (46cm) wide

£13,000-16,000   **DN**

A Chester County, Pennsylvania Chippendale walnut spice box, the moulded cornice over a single door with elaborate line and berry inlay with central eight-point star within a crosshatched circle surrounded by a whimsical scrolling vine and crosshatched border, enclosing an interior with nine drawers, supported by spurred bracket feet.

c1765   *16.5in (42cm)*

£30,000-40,000   **POOK**

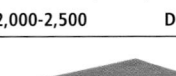

A second half 18thC Colonial rosewood and padouk table cabinet.

15in (38.5cm) wide

£2,000-2,500   **DN**

A mid-late 18thC Indo-Portuguese tortoiseshell and ivory table cabinet, the panelled sides with applied bronze flower-head motifs the fall-front opening to reveal a fitted interior with an arrangement of 11 drawers.

20in (50.4cm) wide

£12,000-15,000   **L&T**

A Victorian walnut table cabinet, the doors opening to three drawers within.

13in (33cm) high

£150-250   **DN**

BOXES

An unusual French mahogany and rosewood travelling pharmacist's case, the rectangular case with a pair of doors, opening to an interior fitted to accommodate small apothecary jars, mixing elements etc., the drawers fitted with a mortar and pestle, some drawers marked for various substances, many original elements remaining.

c1850   *12in (30cm) wide*

£1,300-1,500   **FRE**

A late 18thC American pine red-painted apothecary chest, possibly Middle Atlantic States, the dovetail-constructed beaded case of thirty graduated drawers, retains old labels on drawerfronts, old brass ring pulls, repairs.

30in (76cm) high

£1,300-1,500   **SK**

A late 18th/early 19thC American painted pine apothecary chest, possibly New England, rectangular case of nine drawers, replaced brass pulls, old black-painted surface, the drawer fronts with yellow lettering, imperfections.

34.5in (87.5cm) wide

£1,500-2,000   **SK**

A mid-19thC mahogany apothecary's cabinet, with ten glass medicine bottles, some with contents and original labels, and interior section with a set of scales with brass pans and weights, this section lifting out to reveal a further removable compartmented section with glass mortar, measure, two small pill jars and two further small medicine bottles, with booklet 'Cox's Companion to the Family Medicine Chest, one shilling'.

10.5in (27cm) wide

£350-450   **DN**

A 19thC mahogany apothecary's box, the fitted double doors enclosing a fall-down drawer base, revealing a single drawer and bottle compartments, all containing various sized bottles and containers.

11.5in (29.5cm) wide

£550-750   **WW**

A matched pair of George III mahogany cutlery boxes, of serpentine-fronted form with sloping covers and fitted interiors, each crossbanded in tulipwood, one with additional chequer banding.

14.25in (36cm) high

£700-1,000   **L&T**

A pair of late 18thC George III mahogany and sycamore-strung serpentine-fronted knife boxes, with fitted interiors.

14.5in (37cm) high

£2,500-3,000   **DN**

A pair of George III style mahogany cutlery urns, each with lobed rising upper section revealing a stepped fitted interior, the stiff leaf acanthus-carved body on spreading circular moulded foot, with a separate circular mahogany base.

31.25in (79cm) high

£2,000-2,500 L&T

A pair of 20thC George III style mahogany and boxwood-strung urn lamp bases, each on a spreading foot and octagonal plinth, repair, damage, possibly converted from cutlery urns.

22.75in (58cm) high

£1,500-2,000 DN

A Continental ebonised, mother-of-pearl-inset and amboyna liqueur cabinet, with hinged top, front and sides, the fitted interior with fifteen engraved glasses and four engraved decanters, one decanter broken, lacking one glass.

c1880 *13in (33cm) wide*

£300-500 DN

An Edwardian oak tantalus, with mirrored back and drawer below, containing three associated cut glass spirit decanters, and three drinking glasses.

13.5in (34.5cm) wide

£120-180 ROS

A late 19thC Victorian oak and silver plated metal-mounted tantalus, with three cut glass decanters and stoppers.

15.5in (39.5cm) wide

£200-250 DN

A late 19thC burr oak and brass-mounted tantalus, with three associated glass decanters and stoppers.

16.25in (41.5cm) wide

£350-450 DN

A 19thC and later brass bound oak games compendium, the cover and front doors opening to a fitted interior containing wood chess and draughts pieces, bone dice, dominoes, playing cards and other items, reconditioned.

14in (35.5cm) wide

£700-900 DN

An early 19thC and later oak and oyster walnut-cased cards compendium, the interior later refitted, with playing cards, Bezique markers, die, leather shakers, etc.

12.25in (31cm) wide

£200-300 DN

A silver-plated metal and pietra dure gaming box, of recent manufacture, bearing spurious inscription 'Dunhill'.

13in (33cm) wide

£400-500 DN

A Victorian gilt-tooled leather cased games compendium, inscribed 'W.&J. MILNE, Makers. 126 Princes St. EDINBURGH', with ivory Staunton pattern chess set, draughts counters and other items.

c1880 *12.5in (31.5cm) wide*

£800-1,000 DN

A George IV rosewood and brass-mounted travelling jewellery case, with fitted interior and drawer below.

c1830   12.25in (31cm) wide
£250-350   DN

A Regency satinwood bijouterie box, the hinged lid centred by a reserve depicting Mercury in his chariot being drawn by swans, opening to reveal a compartmented interior, the sides with loop handles, raised on bun feet.

c1820   9in (23cm) wide
£250-350   FRE

A late 19thC Boulle-work brass and faux tortoiseshell jewellery casket, with two concealed drawers beneath the fitted interior.

                              10in (25cm) wide
£1,200-1,500   DN

An 18thC and later Anglo-Indian ivory, tortoiseshell, and penwork casket, the tortoiseshell panels banded by ivory and centred by cartouches, the cover with figures flanking a mother-of-pearl heart, flattened ivory bun feet.

c1745   7in (18cm) wide
£900-1,100   FRE

A Georgian tooled leather trunk, bearing the label 'Edward Smith', with elaborate brass tack decoration of crowns, tulips, and the initials 'G.R.' (George Rex).

c1760   40.5in (103cm) wide
£1,000-2,000   POOK

A late 18thC George III carved and stained wood box, in the form of a Doric columnar pedestal, probably for a bottle, the upper section and capital hinged as the cover, hinge bereft.

                              13in (33cm) high
£200-300   DN

A George III mahogany table top book press, the base with drawer.

c1800   21.25in (54cm) high
£450-650   DN

A George III kingwood, marquetry and crossbanded jewellery and dressing casket, with fully fitted interior.

c1800   12in (30cm) wide
£900-1,100   DN

An early 19thC and later polychrome-painted domed casket, probably Scandinavian.

A late 19thC Swiss carved wooden tobacco box, in the form of the head of Shylock, the cover carved as a hat, with scrolling hair and beard, flanked by two receivers.

                              16.75in (42cm) high
£700-900   L&T

A late 18thC George III mahogany cutlery tray, of rectangular form, with brass handle above two serpentine divisions.

16.25in (41cm) wide
£250-350   DN

19.75in (50cm) wide
£300-400   DN

A 19thC Swiss carved softwood box, modelled as chickens perched on a wheat sheaf, opening to reveal a plush-lined interior.

11.75in (30cm) wide

£700-900 L&T

A Victorian coromandel and brass bound toilet box, by Toulmin & Gale, the hinged cover with an inset plaque initialled 'A', with a compartmented interior and drawer to the side and front.

12.25in (31cm) wide

£250-350 WW

An Austrian or German oak domestic posting box, the cover carved in relief with a maiden with a hand mirror within a foliate reserve above the slot, with cavetto edges, the front with pierced and relief-carved foliage around a roundel with a bird, with glass backing.

c1880 *14.25in (36cm) wide*

£120-180 DN

A late 19thC Victorian mahogany bookrest.

18.5in (47cm) long

£150-250 DN

An unusual Victorian period ebonised panelled casket, the cavetto hinged top, front, sides and back comprising small glazed watercolours of landscapes, with a lined interior and bracket feet, underside bears makers label, 'J.P. White, Cabinet Manufactory, College Hill, Shrewsbury'.

11.5in (29cm) wide

£450-650 L&T

A 19thC Chinese painted tea chest, the top decorated with flowers and a butterfly, the front with figures.

12.25in (31cm) wide

£120-180 WW

An Ottoman mother-of-pearl and horn casket, having a high canted lid, the exterior covered with mother-of-pearl and horn parquetry.

12in (30.5cm) wide

£350-550 FRE

A late 19thC continental thuyawood, crossbanded and brass bound serpentine-fronted cigar cabinet.

11in (28cm) wide

£300-400 DN

BOXES

A Louis XV lacquer and gilt-bronze-mounted inkstand, the shaped base decorated with a wild boar and foliage, with two inkwells and a seated Buddha, raised on four scroll feet.

c1760   *19in (48cm) wide*
£2,000-3,000   **FRE**

A French gilt-metal-mounted fruitwood desk stand, with central foliate cast handle flanked by cut glass ink and pounce pots with foliate cast covers, the rectangular section base with twin concave pen recesses and a drawer below, on four winged paw feet.

c1830   *10.25in (26cm) wide*
£120-180   **DN**

A George IV or William IV ebony, ebonised and Boulle style brass marquetry deskstand.

c1830   *14in (35.5cm) wide*
£400-600   **DN**

A Victorian silver-gilt and malachite inkstand, by John Eldershaw Brunt, London, shaped rectangular stand cast and chased with naturalistic flowers, foliage and bees, fitted with two silver-gilt-mounted and lined inkwells, hinged domed covers, foliate scroll handles leading to floral swags, acorn finials, dated.

1837   *11in (28cm) wide*
£20,000-25,000   **SOTH**

A mid-19thC Continental gilt-bronze-mounted marmo nero Belgio inkstand, with raised handle above a cylindrical decorated porcelain inkwell, with foliate cast cover, flanked by two cut glass wells with foliate cast covers, the rectangular base with concave pen recess, on four foliate cast feet, elements associated.

12.25in (31cm) wide
£150-200   **DN**

A Napoleon III gilt-metal-mounted inkwell, of cubic form, the cover applied with a laurel and oak leaf wreath, the sides with winged figures and hippocamps against a black enamel ground.

c1860   *4in (10cm) high*
£350-450   **FRE**

A late 19thC Régence style gilt-brass-mounted, rosewood, ebony and brass boulle marquetry encrier, fitted with two pen rests centred by a handle and inkpots above a single drawer, the whole veneered with boulle marquetry, raised on paw feet.

14in (35.5cm) high
£800-1,200   **FRE**

A late 19thC Louis XV style ormolu and tiger's eye desk ornament, modelled as a kneeling cherub holding aloft a globe, raised on a canted stepped pedestal base.

9.5in (24cm) high
£3,000-4,000   **L&T**

A 19thC gilt-bronze figure of Cupid with a bow and a dead bird, on a rosewood-veneered plinth with gilt-metal mounts.

7in (18cm) high
£150-200   **GIL**

A late 19th/early 20thC Japanese bronze and ivory-mounted desk stand, cast with two bull elephants, the animals portrayed in combat, on a naturalistically cast base, with recess for pens at the front and lidded compartment for ink to the right, lacking inkwell from within.

17.25in (44cm) wide
£800-1,000   **DN**

A late 19thC French bronze model of a seated mariner, probably a desk stand, portrayed reclining on a barrel, smoking a pipe, a capstan behind him.

6.5in (16.5cm) high
£150-200   **DN**

A late 19thC Swiss carved softwood novelty inkstand, modelled as a collared Labrador, the head hinged to reveal an ink bottle aperture, the paws holding the trunk-form pen tray.

10.5in (27cm) wide
£800-1,200   **L&T**

An 18thC French fruitwood finely carved heraldic snuff box

c1790   3in (8cm) wide

£400-500   RDER

An 18thC snuff box bellows, with inlaid brass studs 'Forget Me Not'.

c1790   5.25in (13cm) wide

£400-500   RDER

An 18thC Dutch boxwood snuff shoe.

c1790   3.5in (8.5cm) long

£600-700   RDER

ESSENTIAL REFERENCE: SNUFF TAKING

The widespread taking of snuff in the Western world dates from the beginning of the 18thC, though it is likely that the habit was practised before this.

- Early snuff boxes were similar to tobacco boxes in form, except for the lids which were hinged (rather than lift-off) which prevented much accidental spillage. John Sandy's 'hidden hinge' snuff box, which completely prevented spillage, was not invented until late in the 18thC. This snuffbox prevented snuff from leaking into the owner's pocket.

- Due to the popularity of snuff-taking, vast quantities of gold and silver snuff boxes were produced in the late 18thC and the early 19thC. New mechanical techniques ensured a plentiful supply of relatively inexpensive sheet silver from which these boxes were made. Decoration varied from simple engine-turning to more extravagant boxes depicting hunting scenes etc in enamel. Wooden and coquilla nut snuff boxes were also extremely popular, and are now very collectable. Some were carved with erotic designs.

- 'Table snuff boxes', or snuff mulls, measuring 3.5-4.75in (9-12cm) were probably used after dinner, when a host would offer guests snuff from a communal box.

- By the mid-19thC, the snuff taking habit had begun to decline.

An 18thC French coquilla nut man with cap snuff box.

c1790   Profile 2.75in (7cm) wide

£800-1,000   RDER

An 18thC Dutch brass tobacco box, with rare rasp in lid.

c1790   5in (12.75cm) long

£250-350   RDER

A French erotic snuff box, with straw interior.

c1800   2.5in (6cm) diam

£300-500   RDER

A 19thC 'Robinson delivers Friday from the Cannibals' transfer print papier mâché snuff box.

The print is reversed – has to be read in a mirror

c1820   3.5in (9cm) diam

£300-400   **RDER**

An early Tunbridge Ware snuff box, with print of Brighton Pavilion.

c1820   1.75in (4.5cm) diam

£80-120   **RDER**

A matched pair of early 19thC timber snuff boxes, of boot form, the timber boot reveals a hollowed interior from a sliding cover, the cover and boot inlaid with brass.

6in (15cm) long

£400-500   **FRE**

A Stobwasser papier mâché painted portrait snuff box, inscribed 'Mlle Ludens, la favourite de P.P. Rubens', of Susanna Lunden after Debucourt's engraving of Rubens painting, signed, numbered 6868 lid and base.

It is most important that lid and base have the same number.

Johann Heinrich Stobwasser (1740-1829) was a German japanner who specialised in small objects, notably boxes very finely painted with portraits, landscapes, mythological scenes etc.

c1825   3.75in (9.5cm) diam

£1,400-1,600   **RDER**

An early 19thC papier mâché theatrical snuff box of Kean, possibly playing Iago.

Edmund Kean (1789-1833), was an unrivalled tragic actor. His successes included Shylock, Richard III, Hamlet, Othello, Iago and Lear.

4.25in (10.5cm) diam

£700-900   **RDER**

A 19thC French pressed boxwood box, 'Mme Angot et Nicolas'.

These snuff boxes date back to the Directoire period, and the successful opera-comique 'Madame Angot ou la poissarde parvenue'. The play was performed in 1797 at the 'Theatre 'd'Emulation'. The author, Antoine Eve, known as Maillot, was paid five hundred francs. The takings of the play were five hundred thousand francs, a considerable sum at the time. Madame Angot is the kind of common, vulgar, ill-mannered woman who suddenly becomes rich.

c1830-40   3.25in (8cm) diam

£400-500   **RDER**

A Scottish treen stippled toad sycamore snuff box, with glass eyes.

c1840   2.5in (6cm) long

£400-500   **RDER**

A Tunbridge snuff box.

c1840   1.25in (3cm) diam

£60-80   **RDER**

A rare Tartan Ware curved snuff box, the cover painted with a dog and two puppies, with wooden hinge, in red, green and yellow striped tartan, one end restored.

3.75in (9.5cm) wide

£150-250   **DN**

A 17thC English hardwood wassail bowl, probably Lignum Vitae, ribbed and waisted.

8in (20.5cm) high

£900-1,100   DN

An 18thC large American boat-shaped burr bowl, with fine old patina.

17.75in (45cm) wide

£2,500-3,500   POOK

A 18thC North American delicate burlwood boat-shaped bowl, from the Shelley Collection.

11in (28cm) long

£12,000-15,000   POOK

A treen single handled scoop, with incised stylised tree decoration.

4.75in (12cm) high

£200-300   WW

A large 18thC burr oak bowl.

21in (53.5cm) diam.

£2,000-2,500   WW

An 18thC treen bowl, of oval form.

18in (46cm) wide

£300-500   WW

A late 18th/19thC American carved round burl bowl, with flat bottom.

12in (76cm) diam

£400-600   POOK

A late 18th/early 19thC American burl bowl, with fine old patina.

13in (33cm) diam

£2,000-3,000   POOK

A 19thC burl timber bowl, of circular form, with a simply turned rim, restored bottom.

16in (40.5cm) diam

£450-550   FRE

A Scandinavian stained birch treen bowl, the adzed body with tramline decoration and broad flange handle, opposed by a small shaped lug.

10.25in (26cm) wide

£350-450   **L&T**

A dated Victorian carved coconut shell vessel, carved to one side with a ship under sail and inscribed 'FANTEE', the other side carved with a Jack Tar holding a Union Jack, a spout at one end with a caricature, a paper label within inscribed 'carved by an old sailor on the Barque Fantee on a voyage from West Africa about 1852'.

1852   *4.75in (12cm) long*

£120-180   **DN**

A mid-Victorian staved wooden cream pail, of laburnum and sycamore, inscribed 'From the Athole Plantations, Dunkeld. Cam' ye by Athole, lad wi' the Philabeg, Down by the Tummel, or banks o' the Garry, Saw ye the lads, wi' their bonnets an' white cockades, Leaving their mountains to Follow Prince Charlie. Anderson. Bookseller. Dunkeld.'

24in (10.5cm) wide

£180-220   **L&T**

A late 18thC George III mahogany adjustable candle stand, adapted.

7.75in (20cm) high un-extended

£100-150   **DN**

A George III mahogany cheese coaster.

c1800   *16.5in (42cm) wide*

£450-550   **DN**

An early 19thC Norwegian birch-wood tankard, the dome lid centred by a relief-carved lion motif, the cylindrical sides with a scroll handle with a lion-form thumb piece, raised on conforming lions, carved bracket feet.

10in (25cm)

£600-800   **L&T**

A mid-19thC oak hanging spoon rack, damage, repair.

13in (33cm) wide

£100-150   **DN**

A mid-19thC Scandinavian carved and stained softwood lidded jug, of tapering form and coopered construction, later elements.

11.5in (29cm) high

£150-250   **DN**

A mid-19thC turned mahogany revolving bobbin stand, for eight reels.

11in (28cm) high

£150-250   **WW**

A French architectural model of a staircase, the two story structure has a parquetry floor, baluster column stair case, two hinged doors to the side walls.

c1860

£9,000-11,000 FRE

A pair of matching 19thC carved and turned coquilla nut and treen ornaments, the basket bases with screw-off covers having a screw-off acorn-shaped finial.

7in (17.5cm) high

£700-900 WW

A set of two Victorian skimming ladles, with turned mahogany handles and pierced bowls, one stamped 'JONES, DOWN ST. W. BRIS'.

Longest 25.5in (65cm) long

£400-600 L&T

LEFT: A late 19thC small treen pug dog inkwell, with green glass eyes and bared teeth, with leather collar, lacking interior fittings.

4in (10cm) high

£250-350 L&T

CENTRE: A late 19thC treen pug dog inkwell, with glass eyes and leather collar.

5in (13cm) high

£300-400 L&T

RIGHT: A late 19thC treen pug dog tobacco box, the naturalistic carved head with glass eyes and blackened patination, enclosing a copper-sleeved interior, his neck bound with a leather collar.

7.75in (20cm) high

£800-1,200 L&T

An unusual late 19thC Colonial carved coconut cup and cover, finely carved with cherubs, pierced love hearts, a firing cannon, a tribal warrior and other scenes, mounted on an associated silver stand, hallmarked.

1919 *8.75in (22cm) high*

£800-1,200 L&T

A 19thC timber articulated model, good period patina, sectional model, finely detailed face and torso, over a later stand.

69in (175cm) high

£25,000-30,000 FRE

A carved and painted softwood humidor of Victorian style, in the form of a pug dog's head, the hinged head revealing a void interior, with inset eyes and carved collar.

14in (35cm) high

£1,000-1,300 L&T

A mid-19thC Victorian ebonised wood and ivory-mounted spinning wheel.

36.25in (92cm) high

£300-500 DN

BOXES

A Tunbridge Ware walnut folding writing box, the lid with mosaic view of Eridge Castle, the interior fitted with two sovereign drawers.

15in (38cm) wide

£400-600 **DN**

A Tunbridge Ware rosewood box, with tessera panel of a seated dog.

2.25in (5.5cm) wide

£150-250 **DN**

A Tunbridge Ware rosewood glove box, the domed cover with tessera rose spray, the sides with a deep mosaic band, on black ground.

10.5in (27cm) wide

£250-350 **DN**

A Japanned Tunbridge Ware box, in the manner of Wise, the lid decorated with a chinoiserie scene, the interior lined with turquoise paper.

8in (20cm) wide

£150-200 **DN**

A Tunbridge Ware ebony jewellery box, possibly by Hollamby, the lid with photographic ware image of a 19th century coastal bay on the Isle of Wight, substantial losses to tessera mosaic bands.

11.5in (29cm) wide

£100-200 **DN**

A Tunbridge Ware rosewood jewellery box, with tessera panel of Edward, Prince of Wales, the interior with removable tray.

8in (20.5cm) wide

£150-200 **DN**

A Tunbridge Ware rosewood stamp box, depicting the head of the young Queen Victoria.

1.5in (4cm) wide

£80-120 **DN**

A small Tunbridge Ware holly sewing box, the pin-hinged lid with foliate mosaic panel and van dyke borders.

4.25in (11cm) wide

£80-120 **DN**

A small Tunbridge Ware rosewood jewellery box, the canted cornered lid with tessera mosaic flower spray on a black ground.

5in (12.5cm) wide

£150-250 **DN**

A late 19thC Victorian yew wood and Tunbridge Ware box, the cover with a depiction of a Gothic ruin.

8.25in (21cm) wide

£120-180 **DN**

A Victorian rosewood Tunbridge Ware tea caddy, the tapering body with a band of roses and a hinged dome lid with a castle view, the twin-lidded interior with ebonised handles.

10in (25.5cm) wide

£550-750 **WW**

A Tunbridge Ware walnut folding writing box, the lid with mosaic view of Eridge Castle, the interior with two fitted sovereign drawers.

15in (38cm) wide

£250-350　　　　　DN

A 19thC Tunbridge Ware rosewood box, with tessera panel of a seated dog

2.25in (5.5cm) wide

£100-200　　　　　DN

A late 19thC Italian Sorrento Ware olivewood and marquetry box, decorated with scenes in the Classical taste, the interior stamped 'L.GARIGIULO'.

7.25in (18.5cm) wide

£120-180　　　　　DN

A large Tunbridge Ware rosewood desk stand, with Boyce, Brown and Kemp label, fitted lidded box between a pair of ink bottles

11.75in (30cm) wide

£500-700　　　　　DN

A Tunbridge Ware view of The Pantiles, attributed to Henry Hollamby, in tessera frame, some losses to corners.

8.75in (22cm) wide

£250-350　　　　　DN

A Tunbridge Ware whitewood cylindrical 'Twenty Guineas' counter box, with line decoration, containing three bone dice.

1.5in (3.5cm) high

£80-120　　　　　DN

A Tunbridge Ware walnut 'Cleopatra's needle' thermometer, with ivory vernier scale, floral mosaic and perspective cube marquetry panels.

7.75in (20cm) high

£150-250　　　　　DN

Two Tunbridge Ware rulers, an unusual 12in (30cm) rule with parquetry roundels, losses to one end, and a 9in (23cm) rule, with tessera mosaic panel.

£80-120

A Tunbridge Ware rosewood sovereign ball, inlaid eight-point stars within reeded roundels.

£180-220　　　　　DN

A Tunbridge Ware tessera panel of Shakespeare's Birthplace, Stratford-Upon-Avon, reputedly by Henry Hollamby.

7.5in (19cm) wide

£180-220　　　　　DN

A Tunbridge Ware visiting card case, by Edmund Nye, one side with Berlin Work cartouche and the other side a spray of flowers.

4.25in (10.5cm) high

£400-500　　　　　DN

BOXES

Two Mauchline Ware novelty pin cushions, one in the form of a stool with a view of Stirling Castle from back walk and inscribed 'bought in the Douglas Room of the Royal Palace of Stirling', the other in the form of a pail, with a view of Folkestone Church.

Larger 3in (7.5cm) high

£80-120   **DN**

A Mauchline Ware stained and natural sycamore quaich, with views of 'cottage in which Burns was born' and 'Alloway Kirk', and inscribed 'the dark portions of this wood are warranted to have grown on the banks of the Ayr and the light, on the banks of the Doon'.

4.25in (10.5cm) wide

£100-150   **DN**

A Mauchline Ware photograph frame, of shaped rectangular form, with an oval aperture and easel back, with views of Killiecrankie, Pitlochrie and Ben Vracky.

5.5in (14cm) high

£100-150   **DN**

A Mauchline Ware disc-shaped snuff box, painted with a view 'Dumbarton Castle', with remnants of zinc lining, hair crack to cover.

3.75in (9.5cm) diam.

£80-120   **DN**

A Mauchline Ware staved wood quaich, the body bound with wicker, inscribed to the base and dated.

1852   *4in (10cm) wide*

£80-120   **DN**

An early Mauchline Ware visiting card case with slip top, with lithographic views of landscapes and animals.

4in (10cm) high

£80-120   **DN**

A novelty Tartan Ware parasol-shaped pin cushion, in McBeth tartan.

5.25in (13.5cm) high

£250-350   **DN**

Two Tartan Ware visiting card cases, one with Prince Charlie pattern and photographic image of a lady and child, the other in MacDonald pattern with a wooden hinge.

Larger 4.25in (11cm) high

£400-600   **DN**

Two Tartan Ware cylindrical rolled tape boxes, in McDuff pattern with a photographic image of Widow Wadham and Uncle Toby, the other in Stuart pattern.

Both 2.5in (6.5cm) high

£150-250   **DN**

A Tartan Ware thermometer, in Caledonia tartan, with an ivory centigrade scale and mercury filled tube.

9.75in (25cm) high to suspension loop

£150-250   **DN**

A Tartan Ware brass-handled brush, in Clan Stuart tartan, possibly for brushing dust from wine bottles.

9.75in (25cm) long

£150-250   **DN**

A Tartan Ware 'PORTRAIT ALBUM', in Stuart tartan enclosing photographic portraits of Victorian ladies and gentlemen, the morocco leather spine with gilt-tooled decoration and title.

6in (15cm) high

£300-500   **DN**

A late 15thC Northern French carved walnut figure, dressed in a cloak over armour, his right foot placed on a representation of the devil, with traces of polychrome.

29in (74cm) high

£4,000-6,000   SOTH

A 17thC Italian carved reliquary, in the form of a life-size bust.

23.5in (59.5cm) high

£600-1,000   POOK

A 17thC Spanish polychrome wood figure of a female saint, probably St. Eulalia, her robes richly decorated to stimulate floral embroidery and partly gilt, the eyes inserted and of glass.

65in (165cm) high

£8,000-10,000   SOTA

A late 16th/17thC Continental carved and painted wood model of a female saint, portrayed crowned and holding a Bible, flaking overall.

20.5in (52cm) high

£2,200-2,500   DN

A late 17thC carved oak caryatid figure.

20in (51cm) high

£350-450   WW

A pair of 17thC Italian carved walnut models, probably saints, comprising a semi-robed male figure and a blind-folded female figure, both on later carved walnut triform socles with ebonised and gilt-metal-mounted bases, losses.

Taller 12.25in (31cm) high

£220-280   DN

A set of four English carved and polychromed female figures, representing the Four Seasons.

c1750   *11.5in (29.cm) high*

£1,700-2,000   POOK

A 19thC American carved walnut figure of George Washington, Pennsylvania, with a waistcoat, vest and ruffed cuffs.

19.5in (49.5cm) high

£6,000-8,000   POOK

A pair of carved oak finials, in the manner of Sir Robert Lorimer, depicting opposed praying female figures.

18.25in (46.5cm) high

£350-450   L&T

A 19thC carved oak wall-mounted figure, of a jester in cap and bells, with both hands outstretched and eyes raised, formerly holding an item, now lacking.

17.5in (44cm) high

£650-850   L&T

A pair of Victorian carved oak busts, depicting Mozart and Beethoven, each raised on a socle base.

11.5in (29cm) high

£1,200-1,500   L&T

CARVINGS

An early 19thC fully carved American spread-winged eagle, with an open beak and red tongue, detailed carved feathers, and talons grasping a circular plinth, retaining its original ebonised surface.

45in (115.5cm) wide

£25,000-35,000   POOK

A 19thC American carved and painted wooden eagle wall plaque, the relief-carved spread-winged figure with an American shield, portrayed grasping an olive branch in its talons, flanked by carved and gilt-tasselled American flags.

50.25in (127.5cm) wide

£45,000-50,000   SK

A 19thC carved and painted eagle lectern, the eagle with outstretched wings perched on orb and mounted on a triangular-panelled and shell-carved support and moulded and scrolled base, the back of eagle fitted with wrought iron shelf and support.

74in (188cm) high

£1,200-1,800   FRE

A pair of 16thC carved oak lions, the standing, fully maned lions raised on naturalistically carved scroll bases, with later moulded oak pedestals, probably originally sections of a chimney piece or architectural fitting.

Both 24.5in (62cm) wide

£1,200-1,800   L&T

A 19thC carved wood lion mask, with ring handle to mouth.

£350-450   L&T

A pair of early 19thC carved giltwood lion masks.

10.25in (26cm) high

£2,200-2,500 PAIR   L&T

A 19thC carved pear-wood figure of a lion, the seated lion raised on an oval base inscribed 'O G 1864'.

3.5in (9cm) high

£2,500-3,500   L&T

A 19thC American carved and polychrome-decorated alligator, Pennsylvania, from the Shelley Collection.

13.25in (33.5cm) long

£5,000-7,000   POOK

A late 19th/early 20thC American carved and painted stag figure, by John Reber, Pennsylvania, from the Shelley Collection.

15.5in (39.5cm) high

£2,000-4,000   POOK

A 19thC Swiss 'Black Forest' carved walnut group, depicting fighting stags, one stag attacking another, which has fallen to the ground, within a naturalist forest landscape, in a glazed display case.

19in (48cm) high

£6,000-8,000   L&T

1: A late 19th/early 20thC Swiss carved wood tobacco box in the form of an owl, perched on naturalistic base, with inset eyes.

10.25in (26cm) high

£1,500-2,000   L&T

2: A late 19th/early 20thC Swiss carved wood tobacco box in the form of an owl, standing on naturalistic base with tree trunk veneers.

These figures are often referred to as Black Forest carvings.

12.75in (32cm) high

£1,000-1,500   L&T

A large Indian carved ebonised wooden model of a squatting elephant, with bands of gilt-heightened decoration.

27.75in (70cm) long

£1,500-2,500   L&T

A dated Italian carved and painted family crest, inscribed verso 'Ants. Julianus Imolensis SCVL'.

1681 *38in (95.5cm) high*
£5,500-6,500 **POOK**

An 18thC carved and painted coat of arms, depicting a lion and unicorn with central quartered shield reading 'Honi Soit Qui Mal Y Pense'.

27.5in (70cm) wide
£8,000-10,000 **L&T**

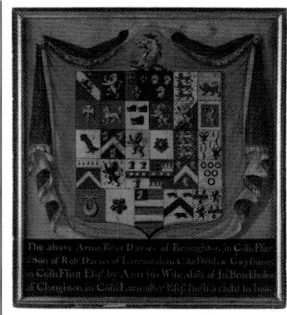

A late 18thC armorial panel, within original frame, the painted coat of arms above an inscription: 'The above Arms, Peter Davies of Broughton…'.

23.5in (59.5cm) wide
£2,500-3,000 **L&T**

A George III carved giltwood coat of arms of the Earl of Darnley, the painted central shield below a crown and flanked by a pair of griffins, verso bears letter from the College of Arms.

12.25in (31cm) wide
£5,000-7,000 **L&T**

An early 19thC painted square coach panel, within a later moulded giltwood frame, depicting two lions holding a central quartered shield, bears motto 'QUONDAM HIS VICIMUS ARMIS'.

11in (28cm) square
£1,300-1,600 **L&T**

A 19thC coach panel within a later ornate giltwood frame, depicting the lion and unicorn flanking the quarter shield of Great Britain inscribed 'QUIS SEPERABIT MDCCXXXIII', some restoration and re-painting.

19in (48cm) wide
£1,300-1,600 **L&T**

A Victorian painted coach panel, now within a fluted giltwood frame, depicting twin lions holding oval coats of arms below a crown, one bears motto 'TRA JUNCIA IN UNO', lower scrolls read 'VIRTUS MILLE SCUTA', some restoration and re-painting.

17in (43cm) wide
£1,300-1,600 **L&T**

A pair of 19thC Persian polychrome-painted and parcel giltwood panels of rectangular form, each decorated with flowers and birds within decorative borders.

30in (77cm) and 32.75in (83cm) wide
£1,000-1,200 PAIR **DN**

A George III carved pine Ionic pilaster capital, later adapted as a wall bracket.

c1770 and later *14.25in (36cm) wide*
£300-400 **DN**

A carved giltwood and gesso wall bracket of Louis XV style, the serpentine simulated marble top on central carved cherub within a double foliate scroll surround.

23.75in (60cm) wide
£1,000-1,200 **L&T**

An early 19thC carved giltwood crown wall mount, formerly part of a larger item.

14.25in (52cm) wide
£550-750 **L&T**

An early 20thC Indian carved hardwood presentation scroll case, the cylindrical hinged case carved in relief with animals and scrolling foliage, opening to reveal a velvet-lined interior, raised on carved lion supports, the rectangular base with ornate fret-pierced apron and angel-form bracket feet.

21.5in (55cm) wide
£750-950 **L&T**

A pair of carved giltwood wall brackets, the shell-carved tops with ornate openwork Rococo-carved supports, one 18thC.

15in (38cm) high
£4,000-5,000 **L&T**

THE CLOCKS MARKET

Whether they are looking to buy a large longcase or a small carriage clock, one of the aspects that concerns most buyers is the name of the clockmaker. The most desirable English longcase and bracket clocks continue to be those made in the late 17thc and early 18thC by names such as Thomas Tompion, Joseph Knibb, Henry Jones, Daniel Quare and Joseph Windmills. However, collectors are also becoming increasingly interested in their apprentices and successors, so prices for clocks by Samuel Aldworth, Brounker Watts, Daniel Delander and William Webster are staying very strong. The same can be said about later 18thC makers such as Ellicott, Vulliamy, Mudge & Dutton, McCabe and Frodsham. Collectors will pay extra for clocks by these and similar makers.

Another important factor is the aesthetics of the clock where the cases have the very best proportions and originality with all components starting life together. Most clocks of this age will have had some restoration and as long as this has been carried out honestly and sympathetically it will not affect the value.

Until relatively recently many collectors confined themselves to London makers, believing their work represented the best quality available. However, buyers are beginning to realise that many makers outside London, particularly those working in the major 18th and 19thC ports, industrial towns and cities, had a clientele who demanded the best clocks and the skills to provide them. As a result, prices are rising for longcase clocks from places such as Liverpool, especially those made by better names such as Joseph Finney and the Condliff family, whose work is equal to that of contemporary London makers. Consequently, ordinary London clocks are not doing as well as they were, and good mahogany longcase clocks are now representing very good value for money.

Carriage clocks made by the renowned makers such as Garnier, Jacot, Drocourt, Le Roy, Margaine and Soldano still remain highly desirable. No matter who the maker, collectors are looking for examples which retain their original escapement and, if possible, the original leather-covered travelling case and key. Case style also influences desirability, with gorge (grooved) cases traditionally more desirable than other case styles such as the corniche. A further selling point is complicated movements such as those with day, date and alarm or moon phase or other unusual features, but that said, the market is still buoyant for clocks with plain dials and simple cases.

The market for the substantial English carriage clocks with chain fusee movements also remains strong, especially the travelling four-glass examples in mahogany or rosewood cases.

Demand for early lantern clocks has been strong and the prices have been boosted after an important lantern clock sold for a world record price of £120,000 at a major London auction in 2008. Here we are seeing the clocks that have been conserved and not over polished achieving the best prices.

Robert Wren, Derek Roberts Antique Clocks, Tonbridge, Kent

LONGCASE CLOCKS

A late 17thC and later arabesque marquetry eight-day longcase clock, the five-finned pillar outside countwheel bell-striking movement, signed 'Jos: Jackman Londini Fecit', case with 19thC restoration.

Joseph Jackson is recorded as working from 1690-1716.

81in (206cm) high

£4,000-5,000   DN

A Queen Anne walnut and arabesque marquetry quarter chiming eight-day longcase clock, the substantial six-finned pillar movement with anchor escapement, chiming the quarters on a graduated nest of six bells and with inside countwheel hour strike on a further bell, the dial with calendar aperture, ringed winding holes and subsidiary seconds dial, signed 'Tho: Carter, London'.

Thomas Carter is listed as being admitted to the Clockmakers Company in 1690.

c1700   95.25in (242cm) high

£20,000-30,000   DN

A walnut marquetry month-going chiming longcase clock, dial signed 'Char Cabrier, London', the three-train movement with six ring-turned knopped pillars, bell-striking and chiming the quarters on six bells, five wheel trains, movement and case associated.

c1705   98in (38.5cm) high

£20,000-30,000   SOTH

A Queen Anne oak thirty-hour longcase clock, the posted countwheel bell-striking single handed movement with rectangular section-steel uprights, and signed 'Luke Wise, Reading'.

Luke Wise is recorded as working in Reading c1686-1710.

c1710   80.75in (205cm) high

£1,500-2,000   DN

An early 18thC ebonised thirty-hour longcase clock, the four-finned pillar outside countwheel bell-striking single-handed movement, with brass dial with calendar aperture, the chapter ring with sliced sword hilt half hour markers and signed 'Geo: Booth Manchesft'r'.

George Booth is recorded working c1758-88, however various details within the construction and decoration of the movement, dial and case of this clock suggest a date of manufacture within the first 20 years of the 18thC.

80in (204cm) high

£1,500-2,000   DN

CLOSER LOOK: GEORGE II LONGCASE CLOCK

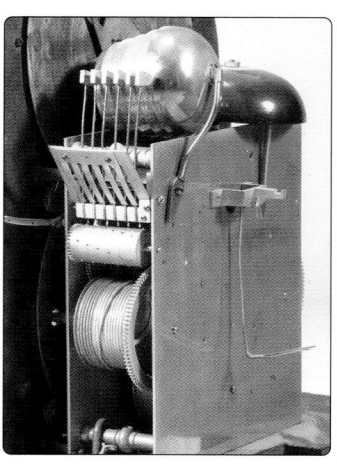

The French script for the days of the week within the arch suggests that this clock was originally made for a French client.

The case features an ogee caddy above break-arch cornice with foliate scroll blind fretwork infill to frieze and integral pilasters to hood door.

The trunk has a herringbone banded burr figured door and panel inlaid sides on conforming base with double skirt.

James Hubert is recorded as working in London 1712-30.

A George Graham walnut longcase clock, dial signed along the lower edge 'Geo: Graham, London', with seconds dial and calendar aperture with pin hole adjustment, the movement with five latched knopped pillars, dead beat escapement with bolt and shutter maintaining power, rack striking on a bell, punch numbered '724', restored case.

c1735   91in (231cm) high

£55,000-65,000   SOTH

A George II walnut eight-day longcase clock, with trip repeat, the five finned pillar rack and bell-striking movement, the seconds dial, signed 'Tho. Baker Portsmouth', the case with break-arch moulded cornice and frieze and integral pilasters to the hood door above herringbone banded break-arch trunk door.

c1740   85.5in (217cm) high

£8,000-10,000   DN

A George II burr-walnut quarter chiming eight-day longcase clock, with day of the week to arch, the substantial five-finned pillar movement with anchor escapement, chiming the quarters on a graduated nest of six bells and rack striking the hours on a further bell, the brass break-arch dial with calendar aperture and subsidiary seconds dial, the arch with days of the week titled in French, signed 'James Hubert, LONDON'.

c1725   93in (236cm) high

£11,000-15,000   DN

CLOCKS

An early 18thC and later inlaid mahogany month-going longcase clock, the dial with calendar aperture and recessed subsidiary seconds dial with subsidiary ring calibrated for the lunar month and penny moon, composite.

91.25in (232cm) high

£2,000-2,500   DN

A mid 18thC red and gilt-japanned eight-day longcase clock, by Robyat, London, the twin train movement striking on a bell, the brass dial with subsidiary seconds dial, the trunk door decorated with chinoiserie scenes.

95.5in (242cm) high

£4,000-5,000   L&T

A George II oak eight-day longcase clock, with four-pillar rack and bell-striking movement, the brass dial with calendar aperture and subsidiary seconds dial, signed 'Thomas Russell, BEDFORD'.

c1750   79in (201cm) high

£1,100-1,400   DN

A mid-18thC George II walnut eight-day longcase clock, with four-finned pillar outside countwheel bell-striking movement, the brass dial with calendar aperture, subsidiary seconds dial, signed 'Jno. Ingram, Spalding'.

81in (206cm) high

£2,000-2,500   DN

A George III oak thirty-hour longcase clock, with four-finned pillar outside countwheel bell-striking movement, the dial signed 'Wooley Codnor'.

James Woolley (c1695-1786) was a renowned provincial clockmaker.

c1750   81in (206cm) high

£2,500-3,000   DN

A George II oak thirty-hour longcase clock, the posted countwheel bell-striking movement with columnar uprights, dial with calendar aperture and signed 'Edward Bilbie CHEWSTOKE'.

c1750   77.5in (197cm) high

£1,200-1,500   DN

A George III mahogany longcase clock, the arch top dial signed 'John Smithyes, Great Saffron Hill, London' above a strike/silent dial, the chapter ring central date and seconds dial, with two-train five pillar movement with alarm mechanism.

92in (233.5cm) high

£6,500-7,500   DUK

A George III scarlet-japanned eight-day longcase clock, with five-pillar rack and bell-striking movement, the dial signed 'John Mason, LONDON', with silvered rocking Chronos figure, case re-decorated.

c1770   86.5in (220cm) high

£1,800-2,200   DN

A George III oak eight-day longcase clock, with four-pillar rack and bell-striking movement, the dial signed 'Rich'd Tyler, WALLINGFORD' on reduced plinth base.

Richard Tyler is recorded as working in Wallingford 1740-82.

c1770   81in (206cm) high

£700-1,000   DN

A George III oak eight-day longcase clock, with four-pillar inside countwheel bell-striking movement, the dial signed 'John Brice DEAL'.

John Brice is recorded as working in Sandwich, Kent c1795.

c1780   79in (201cm) high

£900-1,200   DN

A George III oak thirty-hour longcase clock, the countwheel bell-striking movement signed 'Anthony Lynch, NEWBURY'.

Anthony Lynch is recorded as working in Newbury c1781.

c1785   77in (196cm) high

£800-1,000   DN

An 18thC Dutch marquetry and burl veneer longcase clock, the sarcophagus top with blind fretwork frieze enclosing an eight-day brass face, signed 'Johs Uswald Amsteldam', with dioramic rocking ship harbour scene and two-bell mechanism.

94.5in (240cm) high

£12,000-15,000   POOK

An 18thC Dutch burl veneer longcase clock, the moulded cornice over a frieze with blind fretwork enclosing a brass face, two-bell, eight-day works with silver dial, with line-inlaid door and chamfered stiles.

99in (251.5cm) high

£3,500-5,000   POOK

A late 18thC Dutch burr walnut longcase clock, the brass dial signed 'Johannes Van Wyk en Zoon Amsterdam', with date, day, month, moonphase and the ships automaton in the arch rocking to and fro' connected to the going train of the anchor movement, rack Dutch quarter striking on two alternating bells, alarm removed, associated to the burr walnut-veneered case, with bell top surmounted by a giltwood Atlas and two angels.

106.75in (271cm) high
including Atlas

£10,000-12,000   SOTA

A George III oak eight-day longcase clock, the four-pillar rack and bell-striking movement with brass dial with subsidiary calendar and seconds dials and signed 'Rich'd Boxall Godalming', the arch with 'STRIKE/SILENT' dial.

c1790   80.75in (205cm) high

£1,100-1,300   DN

A late 18thC mahogany eight-day longcase clock, by Charles Graham, Edinburgh, the twin train movement with anchor escapement, with moon phase to arch, the shaped trunk door flanked by inset brass pilaster columns.

110 in (279cm) high

£1,600-2,000   L&T

A late 18thC George III mahogany eight-day longcase clock, with centre seconds and moonphase to arch, the five-pillar rack and bell-striking movement with deadbeat escapement, the brass break-arch dial with arched calendar aperture and silvered nameplate 'BENJ'N ROSE, SWATHLING', the arch with rolling moonphase behind scroll-engraved lunettes.

82in (208cm) high

£2,500-3,000   DN

An 18thC and later George III green-japanned longcase clock, the four-pillar anchor escapement movement signed 'Rich Mason, St. Albans', with strike silence above a seconds dial.

82in (208cm) high

£4,500-5,500   **FRE**

A George III mahogany longcase clock, by Harvey of Weymouth, the arch top dial with a rotating ball moon phase dial, with subsidiary seconds dial and date aperture, the eight-day movement striking on a bell.

90in (228.5cm) high

£4,500-5,500   **DUK**

A Grandmother clock, the eight-day movement with anchor escapement, the dial chased with foliage, the arched roundel inscribed 'Tempus Fugit', in Georgian style mahogany case.

60.5in (153.5cm) high

£2,500-3,500   **HT**

A Regency mahogany eight-day longcase clock, with five-pillar rack and bell-striking movement, with dial with subsidiary second dials and signed 'William Samuel Archer, Hackney', the break-arch pedimented case with fretwork crest and canted angles to hood above break-arch door, on flush-shaped panel-fronted plinth base with double skirt.

c1820   *87.5in (222cm) high*

£3,000-4,000   **DN**

An early 19thC mahogany eight-day longcase clock, by Andrew Smith, Tranent, the twin train movement with anchor escapement, the painted dial with subsidiary seconds and date dial.

81in (206cm) high

£1,500-2,000   **L&T**

An early 19thC mahogany and crossbanded longcase clock, the twin movement with anchor escapement striking the hours on a bell, the dial signed 'J. & G. Leithhead, Galashiels'.

85.75in (218cm) high

£1,000-1,500   **L&T**

A William IV mahogany drumhead longcase clock, the twin train movement with anchor escapement striking the hours on a coiled gong, signed 'P. Martin, Glasgow'.

81.5in (207cm) high

£1,100-1,300   **L&T**

A Scottish William IV mahogany longcase regulator, by John Clark, Forfar, the movement with dead-beat anchor escapement, maintaining power and striking on a gong.

80.75in (205cm) high

£1,500-2,500   L&T

An oak longcase regulator clock, with subsidiary seconds dial, the eight-day movement striking on two bells and a gong, brass cased weights and ebonised pendulum, the dial inscribed 'Willliam Tritschler, Carlisle'.

20.5in (52cm) wide

£2,000-2,500   A&G

A 19thC mahogany longcase clock, the four-pillar anchor escapement movement with a strike silent above a chapter ring with Roman and Arabic numerals, signed 'Edward Clarke London'.

87.5in (222cm) high

£1,500-2,000   FRE

A 19thC carved and stained oak longcase clock, the twin train movement with anchor escapement, the leaf scroll pediment centred by a cockerel, the silvered dial with subsidiary seconds and calender dial, the lion mask carved trunk door between fruiting vine pilasters and leaf scroll-carved sides.

90 in (229cm) high

£1,000-1,300   L&T

An early 20thC green-japanned quarter chiming eight-day grandmother clock, the triple train movement with platform lever escapement and chiming the hours and quarters on five gongs, with 'CHIME/SILENT' dial to arch.

67.75in (172cm) high

£1,500-2,000   DN

A William III ebonised bracket clock, the five-finned pillar twin fusee rack and bell-striking movement with verge escapement, pull quarter repeat work removed, signature erased.

c1695   *14.5in (37cm) high*
excluding handle

£5,000-7,000   **DN**

A French boulle marquetry bracket clock, by Francois Rabby, Paris, the caddy top with flame finials above larger foliate finials and a balustrated frieze, the anchor escapement striking on a bell, the backplate engraved 'Rabby Paris'.

c1700   *23.5 in (60cm) high*

£5,000-7,000   **L&T**

A George III ebonised bracket clock, the five-pillar twin fusee movement now with half deadbeat escapement, the dial with blanked off false bob aperture, calendar aperture and signature plaque 'Chater & Sons, LONDON', the arch with 'Strike/Silent' ring.

c1760   *15.5in (40cm) high*

£2,300-2,600   **DN**

An early 18thC Régence ormolu-mounted tortoiseshell and brass boulle marquetry bracket clock, the dial with enamelled Roman numerals decorated with winged infants, set in arched case surmounted by Father Time.

14in (35.5cm) high

£1,000-1,300   **FRE**

A George III mahogany bracket clock, the five-pillar twin fusee rack and bell-striking movement with trip repeat, with verge escapement, the brass dial with calendar aperture and silvered nameplate 'Will'm Wall, Richmond' beneath 'Strike/Silent' dial.

c1775   *19.5in (50cm) high*

£6,000-7,000   **DN**

A George III ebonised bracket clock, by John Carter, London, the dial with silvered chapter ring and subsidiary silent/strike dial, the striking eight-day twin chain fusee movement with anchor escapement.

19.25in (49cm) high

£2,500-3,000   **L&T**

A late 18thC American Charlestown, South Carolina mahogany bracket clock, the works with white painted face and engraved back plate, signed 'Josh'a Lockwood Charles Town'.

17in (43cm) high

£4,500-5,500   **POOK**

A rare 18thC Chinese Export padouk bracket clock, the arched face painted with a port scene, with a single train fusee movement with a foliate engraved backplate.

27in (69cm) high

£2,500-3,000   **L&T**

A Regency rosewood bracket clock, by James McCabe, the twin train eight-day movement striking the hours and half hours on a bell, the dial serial no.1337.

17in (44cm) high

£7,000-9,000   **L&T**

A late 18thC Austro-Hungarian ebonised quarter striking bracket clock, the four-pillar triple train movement with verge escapement, trip repeat and visible stopwork to the backplate, the dial with false bob aperture, with silvered boss bearing signature 'Chater, London' flanked by subsidiary dials 'Nicht Repl:/Repedit', 'Schlagt/Sch: Nicht'.

15.75in (40cm) high

£900-1,200   **DN**

A Regency bracket clock, by John Caney, the eight-day twin train fusee movement on a bell, the arched case a stepped top surmounted by a pineapple finial and side sound frets, the white painted dial signed 'John Caney, 33 Cheapside, London'.

19.75in (50cm) high

£2,000-2,500   **L&T**

A Regency rosewood bracket clock, by Payne, the eight-day twin fusee movement with anchor escapement and striking on two bells, the white painted dial signed 'Payne, New Bond Street, London'.

24in (61cm) high

£3,500-4,500   **L&T**

An early 19thC Swedish giltwood bracket clock, by Emil Lagerstrom, Enkoping, the twin train movement striking on a bell, on bracket suspending fruiting terminals and with acanthus-carved centre.

29.25in (74cm) wide

£4,000-5,000   **L&T**

A George III mahogany bracket clock, with trip repeat, the five-pillar twin fusee rack and bell-striking movement with anchor escapement, the dial signed 'Younge & Son, London'.

c1820   *15.75in (40cm) high*

£2,000-2,500   **DN**

A William IV brass-inlaid mahogany small bracket clock, the five-pillar twin fusee gong-striking movement with anchor escapement signed 'VINER NEW BOND STREET LONDN', some damage.

c1835   *13.75in (35cm) high*

£2,800-3,200   **DN**

A Victorian Gothic Revival bracket clock, by J. W. Benson, with an eight-day fusee movement, the silvered dial signed 'J. W. Benson, Ludgate, London'.

23.5in (60cm) high

£1,100-1,400   **L&T**

A 19thC Victorian gilt-metal-mounted quarter chiming bracket clock, the substantial four-pillar triple fusee movement chiming the quarters on nine bells and striking the hours on a gong with rise/fall regulation, the brass dial with 'FAST/SLOW', 'CHIME/SILENT' and 'CHIME ON EIGHT BELL/WESTMINSTER CHIME' subsidiary dials, unsigned.

28.75in (73cm) high

£2,200-2,500   **DN**

A large late 19thC mahogany and gilt-metal-mounted bracket clock, unsigned, with triple fusee movement, quarter chiming Westminster and eight Bells, with a mahogany wall bracket.

Clock 26.25in (67cm) high

£3,000-3,500   **DN**

A late 19thC bracket clock, by Payne & Co., no. 4560, fitted eight-day movement striking on a gong, made in New Bond Street, London.

20in (51cm) high

£450-650   **A&G**

A late 19thC bracket clock, the two train movement by Winterhalter & Hoffmeyer, with 'SLOW/FAST' and 'CHIME/SILENT' dials.

22in (56cm) high

£1,200-1,500   **DN**

An American mahogany pillar and scroll shelf clock, by Erastus Hodges (1781-1847), with thirty-hour 'east-west' wooden movement, iron weights and pendulum, damage.

30.5in (77.5cm) high

£8,000-10,000   SK

An early 19thC French Empire mantel clock, with eight-day outside countwheel bell-striking movement, dial signed 'Cleret a Orleans'.

19.25in (49cm) high

£600-800   DN

An American Massachusetts pine and maple cased transitional shelf clock, by William Sherwin, thirty-hour time and strike, weight powered movement.

c1830   30.5in (77.5cm) high

£3,500-4,000   SK

A William IV rosewood small five-glass mantel clock, with trip repeat, with five-pillar twin fusee bell-striking movement, unsigned.

c1830   10.5in (27cm) high

£2,000-2,300   DN

A mid 19thC Victorian brass skeleton timepiece, unsigned, the four-pillar single fusee movement with half-deadbeat escapement, with later ebonised wood base.

9.5in (24cm) high

£350-450   DN

A mid 19thC French Louis XV style ormolu mantel clock, the outside countwheel bell-striking movement stamped 'HY. MARC, PARIS' to backplate.

14.5in (37cm) high

£400-600   DN

ESSENTIAL REFERENCE: THOMAS COLE

A Victorian patinated and gilt brass tripod timepiece, the single train movement with six-wheel train and deadbeat escapement set between stepped plates, the dial with subsidiary seconds dial and signed 'THO'S COLE, LONDON', supported on triform frame with turned and carved ivory finial and supporting the pendulum with heavy silvered ball bob from the centre, on base applied with adjustable silvered calendar.

A late 19thC Louis XV style gilt and patinated bronze mantel clock, modelled as a cherub supporting the movement atop a fluted classical pedestal, the white enamelled dial signed 'Frd. Berthoud, A Paris'.

21.75in (55cm) high

£4,000-5,000   L&T

Thomas Cole was born in Nether Stowey, Somerset in 1800, the second son of the renowned and learned local clockmaker James 'Philosopher' Cole. His brother James Ferguson Cole, who was two years older, learned the trade from his father before moving to London in 1821 to become one of the country's most eminent horologists. Thomas Cole joined his brother in London from 1823 until 1829 when they went their separate ways and by 1845 he was advertising himself as a 'designer and maker of ornamental clocks'. He exhibited at the Great Exhibition in 1851 as well as in Paris in 1855 and again in London in the 1862 British International Exhibition. He died from typhoid fever in 1862. The current example displays the originality and quality of design coupled with the finest workmanship for which Thomas Cole became famous.

c1860   19.25in (49cm) high

£10,000-12,000   DN

A 19thC French gilt-bronze and metal mantel clock, modelled as Napoleon firing a cannon, map to his feet inscribed, 'Montezan'.

15.75in (40cm) wide

£1,200-1,500 **L&T**

A Louis XV style ormolu mantel clock, the eight-day bell-striking movement signed 'HY. MARC A PARIS'.

c1870 *14.5in (37cm) high*

£800-1,000 **DN**

A late 19thC German cuckoo clock, fitted eight-day twin fusee movement, striking on a single gong.

19.5in (50cm) high

£1,000-1,200 **A&G**

A late 19thC French gilt-bronze and enamel clock, in the Persian taste.

11.5in (29cm) high

£1,000-1,200 **L&T**

A late 19thC Louis XV style gilt bronze mantel clock.

20.5in (52cm) high

£700-1,000 **L&T**

A late 19thC French boulle and ormolu mounted shelf clock, the works signed 'H&F Paris'.

29in (74cm) high

£800-1,000 **POOK**

A late 19thC Black Forest carved shelf clock, with carved wolves, birds, etc.

28.25in (72cm) high

£1,300-1,600 **POOK**

A 19thC French gilt bronze-and slate shelf clock, the works stamped 'Marti'.

26.5in (67.5cm) high

£700-1,000 **POOK**

A late 19thC French black slate and brass mantel clock, marked 'Lloyd Payne & Amiel Paris Make', the bronze panel sides with Arcadian scenes.

17.75in (45cm) wide

£850-950 **L&T**

A late 19thC Anglo-French brass timepiece, the eight-day movement with platform lever escapement, with a globe which rotates giving the time.

11.75in (30cm) high

£1,500-1,800 **DN**

A 19thC French mantel clock, the silk suspension movement striking on a bell and signed 'Ch. Duillet'.

14.25in (36cm) high

£400-600 **HT**

A late 19thC French brass and patinated bronze small novelty lighthouse timepiece, unsigned, the eight-day movement with a form of a double-wheel duplex escapement.

9.75in (24.5cm) high

£1,300-1,500 **DN**

A late 19thC French brass novelty windmill timepiece, with aneroid barometer and thermometers, the eight-day movement with platform escapement.

17in (43cm) high

£1,500-2,000 **DN**

A French 'Japonisme' gilt-bronze and champlevé enamel clock, the sides decorated with berried branches, insects and birds, surmounted by a lion dog.

9.75in (25cm) high

£600-800 **L&T**

A French bronzed spelter elephant novelty swinging mystery timepiece, the movement with tic-tac escapement, internal short bob pendulum.

c1900 *11in (28cm) high*

£450-650 **DN**

A late Victorian oak four-glass mantel clock, the four-pillar single fusee movement with anchor escapement, the dial signed by retailers 'R. H. HALFORD & SONS'.

c1900 *11.45in (29cm) high*

£800-1,000 **DN**

An Edwardian mounted tortoiseshell timepiece, by William Comyns, with piqué-inlaid decoration, and in fitted leather case, with marks for London, stamped 'CARRINGTON & CO.', initialled.

1906 *5in (13cm) high*

£1,000-1,500 **L&T**

A Tiffany & Co. enamelled miniature timepiece, and key, signed indistinctly, stamped 'ARGENT DORE 0,925 STERLING SILVER 84' and numbered 4236.

2.75in (7cm) high

£700-1,000 **L&T**

A tortoiseshell and piqué-decorated table clock, with silver frame, white enamel dial and French movement, with marks for London.

1913 *4.25in (11cm) high*

£1,200-1,800 **L&T**

An early 20thC Bulle electric mantel timepiece, the movement with locking crown wheel and contacts for the electromagnetic coil pendulum, the chapter ring inscribed 'Georges Bernard, DINARD'.

13in (33cm) high

£500-800 **DN**

A Swiss gilt-brass inclined plane gravity timepiece, Imhof for the Musée International d'Horlogerie, La Chaux-de-Fonds, Switzerland, with fifteen-jewel movement and white dial set onto an inclined mahogany plane annotated with days of the week, in original box with instruction manual and spare inclined plane stand.

24in (61cm) wide

£650-850 **DN**

An early 20thC French red-japanned 'floating turtle' novelty mystery timepiece, attributed to Grubelin for Dreyfous, Paris, the eight-day movement with platform lever escapement operating horizontal ring magnet to move the floating turtle within the pewter dish annotated with Roman numeral chapters and Arabic quarters to rim.

11.5in (29cm) wide

£2,300-2,800 **DN**

A 19thC French gilt-bronze and marble clock garniture set, the clock with works signed 'Paillard Paris', the candelabra each with six candle-arms and three putti-supports.

Clock 29in (74cm) wide

£6,000-8,000   POOK

A late 19thC French white marble and gilt-metal mounted clock garniture, in the Empire taste, with eight-day twin train movement striking the hours and half hours on a bell, indistinctly signed, the backplate stamped 'S.C. Paris'.

Clock 21in (53.5cm) high

£1,000-1,500   L&T

A 19thC French ormolu and white marble clock garniture, the twin train eight-day movement striking the hours and half hours on a bell, the backplate stamped 3887, with a pair of candelabra.

Clock 13in (33cm) high

£1,800-2,200   L&T

A 19thC French porcelain and gilt-bronze clock garniture, the inset 'jewelled' porcelain panels painted with scenic views and rural scenes, with a pair of Classical style ewers.

Clock 15in (38cm) high

£1,200-1,500   L&T

A French gilt-bronze and porcelain clock garniture, the porcelain dial surmounted by an orb finial with a berried knop and a portrait of a beauty below, with flanking griffin mask handles, the urns decorated with reserves of figures in 18thC costume, all on a bleu celeste ground.

c1890   *Clock 17.5in (44.5cm) high*

£1,500-2,000   FRE

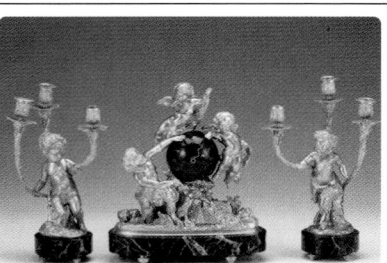

A late 19thC gilt-bronze and marble three-piece clock garniture, with Bacchus and two cupids centred by a globular blue-enamelled clock, on a veined green marble oval base, with a pair of gilt-bronze figural candelabra, one a bacchic child, the other a satyr.

Clock 15.5in (39.5cm) high

£3,000-4,000   FRE

A Louis XVI style gilt-bronze and Carrara marble clock garniture, the enamelled dial with Roman numerals surmounted by a recumbent baccante and supported by winged infants atop goats hung with a lambrequin and bacchic vines, the matching urns with berried knops and mask handles cast.

c1900   *Clock 19in (48cm) high*

£4,000-6,000   FRE

A French gilt-bronze, porcelain and champlevé three-piece clock garniture, the porcelain dial surmounted by an urn finial, with flanking painted plaques depicting flower girls, the urns decorated with Classical figures.

c1900   *Clock 18in (45.5cm) high*

£5,000-7,000   FRE

A Regency rosewood clock, the gilt foliate-engraved face with a silvered engine-turned dial, the case surmounted by carrying handle.

9in (23cm) high

£4,000-5,000   L&T

A repeating carriage clock, signed 'Charles Frodsham', two-train fusee movement, underslung ratchet tooth lever escapement with compensation balance and maintaining power.

c1860   *8.5in (21.5 cm) high*

£14,000-16,000   SOTH

A French champlevé-enamelled carriage clock, the eight-day gong-striking movement with silvered platform lever escapement.

4.75in (12cm) high

£1,800-2,200   DN

A late 19thC French gilt-brass and enamel carriage clock, retailed by Cooke & Kelvey, Calcutta, the repeating lever escapement movement striking on a wire, with a leather travelling case.

8in (20cm) high

£1,500-2,000   L&T

A late 19thC French brass carriage clock, with push-button repeat, unsigned, the eight-day gong-striking movement with silvered platform lever escapement.

5.25in (13.5cm) high

£400-600   DN

A late 19thC French brass carriage clock, unsigned, the eight-day two-train gong-striking movement with silvered platform lever escapement, with original leather case.

6.5in (16.5cm) high

£350-550   DN

A late 19thC French carriage clock, by Drocourt for J. W. Benson, London, the two-train gong-striking movement with silvered platform lever escapement.

5.75in (14.5cm) high

£900-1,200   DN

A late 19thC French carriage timepiece, possibly attributable to Brunelot, Paris, the eight-day movement with silvered platform lever escapement.

6in (15cm) high

£750-950   DN

A late 19thC French brass carriage clock, by C. A. Richard & Cie, the eight-day two-train gong-striking movement with replaced platform lever escapement and push button repeat, excluding handle

5.75in (14.5cm) high

£450-550   DN

A late 19thC French lacquered brass carriage clock, with two-train gong-striking movement, the dial signed and retailed by 'GOLDSMITHS & SILVERSMITHS Co. Ltd', in a corniche type case.

5.5in (14cm) high

£450-650   DN

A late 19thC French brass carriage timepiece, by Henry Jacot, the eight-day movement with replaced platform lever escapement, in a corniche type case.

5.75in (14.5cm) high

£170-200   DN

An early 20thC brass-cased four-glass carriage clock, with French repeat movement striking on two gongs, retailed by Howell & James Ltd., London.

6in (15cm) high

£200-300   ROS

ESSENTIAL REFERENCE: LANTERN CLOCK

Lantern clocks were made almost entirely of brass and comprised a square case on ball or urn feet, a large circular dial with a chapter ring extending beyond the width of the case on early examples, a single hour hand, and a large bell and finial. They usually had ornate pierced fretwork on top of the frame.

Because of their relatively simple construction, lantern clocks were frequently copied in the 19thC and have been faked in modern times.

Patina and oxidation, symmetrical engraving on the centre dial and the clear resonance of the bell help identify a genuine piece.

The characteristic pierced fretwork crown on a lantern clock should fit well into the original feet holes. If not, it has been replaced; sometimes because of damage to the original, but occasionally with a crown bearing the signature of a maker to enhance value.

A Charles II brass lantern clock, the posted countwheel bell-striking movement formerly with verge escapement and pendulum swinging between the trains, now with anchor escapement, the dial with vestigial alarm disc, signed 'Thomas Wheeler Londini Fecit'.

Lantern clocks are weight-driven wall clocks, shaped like a lantern, which were first seen in the UK c1620.

c1680   15in (38cm) high

£3,000-4,000   **DN**

A 20thC Continental painted white metal peddler clock, with pendulum and key.

15.5in (39.5in) high

£220-280   **ROS**

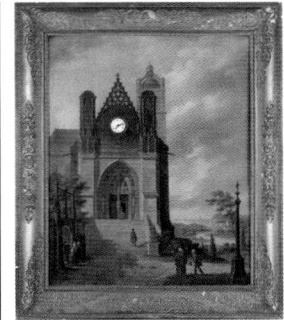

A 19thC picture clock, depicting a coastal view with figures beside a church, the church set with a clock movement, oil on canvas, in original gilt wood and gesso frame.

39in (99cm) high

£400-600   **L&T**

An early 20thC American folk art carved wooden automaton clock, the electric powered clock animating fourteen carved figures.

27.75in (70.5cm) high

£11,000-15,000   **SK**

CLOSER LOOK: MUSICAL DIORAMA

The diorama is modelled as a coastal town with a crenellated tower and watermill flanking a bridge with other gabled buildings behind.

The music is played via a pinned cylinder and steel comb mounted within the base.

The scene is set under a glass dome which has a landscape painted to the rear.

The moulded ebonised wood base incorporates operating plungers and pull-wind cord to left-hand side.

There is an automata of a procession of cavalry over the bridge, turning water wheel to the mill and paddle steamer which rocks back and forth to the foreground.

A late 19thC musical automaton diorama, unsigned.

20.75in (53cm) high

£1,500-2,000   **DN**

A Jaeger-Le Coultre Atmos timepiece, in a fitted case.

Jean Leon Reutter, a French engineer, was working on utilising the change in temperature and atmospheric pressure to wind a clock early in the 1920s. Patents were taken out in 1928 and 1930. The early models were not particularly successful commercially. They had a glass tube which held mercury, a liquified gas and a saturated vapour. The differences in pressure caused a rocking movement in the tube. The movement was transferred to the winding mechanism by a ratchet wheel. Later, ethyl chloride was substituted as a reagent. The Atmos clocks were manufactured by the Swiss firm of Jaeger-Le Coultre. They were marketed in the UK from 1934 by De Trevars Ltd. of Regent St. London W.1.

8.75in (22cm) high

£500-700   SWO

A Jaeger-Le Coultre travelling clock, with satin finished dial, hinged cover which doubles as an easel-back stand, with pouch, box and documents.

1.75in (4.5cm) long

£150-200   L&T

WALL CLOCKS

A George II thirty-hour posted wall clock, the movement with rectangular section posts, the anchor escapement and countwheel strike on a bell mounted above the top plate, with hook and spike wall mounting to rear.
c1730
11in (28cm) high

£1,500-1,800   DN

A French Louis XVI Ormolu Cartel wall timepiece, the enamel dial signed 'Le Nepveu Paris', movement with tapered plates and tic-tac escapement, silk suspended sunburst pendulum, repeating work removed.

17.25in (44cm) high

£2,500-3,000   SOTA

A George III mahogany tavern timepiece, the five-pillar weight-driven movement with five-wheel train, anchor escapement and tapered plates, with salt-box type case, lacking brass bezel and minute hand.
c1790
38.5in (98cm) high

£2,000-2,500   DN

A late 18thC George III black japanned tavern timepiece, the four-pillar weight-driven movement with anchor escapement and tapered plates, the salt-box type case with fretwork ears, the recessed panel door painted with a Lakeland view with pavilion, with pendulum adjustment flap to right-hand side.

46in (117cm) high

£2,500-3,000   DN

An American Federal mahogany banjo clock, possibly Simon Willard & Son, Massachusetts.
c1815
33in (84cm) high

£2,500-3,500   POOK

An American 'banjo' clock, attributed to Aaron Willard, Jr., Boston, the reverse-paintings on glass with 1812 battle scene and four captains' names, eight-day brass weight-powered movement with 'T-bridge' suspension.

c1815   *42in (106.5cm) long*

£5,000-7,000   **SK**

A Regency Edinburgh mahogany wall clock, the enamelled roman dial with single train movement, signed 'A. Philipp Edinburgh'.

     59in (150cm) high

£2,000-3,000   **L&T**

A large American Federal mahogany and eglomise wall clock, with mirror plate and panel showing buildings on a village green, without works.

c1820   *62in (157.5cm) long*

£750-1,000   **FRE**

A Victorian mother-of-pearl-inlaid rosewood dial timepiece, the four-pillar single fusee movement with anchor escapement, signed 'G. ESPLIN, WIGAN'.

c1840   *17.5in (44cm) diam*

£450-550   **DN**

A Victorian rosewood and mother-of-pearl marquetry drop dial wall clock.

c1860   *22.5in (57cm) high*

£450-550   **DN**

An unusual mid-19thC Austrian large oak wall regulator, the single train movement with deadbeat escapement, A-shaped plates and Huygens endless rope system winding via a large wheel and click mounted on the backboard, the dial with subsidiary seconds and calendar dials and signed 'Josef Kotek'.

     56in (142cm) high

£900-1,200   **DN**

A late 19thC American Ithaca calendar clock.

     60.5in (153.5cm) high

£3,000-5,000   **POOK**

A late 19thC American Boston, Massachusetts No. 60 wall regulator clock, by Edward Howard.

     92in (233cm) high overall

£20,000-25,000   **POOK**

A large Vienna style wall clock, with a single train movement with long pendulum with brass-faced bob.

     72in (183cm) high

£1,500-2,000   **DUK**

A 19thC Black Forest wall clock, the case inlaid with mother of pearl roundels.

£150-180   **ROS**

A late 19thC Black Forest carved wall clock.

     47in (119.5cm) high

£3,000-3,500   **POOK**

THE BAROMETER MARKET

The market for barometers has consolidated. While buyers remain relatively selective, prices are strong for the right pieces. There has always been a market for classic examples and those by the best makers, and this continues. A barometer which shows quality in its design, construction and mechanism will always find a buyer, and this has not changed. For example, a good, early, fine mercury stick barometer by a famous maker such as John Patrick or Daniel Quare is relatively rare and likely to be of a high quality, so prices for such pieces are strong due to their historical importance.

The same can be said for later pieces which present themselves as the best of their period, hence 19thC examples by makers such as Adie and Dollond are commanding good prices. However the same cannot be said for mid to late 19thC barometers of average quality by lesser makers. Examples which are more standard in their design and function are not doing as well as they were. On the other hand, wheel barometers with an unusual layout – upside down examples or those with the dial in the centre – are doing well with buyers prepared to pay for innovation or novelty. Prices for polytechnic and Fitzroy barometers in original condition are gaining strength.

Particularly hard hit are the more ordinary mercury barometers which people are nervous of buying because of ill-founded fears that new laws may prohibit the sale and even the repair of instruments containing mercury. Exports to the US have suffered considerably as a result. Consequently, the market for aneroid barometers has grown stronger. Finally, condition and originality have always had a bearing on value, in today's selective market such factors are becoming increasingly important.

Leighton Gillibrand, Dreweatts, Bristol

STICK AND CISTERN BAROMETERS

A late 17thC walnut cistern tube stick barometer, with cross-grain moulded ogee outline arched pediment above caddy-moulded panel-veneered case, the scale annotated for 'Sumer' and 'Winter', with signature 'Henry Wynne' London.

40.5in (103cm) high

£3,500-4,500   DN

A William and Mary walnut cistern tube stick barometer, in the manner of John Patrick.

c1695   *47.25in (120cm) high*

£2,500-3,500   DN

A Queen Anne walnut cistern tube stick barometer, with thermometer, attributed to Stephen Davenport or John Patrick, London, with restored paper scale calibrated from 0 at the top down to 90.

c1715   *39in (99cm) high*

£3,500-4,500   DN

A George II mahogany cistern tube stick barometer, by Edward Scarlett, London, with silvered vernier scale and bayonet-shaped tube, the mercury thermometer signed.

c1740   *35.75in (91cm) high*

£3,000-4,000   DN

A fine George III mahogany cistern tube stick barometer, with hygrometer or Triple Weather Glass, the vernier scale with arched hygrometer scale above Fahrenheit and Reaumur mercury thermometer and signed 'B. Martin, London'.

c1760   *37in (94cm) high*

£3,500-4,500   DN

A George III mahogany cistern tube stick barometer, vernier scale signed 'J. Bird, London'.

c1760   *44in (112cm) high*

£2,500-3,000   DN

A George III mahogany cistern tube stick barometer.

c1765   *37in (94cm) high*

£1,500-2,000   DN

A George III mahogany cistern tube stick barometer with hygrometer, by Henry Pyefinch, London.

c1770   *39.75in (101cm) high*

£1,500-2,000   DN

A George III mahogany cistern tube stick barometer, silvered vernier register signed 'Dollond, London'.

c1770   *39.5in (100cm) high*

£2,500-3,000   DN

A fine George III mahogany cistern tube stick barometer, with whalebone hygrometer and ivory cistern float.

c1770   *43.75in (111cm) high*

£4,000-5,000   DN

A rare George III Irish mahogany cistern tube stick barometer, the brass vernier scale signed 'LYNCH DUBLIN'.

c1770   36.5in (93cm) high
£2,000-2,500   DN

A George III mahogany cistern tube stick barometer, the silvered vernier scale with Fahrenheit mercury thermometer and signed 'G. ADAMS, Fleet Street, LONDON'.

c1780   38in (96cm) high
£3,500-4,500   DN

A George III mahogany cistern tube stick barometer, the silvered vernier scale with Fahrenheit mercury thermometer and signed 'G. ADAMS, Fleet Street, LONDON'.

c1780   38in (96cm) high
£3,500-4,500   DN

A George III brass-inlaid mahogany cistern tube stick barometer, by Edward Nairne, London, the silvered scale with vernier, signed.

c1780   36.25in (92cm) high
£2,200-2,800   DN

A rare George III mahogany multiple-tube barometer, by Baptista Ronchetti & Co, Manchester.

c1785   23in (58.5cm)
£1,600-2,000   DN

A George III mahogany cistern tube stick barometer, by B. Storr, Beverley.

                39 in (98cm) high
£1,000-1,500   L&T

A George III mahogany and chequer-strung cistern tube stick barometer, by Balthazar Knie.

40in (102cm) high

£1,500-1,800   L&T

A George III mahogany cistern tube stick barometer, by Thomas Blunt, London.

c1800   *36.5in (93cm) high*

£3,000-4,000   DN

A rare George III inlaid mahogany double angle tube bulb cistern stick barometer, calibrated in barometric inches from 28 to 31 and signed 'W'm Robb MONTROSE'.

c1800   *37in (94cm) high*

£2,500-3,500   DN

A George III inlaid mahogany cistern tube stick barometer with hygrometer, by Baptista Ronchetti, Manchester.

c1800   *43.75in (111cm) high*

£2,000-2,500   DN

A George III mahogany cistern tube stick barometer, the silvered dial inscribed 'Joseph Teste, No. 54 Leather Lane, Holborn, London'.

39.5in (100cm) high

£2,000-2,500   L&T

A rare George III inlaid mahogany contra-barometer, with silvered scale engraved 'Double BAROMETER' and signed 'T. Thomson EDIN'R'.

c1805   *41.5in (105cm) high*

£5,500-6,500   DN

A George III mahogany cistern tube stick barometer, by Charles Beilby, Bristol.

c1805   *39.5in (100cm) high*

£3,500-4,000   DN

A George III mahogany cistern tube stick barometer, signed 'Jones 241 Oxford Str't, LONDON', with Fahrenheit alcohol thermometer.

c1810   *37.75in (96cm) high*

£2,000-2,500   DN

A George III mahogany cistern tube stick barometer by Hobdell, Oxford.

35.75in (91cm) high

£1,000-1,200   L&T

A 19thC English mahogany marine stick barometer, by Spencer & Co.

36in (91.5cm) high

£1,000-1,500   POOK

A George III mahogany bulb cistern tube stick barometer, the brass vernier dial signed 'Tho's Rubergall 24 Coventry Str.'t., LONDON'.

This was reputedly owned by William Wordsworth, the English Romantic poet.

c1825   *35.75in (91cm) high*

£4,000-5,000   DN

A George IV mahogany stick barometer, inscribed 'J. AMADIO'.

39.5in (100cm) high

£1,500-1,800   L&T

BAROMETERS

A George IV inlaid mahogany bulb cistern tube stick barometer, the paper scale signed 'CHARLES HOWORTH HALIFAX'.

c1830   40.25in (102cm) high

£600-800   **DN**

A fine William IV/early Victorian mahogany slender bowfronted cistern tube stick barometer, signed 'W'M HOLMES, LONDON'.

c1840   38.25in (97cm)

£4,000-5,000   **DN**

A rare William IV mahogany double bulb cistern tube angle barometer, with brass sliding pointers and signed 'SAMUEL LAINTON, MAKER, HALIFAX' , the trunk with exposed tubes retained by domed bosses at the angle of each tube, with Fahrenheit scale mercury thermometer.

c1830   38.25in (97cm) high

£10,000-12,000   **DN**

A mahogany-cased balloonist's barometer, the front door enclosing a Guy-Lussac type of wide bore siphon tube with Bunten air trap mounted against an adjustable ivory scale calibrated from 5 to 31 inches, with manual vernier and signed 'H. NEGRETTI, 19 Leather Lane, HOLBORN'.

c1845   38in (97cm) high overall

£2,500-3,000   **DN**

An early Victorian carved mahogany cistern tube stick barometer, with vernier, Fahrenheit and Reaumur scale mercury thermometer and signed 'WATKINS & HILL, 5 Charing Cross, London'.

c1850   41.25in (105cm) high

£3,000-3,500   **DN**

A 19thC mahogany ship's barometer, by Spencer Browning & Rust, London.

37in (94cm) high

£2,200-2,600   **L&T**

A Victorian carved and spiral-turned mahogany bowfronted marine stick barometer.

c1860   38.25in (97cm) high

£2,500-3,000   **DN**

A Victorian burr-walnut stick barometer, marked 'Smith Beck & Beck, 31 Cornhill, London'.

36in (91.5cm) high

£1,000-1,300   **DUK**

A Victorian rosewood marine stick barometer, signed 'LAWSON & CO, 277 WAPPING, LONDON'.

c1865   36cm (92cm) high

£1,600-1,900   **DN**

An early 20thC Edwardian inlaid mahogany bowfronted cistern tube stick barometer.

38.25in (97cm) high

£1,500-1,800   **DN**

A late 18thC inlaid mahogany mercury wheel barometer, signed 'Ja's Gatty No 130 High Holborn, LONDON'.

37in (94cm) high

£2,000-2,500   DN

A rare inlaid and crossbanded mahogany mercury wheel barometer, attributed to Christopher Bettally, London.

c1790   37.5in (95cm) high

£3,500-4,000   DN

CLOSER LOOK: WHEEL BAROMETER

The stepped caddy pediment is an unusual feature. Other examples of this style of barometer made by John Hallifax have a simple, domed pediment.

The restrained design of the trunk is enhanced by book-matched walnut veneers.

The form and design, with its centrally placed dial, is very rare.

The reading ring is well engraved, with a central brass panel engraved with a foliate panel and the name of the maker.

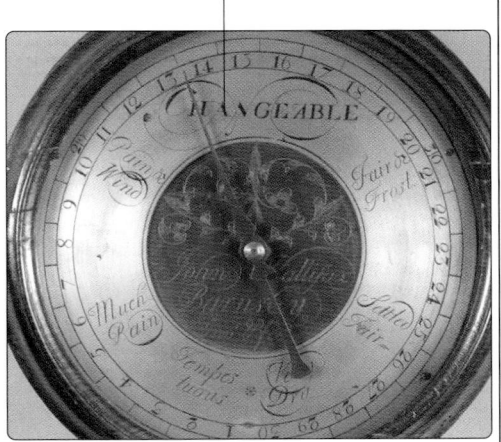

A rare George II walnut siphon tube wheel barometer, with a 7.5in (19cm) register calibrated in inches and also divided 0-30 corresponding to the decimal divisions of the barometric inches, the brass centre signed 'John Hallifax Barnsley Inv:f fecit'.

c1730   45in (114cm) high

£20,000-25,000   DN

A George III satinwood mercury wheel barometer, the 10in (25.5cm) silvered register calibrated in inches and signed 'Anone No. 26 High Holb'n, London' beneath hygrometer and arched Fahrenheit scale alcohol thermometer.

c1805   41.5in (105cm) high

£900-1,200   DN

A George III inlaid mahogany mercury wheel barometer, the 8in (20.5cm) silvered register calibrated in inches and signed 'P. Gally, London' the Fahrenheit scale alcohol thermometer flanked by foliate inlaid oval paterae.

c1810   39in (99cm) high

£1,100-1,300   DN

A rare George III mahogany upside-down mercury wheel barometer, the silvered register calibrated in inches above ivory setting pointer adjustment disc with spirit level signed 'JAMES LIONE No 81 high Holbn'n, LONDON'.

c1810   37.5in (95cm) high

£5,000-6,000   DN

A George III mahogany mercury wheel barometer, the 8in (20.5cm) silvered register calibrated in inches and signed 'P. Manticha, LONDON', with brass setting pointer to glass beneath arched Fahrenheit scale alcohol thermometer.

c1815   36in (92cm) high

£550-650   DN

A Regency inlaid mahogany mercury wheel barometer, the 8in (20.5cm) silvered register calibrated in inches, signed 'G. Testi & Co, Chester' with Fahrenheit scale alcohol thermometer.

c1820   38.5in (98cm) high

£700-900   DN

A Regency mahogany mercury wheel barometer, the 8in (20.5cm) silvered register calibrated in inches and signed 'A. Alberti, Sheffield'.

c1825   39in (99cm) high
£650-750   **DN**

A William IV large rosewood wheel barometer with timepiece, the clock dial signed 'French Royal Exchange, London' with pillar single fusee movement with platform lever escapement to front-plate, with Fahrenheit scale mercury thermometer and hygrometer similarly signed.

c1830   49.25in (125cm) high
£2,200-2,800   **DN**

A William IV mahogany mercury wheel barometer, by Francis Amadio & Son for John Mangiacavalli, London.

c1835   37.75in (96cm) high
£1,500-2,000   **DN**

A satinwood crossbanded mercury wheel barometer signed 'C. Maspolli, Manchester, Warranted'.

c1840   49.5in (126cm) high
£1,400-1,800   **DN**

An early Victorian brass-mounted mahogany mercury wheel barometer, with bowfront mercury Fahrenheit scale thermometer flanked by brass pilaster and hygrometer, with spirit level signed 'Gardner & Dowling, Belfast'.

c1840   43.75in (111cm) high
£900-1,100   **DN**

An early Victorian rosewood combination drop-dial wall clock and mercury wheel barometer, the register inscribed 'P. BREGAZZI Patentee Nottingham No. 44', with registration kite mark for 25 September 1843 to the Royal Coat of Arms, with a drop-dial wall clock with four-pillar single fusee movement.

c1843   41.25in (105cm) high
£3,000-4,000   **DN**

An early Victorian mahogany mercury wheel barometer, the 10in (25.5cm) register calibrated in inches and signed 'DOLLOND, LONDON', with bowfronted Fahrenheit scale, alcohol thermometer, the base with hygrometer.

c1845   40.5in (103cm) high
£2,300-2,600   **DN**

A Victorian mahogany mercury wheel barometer, register signed 'Watkins & Hill 5 Charing Cross London' and inscribed 'REGISTERED 1586 SEPT'R 14TH 1848 No. 201', lacking setting pointer adjustment disc.

c1848   39in (99cm) high
£800-1,200   **DN**

A Victorian oak combined stick and wheel barometer, the register signed 'N. Whitehouse 2 Cranbourn Str. Leicester Square', with brass setting pointer adjustment disc and Fahrenheit scale mercury thermometer to the shaped base section beneath.

c1850   36.5in (93cm) high
£2,000-3,000   **DN**

A late 19thC French walnut banjo clock and barometer pair, the clock with twin train movement striking on a coiled gong.

39in (99cm) high

£2,000-3,000   **L&T**

A rare George III mahogany mercury dial barometer, the register calibrated in inches and signed 'Chamberlain, Portsea', with hygrometer and arched-top Fahrenheit scale alcohol thermometer.

c1810   *42.5in (108cm) high*

£3,500-4,500   **DN**

A rare George III mahogany mercury dial barometer, the register calibrated in inches signed 'S. BREGAZZI, Derby' and with Fahrenheit scale alcohol thermometer.

c1815   *40.25in (102cm) high*

£4,000-5,000   **DN**

POCKET BAROMETERS

A late 19thC nickel finish aneroid pocket/travelling barometer, in original hinged open-fronted leather-covered easel case with hinged strut to rear.

2.75in (7cm) diam

£200-300   **DN**

A late 19thC gilt brass aneroid pocket barometer with altimeter scale, thermometer and compass, the register calibrated in millimetres and inscribed 'Lufft, RUDOLFO HAMMERSLEY, AGUSTINAS ESQ. SANDERA, COMPENS. No 6904'.

2in (5cm) diam

£500-600   **DN**

A late 19thC pocket travelling compendium of aneroid barometer with altimeter scale, mercury thermometer and compass, the altimeter scale calibrated to 10,000 feet within rotating bezel with steel pointer, in gilt-brass watch-form case with velvet-lined leather-covered carrying case.

3in (7.5cm) wide when closed

£550-650   **DN**

BAROMETERS

A late 19thC gilt-brass-cased compensated aneroid surveyor's pocket barometer, with altimeter scale, in original leather outer case.

3in (7cm) diam

£150-200   DN

A late 19thC Swiss pocket compendium with aneroid barometer with altimeter scale, compass and thermometer, the barometer inscribed 'IND'IE GENEVOISE D'OPTIQUE 10 GRAND QUAI, GENEVE', with rotating altimeter scale calibrated to 4,500 metres, in wall-form leather-covered case, thermometer is broken.

4.5in (11cm)

£270-300   DN

A late 19thC gilt-brass aneroid pocket barometer with altimeter scale, thermometer and compass, the altimeter scale calibrated to 20,000 feet, in a watch-form case with small mother-of-pearl compass.

2in (5cm) diam

£450-550   DN

A patinated brass aneroid surveyor's pocket barometer with altimeter scale, the register inscribed 'J.H. Steward Ltd, 406 Strand, 457 West Strand, LONDON, 5674, COMPENSATED, Temp Alt'e Scale 50 (degrees) Fah't', with original leather-covered case.

c1900   *2in (5cm) diam*

£150-200   DN

An early 20thC brass aneroid pocket weather foreteller or Weather Watch, annotated 'FALL', 'STEADY' and 'RISE' and inscribed 'PATENT 6276/15R/137, NEGRETTI & ZAMBRA'.

2.25in (5.5cm) diam

£1,000-1,500   DN

ANEROID BAROMETERS

A late 19thC ebonised and brass-cased desk clock barometer, the timepiece with eight-day French cylinder movement, with an aneroid barometer with mercury tube Fahrenheit thermometer signed 'NEGRETTI & ZAMBRA, LONDON'.

7.5in (19cm) high

£300-400   DN

A brass and ebonised wood-cased Bourdon aneroid barometer, the paper register inscribed 'E. BOURDON AND RICHARDS PATENT PARIS, METALLIC BAROMETER' and with 1849 Paris Exhibition Gold Medal and London 1851 Council Exhibition Medal roundels, .

c1865   *13in (33cm) diam*

£300-350   DN

A Victorian gilt and silvered brass aneroid barometer, in the form of a kettle drum, the underside with kite mark and stamped 'G.B. &Sons'.

c1870   *31.75in (12.5cm) high*

£300-400   DN

A walnut-cased aneroid desk Atmos Barometer, with two-part vacuum chamber, opposing Fahrenheit and Centigrade scale, curved mercury tube thermometer and plaque inscribed 'ATMOS BAROMETER'.

c1880   *8.5in (21.5cm) wide*

£2,000-2,500   DN

A silver-mounted desk compendium of aneroid barometer, goliath watch and thermometer, silver mount heavily worn.

c1890   *8in (20cm) wide*

£130-180   DN

A late 19thC oak-cased barograph, with six-part vacuum chamber within lacquered brass armature operating inked pointer for the rotating paper scale lined drum.

15in (37.5cm) wide

£600-900   **DN**

An early 20thC thermobarograph, with seven-part vacuum chamber, operating inked pointer for the paper scale lined drum and secondary pointer to record the temperature.

14.75in (37cm) wide

£750-850   **DN**

An oak-cased barograph, with four-part vacuum chamber, with inked pointer for the rotating paper scale lined drum, the base plate signed 'GRIFFIN & TATLOCK, LONDON No F.6135".

c1915   *13.5in (34cm) wide*

£350-400   **DN**

A chrome plated barograph, with two-part vacuum chamber within electroplated armature operating an inked pointer for the paper scale, with a curved mercury tube thermometer.

c1925   *14in (35cm) wide*

£1,300-1,800   **DN**

An ebonised cased micro-barograph, with thirteen-part vacuum chamber with inked pointer for the paper scale lined drum and inscribed 'SHORT AND MASON, LONDON... No. 957/45.

c1925   *14.25in (36cm) wide*

£500-600   **DN**

A mid 20thC mahogany cased barograph, with eight-part vacuum chamber within lacquered brass armature operating inked pointer for the rotating paper scale lined drum.

14in (36cm) wide

£450-550   **DN**

A late 18thC Ramsden brass telescope, inscribed 'RAMSDEN, LONDON', thumbwheel rack and pinion fine focusing, single drawtube focusing, 2in (5cm) subject lens, dust cap, dent to body, two lenses replaced.

22in (56cm) long

£1,500-2,500   **FRE**

A 19thC brass portable telescope, by W. Harris & Co, with a 3.5in (9cm) objective lens, thumb-operated fine turning, brass dust cover, tripod, timber adjusting handle, original box.

42in (106.5cm) long

£1,500-2,000   **FRE**

A Dollond floor telescope, with thumb-operated fine focus, 2in (5cm) objective lens, timber tripod stand, signed 'Dollond, London' to tube.

c1840   *37.5in (95cm) long*

£1,200-1,800   **FRE**

A 19thC brass floor telescope, 2in (5cm) objective lens, dust cover, timber tripod stand.

58in (147.5cm) long

£2,500-3,000   **FRE**

A composite 19thC brass telescope, signed on the backplate 'T & R. Willats, 98, Cheapside, London'.

17.75in (45cm) high

£400-500   **ROS**

A late 19thC hand-held 1.5in (4cm) refracting telescope, with four draws, the first signed 'DOLLOND, LONDON' with lens covers.

8.25in (21cm) long closed

£350-400   **DN**

A set of two similar early 20thC leather-covered brass three draw telescopes, by Broadhurst, Clarkson & Co., Ltd.

33.25in (84.5cm) long extended

£100-150   **ROS**

A set of two similar early 20thC wood and brass three-draw telescopes.

33.25in (84.5cm) long extended

£80-120   **ROS**

An early 19thC brass spyglass, by Cox, London, with a removable dust cover, an eight-draw tube, coarse focus, tortoiseshell grip, and a 1.5in (4cm) lens.

31in (79cm) long

£600-800 FRE

A brass spyglass, coarse focus from an eight-draw tube, 1.5in (4cm) subject lens, new blue shagreen skin hand grip.

c1850 *24in (61cm) long*

£800-1,000 FRE

A 19thC brass spyglass, by Cox, Devenport, removable dust cap, tortoiseshell hand rest, seven pull draw tube, 1.5in (4cm) subject lens, and a slide cover eye piece.

22in (56cm) long

£500-700 FRE

A brass spyglass, by Rojs & Co. Regency Street Piccadilly, three-pull draw tube, swinging cover over eye lens, 1.5in (4cm) subject lens, pop dust cover, tortoiseshell hand grip.

c1850 *24in (61cm) long*

£600-900 FRE

A late 18thC style lacquered brass Culpeper type microscope, in original fitted pyramid case, with a quantity of accessories including three other objective lenses and three bone slides.

£650-750 GORL

An early 19thC Bate 'Jones Most Improved' type brass compound microscope, signed, substage condenser and plano/concave mirror, six objectives, three lieberkuhns, live box, and cone.

16in (40.5cm) high

£3,500-4,500 FRE

A late 19thC brass compound monocular microscope, with rack-and-pinion focusing, micrometre screw adjustment, signed 'J. Swift & Son, London.' in a case with extras.

12.25in (31cm) high

£200-250 DN

A 19thC lacquered brass binocular microscope, by' C. Collins, Optician, 157, Gt Portland St, London'.

19.75in (50cm) high

£350-400 ROS

An exceptional early 18thC brass circumferentor, inscribed 'Willz Collier Fecit', the silver-plated compass dial finely inscribed with direction and decoration of foliate scrolls, enclosed by a dome glass cover and brass dust cover, the outer arch pierced and supported by six arms, with original mahogany, ebony and parquetry box.

13.5in (34cm) diam

£11,000-14,000 FRE

A mid 18thC French cube dial, by D. Beringer, small magnetic compass on paper gore-covered dial applied with four adjustable tin dials, for various latitudes.

8in (20.5cm) high

£600-800 FRE

SCIENTIFIC INSTRUMENTS

An 18thC brass pocket compass, the small dial has a single magnetic needle, with an attached sundial, and a screw-on dust cover.

1.5cm (4cm) diam

£200-250   FRE

A silver pocket compass, London, fully hallmarked.

1849 1.5in (4cm) diam

£100-150   FRE

A brass pocket equinoctial dial, the brass case houses a magnetic needle, applied to the right side is an arch measuring 80 degrees, inscribed to the rear.

c1760

£1,000-1,500   *2in (5cm) diam*   FRE

An 18thC probably German brass ring sundial, the exterior engraved with calibrations for the months, lacking pinhole adjustment and suspension loop, the internal surface with double hour scales, in excavated condition.

10cm (4cm) diam.

£300-500   DN

A 19thC brass equinoctial ring dial, 90 degree arc to base, and measuring panel to interior.

3in (7.5cm) diam

£650-850   FRE

A Chinese metal and enamel travelling sundial, with an integral compass.

4.5in (11.5cm) high

£200-250 WW

A brass table dip needle, by Philip Harris, the circular face encloses the dip needle and measured dial.

c1900 *8in (20.5cm) high*

£500-800 FRE

An early 19thC mahogany-cased two-day marine chronometer, with a gimbal-mounted silvered dial, subsidiary seconds and up/down dial, with retaining screw, signed on the dial 'McLachlan, London'.

6.75in (17cm) wide

£2,000-3,000 L&T

An early 20thC ivorine pocket weather forecasting calculator, signed 'NEGRETTI & ZAMBRA, LONDON', the middle for 'BAROMETER AT SEA LEVEL' and the centre pierced with three sectors annotated 'FALLING', 'STEADY' and 'RISING' and inscribed 'PAT. NO. 6276/15', in original box with instructions titled 'WEATHER FORECASTER'.

14in (5.5cm) diam

£85-100 DN

An early 20thC brass table weather forecasting calculator, formed as three discs, the outer calibrated in inches for the barometer reading to the top edge and for wind direction to the lower edge, the middle ring is annotated for 'STEADY', 'RISING' and 'FALLING', the centre with instructions for use, inscribed 'NEGRETTI & ZAMBRA, LONDON, PATENT 6276, 1915'.

4.75in (12cm) diam

£800-1,000 DN

A japanned metal hair hygrometer, with four-inch ceramic register calibrated for 'RELATIVE PERCENTAGE HUMIDITY' and signed 'NEGRETTI & ZAMBRA, LONDON'.

The instrument uses the relative expansion and contraction of hair with changes in moisture in the air to measure relative humidity.

c1935 *4.25in (11cm) diam*

£30-50 DN

A carved wood weather house, with polychrome-printed silhouettes of male and female figures each in the 16thC style dress, the instrument is a form of hygrometer, as the twisted gut suspension absorbs moisture it expands causing the beam onto which the figures are mounted to pivot.

c1900 *8in (20cm) wide*

£40-80 DN

A mid-19thC mahogany-cased brass portable dipleidoscope, the brass bed with three levelling screws mounted with angled prism, bubble level and magnetic compass needle.

4in (10cm) wide

£1,000-1,400 DN

A 19thC French medical shock machine, supported on a mahogany rectangular base are four gilt-metal conductors attached to two supporting brass bars, and a velvet-covered head rest.

A boxed set of rare mechanical slides, including twelve glass colour slides of England, the timber viewer is operated by a swing handle.

c1860

£700-900 FRE

10in (25.5cm) long

£250-300 FRE

A 19thC magnifying glass, the sliding magnifying glass cased in carved shell with silver mounts.

3.5in (9cm) diam

£100-150   **FRE**

A 19thC John Brown amputation set, comprising a timber-handled saw, two spare blades, steel grips, cases.

18in (45.5cm) long

£200-300   **FRE**

A set of twelve eye surgery instruments, Weiss, the steel blades are set to ivory handles, in a fitted leather box.

c1850   Longest 5in (12.5cm) long

£80-120   **FRE**

A set of thirteen 19thC Philharmonic tuning forks, J. Walker, encased in a fitted box.

Longest 6in (15cm) long

£100-150   **FRE**

A 19thC draftsman's set, complete ivory and steel set comprising approximately 25 pieces, including watercolours enclosed under the instrument tray, in a brass-inlaid rosewood box with key.

13in (33cm) wide

£1,000-1,500   **FRE**

A George III table celestial globe, by J & W Cary, London, on a moulded and turned mahogany tripod base.

1802   19in (48cm) high overall

£2,500-3,000   **WW**

A pair of terrestrial and celestial table globes, by G. & J. Cary, London, the maps coloured, the terrestrial globe with losses to southern Italy and Greece, minor losses and abrasions elsewhere, the celestial globe with restored section to South and section rebuild to North, the supporting rings of brass, on original stands of mahogany and ebonised wood, the rings also with small losses and abrasions.

1828   12in (30.5cm) diam.

£4,000-5,000   **SOTA**

A William IV Newton's terrestrial globe, with printed segments and a label 'Newton's New and Improved Terrestrial Globe Accurately Delineated From the Observations of The Most Esteemed Navigators and Travellers To The Present Time, London, Published 1st January 1832'.

43.5in (110.5cm) high

£15,000-20,000   **WW**

A Victorian armillary sphere, the central terrestrial globe bounded by an arrangement of calibrated brass horizons and outer celestial ring marking the constellations, on a short turned cabochon-carved column and pierced scrolling tripod base.

44in (112cm) high

£4,000-5,000   **L&T**

An American 19thC terrestrial globe, by Gilman Joslin, Boston, of typical sphere form, constructed of twelve colour paper gores, with a brass meridian, over a timber stand.

18in (46cm) high

£1,000-1,500   **FRE**

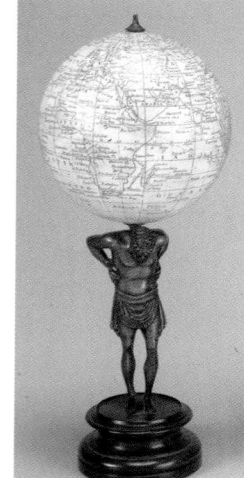

A late 20thC decorative 8in (20.5cm) terrestrial globe on a patinated bronze figural stand, unsigned, the twelve gores printed with a facsimile of Woodward's map, supported by a figure of Atlas on a circular grained wood base.

20.75in (53cm) high

£200-300   **DN**

Edward Everard Arnold (New Orleans, 1824-1866), 'Sch'r H.B. Metcalf, Capt'n Charles L. Murden', signed and dated 'Arnold 1859 pinxt', oil on canvas, two patch repairs, scattered retouch, minor paint losses.

40in (101.5cm) wide

£13,000-16,000   **SK**

Ralph Eugene Cahoon, Jr. (Cotuit, Massachusetts, 1910-1982), signed, oil on masonite depicting sailors netting fish and mermaids.

27.75in (70.5cm) wide

£12,000-15,000   **SK**

Raffael Corsini (Turkish, active 1830-1880), 'Barque Juniata, Capt. Joseph Cheever Entering Smyrna April 22th 1852', signed, gouache on paper, in original walnut veneer frame.

23.5in (59.5cm) wide

£14,000-16,000   **SK**

Antonio Nicolo Gasparo Jacobsen (American/Danish, 1850-1921), portrait of the British steamer 'Circassia', signed and dated 'A Jacobsen 1881', oil on canvas, vessel identified on bow and pennant.

60in (152.5cm) wide

£16,000-20,000   **SK**

19thC American School, portrait of a four-masted ship, unsigned, oil on canvas, framed.

30in (76cm) wide

£1,500-2,000   **FRE**

A 19thC Chinese School, oil on canvas, ''CENTENNIAL' HONG KONG. SEPT. 1878', unsigned, titled below, in a Chinese carved wooden frame, minor craquelure.

32.25in (82cm) wide

£12,000-15,000   **SK**

TEXTILES

A sailor's embroidered woolwork picture, of the 'Prince Consort', the battleship in full regalia, draped with flags, above a crowned banner.

33.75in (86cm) wide

£4,000-6,000   **L&T**

A Victorian sailor's woolwork picture of ship, flying the red ensign, entitled 'HMS QUEEN 1850' within a simulated rosewood frame.

28in (71cm) wide

£3,000-4,000   **L&T**

A mid-19thC sailor's woolwork picture of a naval gunboat, steam and sail, with raised padded embroidered sails and black cotton rigging, silver thread anchors.

Framed 15in (39cm) wide

£500-600   **KT**

A mid-19thC embroidered woolwork picture of HMS 'Marlborough', the 131 gun steam and sail ship flying blue and red ensigns.

Framed 14in (36cm) wide

£600-800   **KT**

A late 19thC sailor's woolwork, worked with a three masted merchantman on an emerald green scudding sea, the hull worked in black and red with grey and white guns holes and port holes.

Framed 22in (56cm) wide

£700-900   **KT**

A mid-19thC embroidered sailor's woolwork, worked with four ships of the line, with black cotton rigging, black beaded gun-ports, on a scudding sea and calm sky in shades of green.

Framed 18.5in (47cm) wide

£1,100-1,400   **KT**

A 19thC American engraved whale's tooth, depicting an eagle, American shield and flags, and Christ upon the cross, inscribed 'M.T.' and 'M.D.S.', some areas with red sealing wax, on a rosewood base.

7in (18cm) high

£6,000-8,000   **SK**

A powder horn, with engraving and inscription 'MARCH ye A 1762 CROWN POINT STEPHEN DYAR,' surrounded by vessels flying British flags, and carved wooden butt plug.

A genealogical search indicates that Stephen Dyar (Dyer, Dier) was born in Weymouth, Massachusetts, October 20, 1741, to Joseph and Jane (Stephens [Stevens]) Dyar. He married Leah Bate(s) October 25, 1764. In the Massachusetts Soldiers and Sailors in the Revolution, Dyar was enlisted as a Minute-man in various lengths of service between April 19 1775 and April 26, 1778.

c1762   *11.5in (29cm) long*

£3,000-4,000   **SK**

A 19thC carved and engraved whale's tooth, depicting a three-masted bark with carved hull, and the initials 'P.M.' engraved in script.

6in (15cm) long

£2,000-2,500   **SK**

A scrimshaw horn, of Masonic Interest, decorated with sailing ships and the City arms of Edinburgh and Glasgow above views of notable buildings: St. Giles Cathedral, Holyrood Palace, Edinburgh University, Tron Church, St. Andrew's Church, St. George's Church, Nelson Monument, Melville's Monument, George Herriot's Hospital, Royal Institution, Register Office, with a lower banding of Masonic emblems and symbols, signed: 'carved by D. Gourlay, Plumber aged 68'.

15in (38cm) long

£1,200-1,600   **L&T.**

A French and Native American war powder or blowing horn, inscribed 'George Losch Anno 1762', carved with the Royal Coat of Arms, New York, a hunter with dogs and a deer, and 'Map of America' showing the river and military forts from Albany to Lake Champlain and Lake Ontario, heightened with black and red.

Provenance: This horn may have been made for George Losch, a gunpowder maker of Philadelphia County, who, along with Oswold Eve, signed an agreement to furnish 'good strong and well seasoned' gunpowder in one year's time to the Committee of the Secrecy of the Continental Congress, January 11, 1776. The committee members included Benjamin Franklin, Robert Morris and Silas Dean.

12in (30.5cm) long

£8,000-10,000   **FRE**

A scrimshaw-decorated walrus tusk, incised to one side with a clipper.

18.5in (47cm) long

£600-800   **L&T**

An early 19thC midshipman's training model, of a fully rigged tea clipper, the absence of sails clearly delineating the positions of masts, rigging and supporting chain mounts, made in dark stained pine and beech.

96.75in (246cm) wide

£2,500-3,500 L&T

A painted pine ship model, of a Mediterranean trading vessel, the painted deck with naturalistically modelled cranking wheels, ships wheel and bell, with full rigging, on a trestle stand.

83in (211cm) wide

£2,500-3,500 L&T

An early 20thC gaff-rigged pond yacht, with a painted hull and planked deck, with a later two-wheeled carriage.

66.5in (169cm) high

£1,200-1,500 L&T

A silver model, of a four-masted English Royal galleon the 'Mary Rose' by Alfred James, Francis William & Arthur Walter Pairpoint, London, in full sail with men on deck, cannons and flying pennants, on a four-wheel base, on a mahogany plinth with title plaque and an oak carrying case 58.75oz (1828g).

The 'Mary Rose' was launched in 1511 and served as flagship in King Henry VIII's fleet. She was one of a new type of purpose-built warship equipped with gunports to enable artillery broadsides to be fired. She was sunk on 19th July 1545 off Portsmouth during a battle with the French fleet which had attacked the English coast. After many years of excavation, the ship was finally raised from the sea bed in 1982.

1920 *19in (48.5cm) long*

£2,500-3,000 DN

A working pond model of a yacht, Birkenhead, gaff-rigged, timber body, cotton/silk sail, with timber stand.

c1920 *24in (61cm) high*

£500-800 FRE

An American 'from scratch' pond model of a yacht, timber body and keel, with two linen sails, on a timber stand.

c1940 *20in (51cm) high*

£350-500 FRE

An American 20thC cased painted near-scale ship model, made by Peter Ness, 'The Flying Cloud, New York'.

41.5in (105.5cm) wide

£800-1,000 FRE

An early 20thC painted wood half model, of a ship mounted on a moulded mahogany backboard, labelled 'Maria a Hinde. Built by Workman Clarke & Co. Limited Belfast 208 29 13 11 hold'.

64in (162cm) long

£2,200-2,600 L&T

A large early 20thC painted wood half model, of a ship on a moulded maple backboard.

92.25in (234cm) long

£2,000-2,500 L&T

An early 20thC painted wood half model, of a ship mounted on a mahogany backboard, labelled 'S. S. William Hinde 160x22 6x11 9 hold. Built by Workman Clark & Co. Limited Belfast'.

51.25in (130cm) long

£3,000-3,500 L&T

'There is No Second', Schooner Yacht America, Isle of Wight 1851', diorama, by William E Hitchcock (1928-2006, Massachusetts), in a moulded giltwood frame.

The yacht 'America' was designed by George Steers for The New York Yacht Club in 1851, in an effort to challenge the British, who had a reputation for yachting supremacy. The 'America' raced in England against fifteen yachts in the annual 53-mile race around the Isle of Wight, conducted by the Royal Yacht Squadron, and won by two minutes. She won the next race, against England's fastest the 'Titania', by nearly an hour. When Queen Victoria was told of the triumph, she asked who was second; the famous reply was: 'There is no second, your Majesty.' A cup was presented to the New York Yacht Club, who offered it to any yacht capable of defeating them, a challenge which has become known as the 'America's Cup'.

33in (84cm) long

£500-1,000 SK

A late 19thC ship diorama, half black model of a five-masted ship, in a glazed case, corrosion of small metal parts.

37in (94cm) wide

£1,800-2,200 SK

An American diorama by Erik A. R. Ronnberg Sr., 'Arctic Steam Whalers off Herschel Island c1890', signed.

1986 *56.5in (143.5cm) wide*

£1,000-1,300 SK

Robert F. Kurtz, diorama of the schooner 'William M. Yerkes', the model taken from an oil painting by S. F. M. Badger, in a glazed moulded mahogany frame with gilt liner.

1983 *22.25in (56.5cm) wide*

£800-1,200 SK

A brass-hooded and gimballed binnacle, by Calvin & Winfrid O. White Co., Boston and New York, fitted onto a full-sized mahogany circular pedestal, on rectangular plinth, cast iron compensating arms, pedestal with copper plate.

£750-1,000 FRE

A ship's brass pedestal-mounted telegraph, by J.W. Ray & Co., Liverpool and London, from a large steamship.

46in (117cm) high

£450-650 FRE

A mid-to late 19thC German Universal Skaphe sundial, by A. Meisser, Berlin, patented by H. Schmeisser, with copper hemisphere on a cobalt-glazed ceramic stand.

6in (15cm) high

£750-1,000 FRE

A 19th/20thC portable brass foghorn, by H.R. Holland, with leather strap and adjustable horn.

20.25in (51.5cm) long

£200-300 FRE

A pair of 19th-early 20thC port and starboard copper lamps, by Stuurboord and Bakboord, with clear glass lenses.

13.75in (35cm) high

£150-200 FRE

Left: An early to mid-20thC Japanese copper and brass diving helmet.

18.5in (47cm) high

£750-1,000 FRE

Right: A late 19th/early 20thC brass and copper diving helmet, by A.J. Morris & Co., Boston, Massachusetts.

18in (45.5cm) high

£2,200-2,800 FRE

A late 19thC shellwork shadowbox, from Barbados, with exotic shells.

The poem on reverse reads 'All the royal gems of the world's kingdoms, Don't compare with Poseidon's humblest creatures, Whose perfection and color are without equal, And are there to be found on our coastal beaches.', comes with printed label 'New Curiosity Shop McGregor St, Barbados W.I. ...Fancy Work ....'

16in (40.6cm) wide

£2,500-3,000 FRE

A Victorian sailor's shell double valentine, in an octagonal hinged glazed case, one side with 'SOUVENIR FROM BARBADOS', the other with a galleon.

28.5in (72cm) wide open

£5,000-6,000 L&T

THE MUSIC BOX MARKET

The inspiration for the design of the familiar cylinder musical box may be found in some of the more complex musical clocks of the 18th century. These clocks could play simple tunes provided by a series of tuned bells that were struck by small hammers which were, in turn, activated by a rotating, pinned cylinder.

At the end of the 18th and during the early 19th century, technology allowed the bells to be replaced with a steel comb consisting of tuned teeth. As this was a much more compact arrangement, more notes could be provided in a given space allowing the musical arrangers greater opportunities to produce elaborate music.

Technical developments, mostly made by Swiss engineers, throughout the 19th century reduced the cost of these machines to such an extent that many households could afford this form of entertainment.

By the mid 1880s, German engineers had developed a more robust system where the musical information was provided via an easily interchangeable disc rather than the more vulnerable, and mostly fixed, cylinder. This system had many advantages, including the opportunity to allow the manufacture of a large selection of titles.

The early 20th century saw the introduction of many marvellous technical advances. Recordings of live music and the introduction of the wireless eventually made the musical box redundant.

Condition is of the utmost importance when considering values. Interest in antique musical boxes has increased over the past 40 years and restoration techniques have been developed to enable a musical box to provide a performance today that is equal to that when it was first produced.

Stephen Kember, Tunbridge Wells, Kent

MUSIC BOXES

A Swiss '2 per turn' cylinder musical box, Nicole Frères, serial no. '43038', playing 12 airs, movement overhauled, case repolished, cylinder 12in (30.5cm) long.
c1860   *22in (56cm) wide*
£4,000-5,000   **PGO**

A Swiss cylinder musical box, movement overhauled, original tune sheet, cylinder 9in (23cm) long.

c1870-1890   *20in (51cm) wide*
£2,000-2,500   **PGO**

An eight-air cylinder musical box, by Ami Rivenc, original tune sheet, original finish to case, movement restored.
c1880   *14in (35.5cm) wide*
£1,800-2,200   **PGO**

A French cylinder musical box, by L'Epee, No. '54846', playing six airs, case refinished, movement over-hauled. cylinder 8in (20.5in) long.
c1885   *16.75in (42.5cm) wide*
£1,800-2,200   **PGO**

A burr walnut crank-wound interchangeable cylinder table musical box, by Nicole Frères, Geneva, each of the eight 16in (40.5cm) pinned cylinders playing a choice of six airs on a double steel comb mounted onto an engine-turned brass bed stamped '43600', flanked by 'Start/Stop' and 'Change/Repeat' levers and crank wind, with an ebonised box containing three further cylinders.
c1880   *the table 46.75in (119cm) wide*
£5,000-7,000   **DN**

A late 19thC Swiss burr thuya wood musical box, with a row of six graduated bells and a 16in comb playing ten airs, with winding handle and two levers, on later inlaid stand , the playing card numbered '5079'.
31.5in (80cm) wide
£4,000-6,000   **L&T**

A late 19thC Swiss eight-air musical box, with 11in (4.25cm) cylinder playing on hooked teeth, no. 3522 in inlaid rosewood case.

20in (50cm) wide
£500-700   **GORL**

A Swiss alternate tip buffet-cased cylinder musical box, by Mojon Manger & Co., double main spring barrel playing twelve airs, movement overhauled, case repolished.

1895   *30.5in (77.5cm) wide*

£4,500-5,500   PGO

A Swiss musical box, playing ten airs, in figured walnut and rosewood case, stamped no. '16635', unrestored.

22.5in (57cm) high

£700-900   A&G

A musical box, by Polyphon, original finish to case, supplied with a quantity of original discs and original packing crate, movement serviced.

c1900   *Disc 8.25in (21cm) diam*

£1,000-1,500   PGO

A Britannia smokers cabinet disc musical box, by B. H. Abrahams, of St. Croix, Switzerland, movement overhauled, original finish to case, supplied with ten discs.

c1900   *21in (53.5cm) wide*

£1,800-2,200   PGO

A Swiss '3 bells in sight' cylinder musical box, by B. H. Abrahams of St Croix, Switzerland, original tune sheet and retaining spandrels, original escutcheon plate, enamelling to butterflies and carry handles, red replacement bell rosettes.

c1900   *18in (45.5cm) wide*

£1,800-2,200   PGO

A Regina 15.5 inch mahogany music box, with serpentine top, crank-activated mechanism, with 85 discs, with 'Regina' decal and 'C.J. Heppe & Son, Philadelphia' label to the underside.

22in (56cm) wide

£2,000-3,000   FRE

An 18ct gold half hunter pocket watch, cuvette inscribed 'PARKINSON & FRODSHAM… LONDON', the reverse with blue enamelled floral border around a monogrammed shield-shaped cartouche.

1.25in (3.5cm) diam

£400-500　　　　　L&T

An open face pocket watch, 18ct gold, the white dial and movement signed 'W Batty & Son, Manchester 53248'.

£600-800　　　　　CHT

A metal-cased Jaeger-LeCoultre pocket watch, open faced with date and alarm, circular champagne dial with black Roman numerals, the centre section as an alarm dial, with further date aperture, the base fitted with a folding strut, movement number 1967826, movement stamped 'K911' to the reverse, the case numbered 11003 and 1186679, with original black leather slip.

£500-800　　　　　ROS

A Belle Époque diamond set fob watch, the front millegrain collet set to the centre with an old European cut diamond, set with single cut diamonds and borders of channel set calibre cut onyx.

Fob 2in (5cm) long

£600-800　　　　　L&T

An Art Deco platinum and diamond cocktail watch, with single cut diamond set bezel, fitted to a mesh link strap, clasp stamped '9ct'.

6.5in (16.5cm) long

£1,000-1,500　　　　　L&T

An Art Deco cocktail watch, calibre cut emeralds and single cut diamonds.

£1,000-1,300　　　　　L&T

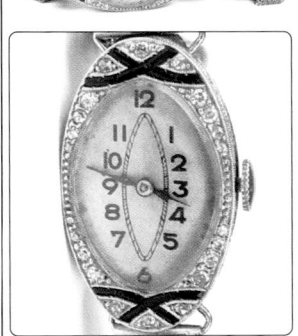

An Art Deco lady's platinum cocktail watch, the case inset with old cut diamonds and shaped baguette cut onyx, fitted with 9ct gold mesh strap.

£250-300　　　　　ROS

An Art Deco cocktail watch, set with single cut diamonds, to a ribbon strap, mounts stamped 18ct.

£800-1,200　　　　　L&T

An Art Deco style diamond and sapphire-set 14ct white gold cocktail watch, inscribed.

£450-550　　　　　CHT

A Baume & Mercier gentleman's gold wrist watch, stamped '750', '18K' and numbered '205688 35041'.

Dial 1.5in (3.5cm) diam

£1,000-1,500　　　　　L&T

A Baume & Mercier lady's 18ct gold wrist watch, numbered '404523 38244T2'.

Dial 1in (2.5cm) wide

£600-800　　　　　L&T

A 1970s Swiss Bulova lady's wristwatch, white gold, with 16 diamonds, silver clockface, blackened hands, quartz clockwork, matted original bracelet.

1in (2.5cm) wide

£200-300　　　　　KAU

A 'Must de Cartier' lady's wristwatch, the winder fitted with sapphire cabochon.

£300-400　　　　　ROS

A 'Must de Cartier' lady's tank watch, silver gilt case, fitted with original black leather strap, case number cc21050.

£500-800　　　　　ROS

A 18ct gold Cartier tank wristwatch, the dial having two faces for different time zones, the tonneau-shaped case with two sapphire cabochon crowns, the dial, movement and case signed, boxed.

£2,500-3,500　　　　　CHT

A 1960s Dunhill gentleman's silver wristwatch, marked on back 'Swiss Chronometer', with original black leather strap.

£850-1,100　　　　　BLO

A lady's diamond Jaeger-LeCoultre cocktail watch, the bracelet box set with round brilliant cut diamonds.

£3,500-5,000　　　　　L&T

A gold Jaeger-LeCoultre gentleman's 18ct gold wristwatch, 18ct gold, automatic movement, the dial, movement and case signed 'Jaeger-le-Coultre'.

£500-800　　　　　CHT

A Longines gentleman's wristwatch, 9ct gold, the silvered dial with subsidiary seconds dial and Roman numerals.

£150-200　　　　　CHT

A Longines gentleman's gold wristwatch, 14ct gold, automatic movement, with subsidiary seconds, the dial, movement and case signed 'Longines'.

£500-600　　　　　CHT

A Longines gentleman's wristwatch, 9ct gold case, the champagne dial with Arabic numerals, baton indices and subsidiary seconds dial, with original guarantee.

£250-350　　　　　CHT

An Omega 18ct white gold lady's bracelet watch, diamond set lugs, the square silvered dial with baton markers, cal. 484 seventeen jewel movement, triple signed.

.75in (1.5cm) diam

£500-700　　　　　GHOU

An 1960s Omega gentleman's 18ct gold wristwatch, cal. no. 600, 17 jewels, centre seconds with date, brown leather strap, working condition, dial needs clean or replacement.

£350-450　　　　　BLO

A 1980s Swiss Omega Seamaster-Cosmic gentlemen's wristwatch, stainless steel, silver clockface.

1.25in (3cm) diam

£250-350   **KAU**

A Patek Philippe gentleman's 18ct gold wristwatch, signed face, Buren Grand Prix movement, in 18ct gold hallmarked case by Dennison of England, with black strap with 14ct gold buckle, good clean working order.

£550-650   **BLO**

A Piaget lady's 18ct gold wristwatch.

£400-500   **ROS**

A gentleman's 14ct yellow gold case wristwatch, by Audemars Piguet, Case no. 8765, including an 18ct yellow gold wide mesh flexible bracelet.

£3,000-4,000   **FRE**

A Rolex 'Oyster Perpetual Explorer' gentleman's stainless steel bracelet watch, reference number '5500', serial number '891137'.

1.25in (3.5cm) diam

£1,400-1,600   **GHOU**

A Rolex Oyster gentleman's wristwatch, perpetual day-date movement, 18ct yellow gold flexible bracelet.

£5,000-6,000   **FRE**

A Rolex 'Oyster Perpetual Datejust' stainless steel gentleman's bracelet watch, the silvered dial with baton markers, sweep centre seconds and date aperture at 3 o'clock, twenty-seven jewels, reference number '16030', serial number '891137', plain bezel, screw back and conforming bracelet.

1.25in (3.5cm) diam

£700-900   **GHOU**

A Tudor Rolex Oyster gentleman's wristwatch, on stainless steel Rolex jubilee bracelet, the dial, movement and case signed.

£150-200   **CHT**

A Tissot gentleman's wristwatch, in a stainless steel case, the square silvered dial with baton indices, the movement, case and dial signed 'Tissot'.

£80-120   **CHT**

A Vacheron & Constantin gentleman's 18ct gold wristwatch, the movement, case and dial signed 'Vacheron & Constantin'.

£1,200-1,500   **CHT**

THE SILVER MARKET

Whether they are buying a mid-19thC tea service or a provincial silver spoon, collectors are becoming far more interested in the history of the silver they are buying. They want to know about the inscriptions, crests and monograms on salvers, mugs and trophies as well as the social history behind spoons and other wares. This means that pieces with provenance are becoming increasingly desirable.

Of course, quality remains important to buyers, as does condition. It is also noticeable that people are looking for good, clear, tidy hallmarks. As ever, any enamel work must be pristine as restoration to even the slightest damage is virtually impossible.

The market for collectables such as small boxes, card cases and vinaigrettes continues to grow, with condition becoming more important. The demand for 19thC silver is still quite strong

and the recent dearth of good Georgian silver on the market means that when pieces do come up for sale there is a lot of interest.

20thC tea services, trays and salvers are rarely worth more than the bullion price unless they are stylish, Art Deco examples, or of great artisitic merit, in which case they are increasing in value. Pieces by the big names of 20thC design such as Archibald Knox are also doing better than those by less well known names unless, of course, they are particularly stylish.

Its rarity makes a big difference to the value of provincial Scottish silver. Buyers look for the less common hallmarks but are also willing to pay for pieces in good condition. Again, the political and social history behind any piece of Scottish silver will make a difference to its value.

Trevor Kyle, Lyon & Turnbull, Edinburgh

A Dutch silver beaker, by David Reyniers, Dordrecht, engraved below the flared rim with strapwork, fruit clusters and scrolls partly terminating in masks and possibly later engraved with ships below, the base inscribed with the initials 'NMIP', fully marked at the base, 11.25oz (350g).

1614　　　*7in (17.5cm) high*

£4,000-6,000　　　**SOTA**

A Dutch silver beaker, by Herman Maetyssen, Deventer, date letter 'L', the body engraved with strapwork and scrolling foliage and a fruit cluster below a phoenix, with the initials 'BA' and 'GK' and two housemarks within a shield, fully marked at the base, 15.8oz (493g).

c1634　　　*7.5in (19cm) high*

£22,000-28,000　　　**SOTA**

A Dutch silver beaker, Jan Lubbers Langeweerd, Groningen, engraved with the personifications of Hope, Faith and Charity inscribed on one side with 'LUE', housemark 'AILIENS', the base applied with a corded girdle above cast bands, fully marked below, 5.9oz (183g).

1636-37　　　*5.25in (13.5cm) high*

£8,000-12,000　　　**SOTA**

A set of six Victorian silver straight tapering beakers, by William Ker Reid, London, with a moulded spreading foot and engraved with armorials, the interiors gilt, 27.5oz (855g).

1848　　　*4in (10cm) high*

£4,000-5,000　　　**DN**

A French silver gilt engraved 'Freesia' beaker, by Puiforcat, moulded and engraved with bands, on a reeded circular foot, first standard mark, engraved '1928-1978', 7.5oz (237g).

3.5in (9cm) high

£200-300　　　**DN**

A William IV silver goblet, by Robert Garrard II, London, with a reeded rim, 8oz (254g).

1833　　　*6.5in (16cm) high*

£800-1,000　　　**DN**

A Victorian silver campana shaped goblet, by William Horton, London, 8.5oz (266g).

£400-500　　　**DN**

A Savage, Lyman & Co. of Montreal embossed and engraved sterling silver presentation goblet, with band of maple leaves, engraved circular monogram and motto, the interior with gold wash, the foot with beaded ring and with stamped maker's marks.

The motto 'Tria Juncta In Uno' and the armorial under the encircled monogram are those of the Order of the Bath. Meaning 'Three Joined In One', the motto refers to the union of England, Scotland and Wales. Created by George I in 1725, it is the fourth highest order of chivalry. This goblet was most probably produced for a Canadian recipient of the honour, or an existing member who moved to Canada.

6.25in (16cm) high

£1,000-1,500　　　**TCF**

A George II sterling silver tankard, possibly Jason Kingman or John Kentish, London, the domed lid above a bulbous body with scrolling loop handle, the repoussé decoration possibly of a later date, 26oz (737g).

1772   *8.25in (21cm) high*

£1,500-2,000   **FRE**

A late George III sterling silver tankard, of traditional form with a curved spout and bands of ribbed decoration, marks rubbed, possibly stamped 'JE', 25oz (708.5g).

1808   *7in (17.75cm) high*

£400-500   **FRE**

A late George III sterling silver tankard, Nicholas Hearnden, London, with a hinged, domed lid, decorated throughout with a ribbed design, 14oz (397g).

1814   *6.75in (17cm) high*

£1,200-1,800   **FRE**

A Victorian silver embossed baluster beer jug, by Martin, Hall & Co., Sheffield, with flowers, foliage and scrolls, a mask spout, a double-scroll handle and a domed cover with a chair-back thumb piece, with a presentation inscription, 24.25oz (755g).

1861   *8in (20.5cm) high*

£600-800   **DN**

A Victorian sterling silver flagon, Robert Roskell, Allan Roskell & John Mortimer Hunt, London, the lid and rim chased with a band of oak leaves, the spout moulded as a satyr mask, the scrolling handle moulded with berries, the spreading body decorated with a continuous band of strapwork and rinceaux, the interior silver gilt, 82oz (2324.5g).

1883   *12in (30.5cm) high*

£4,500-5,500   **FRE**

A George II Exeter provincial silver pint mug, maker's mark 'JC' (untraced) and engraved beneath 'DD' over 'JY', the front later engraved with a crest, 12.5oz (389g).

1747   *5in (13cm) high*

£700-1,000   **DN**

A George III silver mug, by Thomas Wallis I, London, and later embossed with flowers, leaves, scrolls, rocaille and a cartouche, the foot rim repaired, 10.5oz (330g).

1776   *4.75in (12cm) high*

£300-400   **DN**

A George III mug, by Robert Pinkney and Robert Scott II, Newcastle, with baluster-shaped body and engraved initials, with scrollwork handle, on spreading foot, 12.25oz (347g).

5.25in (13.5cm) high

£450-550   **A&G**

A George III provincial silver two-handled pedestal cup, by John Langlands I & John Robertson I, Newcastle, later embossed with flowers, foliate scrolls and rocaille cartouches, 14.75oz (463g).

6.5in (16.5cm) high

£300-400   **DN**

A Victorian silver baluster mug, by George Unite, Birmingham, embossed with an oval reserve and floral swags under a husk band, with a leaf-capped S-scroll handle, on a circular pedestal foot, 10.25oz (319g).

1870   *6.25in (16cm) high*

£200-300   **DN**

A Gorham martelé silver child's cup, 'Morning Glory' pattern, 7 oz (198.5g).

c1899   *3in (7.5cm) high*

£1,200-1,800   **FRE**

A Britannia silver and silver-gilt repoussé cup and cover, George Lambert, London, the knop in the form of a standing nude.

1900   *12in (30.5cm) high*

£1,000-1,500   **FRE**

An English silver miniature trophy, of double-handled cup form with foot, engraved 'The Earl Grey Challenge Cup for Hunt and Military Teams Presented By His Excellency The Governor General 1909', with double curved detail to base of handles, the base stamped with SSH & Co maker's mark and Sheffield hallmarks.

1911   *4in (10cm) high*

£120-180   **TCF**

A silver punch bowl by The Goldsmiths and Silversmiths Co. Ltd, London, the ebonised stand with a silver panel inscribed 'Presented to Lieutenant Colonel W. Anthony, C.M.G. by His Highness The Khan of Kalat in recognition of his valuable services in the promotion of Horse Breeding, 1923-1925', 68.5oz (2136g).

16.5in (42cm) wide

£650-750   **DN**

A silver vase-shaped trophy cup and cover by Mappin & Webb, Birmingham, in George III Neo-classical style with reeded borders and twin handles, with a cast urn of flowers and husk swag band, the cover with an urn finial, 43.75oz (1366g).

1926   *15in (38cm) high*

£600-800   **DN**

ESSENTIAL REFERENCE: JEAN BATTEN

Jean Gardner Batten (1909-1982) was one of the most illustrious and glamourous aviatrix heroines of the 1930s, and a national hero in her native New Zealand.

- Born in Rotorua, New Zealand, she was inspired by the pioneering flights of Charles Lindberg and Charles Kingsford Smith.
- Determined to become a pilot, Batten moved to London in 1930 to take flying lessons, qualifying for both her private 'A' license and commercial pilot's license in 1931. That year, Amy Johnson set the record for flying from England to Australia in 20 days, and Batten embarked on a course to beat that record.
- In 1933 Batten made two failed attempts at Johnson's record. She succeeded on her third attempt, flying the 10,500 miles from London to Darwin in 14 days and 22 hours, smashing Johnson's record by 6 days. Her return flight to England made her the first ever pilot to fly the round trip of England-Australia-England.

A silver flying trophy cup and cover by Asprey & Co., Ltd, London, the cover with an orb and eagle finial, on a tapering stem and a round base, on an ebonised socle with an inscribed silver plaque 'Blind Flying Challenge Cup, Presented by Lady Hay Drummond-Hay, President of the Women's International Association of Aeronautics, 1936' and 'Jean Batten, 1937-8', 19oz (593g).

15.5in (39cm) high

£3,500-4,500   **DN**

TEA AND COFFEE WARE

A Queen Anne octagonal teapot and stand, teapot designed by Anthony Nelme, London, the burner and stand designed by John Fawdery, London, armorial-engraved baluster, covered spout with scroll thumb piece, associated crested stand with scroll supports, 27oz (869g).

Teapot 1709, burner and stand 1710
8.75in (22cm) high altogether

£18,000-22,000   **SOTH**

A George III sterling silver teapot on stand, by George Hindmarsh, London, the lid with a floral garland, the oval body with repoussé floral trails surrounding cartouches, above a hinged stand, raised on shell feet, 31oz (879g).

1781   *10.25in (26cm) high*

£1,500-2,000   **FRE**

A George III silver shaped oval teapot, by Robert & David Hennel, London, engraved with leafy and meander borders, engraved with a monogram and crest, 16.75oz (521g).

1796   *11.75in (30cm) long*

£400-500   **DN**

A George III silver shaped oval teapot, by Peter & Anne Bateman, London, with an ivory handle and finial and fluted, engraved sides, 13.25oz (417g).

1797   *10.5in (26.5cm) long*

£250-300   **DN**

A George IV silver compressed round teapot, by John Edward Terry, London, with a leaf-chased rim and scroll handle, and embossed with flowers, leaves, scrolls and cartouches engraved with crests, the domed cover with a bud and leaf finial, on four leaf and paw feet, 24.25oz (758g).

1826   *11in (28cm) long*

£400-500   **DN**

A George IV Irish silver oblong teapot, by Charles Marsh, Dublin, with a nulled border, a domed cover with a hazel nut and leaf trefoil lineal, a scroll handle and ball feet, the body engraved with wriggle bands and cartouches, one with script initials, 26.5oz (823g).

1821   *12in (30.5cm) high*

£400-500   **DN**

A William IV silver bullet-shaped teapot, and a straight sided hot-water jug, by Richard Sibley, London, the teapot with a leaf-capped broad-fluted spout, engraved with an armorial, the hot-water jug engraved with an armorial, 20.5oz (637g).

Both 1832   *The teapot 5.5in (14cm) diam.*
                       The jug 7in (18cm) high

£500-600   **DN**

A Victorian silver compressed round teapot, by Robert Hennell III, London, embossed with flowers and foliate scrolls on a matt ground, with a leaf-capped handle and spout, a floral-embossed domed cover with a flower finial and four leaf-chased scroll feet, 23.5oz (729g).

1840   *6.75in (17cm) diam*

£350-450   **DN**

A Victorian silver circular tapered teapot, maker's mark 'R&H', Sheffield, the domed cover with a scroll and lobed finial, a C-scroll handle and an engraved tower crest, 20oz (623g).

1850   *11in (28cm) long*

£300-400   **DN**

A mid-19thC American silver tea-kettle on stand, retailed by Bailey & Co., chased with a continuous chinoiserie landscape, with a leaf-cast spout, the stand ending in shell feet, 83oz (2353g).

10in (25.5cm) high

£2,000-3,000   **FRE**

A Victorian silver baluster teapot, by William Moulson, London, engraved with a variant of the Cellini pattern, the domed cover with a lobed finial, with a loop handle, 21.25oz (660g).

1858   *9in (23cm) long*
£250-350   **DN**

A Victorian silver shaped oval straight-sided teapot, by Robert Harper, London, engraved with foliate scrolls, ovolo borders and a helm crest, the cover with a lobed oval finial, with an ivory loop handle, 11.25oz (352g).

                                      8.75in (22cm) long
£350-450   **DN**

A Victorian sterling silver teapot, probably William Chawner, London, retailed by Munday, 6 Gt. Portland St., with a roundel knop and leaf-cast handle with bone spacers, the body decorated with floral bouquets and foliage, raised on scrolled toes, 27oz (765.5g).

1884   *5.5in (14cm) high*
£400-500   **FRE**

A George II silver straight tapering coffee pot, by Peter Archambo I, London, engraved with a crest and armorial, 28.5oz (891g).

1729   *9in (23cm) high*
£4,000-5,000   **DN**

A George II sterling silver coffee pot, by Thomas Heming, London, with acorn knop and treen handle, spout chased with shells, body decorated with floral cartouches, raised on a circular foot, 31oz (879g).

1752   *11.25in (28.5cm) high*
£1,200-1,800   **FRE**

A George II sterling silver coffee pot, by William Cripps, London, of plain baluster form with a pineapple finial, the body centred with an armorial crest, having a woven split reed handle, raised on a circular foot, 16oz (453.5g).

1753   *10in (25.5cm) high*
£1,000-1,500   **FRE**

A George III sterling silver coffee pot, probably Charles Wright, London, the body entwined with foliate trails and acanthus leaves, wooden handle, 30oz (850.5g).

1759   *11in (28cm) high*
£1,000-2,000   **FRE**

A George III sterling silver coffee pot, London, of baluster form centred by an armorial crest and having a leaf cast spout, the lid with an acorn finial, shaped wood handle, raised on a circular foot, marks rubbed, 26oz (737g).

1762   *10in (25.5cm) high*
£1,000-1,500   **FRE**

A George III silver baluster coffee pot, by William Grundy, London, with a double scroll ebonised handle, on a circular foot, engraved with an armorial, 30.5oz (955g).

1770   *10.5in (24.5cm) high*
£1,200-1,800   **DN**

A George II silver straight tapering small coffee pot, the maker's mark indistinct, London, with a shallow domed cover with a bell finial, and an ebonised double scroll handle, 12.5oz (395g).

1773   *6.75in (17cm) high*
£350-450   **DN**

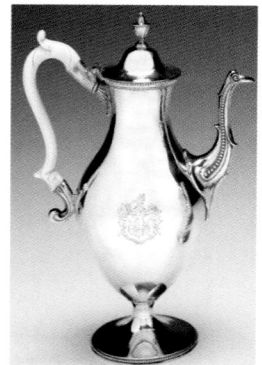

A George III sterling silver coffee pot, by John Denzilow, London, with an urn-form finial and bone handle, beaded spout and circular foot, 29oz (822g).

1784   *12.5in (32cm) high*
£1,200-1,800   **FRE**

A French silver coffee pot, by Francois-Thomas Bernard, Paris, with an acorn knop, the leaf-cast spout with a ram's mask tip, the rosewood handle ending in a female mask, raised on a circular foot cast with leaf-tips, 34oz (964g).

c1838   13in (33cm) high
£1,500-2,000   **FRE**

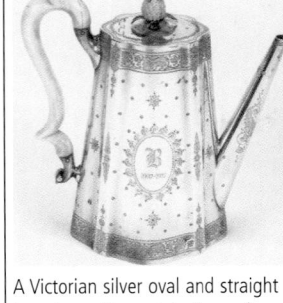

A Victorian silver oval and straight tapering coffee pot, by Samuel Smily, London, with an ivory double scroll handle and pineapple finial, inscribed 'B 1902-1927', and stamped beneath 'Goldsmiths Alliance Limited, Cornhill, London', 27.5oz (856g).

9.25in (23.5cm) high
£400-500   **DN**

A late 19thC American silver coffee pot, decorated throughout with Rococo motifs, the rim and foot with a Greek-key border, monogrammed, 35oz (992g).

12cm (30.5cm) high
£1,000-1,500   **FRE**

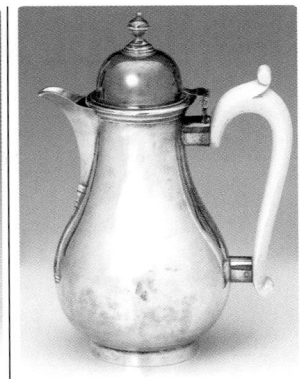

An Edwardian, Queen Anne-style sterling silver coffee pot, Goldsmiths & Silversmiths Co., London, of panelled form with a domed lid and finial, the curved spout opposed by an ebony loop handle, 24oz (680g).

1909   11.75in (30cm) high
£300-400   **FRE**

A George III silver vase-shaped cream jug, by John Bull, London, engraved with leaves, bands and a cartouche, 3.25oz (107g).

1790   5.5in (14.5cm) high
£250-350   **DN**

A George III Irish silver oval milk jug, by Gustavus Bryne, Dublin, with a shaped and moulded rim, a reeded loop handle and fluted sides engraved with floral bands and wreath cartouches, 4.5oz (147g).

1802   4.75in (12cm) high
£180-220   **DN**

A Victorian silver baluster-shaped hot-water jug, by Edward & John Barnard, London, with a scroll handle and a domed cover with an ivory finial, stamped beneath 'Widdowson & Veale, Strand', 25.5oz (797g).

1866   9.5in (24cm) high
£400-500   **DN**

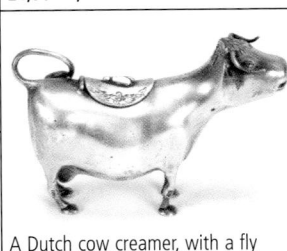

A Tiffany & Co. sterling silver water jug, the hinged lid with a leafy knop above spout with strainer, the entire body with repoussé foliate and leafy decoration, raised on a circular foot, the underside with an elaborate monogram, 26oz (737g).

c1886   8.25in (21cm) high
£1,500-2,500   **FRE**

A Victorian silver vase-shaped hot-water jug, by Edward Hutton, London, 18.75oz (584g).

1887   11.75in (30cm) high
£500-600   **DN**

ESSENTIAL REFERENCE: JAPONISME

Japonisme – or Japonaiserie – was a decorative style inspired by Japanese designs. The exhibitions of Japanese art and design which followed the re-commencement of trade with the West in the 1850s influenced many designers.
- Popular motifs included chrysanthemums, birds and flowers, and stylized branches.
- Metalworkers often produced silverware featuring Japanese motifs or with mixed metal decoration.

An American silver Japanese style pitcher, by Tiffany & Co., with a globular body and a cylindrical neck, hexagonal spot-hammered and applied and engraved with bamboo, a fly caught in a spider's web and a dragonfly, with an angular loop handle, stamped marks and nos. '5066', '1254', 34.75oz (1080g).

8.5in (21.5cm) high
£9,000-11,000   **DN**

A Dutch cow creamer, with a fly finial, the curling tail forming the handle, .833 standard, 5.5oz (178g).

5.25in (13.5cm) long
£400-500   **DN**

A George IV silver compressed round teapot, by John Houle, London, part-fluted flush-hinged cover on four leaf-chased feet, the body engraved with a crest, with a silver milk jug, the marks worn, with a gadrooned rim and leaf-chased scroll handle and an old Sheffield plate sugar basin, 9.25oz (288g).

1821   Teapot 6.5in (16.5cm) diam
£350-450   DN

An American six-piece silver tea service, by Edward Lownes, Philadelphia, including two teapots, a hot water pot, waste bowl, creamer and covered sugar bowl, lid of sugar slightly different, the waste bowl, covered sugar base, one teapot and hot water pot bear maker's mark, some very small dents, no noticeable repairs or re-solders, 178oz (5046g).

c1825
£2,500-3,500   FRE

A William IV silver compressed round and melon fluted three-piece tea service, probably by William Barett II, London, chased with floral panels, the conforming domed cover with a flower finial, with a leaf-capped loop handle, on four flower and shell feet, 47.5oz (1478g).

1831   Teapot 12.25in (31cm) long
£500-600   DN

A Victorian silver four-piece baluster-shaped tea and coffee service, by Joseph & Albert Savory, London, engraved with C-scrolls, foliage and diaper panels, engraved with intials 'F.O.S.', 75.5oz (2358g).

1845-6   Teapot 10.5in (26.5cm) long
£1,200-1,800   DN

A four-piece American sterling silver tea/coffee service, comprising a coffee pot, teapot, milk jug and covered sugar bowl, 85oz (2410g).

c1850   Coffee pot 11.5in (29cm) high
£1,000-1,500   FRE

An American sterling silver three-piece tea and coffee service, P. B. Sadtler & Son, Baltimore, comprising a coffee pot, a teapot and a sugar bowl, chased and embossed with flowers, foliage and vignettes of castles and bridges, centred by monogrammed cartouches and raised on socle bases, the coffee pot unmarked, 95oz (2693g).

c1850   Coffee pot 11.75in (30cm) high
£1,500-2,000   FRE

A French silver cream jug, sugar bowl and a twin-handled bowl and cover, by A. Aucoc, each of baluster form with a central moulded girdle, post 1838 1st standards departments mark, 26.75oz (838g) (the jug loaded).

Cream jug 5.25in (13.5cm) high
£250-350   DN

A Victorian sterling silver four-piece tea and coffee service, by James Dixon & Sons, Sheffield, comprising a coffee pot, teapot, sugar bowl and cream jug, each with a gadrooned rim and raised on ball feet, the pots with treen handles and knops, 63oz (1786g).

1866   Coffee pot 9in (23cm) high
£1,000-1,500   FRE

A Victorian silver baluster-shaped four-piece tea and coffee service, by Samuel Smily, London, with beaded leaf scroll handles, leaf and scroll-chased borders and feet, scroll cartouches engraved with etoille crests, each marked beneath 'Goldsmiths Alliance Limited, Cornhill, London', 94oz (2922g).

1870   Coffee pot 11in (28cm) high
£2,500-3,500   DN

A 19thC French silver and ivory tea and coffee service, Paris, comprising a tray, coffee pot, teapot, hot water kettle-on-stand, sugar bowl and cover, cream jug and waste bowl, each with a berried finial, the rim hung with ribbon-tie garlands, the base decorated with alternating flaming and flower-filled urns, the pots and cream jug with leaf-carved ivory handles, makers mark 'CD' centred by a bee and three stars, 391oz (11,084g) all in.

Hot water kettle 17.25in (44cm) high
£10,000-15,000   FRE

A Victorian four-piece sterling silver tea and coffee service, London, comprising a pyriform coffee pot, a globular teapot, both with bird finials to the covers, an open sugar bowl and a creamer, all with scroll handles and beaded edges, maker's mark 'GB', 71oz (2013g).
1871
£1,000-1,500 FRE

A Victorian four-piece tea set, of tapering oval form with straight spouts, chased with foliage around blind oval cartouche and foliate bands, Sheffield and London, 73oz (2270g).

1879, 1880.
£1,200-1,800 HT

A late 19thC American Gorham sterling silver five-piece tea and coffee service, comprising a teapot, coffee pot, creamer, covered sugar and waste bowl, with lobed foliate decoration, monogrammed 'M', 95oz (2693g).

Coffee pot 10in (25.5cm) high
£1,200-1,800 FRE

A late 19thC Chinese silver eight-piece tea and coffee service, comprising a teapot, coffee pot, tea kettle on stand, lacking handle, covered sugar bowl, creamer, slop bowl, hot water pitcher, sugar tongs and a tray, each of simulated bamboo form with applied bamboo decoration, signed, 182oz (5160g).
Tray 27.5in (70cm) wide
£3,500-4,500 FRE

An American Gorham martelé sterling silver after-dinner coffee service, comprising a coffee pot, sugar bowl and cream jug, each of baluster form chased throughout with foliage enclosing cartouches, the coffee pot with bone spacers to handle, marks for 'Wendell G. Arnold, Silversmith', 37oz (1049g).
1898 *Coffee pot 12in (30.5cm) high*
£4,500-5,500 FRE

A late Victorian silver three-piece oblong 'bachelors' tea service, by Charles Stuart Harris, London, each profusely embossed with flowers, leaves, scrolls, diaper and cartouches, on ball feet, the teapot with a composition handle and finial, 25.25oz (786g).
1898 *Teapot 8.5in (22cm) long*
£250-350 DN

An Edwardian silver four-piece tea set, with gadrooned shell-mounted rims and raised on ball feet, 68oz (2114g).
1906, 1907, 1911
£700-1,000 HT

A silver four-piece circular pedestal tea service, in the Regency style by D. & J. Wellby Ltd, London, each with shell and gadroon shoulders, egg and dart rim and double snake handle, on a reeded circular foot, 87oz (2708g).
1910-11 *Teapot 11.25in (28.5cm) long*
£1,000-1,500 DN

An early 20thC American seven-piece Reed and Barton silver tea and coffee service, comprising a teapot, coffee pot, kettle-on-stand, creamer, covered sugar bowl and a tray, 291oz (8250g).
Tray 27in (68.5cm) wide
£2,500-3,500 FRE

A Tiffany & Co. sterling silver tea and coffee service, comprising a teapot, coffee pot, cream jug, covered sugar bowl, waste bowl and two-handled tray, of rectangular form, with canted edges, the teapot and coffee pot with bone rings to handles, 220oz (6237g).
1913 *Coffee pot 8.5in (21.5cm) high*
£5,000-6,000 FRE

A silver four-piece oval tea service, by Mappin & Webb, Birmingham, with pierced borders and scroll handles, each on four leaf and paw feet, engraved with a monogram, the service 54.25oz (1688g).
1915 *Teapot 12in (30.5cm) long*
£600-800 DN

A 20thC sterling silver tea and coffee service, Elkington & Co., Birmingham, comprising a teapot, coffee pot, hot water kettle-on-stand, covered sugar bowl, waste bowl and cream jug, each of lobed form, the pots all with wooden handles, 170oz (4819.5g).

1920 *Kettle 9.5in (24cm) high*

£1,500-2,000 **FRE**

A 20thC Continental silver tea and coffee service, comprising a coffee pot and teapot with pheasant head spouts, a covered sugar bowl and a creamer, of lobed melon form, the covers with acorn finials, stamped '800'.

Coffee pot 9in (23cm) high

£500-800 **FRE**

A 20thC Cartier silver-gilt coffee service, comprising a coffee pot with ebony handle, cream jug and covered sugar bowl monogrammed 'S', together with an associated Reed & Barton sterling silver-gilt circular salver, 86oz (2438g).

Coffee pot 12in (30.5cm) high

£1,500-2,000 **FRE**

A silver four-piece canted oblong tea service, by James Deakin & Sons, Sheffield, with shaped handles and foliate scroll feet, 58.5oz (1825g).

1923-24 Teapot 11in (28cm) high

£400-600 **DN**

FLATWARE

A George III silver rectangular snuffer stand, the maker's mark worn, London, with a gadrooned border, scroll handle and four hoof feet and engraved with a crest, and with a scratch weight '8=12' beneath, 8oz (252g).

1764 *7in (18cm) wide*

£350-450 **DN**

A set of four George III sterling silver shell-form dishes, London, each with an armorial crest, raised on shell feet, marks rubbed, 15oz (425g).

1768 *4.5in (11.5cm) wide*

£500-700 **FRE**

A late 19thC American set of four Kirk & Sons sterling silver compotes, with chased and embossed decoration, 96oz (2721g).

9.5in (24cm) wide

£3,500-4,500 **FRE**

A pair of sterling silver bonbon dishes, London, each reticulated shell-form dish with a figural handle, raised on dolphin supports, makers mark 'EJG', 22oz (624g).

1908 *5.5in (14cm) wide*

£1,000-1,500 **FRE**

A set of four silver shaped round compotes, by The Goldsmiths & Silversmiths Co. Ltd, London, each embossed with floral swags on a matt ground, with shell and scroll borders and engraved with a monogram, 73.25oz (2283g).

1908-1913 Largest 11in (28cm) diam.

£1,500-2,000 **DN**

A pair of Tiffany & Co. sterling silver tazzas, each with strawberry-cast border, raised on a circular foot, monogrammed, 29oz (822g).

c1916 8in (20.5cm) diam

£1,000-1,500 **FRE**

A set of four 20thC Continental silver shell-form condiment dishes, J. Piault, in the Rococo style, monogrammed, 47oz (1332g).

7in (18cm) long

£400-500 **FRE**

An American sterling silver oval dish, with embossed scrolling and floral pattern and pierced rim, the bowl with engraved 'AB' monogram and the back stamped 'STERLING 925 1988', with '1355' in a diamond.

7in (18cm) wide

£100-150 **TCF**

BASKETS & BOWLS

A George II silver basket, by Paul Lamerie, London, the centre armorial engraved, on cast and chased supports, flower garlands between, the oval bat pierced and engraved with scrolls and foliage, the rim interrupted by shells and mounted at each end with putti heads against shells, the swing caryatid handle cast and chased with flowers, engraved with scratchweight '61 = 1/4', 59oz (1856g).

1739   14in (37.5cm) wide

£180,000-220,000   SOTH

A George III sterling silver pierced basket, by William Plummer, London, the ornate openwork panelled sides with a swing handle and shell-cast rim, raised on a pierced Rococo scroll foot, 38oz (1077g).

1760   14.5in (37cm) wide

£2,000-3,000   FRE

A Dutch silver sweetmeat basket, by Johannes Schiotling, Amsterdam, the oval body pierced and engraved with geometrical patterns, applied with garlands and ribbon-tied medallions with double portraits, the interior divided into four pieces, fully marked, including 1795 control mark for Rotterdam, 11oz (345g).

1777   7in (17.5cm) wide

£8,000-10,000   SOTA

A Dutch silver sweetmeat basket, by Johannes Schiotling, Amsterdam, of shaped oval form on four claw-and-ball feet, the sides pierced and engraved with geometrical patterns, with beaded rims, central flowers and foliage beneath, fully marked below, including a 1795 control mark for Gouda, 10.7oz (334g).

1783   6in (15.5cm) high

£8,000-10,000   SOTA

A Dutch silver basket, by Antonie van Luthervelt, Utrecht, with twig handles at the side, together with a detachable wirework bottle frame, both also struck with a 1795 control mark for Utrecht, fully marked and engraved 'L:A:V:V:', 34.4oz (1070g).

1798   11.5in (29cm) wide

£6,500-8,500   SOTA

A Regency sterling silver basket, by William Bateman, London, of oblong form with a gadrooned edge and reeded swing handle, the sides with foliate-embossed and chased decoration, 33oz (935g).

1815   13in (33cm) wide

£1,500-2,000   FRE

A French silver jardinière, the shaped oval body on four supports, the rim openworked and applied with medallions and garlands, with two handles, with original metal liner, 93.8oz (2660g).

c1880   19.25in (49cm) wide

£12,000-15,000   SOTA

A silver lobed oval cake basket, by Walker and Hall, Chester, with a beaded and gadrooned inter-woven swing handle and shaped rim, a lobed oval bowl with foliate pierced round panels and engraved with foliate scrolls on a beaded oval foot, 28.5oz (888).

1907   14in (35.5cm) long

£500-600   DN

A 20thC sterling silver centrepiece on stand, by Charles & Richard Comyns, London, of oval form with a pierced Vitruvian scroll rim above ribbon-tied medallions, with flanking ram's mask handles raised on foliate-cast feet, the stand with conforming decoration throughout, each monogrammed with a coat of arms, 73oz (2069g).

1925   15in (38cm) wide

£2,000-3,000   FRE

A Belgian silver brandy bowl, makers mark 'GL', Maaseik, the openworked handles decorated with flowers, marked below, 8.2oz (256g).

c1690   10.25in (26cm) wide

£8,000-10,000   SOTA

A William III Britannia standard silver monteith, by Anthony Nelme, London, lion mask pendant handles, the body embossed and chased on either side with a cartouche, on armorial engraved on a scalework background, the other engraved with initials 'WH', the collar with shaped mask and scroll border, 57oz (1796g).

1699   11.5in (29cm) diam

£27,000-30,000   SOTH

METALWARE

A George IV Irish silver round bowl on foot, maker's marks for William Law and possibly William Nelson, Dublin, half reeded, the everted rim with reeded scroll and shells, engraved with a belted crest and motto, 18.5oz (578g).

1820   *8.25in (21cm) diam*

£1,800-2,200   DN

A George IV Irish silver wine cooler, probably Edward Twycross, Dublin, with repoussé cartouches surmounted by eagles, the handles chased with shells and foliage, with a later silver-plated liner, 71oz (2013g).

1825   *11in (28cm) high*

£2,500-3,000   FRE

A Victorian sterling silver rose bowl, possibly Adams & Foster, London, with a silver-gilt bowl and hung with rose garlands, raised on a circular foot, 49oz (1389g).

1860   *12.5in (32cm) diam*

£2,000-3,000   FRE

An American silver footed bowl, with applied cast scallop shell and foliate feet, the bowl with engraved acanthus leaf border, rope-twist rim and applied stylised floral and foliate border to base.

The base is marked with a capital 'S' in a circle, perhaps indicating The Shepard Manufacturing Co. of Massachussetts.

c1860   *5.5in (14cm) high*

£800-1,200   TCF

A Victorian silver gilt oval bowl London, retailed by Dobson, 32 Piccadilly, the ornate part-fluted and foliate-pierced sides with ram's mask and loop handles and ruby glass liner, raised on a spreading oval foot, 26oz (737g).

1873   *11in (28cm) wide*

£800-1,200   L&T

A Tiffany & Co. sterling silver porringer, with a pierced foliate handle, decorated throughout with repoussé flora and fauna, 9.1oz (258g).

c1880   *9in (23cm) wide*

£350-450   FRE

A 19thC American silver repoussé punch bowl, The Loring Andrews Co., Cincinnati, chased and embossed with foliage, fruit, exotic birds, shells and vignettes of castles, raised on a conforming domed foot, 40oz (1134g).

11.75in (30cm) wide

£3,000-4,000   FRE

A Victorian silver Monteith, London, of typical form, the fluted sides with twin scroll handles, chased and embossed with dolphins and foliage, raised on a circular foot, 41oz (1162g).

1885   *12.25in (28.5in) diam*

£2,500-3,500   L&T

A pair of late 19thC American Dominick & Haff sterling silver bowls, retailed by J. E. Caldwell & Co., Philadelphia, the lobed bowls with openwork foliate-chased borders, 46oz (1304g).

12in (30.5cm) diam

£600-800   FRE

An American sterling silver foot centrepiece bowl, retailed by Bailey, Banks and Biddle, with an elaborate foliate-pierced rim and lobed basin, raised on a circular foot similarly chased, 92oz (2608g).

7in (18cm) high

£2,500-3,500   FRE

A large Victorian sterling silver punch bowl, by Charles Stuart Harris, London, 72oz (2041g).

1893   *5in (38cm) diam*

£1,800-2,200   FRE

A late Victorian small silver punch bowl, by Job Frank Hall, London, embossed with acanthus and engraved 'Roseberry from Louisa & Lucy Cohen, May 7 1897', with a glass liner, 10.75oz (335g).

1896   *7.25in (18.5cm) diam.*

£200-300   DN

A Victorian sterling silver reticulated bowl, London, the shaped openwork sides decorated with exotic birds amongst scrolling foliage, centred by a vacant cartouche, raised on four openwork shell feet, 35oz (992g).

1897   *11.75in (30cm) diam*

£1,000-2,000   **FRE**

A Victorian sterling silver monteith bowl, Birmingham, the pierced undulating rim above a repoussé band of masks, raised on a circular foot, marks rubbed, 53oz (1502g).

1898   *10.5in (26.5cm) diam*

£1,800-2,200   **FRE**

An American Whiting sterling silver bread bowl, in the martelé style, the rim with poppy repoussé decoration, 14oz (397g).

14.5in (37cm) wide

£250-350   **FRE**

An Edwardian sterling silver pierced urn, Chester, of flattened campana form, the gadrooned, rim over a reticulated scrolling band and lobed body , 45oz (1275g).

1907

£1,500-2,000   **FRE**

An early 20thC American sterling silver and silver gilt-plated 'Vitruvian' pattern flower-arranging bowl, retailed by W. W. Wattles & Sons, 61oz (1729g).

15.5in (39.5cm) wide

£800-1,200   **FRE**

An American Gorham sterling silver centrepiece bowl, the wide everted rim decorated with C-scrolls and floral garlands, 56oz (1587g).

c1914   *16in (30.5cm) diam*

£800-1,200   **FRE**

A pair of Irish George III sterling silver covered vegetable dishes, by William Hamy & J. Scott, Dublin, each of rectangular form with a berried leafy knop, the handles moulded as palm fronds, raised on fluted tapered legs ending in claw-and-ball feet, 44oz (1247g).

1810   *9.5in (24cm) wide*

£5,000-7,000   **FRE**

A Regency sterling silver soup tureen and cover, by John Houle, London, of oval form with a gadrooned rim and leaf-cast handles, the cover with a detachable foliate handle, the lobed body raised on four leaf-cast feet with scrolled toes, 144oz (4082g).

1811   *16in (40.5cm) wide*

£6,000-8,000   **FRE**

A George IV silver hot water urn, by Smith, Tate, Hoult & Tate, London, with shell-cast gadrooned rim and collar, the lobed body engraved with a family crest above a spigot, upon a square, gadrooned base and raised on anthemion-cast paw feet, 178oz (5046g).

1820   *16.25in (41cm) high*

£4,500-5,500   **FRE**

An early 19thC French silver-gilt soup tureen, the cover with a leaf-cast acorn finial and etched and chased with anthemion hung with drapery and with a leaf-cast rim, the handles cast with swans, all raised on a circular foot, 88oz (2495g).

16.75in (42.5cm) wide

£5,000-6,000   **FRE**

A pair of Victorian sterling silver covered entrée dishes, by Robert Garrard, London, each of lobed domed form surmounted by a griffin finial and engraved with a coat of arm bearing the motto 'mea Gloria fides', the underplate of conforming shapes with a ribbon tied rim, 103oz (2920g).

1854   *11in (28cm) diam*

£5,000-6,000   **FRE**

A pair of American Samuel Kirk & Sons silver repoussé covered entrée dishes, chased and embossed with scrolling foliage and vignettes of castles, houses, bridges, birds and rowboats, raised on four scroll feet, 94oz (2665g).

c1860   13.5in (34cm) wide

£7,000-9,000   FRE

An American sterling silver covered vegetable dish, with removable handle and engraved with a family crest, 46oz (1304g).

13in (33cm) wide

£400-500   FRE

A Peruvian silver covered tureen, with a leafy knop and loop handles, raised on claw-and-ball feet, 74oz (2098g).

12.5in (32cm) wide

£400-500   FRE

A late George II silver sauce boat, by David Mowden, London, with a shaped rim, a flying scroll handle, pad feet and later embossed with flowers and scrolls, 3oz (94g).

1755   5.25in (13.5cm) high

£90-120   DN

A pair of George III silver sauceboats, probably William Skeen, London, on three shell-and-hoof feet, gadrooned rim, leaf-capped flying scroll handle, 25oz (804g).

1766   7.5in (19cm) long

£4,000-5,000   SOTH

A pair of George III silver sauceboats, probably by John Arnell, London, each with a leaf-capped flying scroll handle, a repair near one handle, 18.5oz (582g).

1775   6.75in (17cm) long

£1,000-1,500   DN

A pair of George III oval pedestal sauceboats, maker's mark rubbed, possibly Charles Fuller, London, with reeded rims, loop handles and on oval bases, engraved with a double crest and a monogram, 16oz (504g).

1814   7.25in (18.5cm) long

£800-1,200   DN

A pair of Victorian silver oval sauceboats, by Martin, Hall & Co., Sheffield, with shaped rims, leaf-capped flying scroll handles, anthemion and trefid feet and engraved with a crest, 17.75oz (559g).

1898   7.5in (19cm) long

£600-800   DN

SALVERS

A pair of George III silver waiters, by Richard Rugg London, each centred by a coat of arms, within an ornate trellis-pierced and foliate-chased border, raised on three scroll feet, 30oz (850g).

1762   7.75in (20cm) diam

£1,200-1,800   L&T

A George III sterling silver salver, by John Parker & Edward Wakelin, London, having a shaped gadrooned border bearing an armorial crest, the reverse inscribed 'No. 83, 18-12', 17oz (482g).

1768   9.5in (24cm) diam

£300-400   FRE

A George III silver salver, of plain circular form with beaded border, raised on claw and ball feet, marks for Hester Bateman, London, 31oz (964g).

1782   12in (30.5cm) wide

£1,000-1,500   HT

A pair of George III silver waiters, by Robert & Thomas Makepiece, London, of oval form with a moulded edge, engraved armorial raised on four scroll feet, engraved crest to underside, 42oz (1191g).

1793   10.75in (27.5cm) wide

£2,000-3,000   L&T

A pair of George III oval silver waiters, London, with gadrooned rims and central armorial and crest to edge, raised on conforming scroll feet, makers mark 'WB', 40 oz (1134g).

1799 *11in (28cm) wide*

£1,500-2,000 **L&T**

A George III silver waiter, the centre chased with an initial within a scroll and floral festoon border, on bracket feet, marks for Peter and William Bateman, London, 17.5oz (544g).

1805 *10in (25.5cm) wide*

£350-450 **HT**

A pair of George III oval silver waiters, London, with gadrooned rims and conforming scroll feet, makers mark 'J.C.', 44oz (1247g).

1807 *12in (30.5cm) wide*

£2,500-3,000 **L&T**

A George III sterling silver salver, London, bearing armorial crest, makers mark 'BS.IS', 37oz (1049g).

1810 *12.5in (32cm) diam*

£600-800 **FRE**

An American Gorham sterling silver fish platter, of oval form with a leaf-cast border, the raised ends mounted with figures of jockeys astride hippocamps, 70oz (1984g).

1913 *28in (71cm) long*

£5,500-6,500 **FRE**

A pair of George IV silver waiters, London, of oblong form, with gadrooned rims, raised on four acanthus-cast paw feet, makers mark 'W.B.', 40oz (1134g).

1820 *10.5in (27cm) wide*

£1,000-1,500 **L&T**

A pair of Continental silver gilt circular plaques, profusely embossed with swag, ribbon and bellflower decoration intersected by bust profiles, with ribbon and pole border.

11in (28cm) diam

£250-350 **A&G**

A set of four sterling silver-gilt dishes, Garrard & Co., London, each of scalloped form centred by a coat of arms.

1921 *7.5in (19cm) diam*

£1,500-2,000 **FRE**

A pair of George III silver card trays, London, Storey & Elliot, of shaped circular form with shell and gadrooned cast rim, centred by an engraved armorial crest, raised on three scroll feet, 22oz (624g).

1810 *6.75in (17cm) diam*

£1,000-1,500 **L&T**

A Victorian sterling silver tea tray, by Richard Martin & Ebenezer Hall, Sheffield, with pierced galleried sides and engraved decoration, 174oz (4933g).

1893 *22.75in (58cm) wide*

£6,000-8,000 **FRE**

A silver tea tray, by Hawksworth, Eyre & Co. Sheffield, of oblong form, the shell and scroll-cast rim with twin double scroll handles, 110oz (3118g).

1915 *26.25in (67cm) wide*

£2,000-3,000 **L&T**

A large American Gorham sterling silver tray, of shaped oval form with a reeded border, monogrammed, marked, 84oz (2381g).

1917 *23in (58.5cm) wide*

£1,000-1,500 **FRE**

A Scottish silver-mounted oak sugar caster, by Ferguson & MacBean of Inverness, marked 'F&M', camel, 'INV's, Edinburgh 1891-92.

Ferguson & MacBean's work often specialised in items of historical revivalism as with the Celtic knotwork here. The silver studs to the knotwork borders, the use of stained hardwood is reminiscent of their high quality dirk handles. From the quality it must be assumed that the wooden body was specially commissioned from a wood carver and mounted in-house.

6.5in (16.5cm) high

£2,000-2,500   **L&T**

A 20thC American Gorham sterling silver tea tray, of rectangular form with a scrolling floral cast border and open carrying handles, monogrammed, 108oz (3062g).

28in (71cm) wide

£1,500-2,000   **FRE**

A silver tray, by Thomas Bradbury & Sons, Sheffield, with a moulded border, re-entrant corners and engraved with a presentation inscription, 115oz (3758g).

1935   26.5in (67cm) long

£1,000-1,500   **DN**

A Sheffield silver tray, of oval form, the loop handles moulded with stiff leaves, chased with a band of scrolling foliage, 84oz (2612g).

1939.   24.5in (62cm) wide

£1,200-1,800   **HT**

A pair of continental silver pepperettes, each modelled as a partridge, 9oz (255g).

c1910.   4in (10cm) high

£1,800-2,200   **L&T**

A set of four late Victorian novelty salts, by Saunders & Shepherd Ltd, modelled as miniature cradles, with marks for Birmingham, and matched spoons, (London), 3.5oz (99g) total.

1896   2.25in (6cm) long

£400-500   **L&T**

A pair of Victorian novelty cartridge-form peppers, by Horace Woodward & Co. Ltd, with marks for London 2oz (57g).

1887   2.5in (6cm) high

£2,000-2,500   **L&T**

ESSENTIAL REFERENCE: TRAPRAIN LAW

In 1914 a hoard of more than 150 pieces of native and Roman silver was found at Traprain Law near Edinburgh. It included spoons, bowls and other tableware, some with Christian symbols.

- Four coins were discovered which help to date the find to some point in the 5thC AD. The quality of some of the items suggests that they may have come from as far afield as Rome, Ravenna, or possibly Antioch or Constantinople.
- It may be that the silver represented a payment from the Romans to secure the support of the local Votandini tribe.
- Most of the pieces had been cut up, and one of the few whole objects was a triangular bowl now displayed at the National Museum of Scotland.
- Much of the haul was restored and copies were made under licence and sold to the public.

A pair of silver Traprain salts, with marks for Edinburgh, with incuse marks for 'Brook and Sons, of George Street' and mark of an 'S' in a diamond punch, 3.5oz (99g).

1930, 1934   3in (7.5cm) wide

£250-350   **L&T**

A rare strawberry-form nutmeg grater, Birmingham, by Hilliard and Thomason, the semi-matt-finished naturalistically formed body with hinged opening and pierced hinged steel grille.

1860   1.5in (4cm) long

£7,500-8,500   **L&T**

A Canadian sterling silver stilton scoop, with gilt washed interior and barley-twist handle, stamped 'STERLING 3' and with a flower motif, together with original fitted box marked 'G. Seifert QUEBEC'.

8.75in (22cm) long CAD

£200-300   **TCF**

A set of Birks sterling silver bright cut flatware.

This hand-engraved pattern was introduced in 1894. Standard knives would have had mother-of-pearl or ivory handles, so a fish knife has been added.

Large spoon 8.75in (22cm) high

£40-60   **TCF**

A pair of South or Central American silver-coloured metal salad servers, with stylised eagle terminals and eagle displayed engraved bowl, unmarked, 5oz (160g).

9.75in (25cm) long

£70-100   **DN**

A George III silver toasting fork, with the maker's mark 'IP' only, possibly John Priestman, and engraved with a crest, the turned ebonised handle with a reeded suspension ring.

c1790   *37in (94cm) long*

£1,200-1,800   **DN**

CLOSER LOOK: HUGH ROSS SPOON

The cylindrical top section features a scroll-and-urn type finial.

This spoon is a rather unusual pattern for Scottish silver and in particular for a piece of provincial manufacture. Despite being known mainly for his high quality flatware, Hugh Ross of Tain (c1680-1732) was the maker of some very choice and unusual pieces. Because of the varied and interesting surviving work, he could be considered one of the finest provincial silversmiths of his day.

The centre section of the stem is decorated with intricate scrollwork.

The long oval bowl has an applied leaf emanating from the heel.

A Scottish provincial fancy-back masking spoon, by Hugh Ross I of Tain, marked 'HR' conjoined and within oval punch 0.7oz (20g).

7.75in (19.5cm) long

£2,500-3,500   **L&T**

A Victorian silver embossed round dessert service by Wakeley and Wheeler, London, in a fitted leather-bound case, 8.75oz (277g).

Sugar bowl 3.25in (8.5cm) diam

£350-450   **DN**

A silver Scottish punch ladle, Edinburgh, by John Main, struck with maker's mark only to underside, of traditional form, with turned and knopped wooden handle to the plain oval shallow bowl.

c1720   *14.75in (37.5cm) long*

£350-450   **L&T**

A George III gilt punch ladle, by Robert Gray & Sons of Glasgow, 4.5oz (140g). *Robert Gray & Sons were the most important makers outside Edinburgh. They had perhaps the largest range of private dies for Kings and Queens pattern variants.*

1810-11   *17in (43cm) long*

£1,600-2,000   **L&T**

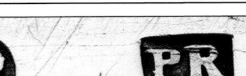

A scarce set of George III knives, by Patrick Robertson, Edinburgh, the stylised Rococo motif scroll pistol-grip handles with engraved crest and motto, the silver blades marked thistle, duty head, PR, with shaped top edge and rounded points.

Silver Scottish knives are unusually scarce, particularly with silver blades. They are more commonly found with steel blades which can quickly deteriorate and this may explain the reason for the small survival rate.

c1785   *8.25in (21cm) long*

£1,200-1,800   **L&T**

A scarce Scottish provincial hair pin, the pin with twisted central section, the finial with simple prick engraved decoration, marked 'ABD', 0.3oz (10.6g).

c1750-60.   *6.75in (17cm) long*

£600-800   **L&T**

A Charles II trefid spoon, by William Law of Edinburgh, makers mark of 'WL' conjoined with crown above and pellet below, the trefid end with engraved initials 'AG / SB' to reverse of terminal, the slightly tapering stem with shaped stylised foliage terminal to bowl with long rat tail to centre, 1.7oz (52.9g).

William Law first appears within the Edinburgh Goldsmiths records on 14th March 1662 where he is commanded to make as his assay 'ane silver coupe with ane cover graven and ane voupe in Robert Lawis shop', his overseers were Edward Cleghorne, Alexander Scott and Alexander Reid. He is then admitted as a master and freeman of the trade on 14th June 1662. Law's mark is also encountered as a Deacons mark as he was elected Deacon from 1667.

7.75in (20cm) long

£3,000-4,000 L&T

A rare Scottish provincial apple corer, by Joseph Pearson of Dumfries, with long hemispherical scoop with simple reeded socket mount to a turned stained wood handle, makers mark 'IP' only.

This is the only recorded example of a Scottish provincial apple corer, while it is a standard form for an English example. The placement of the marks and original provenance strongly suggest a local manufacture to Dumfries and therefore Joseph Pearson.

c1800 6in (15.5cm) long

£500-600 L&T

OTHER SILVERWARE

A sterling silver tea caddy, London, retailed by Goldsmiths & Silversmiths Co., of canted square form with a cylindrical cover and ball knop, 8oz (227g).

1937 5in (12.5cm) high

£250-350 FRE

A sterling silver caddy, London, retailed by Munsey & Co., Ltd, Cambridge, of panelled octagonal form with a wooden knop and beaded decoration to the rim and base, makers mark 'CE', 19oz (539g).

1913 5.25in (13.5cm) high

£500-600 FRE

ESSENTIAL REFERENCE: CASTLE TOPS

Embossed or engraved silver card cases, snuff boxes or vinaigrettes decorated with views of famous landmarks such as castles and historic houses are known as 'castle tops'.

- They were made from the 1830s, many as souvenirs for wealthy tourists. Early examples feature a scene on both sides of the box, later ones usually have a scene on one side only.
- One of the most renowned makers was Nathaniel Mills, who was based in Birmingham.
- The quality of Mills' work is such that the relief decoration can stand up to 0.25in (1cm) away from the surface of the box.
- Landmarks featured include Windsor Castle and Westminster Abbey. The more unusual or famous the subject, the greater the value of the box is likely to be.
- Other decoration may include chasing with flowers, leaves and C-scrolls.

A Scottish gilt table snuff box, by Peter Ross of Aberdeen, marked 'PR', struck twice, 5.2oz (147g).

This box imitates but falls short of the high quality examples being produced in Birmingham by makers such as Nathaniel Mills.

c1820 3.25in (8.5cm) wide

£800-1,200 L&T

An early Victorian 18ct gold snuff box, by Nathaniel Mills, Birmingham, the lid chased with Warwick Castle, with an inscription, dated 1839, to the Right Honourable George Guy, Lord Brooke.

2.75in (7cm) wide

£4,500-5,500 L&T

A Victorian silver table snuff box, by William Elliott, London, of rectangular form, the hinged lid chased and embossed with a hunting scene depicting hounds attacking a wild boar within an oak leaf and acorn border, the sides and base with engine-turned decoration, 11oz (312g).

1849 4.25in (11cm) wide

£800-1,200 L&T

A 19thC probably Swedish silver snuff box, gilt to the interior.

3in (7.5cm) wide

£50-80 FRE

A late 19thC Continental, probably Dutch, silver marriage box, decorated throughout with reserves of floral garlands and marked at the corners with figures within porticos, 16oz (454g).

5.5in (14cm) wide

£800-1,200 FRE

A 19thC Northern European silver snuff box, marked '0.800', the rectangular box enamelled to the lid to show a white horse.

3in (7.5cm) wide

£150-200 FRE

A late 19thC Continental silver oval patch box, apparently unmarked, the hinged cover engraved with dancing figures amidst Renaissance motifs.

3.25in (8.5cm) wide

£350-450 L&T

A Continental silver oval box, import marked for Chester 1911, embossed with Arcadian lovers, the sides with martial trophies and foliage, 3oz (94g).

4in (10cm) wide

£100-150 DN

A sterling silver jewel box, London, the hinged top with wavy etched decoration opening to a velvet line interior raised on bun feet, makers mark 'CD'.

1922 *6in (15cm) wide*

£300-400 FRE

A George III silver inkstand, London, of boat shape form, with a bead-moulded rim, surmounted by three cut glass bottles and raised on pierced, bladed bracket feet, makers mark 'W.P.', 28oz (794g).

1784 *11in (28cm) wide*

£800-1,200 L&T

A Victorian silver desk stand, by Joseph & John Angell, London, with two pen recesses, on four acanthus feet, and with a central round sand box with a shaped-round taperstick cover flanked by two silver mounted cut glass ink wells, 17.25oz (538g).

1840 *9.75in (25cm) wide*

£500-800 DN

A Edwardian sterling silver and cut glass standish, by George Jackson and Edward Fullerton, London, with an elaborately pierced three-quarter gallery incorporating a letter stand, the whole edged with shell-work and centred by two cut glass ink pots with silver lids and collars and a pen tray, raised on claw-and-ball feet, 21oz (595g).

1909 *10in (25.5cm) wide*

£1,200-1,800 FRE

A Georgian style silver desk inkstand, by Millar and Wilkinson London, of rectangular form with shaped rounded ends, beaded edge, bright cut and pierced fern leaf pattern sides, two Bristol blue glass inkwells and central frame for a chamberstick, lacking, and replaced by a continental box and cover, the whole on claw-and-ball feet, 20oz (567g).

1911 *10in (25cm) wide*

£700-1,000 L&T

A sterling silver standish, by D. & J. Welby, London, of rectangular form with bail handles to the sides, the compartmentalised hinged top opening to reveal an ebonised wood pen rest, glass inkwells and sandpot, raised on bracket feet.

1925 *9.75in (25cm) wide*

£1,500-2,000 FRE

A pair of Britannia standard silver picture frames, London, with shell and foliate scroll-chased and embossed decoration.

7.75in (20cm) wide

£1,000-1,500 L&T

A pair of Britannia standard silver photograph frame, London, of upright form. oval to centre, the ground with raised rose detail and splay feet, maker's mark 'M&LS'.

6.5in (16.5cm) wide

£600-900 L&T

A Victorian silver-mounted dressing table mirror, by William Comyns & Sons Ltd, London, the openwork border centred with a grotesque mask with urns, fruit, mermaids and putti amidst scrolling foliage and a vacant reserve below, with a bevelled plate, the easel back covered with fabric.

16in (41cm) high

£1,200-1,800   DN

A George III silver table bell, London, possibly John Reily, well-turned baluster handle, the bell with threaded detail and gadrooned edge.

1817   *4.5in (11.5cm) high*

£1,200-1,800   L&T

A silver table bell, London, of traditional form, ivory baluster handle.

1933

£400-600   L&T

A French silver and cut glass jam pot, Ambroise Mignerot, Paris, the cover with a plumed knop above a cut glass insert, the body with griffin-form handles, decorated with a band of flower maidens alternating with vines, 20oz (623g).

11in (28cm) high

£1,000-1,500   FRE

A silver round tapered vase, maker's mark worn, Sheffield, with twin lion mask hinged handles and a shaped rim, 24.75oz (769g).

1911   *11.75in (29.5cm) high*

£400-500   DN

A Victorian, George III style sterling silver epergne, possibly Joshua Vander, London, after a design by Thomas Pitts, on four openwork cartouche feet, the foliate-chased swag aprons surmounted by a pierced shaped oval basket with a scroll and leaf-cast rim, from which emanate eight outscrolling branches, four supporting pierced baskets, the remaining four hanging, 165oz (4678g).

1890   *26in (61cm) high*

£18,000-22,000   FRE

A mid-18thC and later assembled English silver and cut glass cruet set, comprising a stand, marks for 'Sam Wood, London, 1751', one larger and two smaller casters, marks for 'Davis Thompson, London 1751', two stoppered bottles with silver collars, marks for 'Birmingham, 1881', 35oz (992g).

8in (20.5cm) high

£800-1,200   FRE

A six-piece silver condiment set, Sheffield, Walker and Hall, with leaf-clasped legs and paw feet, comprising four circular salts and a pair of lidded mustard posts, with liners and associated spoons, 58oz (1644g).

£1,200-1,800   L&T

A set of six late George III silver parcel-gilt egg cups, by William Eaton, London, each with moulded girdle and a round foot with an egg and dart border, each engraved with a crest, 14.75oz (463g).

2.75in (7cm) high

£600-800   DN

A pair of Elizabeth II silver gilt wine coasters, by Roberts & Belk, Sheffield, profusely embossed with vine, shells and flowers.

1972   *6in (15cm) diam*

£400-500   A&G

A George III silver wine funnel, by Peter & Anne Bateman, London, 2.5oz (81g).

1796   *4.25in (11cm) high*

£300-400   DN

A pair of mid-20thC French silver wine caddies, each of woven basket form with twist handles, the first example marked 'Christofle', the other marked 'Boulenger', 22oz (624g).

Longer 11in (28cm) long

£150-200 **FRE**

A silver shaving mug and brush, by Levi & Salaman, Birmingham, the mug with a hinged cover, broad scroll handle and gilt interior, the brush of inverted baluster form.

1902 *The mug 4.75in (12cm) high*

£400-500 **DN**

A set of three George III 'Ships Decanters' labels, by George Fenwick, Edinburgh, with integral suspension loops, suspended by belcher link chains, inscribed for 'PORT', 'SHERRY' and 'CLARET', 0.75oz (23.7g).

1806-7 *3.75in (9.5cm) wide*

£1,200-1,500 **L&T**

A Scottish provincial spirit label, by William Constable, Dundee, with reeded border, incised 'BRITISH WINE', suspended from a belcher link chain, marked Edinburgh 1817-1818, 'WC', duty head, 0.3oz (10g).

1817-18 *1.5in (4cm) wide*

£300-400 **L&T**

A pair of Scottish provincial spirit labels, by Alexander Cameron of Dundee, inside 'SHERRY', suspended from integral suspension loops by a belcher link chain, marked 'C', thistle, pot of lilies, 'AC', thistle, 0.3oz (9g).

c1825 *1.75in (4.5cm) wide*

£600-800 PAIR **L&T**

A Scottish provincial spirit label, by John Blair of Dundee, incised for 'MADEIRA', suspended from a belcher link chain, marked thistle, pot of lilies, 'JB', thistle, pot of lilies, 0.3oz (10g).

c1830 *1.75in (4.5cm) wide*

£600-800 **L&T**

A Scottish provincial caddy spoon, by 'WL', possibly William Leighton, Dundee, pot of lilies struck twice, of Fiddle pattern with large fluted shell bowl, marked 'WL', 0.4oz (12g).

3.75in (9.5cm) long

£600-800 **L&T**

A Scottish provincial caddy spoon, Dundee, pot of lilies struck thrice, of Old English pattern with deep scoop shell bowl, marked 'D', 0.4oz (12g).

3.25in (8.5cm) long

£400-500 **L&T**

A Scottish provincial caddy spoon, by Alexander Cameron, Dundee, of Fiddle pattern, with scoop shell bowl, marked 'AC', 'C', thistle, pot of lilies, 0.4oz (11g).

3.75in (9.5cm) long

£500-600 **L&T**

METALWARE

A George III Scottish provincial shoe buckle, by James Wildgoose, Aberdeen, with simple reeded design, the clasp and tongue of shaped semi-circular design with arrow head terminals, marked 'IW', 0.2oz (6g).

c1770   1.75in (4.5cm) wide

£200-300   **L&T**

A pair of Scottish provincial shoe buckles, by William Scott, Dundee, the borders with diamond spacers, the inner and outer borders both with beaded details, with shaped steel tongues, marked 'WS', pot of lilies, total weight 3.9oz (121g).

c1780   3.25in (8cm) wide

£600-800   **L&T**

A pair of George III shoe buckles, by Robert Gray, Glasgow, Edinburgh, with flower-head-, scroll- and leaf-chased details, with shaped steel tongues, date letter lacking to both.

c1790   2.75in (7cm) wide

£800-1,200   **L&T**

A Scottish belt buckle, attributed to Alexander Ritchie, Iona, formed as vine leaf and branch form, marked 'CS*FS', Chester, Rg. No. 391329, 3.7 oz (105g).

1905-1906,   5.5in (14cm) wide

£300-400   **L&T**

A cased set of six Victorian menu holders, probably by William Hutton, each in the form of a woodcock or a grouse upon a turned silver gilt base.

1906   1.5in (4cm) high

£1,200-1,800   **LAW**

A set of six Edwardian place card holders, with polychrome enamel decoration to the front, depicting game birds and a fox, with marks for Chester, 9.5oz (269g).

1903   1.5in (3.5cm) high

£3,500-4,500   **L&T**

A pair of Victorian menu stands, by L. Emmanuel, each of easel back form, modelled as a fox running past a gate, with marks for Birmingham, 1.5oz (42g).

1895   2in (5.5cm) high

£1,000-1,500   **L&T**

A late Victorian novelty vesta case, London, maker's mark 'J.B.A.B.', of plain form, designed as a shoe, with hinged cover and suspension ring.

1878   2.75in (7cm) long

£1,200-1,800   **L&T**

An Edwardian vesta case, maker Samson Morden & Co., Chester, the flat hinged cover inscribed 'HIS MASTER'S VOICE', above the associated cast motif, additionally inscribed to the under of cover 'WITH THE COMPLIMENTS OF THE GRAMOPHONE CO LTD'.

1907   1.75in (4.5cm) wide

£1,000-1,500   **L&T**

A late Victorian novelty vesta case, maker probably G. Loveridge & Co., Birmingham, designed as a footballer's leg and a ball, initialled in script, also inscribed 'C. & M. PATENT'.

1884   2.25in (5.5cm) long

£1,500-2,000   **L&T**

A Victorian tobacco pipe case, by M. C. &Co., Edinburgh, the case in the form of the pipe, with pull-off stem held in place by steel pricker, the hinged 'bowl' section with pinned clasp, engraved with conjoined gothic initials 'CBF', with pipe, 1.5oz (46.7g).

This maker's mark unrecorded in the records of the Edinburgh Assay Office.

5in (13cm) long

£700-900   **L&T**

A Victorian patent silver cigar tool, by Jane Brownett and Alexander Jones, London, with a fold-out steel blade and piercer and a hinged flap to enable it to be used as a rest, engraved with an Earl's coronet and cypher, and stamped with a registration lozenge.

1880   2in (5cm) long

£250-350   **WW**

A souvenir thimble, 'GREAT YARMOUTH', by Henry Griffith and Son, Birmingham.

1930

£50-70   **WW**

A German silver-coloured metal circular sugar bowl, pierced with buds and foliage, with an undulating floral C-scroll rim, on three scroll feet, with a shaped clear glass liner, 12.5oz (390g).

6in (15cm) diam

£150-200 DN

A Chinese silver-coloured metal bowl, embossed with dragons and characters on a matted ground between stiff leaf borders, unmarked, 14oz (441g).

6.5in (16.5cm) diam

£180-220 DN

A set of six Far Eastern silver-coloured metal dishes, with flower-embossed panelled borders, stamped '800' and 'K.S.', 22.25oz (696g).

4.5in (11.5cm) diam

£150-200 DN

A late 19thC Continental Renaissance Revival silver-coloured pilgrim flask wine flagon, embossed to one side with a central princely figure in late 17thC costume with warriors and arms at the cardinal points on a scrolled ground, and a pseudo crest to the other side, the lid embossed with a grotesque mask, 45oz (1285g).

15.25in (38.5cm) high

£1,500-2,000 DN

An Anglo-Indian silver-coloured metal wine bottle cover, pierced with birds and animals amidst foliage and with similarly engraved cartouches, with a bottle-top hung from chains and a removable base, 17.25oz (541g).

12in (30.5cm) high

£250-350 DN

An early 20thC Chinese silver-coloured metal cocktail shaker by Hing Ching, straight-tapered and chased with flower sprays on a hammered ground, 15.75oz (493g).

9in (23cm) high

£450-550 DN

A Spanish, silver-coloured metal desk stand, Madrid, with a bell topped box, two with swan finials to the covers and another with a parrot, the rectangular base with bowed ends and a pierced gallery, assayer's or maker's mark 'N CHANEROI', the bell lacking the clapper, 27.75oz (865g).

1822-23 *9in (23cm) long*

£1,800-2,200 DN

A set of twelve late 19thC Chinese small silver-coloured metal wine cups, each applied with a dragon, makers mark 'WA' not traced, 9.25oz (288g).

c1900

£250-350 DN

An Irish silver-coloured metal hour glass, maker's marks of Edward Twycross and Edward Power of Dublin (maker's marks only), with three shaped supports, the cover with initials 'EC' and the base with a crest, 1.25oz (43g).

3in (7.5cm) high

£550-650 DN

A white metal mounted novelty scent bottle, modelled as a fish with shagreen body and hinged head with stone set eyes, containing a glass scent bottle.

14in (35.5cm) long

£2,000-2,500 L&T

An Edwardian silver napkin ring, with a polychrome-enamelled dolphin boss, by an unascribed maker, 'DG', Birmingham.

1905

£100-150 WW

An early 20thC Continental silver scent bottle case, modelled as a fish, with naturalistic imbrication, the hinged head inset with red glass eyes, import marks for London.

c.1900 *3in (8cm) wide*

£150-180 ROW

A novelty Victorian smoker's companion in the form of a pig, her curly tail a removable smoker's tool, standing by a 'trough' for matches, upon a painted wood base, by JB, possibly John Brumfit.

1885 *3in (8cm) wide*

£200-300 LAW

A silver bulldog, by Berthold Muller, standing solidly and with a removable head.

1910 *5.5in (13.5cm) long*

£1,000-1,500 L&T

SILVER PLATE

A silver-plated circular-pedestal large punch bowl, embossed with fruiting vine on a matted ground, with a conforming pierced band and a cable rim.

16.5in (42cm) diam.

£600-800   **DN**

A French plated round tureen on foot and cover, by Christofle, with twin bifurcated leafy handles, the domed cover with a bead outlined finial.

13.75in (35cm) wide

£150-200   **DN**

A pair of 19thC plated two-handled pedestal wine coolers, of lobed form with C-scroll handles and scroll outlined rims, each engraved with an armorial.

14.5in (36.5cm) high

£800-1,200   **DN**

A Sheffield plate hot water-heated covered roast server, of typical form with floral cast handles and egg and dart border, on outscrolling feet.

12in (30.5cm) high

£600-800   **FRE**

An early 20thC silver-plated revolving supper set, with four Bakelite turned handles, with covered tureen, four entrée dishes, four blue-glass-lined salts and four Georgian-style casters.

21.5in (54.5cm) high

£800-1,200   **FRE**

An American silver plate centrepiece, possibly by The Meriden Britannia Co., the centre column surmounted by a lobed dish and four arms with lobed dishes, supported on four columnar supports, further raised on a base mounted with the figures of Neptune, Galatea and sea creatures, bears a presentation plaque from the government of Bolivia.

40in (101.5cm) high

£8,000-12,000   **FRE**

A late 19th/early 20thC silver-plated metal and ebonised wood mounted mechanical wine pourer, with Archimedes screw mechanism.

11.5in (29cm) high

£250-350   **DN**

A mid-20thC French silver plate mint julep serving set, comprising six cups and an undertray, each with applied hunting motif.

Tray 13in (33cm) wide

£300-400   **FRE**

A set of twelve small pattens by Christofle, of threaded serpentine form engraved initials 'A T' to centre.

6in (15cm) diam

£250-350   **L&T**

A pair of Regency 'tôle-peinte' chestnut urns, the black grounds decorated in gilt with scrolling foliage and insects, with peaked lid and lion's mask and loop handles, raised on a socle foot.

11.75in (30cm) high

£1,800-2,500 **L&T**

A pair of painted metal cover urns, of Classical urn form, the domed covers surmounted by an acorn finial, finely painted with gilt leaf wreathes to the cover, a village scene to the urn, with free-hanging ring handles to the shoulder supported by a lion mask, over circular bases.

c1830 *12in (30.5cm) high*

£1,800-2,200 **FRE**

A pair of early 19thC Regency tôle tea canisters, of cylindrical form with sectioned tapered covers, the central panel decorated with Chinese figures and characters on a gold field against a red painted ground.

18.75in (48cm) high

£1,200-1,800 **FRE**

A pair of 19thC tôle painted canisters, numbered '1' and '4', on a green ground, converted to lamps.

12.5in (32cm) high excluding fittings

£250-350 PAIR **FRE**

A late 19thC Victorian japanned, parcel gilt and mother-of-pearl-inset tin tea canister, of cylindrical form, decorated with figures in a boat before a church.

c1890 *18in (45.5cm) high*

£450-550 **DN**

A pair of Regency tôle painted bird cages, of pagoda form, the ornate stepped fluted tops with pineapple finials, over open wirework cylindrical sides.

51in (130cm) high

£8,000-12,000 **L&T**

A 19thC American Pennsylvania red tôle coffee pot, with yellow and ivory floral decoration and goose neck spout, from the Shelley Collection.

10in (25.5cm) high

£12,000-15,000 **POOK**

A 19thC American New York black tôle document box, possibly by Butler, with bird and floral decoration, from the Shelley Collection.

9.25in (23.5cm) wide

£8,000-12,000 **POOK**

METALWARE

An American pewter pint mug, attributed to Robert Bonnynge, Boston, with solid moulded S-scroll handle and moon-face terminal, likely owner's initials 'AF' impressed on handle top.

1731-63   *4.5in (11.5cm) high*

£7,000-10,000   **SK**

A rare American pewter lidded pitcher, attributed to Johann Phillip Alberti, Philiadelphia, (1754-80), with heart shaped spout, the body with double C-scroll handle, inscribed 'MM Georg Leonart Muller 1763', from the Shelley Collection.

Muller appears to have lived in Lebanon and was a member of Hill Evangelical Lutheran Church.

7.75in (19.5cm) high

£18,000-22,000   **POOK**

A rare American pewter flagon, attributed to Johann Phillip Alberti, Philadelphia, (1754-80), with a ball-shaped thumb piece, a lid with heart-shaped spout and body with double C-scroll handle and inscription 'Georg-Kichen 1763', from the Shelley Collection.

15in (38cm) high

£25,000-30,000   **POOK**

An American Queen Anne pewter teapot, attributed to Johann Phillip Alberti, Philadelphia, (1754-80), with bright-cut chased vines and floral and bird decoration, from the Shelley Collection.

6.25in (16cm) high

£18,000-22,000   **POOK**

A mid-to late 18thC American pewter chalice, attributed to Johann Christoph Heyne, Lancaster, Pennsylvania (1752-81), from the Shelley Collection.

8.75in (22cm) high

£15,000-20,000   **POOK**

A set of five American graduated pewter measures, New York City (1770-1800), together with a gallon-size measure, New York City (1760-80), impressed with an 'A' on the rim, from the Shelley Collection.

Tallest 13in (33cm) high

£7,000-10,000   **POOK**

A late 18th/early 19thC American pewter chalice, attributed to William Will, Philadelphia, (1764-98), from the Shelley Collection.

7.75in (19.5cm) high

£3,500-4,500   **POOK**

BRASS

A German brass covered flagon in Gothic style, the gourd-shaped body supported by a trumpet-base inscribed 'Gewidmet von Lehrer kolleg. Misburg. 1904', tall incurved neck, applied with dragon spout and dragon handle, golden patina.

16in (41cm) high

£1,500-2,000   **SOTA**

A Victorian brass fish tank, the castellated top above glazed panel sides, flanked and divided by cluster columns, on a plinth base.

21.75in (55cm) wide

£800-1,200   **L&T**

A pair of rare 18thC brass Indian palace guards, modelled as a pair of archaic tigers standing on hind legs, set with red glass eyes, inscribed stripes to body.

7.5in (19cm) high

£500-800   **FRE**

An early 19thC European brass travelling lamp, the hinged door with a beaded top edge to a central holder and two apertures, an embossed star back and oval chimney, the back with a folding stand.

5.5in (14cm) high

£120-180   **WW**

A brass alms dish, with embossed decoration, the centre with Samson and the lion and a text border 'Vis Vitae Transeat In Exemplum', the reverse with a later hook.

14.25in (36cm) diam.

£200-300   **WW**

A late 19thC brass fireman's helmet, from the Merral's Mill Fire Brigade, Haworth, the high comb embossed with acorns and oak leaves, pierced and moulded badge, leather and brass chain chin strap.

The Merral's Mill Fire Brigade was disbanded in 1898.

10in (25.5cm) high

£600-800   **HT**

COPPER

A Victorian copper triple-tier mould, stamped 'PC' for Powys Castle.

8.25in (21cm) high

£200-300   **HALL**

A 19thC copper boiler of oval form having twin loop ring handles on a moulded base.

24in (61cm) diam.

£600-800   **LOC**

A Victorian copper wall-mounting jardinière, with balloon back decorated with crown and twin-headed spread bird above cylindrical pan.

£120-180   **LOC**

A Dutch copper log bin, embossed 'A.M. 1684'.

20.75in (53cm) high

£400-600   **DN**

A Victorian copper and brass tea urn of typical form.

21.75in (55cm) high

£100-150   **ROS**

OTHER METALWARES

A late 18thC American tin wrigglework coffee pot, by Willoughby Shade, Tulpehocken, Pennsylvania, the body elaborately decorated with birds, flowers, etc., inscribed 'Hannah Reinert' and stamped on the handle 'W. Shade', from the Shelley Collection.

10.5in (26.5cm) high

£6,000-8,000   **POOK**

A set of rare 18thC lock picks, twelve adjustable iron key arms lead from a single iron rod, leather case.

£250-350   **FRE**

A pair of late George III polished steel sugar cutters.

9.5in (23.5cm) long

£150-200   **WW**

THE GLASS MARKET

Anyone who has broken a wine glass will appreciate the rarity of an early drinking glass and wonder how something so fragile can survive so long. It is perhaps not surprising then that glasses from the 18th century, especially heavy balustroids and wine glasses with intricate air twist stems, continue to find buyers willing to pay for their longevity and beauty.

Collectors continue to look for pieces which required a high level of craftsmanship in their manufacture. Introducing and manipulating air, colour and mercury twists within fragile stems, crafting knops and balusters, and drawing out bowls and feet all required a level of skill which meant these pieces were made in relatively small numbers and sold as luxury items in their day and they remain desirable and valuable pieces today.

On all glass, any damage should be avoided as it will almost always lower value considerably. Repairs are costly. It is always better to buy from a reputable source who can give you a detailed receipt detailing what you have bought.

Also in demand are rummers (a type of goblet) and early 19th century decanters. Decanters should have their original stopper; check that the design and decoration fit with that of the decanter itself and that the stopper fits the neck properly. Many decanters and stoppers are numbered. The value of a decanter lacking its original stopper will be around half one that retains its original stopper.

Early 19th century coloured glass represents particularly good value for money at the moment, especially Bristol green and blue examples.

While the past year has not seen any landmark sales of pre-20th century glass, high prices continue be paid for mid 19th century paperweights by Baccarat, St Louis and others, and original enamelled 'Mary Gregory' glasses. By comparison, 18th century Continental glass is underrated and good value.

Mid to late 19th century Bohemain glass is another area that continues to do well. Again, buyers are looking for pieces in excellent condition and which show exceptional craftsmanship in every area of design and creation: from the blowing and casing of the glass (encasing a layer of clear glass with a layer of coloured) to the level of detail in the cutting and finishing of the decoration. Running a thumb over the surface of the glass will show how deep the cutting is; the deeper and finer the better the quality of the piece is likely to be. Any engraving should add fine detail to the subject matter and create a sense of realism.

The fact that much early glass was handmade means no two pieces will be exactly the same. This adds a charm to a pair or set of similar pieces which will not be seen in more recent mass produced items. As well as age, value for money has a part to play in the desirability of antique glass – many examples are more affordable than a modern copy despite their age.

Jeanette Hayhurst, Jeanette Hayhurst Fine Glass, London

An English wine glass, bell bowl on teared six-sided moulded pedestal stem, with domed and folded foot.

c1720-30   6in (15cm) high
£1,400-1,600   **JH**

An English baluster wine glass, bell bowl, triple annulated knop over teared inverted baluster and base knops, folded foot.
c1720-30   6in (15cm) high
£750-850   **JH**

An English light baluster wine glass, round funnel bowl over angular ball and inverted baluster knops, domed foot.
c1730-40   6.75in (17cm) high
£1,000-1,200   **JH**

An unusual English bucket bowl balustroid wine glass, teared triple-knop stem, folded foot.

c1730-40   5.75in (14.5cm) high
£400-500   **JH**

An English wine glass, drawn trumpet bowl, plain stem, on high conical folded foot.

c1730   6in (15cm) high
£140-160   **JH**

An English wine glass, round funnel bowl engraved with a flower and bird in flight, plain stem, folded foot.

c1730-40 *6in (15cm) high*

£140-160   JH

An English composite stem wine glass, drawn trumpet bowl with plain stem section over knopped multi-spiral air twist stem.

c1740-50 *7in (17.5cm) high*

£650-750   JH

An English wine glass, waisted bucket bowl on double series air twist stem with mercury corkscrew tape surrounded by four-ply band.

c1745-50 *6.25in (15.5cm) high*

£550-650   JH

An English wine glass, round funnel bowl engraved with a fruiting vine, on air twist stem with two mercury spirals.

c1745-50 *6in (15cm) high*

£400-500   JH

An opaque twist wine glass, the flute-moulded ogee bowl supported on a double series stem and conical foot.

c1770 *5.25in (13cm) high*

£350-450   DN

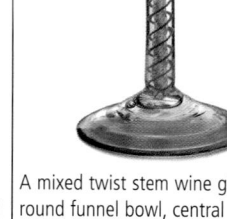

A mixed twist stem wine glass, round funnel bowl, central air twist stem, the gauze surrounded by two opposing white tapes.

c1760 *6in (15cm) high*

£550-650   JH

An English wine glass, lipped ogee bowl, on multi-spiral opaque twist stem with central swelling knop.

c1760 *5.75in (14.5cm) high*

£500-550   JH

A pan-top wine glass, on double series opaque twist stem, with central gauze surrounded by two tapes.

c1765 *6in (15cm) high*

£450-550   JH

An opaque twist wine glass, the ogee bowl supported on a double series stem and conical foot.

c1770 *5.25in (13cm) high*

£250-350   DN

An ovoid bowl wine glass, engraved with a hunting scene and a castle, on hexagonal facet-cut stem.

c1765 *5in (12.5cm) high*

£600-680   JH

A pair of late 18thC facet-stemmed short wine glasses, bowls engraved and polished, stems cut with diamond facets, on conical feet.

c1790

£400-500   DN

A wine glass, on hexagonal facet-cut stem.

c1775 *5.75in (14.5cm) high*

£110-130   JH

An English ale glass, drawn trumpet bowl engraved with hops and barley, plain stem, folded foot.

c1730-40   *7in (17.5cm) high*
£180-220   **JH**

A large English champagne and ale glass, the bowl engraved with fruiting vine stock and ears of barley, on a multi-spiral air twist stem.

c1745-50   *8in (20cm) high*
£850-950   **JH**

One of a pair of champagne or ale glasses, elongated ogee bowl, with hexagonal facet-cut stem with central swelling knop.

c1765   *7in (17.5cm) high*
£500-600 PAIR   **JH**

A late 18thC English dwarf wrythen ale glass, on a rudimentary stem.

5.5in (12.5cm) high
£50-60   **JH**

A late 17thC pale-green tint roemer, the ovoid bowl on a hollow stem applied with prunts beneath a milled band and high spun foot, cracked.

£250-300   **DN**

An English square-based rummer, the bowl with engraved and polished band and slice cutting.

c1800   *5.25in (13.5cm) high*
£120-140   **JH**

One of a pair of English square-pedestal-based rummers, the bowls engraved with swags and birds on a perch.

c1800   *5.25in (13.5cm) high*
£250-300 PAIR   **JH**

An English press-moulded rummer, made in imitation of a cut glass example, with imitation polished printies.

c1860-70   *5.5in (14cm) high*
£25-35   **JH**

An early 19thC English rummer, ovoid bowl, capstan stem.

5.5in (12.5cm) high
£60-70   **JH**

An early 19thC English barrel rummer, on bladed knop stem.

4.75in (12cm) high
£50-70   **JH**

An English cordial glass, fluted round funnel bowl with solid base, double series opaque twist stem with central gauze surrounded by two flat tapes.

c1765   *6.25in (15.5cm) high*
£700-800   **JH**

An English drawn trumpet double series cordial glass, with bowl with engraved border, the stem with central air core surrounded by multi-spiral tapes.

c1745-50   *6.25in (15.5cm) high*
£1,000-1,200   **JH**

A rattafia glass, small elongated bowl over double series opaque twist stem, with central gauze surrounded by four tapes.

c1765   *7.25in (18.5cm) high*
£1,100-1,200   **JH**

GLASS

One of a pair of rare, miniature facet stem liqueur glasses, the bowl cut with twelve slice-cut panels, on diamond-cut stem and panel-cut foot.

c1770   *3.5in (9cm) high*

£420-460 PAIR   **JH**

A late 18thC English firing glass, teared trumpet bowl, flared foot.

3.5in (9cm) high

£80-120   **JH**

An English jelly glass, petal moulded.

c1830-40   *4.5in (11.5cm) high*

£20-25   **JH**

An English jelly glass, honeycomb-moulded, domed foot.

c1760   *3.75in (9.5cm) high*

£140-180   **JH**

An English syllabub glass, with pan top, panel-moulded bowl, on panel-moulded domed and folded foot.

c1760   *4in (10cm) high*

£140-160   **JH**

An early 18thC sweetmeat glass, with an ogee-moulded bowl, raised on an octagonal hollow stem and domed moulded foot.

6.25in (16cm) high

£240-280   **WW**

An early 18thC sweetmeat glass with a flat-cut bowl and shaped rim, above an octagonal stem and domed foot.

5.75in (14.5cm) high

£300-400   **WW**

A whisky tumbler, flute cutting with mirror cutting on base.

c1810   *3.5in (9cm) high*

£50-70   **JH**

A whisky tumbler, with blaze cutting over flutes.

c1810   *3.5in (9cm) high*

£50-70   **JH**

A mid-18thC plain glass tumbler, of gently tapered form.

c1750   *6in (15.5cm) high*

£150-200   **JH**

An early 19thC English glass custard or punch cup, barrel bowl with flute cutting and a stick-down handle.

2in (5cm) high

£25-35   **JH**

A late 19thC English glass custard cup, stick-up handle.

2.75in (7cm) high

£15-18   **JH**

GLASS

One of a pair of Bristol blue decanters, with lozenge stoppers.

c1780-90   11.25in (28.5cm) high
£500-700 PAIR   JH

A pair of late 18thC cut-glass decanters, with bullseye stoppers, the necks with three faceted concentric rings.

11.5in (29.6cm) high
£350-450   WW

A rare, full-sized Bristol blue decanter, with three bladed neck rings and lozenge stopper.

Full-sized Bristol blue decanters are rare.

c1790-1800   11in (28cm) high
£340-380   JH

A pair of early 19thC cut glass decanters, with mushroom stoppers, the bodies faceted and diamond cut, minor chips.

10.75in (27.5cm) high
£200-300   WW

A mallet-shaped decanter and stopper, engraved with diamonds and cut with a band of flutes around the foot.

10.75in (27.5cm) high
£180-220   WW

An early 19thC green glass decanter and disc stopper, of club form.

9.5in (24cm) high
£300-400   DN

A William IV green cut glass decanter and stopper, cut with prismatic steps to its neck above vertical pillars and star-cut base, the original spire stopper cut to match.

c1835   14in (35.5cm) high
£550-650   RGA

One of a pair of shaft and globe decanters, scale-cut neck, lens-, flute-, and diamond-cut body, with hollow blown stopper.

c1860-70   13in (33cm) high
£160-200 PAIR   JH

A Stevens & Williams green-cased decanter and stopper, intaglio cut and engraved with grapes and vine leaves.

c1910   7.5in (19cm) high
£300-340   JH

A mid 19thC Stourbridge yellow- and white-overlaid glass jug, with two matching goblets, decorated with large leaf motifs and with lobed flared feet, few small chips.

Jug 12.25in (31cm) high
£180-220   WW

A claret jug, engraved all over with ears of barley and rye.

The decoration signifies this was made for beer not claret. A beer jug of this sophistication is unusual.

c1870 10.75in (27cm) high
£280-320   JH

A shaft and globe claret jug, with slice-cut neck and lens-cut body, with cut strap handle and hollow blown stopper.

c1880   10.75in (27cm) high
£130-150   JH

GLASS

A pair of English sealed and dated mallet-shaped wine bottles, of olive tint, with string rims, seals stamped MN 1733, some surface scratching.

8in (21cm) 9in (23cm) high

£4,500-5,500 **DN**

An 18thC Dutch green glass bottle, painted with a portrait of Maarten Harpertszoon Tromp, within a foliate border, the decoration probably later.

8.25in (21cm) high

£450-550 **WW**

A Regency oak, burr and rosewood decanter stand, the quadraform stand fitted with four amber glass bottles, with turned wood stoppers, the reeded stem with a pineapple finial.

19in (48cm) high

£3,000-5,000 **L&T**

An 18thC blue glass finger bowl, the body flat-cut with diamonds, applied scallop and gadroon edge silver mount.

5.25in (13.5cm) diam

£500-600 **FLD**

A 19thC ormolu and glass centrepiece, gilt-bronze base with three satyr caryatids joined by a band of vine and grape leaves, supporting a clear cut glass bowl.

11.75in (30cm) high

£600-800 **DRA**

A 19thC New England Glass Co. bride's bowl, with pink overlay Mount Washington cameo on Pairpoint quadruple silver-plated stand, marked on the base 'Pairpoint Mfg. Co'.

7.5in (19cm) diam

£700-1,000 **DRA**

A shallow-cut glass salt, on air-beaded knop stem and shallow-cut foot.

c1760   *2.5in (6.5cm) high*

£70-90 **JH**

An early 19thC heavy diamond-cut glass salt and stand.

There are many salts in this style without a stand. Some had silver stands which have been melted down. Without a stand it is worth £30-40.

2.5in (6.5cm) diam

£100-120 **JH**

A late 18thC boat-shaped glass salt, Van Dyke-cut rim, fluted bowl with notch cutting, on circular foot with square lemon-squeezer pedestal base.

3.25in (8.25cm) high

£60-80 **JH**

GLASS

A Victorian glass cornucopia vase, the cut glass vessel overlaid in blue with cast gilt-metal hand terminal and raised on a marble plinth.

7.75in (20cm) high

£500-600   **L&T**

A late 19thC French Empire style gilt-bronze-mounted cut crystal urn, with twin ram's mask angular handles, raised on a socle base.

12.25in (31cm) high

£1,000-1,500   **L&T**

One of a pair of Continental blue overlay glass shield-shaped vases and covers, each with two clear glass scroll handles cut and engraved with oval panels of sports men and trophies above laurel swags and stepped clear glass base.

c1900   *10.5in (27cm) high*

£8,000-9,000 PAIR   **PART**

A large 19thC Bohemian glass goblet and cover, ten-sided bowl finely engraved with a stag, deer and woodland against the ruby-overlaid ground, on knopped stem and ten-sided foot, cover with spiral rim and acorn finial.

20.25in (51.5cm) high

£3,000-4,000   **GORL**

A pair of Bohemian enamelled glass vases, of cylindrical form with a spreading base, ruby to clear glass decorated in enamels depicting pansies, with gilt highlights.

c1900   *14in (35.5cm) high*

£500-600   **FRE**

A mid-19thC Baccarat glass paperweight, set with a variety of colourful canes, including silhouette canes of a deer, a goat, an elephant, a cockerel, a horse, a dog, and flowers, on a bed of upset latticinio, with date cane.

1847   *3.25in (8.5cm) diam*

£1,500-2,000   **L&T**

A 19thC Baccarat paperweight, scattered millefiori and Gridel silhouette canes on ruffled upset muslin, with signature date cane.

1848   *3in (7.5cm) high*

£1,000-1,500   **DRA**

A Baccarat dated paperweight, set with millefiori canes.

1848   *2.25in (6cm) diam.*

£1,000-1,500   **WW**

A Baccarat dated scattered millefiori paperweight, the clear glass set with assorted coloured millefiori canes, including silhouettes of a horse, a butterfly, a stag, a goat, a cockerel, and a monkey, amongst short lengths of latticinio tubing, dated on a single cane.

1848   *2.25in (6cm) diam*
£1,000-1,500   **DN**

A 19thC dated Baccarat paperweight, scattered millefiori and Gridel silhouette canes on ruffled upset muslin, with signature date cane.

1848   *3in (7.5cm) high*
£1,000-1,500   **DRA**

A Saint Louis paperweight, the clear glass set with tightly packed, brightly coloured short lengths of assorted ribbons and tubing.

3.25in (8cm) diam
£300-400   **DN**

A 19thC cranberry glass table lustre, painted with alternate panels of portraits and flowers between gilt scrolls, hung with ten clear glass lustres, minor wear and chips.

12.5in (31.5cm) high
£650-850   **WW**

A pair of 19thC glass lustre candlesticks, each worked with an etched fan neck, with ten descending lustres, surrounding a tapering column, over a circular base.

9in (23cm) high
£800-1,200   **FRE**

A pair of pale green glass lustres, with enamel decoration and gilded crenulated top, with two tiers of cut prisms.

c1900   *14in (35.5cm) high*
£400-600   **DRA**

A 19thC glass scent bottle and stopper, overlaid in white and painted with a floral garland, some wear to the enamel.

7in (18cm)
£250-350   **WW**

A 19thC French faceted glass casket, with gilt-metal banding, feet and handles, containing two glass scent bottles with stoppers, decorated with gilt stars.

5.5in (14cm) high
£500-600   **WW**

THE JEWELLERY MARKET

Diamonds continue to be more than just 'a girl's best friend' – buyers are willing to pay for large, good quality stones, especially if they are in an attractive period setting. As ever, quality pieces in good condition and which are typical of the era in which they were made sell for good prices.

Early 20thC jewellery tends to be more popular than mid- to late-19thC pieces, possibly because the settings are more delicate. There is still a market for 19thC pieces, but those that sell well are usually exceptionally good examples of their type and in excellent condition. The value of Belle Époque jewellery, dating from c1910-15, looks set to rise as buyers become increasingly enamoured with its light style.

Art Deco jewellery continues to appeal to many buyers, both those looking for period pieces and others who appreciate the modernity of the settings and feel they have a contemporary look despite their age. Many Art Deco jewels are set with diamonds, adding to their desirability in the marketplace.

Buyers are also willing to pay a premium for signed pieces by makers such as Cartier and Boucheron – even plain gold bracelets signed by names such as these will fetch far more than unsigned pieces.

Post-war jewellery, especially Scandinavian pieces from the 1950s, 60s and 70s, is an up and coming collecting area. The majority of the pieces, particularly those made in Sweden, often pass unnoticed at auctions, fairs and in shops. A little research can uncover hidden gems while prices remain reasonable. British jewellery from the same period looks set to follow, particularly pieces by designers such as John Donald.

The market for vintage costume jewellery remains strong but has moved on. While the big names such as Chanel, Dior, Trifari and Schiaparelli continue to attract buyers and high prices, collectors are willing to pay more than previously for a piece which is a great design even if it is not signed.

Emma McMillan, Lyon & Turnbull, Edinburgh

EARLY JEWELLERY

An early 19thC moonstone and diamond brooch, the moonstone panel carved in relief with a running fox, within a rose cut diamond-set border.

1.25in (3cm) wide

£3,000-4,000 L&T

A 19thC French gold-mounted Antique style multi-gem-set intaglio brooch, incised with zodiac symbols, probably by Jules Wiése, stamped 'JW' with French control marks.

2.5in (6.5cm) wide

£1,200-1,500 L&T

An early 19thC diamond brooch/pendant, claw-set with graduated old mine cut diamonds, the border set with rose cut diamonds.

1.5in (4cm) wide

£700-1,000 L&T

An early 19thC diamond bird brooch, with old mine and single cut diamonds, with ruby cabochon-set eye, with three old mine cut diamonds.

1.5in (3.5cm) wide

£2,000-3,000 L&T

A mid-18thC niello decorated plaid brooch, with engraved bosses with knot work, crosshatched and star designs, engraved 'MS 1781', unmarked, 2.7oz (84g).

3in (7.5cm) diam

£900-1,200 L&T

A mid-18thC dated ring brooch, engraved and stamped with semi-circular and prick dot border, with later engraved script initials 'CF' unmarked, 4oz (124.5g).

1795 *3in (7.5cm) diam*

£500-800 L&T

A Scottish plaid brooch, by Charles Jamieson of Inverness, marked 'CJ','INS', dromedary and 'CJ' on its side, engraved with original owner's initials 'DM*KF', 2.5oz (77.75g).

1797 *4in (10cm) diam*

£1,000-1,300 L&T

ESSENTIAL REFERENCE: JACOBITE JEWELLERY

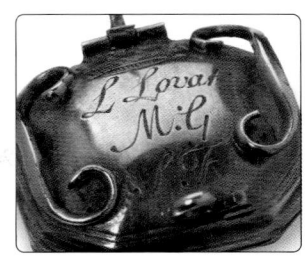

An 18thC memoriam brooch of Jacobite interest, the canted square rock crystal enclosing a lock of hair, in collet-set gold mount with two scroll mounts to reverse and hinged pin, the back of the closed setting engraved with a crown with 'L Lovat / M:G / SF' below.

£2,500-3,000   L&T

A 16thC French gilded bronze and engraved portrait medallion, with burnished mirror verso revealing an open compartment, the portrait depicting Henry III, the border inscribed in capital letters: 'HENRICVS III D G FRANCORVM ET POLANIAE REX 1584'.

4.25in (11.1cm) high

£6,000-8,000   L&T

A Scottish George III memoriam ring, with double enamelled borders inscribed 'Mrs Bailie of Polkemmet. OB '10' apr 1799: AE'48' 'Lord Polkemmet. OB.' 14 MAR. 1816: AE'79', marked 'IG', along with two domed glass-covered lockets of hair.

£500-700   L&T

An 18thC Jacobite secret service ring, the oval cabochon emerald in a simple collet mount with open work to shoulders and simple shank, the reverse of the closed back setting engraved 'CR / III / 1766'.

The significance of this unassuming item of 18thC jewellery is far greater than it appears. Once defeated by the English troops in 1746 at the Battle of Culloden, Prince Charles Edward Stuart (Bonnie Prince Charlie) fled to the safe haven of France to reunite with his father. He and a large proportion of the Scottish population still considered him the rightful heir to the Scottish throne. Even after this final defeat at Culloden, Charles and his father James for many years still held hopes to overthrow the English rule of Scotland and planned for another attack on the throne to claim back their rightful place in Scotland. These plans were not helped by the outlawing of Scottish traditions by the victorious English monarch and the fact that the reprisals for supporting the Jacobite cause included death. The population which backed Prince Charles had to find other ways to show their support in secret and this is where the wealth of poetry and songwriting blooms, the common factor in all writings is the fact that neither James' nor Charles' names were ever uttered but the significance was not lost to their supporters. This theme carried on to the applied arts in crafts such as silver, carvings, glass and jewellery. This ring was used as a 'signature' when travelling with correspondence from Charles. No document could carry a signature or seal, as if the bearer was found in possession of such marked papers by government troops, he would almost certainly have been sentenced to death. Therefore this ring would accompany the messenger to show that documents had originated from Charles and were considered official. This Jacobite secret service provided an invaluable service to Charles who had to keep all his loyal supporters abreast of his plans and movements. The cipher of CR III 1766 is also important as this is the year that Charles' father James died in France. Charles now considered himself the rightful King of Scotland and gave himself the title King Charles III, rather than Prince of Wales, which even in exile he still used.

£15,000-20,000   L&T

19TH C JEWELLERY

A Victorian gold-mounted oval shell cameo brooch, with a glazed locket containing a scroll of hair, inscribed 'JAMES ANTHONY, STEEL MARCH 1864' and signed 'NERI'.

2in (5cm) long

£350-450   L&T

A late 19thC Holbeinesque brooch, with central ruby and seed pearl cluster, and decorated with enamel and seed pearls.

1.5in (4cm) wide

£2,000-2,500   L&T

A gold and Pertabghar enamel brooch, decorated with mythical beasts within foliate scrolls and an outer scroll border.

1.25in (3cm) wide

£200-400   L&T

JEWELLERY

A Victorian shamrock brooch, collet-set to the centre with a rose cut diamond, three petals set with a circular cut sapphire within rose cut diamonds.

0.5in (1.5cm) long

£750-850   **L&T**

A late Victorian heart-shaped brooch, set with an old European cut diamond, a circular cut ruby and sapphire, within a border of half-pearls.

1in (2.5cm) long

£1,000-1,500   **L&T**

A 19thC brooch, with an Earl's crown surmounted by an egret feather, set with old European cut diamonds, with oval cut sapphire, in a case.

2.25in (5.5cm) long

£750-950   **L&T**

A Victorian multi-gem-set brooch, set with three oval and pear cut rubies, and old European cut diamonds, surmounted by a bouton pearl and suspending a large pearl drop.

1.5in (4cm) wide

£2,000-3,000   **L&T**

A Victorian closed crescent brooch, set with graduated circular cut sapphires and an inner border of smaller old European cut diamonds.

1.5in (3.5cm) diam

£800-1,200   **L&T**

A Montrose agate-set brooch, of cross form with applied foliate-engraved crown set with three orange cabochons, unmarked.

c1870   *1.75in (4.5cm) wide*

£250-300   **L&T**

A rare Scottish provincial luckenbooth brooch, by Daniel Ferguson of Nairn, of typical conjoined double heart form with stylised 'Inverness' spectacles surmounting, with all-over finely engraved detail, 0.7oz (24g).

Little is known about the early career and training of Daniel Ferguson, it appears that originally he trained and traded purely as a watchmaker, and established this business in 1837 aged 23. The main output of named works are clocks and watches with signed dials and movements. For this reason and the total lack of known marked pieces, one must assume that whilst capable of making items, Ferguson either retailed or did not mark his items. It should also be noted that only a small amount of work is known with his Inverness mark (DF INVSS) and an assumption that he only marked a small proportion of his work seems fair. So far only three examples of items marked by Ferguson in Nairn have been recorded, no matter the number unrecorded to date these must still be considered amongst the rarest provincial marks in Scotland.

c1840   *3in (7.5cm) high*

£2,000-3,000   **L&T**

A Victorian gold-mounted Scottish pebble brooch, reverse stamped with a registration number, with box stamped 'TESSIERS LTD... LONDON'.

1.5in (4cm) diam

£600-800   **L&T**

A gold pebble-set garter brooch, unmarked.

2.5in (6.5cm) wide

£600-800   **L&T**

A gold-mounted pebble brooch, with panels of agate and hardstones, set with six raised circular cut foil backed crystals, the centre with circular cut citrine, unmarked.

1.25in (3.5cm) diam.

£250-350   **L&T**

A Celtic Revival Tara brooch, by Waterhouse of Dublin, intricately cast with Celtic motifs.

4in (10cm) wide

£500-800   **L&T**

A gold-mounted pebble brooch, with detailed engraved border of Celtic and interlaced designs, between panels with agates and hardstone, the centre applied with engraved saltire with applied crown, unmarked.

1.75in (4.5cm) diam.

£750-850   **L&T**

A Scottish Royal plaid brooch, by William Robb of Ballater, inscribed '19 ERI 04', Edinburgh, 3oz (93.5g).

Presented by King Edward VII to his ghillie on the Balmoral estate on his retirement. The pattern is worn by the Balmoral Highlanders.

1898-99   3.25in (8.5cm) diam

£3,000-4,000   **L&T**

A Scottish provincial grouse claw brooch, in tablet punch, the claw with mounts, the terminal set with an oval cut citrine in top-twisted collet setting, marked 'JAS. RAMSEY / DUNDEE'.

c1900   3.25in (8.5cm) long

£250-350   **L&T**

A Scottish silver plaid brooch, by R. W. Forsyth Ltd., with cairngorm within Celtic knots and scrolls, with marks for Edinburgh.

1910   3.75in (9.5cm) diam

£600-800   **L&T**

A Highland plaid brooch, by Henry Tatton, Edinburgh, with engraved Celtic knotwork panels divided by engraved bosses, the centre claw-set with a circular cut citrine.

1919-20   3.25in (8cm) diam.

£400-600   **L&T**

A Highland plaid brooch, by R. W. Forsyth, Edinburgh, with alternate panels of Celtic knotwork and intertwined Celtic beasts, claw set with a circular cut citrine.

1925   3.25in (8.5cm) diam.

£400-500   **L&T**

A Celtic plaid brooch, by Thomas K. Ebutt, Edinburgh, with engraved Celtic bosses and knotwork panels around a raised claw-set circular cut citrine.

1926-27   3.25in (8.5cm) diam.

£280-340   **L&T**

A Victorian gold Scottish pebble bracelet, with padlock clasp, with glazed hair panel to reverse, inscribed 'SIR WALTER SCOTT'.

8in (20cm) long

£2,200-2,500   **L&T**

A gilt hardstone bracelet, the links composed of granite-backed agate panels with central pyramid agates.

£500-700   **L&T**

A 19thC gold bracelet, composed of faceted belcher links with pierced oval links, with a heart-shaped fob, set with a cushion cut garnet, with a George III quarter guinea dated '1804', in a fitted case.

7.5in (19cm) long

£300-500   **L&T**

A Renaissance Revival demi-parure, comprising hinged bangle and matching pendant earrings, applied with putti and rose cut diamonds around the central oval mother-of-pearl plaque, hand painted with an enamelled portrait, in a fitted case.

Bangle 2.5in (6.5cm) wide

£4,000-6,000   **L&T**

A Victorian gold ruby and rose cut diamond bangle, of hinged design.

2.5in (6.5cm)

£500-700   **L&T**

A Victorian rock crystal pendant, carved as a heart and surmounted by a crown set with four rose cut diamonds and fringed by pearls.

2.25in (6cm) long

£800-1,000   **L&T**

JEWELLERY

A Victorian gold memorial pendant, with panel containing woven hair, inscribed 'WALTERUS. DECR. XI MARGERETA. DECR. 3. 1858' and 'CARLAOTTA. H.J. HOPE SCOTT OCTR. 26 1858 RIP'.

2in (5.5cm) long

£1,000-1,500   L&T

A possibly Indian aquamarine and gold necklace, comprising ten light blue pillow cut stones, the largest 50 carats, for a total of approx. 249 carats, set in 24K gold die-struck setting.

c1900   *16in (40.5cm) long*

£6,000-10,000   POOK

A late 19thC American large sterling silver heart-shaped locket, enamelled with a shield containing three books and the word 'VERITAS'.

2.5in (6cm) high

£125-150   BB

A late 19thC amethyst heart pendant, the large faceted heart-shaped amethyst, approximately 1.5in (4cm) x 1in (3cm) suspended from a rose cut diamond suspension loop, attached to a black silk cord necklace.

£1,800-2,200   DN

An early 19thC multi-gem-set pendant, set with cushion cut gems, including citrine, amethyst, chrysoberyl, rock crystal, aquamarine, garnet and pink topaz.

2.75in (7cm) long

£1,500-2,000   L&T

A Victorian gold-mounted verse crystal intaglio pendant, the high-domed crystal depicting a bird resting on a fruiting branch, within bead borders.

1.5in (4cm) diam

£1,000-1,500   L&T

A Victorian amethyst rivière necklace, composed of oval cut amethysts, suspending matched detachable pear cut amethyst drop, swallow surmount.

15.75in (40cm) long

£1,000-1,300   L&T

A matched Belle Époque suite, the necklace with a single cut diamond-set bow-tied ribbon, with a pearl, surmounting knife bars, collet-set with diamonds, suspending a pearl drop, within diamond-set borders, the earrings similar.

Necklace 20.5in (52cm) long

£3,000-4,000   L&T

A Victorian gold and banded agate Prince Albert memorial stick pin, dated 1861 and a possible gift from Queen Victoria, engraved to the reverse 'in remembrance of the beloved Prince Dec 14th 1861 from VR'.

£850-1,000   DN

A Victorian 18ct gold-mounted gentleman's mourning ring, box-set with an old European cut diamond, with black enamelled panels to the shank.

£2,500-3,000   L&T

A Victorian diamond ring, set with three graduated old European cut diamonds, with rose cut diamonds between and scroll-pierced gallery.

£4,000-6,000   L&T

A pair of Belle Époque pearl and diamond earrings, each composed of a bow-tied ribbon, set with graduated old European cut diamonds, with a pearl drop, within a shaped surround, millegrain collet-set with graduated old European cut diamonds.

1.25in (3cm) long

£3,300-4,000   L&T

EARLY 20THC JEWELLERY

A Guild of Handicraft silver pendant, by C. R. Ashbee, depicting the tree of life with a turquoise enamelled medallion and two hanging natural pearls, monogrammed 'L.C.' on verso'.

Pendant 1.5in (4cm) high

£3,000-4,000

An Art Nouveau Charles Horner silver necklace, set to the front with a greenish-blue enamelled panel, suspending a drop collet set with a circular cut orange gem, made in Chester.

1908   *9.75in (25cm) long*

£250-350   L&T

An Art Nouveau Liberty & Co. enamelled silver pendant, by Charles Fleetwood Varley, the hand-painted enamel plaque depicting silhouetted trees against a sunset, applied with turquoise enamelled foliate motifs, possibly by Jessie M. King, suspending a baroque freshwater pearl drop.

A Victorian landscape and seascape painter, Varley's enamelled scenes were more often set into lids for silver or pewter boxes. Jewellery by Varley is rare and, although unmarked, this piece exemplifies his use of softly enamelled, deep colours within a foliate border, also enamelled in complimentary tones.

2in (5cm) long

£800-1,200 **L&T**

A Theodor Fahrner Jugendstil silver pendant, with simulated ivory pierced panel set with chrysoprase, marcasite and white enamel, signed with monogram 'TF' and stamped '935'.

£500-800 **L&T**

An Art Nouveau 9ct gold necklace, possibly by Sydney & Co., collet-set with graduated circular cut moonstone cabochons, with rope-twist borders, within a wirework surround, suspending a moonstone cabochon drop, suspended from a fancy link chain.

24.75in (63cm) long

£1,800-2,200 **L&T**

An Edwardian 15ct gold pendant, alternately composed of collet-set circular cut amethysts and plain oval links, suspending a seed-pearl-set scroll-form drop, also collet-set with two circular cut amethysts.

20.5in (52cm) long

£700-1,000 **L&T**

An Edwardian necklace, collet-set with graduated circular cut garnets, interspersed by floret-set seed pearls, the front fringed by graduated pear cut garnet drops, to a fine belcher link chain, in a fitted case.

17.75in (45cm) long

£600-800 **L&T**

An Edwardian 9ct gold necklace, with belcher links, set with small spherical opal beads, interspersed by faceted cushion cut rock crystal beads, flanked by opal cabochons.

19.75in (50cm) long

£1,200-1,400 **L&T**

An Edwardian multi-gem-set necklace, the front of scroll design, claw-set with three circular cut pink tourmalines and two cushion cut peridots, set with graduated seed pearls, with a belcher link chain.

15.75in (40cm) long

£1,200-1,400 **L&T**

A Harry Dixon hammered sterling brooch, set with a citrine, hand incised 'HARRY DIXON SF 1933 Sterling 925 9'.

2in (5cm) wide

£250-350 **DRA**

An Edwardian floral brooch/pendant, the central old European cut diamond within border of circular cut demantoid garnets and heart cut opal cabochons.

0.75in (2cm) diam

£1,800-2,200 **L&T**

A Murrle Bennett & Co. 15ct gold brooch, set with a central amethyst cabouchon and collar-set with three seed pearls.

£700-1,000 **FLD**

A Heinrich Levinger Art Nouveau brooch, modelled as a stylised dragonfly with green plique-a-jour wings and cabochon cut, collar-set moonstone body and garnet eyes.

4.25in (10.5cm) long

£2,000-2,500 **FLD**

A Murrle Bennet & Co. 15ct gold brooch, with central set emerald within pierced borders with three seed pearls, with a freshwater pearl drop, stamped to reverse.

£450-550 **FLD**

A Scottish Arts and Crafts hammered silver bar brooch, set with amethyst and corded wirework, stamped maker's mark 'King'.

£100-200 **L&T**

A pair of Edwardian style multi-gem-set earrings, each designed as an insect, with circular cut ruby-set thorax, oval cut opal cabochon-set abdomen and seed-pearl-set wings, suspending a collet-set round brilliant cut diamond drop.

1in (2.5cm) long

£1,000-1,500 **L&T**

An early 20thC platinum-mounted ring, claw-set with an old mine cut diamond.

£4,500-5,500 **L&T**

An early 20thC bracelet, with brilliant cut diamonds, fancy assorted links and single cut diamond spacers.

7in (18cm)

£2,500-3,500   L&T

An Art Deco bracelet, set with graduated round brilliant cut diamonds.

7in (18cm)

£15,000-20,000   L&T

An Art Deco French white gold-mounted bracelet, millegrain collet-set throughout with graduated old European and single cut diamonds, snap fastening and safety chain.

7.25in (18.5cm) long

£7,000-9,000   L&T

An Art Deco style platinum bracelet, collet-set with graduated trap cut emeralds and graduated rectangular panels, each channel-set with three baguette cut diamonds, with snap fastenings and safety clip.

7in (17.5cm) long

£7,000-8,000   L&T

An Art Deco bar brooch, millegrain collet-set to the centre with a round brilliant cut diamond, to a stepped bar, set with borders of single cut diamonds.

2.25in (5.5cm) wide

£3,000-4,000   L&T

A Tiffany & Co. crowing cockerel novelty brooch, set with graduated circular cut rubies and round brilliant and single cut diamonds, signed and stamped '18K'.

2.5in (6cm) long

£1,700-2,000   L&T

An Art Deco brooch, set to the centre with a fancy rectangular cut aquamarine, flanked by graduated old European cut diamonds.

3.5in (9cm) wide

£6,000-8,000   L&T

An Art Deco 18ct white gold cluster ring, the curved front designed as a plaque, with central old mine cut champagne-coloured diamond, within a millegrain surround, pavé-set with graduated old European cut diamonds.

£1,100-1,500   L&T

An Art Deco cocktail ring, the central box-set old mine cut diamond to a domed surround, pavé-set with graduated early brilliant and single cut diamonds.

£3,500-4,000   L&T

An Art Deco platinum ring, the central oval cut sapphire claw-set within a scrolling surround, set with graduated single and baguette cut diamonds.

1in (2.5cm) high

£2,500-4,000   L&T

An Art Deco ring, designed as a broad tapering band, with central channel-set border of graduated rectangular cut sapphires, flanked with brilliant cut diamonds and rectangular cut sapphires.

£1,000-2,000   L&T

An Art Deco cluster ring, millegrain collet-set with three graduated round brilliant cut diamonds, with a surround of invisibly set French cut sapphires, set to each shoulder with four graduated old European cut diamonds.

£2,500-3,500   L&T

A 1930s Art Deco silver and paste ring.

£110-125   TDG

A Belle Époque fob watch, the front millegrain collet-set with an old European cut diamond, set with single cut diamonds and borders of channel-set calibre cut onyx, suspended from a long black cord.

Fob 2in (5cm) long

£550-750   L&T

An Art Deco necklace, the front claw-set to the centre with nine graduated round brilliant cut diamonds, flanked by graduated clusters of three vertically set diamonds and five baguette cut diamonds, the detachable front may be worn as a bracelet and the remaining section as a bandeau.

16.25in (41.5cm) long overall

£20,000-30,000   L&T

A pair of cufflinks, with a bar millegrain-set with single cut diamonds, and set to each end with a collet-set high-domed ruby cabochon.

Terminals 1in (2.5cm) long

£1,500-2,000   L&T

A pair of ruby- and diamond-set cufflinks with baton-shaped terminals.

Terminals 0.75in (2cm) long

£800-1,000   L&T

A pair of French gold-mounted sapphire cufflinks, with channel-set border of calibre cut sapphires, with terminals set with a circular cut sapphire cabochon.

Terminals 0.75in (2cm) long

£1,500-1,800   L&T

A pair of Boucheron cufflinks, collet-set with an oval cut sapphire cabochon, each sapphire of an intense blue hue, signed and stamped 'OR 750'.

Terminals 0.75in (2cm) long

£4,000-6,000   L&T

A pair of sapphire and cowrie shell cufflinks, possibly Trianon.

Terminals 0.75in (2cm) long

£1,000-1,400   L&T

A pair of French white gold and platinum sapphire cufflinks.

Terminals 0.5in (1.5cm) long

£2,000-3,000   L&T

A pair of Boucheron 18ct gold-mounted onyx and ruby cufflinks, numbered 'A3403216'.
Terminals 0.75in (2cm) long
£1,500-2,000   **L&T**

A pair of platinum-mounted sapphire- and diamond-set cufflinks.
Terminals 0.5in (1.5cm) long
£1,400-1,800   **L&T**

A pair of French Van Cleef et Arpels platinum-mounted diamond cufflinks, signed and numbered '42885 BTESGOG'.
Terminals 0.75in (2cm) long
£2,200-2,800   **L&T**

A pair of Bulgari cufflinks, each set with four round brilliant cut diamonds, signed.
Terminals 0.75in (2cm) diam
£2,600-3,000   **L&T**

A pair of novelty cufflinks, attributed to David Webb, each designed as a hexagonal bolt with screw-turned post, unmarked, tests as gold.
Fronts 0.5in (1cm) diam
£1,200-1,800   **L&T**

A pair of Bulgari novelty cufflinks, with two-colour graduated circular button-form terminals, conjoined by belcher links, signed.
Terminals 0.5in (1.5cm) diam
£850-1,000   **L&T**

A pair of early gold-mounted cufflinks, the terminals each set with a rose cut rock crystal above initials in gold scrolling script, within a red border, with closed back setting.
Terminals 0.5in (1cm) diam
£1,500-2,000   **L&T**

A pair of cornelian intaglio-set cufflinks, within a broad bezel conjoined by belcher links, unmarked, tests as gold.
Fronts 0.5in (1cm) diam
£1,200-1,500   **L&T**

A pair of cufflinks, each claw-set with a sugar-loaf cabochon cut emerald, stamped '750' and 'PSN'.
Terminals 0.5in (1.5cm) long
£2,300-2,800   **L&T**

A pair of 14ct white gold cufflinks, each terminal millegrain collet-set with a square cut coral cabochon, within a surround of rose cut diamonds, conjoined by belcher links.
Terminals 0.5in (1cm) long
£1,200-1,500   **L&T**

An 18ct gold-mounted gentleman's dress set, each circular terminal millegrain collet-set with a circular cut sapphire cabochon, within a surround of rose cut diamonds, with blue guilloche enamelled border and outer white enamelled edge.
Terminals 0.5in (1.5cm) diam
£3,500-4,500   **L&T**

A Chanel Maltese Cross pin, with green, red and pink poured glass cabochons in gilt-metal settings.

1990s. *2.5in (6.5cm) wide.*

£90-120 PC

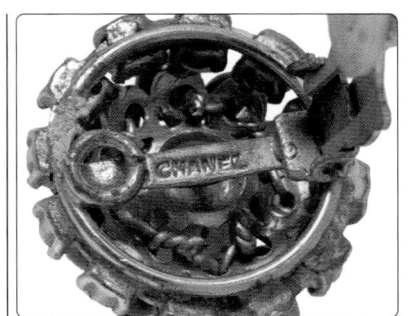

A pair of Chanel earrings, gold tone metal set with faux pearls surrounded faux rubies and faux seed pearls, marked 'Chanel'.

late 1960s *1in (2.5cm) diam*

£150-250 PC

A Coro Duette, 'Quivering Camelias', gilt-metal set with clear and emerald rhinestones and green enamel, the trembling flowers mounted on springs, signed with patent numbers.

1940s *3in (7.5cm) long*

£200-250 PC

A Coro chateleine pin, of a girl walking a dog, gold tone metal set with turquoise, pink and red crystals, signed 'Coro'.

1950s *Girl 2in (5cm) high*

£120-160 PC

An 'en tremblant' flower pin, by Kramer for Dior, rhodium-plated setting with pavé-set rhinestones and a large clear rhinestone in the centre, unmarked.

1960s *2.5in (6.5cm) long*

£60-100 PC

A Christian Dior heart-shaped pin, with co-ordinating star and drop earrings, silver tone setting with oval, round and navette aquamarine, chalcedony, pale green and fuchsia pink prong-set pastes.

1960s *Pin 3.5in (7cm) wide*

£220-260 PC

A Christian Dior wreath pin and co-ordinating earrings, silver tone metal with gold metal decoration, prong-set with clear rhinestones, marked 'ChrDior 1959'.

1959 *Pin 2.5in (6.5cm) high*

£250-350 PC

A Christian Dior swordfish pin, silver tone metal prong-set with clear rhinestones, a red rhinestone eye and dangling faux baroque pearls.

1960s *4.25in (11cm) long*

£180-280 PC

A pair of earrings, Mitchell Maer for Christian Dior, silver tone metal set with black and clear crystal rhinestones with faux baroque pearl drops, signed 'Christian Dior by Mitchell Maer'.

1950s *2in (5cm) long*

£100-150 PC

A rare Christian Dior faceted paste brooch, signed.

1962 *3in (7.5cm) long*

£140-160 TDG

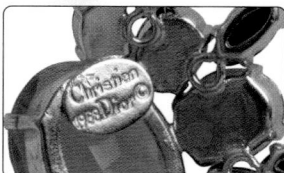

A pair of Christian Dior earrings, silver tone metal with prong-set citrine and clear rhinestones, marked 'Christian Dior 1958'.

1958   *1.5in (3.5cm) long*

£80-120   **PC**

A Stanley Hagler floral pin and earrings set, with petals and leaves of faux pearls and seed pearls, and clear crystal rhinestones, hand-wired to filigree gold-plated backings.

Early 1990s.   *Pin: 3in (7.5cm) long*

£160-200   **PC**

A Stanley Hagler flower pin, with brown plastic leaves, citrine glass beads and a brown onyx cabochon, signed 'Stanley Hagler N.Y.C'.
This unusual design was probably made to order.

1980s   *3.5in (9cm) diam*

£80-120   **PC**

A Miriam Haskell floral and fruit motif pin and earrings, with silvered faux 'black' baroque and seed pearls on a filigree gilt-metal casting.

1950s.   *2in (5cm) long.*

£120-160   **PC**

A Joseff of Hollywood bar pin and earrings, 'Russian gold' setting with faux rubies, signed 'Joseff Hollywood'.

1940s   *Pin 3.5in (9cm) long*

£100-140   **PC**

A Joseff 'Sun God' pin, in 'Russian gold' with clear rhinestone eye tremblers.

1940s.   *3in (7.5cm) diam.*

£250-300   **PC**

A rare Joseff 'Moon God' with ruff pin, 'Russian gold' with clear rhinestone eye tremblers.
Moon god pins without the ruff are almost 1/3rd the price.

1940s.   *2.5in (6.25cm) diam.*

£300-400   **PC**

A Joseff 'Russian gold' chatelaine camel pin, with faux ruby, emerald, citrine, jade and aquamarine crystal cabochons.

1940s.   *1.25in (3cm) wide.*

£250-300   **PC**

A collection of bee brooches, by Joseff of Hollywood.

1940s

LARGE BEE £70, MEDIUM BEE £60, SMALL BEE £30 EACH   **PC**

A Rebajes stylised 'African head' copper pin, with copper wire necklace and earrings.

Late 1940s.   *3in (8cm) high*

£220-260   **PC**

A Regency flower pin and earrings, gold-plated setting with topaz and aurora borealis crystals, marked 'Regency'.

1950s   *Pin 3in (7.5cm) diam,*

£60-100   **PC**

An Elsa Schiaparelli pin and earrings, with prong-set leaves of pale green and pink Lucite on a gold-plated backing.

1950s. *Pin: 3.5in (9cm) long*

£300-400 PC

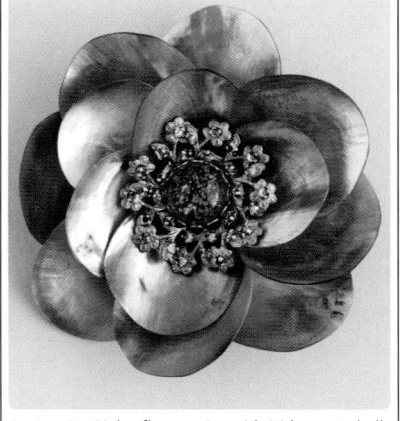

An Ian St. Gielar flower pin, with iridescent shell petals, an amber-red glass centre encircled by topaz crystal rhinestones.

Late 1990s. *3.5in (9cm) diam.*

£160-200 PC

A 1980s Hervé van der Straeten 'Primitive' necklace, the gilt-metal mask applied with gilt-studded ceramic discs forming the hair, pendant cabochon amethyst stones forming earrings, the chain formed from beaten metal medallions, maker's plaque to reverse.

17in (43cm) long

£600-800 KT

A Trifari poinsettia pin, designed by Alfred Philippe, with faux rubies and diamonds configured in imitation of the 'invisible setting' technique developed by Van Cleef and Arpels.

1950s. *2.75in (7cm) diam.*

£650-850 PC

A pair of Trifari carnation earrings, red, green and clear diamante in 'invisible setting'.

1950's *3cm (1.25in) long*

£100-130 PC

A Weiss Christmas tree pin, japanned metal set with green, red, yellow, pink and clear crystal rhinestones, marked 'Weiss'.

1950s *2.75in (7cm) high*

£100-150 PC

A pair of Weiss earrings, prong-set with aurora borealis rhinestones, marked 'Weiss'.

1.5in (3.5cm) long

£45-65 PC

A pair of Weiss earrings, gold tone metal prong-set with green, citrine and clear aurora borealis rhinestones, marked 'Weiss'.

1.5in (3.5cm) long

£40-60 PC

A pair of Weiss earrings, the central pink rough-cut stone surrounded by lilac green and pink baguettes.

3cm (1.25in) long

£50-70 PC

An 18thC Jacobite interest enamel patch box, the lid with portrait of Prince Charles Edward Stuart.

With an accompanying note stating 'This box was presented by Prince Charles Edward to Captain John Burnett of the R H Arty'.

2.5in (6.5cm) diam

£1,500-2,000 L&T

An early George III double partition silver spice box, with crest of a hand with motto 'MANENT OPTIMA CAELO' and script initials 'GM', the interior with engraved galleon with legend 'James Miller Grocer in Canongate 1773', unmarked.

c1775 *3.25in (8.5cm) high*

£1,000-1,500 L&T

An 18thC Gujarat mother-of-pearl round box, with florette on cover picked out in red.

4in (11cm) diam

£2,000-3,000 DN

A George III engraved silver counter box, the pull-off cover with a miniature portrait of a young girl behind glass, unmarked.

c1800 *75in (2cm) diam*

£200-250 WW

A 19thC Continental tortoiseshell pique-gold and mother-of-pearl-inlaid box, the hinged lid inlaid with a mythological scene, opening to reveal an interior with removable tray, the sides decorated with Classical maidens and castles.

5.5in (14cm) wide

£15,000-20,000 L&T

A Victorian gold-mounted agate presentation table snuff box, the lid engraved with the presentation border 'PRESENTED BY COLONEL DUGALD CAMPBELL R.A. TO ARTHUR CAMPBELL WRITER TO THE SIGNET 1848'.

1848 *2.75in (7cm) wide*

£5,000-7,000 L&T

A rare Scottish silver, Castle Douglas provincial snuff mull, by Adam Burgess of Castle Douglas or Dumfries, the cow horn body with carved seal head terminal, the hinged cover with applied thistle design with circular cut amethyst, marked 'AB', ruined castle, 'D', fouled anchor.

It has often been the case that this combination of the makers mark for Adam Burgess and the ruined castle mark signify his time working in Castle Douglas rather than Dumfries. It does seem a little hopeful that the surviving body of work featuring these marks comes from this short period, of eleven months. There can be no firm differentiation, between these periods unless the items are fully hallmarked in Edinburgh, as is often the case, and the time line examined. This maker is generally known for his flatware.

c1835 *4.25in (11cm) long*

£2,500-3,500 L&T

A French rose gold-mounted and lined tortoiseshell box, the cover with central glazed shell cameo carved with a Classical figural scene, with an outer blue-enamelled border, with French control marks.

3.25in (8cm) long

£1,200-2,000 L&T

A Scandinavian silver-mounted cowrie shell snuff box, indistinctly marked.

c1850 *3.25in (8cm) wide*

£120-160 ROS

A gold-mounted agate snuff box, with flat hinged cover and scroll-form thumb piece.

2.5in (6.5cm) wide

£250-350 L&T

A 19thC banded agate-mounted gilt-metal casket, on four ball feet.

6.5in (16.5cm) wide

£600-800   **DN**

A Scottish market agate scent bottle, by J Cook & Sons, Birmingham, the screw-off cap set with a circular cut amethyst.

c1890   *4.25in (11cm) long*

£350-450   **L&T**

A gold-mounted curly horn table snuff mull, the cover engraved and set with a cabochon-banded agate, the body applied with a thistle mount with tools, paw, snuff spoon, rake and ivory mallet, suspended from a belcher link chain, the mounts unmarked.

5in (13cm) long

£4,000-5,000   **L&T**

A gilded multi-gem-set box, the hinged cover decorated with rope-twist scrolls, enamel, seed pearls and other gems, around a cut garnet cabochon, with Swedish import marks.

1.5in (4cm) long

£180-240   **L&T**

A deep blue enamel decorated gold box, apparently unmarked, with hinged cover, and decorated with a diaper pattern.

3.5in (9cm) long

£1,000-1,500   **L&T**

A 19thC French gilt-bronze and agate jewellery casket, scroll-engraved with applied relief pendant mounts and inset with fourteen different agate panels.

5.75in (14.5cm) long

£400-600   **DN**

A French yellow metal and red-enamelled compact, with carved oval jade and rose cut diamond-set thumb-piece, with mirror, two lidded compartments and a lipstick holder inside.

3in (7.5cm) long

£600-900   **L&T**

A white metal-mounted ivory patch box, inlaid and painted to the underside with a miniature portrait of an Elizabethan lady, unmarked.

3.5in (9cm) long

£350-450   **L&T**

A silver-mounted tortoiseshell mechanical nécessaire, retailed by Goldsmiths & Silversmiths Co., London, with fitted interior, the front with a spring mechanism opening to reveal further compartments, marks rubbed.

Nécessaire is a French term for a small box of silver, leather-covered wood, porcelain or enamel which carries everything 'necessary' for a lady's daily requirements.

1912   *7.5in (19cm) wide*

£2,000-3,000   **FRE**

A French red-enamelled compact, with jade and rose cut diamond thumb-piece, with mirror, lidded compartments, lipstick holder inside.

3in (7.5cm) long

£600-900   L&T

A rose gold multi-gem vesta case, decorated to the front with a question marks set with rose cut diamonds, a sapphire and ruby.

1.5in (4cm) long

£400-500   L&T

A gilt-metal-mounted lapis lazulis box, with scroll-form thumb-piece.

3.5in (8.5cm) long

£200-300   L&T

A French gold-mounted jadeite box, with diamond-set thumb-piece, and French control marks, stamped '750'.

3.5in (9.5cm) long

£700-900   L&T

An engraved gilt-bronze singing bird box, numbered 51 and in its original box, with inscription by Chevob & Co (previously Baker-Troll & Co), Geneva, Switzerland.

c1890   *10in (4cm) high*

£5,500-6,500   RGA

A 19thC German sterling silver, enamel and ivory automaton singing bird box, the bird with red, blue and green plumage beneath a carved ivory lid, raised on four ivory bun feet.

4.25in (11cm) wide

£2,500-3,500   FRE

ESSENTIAL REFERENCE: BIRD TABATIÈRES

- The mechanical singing bird tabatières were made as early as the 1780s as a rich man's toy, made from precious metal or tortoiseshell.
- Tabatière is a French word meaning 'snuffbox', but has come to be used to describe all small, high quality boxes, including the 'singing bird' tabatières which originated in Geneva, Switzerland, developed by Pierre Jaquet-Droz towards the end of the 18thC.

A red enamel and gilt-metal singing bird box, on small lion paw feet, the cover in ivory carved with a bird. When the operating lever is activated the lid opens and the bird pops up through the grille and begins to sing. At the same time the bird rotates 180 degrees backwards and forwards, opens and shuts its beak and flaps its wings. It then returns to the box and the lid closes.

c1890   *5cm (2in) high*

£8,000-11,000   RGA

CLOSER LOOK: SINGING BIRD CAGE

The mechanism is very intricate, comprising a clockwork movement which works a series of rods that move the birds' heads from side to side, open and close the beaks and flap the tails and wings, whilst working a bellows which gives the birds their song.

The birds take it in turns to move their heads from side to side and sing.

The vast majority of singing bird cages were made for the home, where they were played on special occasions to amuse the family, but some were made for shop premises and had a penny-in-the-slot mechanism. These examples are much more difficult to find today.

A very rare late 19thC singing bird cage with three birds, operated by a penny-in-the-slot mechanism.

c1890   *58.5cm (23in) high*

£8,000-9,000   RGA

A pair of Elkington & Co. cloisonné vases, depicting birds and grasses, signed to vase and impressed mark under foot.

11in (28cm) high

£17,000-20,000   HT

A 19thC Austrian ebonised and enamel-inset table cabinet, with figure-decorated pediment, two doors concealing three small drawers and long frieze drawer.

9in (23cm) high

£2,000-2,500   L&T

A 19thC French 'Japonisme' champlevé enamel and gilt-bronze jardinière, probably by Barbedienne.

13.25in (34cm) high

£2,000-2,500   L&T

A 19thC Limoges enamel plaque, depicting an Elizabethan court scene, surrounded by enamelled plaques decorated with rinceau and masks, framed.

11in (28cm) high

£2,500-3,000   FRE

ESSENTIAL REFERENCE: CHESS

Chess became very popular in the 18thC and 19thC when many sets were made. These were most often made from carved or turned wood, though ivory, bone and tusks were also used. Ivory and exotic woods, such as rosewood, are the most valuable now, as are examples earlier than the 18thC. The export markets of China and India were particularly strong. Britain, Germany and France were also good producers.

- The official set of the World Chess Federation is known as the Staunton Set. It was designed by Nathaniel Cook for Jacques & Sons in 1849, and was endorsed by and named after Howard Staunton, a famous English Grand Master.
- Sets should be complete and undamaged. Period boxes can add value. The inclusion of a chess board is not necessary.

An American Gorham sterling silver and champlevé chamberstick, with a dolphin-form handle, monogrammed 'VHS'.

c1893   *4in (10cm) diam*

£2,500-3,500   FRE

A large early 20thC Limoges enamel plaque, with a profile bust of Minerva with a plumed helmet, against a scrolling copper-coloured ground.

20in (51cm) wide

£3,500-4,500   FRE

IVORY

An ivory snuff box, the cover painted to show a view from a country house.

c1830   *3.5in (9cm) diam*

£200-250   FRE

A late 19th/early 20thC Viennese enamelled silver and jewel-mounted chess set.

21.75in (55cm) square

£13,000-16,000   FRE

A 19thC Vizagapatam quill and ivory frame, backboard lacking.

8.5in (21cm) wide

£550-650   L&T

A set of six 19thC French ivory figures, each standing on a walnut and ebonised barrel, comprising: a conductor, a flautist, an accordian player, a lute player, a double bassist, and a bagpipe player.

6in (15cm) high

£5,000-6,000   L&T

A pair of 19thC ivory plaques, with carved angels with cupids, representing the Arts, in carved wood frames.

7.25in (18cm) wide

£1,500-2,000   A&G

A 19thC ivory plaque, depicting classical figures, cherubs and dolphins in the sea, in a red leather fitted case.

4.25in (11cm) high

£900-1,200   L&T

A set of three 19thC Indo-Portuguese graduated ivory and tortoiseshell sand glasses.

Largest 10.25in (26cm) high

£4,000-5,000   L&T

A late 19thC Indo-Portuguese turned ivory, tortoiseshell and rosewood chalice.

12in (31cm) high

£4,000-6,000   L&T

A late 19thC carved ivory and yellow metal-mounted Malacca walking stick, the metal mount stamped '18CT'.

35.5in (90cm) high

£800-1,000   DN

MINIATURES & SILHOUETTES

A small oval oil-on-poplar panel profile portrait of a gentleman, Jacob Eichholtz (American 1776-1842), attributed.

9in (22.5cm) high

£4,000-5,000   POOK

A pair of 19thC Indian portraits on ivory, of Shah Jehan and wife Mumtaz Mahal.

4in (10cm) high

£400-600   DN

A miniature watercolour-on-ivory portrait of Jeremiah Kahler, Boston, MA, unsigned, attributed to Henry Pelham (1749-1806), in gold frame.

2in (5cm) high

£2,000-3,000   FRE

A pair of miniature watercolour-on-paper portraits of Charles Sherwin and his wife Hanna, unsigned, attributed to Rufus Porter (American, 1792-1884), the sitters identified in an inscription on the reverse also 'came from Warwick Mass to Windham, Vt.' in original eglomise mats and moulded giltwood frames, foxing and minor toning.

c1830   3.25in (8.5cm) wide

£3,000-4,000   SK

An early 19thC English School watercolour-on-ivory portrait miniature of a gentleman, unsigned, in a gilt metal frame, the reverse enclosing a lock of hair set with three seed pearls.

3in (7.5cm) high

£300-400   **FRE**

A pair of English School portrait miniatures, depicting a man and woman dressed in black and seated by red drapery, framed.

c1830   *3.25in (8.5cm) high*

£250-350   **FRE**

An early 18thC oil on copper English School portrait miniature of a gentleman, unsigned.

2.75in (7cm) high

£1,300-1,600   **FRE**

An 18thC English School portrait miniature, 'Sir Francis Drake', unsigned, watercolour and gouache on vellum, with 'Sir F. Drake 1587'.

4.75in (12cm) high

£300-400   **FRE**

An American School portrait silhouette of William Merritt Chase, signed and dated 'M. P. Parker Fed. 28, 1906,' and inscribed by the sitter.

11.75in (30cm) high

£1,500-2,000   **FRE**

An American School portrait silhouette of Thomas Eakins, inscribed and signed 'My Dear Mrs. Parker many thanks for your skillful silhouette, Thomas Eakins,' framed.

c1905   *9in (23cm) high*

£3,000-4,000   **FRE**

A 19thC English School silhouette group, inscribed James Sword and Fancy, reverse-painted on glass, framed, verso with inscription, 'Harriet B. Buttrick' and printed framer's label, 'Samuel Jennings, Carver, Gilder and Printer Seller, London'.

c1840   *13in (33cm) wide*

£200-400   **FRE**

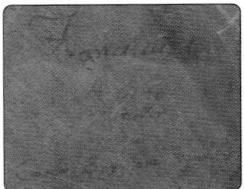

A pair of Continental wax portrait reliefs, probably depicting the King and Queen of Naples, dated and inscribed to the reverse 'Franciscus Pieri fecit', mounted and framed.

1756   *18.75in (47.5cm) wide overall*

£2,000-2,500   **DN**

SEALS

A Georgian multi-gem-set fob seal, with rose cut amethyst-set base, with entwined borders of oval cut rubies and rose cut diamonds.

1.5in (3.5cm) wide

£700-1,000   **L&T**

A late 18thC gold-mounted fob seal/locket, with cornelian inset base, inscribed 'SEMPRE' with miniature by A. Delatour.

Portrait 1in (2.5cm) long

£800-1,500   **L&T**

OBJETS DE VERTU

A 19thC blackamoor fob seal, the head carved from banded agate with an old cut diamond collar and surmount, on a gold base set with a cornelian intaglio carved with an armorial.

1.5in (4cm) high

£3,500-4,000   DN

A large 19thC glass wax seal, with simulated tooled surface, the base marked 'P.R.'.

4in (10cm) high

£250-350   FRE

A 19thC French ivory and silver wax seal, the seal inscribed with 'nec spe nec metu', seal base marked 'P.J.'.

4in (10cm) high

£300-400   FRE

A 19thC silver owl model wax seal, with green glass eyes, ebony and 'O.N/N.O' mark, marked '26, 5, 33'.

2.5in (6.5cm) high

£180-240   FRE

OTHER OBJETS DE VERTU

A late Victorian silver gilt chatelaine, by William Comyns, the clip suspending a pair of scissors with cast sheath (Chester 1896), an aide memoir (Birmingham 1896), a gilt-metal thimble case/pin cushion, and a needle case (Chester 1898).

10.5in (26.5cm) long

£450-650   L&T

A white metal-mounted agate-handled knife, with an impressed leather case.

5.5in (14cm) long

£400-600   L&T

A gentleman's travelling companion, the silver and fishskin case has several inscriptions and dates, including '1727', '1777' and '1875', the case encloses a pencil, toothpick, fruit knife, ear sprout, tweezers, and other items.

4in (10cm) high

£750-1,000   FRE

A Scottish provincial page turner, by Ferguson and Macbean, Inverness, marked 'F&M, camel, INVS', with 'Edinburgh 1896' marks, the handle formed from a roe deer antler, initialled 'R.C.R'.

18.75in (47.5cm) long

£500-700   L&T

A 19thC agate goblet, of campana form and with lobed decoration.

5.5in (14cm) high

£800-1,000   L&T

A 19thC Italian 'marmo giallo' marble tazza, in the Neoclassical style, the reeded bowl with twin scroll handles and lion mask motifs.

8in (20.5cm) wide

£1,800-2,400   L&T

A late 19thC Italian Grand Tour specimen marble pen tray, modelled as a Roman trough, underside bears hand written label dated '1823'.

6.75in (17cm) wide

£600-900   L&T

A 19thC near pair of Neoclassical style gilt-bronze and Sienna marble inkwells, one stamped 'Tiffany & Co.'.

Tallest 5in (12.5cm) high

£500-800   FRE

A novelty miniature gem-set moss agate dish, decorated with enamel, seed pearls and red stone.

4in (10cm) wide

£700-1,000   **L&T**

A pair of 18thC North Italian gilt-brass-framed scenic micro mosaic panels, depicting verdant cappriccio landscapes with temple follies and passing figures, within cavetto moulded frames with beaded inner slips.

6.75in (17cm) wide overall

£40,000-50,000 PAIR   **L&T**

A 19thC Italian micromosaic plaque, depicting St. Peter's Square, Rome.

11in (28cm) wide

£8,000-10,000   **FRE**

A late 19thC Italian silver and micromosaic crucifix, the cross inset with views of Rome and a silver figure of Christ, the reverse inscribed 'Roma' and dated.

1899   *7in (18cm) high*

£550-750   **FRE**

A 19thC King's bronze and ivory brush corkscrew, the ivory brush surmounts a bronze column base with patent label to front.

£350-450   **FRE**

A bronze, brass and timber corkscrew, barrel-shaped handle, brass screw, bronze barrel column base.

c1840   *6.5in (16.5cm) high*

£130-200   **FRE**

A 19thC Italian olivewood corkscrew, timber and iron, with a rectangular double handle grip.

8in (20.5cm) high

£250-350   **FRE**

A 19thC American horn and silver corkscrew, the shaped antler handle is applied with two silver mounts decorated to show vine leaves.

6.5in (16.5cm) high

£400-600   **FRE**

An American sand picture in a bottle, with ship Wm. H. Cook and patriotic eagle, by Andrew Clemens, McGregor, Iowa, dated.

Andrew Clemens was born in Dubuque, Iowa, in 1857. At the age of five he became deaf after a bout of encephalitis. He earned his livelihood by painstakingly arranging coloured sand with a few hand-made tools to make pictures in glass bottles.

1888   *6.75in (17cm) high*

£6,000-8,000   **SK**

A sand glass, with hand-blown glass, supported by three mahogany barley-twist columns, over three bun feet.

c1840   *15in (38cm) high*

£1,000-1,500   **FRE**

A pair of 19thC sand glasses, with hand-blown glass, one is tartanware, the other is of turned mahogany.

7in (18cm) high

£550-750   **FRE**

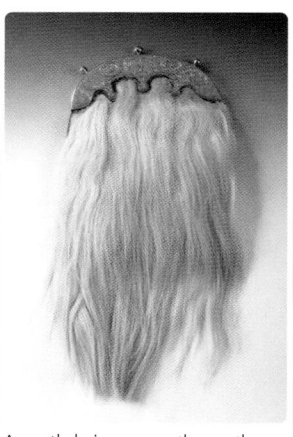

A goat's hair sporran, the cantle with motto 'MANU FORTI', with marks 'FERGUSON BROs/INVss', and marks for Inverness.

c1870.   *6.25in (16cm) wide*

£500-600   **L&T**

A Highland dress sporran, by Wilson and Sharp, Edinburgh, with long link sporran chain.

1928   *75in (20cm) long*

£1,100-1,500   **L&T**

A Victorian novelty purse, formed as a miniature sporran, chased as a horse hair sporran set with orange cabochons, the mounts unmarked.

3.75in (9.5cm) high

£500-600   **L&T**

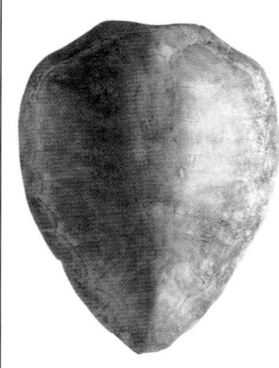

An early 19thC loggerhead 'blond' turtle shell.

36.5in (93cm) long

£3,000-4,000   **L&T**

A lion (*Panthera leo*) taxidermy specimen, head mount.

c1900

£200-300   **GIL**

A Nyala Antelope (*Tragelaphus angasii*) taxidermy specimen, shoulder mount facing right.

£200-300   **GIL**

A Zebra (*Equus quagga*) skin game rug.

£1,000-1,200   **GIL**

An early 20thC American gilt-painted metal money box, modelled after Independence Hall.

9in (23cm) high

£160-200   **FRE**

An early 20thC American rustic tree root frame, composed of gnarled and entwined tree roots applied to a rectangular wooden frame.

39x47in (99x119.5cm)

£2,500-3,000   **SK**

An early 20thC American tramp art double lamp, bank, and storage box.

28.25in (72cm) wide

£4,000-5,000   **SK**

An early 20thC American chip-carved tramp art footed box.

17.75in (45cm) high

£500-750   **SK**

A Regency papier-mâché and gilt-brass table coaster, the pierced wheels previously leathered, one with remains.

12.25in (31cm) wide

£1,500-2,000   **WW**

ESSENTIAL REFERENCE: FABERGÉ MARKS

A guilloché enamelled silver cigarette case, by Fabergé, hallmarked St. Petersburg, 88 standard, workmaster initials of August Hollming, Fabergé in Cyrillic and scratched inventory number '19334'.

c1912   *4.5in (11.5cm) long*

£35,000-45,000   **JACK**

A silver and guilloché enamel desk clock, by Fabergé, workmaster Henrik Wigstrom, scratched inventory number '25483', stamped with the workmaster's initials 'H.W.' and Fabergé in Cyrillic, hallmarked St Petersburg

1908-17   *4in (10cm) diam*

£60,000-80,000   **JACK**

Peter Carl Fabergé (1846-1920) was a Russian goldsmith and jeweller. He took over the family concern in 1870, which soon became the leading jewellers in St Petersberg, receiving the Imperial appointment in 1881.

Branches were later opened in Moscow (1887), Kiev (1907) and London (1906). At the height of its activity, Fabergé employed more than five hundred members of staff.

Motifs were usually inspired by the 18thC French style, though some later products are Art Nouveau in style.

A 20thC blue enamel and silver gilt pill box, with enamel over an engine-turned ground, two diamonds, the cover with a lapis lazuli panel and a further diamond, pseudo Fabergé marks.

1.25in (3cm) high

A Faberge enamel cigarette case, engine-turned ground, diamond-set thumb piece, and marked 'Faberge', work master Henrik Wigstrom, with workmaster's initials, 88 standard, with London import marks.

c1910   *3.25in (8cm) wide*

£14,000-18,000   **FRE**

£800-1,200   **FRE**

A Russian silver and enamel frame, with an engine-turned ground, surmounted ribbon-tied drapery set with a cabochon ruby, 88 standard, pseudo Fabergé marks, with leather case.

4.5in (11.5cm) high

£700-900   **FRE**

A small 20thC Russian silver enamel box, with pseudo Fabergé marks.

£1,300-1,600   *4in (10cm) wide*

A late 19thC Russian silver and enamel cigarette case, from St Petersburg, with foliate champlevé enamel, the lid centred by a view of St Petersburg, the reverse with birds.

4in (10cm) wide

£2,500-3,000   **FRE**

A Russian enamel silver brooch, maker's mark 'XN', designed as a ribbon garter, with applied dates '1877' and '1878', with imperial Queen's crown, with original box.

1.75in (4.5cm) long

£400-500 L&T

A Russian silver gilt and enamel kovsh, possibly by Iuka Khaimovich Lozinskii, modelled with a horse head handle, bearing assay mark for 'A. Romanov' Moscow.

1894 *5in (12.5cm) long*

£1,000-1,500 FRE

A matched set of six late 19thC Russian silver salts, with marks on five for St Petersburg, assay master A. Riktera, with stylised polychrome enamel decoration, each with a blue glass liner.

c1899-1903 *1.5in (3.5cm) wide*

£500-600 SET L&T

A late 19thC Russian spoon and maple spoon, work master MC, the bowl with champlevé enamel decoration, the maple spoon also with champlevé enamel, import marks for '1908'.

c1896-1908 Longest 8in (20.5cm) long

£600-800 L&T

CLOSER LOOK: CLOISSONÉ ENAMEL BOX

An early 20thC Russian silver scent bottle, decorated with purple guilloché enamel and gold, rubies and rose cut diamonds, the stopper with colourless stone.

3.5in (8.5cm) high

£3,000-4,000 L&T

The box is decorated with pan-Slavic motifs. The pan-Slavic revival was a mid-19thC movement based on the study of Russian history and a number of celebrated 17thC works of art.

Fedor Rückert was a Fabergé workmaster and his chief supplier of enamelwares. He was born in Moscow, of German origin, and made articles in Moscow in cloissoné enamel. Fabergé's Moscow signature often obliterates Ruckert's initials. Ruckert also sold his cloissoné objects independently, which explains why a number of his pieces bear no Fabergé signature.

A Russian silver gilt and cloisonné enamel box, with marks for Fedor Rückert, marked to the underside.

c1908-17 *2.75in (7cm) wide*

£75,000-100,000 L&T

Four Russian silver napkin rings, each with polychrome enamel-decorated floral designs, three with workmaster's mark of 'MC' and one 'H', import marks.

c1910 *2in (5cm) wide*

£1,800-2,200 L&T

A Russian silver enamelled miniature kovsch, with 'plique a jour' border and trefid handle, the plain exterior with traces of gilding, with control marks.

1908-1917 *3.75in (9.5cm) long*

£400-500 L&T

A Russian silver and cloisonné enamel-decorated salt, designed as a miniature throne with hinged lid to the seat.

5.75in (14.5cm) high

£2,500-3,000 L&T

A 20thC Russian silver gilt and enamel icon, depicting Christ with saints and apostles, beneath a silver gilt repoussé oklad.

12.25in (31cm) high

£450-650 FRE

A Russian silver gilt and enamel cased tête-â-tête, comprising two cups and saucers, a waste bowl with swing handle, two dishes, two spoons and a strainer, maker's mark in Cyrillic 'LFO', in a fitted case with a Soviet retailer's stamp to interior.

c1925 *Waste bowl 4.25in (11cm) diam*

£4,500-5,500 **FRE**

A cased set of twelve late 19thC Russian silver and enamel teaspoons, retailed by Samuel Kirk & Sons, Baltimore, 84 standard.

£1,500-2,000 **FRE**

A Russian silver gilt enamel cigarette case, by Khlebnikov, St Petersburg, with hinged lid and medallion portrait of Czar Alexander II, vesta case and strike.

1876 *4in (10cm) wide*

£8,500-10,500 **FRE**

A late 18thC/early 19thC Russian multi-panel icon, the central image of the Madonna and Child enthroned and encircled by twelve panels depicting scene from the life of Christ.

10in (25.5cm) wide

£900-1,200 **FRE**

SILVER

An early 20thC Russian silver-coloured tea glass holder, maker's mark 'EC' 84 Kokoshnik mark Moscow 1908-1917, with later .875 standard marks for Moscow.

1927-58

£150-250 **DN**

A 19thC Russian silver-coloured napkin ring, by Stephan Wakeva, possibly for Fabergé, 84 Zolotnik mark St Petersburg, maker's mark 'S.W.'

1896-99 *1.5in (4cm) high*

£250-300 **DN**

A late 19thC Russian silver-coloured tea glass holder, by Alexander Joseph Fuld, Cyrillic maker's mark 'A.F', later engraved in Cyrillic and dated 1925, 84 Zolotnik mark Moscow 1885.

£100-150 **DN**

A Russian silver-coloured cigarette and vesta case, with a concealed vesta case, maker's mark 'A.B.' (possibly Aron Berg), 84 Zolotnik mark.

post-1896 *4in (10cm) long*

£550-750 **DN**

A Russian silver cigarette case, marked '84, B.C. 1869', the gilt interior covered by a hinged lid, of rectangular form.

1869 *5in (12.5cm) wide*

£250-350 **FRE**

An early 20thC Russian niello silver cigarette case, the cover depicting a harness racer and horse.

3.75in (9.5cm) wide

£300-450 **FRE**

A Kasimir Malevich/State Porcelain Factory Russian porcelain plate, in abstract geometric 'suprematist' pattern, signed and dated on back.

1923   9.5in (24cm) diam

£3,500-5,500   SDR

A late 19thC Russian Kornilov St. Petersburg porcelain five-piece tea service, comprising a teapot, covered sugar bowl, creamer, cup and saucer, red factory mark to underside, blue factory mark to cup.

Teapot 4.5in (11.5cm) high

£500-700   FRE

A Russian Kuznetsov ceramic and silver-mounted bowl, the mounts by the Fabergé workshop, work master KV, St Petersburg pre-1899.

3.25in (8cm) diam

£2,200-2,500   L&T

A 19thC Russian lacquer box and cover, the cover painted with figures in a troika pulled by three horses.

5.25in (13.5cm) wide

£300-350   L&T

A 19thC Russian lacquer box and cover, the cover painted with figures in a troika pulled by three horses.

4.5in (11.5cm) diam

£200-300   L&T

A 19thC Russian lacquer box and cover, the cover painted with figures in a troika pulled by three horses.

3.5in (9cm) diam

£200-300   L&T

A Russian lacquer box, underside of the lid bears triple gilt imperial double eagle and Cyrillic inscription.

9.5in (24cm) wide

£700-1,000   L&T

An early 20thC Russian bronze figure group, light brown patina, modelled as a Cossack on horseback kissing a young lady farewell, signed indistinctly 'A.M. Bo**g**'.

10.5in (26.5cm) high

£3,000-3,500   FRE

A Russian bronze equestrian figure group, 'Charging Cossacks', medium brown patina, inscribed 'Cyrillic' and 'Fabr. C. F. Woerffel', on a black marble base.

17in (43cm) high

£3,000-3,500   FRE

A late 19thC bronze 'Pointer', after Nicolai-Ivanovitch Lieberich (Russian, 1828-1883), inscribed 'Lieberich' and with Fabr. CF. Woerffel foundry mark.

13.75in (35cm) long

£850-1,000   FRE

A first half 18thC brass six-light chandelier, with knopped stem and scrolling branches.

25.5in (67cm) wide

£1,800-2,200   DN

A late 18th/early 19thC painted and gilded wooden chandelier, with carved acorn terminals and medial reeded sphere, the arms with carved wooden bead and bud motifs, tin candlecups, red, green and gilt surface, paint losses.

41in (104cm) diam.

£9,000-12,000   SK

A 19thC carved giltwood electrolier, the leaf-knopped baluster decorated in the 'Renaissance' taste.

52.25in (133cm) high

£2,500-3,000   L&T

A 19thC French gilt brass six-branch electrolier, the central knopped stem issuing doves and pierced stiff branches with scroll brackets, the pineapple finial ends with polychrome-decorated shades.

33in (84cm) high

£500-700   WW

An early 20thC Empire style gilt-metal and cut glass electrolier.

27.5in (70cm) high

£1,500-2,000   DN

An American matched pair of tin four-arm candelabra.

c1800   *14.25in (36cm) high*

£2,000-3,000   POOK

A large six-light antler chandelier, formed from interlaced antlers.

63in (160cm) diam.

£1,500-2,000   L&T

An Edwardian brass and opaque glass twin-light billiards electrolier.

59in (150cm) high

£200-300   DN

LIGHTING

A Victorian octagonal bronze hall lantern, the pagoda-form top with a faceted bell-shaped corona, with a gadrooned apron with a pine cone finial.

31.5in (80cm) high

£3,500-4,500   **L&T**

A late 19thC Victorian wrought iron, stained and leaded glass lantern, one foot replaced.

25.25in (64cm) high

£200-300   **DN**

A bronze and gilt-bronze three-light hall lantern, in the manner of Osler, with trailing acanthus and berried finial uprights.

42.5in (108cm) high

£2,000-3,000   **L&T**

An early 20thC George III style gilt-brass and glazed hexagonal hall lantern.

23.25in (59cm) high

£900-1,200   **DN**

A set of six early 20thC brass and opaque glass hexagonal-section lanterns, in the Gothic style.

43.25in (110cm) high

£1,500-2,000 SET   **DN**

A pair of early 20thC George III style brass hexagonal-section hall lanterns, later replaced Perspex panes.

32in (81cm) high

£3,000-3,500 PAIR   **DN**

A set of three 20thC glass hanging lanterns.

18in (46cm) high

£650-850 SET   **DN**

WALL LIGHTS

A pair of French pagoda-shaped 'bird-cage' lanterns, with strands of faceted glass beads.

The overall design closely resembles decorative ceiling lights made by the Parisian firm of Bagues in the 1930s and thereafter.

c1950

33.5in (85cm.) high

£30,000-40,000 PAIR   **PAR**

A pair of George III giltwood girandoles, in the Chippendale style, the shaped divided plates within ornate Rococo scroll-carved frames, surmounted by stylised ho-ho birds.

57in (144.5cm) high

£35,000-50,000   **L&T**

A pair of 19thC brass wall candelabra, cast in Rococo style.

14in (35.5cm) high

£600-800 **FRE**

A pair of Victorian gilt-brass three-branch wall lights, in Gothic taste.

10.25in (26cm) high

£300-500 PAIR **WW**

A pair of 19thC Continental Louis XV style gilt-bronze three-light wall appliqués.

20in (51cm) high

£400-600 PAIR **DN**

A pair of late 19thC American gilt-bronze three-light wall sconces.

20in (51cm) high

£300-400 **FRE**

A pair of 20thC Continental gilt-metal twin-light wall appliqués, each with urn-cast sockets above drip pans.

10in (25.5cm) wide

£600-800 **DN**

A set of two pairs of early 20thC Louis XV style gilt-metal twin-light wall appliqués.

The larger pair 17.25in (44cm) high

£400-600 **DN**

One of a suite of twelve early 20thC gilt-metal wall appliques, each cast with twin scrolling branches supported by a mythical winged and crowned figure on a scrolled fish-tail support, with moulded flame-glass shades.

£5,000-6,000 SET **L&T**

A pair of early 20thC French bronze four-light figural wall appliqués, cast as a male and female Bacchante.

17.75in (45cm) wide

£5,000-6,000 **DN**

SILVER CANDLESTICKS

A pair of late George II cast silver hexafoil candlesticks, by James Gould, London, engraved with armorials, the nozzles unmarked, 42oz (1309g).

1750 *9.25in (23.5cm) high*

£2,000-2,500 **DN**

A set of four late George II cast silver Rococo candlesticks, by John Pollock, London, the bases each with a cartouche engraved with an armorial, 90oz (2797g).

1753 *10.75in (27.5cm) high*

£5,000-7,000 **DN**

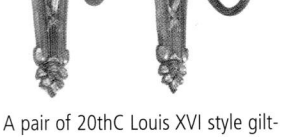

A pair of second quarter 20thC Italian wirework and carved giltwood twin-light wall appliqués, modelled with rising ears of wheat.

18.5in (47cm) high

£300-500 **DN**

A pair of 20thC Louis XVI style gilt-metal wall appliqués.

11.5in (29cm) high

£100-150 **DN**

A pair of mid-18thC Augsburg silver candlesticks, with scalloped bases.

6.75in (17cm) high

£1,800-2,200 **POOK**

A pair of George III silver candlesticks, by John Carter II, London, engraved with a castle crest, loaded.

1768   10.25in (26cm) high
£1,200-1,500 PAIR   DN

A pair of George III cast silver table candlesticks, London, William Cafe.

1774   7.75in (20cm) high
£3,000-4,000   L&T

A pair of William IV silver shaped circular candlesticks, by Hy. Wilkinson & Co., Sheffield, with scroll and leaf outline acanthus knops and capitals, loaded.

1836   8in (20cm) high
£400-500 PAIR   DN

A pair of Polish silver repoussé Sabbath candlesticks, stamped '84 standard', makers mark 'ZM', assay mark 'AT'.

1887   15.25cm (39cm) high
£1,000-1,500   FRE

A pair of Louis XV style gilt-bronze five-light candelabra.

c1890   23.5in (59.5cm) high
£1,800-2,200   FRE

A set of four Victorian sterling silver candlesticks, Hawksworth, Eyre & Co., Ltd, Sheffield, each with columnar standard and Corinthian capital.

1891   7in (18cm) high
£1,200-1,600 SET   FRE

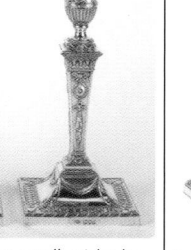

A pair of Victorian candlesticks, by Gold & Silversmiths Co., Ltd, of Classical form with urn-shaped nozzles, swag and paterae square-tapered stems, filled, engraved with inscription 'St. M.T.C. Grand National – 1st Prize, 1900', London.

1899   9.25in (23.5cm) high
£500-700   A&G

A pair of silver square candlesticks, by Hawksworth, Eyre & Co. Ltd. Sheffield, embossed in the Adam style with urns, stiff leaves, oval pendants and rams' masks, loaded.

1905   8.5in (21.5cm) high
£650-850   DN

A pair of silver candlesticks, in George II style, by Fordham & Faulkner, Sheffield, loaded.

1914   9.25in (23.5cm) high
£350-450   DN

A pair of 20thC Continental silver lion-form Sabbath candlesticks, the bases with reserves of Old Testament scenes and applied with frogs and beetles.

7.5in (19cm) high
£800-1,200   FRE

A pair of German silver five-light four-branch candelabra in late 17thC style, import marked for London. 93.25oz (2905g).

1945   12.25in (31cm) high
£3,500-4,000   DN

A pair of silver hexagonal two-branch candelabra, by Richard Comyns, London, 55.5oz (731oz).

1972   10.75in (27cm) high
£1,500-2,000   DN

A Gothic three-knop brass candlestick, retaining old desirable verdigris patination.

c1450

£4,000-5,000   **POOK**

A mid-drip brass candlestick, with 'great bell' base.

c1540   *11in (28cm) high*

£7,000-9,000   **POOK**

A mid-17thC Dutch brass 'Heemskirk' candlestick.

9in (23cm) high

£550-750   **DN**

A first half 18thC Scandinavian copper alloy hexagonal candlestick, later elements.

9.5in (24cm) high

£300-400   **DN**

A pair of Louis XV brass candlesticks.

c1750   *10.25in (26cm) high*

£200-250   **DN**

A pair of German brass pricket candlesticks, inscribed 'Thomas Henning ver Ehret dise Leuchter, Ao:1762 no Aprilis',

1762   *19in (48.5cm) high*

£1,500-2,000   **DN**

A pair of 18thC turned brass candlesticks, with serpentine edged bases.

5.5in (14cm) high

£220-280   **WW**

An American brass, copper and iron gimballed fat lamp, by Peter Derr, Pennsylvania, impressed 'P.D. 1843'.

10.75in (27.5cm) high

£4,500-5,500   **POOK**

A pair of late 19thC Elkington & Co gilt-brass lustre candlesticks, in Grecian taste, fitted for electricity.

9in (23cm) high

£400-500   **DN**

A pair of Victorian brass altar candlesticks, the knopped stems with coloured glass prunts.

24.25in (61.5cm) high

£550-750   **WW**

A pair of late 18thC painted and parcel giltwood and composition candle holders, modelled with standing amorini, chips and losses.

12.5in (32cm) high

£100-150 DN

A pair of Regency bronze lustre candlesticks, with urns issuing anthemion pierced fronds hung with faceted glass drops, each on three monopaedic eagle mask supports.

34cm high c1815

£1,000-1,500 L&T

A pair of Regency patinated and gilt bronze candlesticks, cast as urns on dolphin stems.

5.75in (14.5cm) high

£300-400 DN

A pair of early 19thC Chinese pewter prickets, impressed mark.

11in (28cm) high

£300-400 FRE

A pair of second quarter 19thC Restoration gilt and patinated bronze lustre candlesticks, hung with glass pendants.

£300-400 DN

A pair of 19thC French bronze candlesticks in the Empire taste, the drip pans hung with faceted drops and upheld by Egyptian male figures, with circular rouge marble bases.

9.5in (24cm) high

£600-800 L&T

A pair of 19thC Louis XV style gilt-bronze and Chinese porcelain candelabra, with turquoise glaze figures, on Rococo bases.

10in (25.5cm) high

£2,000-3,000 FRE

A pair of French Empire bronze and gilt-bronze twin-handled metamorphic candlesticks, each with reversible cover, mounted with griffin finial and to the reverse with flowerhead nozzle, raised above an urn with elephant handles.

15in (38cm) high

£5,500-7,500 L&T.

A pair of late 19thC bronze cassolettes, in the form of urns on stands, the domed lids with fir cone finials above ram's head-decorated bodies on triform chain-hung stands with hoof feet.

12.25in (31cm) high

£900-1,200 L&T

A pair of last quarter 19thC French gilt-bronze and 'marmo rouge' griotte mounted twin-light candelabra.

9.5in (24cm) high

£350-450 DN

A pair of 19thC French three-branched candelabra, each modelled as a cherub holding a cornucopia of flowers.

17.25in (44cm) high

£800-1,000   L&T.

Two Empire style bronze and brass candlesticks, modelled as Grecian male and female figures holding torchères.

22.25in (56cm) high

£900-1,200   L&T

A late 19thC pair of French Empire bronze candelabra, with stems formed as Classical maidens, each on marble bases.

17in (43cm) high

£1,000-1,500   FRE

A pair of late 19thC Continental gilt and patinated bronze candlesticks, on green serpentine marble bases.

9.75in (24.5cm) high

£180-220   DN

A pair of late 19thC Louis XV style gilt-bronze twin-light candelabra, cast as scrolling foliage.

13in (33cm) wide

£350-500   DN

An early 20thC French parcel silvered and gilt-bronze three-light candelabrum, the triform base with three addorsed swans.

18in (46cm) high

£220-300   DN

An 18thC Italian carved walnut altar candlestick, with later electrical fitment.

27.5 in (70cm) high

£250-300   DN

A pair of late 17th/early 18thC Italian carved wood, silver and gilt gesso floor standing candlesticks.

68.25in (173.5cm) high

£2,000-3,000   HALL

A pair of French gilt and patinated bronze six-light candelabra, now mounted as lamps.

c1825   *29.5in (75cm) high*

£1,800-2,400   FRE

A pair of 19thC turned oak pricket candlesticks.

27.5in (70cm) high

£450-550   DN

CLOSER LOOK: REGENCY CANDELABRA

Colza lamps were hugely in demand before the dawn of electricity and were subsequently redundant, unless reutilised for electric light.

The upper section is based upon a large two-handled vase and cover acting as the reservoir for the Colza oil used to feed the lamps and utilising the fluted ormolu arms as conduits to the glass-shaded burners.

The arms are embellished with lotus leaves and the vases have acanthus mounts. These reflect the knulling of the bases and the lotus flower finials of the tops, typifying the Neoclassical inspiration of the lights.

The tops of the tripod bases have a circular concave frieze with a running border of florettes and acanthus leaves above a reversed finial with knulled decoration centred by an ormolu knop. The bases reflect this device.

The distinctive design is one often used in Neoclassical schemes, but the detailing reflects the more robust revival of interest in the antique seen in the works of Thomas Hope and George Smith and popularised by Ackermann's widely circulated designs.

In the ancient world cranes represented fidelity and were messengers of the gods. Here, they may be taken from a family crest.

James Smethurst existed for some time as a purveyor of fine furnishings, adding '& Co' to the name of his business after 1814.

Each tripod base has three tapering moulded supports with circular stepped bases and with rams' heads to the top and lion paw feet.

A rare pair of Regency bronze and ormolu three-light candelabra, label of James Smethurst, 138 New Bond Street, consisting of detachable upper lights, which sit upon bronze circular tops with tripod bases.

c1810

£180,000-200,000

72in (183 cm)

PAR

A 19thC bronze Egyptianesque Colza oil lamp, with flaming finial and coiled serpent-mask handle, the bowl cast with a Pharaoh mask, adapted for electricity.

15.25in (35cm) wide

£1,200-1,500   L&T

A pair of Egyptianesque bronze and ormolu Colza oil lamps, probably by William Bullock, with fluted socles and triform platforms with winged monopaedic chimera corner ornaments.

19.75in (50cm) high

£3,000-4,000   L&T

A pair of French Empire bronze and ormolu candelabra, the green-veined marble bases with ormolu mounts, each now with two electric lights.

c1815

£45,000-50,000   PAR

A French Empire period gilt and patinated bronze lamp, the reeded and leaf-cast column raised on a square base with applied mounts, fitted for electricity.

37.75in (96cm) high

£2,500-3,000   L&T

A pair of Charles X gilt and patinated bronze lamps, the reeded columns raised on triform bases with applied swan mounts, fitted for electricity.

21.5in (54.5cm) high

£5,000-6,000   L&T

A mid 19thC Continental painted and parcel-gilt porcelain twin-handled vase, later adapted as a table lamp.

17in (43cm) high

£550-650   DN

A pair of 19thC gilt and patinated bronze lamps, formed as Roman oil lamps, with seated figures depicting 'L'Etude' & 'Philosophie', on square green marble bases.

13.75in (35cm) high

£4,000-5,000   FRE

A pair of 19thC Louis XVI style gilt-bronze mounted 'sang du boeuf' urns, the upright leaf-cast handles ending in female masks, now mounted as lamps.

Urn 17in (43cm) high

£6,500-8,500   FRE

A pair of Chinese famille rose vases, decorated with warriors and nobles in mountainous landscapes, converted to lamps.

32.25in (82cm) high

£3,000-4,000   L&T

A late 19thC Louis XVI style gilt and patinated bronze lamp, with urn-form spiral fluted body supported by three female caryatids.

19in (48cm) high

£1,500-2,500   FRE

A pair of late Victorian gilt-brass table lamps, in the Gothic taste, the knopped and leaf-cast stems on cinquefoil pierced triple leaf-form bases, adapted and wired for electricity.

36.5in (93cm) high

£4,000-5,000   L&T

A pair of French Empire style gilt and patinated metal storm lamps, the glass shades raised by three cabriole supports surmounted by swan finials.

18in (46cm) high

£2,200-2,800   L&T

A late 19thC Elkington silvered metal centrepiece adapted as a table lamp, with three addorsed sphinxes.

12.25in (31cm) high

£180-240   DN

A late 19thC brass table oil lamp, with four adorned columns above a plinth with seated hounds, with later electrical fitments.

22in (56cm) high

£850-1,100   DN

A brass and decorated glass table oil lamp.

c1900   31in (79cm) high including shade

£170-200   DN

A pair of Louis XVI style marble and gilt-bronze-mounted lamps, the stems surmounted by palmette-form fittings and applied with lion mask motifs.

37.5in (95cm) high

£3,000-4,000   L&T

A pair of bronze and gilt-bronze lamps, modelled as figures of the Duke of Wellington and Napoleon, wired for electricity.

26.5in (67cm) high

£1,700-2,200   L&T

A pair of early 20thC carved and painted wood figures of Nubian women, now adapted as lamp bases.

38.25in (97cm) high

£1,000-1,400   L&T

A pair of 20thC gilt and patinated metal table lamps in the Restoration style, each with faux oil burner above a faceted glass reservoir.

26.5in (67cm) high overall

£900-1,200   DN

An early 18thC oak fire surround, the moulded overhanging cornice on ring-turned straight baluster supports above a back composed of fielded panels, above a rectangular mantel shelf, on panelled jambs, adapted.

72in (183cm) wide

£1,200-1,700   **L&T**

A late 18th/early 19thC carved pine and gesso chimneypiece, in the Adam style.

73.25in (186cm) wide overall

£1,700-2,000   **DN**

A Regency or George IV cast iron hobgrate, with foliate cast cresting and uprights.

c1820

£500-750   **DN**

A rare California Clay Products (CALCO) fireplace surround, composed of thirty-nine tiles embossed with Mayan warriors and glyphs.

1920s   *44in (112cm) high*

£1,500-2,000   **DRA**

A George III engraved brass and iron firegrate.

c1780 and later   *32.25in (82cm) wide*

£3,500-4,500   **DN**

A Regency cast iron fire basket, of urn form with loop handles, hung with drapery above an ash drawer.

32in (53.5cm) wide

£1,500-2,000   **FRE**

A William IV iron fire basket, with cast brass mounts, over a rope twist border of four leaf-moulded ball feet.

26in (66cm) wide

£2,500-3,000   **HALL**

A late Victorian cast iron and brass fire grate, with a fan cresting and serpentine front with urn finials.

32.75in (83cm) wide

£600-1,000   **WW**

A 20thC cast iron and brass mounted fire grate, the basket with arched backplate and twin urn finials at the front.

22.75in (58cm) wide

£450-650   **DN**

A George III polished steel bowfront fender.

50in (127cm) wide

£700-900   **WW**

A Victorian pierced brass fender.

46in (117cm) wide

£120-150   **WW**

A late 19thC Louis XVI style French gilt bronze adjustable fender, with swagged spirally fluted urns and flambeau finials.

13.75in (35cm) wide

£450-550   **DN**

A set of six 19thC brass fenders of varying design, damage.

Longest 49in (124cm)

£300-400   DN

A late 19thC Régence style silvered fireplace suite, comprising a pair of urn-form chenets with flame finials and scroll bracket feet, a similar pierced fender, and a three piece fire tool set.

60.5in (153.5cm) wide

£6,500-7,500   FRE

A 19thC brass and wirework fender, with turned steel implement rests.

40.75in (103cm) wide

£200-250   WW

A steel fender, by Sir Robert Lorimer, with scrolling hinged sides, the angles with ball finials above leaf-shaped pad feet.

43in (109cm) wide

£1,800-2,200   L&T

An early 20thC brassclub fender.

64.5in (164cm) wide

£400-500   HALL

A rare pair of New York Federal brass andirons, from the workshop of Richard Wittingham, with ball and finial terminals, with classically engraved plinths.

c1810   *21.75in (55cm) high*

£4,000-5,000   **POOK**

A pair of brass andirons, of a Neoclassical form.

c1820-1840   *12in (30.5cm) high*

£300-600   **FRE**

A pair of wrought iron andirons, the fronts with flattened disc finials.

14.75in (37.5cm) high

£110-140   **WW**

A late 19thC pair of continental gilt metal and cast iron mounted chenets, each with a cloaked putto beside a brazier.

8.75in (22cm) high

£300-400   **DN**

A pair of late 19thC gilt metal chenets, in the Neoclassical style, each with swagged urn above a frieze.

£300-400   **DN**

A late 19thC Louis XV style gilt-bronze fire screen and chenets, of ornate Rococo form.

Fire screen 31in (78.5cm) high

£1,700-2,000   **FRE**

A late 19thC Louis XV style pair of French patinated and gilt-bronze chenets.

13.5in (34cm) wide

£1,200-1,600   **DN**

A pair of late 19thC Victorian cast iron andirons, the uprights cast as the Duke of Wellington.

16.25in (41cm) high

£350-450   **DN**

A pair of firedogs, in the manner of Ernest Gimson, each with cut out circular rosettes, chased with flowering foliage above a pierced panel below on wrought iron stand.

25.25in (64cm) high

£1,000-1,500   **L&T**

A pair of American Roycroft style andirons, made of black enamelled curled elements, complete with cross-bar, unmarked.

Provenance: From the living room at Vancroft, the Wellsburg, W.Va., home designed by the Pittsburgh architects Alden and Harlow and built at a cost of more than $1,000,000 as a hunting lodge for Joseph B. Vandergrift in 1901.

c1901   *36.5in (92.5cm) high*

£1,400-1,800   **CRA**

A rare pair of Roycroft andirons, made of black enamelled curled elements with twisted rings, large orb-and-cross incorporated in design.

c1901   *31in (78.5cm) high*

£3,500-4,500   **DRA**

A pair of American painted fire irons, the iron terminating in a painted iron model of a duck's head, some losses.

c1920   *12in (30.5cm) high*

£750-1,000   **FRE**

An 18thC Northern Europe wrought iron trammell, or 'chimney crane', with a line of ratchet teeth to one side supporting an adjustable arm with mounting ring above an overscrolled pot hook at the lower end, the lever handle with embossed brass collar, with inscription 'WAM/ACNK/ELVET/ANNO 1790'.

94cm high

£600-800   L&T

A late 19thC New York State North Wind face-carved wood, iron, and leather bellows, impressed 'W.R. PRIES 433 CANAL OF N.Y.'.

32.5in (82.5cm) high on stand

£3,500-4,500   SK

A Victorian cast iron doorstop, modelled as a standing elephant.

10in (25cm) long

£500-800   L&T

A pair of late 19thC Victorian painted iron door porters, cast as Punch and Judy.

11.75in (30cm) high

£150-200   DN

An American Central Pennsylvania painted pine fireboard, decorated with angels, tulips and birds.

The source of the decoration comes from the same printed fraktur which inspired the furniture of the Mahantongo Valley.

c1900

61in (155cm) wide

£5,000-6,000   POOK

An American cast iron 'Wedding Dance' stove plate, dated.

1746

26in (66cm) high

£1,300-1,600   POOK

An American Portsmouth, New Hampshire painted leather fire bucket, inscribed 'No2', with the name 'G.K. Haswell F.F.S' (Federal Fire Society) enclosing the date.

1789   *11.75in (30cm) high*

£2,500-3,500   POOK

A George III mahogany and brass banded peat bucket, of navette form, with brass swing handle and liner.

14.5in (37cm) wide

£3,000-4,000   L&T

A pair of late 19th/early 20thC copper and brass log buckets.

15in (38cm) diam

£400-500 PAIR   DN

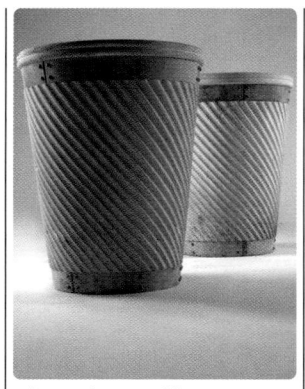

A late 20thC pair of limestone peat bucket planters, of spirally reeded tapering form, each with a bronze bound frieze and base.

26in (66cm) high

£3,000-4,000   **L&T**

CLOSER LOOK: CAST IRON URNS

Each urn would originally have stood upon a cast iron stove with a door to the front to allow coals to be inserted and lit and a vented tray at the bottom to allow a controlled input of oxygen and to collect the spent ash. The urn, while adding a classically decorative element to an otherwise utilitarian article, also assisted in the radiation of heat and incorporated a vent pipe at the rear which would have led out through the wall of the room to a chimney or directly to the outside of the building. The size, elaborate detail and obvious cost of such stoves would only allow their installation in the grandest of houses of the period and as such they are extremely rare.

The body is decorated with a pair of mythical bearded masks united by trailing swags of flowers and a fluted border.

The lower section has conforming cast leaf decoration.

These urns correspond very closely to a pen and grey wash manuscript design in a volume of drawings amongst the Carron papers at the Scottish Record Office with exactly the same dimensions, allowing a confident attribution to the Carron Iron Co, Falkirk, Scotland.

One of a pair of cast irons urns of Classical inspiration, the lids with cast leaf decoration topped by a flame finial, on a flared socle and squared plinth.
c1780.   *39in (99cm) high*

£20,000-25,000 PAIR   **RGA**

A pair of modern cast iron Versailles style garden planters, with 'fish scale' side panels on four lotus cast uprights with pineapple finials, green painted.

24.75in (63cm) wide

£2,500-3,500   **L&T**

A Regency cast iron garden bench, the back with reeded lozenge trellis splats with bifurcated outscrolling terminals.

60in (153cm) wide

£1,800-2,400   **L&T**

A French suite of faux bois furniture.
c1930   *Table 42in (106.5cm) diam*

£900-1,200   **POOK**

A pair of late 20thC limestone garden benches.

59in (150cm) wide

£2,000-2,500 PAIR   **L&T**

An American Gothic Revival cast iron birdhouse, marked 'Miller Iron Works Providence R.I.' and modelled on a house in Roslyn Harbour, NY.
c1868   14in (35.5cm) wide

£900-1,200   **POOK**

A large 19thC cast iron figural fountain, in the form of a female water carrier, formerly painted.

64.25in (163cm) high

£4,500-5,500   **L&T**

A Victorian cast iron and painted model of a greyhound by Coalbrookdale, indistinctly marked to cartouche base, 'B. DALE...', rear with patent lozenge, formerly part of a large item.

19in (48cm) high

£2,000-2,500 **L&T**

A late 19thC patinated bronze garden fountain, cast as a nubian youth holding aloft a water lily flower stem, the base cast with water lily leaves.

21.25in (54cm) high

£500-800 **L&T**

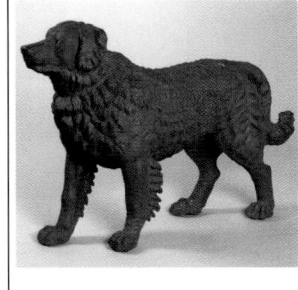

A late 19thC American cast iron Newfoundland dog garden ornament, in the full round, painted dark grey.

54.5in (138.5cm) long

£30,000-35,000 **SK**

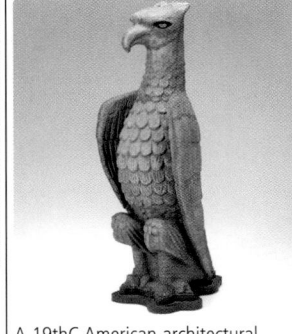

A 19thC American architectural model of an eagle, standing over a black painted plinth base.

33in (84cm) high

£800-1,000 **FRE**

A late 19thC Victorian foliate cast iron finial, cast in two halves.

37.5in (95cm) high

£200-300 **DN**

A pair of early 20thC lead models of putti, emblematic of Spring and Summer.

25.5in (65cm) high

£900-1,200 **DN**

MARBLE

A pair of 19thC Cornish marble sphinx, attributed to the London Serpentine Company.

28in (71cm) wide

£1,200-1,800 **L&T**

A pair of carved Travertine marble sphinxes.

35.25in (89.5cm) wide

£900-1,200 **FRE**

A pair of 19thC Louis XV style gilt-bronze mounted marble urns on pedestals, each of campana form with an oak leaf carved rim with an egg and dart collar, the handles cast with grotesque masks.

57in (145cm) high

£30,000-35,000 **FRE**

A pair of Louis XVI style gilt-bronze and moulded glass pedestals, each with a circular green marble top upon a faceted standard and leaf-cast shaped square base.

39.5in (100cm) high

£2,200-2,800 **FRE**

A pair of Empire style gilt-bronze mounted porphyry pedestals and urns, each urn with a rim cast with bacchic vines above two handles cast as swans, the base cast with rinceaux and medallions.

66in (167.5cm) high

£13,000-16,000 **FRE**

A 19thC specimen marble pedestal, the square top with a cylindrical column support and moulded square base.

44in (111.5cm) high

£1,100-1,500 **L&T**

An Afshar rug, the zigzag field with eleven polychrome lozenge medallions, within cream cartouche border between multiple bands.

74.75in (190cm) long

£350-450   **L&T**

A late 19thC Bakshaish carpet, north Persia.

206in (523cm) long

£10,000-12,000   **FRE**

A large Bakshaish carpet, the camel field with all-over rosette, lozenge and serrated leaf pattern, within blue turtle palmette border, worn.

244in (620cm) long

£3,000-4,000   **L&T**

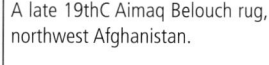

A late 19thC Aimaq Belouch rug, northwest Afghanistan.

89in (226cm) long

£500-600   **FRE**

A Bidjar carpet, the crimson field with all-over palmette, rosette and foliate lattice, within indigo turtle palmette and angular vine border between camel and blue bands.

145in (368cm) long

£2,500-3,000   **L&T**

A large Fereghan carpet, the indigo field with all-over herati pattern, brick-red turtle palmette and vine border between blue bands.

244in (620cm) long

£5,500-6,500   **L&T**

A Hamadan carpet, west Persia.

c1920-30   *120in (305cm) long*

£1,200-1,500   **FRE**

A Hamadan carpet, west Persia.

c1920   *208in (528.5cm) long*

£3,500-4,500   **FRE**

A Persian Heriz room-size rug, with medallion, in tones of red.

c1970   *146in (371.5cm) long*

£450-650   **DRA**

A Heriz carpet, the red field with central indigo and ivory medallion suspending pendants, ivory and red spandrels, within indigo rosette and leafy vine border between blue, red and yellow bands.

148.5in (377cm) long

£900-1,200   **L&T**

A Heriz carpet, the red field with central indigo and red medallion suspending pendants, ivory and red spandrels, within indigo turtle palmette and vine border between red and cream bands.

129in (328cm) long

£550-750   **L&T**

A Heriz rug, with a blue medallion on a red field with navy border.
c1920   *68in (173cm) long*
£1,500-2,000   **POOK**

A Heriz room-size rug, with central medallion on a red field with navy border.

The town of Heriz to the north-east of Tabriz, produces distinctive carpets with patterns based on formal town designs.

Both all-over and medallion designs are woven.

Heriz carpets are characterised by their angular rendering of the design elements. The medallions are often star-like in form.

c1930   *134in (340.5cm) long*
£1,400-1,800   **POOK**

An Isfahan carpet, the ivory field with central red and blue medallion suspending pendants, within red palmette and leafy vine border between indigo and ivory bands.
216in (550cm) long
£3,000-4,000   **L&T**

A Persian Kashan rug, with floral pattern in rose tones, some areas of wear.
c1910   *82in (208cm) long*
£500-600   **DRA**

A Kashan carpet, central Persia.
c1920   *165in (419cm) long*
£2,200-2,800   **FRE**

A Kashan carpet, central Persia.
c1920   *157in (399cm) long*
£3,000-4,000   **FRE**

A late 19thC Kashan silk prayer rug, central Persia.
81in (205.5cm) long
£3,000-4,000   **FRE**

A silk Kashan prayer rug, the ivory field with claret vase issuing tree-of-life pattern, claret spandrels, within claret palmette and floral border between peach and light blue bands.
79.5in (202cm) long
£1,500-2,000   **L&T**

A Kashan silk rug, the ochre field centred by an urn issuing a spray of flowers, within navy spandrels, conforming border and guard stripes.
82in (208cm) wide
£2,000-2,500   **DN**

A Kashan prayer rug, the indigo field with floral tree-of-life-pattern, red spandrels, within indigo floral cartouche border between cream bands.
77in (196cm) long
£1,000-1,400   **L&T**

A Kashan part-silk prayer rug.

92.5in (235cm) long
£300-400   **DN**

TEXTILES

A Kashan silk rug.

78in (198cm) long

£2,600-3,000   DN

A Lavar Kerman room-size rug, with central medallion and floral pattern.

c1910   108in (274.5cm) long

£4,000-5,000   POOK

A Kerman carpet, southeast Persia, with 'JERREHIAN BROTHERS' printed cloth label on back of carpet at each end.

c1930-40   240in (609.5cm) long

£4,000-4,500   FRE

A Persian Kerman palace-sized carpet, hand-woven wool with all-over stylised florals on a burgundy ground.

1940s   266in (675.5cm) long

£9,000-12,000   JACK

A late 19thC Kurdish long rug, northwest Persia.

109in (277cm) long

£500-750   FRE

A mid-19thC Kurdish rug, northwest Persia.

69in (175.5cm) long

£1,000-1,500   FRE

A Persian Mahal carpet, the red field with all-over palmette and vine lattice.

149.5in (380cm) long

£1,000-1,300   L&T

A Mahal rug, northwest Persia.

1930s   84in (213cm) long

£200-300   WW

A Qashqai carpet, the indigo field with three ivory and red hooked lozenge medallions, red spandrels, within ivory palmette and scrolling vine border between red and blue bands.

107.5in (273cm) long

£900-1,100   L&T

A Qashqai rug, the plain brown field with central ivory medallion, plain indigo spandrels with inscription to each end.
These rugs are produced in Fars province, Southwestern Persia.

86.5 in (220cm) long

£500-750   L&T

A Sarouk rug, west Persia, Mahajeran type design.

c1920   91in (231cm) long

£1,600-2,000   FRE

A Sarouk carpet, west Persia.

c1930-40   248in (630cm) long

£1,500-2,000   FRE

A late 19thC Sarouk Fereghan carpet, west Persia.

155in (393.5cm) long

£4,000-5,000   **FRE**

A Sarouk Fereghan rug, the rose field with central ivory stepped lozenge medallion suspending pendants, within shaped indigo palmette and floral vine border with outer rose band.

85.75in (218cm) long

£2,400-2,800   **L&T**

A late 19thC Serapi carpet, northwest Persia.

138in (350.5cm) long

£2,500-3,000   **FRE**

A Serapi runner, the red field with five indigo linked elongated lozenge medallions, within blue, cream and red stylised vine borders.

154.25in (392cm) long

£700-900   **L&T**

A Serapi rug, with central medallion on an ivory field with blue corners and red border.

c1910   *78in (198cm) long*

£5,000-6,000   **POOK**

A Shahsevan kelim, the indigo field with all-over pattern of polychrome serrated hexagons.

135.75in (345cm) long

£1,000-1,500   **L&T**

A Shiraz carpet, southwest Persia.

1940s   *111in (282cm) long*

£250-300   **WW**

A Tabriz carpet, northwest Persia.

c1900   *171in (434.5cm) long*

£3,500-4,000   **FRE**

An early 20thC Tabriz rug, northwest Persia, outer end of rug with a linen border with woven inscription: 'JERREHIAN BROTHERS/RUGS OF QUALITY'.

83in (211cm) long

£1,500-2,000   **FRE**

A late 19thC Tabriz silk prayer rug, northwest Persia.

64in (162.5cm) long

£3,000-4,000   **FRE**

A late 19thC Tabriz silk prayer rug, northwest Persia.

68in (172.5cm) long

£4,000-5,000   **FRE**

TEXTILES

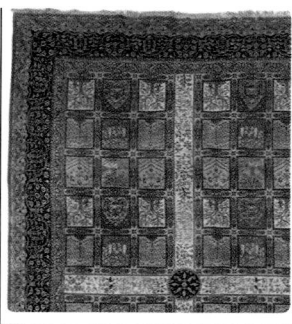

A large Tabriz style garden carpet, the cruciform field with central foliate roundel and fifteen rectangular tree and vase panels to each quarter, within indigo scrolling floral vine border between palmette bands.

240in (610cm) long

£2,500-3,500   L&T

A large Tabriz carpet, the rose field with all-over pattern of palmettes, flowers, vine and strapwork, within café-au-lait cartouche and floral vine border between green bands.

236.25in (600cm) long

£12,000-15,000   L&T

ESSENTIAL REFERENCE: TABRIZ

Following the Safavid conquest of Persia (now Iran), four royal workshops for weaving carpets and textiles were established in Kashan, Kerman, Isfahan (now Esfahan) and Tabriz. These grew into the four great centres of production.

- The earliest Persian carpets, produced in the 15th/16thC, are associated with Tabriz.
- Tabriz rugs generally use the symmetric (Turkish) knot.
- Tabriz designs are the most diverse in Persia, including a wide variety of curvilinear and geometric patterns. These include several variations of the medallion-and-corner design, panelled garden, vase, hunting, pictorial, etc.
- The palette of Tabriz rugs is also extremely varied, including very vivid and pastel colours.

A Persian Tabriz room-size rug with central medallion, in tones of red.

c1970

£700-1,000

150in (381cm) long

DRA

An unusual Persian Tehran Masonic rug, the plain cream field woven with central masonic devices and inscribed 'Lodge of Teheran 1541' in Persian above and English below.

41.75in (106cm) long

£550-750   L&T

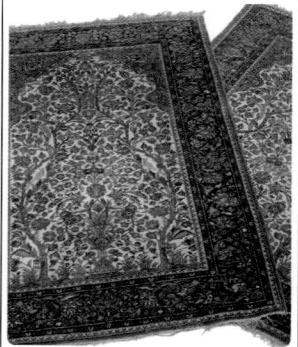

A pair of Tehran prayer rugs, each with an ivory field centred by flowering trees below a red mihrab, within a blue border and multiple guard stripes.

82in (208cm) wide

£600-800   DN

A Zeigler Mahal carpet, the abrash camel field with all-over herati pattern, within rust-red rosette and floral vine border between blue and camel bands.

166in (422cm) x 148.5in (377cm)

£5,000-6,000   L&T

A large Zeigler carpet, the rust-red field with small blue and ivory medallion and large palmette and scrolling leafy vine pattern, within indigo palmette and floral vine border between olive and cream bands.

206.75in (525cm) x 148.5in (377cm)

£7,000-9,000   L&T

A woven wool carpet, in Zeigler style, retailed by Liberty, the deep orange field decorated with foliage in camel and cream tones, within conforming borders and cream guard stripes.

169.25in (430cm) wide

£4,000-6,000   DN

A Zeigler style carpet, the cream field with all-over large palmette and vine pattern, within brown palmette and angular vine border between brown bands.

171.25in (435cm) long

£4,000-5,000   L&T

A Northwest Persian runner, with seven medallions on a brown field with red border.

c1910   *137in (348cm) long*

£1,700-2,000   POOK

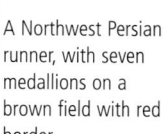

A North Persian pictorial rug.

c1920   *79in (200.5cm) long*

£2,000-3,000   FRE

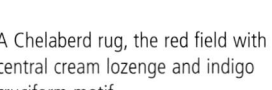

A Chelaberd rug, the red field with central cream lozenge and indigo cruciform motif.

67.75in (172cm) long

£750-1,000 **L&T**

A Chi Chi rug, northeast Caucasus.

c1900 *74in (188cm) long*

£2,000-3,000 **FRE**

A Gendje rug, the brown field with all-over lattice and star pattern.

87in (221cm) long

£800-1,200 **L&T**

A late 19thC Karabagh rug, south Caucasus.

95in (241.5cm) long

£1,000-1,300 **FRE**

A Chelaberd rug, the red field with central ivory lozenge and green cruciform medallion flanked by ivory eagle's wings.

80.25 in (204cm) long

£1,500-1,800 **L&T**

A late 19thC Kasim Ushag rug, south Caucasus.

97in (246.5cm) long

£1,500-2,000 **FRE**

A Caucasian Kazak rug, in indigo and madder red.

c1930 *103in (260cm) long*

£900-1,100 **DRA**

A Kazak long rug, with repeating medallions on a blue field with running dog border.

c1910 *78in (198cm) long*

£1,500-2,000 **POOK**

A Kazak throw rug, with three medallions on a red field with ivory border.

c1900 *86in (218.5cm) long*

£1,500-2,000 **POOK**

A Kazak throw rug, with three medallions on a blue field with red and blue borders.

c1910 *104in (264cm) long*

£1,500-2,000 **POOK**

A Kazak long rug, the indigo field with two elongated red and ivory medallions.

108.5in (276cm) long

£1,500-2,000 **L&T**

A Moghan Kazak rug, the field with four blue rectangles containing polychrome stepped, hooked lozenge medallions.

71.75in (182cm) long

£1,500-2,000 **L&T**

TEXTILES

ESSENTIAL REFERENCE: KAZAK

Rugs from the Kazak district in western Caucasus, Eurasia, are epitomised by bold and open designs,

- Wool pile is long and usually much more loosely woven than rugs of the North and East of Caucasus. This results in striking, less detailed designs. These designs are often based on early classic Persian and Anatolian forms.
- With a primarily village-orientated nature of production, Kazak mainly produces small rug-sized pieces and runners, which also display the bold designs to best effect.
- The best Kazak rugs are woven with bright vibrant colours that are not conflicting. Pieces made after 1800 may include harsh chemical dyes, like oranges and purples, which stand out from the traditional, natural colours.

A Kazak throw rug, with four medallions, and red and white striped border.

c1900   *98in (249cm) long*

£2,500-3,000   **POOK**

A Kuba rug, east Caucasus, dated '1323'.

1905   *109in (277cm) long*

£1,500-2,000   **FRE**

A Kuba rug, the abrash brown field with three ivory and red medallions.

49.25in (125cm) long

£450-650   **L&T**

A late 19thC Lenkoran rug, southeast Caucasus.

119in (302.5cm) long

£1,800-2,200   **FRE**

A Lenkoran long rug, southeast Caucasus.

c1900   *119.5in (304cm) long*

£1,000-1,300   **WW**

A late 19th/early 20thC Lenkoran area runner, southeast Caucasus.

150in (375cm) long

£500-750   **WW**

A late 19thC Perepedil rug, east Caucasus.

57in (145cm) long

£1,500-2,000   **FRE**

A Peshawar Serapi room-size rug with geometric floral pattern in rust-coloured pattern.

120in (305cm) long

£750-1,000   **DRA**

A late 19thC Shirvan rug, east Caucasus.

59in (150cm) long

£1,200-1,600   **FRE**

A Shrivan rug, the navy field centred by red and ivory abstract medallions, within a chevron and flowerhead-decorated border within multiple guard stripes.

86.5in (220cm) long

£750-950 DN

A Shirvan rug, the ivory field with all-over red and blue stylised pattern.

70.5in (179cm) long

£1,500-2,000 L&T

A late 19th/early 20thC Shirvan rug, southeast Caucasus.

86in (219cm) long

£1,800-2,200 WW

A Caucasian Soumac carpet, the red field with three columns of seven polychrome hooked lozenge medallions.

105in (267cm) long

£1,200-1,600 L&T

A Caucasian runner, with repeating medallions and human figures on a red ground with multiple borders.

c1910 *66in (167.5cm) long*

£500-750 POOK

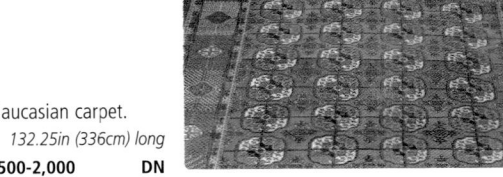

A Caucasian carpet.

132.25in (336cm) long

£1,500-2,000 DN

TURKISH RUGS & CARPETS

An early 19thC Beshir prayer rug, south Turkestan.

82in (208.5cm) long

£2,000-3,000 FRE

An early 20thC Kazak khilim, Turkestan.

152in (386cm) long

£450-650 FRE

A late 19thC Oushak carpet, west Anatolia.

138in (350.5cm) long

£4,000-5,000 FRE

A 19thC Saryk Turkoman chuval, east Turkestan, cotton highlights.

61in (155cm) wide

£1,000-1,500 FRE

A Tekke kapunuk, the U-shaped band with red and indigo serrated scrolls on an ivory ground, within inner ivory hatched and outer X-bands, with original tassels.

46.5in (119cm) long

£3,000-3,500 L&T

A Tekke Ensi rug.

67.75in (172cm) long

£300-400 DN

An Ushak carpet, the red field with all-over large blue palmette and cruciform motif pattern, reduced and border re-sewn to one side.

183.5in (466cm) long

£3,000-3,500   L&T

A large Ushak carpet, the red field with all-over pattern of large light blue palmettes and cruciform motifs.

275.5in (700cm) long

£4,500-5,000   L&T

A large Ushak carpet, the red field with all-over serrated blue medallion, palmette and serrated leaf pattern, within blue lozenge, tulip and foliate vine border between orange bands.

245in (622cm) long

£8,000-10,000   L&T

A late 19th/early 20thC Turkestan Chyrpy, probably Uzbek.

43in (109cm) long

£200-300   FRE

A late 19th/early 20thC Turkestan Chyrpy, probably Uzbek.

41in (104cm) long

£200-300   FRE

A late 19thC Yomud asmalyk, west Turkestan.

45in (114.5cm) wide

£500-700   FRE

A mid-to late 19thC Yomud Group chuval, west Turkestan.

43in (109cm) wide

£600-800   FRE

A late 19thC Yomud Group khordjin, west Turkestan.

37in (94cm) wide

£500-1,000   FRE

A Yomut juval, the red field with three columns of three guls, original back.

45.75in (116cm) x 29.5in (75cm) high

£150-200   L&T

A 19thC Western Turkoman tentband (Ak Yup), west Turkestan.

The present tentband is knotted on adjacent warps, like a piled rug, rather than on alternating warps as is typical of mixed technique tentbands. As such, the knots are viewable from the back of the tentband.

438in (1,112.5cm) long

£3,500-4,500   FRE

A Turkish silk rug, the rose field with all-over palmette and leafy vine pattern.

62.5in (159cm) long

£750-950   L&T

OTHER RUGS & CARPETS

A Chinese saddle cover, comprising two sewn shaped ivory panels, each with central deer and two leather bosses.

52.25in (133cm) long

£300-500   L&T

An 18thC Chinese wool carpet, dark blue edge, ivory ground with light blue lotus flowers issuing leaves.

96in (30.5cm) long

£1,500-2,000   FRE

A Chinese, late Qing Dynasty rug, central medallion of eight floral sprigs to a blue ground within two diaper borders.

102in (259cm) long

£750-1,000   FRE

A 19thC Chinese voided velvet carpet, the mid-brown velvet woven with purple and coral-pink peonies and scrolling foliage.

82.5in (210cm) wide

£600-900   KT

A 19thC Tibetan tiger rug, of rectangular form, woven wool pink and brown striped tiger on a blue ground.

55in (139.5cm) long

£4,500-6,500   FRE

A late 19thC Tibetan rug, depicting two multi-colour dragons chasing a flaming pearl and ruyi clouds.

72in (183cm) long

£400-700   FRE

TEXTILES

A Laristan carpet, north India.

c1920   *165in (419cm) long*
£2,000-2,500   FRE

An Indian carpet.

c1940   *142in (360.5cm) long*
£1,200-1,600   FRE

An Afghan rug.

126in (320cm) long
£450-650   DN

A late 18th/early 19thC Ladik prayer rug, central Anatolia, inscribed in Armenian 'GLR' and includes a 'cross of Jerusalem' in the stepped mihrab.

62in (157.5cm) long
£1,500-1,800   FRE

A Konya long rug, central Anatolia.

c1875   *124in (315cm) long*
£1,800-2,200   FRE

A woven carpet in Aubusson style, of recent manufacture.

165in (419cm) wide
£1,000-1,500   DN

A 20thC woven carpet, the brown field with an acanthus scroll-decorated border, bearing label to underside 'TUBERVILLE SMITH & SON LTD'.

220in (560cm) wide
£350-550   DN

TAPESTRIES

A 17thC Flemish tapestry, woven in wool and silk with exotic birds, animals and foliage surrounding an architectural arch, the wide fruit-woven border with oval reserves depicting landscape views, bears Royal coat of arms.

12.25 (285cm) long
£5,000-6,000   L&T

A 17thC continental verdure tapestry depicting the Trojan Horse and robed figures, reduced, faded and with general wear and tears overall.

124in (315cm) wide
£5,500-6,500   DN

A 17thC Continental verdure tapestry, depicting hunting dogs attacking a bear in a wooded landscape, with later brass hanging rod, some wears, tears and fading.

118in (300cm) wide
£1,200-1,600   DN

A mid-18thC French Beauvais tapestry panel, designed by Jean Baptiste Oudry, with an owl being tormented by other birds, originally a sofa back, condition poor to the centre.

49.25in (125cm) long
£3,500-4,000   L&T

A mid-18thC framed Beauvais chinoiserie tapestry panel, some wear and restoration to the background.

37.5in (95cm) high

£1,400-1,800   **L&T**

A mid-18thC French framed embroidered oval panel, worked in tent stitch with coloured wools, depicting the Rape of Proserpine, probably original chair back centre (some reworking to the background).

19in (48cm) wide

£550-750   **L&T**

An 18thC Flemish verdure tapestry panel, decorated with trees and foliate in shaded blue-green and ochre around a central castle, the foreground with two fighting hounds, within a replaced outer slip and a canvas backing, probably reduced from a larger tapestry.

84.5in (215cm) wide

£1,200-1,800   **L&T**

A mid-19thC French Aubusson part-silk tapestry.

93.5in (237cm) long

£2,500-3,500   **WW**

NEEDLEWORK

A late 17thC needlework panel, worked in coloured wools in petit point, depicting a hunting scene within borders, with later applied binding to the edges.

65.75in (167cm) wide

£1,300-1,600   **DN**

A set of four Jacobean raised work embroidered wall hangings, decorated with vertical branches in shaded brown issuing blue leaf palmettes and leaf scrolls with madder rosettes and stylised tulips, mounted on a later twill self-coloured backing and edged with a later green fabric slip, comprising two narrow strips and two square portions.

80in (203cm) long

£3,500-4,500 SET   **L&T**

An early 18thC needlework panel, worked with a lady shepherdess and gentleman in an idealised landscape with buildings to the distance.

20in (51cm) wide

£1,000-1,300 **DUK**

An American Philadelphia wool-on-linen needlework, depicting a bird perched on a floral tree atop a grassy landscape.

c1750 *11.75in (30cm) high*

£11,000-14,000 **POOK**

An American canvaswork picture, probably Boston, depicting a shepherdess, sheep, spotted dog, cow and exotic bird in tree, and brick house beyond, worked in polychrome wool yarns, in original frame.

c1750 *16in (40.5cm) high*

£25,000-30,000 **FRE**

A mid-18thC English pictorial needlework, with two figures in a pastoral setting with animals and birds.

18in (45.5cm) high

£2,800-3,400 **POOK**

A mid-18thC needlework picture, the central oval depicting a pastoral scene of a shepherd and shepherdess with gambolling lambs, the shepherd playing a flute, enclosed by flowerhead and foliate motifs, within a moulded maple frame.

35.25in (80cm) high

£1,500-2,000 **L&T**

A mid-18thC American wool needlework and felt picture, possible Pennsylvania, depicting a landscape with stag, doe and fawn below a tree with a dove.

12.5in (32cm) wide

£1,700-2,000 **POOK**

A framed mid-18thC embroidered picture worked in tent stitch with coloured wools, depicting Tobias leaving home for Medea (slightly worn and reworked in parts).

22.75in (58cm) high

£700-900 **L&T**

A mid-18thC French tent stitch needlework, depicting figures in a landscape within a floral border.

32.5in (82.5cm) high

£2,000-3,000 **POOK**

An early 19thC English wool and silk-on-linen needlework picture, depicting a woman seated in front of her house with dog, fisherman, butterfly, cherry tree and perched peacock, with a gilt-lined ogee frame.

22in (56cm) wide

£9,000-11,000 **POOK**

A 19thC American wool-on-cloth trapunto needlework picture, with birds perched in a cherry tree, retaining paper label verso, inscribed 'Miss Elizabeth L. Baker, Bernardsville, New Jersey'.

30.5in (77.5cm) high

£2,500-3,000 **POOK**

A 19thC wool- and chenille-on-silk needlework picture.

22.5in high

£150-200 **POOK**

A 19thC woolwork picture of two hounds amongst foliage, signed 'Linwood', with gilt frame.

17.25in (44cm) wide overall

£600-800 **DN**

An 18thC silk needlework, depicting a central urn with flowers.

7.5in (19cm) square

£1,300-1,600   POOK

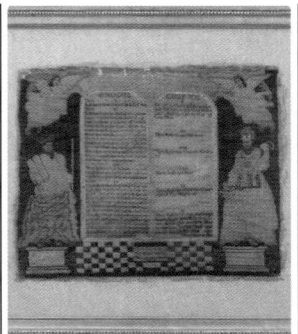

A silk-on-linen needlework, with trumpeting angels and seated figures flanking the ten commandments, dated.

1744   15.5in (39.5cm) wide

£450-650   POOK

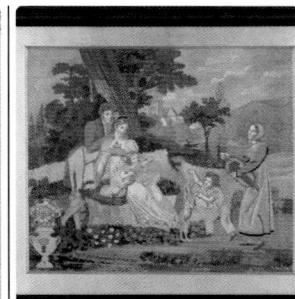

An early 19thC English silk, chenille and paint-on-silk pictorial needlework, depicting a young husband and wife with their two children, dog and nanny in a landscape, signed in stitch under mat 'Viclor'.

13.5in (34.5cm) wide

£2,500-3,500   POOK

A silk-on-linen needlework wrought by Miss Margaret Smith, the central brick house flanked by trees with animals and figures on a green lawn within a floral vine border.

16.5in (42cm) high

£3,000-4,000   POOK

SAMPLERS

One of a pair of needlework samplers in silk on linen inscribed, 'Nancy Martindale 1761' on one, the other '1759' with alphabets, numbers, flowers, scenes, figures, trees and animals.

16in (41cm) high

£1,500-2,000 PAIR   POOK

CLOSER LOOK: NAPOLEONIC WAR SAMPLER

The brown linen ground is worked with a soldier and a sailor with Britannia medallion to the centre and a lion and unicorn beneath. This eye-catching central image adds to the sampler's appeal.

The overall design is well balanced and finely stitched.

The borders and the panels either side of the main verse are formed of entwined flowering vines.

Text that comments on current affairs is highly desirable. Here the mottoes read: 'Britain Rule Nia' (Britannia Rule), 'God Save the King', 'O the Roast Beef of Old England', the upper verse 'if the French should invade us they shall be taught, How dearly one inch of our isle must be bought, Hand and Heart one and all for the land that is free, And we'll soon drive those Plunderers into the sea, Britons strike home hearts of oak'.

A rare Napoleonic war sampler, 'Briton's Protection', by Mary Millward.

1804   Framed 20in (51cm) high

£4,000-5,000   KT

A needlework sampler, worked in silk threads on a loosely woven wool ground, signed and dated 'Mary Vowles, November 21 1794 FINIS', in a later moulded wood frame, small losses to backing fabric.

17in (43cm) wide

£1,200-1,400   SK

An embroidered sampler, by Ann Spencer and also bearing the name of her teacher 'Mrs C Hall', worked in couched and looped silks and in Algerian eye and cross stitch, with large trees and pots of harebells, the ground scattered with little birds and beasts with 'Lord of All Power' verse to the centre.

c1800   Framed 14.25in (36cm) wide

£600-900   KT

An embroidered sampler, by Amy Langdon, 'Life how short, Eternity how long', the cream wool ground completely smothered with tiny figures, animals, a central red house, parrots, butterflies, roosters, angels, carnation and daisy border.

1802   18.5in (47cm) wide

£3,000-4,000   KT

TEXTILES

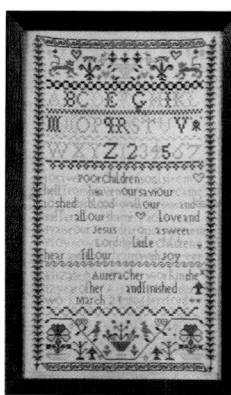

A needlework sampler, worked with silk threads on a linen ground, signed and dated 'Elizabeth Auteracher worked in the 12 year of her age and finished this work March 28 1806 Hereford', in a contemporary mitred oak frame.

21.25in (54cm) high

£150-180   **SK**

A needlework sampler, silk threads on a linen ground, signed and dated 'Hannah Hildreth Aged 9/1808', in a moulded giltwood frame, minor toning and foxing.

18.25in (46.5cm) high

£2,000-3,000   **SK**

A needlework sampler, worked in silk threads on a linen ground, signed and dated 'Mary Francis aged 9 years in the year 1811', in a contemporary wood frame.

22in (55.5cm) high

£900-1,100   **SK**

A needlework sampler, 'Mary H. Bateman Born Aug. 6 1818 Aged 10 yrs.,' stitched with silk on linen with the verse 'May truth and virtue guide thy heart, Nor hope nor peace nor joy depart.'

16.5in (42cm) wide

£2,000-2,500   **SK**

A needlework sampler, framed.

c1820   *15.25in (39cm) wide*

£220-280   **DN**

A needlework sampler worked in wool threads on a linen ground, signed and dated 'Sarah Greens Sampler Aged 12 1824', in a later moulded wood frame, toning, stitch losses.

16.5in (42cm) high

£500-750   **SK**

A needlework sampler, 'Jane Halsey March 10 1825,' in silk on wool, depicting a large building, likely an academy, surrounded by a fence, plants and birds.

13in (33cm) wide

£800-1,000   **SK**

A large pictorial needlework sampler, in silk on linen, with several monograms, likely members of Louisa's family, and geometric floral and strawberry borders, signed 'Louisa Lamberts 1831,'.

24.5in (62cm) high

£2,500-3,000   **SK**

An unusual early 19thC needlework sampler, showing a kneeling figure of a black slave in chains above a field of sheep and inscribed 'Pity the negro slave, emancipated in 1832, Hannah Shiels', in mahogany frame.

10.25in (26cm) high

£4,000-5,000   **L&T**

An embroidered pictorial sampler, by Ann Chapman, with short verse on the theme of mortality, large central Georgian house with climbing plants, within a parkland with rose arbours, lawns with a seated girl and her dog, an elegant young lady with a basket and presumably their parents to either side – a stout black garbed gentleman with his stick, and a bonneted lady with her kerchief, worked in silks on a cream wool ground.

1839   *Framed 17.25in (44cm) wide*

£3,000-4,000   **KT**

An English silk-on-linen needlework, wrought by Ann Bayley Pettipher, religious verse, Native American figures, trees and pastoral scenes, dated.

1858   *13in (33.5cm) wide*

£750-1,000   **POOK**

OTHER TEXTILES

A set of late 17thC English crewelworked bedhanging, heavily re-worked in the 1920s, comprising two large square curtains, two narrow curtains, a long fringed pelmet, three valance panels, two of which are 1920s.

89.75in (228cm) long

£8,000-10,000 SET   **KT**

A late 17thC 'bearing' or christening cloth, of pale blue/silver satin, with deep border of gold and silver bobbin lace, backed in pale blue silk, with hand-written note attached to one corner 'Christening cloth, Newton'.

75in (190cm) long

£900-1,200   **KT**

A late 17th/early 18thC English stumpwork, with spread-winged eagle, snakes and stylised floral and fruit trees.

11.75in (30cm) wide

£1,100-1,400   **POOK**

A Queen Anne pictorial beadwork, the centre with vibrant blue, green, yellow, brown and tan pot with numerous intricate flowers flanked by recumbent stag, unicorn, lion and tiger

c1710   *15.5in (39.5cm) wide*

£2,000-2,500   **POOK**

A pair of embroidered and false-quilted cushions, the linen ground delicately worked in fine chain stitch with meandering foliage and exotic blooms, the reverse of linen covered with a lattice of yellow false-quilting stitch.

c1700-10   *Larger 19in (48cm) wide*

£5,500-6,500   **KT**

A pair of chinoiserie embroidered cushions, the linen ground embroidered with central phoenix motifs, the corners with oriental ladies below large parasols, the reverse with a lattice of fine chain stitch within foliate borders.

c1700-10   *18in (46cm) wide*

£1,500-2,000   **KT**

An early 18thC Italian embroidered mirror surround, with raised work central rocaille and acanthus scrolls worked mainly in couched silver threads, mounted onto crimson velvet, inset with an antique mirror plate, later braid border.

36in (90cm) square

£1,000-1,300   **KT**

A Continental stitching sample, inscribed 'Anno 1734', with various blocks of flame stitch, herringbone, tent stitch, eye stitch, etc., alphabet, flowers, potted fruit trees, birds, and flower-filled urn.

£2,500-3,000   **POOK**

An unusual mid-18thC American needlework and felt picture, depicting a colourful bird perched on a cherry tree with lawn and flowers, the felt outlined in stitches.

£3,000-5,000   POOK

An 18thC linen panel with crewelwork embroidery, worked in coloured wools upon a joined cream linen panel, the central cartouche with initials 'IAWR' below a coronet, surrounded by stylised flowers and pomegranates.

65in (165cm) long

£800-1,000   DN

An early 19thC American folk art needlework embroidery, with rows of human figures.

20in (51cm) wide

£2,000-3,000   POOK

A French copper-plate printed bedcurtain, with the 'Apotheosis of Franklin and Washington' printed in red on a cotton ground, comprised of three panels.

c1785   *87in (221cm) wide*

£4,000-5,000   FRE

A pair of silk portières woven with Glasgow rose pattern in jade green and black, some discolouration.

88 in (224cm) long

£350-550   DRA

An early 19thC printed cotton handkerchief, printed in green with 'Dr. B. Franklin's Maxims or Moral Pictures for Youth'.

17.5in (44.5cm) wide

£1,000-1,500   FRE

A Carlisle, Pennsylvania appliqué tablecloth, with colourful baskets of tulips and tulip trees.

c1900

£350-450   POOK

COSTUMES AND COUTURE

An 18thC infant bodice of 1720s silk lampas, the ground of light brown satin woven with yellow and blue leaf shapes, berries and lace patterns, lined in raspberry pink silk, adorned with gold bobbin lace, back laced.

13in (33cm) long

£900-1,100   KT

A pair of stays, of pale brown linen with green top-stitched detailing, green and white Chinese damask satin centre panel, back laced.

c1760

£1,500-2,000   KT

A figured black silk gentleman's suit, the black silk ground woven with fine green stripes and small pink and blue lozenges, lined in ivory silk, matching breeches with small-fall front, the ivory satin waistcoat embroidered with wild flowers and oak leaves.

c1790

£5,000-6,000   KT

A late 1870s/early 1880s Worth labelled blue dolman jacket, with velvet collar, with engine-turned mother-of-pearl buttons to fasten, lined in navy self-striped satin, with vestigial blue satin hood with ribbon trim.

This has the printed gold-on-black Worth label which was used during the c1870-1885 period.

Chest 36in (92cm)

£550-750   KT

A Worth ball gown, with signature label to waistband, of pink damask satin woven with large bearded irises and swags of interlaced ribbons.

c1900

£2,300-2,800   KT

An Edwardian cream lace and embroidered tea dress, with elaborate naturalistic stumpwork embroidery with a centralised exotic bird motif, surrounded by stylised flora and fauna, glass buttons at shoulders and one side.

£300-400   FRE

A Liberty & Co. black and gold damask evening mantle, woven with leaf clusters against a chequered ground, large knotted tassels to the sleeve openings, large gilt thread buttons and fringed hem, un-lined, labelled 'Liberty & Co, Paris & London'.

c1915

£650-850   KT

A blue satin jacket for a Captain of the Guard, from Diaghilev's Ballet Russes 'La Boutique Fantasque', first performed 1919, designed by André Derain.

£350-450   KT

ESSENTIAL REFERENCE: BALLET RUSSES

The Ballet Russes (French for the 'Russian Ballet') was established in 1909 by Russian impresario Serge Diaghilev (1872-1929). The vitality, colour and movement in Russian ballet created a sensation in Western Europe, and its influence can be seen in almost every area of the arts in the Art Deco period.

- The dancers were associated and trained with the Tsar's Imperial Ballet of St. Petersburg. It used many of the works of the great choreographer Marius Petipa.
- The sets designed by Léon Bakst were brilliantly coloured and featured a medley of Persian, Oriental and Russian influences. These inspired interior designers to move away from the restrained palette of the previous era. Textile designers embraced the colourful geometric patterns seen in the ballet.
- Two of the Ballet Russes's dancers, Ida Rubenstein and Vaslav Nijinsky, became the models for the 'Russian Dancers' by Demêtre Chiparus, the master of bronze and ivory sculpture.
- Art Deco furniture designers inspired by the ballet used colourful and exotic materials like Macassar ebony and palisander enriched with ivory, shagreen and lacquer in bold patterns such as sun-rays and checks.

A Lezghin outfit, for Diaghilev's Ballet Russes 'Thamar', first performed 1912, designed by Leon Bakst, comprising fuchsia pink satin frock-coat edged with silver braid stencilled with diamonds, hanging sleeves with inner blue satin sleeves striped with yellow silk, calico lining inked 'Frank George Heops', with a pair of yellow satinised cotton Turkish trousers adorned with silver braid and green ribbons, with inked label written in Russian, green satin belt with inked names 'Andreef, Bor, Alg'.

£13,500-15,500   KT

A 1920s Art Deco beaded dress, silk straight caftan sheath with shoulder-grazing sleeves, beaded with short cut bugle beads.

£250-350   FRE

A 1920s black silk floral medallion-jacquard Art Deco gown, unlabelled.

£250-500   FRE

A late 1930s/1940s Jeanne Lanvin black silk jersey 'Goddess' gown, with large woven silk label, numbered '2590.5'.

Bust approx 36in (91cm)

£1,300-1,600   KT

A rayon cream twill beaded skirt suit, pencil skirt with nipped-waist fitted jacket, 'key hole' neckline, with a trailing bellflower beaded motif in red, blue and gunmetal-grey on the back of the collar and left shoulder, unlined and unlabelled.
1940s

£150-200   FRE

A Jeanne Lanvin emerald green tulle ball gown, the boned strapless bodice with ruched and shirred panels, the separate petticoat with bouffant section to left hip to raise the skirt higher at that point to give an asymmetric hemline, labelled and numbered '6653'.

Summer 1949   *Bust 34in (86cm)*

£2,600-3,000   KT

An early 1950s Paquin black velvet and organza halter-necked gown, the slim fitted bodice with cross-over pleats of organza to the décolleté, with large organza bow to the back, bearing the Paquin 'Les Couturiers Associès' label.

Bust 36in (91cm)

£2,000-2,500   KT

An early 1950s Madame Grès black and white taffeta ball gown, with a play of black against white, labelled 'Grès, 1 Rue de la Paix, Paris'.

Bust 34in (86cm)

£1,500-2,000   KT

A Christian Dior goffered silk organza and velvet evening gown, the bodice with boning but not corseted, of cream organza with flounce of black organza emerging from the black velvet band below, stiffened inner petticoat, labelled and numbered '10893', and also labelled behind the main label '188337'.
1951   *Bust 32in (82cm)*

£8,000-10,000   KT

An early Hubert de Givenchy orientalist dinner gown, comprising button-fronted bodice, cut wide at the shoulders, the over-skirt with nipped-in waist of beetle-wing black and green changeable silk, together with a black silk petticoat, labelled and numbered '3328'.
1952   *Bust 34in (86cm)*

£2,200-2,800   KT

A 1950s Jean Patou black wool crêpe cocktail gown, with corseted inner bodice.

Bust 34in (86cm)

£750-950   KT

A mid-1950s Madame Grès ball gown, the elaborately boned strapless bodice edged in garlands of silk blossom and roses, the dress formed from four layers of white and yellow chiffon, organza and taffeta and a final translucent overlay of glistening white horsehair which gives glimpses of the primrose yellow layers below and also ensures a perfect silhouette, labelled 'Grès, 1 Rue de la Paix, Paris'.

Bust 34in (86cm)

£3,500-4,000   KT

A Christian Dior shocking pink party dress, silk taffeta with silk gauze lining in the skirt, with large applied bow detail at front and an attached stand-up shawl, labelled 'Christian Dior New York.'

Fall 1958

£250-400 FRE

A late 1950s Simonetta stencilled satin and cut velvet evening coat, label removed.

£3,000-4,000 KT

A Pierre Balmain ball gown and matching evening coat, labelled and indistinctly numbered, the boned strapless bodice with ruched folds of ivory satin emphasising the curves of the breast in contrast to the tiny, fitted waist and enormous satin skirt with five internal layers of silk, tulle and horsehair petticoats, embroidered and appliquéd overall, faintly numbered '24, 418'.

1955 *Gown bust 34in (82cm)*

£20,000-25,000 KT

A late 1950s Pierre Balmain oyster satin evening gown, labelled and numbered '84-466'.

34in (86cm)

£3,500-4,500 KT

A Jean Dessès chine rose-print taffeta cocktail dress, detached label, with corseted inner bodice, with inner and outer taffeta skirts and layers of tulle petticoats, the overskirt draped and caught in place with a massive bow to one side, matching belt.

c1959 *Bust 38in (96cm)*

£1,800-2,400 KT

A late 1950s/early1960s Balenciaga oyster taffeta evening coat, no fastenings, the sleeve and front panels cut in one piece, the back and rear sleeves also cut in one piece, labelled 'Eisa'.

Chest 52in (132cm)

£4,000-5,000 KT

A Balenciaga petrol blue silk ball gown, hem encrusted in a 2in (5cm) wide band of tiered beading with moulded white lily of the valley and globular beads, crystal discs and cream silk buds, labelled and numbered '93027'.

c1958-60 *Bust 34in (86cm)*

£1,700-2,000 KT

A Victor Saks leopard coat, with mink cuffs and collar.

1960s *Bust 40in (101cm)*

£800-1,000 FRE

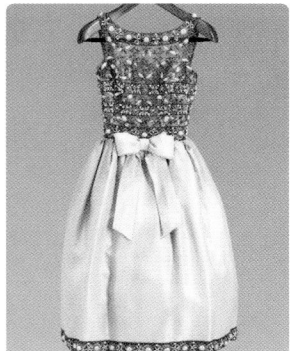

A 1960s Bob Bugnand party dress, with rhinestone-, branch-coral- and mother-of-pearl-encrusted bodice, tussah silk tulip-shaped skirt with matching beadwork at hem, labelled 'Bob Bugnand, Paris'

Size 0-2

£400-600 FRE

A 1960s black feathered column gown, with silk ribbon straps decorated with bows, back zip closure.

Size 6-8

£500-750 FRE

CLOSER LOOK: MARILYN MONROE'S CAPRI TROUSERS

Monroe's status as one of the most iconic images of the 20th century, her links with JFK, along with the inclusion of two photographs apparently showing her wearing these trousers add to their desirability.

The label reads: 'Designed by Jax'. Jax was one of Marilyn Monroe's favourite designers and she also owned dresses by him.

The narrow, fitted look was typical of Jax's designs.

Marilyn Monroe's cream slubbed silk Capri pants, together with an image of Marilyn Monroe, seemingly wearing these trousers, taken by Willy Rizzo in 1961, and another by George Barris taken in one of her last photo sessions in June 1962, two months before her death.

c1961-62 *Waist 25in (64cm)*

£5,000-6,000 KT

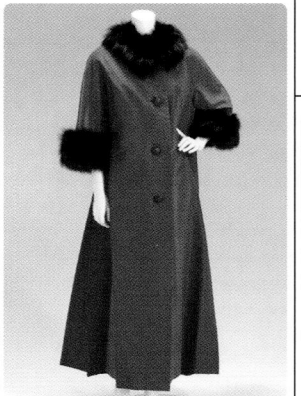

A 1960s Guy Laroche violet silk fox-trimmed opera coat, bright violet-red silk with large decorative buttons and black fox collar and cuffs, labelled 'Guy Laroche Paris'.

£200-300 FRE

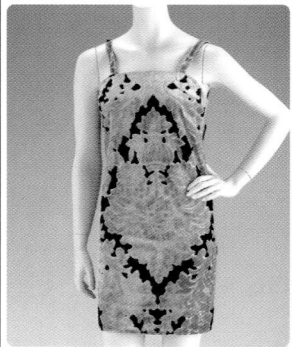

A 1960s Rudi Gernreich tapestry mini dress, labelled 'Rudi Gernreich'.

£200-300 FRE

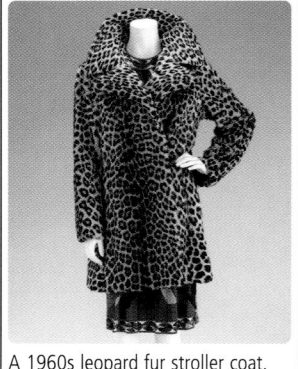

A 1960s leopard fur stroller coat, labelled 'Patchin Furs'.

Size medium

£1,500-2,000 FRE

A Cristobal Balenciaga primrose yellow silk ball gown, labelled, number is indistinct.

c1960 *Bust 36in (91cm)*

£3,000-4,000 KT

A Balenciaga hot pink and fuchsia matelassé cocktail ensemble, the sleeveless gown with jewel-neckline, the matching coat with three-quarter sleeves and fold-over lapels, labelled and numbered '33030'.

c1960 *Bust 36in (92cm)*

£3,000-3,500 KT

A Madame Grès navy pleated jersey evening gown, the fitted bodice with split to centre front and with vertical splits, labelled.

c1960 *Bust 34-36in (86-91cm)*

£4,000-5,000 KT

An early 1960s Princess Galitzene feather-sequinned mini dress, the black silk ground entirely smothered in spiky pierced elliptical black sequins, labelled 'Irene Galitzene, Roma'.

Bust 34-36in (86-91cm)

£2,500-3,000 KT

A Pierre Cardin jewelled evening gown, entirely covered in gold and silver sequins in a giant hounds-tooth check repeat and further embellished with large rose-cut and elliptical pastes, labelled 'Pierre Cardin Paris'.

c1965 *Bust 34in (87cm)*

£5,500-6,500 KT

A rare Yves Saint Laurent 'African' Collection mini-dress, the beige silk/linen under-dress covered with a tunic of latticed wooden beads, lined in beige silk, labelled and numbered '14635'.

1967   *Bust 32in (82cm)*

£13,000-15,000   **KT**

A 'Souper Dress', printed paper, probably Mars of Asheville, printed with the Andy Warhol design, original label with care instructions to neck.

c1968   *Bust 34in (86cm)*

£2,000-2,500   **KT**

A 1960s-70s Jean Lanvin haute couture evening gown, grass-green silk twill full-circle skirt, wide beaded 'grapevine' motif hunter green corset waist, unlined, labelled 'Jeanne Lanvin – Paris' and '49 01(?)' handwritten verso.

£700-1,000   **FRE**

An Emilio Pucci strapless beaded and jewel-encrusted evening gown, printed fine silk chiffon, heavily beaded with iridescent sequins, faceted crystal beads, and rhinestones, marked on a large black label 'EMILIO PUCCI / Firenze.'

£600-900   **FRE**

A Norman Norell beaded evening gown, sleeveless fitted full-length sheath decorated with ivory bugle beads and turquoise and magenta paisley designs, labelled 'Norman Norell' and 'Marsal'.

c1970   *Size 2-4*

£500-750   **FRE**

A Christian Dior brocade and beaded hostess gown, in Persian paisley brocade, labelled 'Boutique Christian Dior Paris / Made in France', and stamped '1754205'.

c1970   *Size 6-8*

£250-350   **FRE**

A 1970s Emilio Pucci silk jersey dress, labelled 'Emilio Pucci/Florence Italy' and 'Exclusively for Saks Fifth Avenue'.

Size 8

£250-350   **FRE**

A Hubert de Givenchy evening gown, of emerald green chiffon smothered in tiny pink and green floral sequins and adorned with paste tassels with shocking pink, green and mauve feathers, labelled and numbered '41763'.

c1970   *Bust 34in (86cm)*

£1,500-2,000   **KT**

A Christian Dior silk satin evening coat, labelled 'Christian Dior Paris/Automne 1971'.

Size 4

£200-250   **FRE**

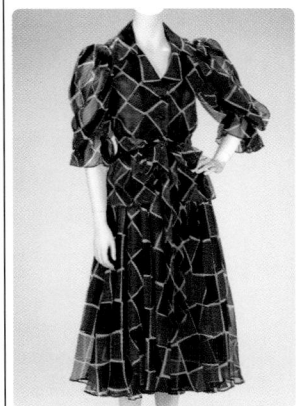

A 1970s Yves Saint Laurent silk organza harlequin print shirtwaist dress.

Bust 34in (86cm)

£350-550   **FRE**

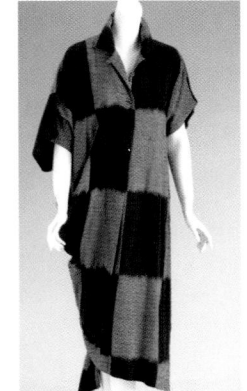

A 1980s Issey Miyake cotton kasuri dress, labelled 'Issey Miyake'.

Size small

£250-300   **FRE**

TEXTILES

A late 17thC French tapestry purse, woven in polychrome silk and metal thread, with central motif of a small brown dog below two birds bearing bunches of coloured grapes, simple silver knots and pink floss silk tassels to the corners, lined in blue silk.

4.75in (12cm) wide

£1,000-1,400 KT

An early 20thC Orientalist micro-beaded purse, enamel Etruscan Revival frame with cut glass and cabochon jewels, the body of the purse beaded in the style of Persian prayer rug with tiny faceted metal beads.

£200-250 FRE

The gold-painted wicker is in excellent condition with no wear or flaking.

The green velvet has faded a little but the red velvet cherries which embellish it retain their vibrant colour.

The green rhinestones add sparkling highlights.

The lining appears to be as-new with no marks or tears.

A Midas of Miami gold-painted wicker and green velvet handbag.

1950s *12in (30.5cm) wide*

£150-250 PC

A 1920s-30s Art Deco bag, fine-beaded with a celluloid frame.

£300-400 TDG

A 1920s French Egyptian Revival microbeaded purse, blackened silver frame with a chain handle, depicting a Pharaoah and servant, with various hieroglyphics and symbols surrounding, beaded fringe.

£250-350 FRE

A 1920s-30s micro-beaded 'landscape' framed purse, with detailed romantic landscape depicting a house on a hill in a picturesque garden with a stream and two figures fishing, with a silver etched frame.

£250-350 FRE

A 1930s-40s Lederer of Paris natural alligator box purse, modified picnic basket shape with a lift-lid, opening to reveal an apple-green kid-lined interior, fitted with a matching mirror and case, and coin purse containing original 'Lederer' tag and also reading 'Porte Bonheur de Paris' with an attached drilled ten centime coin dated 1939.

£250-300 FRE

A 1940s python handbag, hinged vanity wing with mirror and pouch.

£200-275 TDG

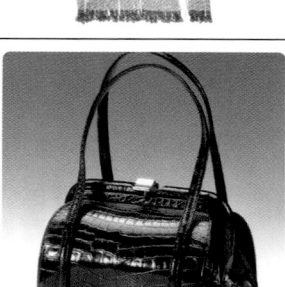

A 1950s black Coblentz alligator purse, small 'doctor's bag' shape with two loop handles and gold latch, lined in black and embossed 'Coblentz Original' in gold.

£300-400 FRE

An early 1960s Hermès forest-green leather handbag, lined in soft green leather and with separate coin purse and mirror, with angular gilt-brass lifter-clasp stamped 'Hermès Paris'.

10in (26cm) long

£600-800 KT

A rare Pierre Cardin black and white bag.

c1960s

£180-220 TDG

A Cartier black alligator purse in fitted case, trapezoid shaped with calfskin lining, envelope flap with large gold bracelet handle, embossed on the interior 'Cartier / New York, Paris, London, Caracas / Made in France', with red satin-lined Cartier storage case.

£2,000-3,000 FRE

A large 1960s French black alligator handbag or lady's briefcase, with an open pocket at the back with a separate document purse that pulls up, attached, kid-lined interior, by Reine Astrid.

£1,200-1,600 FRE

An Emilio Pucci velvet purse, shaped like an oversized coin purse, with a clamshell snap closure and loop top handle, with coral leather piping and trim.

1960s-70s

£250-300 FRE

A Hermès crocodile handbag, 'Crocodylus porosus', soft black kid leather lining with side pockets, mirror and coin purse.

c1970 *11in (28cm) wide*

£850-1,050 KT

A 1970s Louis Vuitton train case, signature canvas travelling cosmetic and toiletry case, fitted with a slide-in bottle holder and a small suitcase-shaped box, with brass signed hardware and leather trim and luggage tag.

14in (35.5cm) wide

£700-1,000 FRE

CLOSER LOOK: HERMÈS KELLY BAG

Hermès made its first Kelly bag in 1935 as a more refined version of a saddlebag it had created three years earlier. It was known as the 'small tall bag with straps' until 1955 when it was renamed the 'Kelly bag' to commemorate Grace Kelly's marriage to Prince Rainier of Monaco. Its fame was boosted a year later when Princess Grace was photographed on the front cover of Life magazine, holding the bag, it was rumoured, to hide her pregnancy. Today it is celebrities such as Victoria Beckham who are seen carrying this classic bag.

The sections are saddlestitched together by hand at the Hermès workshop in Paris. A bag takes 20 hours to make.

Kelly bags fasten at the front with a padlock and rotating clasp; the lock is stamped 'Hermès-Paris'.

Kelly bags are so desirable there is always a waiting list for them. Add to this the fact that they improve with age, it is no wonder that the market for Kelly bags is consistently strong.

A Hermès sable crocodile Kelly bag, lined in soft kid leather, with matching padlock, two keys and fob stamped in gold and also to a gilt edged closure strap.

c1966 *11.5in (29cm) long*

£4,000-6,000 KT

A Pucci silk abstract printed purse, with heavy gold chain handle, opening to reveal two equally-sized accordion-sided sections lined in leather.

1970s *8.5in (21.5cm) long*

£250-350 FRE

A Chanel black alligator purse, exterior pockets on both sides and interior zip pockets, embossed 'Chanel' and 'Made in Italy' in gold on interior, and with hanging Chanel logo charm.

£1,200-1,800 FRE

A Chanel quilted purse, soft black kidskin with front-flap and logo-latch, lined in burgundy leather and embossed 'Chanel' and 'Made in France' in gold on the interior.

£750-950 FRE

A Judith Leiber snakeskin purse, undyed python pouch-style evening bag with hinged frame closure, long shoulder strap which can tuck into the bag to form a clutch, with 'Judith Leiber' etched gold plate label.

£300-400 FRE

A Lana Marks 'Princess Diana' alligator purse, rich cognac front-flap top-handled bag with magnetic closure, alternate long shoulder strap, two main interior compartments.

£2,000-2,500 FRE

A 1980s Judith Leiber crystal minaudière, kidney bean-shaped with pave crystal surface, gold and semi-precious cabochon latch, fitted with coin purse, mirror comb and attached chain.

£350-450 FRE

A Chanel pebble-textured leather purse, rich wine leather front-flap design with decorative 'quilt' topstitching, brass logo turn-lock closure and hardware, chain shoulder strap, lined in logo jacquard and labelled 'Chanel/Made in Italy'.

£400-500 FRE

Audubon, John James, 'Mississippi Kite', London, R Havell, hand-coloured engraving with aquatint and etching, plate CXVII from 'The Birds of America', with J. Whatman Turkey Hill watermark.
1831

£1,600-2,000   **FRE**

Barbault, Jean, 'Les plus beaux monuments de Rome ancienne', Rome, de l'imprimerie de Komarek, 69 [of 73] plates, near-contemporary pasted paper boards, contemporary calf backstrip, worn.
1761

£1,000-1,300   **L&T**

Burns, Robert, 'Poems, Chiefly in the Scottish Dialect', second edition, first Edinburgh edition, minor spotting, original boards, uncut, rebacked, chipped and soiled, joints and spine cracked.
1787

£1,500–2,000   **BLO**

Cambridge, Richard Owen, 'The Works', first collected edition, fifteen engraved plates and one facsimile, later half calf over marbled boards, a little rubbed.
1803

£250-300   **BLO**

Churchill, Sir Winston, 'The Story of the Malakand Field Force', first edition, six maps, foxed at beginning, original cloth, gilt, rubbed.
1898

£2,000-2,500   **BLO**

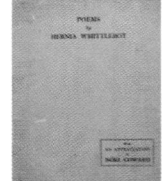

Coward, Nöel, 'Hernia Whittlebot Poems...with an appreciation by Nöel Coward', one of only 24 copies, signed inscription from Coward on verso of title, occasional light finger-marking.
1923

£550-750   **BLO**

Curtis, Edward S. 'The North American Indian', Volume II, 'Pima, Pagago, Quhatika, Mohave, Yuma, Maricopa, Walapai, Havasupai, Apache, Mohave', limited to 500 sets.
1908

£5,000-6,000   **SK**

Dickens, Charles, 'A Christmas Carol', first edition, trial issue, hand-coloured etched frontispiece and three plates by John Leech, illustrations, some foxing, rebacked preserving original spine, a little rubbed and faded, preserved in modern cloth drop-back box.
1843

£3,500-4,500   **BLO**

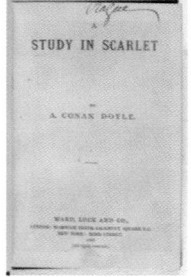

Doyle, Arthur Conan, 'A Study in Scarlet', London, Ward, Lock and Co., first edition, first impression, six plates, late 19thC green pebbledash cloth, faint library stamp on endpapers, adhesion to page 8-9, lacking the two pp. advertisements at the beginning.
1888

£8,500-9,500   **L&T**

Hardy, Thomas, 'The Woodlanders', first edition, three volumes, half-titles, original dark green bead-grain cloth, volume one neatly repaired at head of lower joint, with minor rubbing to extremities, preserved in cloth drop-back box, a little rubbed and soiled.
1887

£2,200-2,600   **BLO**

Kane, Paul, 'Wanderings of an Artist among the Indians of North America, from Canada to Vancouver's Island and Oregon through the Hudson's Bay Company's Territory', London, Longman, Brown, Green et al, folding map, eight colour plates, original brown cloth gilt, inner hinges weak, some leaves loose, contemporary owner's ink inscription on title page.
1859

£1,000-1,200   **L&T**

Kipling, Rudyard, 'The Jungle Book' and 'The Second Jungle Book', first edition, original gilt-pictorial, letters and decorated blue cloth, full-page and text illustration, together in custom 1/2 scarlet morocco and cloth slipcase.
1894 and 1895

£1,200-1,500   **FRE**

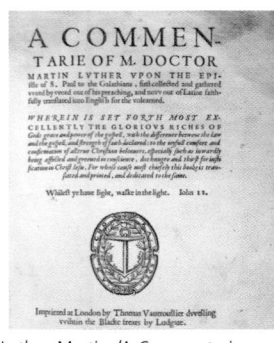

Luther, Martin, 'A Commentarie ...upon the Epistle of S. Paule to the Galathians', first English edition, Thomas Vautroullier, device on title, lacks *2 (? blank), some small tear, contemporary calf, gilt ornament on covers, rubbed, ends of hinges cracked, original ties.

1575

£2,300-2,700   **BLO**

Manson, James A, 'Sir Edwin Landseer', London and New York, the Walter Scott Publishing Co., Ltd. and Charles Scribner's Sons, photogravure frontispiece, 21 engraved plates, dark green morocco bound to a Cosway style for Sotheran & Co., gilt ruled and tooled turn-ins, marbled endpapers, slipcase.

1902

£6,000-8,000   **BLNY**

Orme, Edward, 'Orme's Graphic history of the life, exploits and death of Horatio Nelson', London: printed for, published and sold by Edward Orme… and by Longman, Hurst, Rees, and Orme, very rare earliest undated issue, engraved portrait, nine hand-coloured aquatint plates, one full-page facsimile of Nelson's handwriting, contemporary half maroon morocco, with original printed label on upper cover.

1806

£2,500-3,000   **L&T**

Planché, James Robinson, 'Costume of Shakespeare's Tragedy of Hamlet [...Othello and Comedy of the Merchant of Venice]', title vignette hand-coloured and heightened with gold, 36 hand-coloured plates by G. Scharf, contemporary half calf, covers almost detached.

1825

£700-1,000   **BLO**

Rackham, Arthur and Barrie, J. M., 'The Peter Pan portfolio', London, Hodder & Stoughton, number 471 of 500 copies, signed by the publishers and the engravers, twelve colour plates, original box.

1912

£3,000-3,500   **L&T**

Shakespeare, William, 'Macbeth', edited by William Davenant, eight edition, browned and spotted, margins trimmed with partial loss, modern half calf over marbled boards, new endpapers.

1710

£750-1,000   **BLO**

Verne, Jules, 'The Will of an Eccentric', first edition, Sampson Low & Co., plates, fold-out 'Noble Game of the United States of America'.

1900

£1,000–1,500   **BLO**

Verne, Jules, 'From the Earth to the Moon...and a Trip Round It', first English edition, Sampson Low & Co., original blue pictorial cloth decorated in gilt and black.

1873

£4,500-5,000   **BLO**

MODERN FIRST EDITIONS

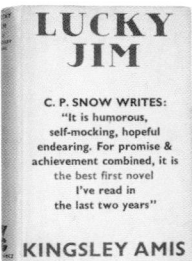

Amis, Kingsley, 'Lucky Jim,' first edition, minor spotting to extreme edge of some ff., original boards, dust-jacket slightly darkened at spine, small closed tear near head of spine.

1953

£2,000-2,500   **BLO**

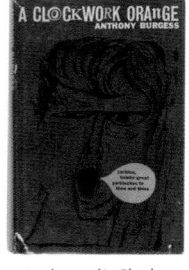

Burgess, Anthony, 'A Clockwork Orange', first edition, first issue, original boards, slight damage to spine, original dust-jacket, worn at corners, torn at foot of spine.

1962

£750-1,000   **BLO**

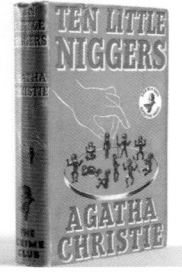

Christie, Agatha, 'Ten Little Niggers', London, for the Crime Club, by Collins, first edition, original orange cloth, dust jacket priced '7s 6d.', some short closed tears.

1939

£2,500-3,000   **L&T**

Christie, Agatha, 'The Mysterious Affair at Styles', first edition, light creasing to last f., contemporary inscription on front free endpaper, original decorated brown cloth, slight splitting to lower joint.

1921

£2,000-2,500   **BLO**

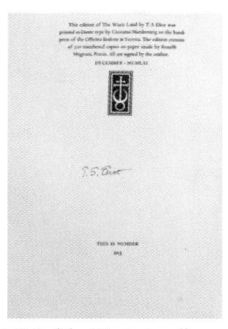

Eliot, T. S., 'The Waste Land', number 203 of 300 copies signed by the author, printed by the Officina Bodoni in Verona for Faber & Faber, original vellum-backed marbled boards, top edge gilt, others uncut, board slip-case a little rubbed with splits to joints, 4to.
1961
£1,700-2,000 BLO

Faulkner, William, 'Pylon', first trade edition, New York, original blue and black cloth, dust-jacket, chipped at head of spine, slight rubbing to fore-edges and upper joint, minor browning on lower panel.
1935
£200-250 BLO

Fleming, Ian, 'Casino Royale', first edition, first impression, full-page inscription from the author on front free endpaper, original boards, slightly cocked, first state dust-jacket without Times review, slightly chipped at head of spine.

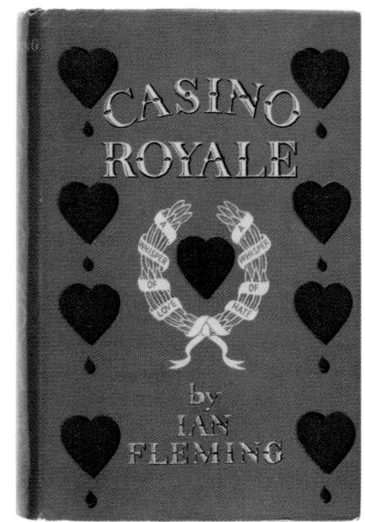

The inscription reads 'To / the power behind / the publishers' throne! / from / the author / May 1953', presumably referring to somebody related to the publishers Jonathan Cape. 'Casino Royale' is always a desirable first edition and this example is in excellent condition which makes it even more collectable.
1953
£25,000-30,000 BLO

MILLER'S COMPARES

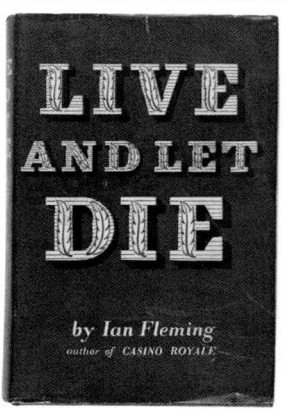

Fleming, Ian, 'Live and Let Die', first edition, original boards, first issue dust jacket without credit to Kenneth Lewis, a few light small marks/scratches but otherwise a very good example, 8vo.

1954
£8,000-9,000 BLO

Fleming, Ian, 'Live and Let Die', first edition, first state dust-jacket, slightly rubbed at joints, rubbed at corners with minor fraying to spine ends, two small closed tears, otherwise a very good example, 8vo.
1954
£11,500-12,500 BLO

First editions of Ian Fleming's James Bond novels are highly desirable. While condition is important to collectors, a signed copy – especially one dedicated to a close friend or colleague – will be hotly contested at auction.

These two copies of 'Live and Let Die' are in similar, good condition. The edition on the right has the first state dust jacket and a full-page inscription from Fleming on the front free endpaper. It reads: 'To Donald Crowther, Who helped with the coin!, from the author 1954'.

Donald Crowther seemingly worked at Spink, the London dealer and auctioneer in coins, medals, stamps, banknotes at this time, and must have advised Fleming on the 17thC gold coins being sold by 'Mr Big' in the plot of 'Live and Let Die'. The inscription adds to the connection between the author and the recipient and so the value increases.

Fleming, Ian, 'Moonraker', first edition, issue with 'shoot, signed presentation inscription from the author on front free endpaper, original boards, dust-jacket, slightly rubbed at corners, spine slightly dulled.

The inscription reads: 'To E.B. Strauss, This 'Tagebuch eines, halbwüchsigen Spiones'!, Ian Fleming, 1955'.
1955
£10,000-12,000 BLO

Fleming, Ian, 'For Your Eyes Only', first edition, signed inscription from the author on front free endpaper, original boards, dust-jacket.

The inscription reads 'To Maureen, 'Just across the corridor'!, from Ian Fleming'. A pencilled note at the front indicates that Maureen worked across the hall from his office, possibly at Kemsley Newspapers.
1960
£7,500-8,000 BLO

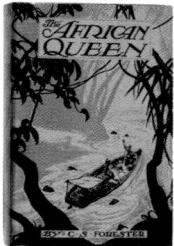

Forester, C.S., 'The African Queen', first American edition, Boston, ink name on front free endpaper, original textured cloth, dust jacket, skillful restoration to spine ends, corners and upper joint.
1935
£750-850 BLO

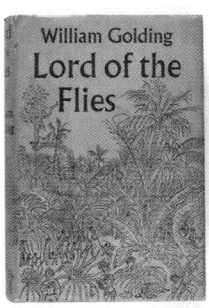

Golding, William, 'Lord of the Flies,' London, Faber and Faber, first edition, original red cloth, dustwrapper discoloured, small tear on upper hinge.

1954

£1,500-2,000   **L&T**

Greene, Graham, 'Babbling April', Oxford, Basil Blackwell, original purple-grey boards, minor wear.

1925

£2,500-3,000   **FRE**

Haggard, Sir Henry Rider, 'King Solomon's Mines', neatly repaired without loss, original red cloth, rubbed, a few small stains to upper cover, spine faded and chipped, lower joint repaired.

1885

£1,100-1,300   **BLO**

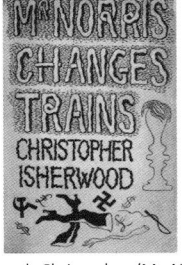

Hemingway, Ernest, 'The Old Man and the Sea', first edition, first issue with 'A' and publisher's seal on copyright page, New York, original cloth, dust jacket, small closed tear near head of spine.

1952

£900-1,200   **BLO**

Isherwood, Christopher, 'Mr. Norris Changes Trains', first edition, Hogarth Press, light spotting to endpapers, original cloth, faded at spine and fore-edges, dust-jacket, neat restoration to edges and corners.

Scarce in dust jacket
1935

£1,200-1,500   **BLO**

Joyce, James, 'A Portrait of the Artist as a Young Man', first edition, New York, contemporary inscription on front free endpaper, original cloth, gilt lettering on spine slightly dulled.

1916

£1,200-1,500   **BLO**

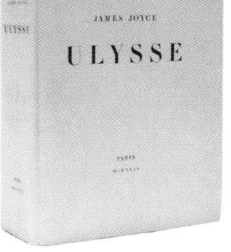

Joyce, James, 'Ulysses', first edition in French, Paris, La Maison des Amis des Livres, from an edition of 100 copies on vélin d'Arches, original printed card wrappers, a fine copy, glassine dust jacket, torn and creased at fore-edges, in modern half calf drop-back box.

1929

£1,500-2,000   **BLO**

Lawrence, D. H., 'Sons and Lovers', first edition, with twenty pages of publisher's catalogue, ink name on front free endpaper, original blue cloth lettered in gilt, very slightly cocked.

1913

£700-1,000   **BLO**

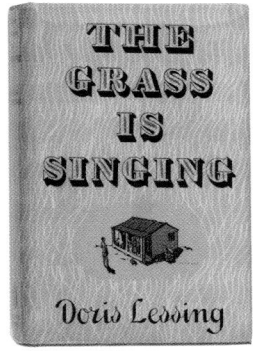

Lessing, Doris, 'The Grass is Singing', first edition, original cloth, dust-jacket.

Lessing won the Nobel Prize for literature in 2007. This is her first novel.

1950

£450-550   **BLO**

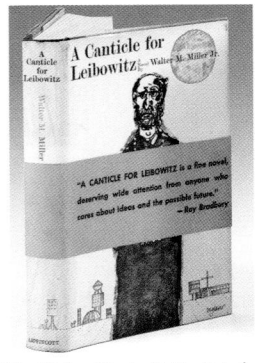

Miller, Walter M., Jr., 'A Canticle for Leibowitz', Philadelphia & New York, J. B. Lippincott, first edition, original pink cloth, black cloth shelf back, light wear, with orange wrap-around label.

1960

£500-750   **FRE**

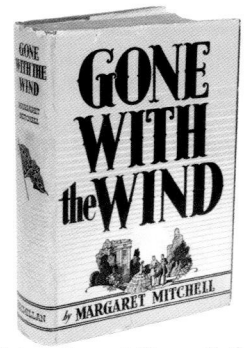

Mitchell, Margaret, 'Gone with the Wind', first edition, The MacMillan Company, New York.

This is the first edition, first issue of this Pulitzer prize winner for Literature in 1937.

1936

£1,500-2,000   **BLNY**

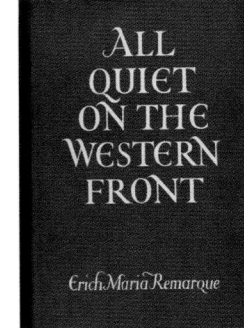

Remarque, Erich Maria, 'All Quiet on the Western Front', first English edition, original cloth, dust jacket, subtle restoration to fore-edges, spine ends and part of top edge of upper panel, spine lettering darkened.

1929

£600-800   **BLO**

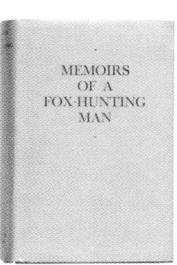

Sassoon, Siegfried, 'Memoirs of a Fox-Hunting Man', first edition, light spotting to endpapers, original cloth, dust jacket.

1928

£850-1,100   **BLO**

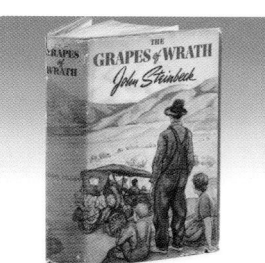

Steinbeck, John, 'Grapes of Wrath', New York: Viking, first edition, original pictorial grey cloth, light edge wear, several deep chips to dust jacket.

1939

£300-400   **FRE**

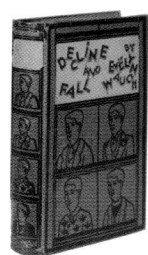

Waugh, Evelyn, 'Decline and Fall', first edition, plates by the author, original patterned cloth, dust jacket faded, spine faded and lower panel detached.

1928

£3,000-4,000   **BLO**

Wells, H.G., 'The Island of Doctor Moreau', first edition, first issue, 33 pages of advertisements, frontispiece, original pictorial cloth, slight darkening to spine and corners, slightly cocked.

1896

£550-750   **BLO**

Wells, H.G., 'The Invisible Man', first edition, first issue, two pages of advertisements, minor browning to endpapers and edges, original pictorial cloth lettered in gilt, spine and part of lower cover faded.

1897

£750-950   **BLO**

Wilde, Oscar, 'The Importance of Being Earnest', first edition, one of 1,000 copies, original salmon cloth with gilt designs by Shannon, slightly bumped and rubbed at corners.

1899

£1,100-1,400   **BLO**

Wodehouse, P.G., 'My Man Jeeves', first edition, first issue, Butler and Tanner printers, original brown cloth, frayed at spine ends with slight loss, undated.

1919

£250–350   **BLO**

Yeats, William Butler, 'The Countess Kathleen and Various Legends and Lyrics', first edition, Arthur Symons' copy with his ink inscription on front free endpaper.

1892

£2,200–3,000   **BLO**

CHILDREN'S BOOKS

Baum, L. Frank, 'The Life and Adventures of Santa Claus', coloured title and 11 plates, original red pictorial cloth, inscribed L. Frank Baum / Hollywood / April 1907'.

1902

£3,000-3,500   **BLNY**

Bewick, Thomas, 'A New Lottery Book of Birds and Beasts for Children to Learn their Letters by as soon as they can Speak', first edition.

1771

£4,500-5,500   **BLNY**

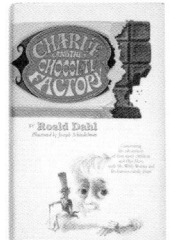

Dahl, Roald, 'Charlie and the Chocolate Factory', first edition, first issue, New York, illustrations by Joseph Schindelman.

1964

£2,000-2,500   **BLO**

Disney Studios, 'The Pop-Up Mickey Mouse', New York, Blue Ribbon Books, original edition, original colour pictorial boards, three colour pop-up illustrations.

1933

£100-150   **FRE**

Greenaway, Kate, 'Mother Goose or the Old Nursery Rhymes', first edition, London and New York, George Routledge & Sons, printed in colour from woodblocks by Edmund Evans.

First edition, first state in the rare pictorial cloth binding with no table of contents and no Evans seal added to the recto of the rear endpaper, plus all three textual errors. One of Kate Greenaway's loveliest publications for children.

1881

£1,000-1,500   **BLNY**

Milne, A. A., 'Winnie-the-Pooh', London, Metheun & Co., illustrated by Ernest H. Shepard, folding map at rear, original dark blue boards, number 182 of 350 copies signed by Milne and Shepard in 1926, jacket lightly rubbed, spine faded.

1926

£3,500-4,500   **BLNY**

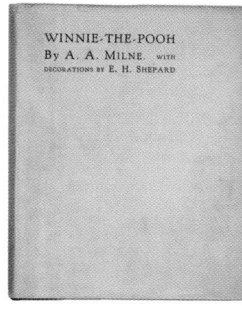

Nicholson, William, 'An alphabet', London, Heinemann, 26 plates, original decorative boards, some rubbing to edges, owner's ink inscription on front endpaper.

1898 [1897]

£700-900   L&T

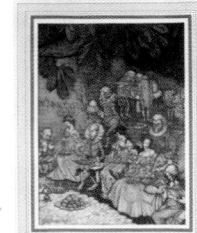

Potter, Beatrix, 'The Tale of Peter Rabbit', London, first edition, first printing, privately printed by Strangeways, coloured frontispiece, 41 full-page line illustrations, all after Potter, inscription by C.E. Cobb dated June 1902.

1901

£25,000-35,000   BLNY

Rowling, J. K., 'Harry Potter and the Order of the Phoenix', London, Bloomsbury, first edition, presentation copy, inscribed on title-page 'To Chantelle, lots of love, J. K. Rowling X', original cloth, dust jacket, unread in mint condition.

2003

£1,200-1,500   L&T

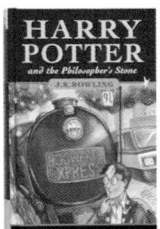

Rowling, J. K., 'Harry Potter and the Philosopher's Stone', first edition, very slight darkening to ff, original pictorial boards, tiny nicks to the tips of the fore-corners and foot of spine corners, slightly cocked.
One of only 500 first edition copies released.
1997

£16,000-20,000   BLO

Sendak, Maurice, 'Where the Wild Things Are', first edition, New York, Harper & Row, coloured illustrations after Sendak.

First edition with the very rare first issue dust-jacket

1963

£2,200-2,600   BLNY

Tolkien, J.R.R., 'The Hobbit', first edition, full-page illustrations and map endpapers by the author, gilt figure of 'Smaug' to foot of upper cover.

1937

£3,000-3,500   BLO

DOCUMENTS

Byng, John, Admiral, executed by firing squad on the quarter-deck of HMS Monarque for neglect of duty (1704-57), 'Journal of Byng's Command of the Mediterranean Fleet in 1748', autograph manuscript, 121pp., numerous ink corrections, paper watermarked with Arms of Great Britain over 'GR', c1740s, wrappers with inscription.
c1740s

£17,000-20,000   BLO

Dickens, Charles, a cheque drawn on Messrs. Coutts and Co. for £500, paid to 'Self', signed by 'Charles Dickens', 'Twenty Ninth October 1864'.

£1,200-1,500   L&T

Staffordshire, Robert de Wicliff and Antony St. Quintin, quitclaim to John Depden all rights in the manor of Hanlay [Hanley], manuscript in Latin, on vellum, folds, a little browned, two red wax seals, one fine impression and the other cracked and with slight loss, Helagh (Yorkshire), 2nd October 1393.

Hanley, a suburb of Stoke-on-Trent.

6.5in (16.5cm)

£850-950   BLO

A grant by Sir William Phelipp, John Barney and others of the manor of 'Cokefeldhalle', Yoxford, Suffolk to John Manning, manuscript on vellum, in Latin, folds, four wax seals with remarkably fine and clear impressions, witnessed by Simon Felbrigg, John Heveningham, John Fastolf and others, 21st July 1428.

10.75in (27.5cm) wide

£800-1,000   BLO

Robinson, W. Heath, five advertisements for the Duroid Co., printed from the original blocks.

£250-350   **L&T**

Morley, Alan, a collection of four Nosey Parker strip cartoons, numbers 393, 400, 440 and 503, pen, ink and blue pencil, each approximately twelve cells.

Each 9in (23cm) wide

£400-600   **L&T**

A set of twelve original ink 'Beau Peep' strip cartoons, as published in The Daily Star, numbered Sat. 132, Wed. 63 – Sat. 66, Mon. 31 – Sat 36.

£200-300   **L&T**

A set of ten signed original ink cartoons of cats, by Paul Wood, Jack Blyth, Wright, Dicky Howett, Richie and Pep, on paper or card, one numbered in ink in margin.

£200-300   **L&T**

A set of ten signed original golf cartoons, by Chris Wright, Jack Blyth, Sax, and Wing, ink on paper or card, three with number in ink in margin.

£200-300   **L&T**

Watkins, Dudley, 'Oor Wullie' and 'Ma & Pa Broon', both pen and ink over pencil, signed by Watkins.

Dudley Dexter Watkins (1907-69) was a comic artist, employed by publisher DC Thomson, who made his name drawing two comic strips for the Scottish Sunday Post newspaper: 'Oor Wullie' and 'The Broons'. Both were launched in a comic supplement published by the newspaper on March 8 1936. 'Oor Wullie' follows the adventures of an eight- or nine-year-old boy who gets into trouble, eats too many sweets and does his best to avoid girls. Most strips begin and end with him sitting on his trademark upturned metal bucket. 'The Broons' is a domestic comedy about a large family and presents a warm-hearted picture of urban Scottish life. The Broons all 'spoke' in broad Scottish dialect and rapidly became popular – by 1971 the Sunday Post had an estimated readership of just under three million, or 79 per cent of the adult population of Scotland.

1938

£5,500-6,000   **L&T**

Collins, Dennis and Dodd, Maurice, ten original ink strip cartoons on card of 'The Perishers', numbers L89-L98, each numbered and dated in the margin, stamped on verso 'Slade London'.

1977

£450-550   **L&T**

Fisher, Harry Conway 'Bud', 'Mutt and Jeff', original pen and ink cartoon drawing in five panels on card, depicts Jeff and a doctor attending an ailing Mutt, light fading, corners chipped, some minor scattered rubbing.

Created in 1907, Mutt and Jeff was the first successful daily comic strip in the United States and thus the beginning of a particularly American popular art form that reached millions through the massive circulations of the Pulitzer and Hearst newspaper empires. Lanky Mutt and short Jeff soon passed quickly into the American vernacular, becoming the basis for early films as well as comic books. The strip ran for nearly 75 years, though Fisher himself had stopped drawing the strips by 1932, when he had become wealthy enough to let another artist work under his license.

28in (72cm) wide

£250-350   **BLNY**

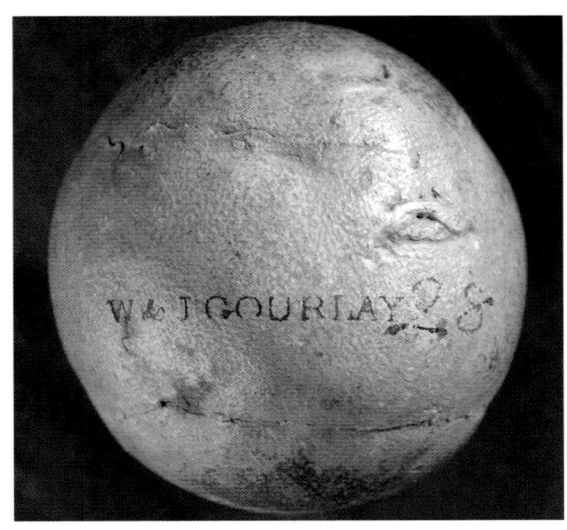

A W. & J. Gourlay feather golf ball, stamped with the maker's name and numbered 28, in ink, in mint condition.

£5,400-6,500   L&T

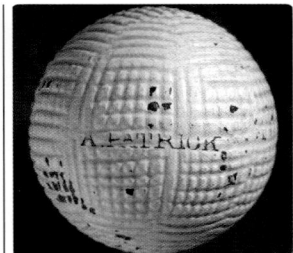

An Alex Patrick of Leven hand-hammered gutty ball, stamped 'A. Patrick' retaining most of the original paint.

£6,500-8,500   L&T

A 'Henley Union Jack' pattern gutty ball, in mint condition.

£4,200-4,800   L&T

A Stowe Woodward 'Burbank' rubber-core ball, patterned with swirling-pattern grooves.

£1,200-1,800   L&T

A US Rubber Co. 'Tiger 1' yellow rubber-core ball, with circlet pattern.

£150-200   L&T

A Hutchison & Main, Springvale 'Hawk' bramble-pattern gutty ball, in original wrappers.

£380-420   L&T

A Tom Morris beech-headed longnose spoon, the scared head stamped 'T. Morris', horn insert to sole, lead counterweight, hickory shaft.

£1,300-1,700   L&T

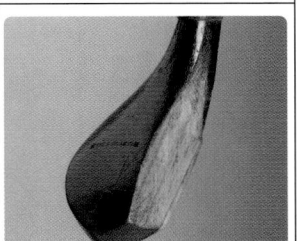

A James J. Hutchison longnose playclub, the scared beech head stamped 'Hutchison', with horn insert, lead counterweight, hickory shaft, head cracked.

£480-550   L&T

A Robert Forgan longnose putter, the scared beech head stamped 'R. Forgan' and Prince of Wales feathers, horn insert to sole, lead counterweight, the hickory shaft stamped 'R. Forgan & Son, St. Andrews'.

£850-950   L&T

A Cochranes Ltd Mammoth niblick, Edinburgh, with dot-pattern face, hickory shaft.

£6,000-7,000   L&T

An American Harry C. Lee & Co. backward putter, New York, aluminium head, hickory shaft.

£2,000-2,500   L&T

A Baltimore Putter Co. 'Triangular' putter, multifaceted adjustable putter, hickory shaft.

£1,600-2,000   L&T

'Glasgow from the Green with Golfers in the Distance', by A. R. Grieve, signed, inscribed and dated on the reverse, watercolour.

1879   14.5in (36.5cm) wide

£1,200-1,800   L&T

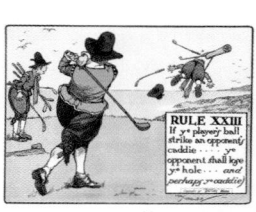

Charles Crombie, 'The Rules of Golf Illustrated', London, Derby & Sons, with 24 colour lithographs, lettered cloth-backed boards, minimal soiling, boards slightly rubbed and soiled.

This elaborate album was issued by 'Golf Illustrated' to advertise Perrier. A limited edition of plate-marked proofs was also issued.
1905

£850-950   **BLNY**

A George Pietzcker sepia photograph, depicting the 1931 America Ryder Cup Team, including Sam Ryder and Walter Hagen.

16in (40.5cm) high

£8,000-9,000   **L&T**

A Ryder Cup Official Souvenir programme, Southport, The Fourth International Golf Match, Monday & Tuesday, June 26-27, 1933, internally signed by Arthur J. Lacey, John Henry Taylor and Syd Easterbrook.

£1,000-1,500   **FRE**

A copy of Time Magazine, Vol. XVI no. 12, September 22, 1930, with a portrait of Robert Tyre 'Bobby' Jones Jnr to the cover.

£300-400   **L&T**

A late Victorian silver and enamel golfing vesta case, London, the obverse with an arched rectangular enamelled panel of a golfer at the top of his back swing, the reverse with cursive initials.
1891   *2.25in (5.5cm) high*

£1,900-2,200   **L&T**

An Augusta National Golf Club 1939 Master's Tournament Series Ticket, March 26th-April 2nd, no. 298, signed by the winner Ralph Guldahl to the obverse and Sam Snead to the reverse.

£3,200-3,800   **L&T**

A Dunaverty Golf Club white metal medal, the obverse relief decorated with ribbon-tied crossed clubs and balls, the reverse inscribed 'Dunaverty Golf Club, 1889… Won by Mr William Reid', with cast surmount and right suspension, cased.

1.5in (4cm) diam

£580-700   **L&T**

A Gorham sterling silver and enamel vesta case, decorated to the obverse with a golfer lining up a putt.

2.25in (5.5cm) high

£4,200-5,000   **L&T**

A Copeland Late Spode pottery jug, relief-decorated in white with a scene of golfers in the round, on an olive-green and beige ground.

4.25in (11cm) high

£420-550   **L&T**

A Royal Doulton 'Colonel Bogey Whisky' water jug, the salt-glazed baluster body relief-decorated with a crest inscription and ornamental band and transfer-printed with two golfing scenes.
c1904   *7.5in (19cm) high*

£1,400-2,000   **L&T**

A Royal Doulton, Burslem blue and white transfer-printed plate, decorated with a golfing scene.

c1888   *12in (30.5cm) diam*

£5,000-7,000   **L&T**

Garrincha's 1962 World Cup final shirt, a match-worn Brazil No. 7 international jersey, some damage.

Manoel Francisco dos Santos (1933-83), known by his nickname Garrincha (Little Bird), was an outstanding Brazilian right winger and influential member of the 1958 and 1962 World Cup winning teams.

£15,000-20,000   GBA

A pair of black leather football boots, worn by Stanley Matthews in 1953.

These are a pair of Co-Op boots that were supplied to Matthews in exchange for his appearances in their stores to sign autographs.

£1,500-2,000   GBA

A leather football, with removable lid and internal ceramic pot.
c1920

£500-600   RGA

A signed Manchester United 1968 European Cup final LP record, produced by Instant Records, with commentary from the match against Benfica at Wembley Stadium, the sleeve designed in the shape of a football and signed in blue biro by the 11 Manchester United finalists Alex Stepney, Pat Crerand, Bill Foulkes, John Aston, David Sadler, Shay Brennan, Nobby Stiles, Tony Dunne, Brian Kidd, George Best and Bobby Charlton.

£1,800-2,200   GBA

An F. A. Cup Final programme for Tottenham Hotspur v Wolverhampton Wanderers, played at Stamford Bridge Chelsea 23rd April 1921.

£2,300-2,800   GBA

'Pelé: Edson Arantes do Nascimento', a deluxe large-format limited edition book, published by Gloria Books with each copy personally signed by Pelé.

£550-650   GBA

A large sgraffito-technique Chelsea Football Club crest roundel, suitable for use as a table top.

This unique piece was owned by Raphael Djanogly OBE and was made at the time of the club's historic 1954-55 Championship winning season. The club crest was introduced under Ted Drake's management in 1953 as part of his modernisation plans for the club.

42in (107cm) diam

£2,000-3,000   GBA

A important bronze plaque presented to Jules Rimet by the French Football Federation in 1931, designed by Abel La Fleur, the plaque signed 'Abel La Fleur - Sculp't.

21.75in (55cm) high

£4,000-6,000   GBA

A large spelter group of two footballers, signed Ulysse, the players modelled chasing the ball side-by-side, one with the ball 'mid-air' on his right foot.

16.5in (42cm) high

£300-400   GBA

A large spelter figure of a footballer, signed S. Kinsburger, modelled running with the ball at his right foot.

19in (49cm) high

£250-350   GBA

A chromium-plated figure of a footballer, modelled taking a powerful right foot shot, the ball sculpted separately on the marble base.

11.5in (29cm) high

£150-200   GBA

A red silk jockey's jacket, worn by Jem Mason, mounted in a display case with caption reading 'Jacket Worn by J. Mason, who rode Mr J. Elmore's 'Lottry', winner of the First National on this course'.

These silks were displayed in the County Stand at Aintree racecourse.

34in (86.5cm) high

£2,500-3,000 **GBA**

A 1950s jockey's jacket, in the famous Crazy Quilt colours, by Boyce & Rogers of Newmarket.

These colours were first registered in 1950 to Chesney Allen, a member of the Crazy Gang.

£500-700 **GBA**

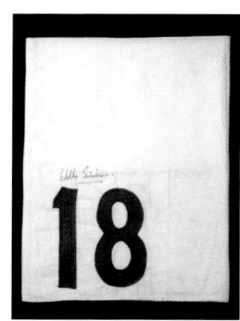

Shergar's no. 18 number cloth from the 1981 Derby Stakes, signed by his jockey Walter Swinburn.

Shergar is one of the most famous horses of the 20thC. Having been retired to a stud in County Kildare, he was stolen and held to ransom. He was never seen again and is presumed to have been killed.

£4,500-5,500 **GBA**

A racing plate worn by Brown Jack when winning his historic sixth consecutive Queen Alexandra Stakes in 1934, mounted with a silver plaque.

1934 *8in (20cm) high*

£850-950 **GBA**

A Trigo 1929 Derby silk commemorative scarf, mounted, framed and glazed.

37.5in (95cm)

£80-120 **GBA**

A Blenheim 1930 Derby silk commemorative scarf.

£85-95 **GBA**

A 1912 Grand National souvenir display, created and signed by Arthur F. Meyrick, comprising hand-coloured photographs of the 1912 Grand National winner 'Jerry M', Sir Charles Assheton-Smith (owner), Robert Gore (trainer) and Ernie Piggott (jockey), mounted with two locks of the horse's hair, in a modern frame.

22in (56cm) wide

£400-600 **GBA**

Jason Lowes, 'Desert Orchid', signed, watercolour and gouache, additionally signed to the mount by the trainer David Elsworth.

This original work has been reproduced as a limited edition print of 55, all signed by David Elsworth.

20.25in (52cm) wide

£1,500-2,000 **GBA**

The historic Aintree Racecourse mounting bell, inscribed 'Aintree Racecourse, 1831'.

This bell signalled to the jockeys to mount their horses.

13.75in (35cm) high

£10,500-12,500 **GBA**

A bronze, 'Gladiateur', by Pierre Lenordez (1815-1892), signed, mid-brown patina, the plinth cast with a panel inscribed with details of the 19thC French racehorse.

13.75in (35cm) wide

£5,500-7,500 **GBA**

The silver trophy, for the 1881 Chesterfield Cup at Goodwood, in the form of a sculptural group by Hunt & Roskell titled 'Sir Roger de Coverley and the Gypsies, Spectator,' hallmarked London, on a naturalistic base with a title plaque, inscribed 'Goodwood 1881', with the original oak fitted carrying case, with key.

Trophies such as this were often the prize for races at this time, rather than cash. This is typical of the style of trophies offered, where a horse usually formed part of the design but rarely in a sporting context.

1881 *Group 18.5in (47cm) long*

£23,000-28,000 **GBA**

A stuffed pike, mounted in a naturalistic setting with painted backboard, ebonised and gilt-lined, glazed, bowfront case, the back with attached advert for 'Geo. Bazeley, Taxidermist, Northampton'.

49in (124.5cm) wide

£600-800   **L&T**

A stuffed bream, by J. Copper & Sons, London, in a naturalistic setting with painted backdrop, a label to the interior inscribed 'Bream, 3lbs. 10ozs., Caught by H. Taylor, River Severn, at Upton on Severn, Sept. 25th 1927', ebonised and gilt-lined, glazed, bowfront case.

26.5in (67cm) wide

£800-1,200   **L&T**

A stuffed chub, by W. F. Home, London, in a naturalistic setting with painted backdrop, the ebonised and gilt-lined, glazed, bowfront case inscribed, 'Chub, 3lbs., Caught at Broxbourne by W. Perry, 15th Oct. 1924'.

22.5in (57.5cm) wide

£450-550   **L&T**

A stuffed chub, by W. R. Pape, Newcastle-upon-Tyne, mounted against grasses on a painted backdrop, inscribed, 'Cheshunt, 'Old Lea', July, 1933, Wgt 3lb. 12ozs., re-cased 1956', in an ebonised glazed case.

24.5in (62cm) wide

£150-200   **L&T**

A Hardy 'Perfect' all-brass salmon fly reel, pierced brass foot, turk's head locking nut above tension adjuster to rim, dished backplate, the faceplate stamped horizontal, oval, horizontal and rod-in-hand logs, Hardy replacement ebonite handle.

4in (10cm) diam

£1,000-1,500   **L&T**

A very rare 1896 Pattern Hardy brass and alloy 'Perfect' 4.5in (11.5cm) Salmon Fly Reel, seldom seen variant with backplate, frame and foot cast integrally in alloy and with dished alloy drum with large and small perforations, all left in 'bright' finish.

1895-97

£1,000-£1,500   **MM**

A brass race check winch, made by J. Bernard & Son, London, with folding horn handle.

3.75in (7cm) diam

£600-800   **TEN**

A Hardy's 2.75in 1982 Special Edition 'Perfect' brass fishing reel, from the centenary boxed rod and reel set, in leather case with sterling silver presentation plate.

£1,500-2,000   **MUR**

A Hardy brass and alloy Perfect 3' reel.

£400-500   **BRI**

A pair of original New York Yankee Baseball Stadium chairs, painted blue, with plaque on back reading 'Yankee Stadium 50th Anniversary 1923-1973.'

32.5in (82.5cm) high

£850-950   **DRA**

A New York Yankees 1939 World Series signed baseball, with 22 signatures including 19 players who include Joe DiMaggio.

£600-800   **DRA**

A silver cigar case presented to pugilist Tom Sayers in 1860, manufactured by Hilliard & Thomason, the body engraved 'Presented by L. Abrahams to Tom Sayers, The Champion of the World', hallmarks for Birmingham, 1860, hinged lid.

Thomas Sayers was born in the deprived slum district of Pimlico, Brighton on 25th May 1826. He is considered one of the most brilliant pugilists known and was involved in contests lasting up to 85 rounds. He became the bare knuckle Champion of England when he beat 'The Tipton Slasher' in 1857. He was elected into the Boxing Hall of Fame in 1954. Abrahams was named in contemporary newspapers as Sayer's promoter.

5.25in (13.5cm) high

£2,600-3,000   **GBA**

A Bank of England £5 banknote signed by Muhammad Ali.

£250-300   GBA

A Nigel Mansell nomex race-suit, worn during the 1987 F1 season when driving the Williams-Honda FW11B, made by 'Stand 21', with embroidered name on the belt, Union Jack and all sponsors patches.

In the 1987 season Nigel Mansell won six Grand Prix and once more finished second in the Drivers' World Championship, following the famous incident with the exploding rear tyre in Australia in 1986.

£3,000-5,000   GBA

A mahogany cabinet made from the hull of a boat, the hinged door inscribed 'O.U.B.C. Eights 1895, Magdalen College, Head of the River' and with names, the interior with two drawers and a shelf with painted college arms.

16in (40.5cm) high

£1,500-2,000   WW

A Victorian velvet rugby cap, presented to Alfred Ash for the Yorkshire Challenge Cup Final 1887, mounted in a stained wood frame.

£800-1,200   HT

A large French spelter figure of a rugby player, signed Lemoyne, modelled about to take a kick.

17in (43cm) high

£200-300   GBA

The silver-gilt Lonsdale Belt for the Lightweight Championship of Great Britain, won outright by Dave Charnley in 1963, hallmarks for Mappin & Webb, Sheffield, 1956.

32in (81.5cm) wide

£8,500-9,500   GBA

A large Bähr & Pröschild bisque shoulder head doll, with brown sleeping eyes, the open mouth with teeth, a dimple to the chin, earrings, replaced dark brown real hair wig, leather body with bisque forearms, wearing an old white dress, one brown leather shoe, marked '410'.

c1900   *24in (60cm) high*

£380-420   **WDL**

A large German B. S. W 'Wendy' bisque character doll, with deeply moulded mouth, brown glass sleeping eyes and moulded eyebrows, on a pink jointed composition body, wearing a blonde antique mohair wig and old, if not original, clothing, shoes and socks, marked on rear of head '2033', and in a heart 'B S W 537', small professional restoration of one finger on each hand.

23in (58.50cm) high

£18,000-22,000   **JDJ**

A Heubach 9573 Googley doll, with blue glass sleeping eyes, on typical composition body with moulded shoes and socks, retains original brown mohair wig, straw bonnet and red and white print dress.

7in (18cm) high

£450-550   **JDJ**

A German Heubach Koppeldorf 300.3 doll, with open/close eyes and mouth showing two teeth and a tongue, in knitted jacket.

c1920-25   *18in (45.5cm) high*

£150-250   **HB**

A Heubach doll, in all-original clothing, with shoulder plate attached to a cloth body, dressed in a white suit and straw hat.

c1900   *20in (51cm) high*

£250-350   **HB**

A Jumeau first series portrait doll, with glass eyes, original wig with curls, marked shoes and original green dress, with original spring in head, on eight-ball-jointed Jumeau body, marked with '3/0' in neck socket, body shows minor wear.

13in (33cm) high

£7,000-8,000   **JDJ**

A rare large French Têtê Jumeau, the unmarked size 16 pale bisque doll, with curly wig with long tails, original cork pate marked '16', brown paperweight eyes, open mouth, large composition/wood body, in glass case.

36in (91.50cm) high

£2,200-2,800   **JDJ**

A Kämmer & Reinhardt bisque head doll, with sleeping eyes, modelled and painted eyebrows, open mouth with teeth, pierced ears with earrings, dimples in the chin, with a blonde real hair wig with plaits, marked '191' and 'Ehlert'.

20in (50cm) high

£500-600   **WDL**

A Kestner 'Bru' doll, with sleeping eyes, open-closed mouth with moulded teeth, multi-balled composition body with jointed ankle, with antique clothing and original wig with plaster pate, minor wear and paint touch-up to body.

18.50in (47cm) high

£1,800-2,200   **JDJ**

A Kestner character baby doll 152, with open/close eyes and mouth with moulded tongue and teeth, dressed in a long white dress.

c1915-20   *13.75in (35cm) high*

£450-500   **HB**

A rare Simon & Halbig bisque head doll, with open mouth, replaced brown eyes, painted lashes, brown real hair wig, body in fifteen parts, wearing a short velvet suit, an old white shirt, an old embroidered straw hat and old red leather boots.

32in (80cm) high

£400-500   **WDL**

TOYS

A pre-Greiner papier-mâché head doll, with glass eyes, stitched leather arms and hands, in original clothing.

c1860.   *29in (73.5cm) high*

£250-300   DRA

An extremely rare Kaulitz doll, with papier-mâché head and painted brown eyes, red cheeks and a ginger wig, wearing an old blue dress, brown leather shoes, an old straw hat, stamped in red 'Germany'.

18in (45cm) high

£1,600-2,000   WDL

A wax head doll, with blue sleeping eyes, the open mouth with four teeth, a blonde original mohair wig, thirteen-part body, the left thumb missing, wearing old shoes and socks.

c1900   *11.25in (28cm) high*

£280-320   WDL

A mid-18thC English wooden doll, the gessoed face with large black glass eyes, wooden body articulated at elbows, hips and knees, with mortise and tenon joints, which enable a life-like movement, refined carving of the ankle bones, feet and hands, retains dark brown human hair wig which is topped by a lace mantua over a red silk brocade dress, beneath her dress are a plain chemise and an off-white quilted petticoat, stockings and red leather shoes with ties.

28in (71cm) high

£18,000-22,000   JDJ

DOLLS HOUSES

A late 19thC English painted and paper-covered Victorian dolls house, the three-storey house opens at the front to reveal four papered rooms, on a platform base, with assorted furniture.

32.5in (82.5cm) high

£10,000-15,000   FRE

An American New York Eloise dolls house, in the shape of the Plaza Hotel, with a hand-cranked elevator, with a group of dolls house furniture to include two Chinese Chippendale chairs, a washstand, a marble-top table, painted bed etc.

c1910   *26.75in (68cm) wide*

£4,500-5,500   POOK

A 'Mystery House' dolls house, distributed by F. A. O. Schwartz, with eight rooms, two hallways, stairway, windows, porch, mouldings, period interior restored with antique fabrics, originally owned by Annie Pinkway Watt of New York City.

c1900   *54in (137cm) wide*

£6,000-7,000   BER

An early 20thC German M. Gottschalk dolls house, front section opens in two pieces to expose six rooms plus a closet, retains original wallpaper and flooring, second floor has spectacular crested arches.

37in (94cm) high

£4,000-5,000   JDJ

A late 19th/early 20thC painted card and paper model of Stowe House, depicted with trees either side of a lake in the foreground, in a rectangular-section glass display case, with ebonised wood base.

19in (48cm) wide

£160-200   DN

A late 19thC Viennese enamelled and gilt-metal suite of dolls house salon furniture, comprising settee, three chairs and a table, all decorated with scenes of courting couples.

The settee 3in (7.5cm) wide

£450-550   DN

A pair of patinated lead maquettes, cast from models by George J. Frampton, made for Queen Mary's Dolls House, raised on L-shaped faux marble pedestal bases, one bearing monogram 'CF' and dated.

1922   *10.25in (26cm) high*

£800-1,200   L&T

A German painted Noah's Ark, with forty-two animals,

c1900   40in (101.5cm) wide
£2,300-3,000   POOK

A late 19thC German painted pine Noah's Ark and seventy-two carved animals, with fabric hinged lid, wire latch, with stencilled windows, trim and roof, and hand-painted dove, containing hand-carved and painted animals and two female figures, with minor imperfections.

24in (61cm) long
£1,200-1,800   SK

A painted and carved miniature circus bandwagon and bandstand, by Frank Goldquist, Savannah, Illinois, dated March 9, 1948, the horse-drawn wagon with two drivers and eleven musicians together with a bandstand with carved musicians.

20in (51cm) long
£1,200-1,800   FRE

Two carved and painted miniature calliope wagons, by Frank Goldquist, Savannah, Illinois, dated Sept 20, 1951, and Oct 10, 1964, the first with a carved driver, the second a plastic driver.

Largest 19in (48.5cm) long
£1,000-1,500   FRE

An English carved and painted wood rocking horse, with real hair mane and tail, sheepskin saddlecloth, leather saddle, stirrups and bridle, raised on square-section pillar stand.

£550-650   A&G

An early 20thC large carved rocking horse, by F.H. Ayres, restored by Brian & Jean Tildesley.

48in (122cm) high
£4,800-5,200   RGA

A small rocking horse, restored, in very good condition.

PROVENANCE: This horse was acquired from Marguerite Fawdry, owner of Pollocks Toy Museum in Scala Street, London and the author of 'The English Rocking Horse'.

c1910   29in (73.5cm) high
£2,000-2,500   RGA

An early Lines Bros. painted wood and fabricated metal pedal car, with buff-coloured bodywork and green-painted wheel arches and upholstery.

1942   55in (140cm) long
£1,600-2,000   A&G

An Austin A40 fabricated metal pedal car, in sky blue.

58in (147cm) long
£1,000-1,500   A&G

A Viktor Schreckengost enamelled steel pedal car, of aeroplane form.

47in (119cm) wide
£1,700-2,200   SDR

A 1930s Industrial Modernism child's bicycle, painted metal, bears mark to both sides 'Kiddy Bike/Safe and Sound'.

40in (102cm) wide
£220-280   L&T

A late 20thC Japanese Chevrolet Corvette, white-lacquered and lithographed tinplate, battery-driven, with illuminated rear window, signed 'Corvette', 'Chevrolet' and 'Made in Japan', maker's mark Taiyo.

10.25in (25.5cm) long

£18-22   KAU

A Japanese Irco musical Cadillac, boxed example, battery-operated, plays music when moving forward, colourful graphics on box lid.

9in (23cm) long

£100-200   BER

A Japanese SSS sight-seeing tin bus, white with nickel side trim, features interior red seating, rubber tyres and friction driver, boxed.

7.75in (19.5cm) long

£100-200   BER

A pair of Hauser military vehicles, tin and lithographed in olive, one in blue camouflage, includes six-wheel Krupp truck and anti-aircraft truck, with replacement wheels and breaks to windshields, missing some smaller accessories.

11in (28cm) long

£200-300   BER

A Tipp and Co. Hindenburg dirigible, boxed example, lithographed tin, painted in silver overall with celluloid propellers, swastika markings to fin and box.

The Hindenburg ran the first scheduled transatlantic flights, and remains the largest aircraft ever to take to the skies. It burst into flames in 1937, marking the end of commercial dirigibles.

11in (28cm) long

£1,300-1,600   BER

A small river boat, by Uebelacker of Germany, hand-painted tin, red and white hull, simple details to deck features canopy top on rear deck area, single stack, figurehead and brass plate on stern, repainted.

9in (23cm) long

£250-350   BER

A Martin orange vendor, lithographed and hand-painted tin, open cart contains embossed orange display, figure wears cloth shirt, spoke wheels painted red.

7.5in (19cm) long

£500-700   BER

A Spanish lithographed tin toy, with two bear cubs riding with larger bear driving motorcycle.

9in (23cm) long

£1,000-1,500   BER

A German lithographed tin toy, by Tipp & Co. depicting boy with blackboard, clockwork movement.

8in (20cm) high

£900-1,200   BER

CLOCKWORK

A Renault lithographed tin biplane, by Carl Rossignol of France, very colourful graphics, features seated pilot, three propellers, disc wheels, clockwork mechanism, repaint to propellers, minor break to fin bracket.

13.5in (34.5cm) wide

£300-400   BER

A lithographed tin biplane, by Distler of Germany, in red overall, single propeller, wing reads 'JD 2755', fuselage contains windows on sides, disc wheels, clockwork-driven, resoldered propeller, one wing replaced.

16.5in (42cm) wide

£300-350   BER

A hand-painted tin German Märklin zeppelin, in white with silver gondolas, striking scale and design, complete with celluloid propellers and clockwork mechanism, some overpaint to body.

c1910   *12in (30.5cm) long*

£2,000-2,500   BER

A rare German Bing limousine, dark blue, with green lining, black roof, orange hubs, includes chauffeur, clockwork motor, steerable front wheels and, unusually, cable for remote-control steering, which requires reattachment, both rear doors open, some surface corrosion.

c1920   10.5in (27cm) long
£470-550   VEC

A lithographed tin limousine, by Karl Bub of Germany, in maroon with light red striping and black roof, features full running boards, nickel head lamps, seated chauffeur, opening side doors, spoke wheels, clockwork driven, figure repainted, replaced lamps and bracket, wear to roof.

                14in (35.5cm)
£750-850   BER

A convertible B2 Torpedo open tourer, by Citroën of France, with nickel plate grill, full running boards, simulated soft top lays across back seat, celluloid windshield, clockwork driven.

c1920s   14.25in (36cm) long
£800-1,200   BER

A hand-painted luxury limousine, by Carette of Germany, in white with blue striping and roof, red-trimmed window frames, embossed seating painted brown, bevelled glass windows, nickel plated headlamps, rubber tyres, spoke wheels, roof rail rack and clockwork driven, roof rail repainted, lamps replaced, dent to hood and roof.

This model is the largest in the series.

                16in (40.5cm) long
£2,500-3,000   BER

A rare Converse touring car, with fold-down canvas roof, heavy-gauge tin blue body with yellow running boards and red embossed seating, wooden dummy lights, spoke wheels, celluloid windscreen and clockwork mechanism with centre body crank position, break at windscreen, front wheels loose.

                15in (38cm) long
£1,500-2,000   BER

A Converse pressed-steel covered auto wagon, early example with three bench seats, original fringe surrounding roof with clockwork key at centre, rubber tyres, spoke wheels, paint worn but with traces of red and bright green flooring, black fenders, scarce example, wear to paint.

                10.5in (26.5cm) long
£600-1,000   BER

A Distler lithographed tin fire ladder truck, bright red, with seated fireman, extension ladder and clockwork mechanism.

                11in (28cm) overall
£300-500   BER

A lithographed tin limousine, by Distler of Germany, with electric headlights and rear license, grill reads '603', in yellow with orange trim, blue sides, black rood and running boards, with seated driver, clockwork driven.

                10in (25.5cm) long
£700-1,000   BER

A rare Hans Erbel 'Strawbridge & Clothier' tin windup delivery truck, with original box and shipping label pasted to exterior, crazing to lithography and hand-painted frame.

£3,000-4,000   JDJ

A limousine, by Hans Eberl of Germany, well-modelled lithographed tin example, colourful blues and grey with extensive gold trim highlights, features opening doors, seated driver, roof top luggage rack, side brake, spoke wheels, glass wind shield, clockwork driven, restoration to bottom of one door, roof and fenders.

                13.5in (34.5cm) long
£1,000-1,200   BER

A German Greppert and Kelch lithographed tin open tourer, in rich green and beige with red embossed seating, driver at wheel, clockwork mechanism.

1920s   7.75in (19.5cm) long
£350-450   BER

A Gunthermann tinplate four-door sedan, large scale clockwork model in blue, plated parts, steerable front wheels, lacks bonnet motif, otherwise in good condition, with a fair condition illustrated box.

                11in (28cm) long
£240-300   VEC

A large hand-painted limousine, by Märklin of Germany, in deep blue with light blue pinstripes, features opening doors, glass windows, rear luggage rack and roof top rack, nickel steering wheel, side lamps, headlamps, rubber tyres, ornate spoke wheels and clockwork mechanism.

A very desirable find, for its scale and design this example is arguably the finest made by Märklin.

18in (45.5cm) long

£12,000-15,000   BER

A saloon by Richter and Co. of Germany, depicts seated driver, luggage rack on striped roof, gold running boards, clockwork driven.

This is one of the more colourful and graphic of lithographed early toy autos.

5.75in (14.5cm) long

£1,000-1,500   BER

A lithographed tin ladder truck, by Tipp and Co. of Germany, open bench body with complete railing and three seated firemen, contains driver and ladder on supports, clockwork driven, spoke wheels.

8.5in (21.5cm) long

£500-1,000   BER

A hand-painted tin ocean liner, by Bing of Germany, four-stack model with red and white hull, upper deck cabin, railed sides, ten lifeboats, pilot's cabin, funnels, mast and clockwork mechanism, repainted.

27in (68.5cm) long

£2,500-3,000   BER

A hand-painted tin river boat, by Bing of Germany, with full canopy over entire deck, clockwork driven, side windows and railed sides.

19.5in (49.5cm) long

£1,000-1,500   BER

A Lehmann hand-painted and lithographed tin 'Tut Tut' toy, depicts suited gentleman with horn in mouth riding open auto, clockwork mechanism.

6.75in (17cm) high

£700-1,000   BER

A Märklin red clockwork racer, racing no. 7, cycle type wings to front wheels, lacks wheels to rear and with no clockwork motor, otherwise in good condition.

1934   15in (38cm) long

£300-400   VEC

An English Meccano tinplate racer, black open auto with red interior and fenders, clockwork mechanism, tool and extra screws.

9in (23cm) long

£180-220   BER

A lithographed tin luxury model limousine, by Tipp and Co. of Germany, with beige body and blue bonnet, roof and running boards, electric headlights, opening rear doors and clockwork mechanism, some scratches and denting to roof.

15in (38cm) long

£600-1,000   BER

A hand-painted tin Union ferry boat, by Gebrüder Bing of Germany, with open end deck, large covered cargo and passenger cabin, long stack, clockwork mechanism, restored.

16in (40.5cm) long

£400-750   BER

A hand-painted freighter, by Fleischmann of Germany, exact-scale depiction of ocean freighter, with red and black hull, white deck rail and cabin, grey stack with 'Eggo' decal on funnel, green catwalk, clockwork driven, great deck cap detail, some repaint, replaced flags.

21in (53.5cm) long

£450-750   BER

A hand-painted tin ocean liner, by Fleischmann of Germany, with red and black hull, it features upper deck, full cabin, two stacks, four lifeboats, two masts with ladders, clockwork mechanism, some corrosion, restored.

Modelled after the 'Albert Ballin' transatlantic liner.

19in (48.5cm) long

£750-1,000   BER

A 1920s American Ferdinand Strauss 'Tip-Top Porter', clockwork mechanism, some wear and chips, in good condition.

6in (15cm) high

£140-200   VEC

A lithographed tin 'Jacko the Organ Grinder' toy, by Distler of Germany, clockwork driven, depicts full figure with organ and dancing monkey on top, spoke wheels.

6.5in (16.5cm) long

£1,400-2,000   BER

A hand-painted tin Ferdinand Martin 'Le Petit Livreur' toy delivery boy, depicted pushing cart, wearing a cloth jacket, clockwork action, exceptional condition, boxed.

8in (20.5cm) high

£900-1,200   BER

A hand-painted and lithographed tin Lehmann 'Paddy the Pig' toy, the rider wearing a cloth jacket.

5.5in (14cm) high

£700-1,000   BER

A Lehmann lithographed tin 'Alabama Coon Jigger', with original box, figure holds Lehmann flag in hand, clockwork mechanism, unusual box.

10in (25.5cm) high

£400-500   BER

A Martin 'Piano Player', features cloth-dressed musician seated at tin piano with candles and music sheet, clockwork mechanism, repainted.

5in (12.5cm) high

£600-800   BER

A German 'Black Minstrel' clockwork toy, features a black woman playing a banjo accompanied by her gentleman caller, clockwork mechanism with music contained within the lady's hoop dress, when activated she appears to strum the banjo with her right hand as his upper body and head sway to and fro, while being propelled forward.

7.5in (19cm) high

£4,000-5,000   JDJ

A lithographed tin clockwork balloon salesman, features die-cut tin balloon seller with hand organ and toys, clockwork activates his eyes to roll, his hand to move up and down, and the toys to swing.

6.5in (16.5cm) high

£400-600   BER

A hand-painted tin figure of a minstrel, holding banjo in hand, good detail to large collar, clockwork mechanism.

7.75in (19.5cm) high

£600-800   BER

A Ferdinand Martin 'The Drunkard' toy, hand-painted tin head and hat, lead hands and feet, cloth body, holds wooden bottle and lead cup in hands, clockwork mechanism, rub to face paint.

8.25in (21cm) high

£400-500   BER

A Lehmann tinplate clockwork 'Climbing Monkey' toy.

8.75in (22cm) high

£25-35   ROS

A US Zone German clockwork Chuco 7403 Rolly Bear, brown and black glass eyes, black horizontally stitched nose, yellow felt scarf, felt pads, holding wooden staff, mounted onto two skates, each with four wheels, in near mint condition.

8.25in (20.5cm) long

£400-500   VEC

An Arcade cast iron 1927 Buick sedan, luxury styling, gold trim, black roof and full running boards, spoke wheels, white rubber tyres, spare stencilled, missing driver, otherwise good condition.

8in (21cm) long

£7,000-1,000　　　　　　BER

An Arcade cast iron yellow cab, in classic orange and black with seated nickel driver, painted disc wheels, stencilling on doors.

9in (23cm) long

£1,000-1,200　　　　　　BER

An Arcade cast iron Chevrolet coupé, painted with grey body, black roof and runnings boards, silver trimmed grille, features nickel disc wheels with spare on trunk.

8in (20cm) long

£500-600　　　　　　BER

A Hubley cast iron Hillclimber motorcycle, painted blue, classic depiction of seated racer on cycle, black trunk and motor, well detailed.

7in (18cm) long

£450-600　　　　　　BER

A Kenton cast iron sedan, for Sears, made for familiar store, in large scale, painted red and black, silver spoke wheels, red centres, includes original driver, embossed spare.

12in (30cm) long

£1,000-1,500　　　　　　BER

A Kenton cast iron cement mixer, with nickel rotary cement mixer on body, embossed open frame, white rubber tyres.

9in (23cm) long

£600-1,000　　　　　　BER

A Kilgore 'Tat' aeroplane, with yellow and green paint, cast rib wing, embossed 'TAT' on fuselage.

14in (36cm) long

£1,800-2,200　　　　　　BER

A rare pressed steel American National Mack coal truck, with enclosed green cab with orange hopper body, rubber tyres, painted wheels, orange trim, decals on grille and sides.

25in (64cm) long

£4,000-5,500　　　　　　BER

A very rare Toledo Bulldog Mack circus truck, with orange open cab, green three panel van body, containing lithographed images of caged animals,

26in (66cm) long

£6,500-7,500　　　　　　BER

A pressed steel Toledo 'Bulldog' coal truck with red doorless cab with black open body, chute slide, interior bed, side gate, rubber tyres, disc wheels, original celluloid windscreen, decal on grille.

c1925　　*25in (64cm) long*

£3,000-4,000　　　　　　BER

A 19thC 'Always Did 'Spise a Mule' cast iron mechanical bank, original paint, good condition, patent information on base.

10in (25.5cm) wide

£1,400-2,000　　　　　　DRA

A pre-WWII Dinky no. 22D Delivery Van, 'W.E. Boyce' type 1 with 'Hornby Series' embossed to underside of cab.

A very rare promotional van and the only one known. W. E. Boyce was a cycle shop on Archway Road in London in the 1930s and was apparently still trading under that name into the early 1960s.

£20,000-25,000   VEC

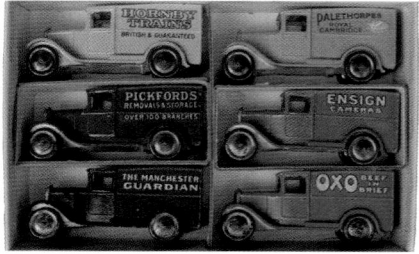

A very rare pre-WWII Dinky no. 28/1 trade box for six type 1 Delivery Vans, containing six vans, including no. 28a 'Hornby Trains', no. 28c 'Pickfords', no. 28c 'Manchester Guardian', no. 28d 'Oxo', no. 28e 'Ensign Cameras' and no. 28f 'Palethorpes', all with 'Dinky Toys' cast to underside of cab roof, all contained within yellow Trade Box with original internal dividers.

£35,000-40,000   VEC

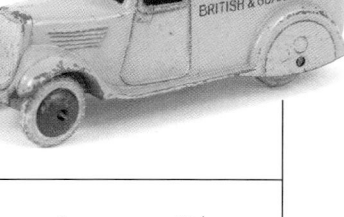

A pre-war French-made Dinky 'Super Streamline' Saloon, 24E type but with no side window framing, thirteen bonnet louvres, red chassis and white Dunlop tyres, with type 1 criss-cross chassis and type 1 radiator grill with diamond, possible repaint, unboxed.

£150-200   DN

A rare pre-war Dinky no. 28A 'Hornby' Delivery Van, type 2, yellow body, smooth blue hubs with white tyres 'Hornby Trains British & Guaranteed' to both sides, slight fatigue with clear glue to underside, in excellent condition, paint and printing to both sides.

£1,000-1,500   VEC

A rare pre-war Dinky no. 28B 'Pickfords' Delivery Van, type 1, dark blue, blue metal wheels, slight distortion to shape, rear brace between wheelarches detached one side, some fading to one side, slight corrosion to same rear corner, in good condition.

£350-400   VEC

A rare Dinky no. 234 Ferrari, blue body, yellow triangle to front, blue plastic hubs, racing no. 5, overall in excellent condition.

£330-400   VEC

A Dinky no. 449 Chevrolet El Camino Pick-up, 'Mickey Thompson Enterprises' decals, promotional give-aways, in near mint condition, with near mint condition box.

£170-220   VEC

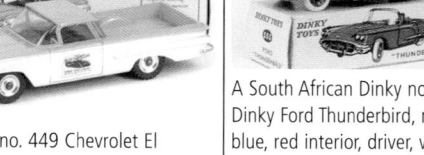

A South African Dinky no. 555 Dinky Ford Thunderbird, metallic blue, red interior, driver, white tyres, slight corrosion to hubs and damage to windscreen, good condition, including box, slight marks to end flap.

£300-400   VEC

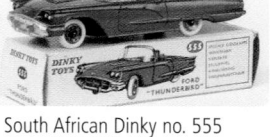

A French Dinky no. 809 GMC US Army 6x6 Truck, military green with tilt, driver, white star to bonnet and sides, spun hubs, in near mint condition, with excellent condition, inner card and excellent condition detailed picture box.

£150-200   VEC

A French Dinky no. 810 Dodge DC56 Military Command Car, military green, plastic tilt, driver, aerial, decals, camouflage net missing, in mint condition, with good condition camouflage effect yellow card box.

£140-200   VEC

A French Dinky no. 824 Berliet Gazelle 6x6 Truck, military green with tilt and spun hubs, in good condition, with good condition detailed picture box.

£80-120   VEC

A Dinky no. 903 Foden Flat Truck with tailboard, violet blue cab, chassis, orange flatbed, mid-blue Supertoy hubs, black treaded tyres, in near mint condition, with near mint striped lift off lid box.

£600-700   VEC

A Corgi no. 241 Ghia L.6.4, lime green, deep yellow interior, cast hubs, in mint condition, with near mint condition blue and yellow carded box, complete with Collectors Club folded leaflet.

£150-200   **VEC**

A Corgi no. 258 'The Saint' Volvo P1800, white, red interior, spun hubs, mint including blue and yellow carded box, superb example.

£350-450   **VEC**

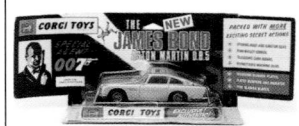

A Corgi no. 270 'James Bond' Aston Martin DB5, silver, tyre slashers, secret instruction pack containing unapplied decal sheet, lapel badge, spare bandit figure and folded leaflet, overall condition is mint, apart from very slight discolouration to door, with first issue wing-flap box.

£500-600   **VEC**

A Corgi no. 321 BMC Mini Cooper S, 'Rallye Monte Carlo', red with red interior, white roof with autograph signatures, spun hubs, racing number 2, in excellent condition, with good condition blue and yellow carded picture box with flash.

£280-320   **VEC**

A Corgi no. 328 Hillman Imp, 'Rallye Monte Carlo', blue body, white side stripe, off white interior, spun hubs, racing number 107, in mint condition, with mint condition display card and correct folded instruction sheet, outer blue and yellow carded box.

£300-400   **VEC**

A Corgi no. 340 Sunbeam Imp, 'Rallye Monte Carlo', blue body, cream interior, spun hubs, racing number 77, in excellent condition, with excellent condition display card and correct folded instruction sheet and good condition outer blue and yellow carded picture box.

£180-220   **VEC**

A Corgi 'Evening Standard' no. 421 Bedford Van, silver, black lower body, flat spun hubs, in near mint condition, with excellent condition blue and yellow carded box complete with Collectors Club folded leaflet.

£180-220   **VEC**

A Corgi no. 474 Ford Thames 'Walls Ice-cream' ice-cream van, with musical chimes, pale blue, cream, spun hubs, in near mint condition, with excellent condition inner pictorial stand, in good condition outer blue and yellow carded box.

£240-300   **VEC**

A Corgi no. 653 'Air Canada' Concorde, white, red, blue, near mint condition, in excellent condition correct issue blue and yellow carded box.

£250-300   **VEC**

A Corgi no. 1101 Bedford S-type Carrimore Car Transporter, rare issue finished with metallic mauve cab, blue trailer, flat spun hubs, in excellent condition, with near mint condition blue and yellow carded lift off lid box, complete with inner packing.

£400-500   **VEC**

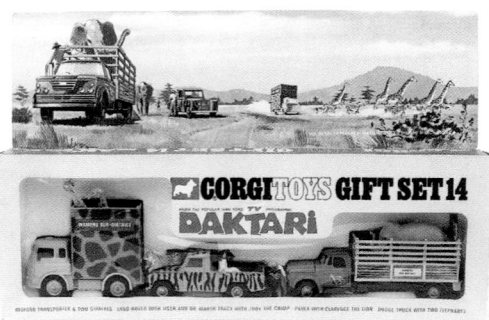

A Corgi no. GS14 'Daktari' Gift Set, comprising Bedford giraffe transporter, Land Rover and cattle truck, plus various figures including Clarence the cross-eyed lion, overall conditions are near mint to mint, inner polystyrene packing is mint, outer blue and yellow picture box is good, although slightly creased, complete with picture header card which is excellent plus.

£400-500   **VEC**

A Corgi no. GS36 'Tarzan' Gift Set, comprising various vehicles and figures, mint condition, in excellent condition window box, although grubby around corners.

£200-250   **VEC**

An unusual Italian Alpia large clockwork trolley bus, wooden bodied, with six plastic wheels, includes opening doors to side and trolley poles, lacks driver mirror and clockwork spring requires attention, otherwise in excellent condition.

20.5in (52cm) long

£2,200-2,800   **VEC**

A rare AR Toys clockwork military ambulance, clockwork operation to rear wheels, red hubs with white tyres, with soldier figure driver, opening rear door with rotary catch, some wear to edges, otherwise in good condition, with a fair condition plain card box.

£300-400   **VEC**

An unusual and rare German Blomer & Schuler flying car, with wings and propeller, futuristic shape with brick-red aluminium body, clockwork operation, with retractable wings and propeller to front, steerable front wheels, scratch above one rear wheel, otherwise in excellent condition.

7.75in (20cm) long

£350-450   **VEC**

A rare Britains no. 9526 Fordson Super Major Spud, black steering wheel, orange metal front wheel and 'Spud' rear wheel, complete with rear attachment, on excellent condition inner sliding plinth, with good condition card outer box, one side flap detached, tuck-in part of end flap missing.

£1,000-1,500   **VEC**

A Budgie Toys no. 298 Alvis Salamander Fire Crash Tender, black base, grey ladders and hose, in excellent condition, with excellent condition carded picture box with colour folded leaflet.

£350-450   **VEC**

A Distler Electro Matic 7500 Porsche, battery-operated large scale tinplate model, removable hood reveals battery compartment, with selector lever to interior, rubber tyres, steerable front wheels, some light wear and corrosion to interior of battery compartment, otherwise in excellent condition, with a good condition colourfully illustrated box and contemporary colour leaflet.

10.25in (26cm) long

£470-550   **VEC**

A very rare G.I.S.E.A. Live Steam Tractor, front-loading fuel tray, brass radiator top, steel chimney, in excellent condition, with yellow plastic funnel and card 'Funziona Con Motore A Bapore', with instructions in Italian marked 'Gisea (Giocattoli Italiani Scintifici E Artistici) Milan', within plain brown card box, paper label to one end.

11in (28cm) long

£550-650   **VEC**

A German JNF tinplate American station wagon, metallic blue, with grey plastic roof-rack, detailed tin-printed interior, plated parts, friction drive with steerable front wheels, supplied with four card suit-cases to roof, in excellent condition.

10.25in (26cm) long

£330-400   **VEC**

A rare Kellerman no. 353 clockwork touring rider and male passenger, red bike, brown rider, blue and brown passenger, tin wheels, passenger rotates from hips as rider turns, in near mint condition, with good condition full colour illustrated card box, and original key.

£750-850   **VEC**

An Italian Lima no. 3001 Auto Pompieri Fire Engine, red plastic body, with tinplate baseplate, battery operated, with yellow ladder, four firemen figures sealed in a plastic bag, some interaction between wheel hubs and tyres, otherwise in near mint condition, with good condition colourfully illustrated box.

8.75in (22cm) long

£300-400   **VEC**

A Japanese Marusan 'Baby Scooter' pat no.4940, with rider and woman passenger, red and grey with 'Silver Pigeon' to rear, friction drive, scooter with clear windscreen, tin blue wheels to front, slight mark on one side, otherwise in near mint condition, with excellent condition box with detail, full colour picture to lid.

£650-750 VEC

A Matchbox Regular Wheels no. 72a Fordson Major Tractor, yellow plastic front and rear hubs with black tyres, in mint condition, with type D colour picture box.

£500-600 VEC

A Matchbox Regular Wheels no. 39b Pontiac Bonneville Convertible, cream interior with red steering wheel, crimson base with grey plastic wheels, in mint condition, with near mint condition type D colour picture box.

£1,200-1,800 VEC

A Matchbox Regular Wheels no. 22c Pontiac GP Coupé, red, grey interior, black base and plastic wheels, in near mint condition, with good condition later issue F style box.

£570-700 VEC

A US Zone German Schuco 'Curvo 1000' motor cycle, blue with grey and cream engine detail, rider with red jacket and tan trousers, gauntlets, helmet, flat spot to front tyre, otherwise in near mint condition, with good condition box, complete with instructions.

5in (13cm) long
£1,200-1,800 VEC

A Western German Schuco 5710 Elektro radio car, cream upper open body, red lower body, gold and cream plastic 'fins' to rear, lithographed interior, dashboard, plated lights, radiator, front and rear bumpers, windscreen frame, 'Schuco' to front of bonnet, one wheel hub corroded, otherwise in excellent condition.

11in (28cm) long
£550-650 VEC

A Limited Edition Solido 'James Bond - Goldfinger' Rolls Royce, from an edition of 100, complete with Goldfinger and Oddjob figures, mint condition including gold tube.

£400-500 VEC

A French VeBe large tinplate fire engine, with clockwork motor, elevation and extending controls to ladder, which is mounted on a revolving turntable, opening door to cab, wired for electric headlights, with tyres and steerable front wheels, some surface corrosion to silver painted ladder, otherwise in good condition with rubber.

15.75in (40cm) long
£350-450 VEC

A Japanese Yonezawa 'Diamond' hood truck, friction drive, red with yellow plastic tilt, detailed tin-printed interior, plated parts, very light wear due to storage, otherwise in excellent condition with some inner packaging, with fair card box with illustrated lift off lid.

15.5in (39cm) long
£430-550 VEC

A pressed steel open-top car, of unconfirmed manufacture, greyish green, with cream interior, clockwork operation to rear wheels, poseable front wheels, rubber tyres, some wear to upper edges but includes tinplate windscreen surround and rear wheel cover.

11in (28cm) long
£330-450 VEC

TOYS

A rare Schuco miniature orange teddy bear, with black stitched face and metal eyes.

2.75in (7cm) high

£100-150   A&G

A rare Schuco miniature pink teddy bear, with black stitched face and metal eyes, faded and worn.

2.75in (7cm) high

£120-180   A&G

A pale gold Steiff centre-seam mohair teddy bear, with boot button eyes, hump back and elongated feet, light brown vertical stitching to nose, Steiff button in ear, original pads.

This bear belonged to Pamela Winstanley (b.1910) and was sold together with photographs and a history of its owner. Centre-seam Steiff are rare as one piece of mohair was sufficient to produced six and a half bear heads, so the head of the seventh bear was made from two pieces sewn together creating a seam down the middle of the head.

21in (54.5cm) high

£5,000-6,000   BWL

A Steiff beige bear with glass eyes, no buttons or tags.

17in (43cm) high

£100-200   BER

A Steiff blonde mohair 'Petsy' teddy bear, blue and black glass eyes, red vertically stitched nose, centre seam, wired ears, fully jointed, felt pads, red clear stitching, hump, inoperative squeaker, mohair thinning and balding in places, pads holed, stuffing shifted at neck and tops of limbs, button with remains of red tag behind.

1928   *11in (28cm) high*

£1,700-2,200   VEC

A Steiff blonde mohair teddy bear, with brown woven nose and boot button eyes, together with a gift certificate, dated.

1908   *14in (35.5cm) high*

£1,500-2,000   HGS

A Steiff small brown mohair bear, lacks button in his ear.

c1907   *10in (25.5cm) high*

£500-600   TCT

An early American blonde mohair teddy bear, by an unknown maker, with original paw pads, glass eyes and stitched nose.

c1908   *11.5in (29cm) high*

£280-320   TCT

An early American blonde mohair teddy bear, by an unknown maker, with original paw pads, black stitched nose and mouth and boot button eyes.

c1908   *10in (25.5cm) high*

£350-450   HGS

A pre-war musical straw-filled teddy bear, covered in long orange plush with tune played by pressing tummy, shaved snout, white and black button eyes, swivel joints, replaced pads.

17in (6.75cm) high

£2,400-3,000 HT

An American golden mohair teddy bear, with glass eyes, horizontally stitched black nose, fully jointed, felt pads, black claw stitching, hump, nose partially re-stitched.

1915-20 *19in (48cm) high*

£250-350 VEC

A blonde mohair bear, with black boot button eyes, vertically stitched nose, fully jointed, black claw stitching, excelsior stuffed, one pad is felt, other three are suede.

14in (36cm) high

£40-60 VEC

An early Steiff 'Affen' monkey soft toy, dark brown felt over non-jointed body, red felt waistband with outstretched legs, holds an orange felt ball between the two front legs, vertical centre seam down front of face, black bead eyes and a stitched horizontal mouth, thick head of hair and beard made from rabbit fur, and a yarn tuft at the tip of his tail.

Pictured in the 1892 Filz-Spiel Weaaren-Fabrik catalogue as number 48.

9.5in (24cm) high

£4,000-5,000 JDJ

A Steiff life-size baby giraffe, mohair body with naturalistic details, with button in left ear.

96in (244cm) high approx.

£2,200-2,800 FRE

A German mohair plush cat, with glass eyes, felt sewn on trousers, embroidered shirt.

c1960 *32in (81cm) high*

£100-200 BER

A black drummer boy automaton, with papier-mâché head, leather eyes, in working order with drum sticks acting as speed regulator.

30in (76cm) high

£10,000-13,000 BER

A Lambert nargileh smoker automaton, by Leopold Lambert, with music playing the figure raises and lowers head, arm, pipe and teacup.

c1885 *21in (53cm) high*

£2,500-3,500 BER

A limited edition Steiff 'Musician Brown', from an edition of 1,200, with button, the wood-wool-stuffed felt figure with mohair hair and beard, cornet missing.

This is a replica of the 1911 'Musician Brown' figure.

1996 *15.25in (38cm) high*

£100-150 WDL

A Goblin Paints advertising figure, entitled 'Paint More Save More', the two goblins holding a paintbrush or a bag of cash, some damage.

19in (48cm) high

£450-550 LA

A set of four 19thC timber puppets, of sectional timber composition, joined cloth costume, naively painted, with stands.

18in (45.5cm) high

£1,000-1,500 FRE

A French clockwork-driven carousel, with figures and horses, tattered silk canopy, label on base.

12in (30cm) high

£1,500-2,000 BER

An English wooden baby carriage.

£800-1,200 GORL

A late 19th/early 20thC painted canvas circus banner, mounted on a wooden frame.

102in (259cm) high

£2,200-2,800 SK

A mid-20thC American painted canvas circus banner. 'Millard & Bulsterbaum 2894 W 8th St. Coney Island, N.Y.' stencilled lower right.

96in (244cm) high

£1,400-2,000 SK

A Fromann & Bunte transformation pack, third edition.

c1870

£100-150 BLO

A late Italian 19thC olive wood playing card box, in the form of a book with inlaid playing cards with sliding interior for four packs of playing cards.

6.75in (17cm) wide

£300-400 BLO

A stone figure, 'Owl', by Latcholassie Akesuk (1919-2000), E7-1055, Cape Dorset.

c1960   10in (25.5cm) high

£8,500-10,500   **WAD**

A stone figure 'Ecstasy', by Abraham Apakark Anghik, Salt Spring Island, signed in Roman, dated.

2001   26in (66cm) high

£3,000-5,000   **WAD**

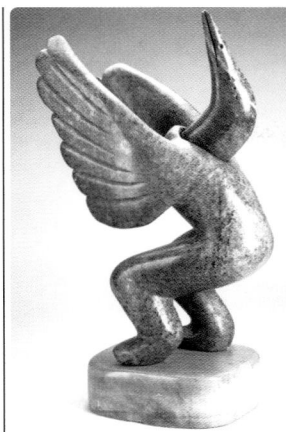

A stone figure, 'Raven Man', by Abraham Apakark Anghik, Salt Spring Island, signed in Roman, dated.

2000   37in (94cm) high

£2,500-3,500   **WAD**

A stone figure, 'Musk Ox', by Barnabus Arnasungaaq, (b1924), E2-213, Baker Lake, signed in syllabics.

12in (30.5cm) wide

£6,000-8,000   **WAD**

A stone figure, 'Hawk', by Kenojuak Ashevak (b1927), E7-1035, Cape Dorset, signed in syllabics.

14in (35.5cm) high

£3,500-4,500   **WAD**

A stone figure, 'Archer', by Abraham Etungat, (1911-99), E7-809, Cape Dorset.

c1960   17in (43cm) high

£6,000-8,000   **WAD**

An antler carving, 'Running Bird', by Luke Iksiktaaryuk, (1909-77), E2-45, Baker Lake.

13in (33cm) high

£7,500-9,500   **WAD**

A stone figure, 'Owl Landing', by Osuitok Ipeelee (1923-2005), E7-1154, Cape Dorset.

1983   15.25in (38.5cm) wide

£2,500-3,500   **WAD**

A stone statue, 'Shaman's Head', by John Kavik (1897-1993), E2-290, Rankin Inlet.

c1970   8.5in (21.5cm) wide

£20,000-25,000   **WAD**

A stone figure, 'Standing Woman', by Sheokjuk Oqutaq, (1920-82), E7-919, Cape Dorset.

c1949   5.5in (14cm) high

£11,000-13,000   **WAD**

A stone figure, by John Pangnark (1920-80), E1-104, Arviat.

9in (23cm) long

£5,000-6,000   **WAD**

TRIBAL ART

A stone statue, 'Many Faces', by John Tiktak, (1916-81), E1-266, Rankin Inlet, signed in syllabics.

12in (30.5cm) high

£25,000-30,000   **WAD**

A stone figure, 'Polar Figure', by Pauta Saila, (b1916), E7-990, Cape Dorset.

16in (40.5cm) high

£4,500-5,500   **WAD**

A stone and ivory figure, 'Dancing Walrus', by Pauta Saila, E7-990, Cape Dorset, signed in Roman.

c1975   17in (43cm) high

£4,500-5,500   **WAD**

A stone figure, 'Mother and Child', by George Tataniq, (1910-91), E2-179, Baker Lake, signed in syllabics and disc number.

11in (28cm) high

£5,000-6,000   **WAD**

A bone figure, 'Drummer', by Charlie Ugyuk, (1931-98), E4-341, Spence Bay.

18in (45.5cm) high

£5,000-6,000   **WAD**

A stone figure, 'Mother and Child', unidentified artist, Arviat.

11in (28cm) high

£8,500-10,500   **WAD**

A stone figure, 'Sedna Mother and Child', unidentified artist, Salluit.

c1950   9in (23cm) high

£11,000-15,000   **WAD**

A stonecut, 'Enchanted Owl', by Kerouac Ashevak (b1927), E7-1035, Cape Dorset, a/p, unframed.

1960   26in (66cm) wide

£25,000-30,000   **WAD**

A skin stencil, 'Polar Bear and Cub in Ice', by Niviaxie, (1908-59), E7-1077, Cape Dorset, 18/30, framed.

1959   22in (56cm) wide

£16,000-20,000   **WAD**

An appliqué wall hanging, by Jessie Oonark (1906-85), E2-384, Baker Lake, stroud, embroidery floss, thread, dated to tag.

1974   73in (185.5cm) wide

£16,000-20,000   **WAD**

An early 20thC Inuit carved ivory cribbage board, with animal heads projecting from the ends and two relief-carved heads on the playing surface.

16in (40.5cm) long

£550-650   **SK**

An Inuit incised ivory tusk, split section, one side with a whaling scene, two traditionally dressed men sitting on a European chair and stool, various animal and plant devices, and a winged fantasy creature, red pigment details.

c1900   *17.25in (44cm) long*

£2,500-3,500   **SK**

A 20thC Inuit ivory seal, age cracks.

6in (15cm) long

£180-220   **SK**

A 20thC Inuit stone carving, bust of a man wearing an animal headdress, appears phallic when viewed from behind, applied metal eyes.

6.75in (17cm) high

£1,300-1,800   **SK**

An Inuit carved wood mask, King Island, with exaggerated facial features and pierced at the eyes, nose and mouth.

c1900   *6in (15cm) wide*

£1,000-1,500   **SK**

A late 19thC Inuit painted carved wood bowl, the ovoid form with red and black rim and five stacked stylised animals on the inside.

11in (28cm) long

£1,500-2,000   **SK**

An early 20thC Inuit coiled basket, the round flat-bottom form with minimal geometric decoration, the lid with walrus ivory knob carved in the form of walrus heads, minor stitch loss.

10in (25.5cm) diam

£300-400   **SK**

NORTH EASTERN TRIBES

A pair of third quarter 19thC Northeast Iroquois beaded cloth and hide child's moccasins, the soft sole forms beaded on the vamps with multicoloured floral and geometric devices using small seed beads, the silk-covered cuffs with larger bead edgings, minor bead loss.

4.75in (12cm) long

£600-800   **SK**

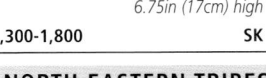

A mid-19thC Northeast beaded cloth bag, red trade cloth, decorated on both sides with multicoloured variations of the C-scroll pattern, remnant silk edging.

5.5in (14cm) high

£400-600   **SK**

A mid-19thC Northeast Micmac quilled birch bark box, the rectangular lidded form with multi-coloured chevron pattern sides and geometric lid, minor quill loss.

5in (12.5cm) long

£400-500   **SK**

A third quarter 19thC Northeast Micmac quilled Rococo Revival chair, the rosewood and walnut slipper chair with traditional polychrome-quilled birch bark panels on the seat and back, wear to quill work.

37in (94cm) high

£1,000-1,500   **SK**

A third quarter 19thC Northeast Huron moose-hair-embroidered birch bark cigar case, with male and female figures smoking pipes and perched birds on foliage, hair loss.

5in (12.5cm) high

£300-500   **SK**

A mid-19thC Northeast Iroquois beaded cloth corn husk doll and cradle, the female wearing traditional clothing of the period, with silver brooch/pin, minor loss.

Doll 11.5in (29cm) high

£6,000-8,000   **SK**

A first quarter 20thC Northwest coast carved and painted wood totem pole, carved with stylised human and animal forms, avian finial, and painted with early commercial colours.

34in (86.5cm) high

£2,000-3,000　　SK

A last quarter 19thC Northwest coast carved wood bear, crouching on a round base, with front paws up and curled at the chest, traces of red and black pigment, cracks.

23.5in (59.5cm) high

£5,500-6,500　　SK

A late 19thC Northwest coast Nootka carved wood mask, the hollow oval form with wide pierced down-turned mouth, round pierced eyes, and flattened nose, red, black and white pigment details, patina of use, written on the inside 'Old Native Dance Mask – Alaska – OR'.

11.75in (30cm) high

£1,200-1,800　　SK

A mid-19thC Northwest coast Haida carved argillite, elaborate form with abstract European ship theme and two European-dress figures, damage, in two pieces.

15.25in (38.5cm) long

£4,000-5,000　　SK

A pair of Algonquin moccasins, one moccasin has loose upper beaded portion.

c1850　　*9in (23cm) long*

£150-200　　ALD

A Northwest Coast Tlingit polychrome twined basket, with multicoloured bands, the outside with multicoloured fret and cross devices, small split.

c1900　　*11.5in (29cm) diam*

£3,500-4,500　　SK

PLAINS TRIBES

A Native American embroidered fringed hide shirt, possibly Northern Plains, the front placard, pocket, cuffs and shoulders decorated with dyed embroidered leaves and flowers.

c1900　　*30in (76cm) high*

£1,500-2,000　　POOK

A late 19thC Central Plains Lakota beaded hide man's vest, beaded on the front and back with multicoloured geometric designs on a white background, minor bead loss.

20in (51cm) long

£1,000-1,500　　SK

A pair of last quarter 19thC Central Plains Arapaho beaded hide woman's high-top moccasins, the hard sole forms with soft uppers stained yellow and red, with multicoloured geometric detailing including a cross on one vamp and a circle on the other, brass beaded fringe along the side panels.

18in (45.5cm) high

£4,000-6,000　　SK

A pair of last quarter 19thC Central Plains Lakota beaded hide possible bags, the rectangular forms beaded on the front and sides with multicoloured geometric devices, tin cone and red horsehair drops from the sides.

21in (53.5cm) long

£5,500-6,500　　SK

A last quarter 19thC Northern Plains Crow tomahawk and beaded hide drop, with ash handle pierced for smoking, a variant spontoon-style brass head, the handle wrapped with otter skin at the top.

Tomahawk 18.5in (47cm) long

£1,000-1,500　　SK

A last quarter 19thC Plains pictograph drawing, titled 'Kills 3 Crows', coloured pencil drawing depicting a warrior on foot counting coup on a wounded warrior, and a man and woman shot with arrows, unframed.

8.25in (21cm) wide

£1,200-1,800　　SK

A Southwest Hopi polychrome carved wood Kokopelli katcina, the cottonwood hump-backed flute player carrying a rattle in one hand and a stick in the other, the body slightly twisted and with male genitalia, the black case mask with long tapered bill, old tag on the back, one arm re-glued.

£1,800-2,200   SK

A Southwest Hopi polychrome carved wood mudhead katcina, with arms to the sides and painted with black, white, red and dull pink pigments.

4.5in (11.5cm) high

£700-1,000   SK

A Southwest Sipikne, Hopi, polychrome carved wood Zuni Sun God katcina, the case mask with black stripes, large red ears, and snout.

2.75in (7cm) high

£800-1,200   SK

A Southwest Cochiti, Pueblo, polychrome pottery story teller figure, Sarafina Ortez, the seated female form with fourteen listeners.

8.25in (21cm) high

£650-850   SK

A Southwest polychrome pottery vessel, Margaret and Luther, Santa Clare Pueblo, the rounded form with stylised bird and rabbit devices on a buff slip.

3in (7.5cm) high

£200-300   SK

A late 19thC Southwest Acoma polychrome pottery pitcher, with handle between two stylised bird heads, one a spout, painted with black and red-brown abstract foliate designs on a cream-coloured ground.

4.5in (11.5cm) high

£500-800   SK

A first half 20thC Southwest Paiute beaded coiled basketry bowl, the outside overlaid in a multicoloured geometric pattern.

5in (12.5cm) diam

£250-350   SK

A Southwest Apache coiled basketry bowl, with concentric five-point star pattern, stains.

c1900   15in (38cm) diam

£500-800   SK

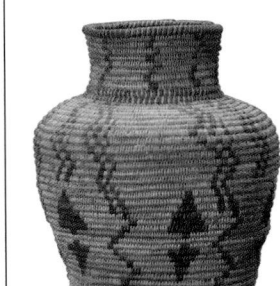

A Southwest Apache coiled basketry olla, with high shoulder and flared rim, decorated with zigzag and triangular devices, stitch loss.

c1900   8.5in (21.5cm) diam

£250-350   SK

A Southwest Navajo, Two Gray Hills, regional weaving, tightly woven with natural and synthetic dyed homespun wood, a storm pattern variant on a variegated grey background, black border.

c1940   75.5in (192cm) long

£1,000-1,500   SK

A last quarter 19thC Southwest Navajo, Germantown weaving, tightly woven with a multicoloured serrated diamond pattern, a two-colour stepped border, and fringe at one end, fading.

52in (132cm) long

£500-800   SK

A Southwest Navajo transitional weaving, natural and synthetic dyed homespun yarn, with serrated diamond, crosses, and arrow devices on a red background, wool loss.

c1900   88in (223.5cm) long

£500-800   SK

A Pre-Columbian Jalisco painted pottery couple, the female with hands on her drum-playing husband's shoulders, both with necklaces and ear ornaments, elaborate headdress, and painted detail.

100BC-AD250   *9.5in (24cm) high*

£600-800   **SK**

A Pre-Columbian Jalisco painted pottery female figure, seated with legs to the side, out-thrust arms, wearing a skirt, headdress, and nose ornament, red pigment detail, nose tip restored.

c100BC-AD250   *10.25in (26cm) high*

£300-400   **SK**

A Pre-Columbian Jalisco seated male pottery figure, the hollow hunch-backed form with hands to the ground, wearing ear discs and a headdress.

c100BC-AD300   *7.5in (19cm) high*

£500-800   **SK**

A Pre-Columbian Jalisco painted pottery figure, the seated female form with a bowl on her shoulder and one resting on her thigh, nose and ear ornaments with black and red body decoration, some restoration.

c100BC-AD250   *15in (38cm) high*

£500-800   **SK**

A Pre-Columbian Nayarit painted pottery figure, the standing female form with upturned arms, ears ornaments, and black and red body paint, restoration.

c100BC-AD250   *16in (40.5cm) high*

£600-800   **SK**

A Pre-Columbian Zacatecas painted pottery female figure, seated with hands to the side and black and red geometric decoration on the upper body.

c200BC-AD200   *11.5in (29cm) high*

£1,100-1,500   **SK**

A Pre-Columbian Colima painted pottery turtle-dog figure, with open spout tail, red shell and dog-like head.

c200BC-AD200   *6.5in (16.5cm) high*

£1,200-1,800   **SK**

A Pre-Columbian Colima painted pottery dog, the plump seated form with flared spout on the top of the head, upturned tail, and incised toothy grin, remnant black and red pigment.

c100BC-AD300   *9.25in (23.5cm) high*

£1,000-1,500   **SK**

A Pre-Columbian Chancay, Peru, painted pottery animal, the bulbous redware form with brown and white paint.

7.5in (19cm) high

£150-200   **SK**

A Pre-Columbian Inca, Peru, blackware stirrup-spout pottery vessel, in the form of a boat with a seated human figure at the helm, incised and relief-carved detail.

c1200-1400   *7.5in (17cm) high*

£200-300   **SK**

A Pre-Columbian painted pottery vessel, a whistling form with strap and spout double body, the front in the form of a seal, with dark brown and white pigment on red body.

6in (15cm) high

£350-450   **SK**

A Pre-Columbian Maya, El Salvador, polychrome cylinder, three elaborately dressed standing male figures on a buff-coloured background with red and black framing lines, surface loss.

cAD650-900   *7in (18cm) high*

£800-1,200   **SK**

A Nok anthropomorphic terracotta figure, from Nigeria, some damage.

300BC-AD200   *8.25in (21cm) high*

£500-800   **BLA**

A Mambila figure, from Cameroon or Nigeria.

16in (41cm) high

£5,500-6,500   **BLA**

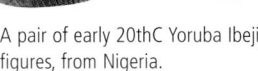

A late 19thC Yoruba reliquary guardian figure, from Nigeria.

18.75in (47.5cm) high

£4,500-5,500   **BLA**

A pair of early 20thC Yoruba Ibeji figures, from Nigeria.

10.5in (27cm) high

£350-450   **BLA**

A 19thC Dogon or Proto Dogon anthropomorphic figure, depicting a hermaphrodite protector.

11.25in (28.5cm) high

£3,500-4,500   **BLA**

An African Baule carved wood male figure, from Ivory Coast, seated on a stool with hands on knees, one palm out, the body and large head with finely carved detail, including a headdress with cowry shell edging and animal hair attachment, red, white, and black pigments, wood loss.

17in (43cm) high

£2,500-3,500   **SK**

An Ibo dance mask crest, from Nigeria.

c1900   *11in (28cm) high*

£800-1,000   **BLA**

A carved wood Idoma fetish mask, from Nigeria.

c1900   *16.5in (42cm) high*

£1,500-2,000   **BLA**

An early 20thC Ejagham helmet mask crest, from Nigeria

15in (38.5cm) high

£1,500-2,000   **BLA**

A 20thC Epa mask, from Nigeria, carved wood with traces of pigment.

44in (112cm) high

£600-800   **FRE**

A Karumba antelope form helmet mask, from Burkina Faso, surmounted with tall horns, forward-curved ears, twine issuing from holes to the edge, polychrome painting.

54in (137cm) high

£200-300   **FRE**

An African Guro carved wood mask, from Ivory Coast, the hollow form with long narrow nose, pierced narrow eyes, scarification marks, and tripartite coiffure, dark patina, cracked.

12.5in (32cm) high

£1,200-1,800   **SK**

An African Benin carved wood kola nut bowl, from Nigeria, the lidded form carved to represent a stylised antelope head, with incised detail, wood loss.

15.25in (38.75cm) long

£500-800 **SK**

An African Kuba carved wood box, from D. R. Congo, the crescent-shaped lidded form with relief-carved geometric decoration on the sides, top, and handle, traces of red pigment.

13.25in (33.5cm) wide

£600-800 **SK**

An African Kuba carved lidded box, from D. R. Congo, with incised geometric patterns, traces of red pigment, dark patina, minor wood loss.

6.5in (16.5cm) high

£450-650 **SK**

An early 20thC Bambara carved wood cane-top, from Mali.

21.5in (55cm) high

£800-1,200 **BLA**

An African Yoruba carved wood shango staff, from Nigeria, with cylindrical handle surmounted by a platform with a kneeling female figure holding a bird in one hand and a gourd shaped item in the other, the axe-shaped projection from head stained black on one side and with kaolin-filled incised lozenges, black surface.

17in (43cm) high

£1,000-1,500 **SK**

A South African Zulu carved wood ball-headed club, part of the shaft covered in fine two-colour braided wire, dark patina.

22in (56cm) high

£500-800 **SK**

An early 20thC Dogon wooden door lock, from Mali.

19in (48cm) high

£600-800 **BLA**

An African Songye wood and metal ceremonial axe, Congo River Basin, the forged steel blade with elaborate open work and single-head projection on both sides, the wood handle covered with a copper sheath, patina of use.

Handle 15in (38cm) long

£800-1,200 **SK**

An Ashanti carved child's stool, from Ghana, the dished seat on an elephant support.

12.5in (31.5cm) wide

£100-150 **WW**

An African Kuba carved horn cup, from D. R. Congo, the gracefully curved form with relief-carved geometric and concentric circle devices, patina of use.

16in (40.5cm) long

£1,500-2,000 **SK**

An African ivory and horn sceptre, the handle with animal hair whisk and brass-braided wire wrap, the finial in the form of a dog head with inlaid eyes and teeth.

Handle 10.5in (26.5cm) long

£500-800 **SK**

A Benin bronze cat head, good cast, handle to back of head.

c1900 *5.5in (14cm) high*

£300-500 **FRE**

A large Yuat Rivershield, from New Guinea, carved wood with pigment and raffia ornamentation through the nose of five faces, one side with raffia tassels attached.

78in (198cm) high

£200-300 FRE

A Mendi village shield, from New Guinea, painted wood, with cloth handles to the rear.

65in (165cm) high

£450-550 FRE

A Mendi shield, from New Guinea, painted wood, rope handle leading to a triangle shape to the front.

60in (152.5cm) high

£300-400 FRE

A carved and painted Sepik River mask, from New Guinea .

9.75in (24.5cm) long

£100-150 WW

A carved wood and painted Sepik River mask, from New Guinea, decorated with feathers and cowrie shells, some losses to the shell decoration.

29in (74cm) long

£200-300 WW

A carved wood and painted Sepik River standing figure, from New Guinea, with cowrie shell eyes.

34.75in (88.5cm) high

£300-400 WW

A Garamut slit drum, from New Guinea, carved sides with carved figural handles.

88in (223.5cm) long

£450-550 FRE

A shell pectoral bride price, with case, from New Guinea, Kina shell with woven red neck band, ornamented with cowrie shells and cuscus fur, covered in red pigment with detailed carrying case.

14in (35.5cm) high

£60-100 FRE

A 19thC Maori inscribed club, with bands of geometric carved decoration, the tip carved with a lion mask, inscribed 'A MIGHTY CHIEF FIRST CUT ME FROM THE TREE AND REDUCED ME TO THE STATE YOU SEE, A WARRIORS ARM SUSTAINED ME IN THE FIELD AND WITH MY HELP HE MADE MANY TO YIELD, COMMITED BY FATE TO CROSS THE BRINY WAVE FOR I WAS BOUGHT BY A SAILOR STOUT AND BRAVE TO OTAHEITE'S ISLE OF FAME, ST SINGAPATAM WAS THE FRIGATES NAME, WALDEGRAVE CAPTN APRIL 29 WE LEFT THE BAY IN THE YEAR 1830 WE SAILED AWAY'.

43.75in (111cm) long

£3,000-5,000 WW

A Baining mask, from New Britain, painted tapa cloth over a cane frame, large abstract head forming circular eyes and a complexly painted pattern to the front, elongated mouth shape, over a wood stand.

42in (106.5cm) high

£500-800 FRE

An early 18thC steel-mounted Italian flintlock holster pistol, the rounded banana-shaped lock with finely chiselled acanthus leaf at the tail and on the frizzen back, elegant shaped cock with floral chiselled cock retaining screw head, trigger cut and scrolled with foliate chiselling, replacement trigger guard, bulbous spurred pommel with chiselled acanthus leaves on both sides and floral butt cap en suite with cock retaining screw, pierced and cut steel blank escutcheon, finely cut foliate side plate, the two-stage barrel octagonal at the breech tapering to a slender muzzle with rubbed classical portrait head at the breech, plain tang, dark walnut full stock carved with foliate scrolls at the barrel tang, trigger guard finial and rear chiselled steel ramrod pipes, rubbed 'Anton Boniscolo' signature and replacement ramrod.

20.75in (53cm) long

£3,000-5,000　　　　　　　　　　　　　　　　　　　L&T

A mid-18thC silver-mounted flintlock three-stage cannon-barrelled turn-off pistol, the dark walnut butt carved with a shell below the engraved barrel tang and with carved tear drops behind the cast silver trophy of arms side plate, engraved silver spurred pommel with grotesque mask butt cap in the form of leaves, rococo escutcheon engraved with a viscount's crest and coronet, signed 'Barbar, London 2' at the breech with 'IB' stamp for James Barbar and engraved acanthus leaves with London proof mark, with Keith Neal collection tag 'P 228' attached to the floral engraved trigger guard.

The crest and coronet is that of Lionel Tollemache (1734-1799), 5th Earl of Dysart. The 5th Earl was responsible for reshaping the gardens at Ham House, Richmond Park Middlesex. Ham House is now in the care of The National Trust given by the Tolleche family in 1948. Jacobus Barbero was apprenticed on October 7th, 1714 for seven years to his father Ludovicus in June 1737. In May 1741 he became Gentleman Armourer to King George II. In 1742 he was appointed Master of Gunmakers Company. The spelling of the name varies between Barber and Barbar. He died in April 1773.

11.75in (30cm) long

£4,500-5,500　　　　　　　　　　　　　　　　　　　L&T

A rare George II flintlock blunderbuss pistol, by Grice, with steel barrel and action, walnut butt and cappings.

c1755 　　　　　*14.25in (36cm) long*

£2,200-2,600　　　　　　　　　RGA

An 18thC paktong flintlock, boxlock, turn-off cannon barrel pocket pistol, with 'PERRY-LONDON' within scrolls on each side of the lock, with full Birmingham hallmarks for '1777' and maker's mark 'CF' for Charles Freeth.

5.75in (14.5cm) long

£3,500-5,500　　　　　　　　　L&T

A 55 bore flintlock boxlock pocket pistol, London proved, the frame engraved with swags and 'Broomhead, London' in ovals, top safety, hidden trigger, plain walnut slab butt, with some original blued finish.

c1800 　　　　*7.25in (18.5cm) long*

£250-350　　　　　　　　　W&W

A George III double-barrelled flintlock highwayman's pistol, by Brasher, with steel barrels and actions, walnut butts, in good condition.

c1810 　　　　　*15in (38cm) long*

£4,500-5,500　　　　　　　　　RGA

A 42 bore flintlock boxlock pocket pistol, by Parker of Holborn, London, hidden trigger, partly chequered walnut slab butt with escutcheon.

c1820 　　　　　*5in (12.5cm) long*

£500-700　　　　　　　　　W&W

A mid-19thC flintlock service pistol, by Dobson and Baker, with steel barrel and action, and walnut butt with brass cappings.

c1840 　　　　　*15in (38cm) long*

£2,200-2,800　　　　　　　　　RGA

A flintlock pocket pistol, with octagonal steel barrel and brass lock, signed Noyes, Warminster, together with various flints and a bullet mould.

£400-600　　　　　　　　　SWO

An Irish 32 bore flintlock pocket pistol, by Dempsey, Dublin, with 4.25in (11cm) steel barrel, sliding safety and roller frizen, complete with ramrod, steel trigger-guard and butt cap, the chequered grip inlaid with a silver-coloured metal escutcheon.

8in (20.5cm) long

£450-550　　　　　　　　　A&G

A Continental 36 bore brass cannon-barrelled and brass-framed flintlock boxlock pocket pistol, top saftey which also locks the frizzen, flattened chequered walnut butt inset with silver studs, octagonal flared finial with flat brass cap.

7.5in (19cm) long

£350-450　　　　　　　　　W&W

A 19thC flintlock holster pistol, the lock struck with an eastern seal mark, with brass trigger guard and butt cap.

£250-350　　　　　　　　　SWO

GARTH VINCENT

ANTIQUE ARMS, ARMOUR & MEDALS

I have customers worldwide
and I am interested in purchasing
single items or complete collections,
advice freely given

Dealer in antique and reproduction
arms and armour for the collector,
investor and interior decorator

Commission buying at auction

Access & Visa accepted

Brochure available

**The Old Manor House
Allington, Nr Grantham
Lincolnshire NG32 2DH
Telephone: 01400 281358
Fax: 01400 282658
Mobile: 07785 352151**

Email: garthvincent@aol.com

Website: http://www.guns.uk.com

ARMS & ARMOUR

An Eastern flintlock pistol, with wirework decoration.

£180-220   SWO

An early 19th Century Belgian Seaservice flintlock holster pistol.

£250-350   SWO

A Belgian Sea Service flintlock holster pistol.

£300-400   SWO

A flintwood Sea Service belt pistol, the lock stamped Woolley, Sargeant & Fairfax, with swivel ramrod and brass butt cap.

£400-600   SWO

An American matched pair of Jacob or Peter Kunz (Kuntz) Kentucky pistols, SN and NSN, octagonal to round smooth barrels of approximately 45 calibre, the brass and side plates are engraved, each butt cap has a pierced finial extending up the grip, the flintlocks are each marked 'C. BIRD & Co PHILADa'.

The curly maple stocks with chequered wrists show the original red violin finish used by Kunz and other gunsmiths who learned their trade in the Lehigh Valley, PA, area. Peter and Jacob Kunz were born in the late 18thC in Whitehall Township, Lehigh City, PA. They later also worked in Philadelphia. The Kunz brothers were awarded a number of Franklin Institute awards for being the most accomplished gunsmiths in Philadelphia and for their fine craftsmanship. Like most gunsmiths, not all of their work was signed. However, pistols are quite easily identified by their characteristics, and this pair is signed 'P Kunz'. Kentucky pistols in matched pairs are extremely rare and desirable.

8.5in (21.5cm) long

£40,000-60,000   JDJ

A 120 bore continental flintlock steel pocket pistol, signed Seglas, London, with tapering barrel, box-lock action signed on the right and inscribed 'London' on the left, engraved bag-shaped butt swelling towards the base and engraved sliding trigger-guard operating a safety-catch also locking the steel, engraving worn throughout.

5.5in (14cm) long

£500-700   TDM

A late 18thC pair of flintlock pistols, probably German, full length walnut stocks carved around the tang and the underside with Rococo scrolls, the gilt brass cast mounts chased with satyr's heads and trophies of war, the trigger guard with an Ottoman crescent length barrel.

13.5in (34.5cm) barrel length

£7,000-10,000   SOTA

A pair of 18thC duelling pistols, saw butt, silver mounted, hallmarked 'MB' for Matthew Boulton, flat pommel engraved with initials 'JG' for Joseph Gosling, his silver coat of arms inlaid into the left side of both pistols, silver ramrod pipes, and original ramrods, the replacement percussion locks signed 'William Powell', converted from flint, in original fitted oak case with various accessories.

1799

£7,000-10,000   L&T

A flintlock blunderbuss, by Aston, Manchester, 14in (35.5cm) long brass barrels, complete with ramrod, brass trigger-guard and butt cap.

29.25in (11.5cm) long

£800-1,200   A&G

A George III flintlock blunderbuss, scrolled brass trigger-guard and Damascus steel barrel, with walnut stock with brass capping, fitted with a spring-loaded steel bayonet, in good condition.

c1810

32in (81.5cm) long

£2,500-3,500   RGA

An early 19thC Dutch colonial flintlock blunderbuss, with swamped steel barrel strongly swelling and fluted towards the muzzle, inlaid with fine brass linear patterns and a central foliate panel, English regulation lock stamped with 'GR' crowned, hardwood full stock boldly carved with flowers on the right of the butt, brass regulation mounts and a pair of steel sling swivels, ramrod and fore-end cap missing, crack and repairs to stock.

44in (112cm) long

£500-700   TDM

An early 19thC percussion cap pistol, cross-hatched walnut stock, some engraving on side panels, sound condition, one screw needing replacement.

7.75in (19.5cm) long

£150-250 **BLO**

An early 19th Century French percussion belt pistol, with indistinct engraved marks to the lock.

£300-400 **SWO**

An American .54 US Marshall's percussion holster pistol, the lock stamped 'MIDDTN CONN.'
c1850

£500-700 **SWO**

A mid 19th Century percussion pistol, by Nock of London.

£350-450 **SWO**

An Irish 12 bore percussion travelling pistol, by Trulock of Dublin, with registration number 'DC-4692', walnut fullstock with plain brass mounts, swivel ramrod.

9in (23cm) long

£180-220 **W&W**

A 22 bore percussion belt pistol, with 4.75in (12cm) long octagonal steel barrel and swivel ramrod underneath, with steel butt cap and fitted with a small magazine.

9.5in (24cm) long

£320-380 **A&G**

A percussion Tower pistol, the lock stamped 'Tower'.

£200-300 **SWO**

An unusual French 34 bore all steel percussion boxlock pocket pistol, with turn-off rifled barrel with St Etienne proof, the frame stamped 'Vincent, Brevete SDGD', hidden trigger.

5.75in (14.5cm) long

£200-300 **W&W**

A pair of 19thC cased percussion pocket pistols, with foliate-engraved hammers, false breeches with silver line inlays, barrel tangs and fire-blued trigger guards, plain silver escutcheons, full walnut stocks with chequered butts, captive swivel ramrods, contained in original mahogany case lined with green baize with small powder flask and associated turn screw, with plain brass shaped escutcheon on case lid, the engraved flat-sided locks with safety slides and signed 'WESTLEY RICHARDS and WESTLEY RICHARDS LONDON', the Westley Richards trade card on the inside of the lid states 'Gun Manufacturer to His Royal Highness Prince Albert, 170 New Bond Street'.

The family of Westley Richards were Birmingham gunmakers of the highest renown during the latter part of the 18thC and throughout the 19thC. William started at 82 High Street, Birmingham in 1812, and opened a London shop at 170 New Bond Street in 1815.

7in (18cm) long

£9,500-11,500 **L&T**

A 19thC double barrel percussion sporting gun, the top rib engraved 'Gasquoine and Dyson, Market Place, Manchester', finely engraved trigger-guard and butt plate tang, in a fitted mahogany case , numbered '1381'.

£1,200-1,800 **L&T**

A pair of percussion pistols, by Falisse and Trapmann à Liege, with round ribbed 4.75in (12cm) Damascus barrels and concealed triggers.

9.25in (23.5cm) long

£1,800-2,200 **GVI**

A fine pair of 19thC French percussion target and duelling pistols, by Jalaber Lamotte of St Etienne (1810-1855), with octagonal 9.75in (25cm) barrels with 0.5in (12mm) polygrove bores, the Damascus steel barrels stamped with French proof marks and stamped with the French barrel maker's name 'Massardite Peiegon', the French walnut stocks stamped with the stocker's name 'A Gonon', the trigger guard and locks engraved with foliage, maker's name inlaid in gold, cased with original accessories.

£4,200-4,800 **GVI**

A fine cased pair of 80 bore silver-mounted percussion travelling pistols, by Westley Richards, London, with Birmingham proof marks and silver hallmarks for 1850, maker's mark 'hs', dated.
1851

£3,000-5,000 TDM

A pair of early 19thC mahogany cased percussion pistols, by Conway of Manchester, with steel barrels and actions, walnut butts with silver cappings, including numerous accessories, the case bearing a retailer's label for 'Williams & Powell, Liverpool'.
c1830 *9in (23cm) long*

£5,500-6,500 RGA

A 19thC English pepperbox percussion pistol, six-barrelled, the rounded German silver action engraved 'Charles Jones, 26 St James Street, London', in a mahogany case, with accessories.
Pistol 7.75in (20cm) long

£1,500-2,500 L&T

A rare 19thC long barrel pepperbox percussion revolver, by Foster of Wisbeach, with a walnut butt with engraved brass cappings.
c1840 *11.5in (29cm) long*

£5,500-6,500 RGA

A four-barrelled 42 bore Mariette self-cocking ring trigger underhammer percussion pepperbox revolver, with turn-off twist barrels numbered 1 to 4, Liege proved, rounded scroll engraved frame, the butt strap stamped 'Mariette Brevete' and numbered '1346', with plain ebony grips.
8.75in (22cm) long

£350-450 W&W

An American six-shot percussion pepperbox pistol, with 3in (8cm) long steel barrel stamped 'Allen & Thurber, Worcester, patented 1837', with scroll-engraved action, the hammer stamped 'Allens Patent', with wood slabs to the grip.
7in (18cm) long

£450-550 BE

A six-shot 120 bore self-cocking bar hammer percussion pepperbox revolver, engraved 'Akrill Beverley'.
7.75in (19.5cm) long

£350-450 W&W

A South American 'Amazons' double barrel percussion pistol.

£180-220 SWO

A single-barrelled 14 bore percussion sporting gun, with a 32in (81cm) long twist barrel, the lock and rounded hammer engraved with scrolls, light walnut halfstock with chequered fore-end and wrist, vacant oval escutcheon on underside of butt, engraved steel mounts, brass-tipped ebony ramrod with concealed worm, surface rust to barrel, otherwise in good working order and condition.
48in (122cm) long overall

£250-350 W&W

A single-barrelled 16 bore percussion sporting gun, by W. Weston, Brighton, with a slender flat topped round 32in (81cm) long barrel from a Wogdon flintlock gun, with oval 'Wogdon' poincon at breech, the breech plug with two platinum lines, the lock and hammer engraved with dog tooth borders and scrolls, the plate with game birds and 'W Weston, Brighton', slender walnut halfstock with chequered wrist, the fore-end with silver cap and barrel wedge plates, steel mounts, the trigger guard with pineapple finial, the bow engraved with game dog and 'Stevens' in panel, the butt plate tang with game birds, small silver escutcheon engraved with crest and finials, in good working order, barrel slightly pitted overall, ramrod rib slightly damaged, minor defects to stock, no ramrod.
48in (122cm) long overall

£350-450 W&W

A Russian Crimean War period .704 calibre Belgian Brunswick military percussion rifle, with a 30.5in (77.5cm) long barrel, bayonet bar at muzzle and hinged rearsight, back action lock stamped 'P J Malberbe à Liege', walnut fullstock with regulation pattern heavy brass mounts including large patch box in butt, the oval escutcheon engraved with crowned cipher of Nicholas I, the butt plate tang engraved with Imperial eagle and 'No. 688', sling swivels, lock and barrel moderately pitted overall, otherwise in good working order, steel ramrod a good replacement.
46in (116cm) long overall

£1,800-2,200 W&W

A .577 calibre three-band Enfield percussion rifle, with a 39in (99cm) barrel with Birmingham proofs, the lock stamped with crown and 'Tower 1866', medium brown walnut fullstock with regulation pattern brass mounts, sling swivels, original steel ramrod.
55in (140cm) long overall

£400-600 W&W

A very rare Colt Paterson No. 3 Belt Model Percussion Revolver, serial number 152, Cal. 34, with 5.5in (14cm) oct bbl with eleven grooves.

According to 'Flayderman's Guide to Antique American Firearms', only about 850 of the No. 2 & No. 3 Paterson revolvers combined were made between 1837-1840.

c1838

£80,000-100,000   JDJ

A rare Samuel Colt presentation cased colt model 1860 army percussion revolver, serial no. 4740, Cal. 44, 8in (20.5cm) round barrel.

This gun was presented to Edwin Oscar Perrin (1822-88) who served in the Civil War under Colonel Kit Carson. He was the Secretary of five Democratic National Conventions and, in 1868, was elected Clerk of the Court of Appeals in New York and reappointed to the same position by the court in 1870.

£35,000-45,000   JDJ

A rare pair of silver-plated Colt single action army revolvers, serial numbers 208657 and 208673, Cal. 45 Colt, with 4.75in (12cm) barrels.

These are the only known matched pair of engraved, silver-plated Colt single action revolvers with backstrap inscriptions.

Barrels 4.75in (12cm) long

£100,000-200,000   JDJ

A .36 calibre rim-fire U.S. Colt model 1871/72 cartridge converted pocket revolver, No. 4038 with 3.5in (1.5cm) blued round barrel stamped 'Colt's Pt. F.A. MFG. Co. Hartford. CT USA', engraved cylinder, case-hardened frame stamped with patent details on the left, case-hardened trigger, polished walnut butt, with matching numbers and retaining much original finish throughout.

8.5in (21.5cm) long

£800-1,200   TDM

A scarce Henry Nettleton-inspected Colt Cavalry single action army revolver, Cal. 45 Colt. serial number 48269, blue and case coloured with 7.5in (19cm) bbl, marked with the date '1878'.

Henry Nettleton was the sub-inspector for only about 3,000 Colt Single Actions under inspector Capt. John E. Greer in 1878.

£15,000-20,000   JDJ

A rare presentation Glahn engraved gold-plated single action army revolver, serial number 354396, Cal. 38-40, single action with 4.75in (12cm) barrel, fitted with rampant Colt medallion pearl grips, the barrel has an engraved presentation which reads 'To Arthur / from a Grateful County'.

There are only twelve gold engraved Colt single action guns from the total 357,859 single action guns manufactured in the first generation.

£80,000-120,000   JDJ

A rare Confederate Augusta Machine Works 12 stop revolver, SN 'L', 7.75in octagonal bbl, brass triggerguard and backstrap, distinctive bulged Augusta stocks.

Probably no more than ten examples of this gun are known.

£35,000-45,000   JDJ

A five-shot RF Smith & Wesson Model 1.5in tip-up SA revolver, with name, address and patent dates and engraved in Gothis script 'Fd Claudin Brevete a Paris, Boulevard des Italiens 38', number '34277', blued finish overall, rosewood grips.

7.75in (19.5cm) long

£500-600   W&W

ARMS & ARMOUR

A Belgian six-shot 7mm DA PF pepperbox revolver, fluted cylinder with rifled barrels, Liege proved, loading gate on the right, folding trigger, chequered walnut grips, ejector rod screwed into the butt.

4.75in (12cm) long

£350-450   W&W

A Belgian six shot 7mm closed frame double action pinfire revolver, the 4in (10cm) long barrel tips up to allow removal of the cylinder, with folding trigger, plain walnut grips, Liege proved, the breech stamped 'Jongen Freres Brevette' and '1382', the frame and cylinder engraved with panels of scrolls, the frame numbered '9632', in good working order, dark patina overall, light pitting to cylinder, one grip chipped.

8in (20.25cm) long overall

£250-300   W&W

An English six-shot 7mm DA solid closed frame PF revolver, engraved 'Coles patent', Birmigham proved, scroll-engraved frame and breech, conventional loading gate but unusual ejector rod attached to the frame and cylinder pin, folding trigger, chequered walnut grips, in an original fitted oak revolver case with brass escutcheon in the lid and blue baize lining.

7.5in (19cm) long

£300-500   W&W

A Bentleys' calibre shot self-cocking percussion revolver, the hammer fitted with patent safety catch, with octagonal rifled 7.25in (18cm) barrel, with chequer grip, engraved 'J. Bentley & Son, Liverpool', patent no. '2955.425'.

12.5in (32cm) long

£600-800   A&G

A rare .177 calibre Accles & Shelvoke 'Warrior' side lever air pistol, second model, the frame stamped 'The Warrior Made by Accles & Shelvoke Ltd Birmingham' and 'F Clarke's Patent Nos Brit 351268 USA 568057', pressed horn grips, in general working order, small welded repairs to air chamber and front grip strap, the latter partly obliterating the serial number, otherwise in good condition.

£250-350   W&W

A .22 calibre pre WWII slant grip Webley Senior air pistol, serial number S11781, the barrel lug stamped '22/S', the rear plug secured by grub screw, no patent dates on barrel link or breech block, in good working order.

£400-600   W&W

A Westley and Richards 12 bore double barrel hammer shot gun, side locks engraved, chequered walnut stock, wooden ramrod, serial no. GT 5521, with 30in (76.2cm) barrels, and fitted within a brass-bound gun case with trade label and a leather case carrier.

33in (84cm) long

£550-650   WW

A 12 bore Holland & Holland Royal side-by-side sidelock ejector, with 27in (68.5cm) replacement barrels, 2.75in (7cm) chambers, gold-lined cocking-indicators, engraved with the initials 'GMKY', chequered ebonite butt plate, serial number A5451.

c1906

£7,000-9,000   L&T

A Wurfflein side-by-side cased rifle/shotgun combination, SN NSN, combination gun has 31in (79cm) round barrels marked 'JOHN WURFFLEIN PHILADA', 38 Cal rifle barrel and approx 20 ga. Shot barrel, engraved right-hand lock is marked 'JOHN WURFFLEIN' and the left-hand lock is marked 'PHILADELPHIA', all iron hardware is finely engraved and the inside of the capbox door is marked 'TK No 6'.

£10,000-15,000   JDJ

A double-barrelled 16 bore underlever pinfire sporting gun, by Reilly, 502 New Oxford Street, London, with 30in (76cm) long twist barrels, with London 15 bore proofs, number 10456.

45.5in (115.5cm) long overall

£500-600   W&W

A German VG5C semi-automatic rifle, SN 7538. Cal. 7.92 X 32 cartridge, spot-welded receiver with no finish and assembled basic block pieces of wood, with the serial number stamped into the buttstock. 4-33961 BK25, complete with canvas sling and magazine, and in working order.

These are very rare as most of the GI's brought home German guns that were more finely made instead of these.

£15,000-20,000   JDJ

A rare WWII Sedgeley Experimental Glove Gun, Cal. 38 S&W, no serial number, metal, with a 4.75x2.5in sheet metal backing with six holes for attaching to back of a heavy glove, small box on top with a sliding safety and an articulated, smoothbore 3in (7.5cm) bbl with a plunger adjacent to the bbl.

This experimental item was probably generated by the Office for Strategic Services for clandestine operations.

£3,500-4,500   JDJ

A 17thC Spanish rapier, cup-hilted, the grip of shaded and reeded ivory, long round-section quillons with two turned knops at the ends, the knuckle guard with central knop and cup-shaped handguard, the slender double-edged blade with central fuller stamped Solingen, with plain oval pommel.

Blade 42in (106.5cm) long

£500-800   **L&T**

A 17thC Spanish rapier, cup-hilted, the grip covered in black horse hair, with wide brass ferules, long round-section quillons with two flared knops at the ends, the knuckleguard with turned knop midway, with cup-shaped handguard, the slender double-edged blade with short central fuller stamped 'SOLINGEN', with plain but shaped pommel.

Blade 40in (101.5cm) long

£500-800   **L&T**

A 17thC Spanish rapier, cup-hilted, the grip tightly bound with a double twist of silver wire, long quillons and knuckle guard with turned terminals at each end, the cup handguard pierced and with scalloped top edge, the double-edged blade of triangular section, with a writhen-turned pommel.

Blade 34in (86.5cm) long

£800-1,200   **L&T**

A scarce early 18thC English officers sword, with copper alloy heart-shaped shell guards, the knuckle guard with two swept-forward guards that join the shell guard midway, and short wrist guard, some small patches of gilding, with single edge lightweight blade with narrow fuller at back edge, damaged edge, wooden grip binding missing.

Blade 30in (76cm) long

£400-600   **L&T**

An early 18thC Scottish basket-hilted cavalry back sword, single edged, the hilt of conventional form with pierced cross guards joined at the pommel by a ring, large bun-shaped pommel, damaged blade edge and tip, deep corrosion on hilt and blade, grip missing.

Blade 31in (79cm) long

£400-600   **L&T**

An 18th Century Scottish basket-hilted sword, with a pierced-bowl hilt, the blade struck twice 'Andria Farara' within three X's, blade bent and cracked.

Blade 31in (79cm) long

£500-700   **SWO**

£4,500-6,500

An early 18thC Scottish basket-hilted broad sword, the wooden grip covered in black dogfish skin, the basket of traditional form with the guard of flat-section bar terminating at the shallow bun-shaped pommel cut with a groove to take the guard, missing wrist-guard with the remains of the leather liner, the broad double-edged blade with four narrow fullers for three quarters of the blade length, stamped with 'ss' blade-smith's mark and with the running wolf motif.

36.25in (92cm) long

    L&T

An early 19thC Gibson, Thompson & Craig scarce stirrup-hilted Flank Company officer's sabre, in associated scabbard, with gilt-metal hilt, chequered ivory grip, the deeply curved blued blade engraved and inlaid in gold with martial trophies, royal arms, and makers' mark.

35 in (89cm) long

£300-500   **L&T**

A 19thC Prussian officer's dress sword, the fish skin grip to a gilt-brass hilt with Prussian eagle, the fullered blade with a steel scabbard.

Blade 30.5in (77.5cm) long

£220-280   **WW**

A Prussian cavalry trooper's sword, broad shallow-curved 32.5in (82.5cm) long blade, stamps on backstrap including date '? 5.87', regulation heavy quality steel stirrup hilt with knucklebow and langets, plain pommel and eared backstrap, ribbed leather grip, in its steel scabbard marked en suite '86.R.1.1', some surface rust.

£450-550   **W&W**

A German State M1889 cavalry trooper's sword, straight pipe black 32in (81.5cm) long blade, double edged at point, with crowned crossed swords mark of 'C K Co', ribbed composition shaped grips, in steel scabbard with opposing hanging rings.

£550-750   **W&W**

A French curassier trooper's M An XI sword, straight 37.5in (95.5cm) double fullered blade, marked on backstrap '…Klingenthal mars (unclear) 1811', regulation brass hilt with flat guard into knucklebow, three sidebars, cap-shaped pommel, brass wirebound leather grip, stamps at forte and on hilt, with steel scabbard with two hanging rings.

£600-700   **W&W**

An 1897 pattern infantry officer's sword, with a dumbbell blade with a broad central fuller etched with a crown foliage, engraved with the maker's name 'W.H. Hall, Sheffield', wire-bound fish skin grip and leather field scabbard complete with original knot and frog.

Blade 32.25in (82cm) long

£220-280   **GVI**

A mid-late 20thC 1897 pattern infantry officer's sword, straight fullered blade by Wilkinson, number '85533' on backstrap, etched with crowned royal arms and cypher with wreath within scrolled frosted panels, regulation plated hilt, the guard incorporating crowned ERII cypher, pommel and chequered backstrap, wirebound fishskin grip, with black leather knot, in its plated scabbard, with leather field service scabbard and chamois-lined black cover.

After 1953   *Blade 32in (81.5cm) long*

£300-500   **W&W**

A 14th King's Hussars officer's sword, 1912 Pattern, by Rogers & Co. London, with a regulation straight single-edged blade, heavy nickle bowl hilt, ribbed fish skin grip, leather-covered scabbard and acorn sword knot, the blade etched with the regimental name and the name of the original owner 'W.A.E Coates ...XIV King's Hussars.'.

Blade 35in (14cm) long

£420-480   **GVI**

A shortsword, the blade by Thomas Gill, Birmingham, with broad blade formed with a serrated back-edge, etched with the maker's details, 'Warranted never to fail' and the date '1792' on the respective sides of the forte, with brass hilt cast with scrollwork in low relief.

18in (45.5cm) long

£400-600   **TDM**

A WWI 1897 pattern infantry officer's sword, straight slender fullered blade, engraved at forte on one side 'Albert Adams 1915', regulation plated hilt, the guard incorporated crowned GVR cypher, pommel and chequered backstrap, wirebound fishskin grip, with leather knot, in its leather field service scabbard and modern chamois-lined cover, in very good condition.

Blade 33in (84cm) long

£300-400   **W&W**

A Royal Navy officer's sword, single-edged blade, etched with a fouled anchor and the royal cipher, with a gilded brass gothic hilt with a wire-bound fish skin grip and original sword knot, contained in original brass-mounted leather scabbard and with original storage bag, engraved with original owner's name, 'J.B. Russell' on the folding guard, in excellent condition.

After 1902   *Blade 31in (12cm) long*

£300-400   **GVI**

A late Victorian Royal Artillery officer's 1821 pattern dress sword, by Meyer & Mortimer, Conduit Street, London, slightly curved, slender, fullered blade, etched with grenade, cannon and winged lightning within scrolled frosted panels and 'By Appointment', with Prince of Wales feathers at forte, regulation triple bar steel hilt with stepped pommel and diced backstrap, wirebound fishskin grip, in its steel scabbard with two hanging rings, the blade retaining most original polish, patina to hilt and scabbard.

Blade 29in (73.5cm) long

£250-350   **W&W**

A Spanish Light Infantry side arm, slightly curved and hollow ground single-edged blade, sharpened for three-quarters of length, engraved on one side 'Arta Faba de Toledo 1891', solid brass hilt of French style with knucklebow and ribbed grip, in good condition.

Blade 27.5in (70in) long

£80-120   **W&W**

A Prussian sidearm with brass grip and a leather scabbard.

£120-180   **SWO**

An early brass-handled dirk, the solid one-piece brass handle with ribbed grip and simple incised linear decoration to pommel, the blade reduced from a sword blade and marked 'ME FECIT', with a triple 'S' mark below.

17.75in (45cm) long

£6,000-8,000   **L&T**

A late 18thC Scottish dirk, with broad blade cut-down from a broadsword, incised with a series of marks on each side including a running wolf, a cross and orb, rootwood grip carved with a naive flowerhead on each face, formed with a pair of tall shoulders, each reinforced with a brass panel and brass disc pommel, in a contemporary leather scabbard with later brass mounts.

20in (50.5cm) long

£1,500-2,000   **TDM**

A highland dirk by Robert Mole & Sons, Birmingham, with etched blade, nickel-mounted hilt with hardwood grip carved with basket-weave designs enriched with nickel nails, associated steel pommel cap cast with a crown, in an associated scabbard with steel mounts cast with thistle foliage, and the hilt and scabbard inscribed '14LD.1' and '14LD.3' respectively.

1900   17.5in (44.5cm) long

£700-900   **TDM**

A Scottish provincial highland dirk, by J. Hodge of Inverness, with basket weave-carved handle with studded grip, claw set with circular cut citrine, the leather covered scabbard with applied mounts with pierced decoration and foliate engraved designs, the top mount with applied crest and motto for clan Fraser, the ensuite knife and two-prong fork set and carved similarly, marked 'J. Hodge'.

c1890   18in (46cm) long

£2,000-3,000   **L&T**

A Victorian gilt-metal-mounted dress dirk, of the 79th Regiment (The Queen's Own Cameron Highlanders), the basket weave-carved wood hilt with circular-cut cairngorm-set pommel, and thistle-, acorn- and foliate-cast mounts, contained in a similarly mounted leather scabbard, fitted with a companion knife and fork with matching pommels.

Dirk 16.5in (42cm) long

£2,500-3,500   **BE**

A late Victorian boy's Highland dirk and sgian dubh suite, the dirk with antler handles set with foil-backed stones to pommels, with spear point blades and two-prong bi knife, together with matching sgian dubh, the mounts unmarked.

A 'sgian dubh' is a Scottish ceremonial dagger.

Dirk 11.75in (30cm) long

£1,000-1,500   **L&T**

A Scottish provincial sgian dubh, by William B. Taylor of Inverness, marked 'W.B.T, INVss', Edinburgh 1919-20, the carved wooden handles with intertwined Celtic knotwork and leaf detail, with pin cap with simple knotwork border, the leather-covered scabbard with Celtic knotwork mounts.

1919-20   7in (17.5cm) long

£450-650   **L&T**

A 19thC American bowie knife, with faceted ivory hilt, the blade etched with various slogans, including 'I can dig gold from quartz, California Bowie Knife,' stamped 'Tiffany, Broadway, New York, U.S.A.'

12.75in (32.5cm) long

£400-600   **SK**

A rare Civil War Bowie knife, made by the C. Roby & Co. of West Chelmsford, MA., the Bowie blade with diamond-shaped flat grind with about 3in of back grind, oval steel handguard with turned, ribbed walnut handle with swelled middle, a brass ferrule and a cast brass eagle head pommel, marked on left ricasso 'C. ROBY & CO. / W. CHELMSFORD / MASS.', left side of blade is etched with crossed cannons and an American shield in a wreath, right side is etched 'US' in a wreath and another panel has crossed swords in a wreath.

1861-65   Blade 9.25in (23.5cm) long

£10,000-15,000   **JDJ**

A plug bayonet for the Royal Guard of James II, with tapering double-edged blade etched with the inscription 'God save King James the 2', stamped with a King's Head mark and with the mark of the London Cutler's company, matching pommel and turned hardwood grip.

c1687   16.5in (42cm) long

£4,000-6,000   **TDM**

A 19thC Persian Jambiya, with curved blade chiselled with foliage over the lower half, carved bone grip decorated with a pair of courtly figures on each side, in its leather-covered wooden scabbard.

17.25in (44cm) long

£300-400   **TDM**

An Argentinian gaucho's dagger, steel blade with stamp, head of Liberty, libertad below, in .900 silver hilt, with 'LSB' monogram in gold, in silver scabbard by J.S. Ferra, superb condition, some minor blade oxidation.

c1900   Blade 6.25in (16cm)

£200-300   **BLO**

An Eastern dagger, with brass-mounted wooden holt, the brass and chased white metal scabbard with two brass suspension rings.

15.5in (39.5cm) long

£120-180 LFA

A Meiji period Japanese tanto, with carved ivory handle and sheath, decorated with numerous figures undertaking various activities, including fishing from a boat, with subsidiary side blade.

12in (30.5cm) long

£1,500-2,500 L&T

A 17thC East European war hammer, with steel head formed of eight pierced shaped flanges, moulded slightly down-curved tapering rear spike, fluted neck, tapering tubular shaft retaining an early leather covering over cord, and modern leather thong.

26.75in (68cm)

£5,800-6,800 TDM

A late 18thC stonebow, by T. Barker, Warrington, with steel bow fitted with an early string with bone spacers, folding fore-sight, figured walnut tiller with turned steel knop-shaped finial, built-in gaffle, signed on the back-sight and engraved with a flower above and beneath.

28in (71.5cm) long tiller

£1,400-1,800 TDM

A Northern Italian close-helmet, the headpiece with a roped comb and pointed visor with a horizontal sight and pierced breathing holes, the neckplates to front and rear.

c1570 *9in (23cm) wide*

£3,500-5,500 FRE

A combed Morion helmet, retaining traces of original coloured finish to the metal.

Helmets of this type were worn by foot soldiers and comparatively few survive outside major collections.

1560

£1,800-2,200 GVI

A 17thC English Civil War cavalry trooper's helmet, with a two-piece skull and rising peak with a three bar face guard, unusual form to the lobster tail, in very good condition.

£2,000-2,500 GVI

An officer cadet's helmet, from the Royal Military College.

c1881-1901 *11in (28cm) high*

£750-850 RGA

An Argentinean officer's 'Pickelhaube', of typical German form with patent leather skull, gilt spike and chinscales and gilt badge in the form of the Argentinean arms, pale blue and gilt rosettes, leather headband and cream silk lining, top of skull slightly depressed, some crazing to patent leather, silk lining split, otherwise in good condition.

c1910

£380-420 W&W

An English Civil War pikeman's suit of armour and helmet, comprising breast plate, back plate, tassets and helmet, the shoulder straps and tassets secured by hooks, in good condition.

c1640

£5,800-6,800 GVI

An early 17thC pair of German etched blue and blued gauntlets, each formed of a strongly flared and pointed cuff made in one piece with a riveted join at the inside of the wrist.

£3,000-5,000 TDM

A rare officer's short-tailed coatee, of Captain John Howie of the 2nd Regiment of Renfrewshire Local Militia, fitted with epaulettes to both shoulders, together with a shoulder-belt plate struck with the regimental badge and title, and an officer's gorget of 1796 Universal Pattern.

1808-14

£1,200-1,800   **L&T**

A WWI German pilot's uniform.

1914-18

£350-450   **SWO**

A rare Royal Air Force lieutenant's khaki service dress tunic, embroidered cloth pilot's wings, gilt Royal Naval Air Service style crown/eagle buttons with roped edge, two buttons missing.

1918-19

£450-550   **W&W**

An early 19thC Ayrshire Yeomanry officer's black leather sabretache, mounted with a silvered metal four-pointed star backing the centre gilt-copper medallion of St. Andrew with the Ayrshire Yeomanry inscription on the border.

£250-350   **L&T**

A 19thC 2nd Royal North British Dragoon Guards (Greys) officer's black leather sabretache, mounted with regimental brass Waterloo Eagle.

£300-400   **L&T**

A 20thC Argyll and Sutherland Highlanders officer's sporran, with red leather purse, silver-plated cantle applied with the regimental motto and devices in gilt-brass, white hair covering with silver bullion tassels and complete with its belt.

10.5in (27cm) high

£1,200-1,800   **TDM**

An officer's copper gilt rectangular shoulder belt plate, of the Leeds, West York, Local Militia, in the centre a silver-plated rose within a crowned oval inscribed 'Leeds West York', below a scroll marked 'Local', rounded corners, hook and two studs fastening, with its original chamois leather liner, lacquered overall, in good condition.

c1810   *3in (7.5cm) high*

£420-480   **W&W**

An officer's silver-plated rectangular shoulder belt plate, of the Third West York Militia, bearing rose within crowned strung bugle with title scrolls below, lacquered overall, plating high spots rubbed, small knock to lower left corner, otherwise in good condition.

£350-450   **W&W**

A Victorian dress powder horn, formed from a flattened section of cow horn, the mounts with chased thistle borders and detail, the centre of the panel set with rectangular cut citrine with chased crest above.

13in (33cm) long

£420-480   **L&T**

A post-1902 officer's gilt and silver-plated shako badge, of the Highland Light Infantry.

£150-250   W&W

A WWI Tribute Cross, the gold paty cross with '22 Loyalty 1914' and 'Presented to W.J. Marshall by F.L.C.'.

This medal was awarded by Sir Frederick Lucas Cooke of London to his workers who enlisted in 1914. It is known to have been awarded in gold, silver and bronze.
1914

£150-200   DNW

An other rank's or bandsman's white metal shako plate, of the 74th Highlanders, in very good condition.

£200-300   W&W

A Victorian officer's die-struck silver-plated small shako plate, of the 16th (Harrogate) West York Rifles Volunteers, in good condition.

£320-380   W&W

An 1874 pattern other rank's brass Glengarry badge, of the 26th (Cameronians) regiment, brass lugs, cleaned and lacquered, in good condition.

£180-220   W&W

An 1874 pattern non-commissioned officer's gilt Glengarry badge, of the 71st (Highland Light Infantry) regiment, lacquered, in very good condition.

£250-350   W&W

An officer's silver-plated helmet plate, of the Sixth West York Militia, rose on original black patent leather, in very good condition.

£180-220   W&W

An officer's silver-plated forage cap badge, of the Fifth West York Militia, in very good condition.

£200-300   W&W

A Patiala Family Order Officer's breast badge, in silver-gilt and red and green enamel, no ribbon, extremely fine.

£550-650   BLO

An officer's cast silver-plated star headdress badge of the Second West York Militia, rose in the title scroll on rayed star, two lugs, in very good condition.
c1830   2.25in (5.5cm) wide

£350-450   W&W

A rare pair of WWII printed cloth badges, of the 202nd (Assam) line of communication area, in good condition.

£80-120   W&W

A scarce Vatican Order of Christ Knights gold and enamel breast badge, with crown in silver-gilt, slight enamel damage at suspension, extremely fine.

The Vatican Order of Christ is awarded in one class only and reserved for Roman Catholic Heads of State.

£400-600   BLO

A military general service medal, with three clasps 'Fuentes D'onor', 'Vittoria' and 'Pyrenees', clasps slightly buckled, edge knock, otherwise in good condition.
1793-1814
£1,000-1,500   W&W

A Peninsular War military general service medal, naming J. Rippen, Eighteenth Dragoons, with one clasp 'Sahagun & Benevente', minor edge bruises, in excellent condition.
1793-1814
£1,200-1,800   DNW

A Peninsular War military general service medal, naming George Small, Serjeant, 57th Foot Regiment, with one clasp 'Albuhera', with riband buckle, edge nicks, in very good condition.
1793-1814
£3,500-4,000   DNW

A Peninsular War military general service medal, naming W. Gunner, Serjeant, 88th Foot, with five clasps 'Talavera', 'Busaco', 'Fuentes D'Onor', 'Ciudad Rodrigo' and 'Badajoz', suspension claw refixed, few edge bruises, in very good condition.
1793-1814
£3,500-4,000   DNW

A rare Army of India medal, naming G. Hunter, 29th Light Dragoons, with three clasps, 'Allighur', 'Laswarree' and 'Capture of Deig', short hyphen reverse, officially impressed naming, edge bruising and contact marks, in very good condition.
1799-1826
£7,000-8,000   DNW

A very rare Army of India medal, naming T. Davis, 76th Foot, with four clasps 'Allighur', 'Battle of Delhi', 'Laswarree' and 'Battle of Deig', short hyphen reverse, officially impressed naming, edge bruising, in good condition.

Only twenty-three of these medals were issued with four clasps, including fourteen to British regiments, and five with this combination of clasps, all of which were awarded to the 76th Foot, known as Lord Lake's 'Handfull of heroes'.
1799-1826
£12,000-18,000   DNW

A rare German second class Iron Cross, the suspension loop marked 'KO', silver with magnetic steel centre, possibly intended for display or exhibition, very fine or better, ribbon worn.
1813
£300-500   BLO

A Waterloo campaign medal, naming Thomas Morris, Second Battalion, 73rd Regiment Foot, naming re-engraved in contemporary large capitals, with replacement silver ball mount and straight bar suspension, some edge bruising and contact marks, in good condition.
1815
£1,000-1,500   DNW

A China campaign medal, naming P. A. Helpman, Lieutenant of H.M.S. Columbine, with replacement silver mount and contemporary gold swivel straight bar suspension, with gold buckle and brooch bar, edge bruising, in very good condition.
1842
£2,000-3,000   DNW

A Sutlej campaign medal, for Modkee 1845, naming Corporal William Sherman, 31st Regiment, with three clasps 'Ferozeshuhur', 'Aliwal' and 'Sobraon', slight contact to Queen's cheek, otherwise in very good condition.
1845-46
£1,000-1,500   DNW

An extremely rare first issue Victorian Royal Marine Meritorious Service Medal, awarded to Sergeant W. Maxwell, Royal Marine, with '1848' on the obverse and with dated edge.
£2,500-3,500   DNW

A very rare Canada general service campaign medal, naming 1673 Private J. Greenhil, First 60th Royal Rifles, with one clasp 'Red River 1870', officially impressed naming, in excellent condition.
1866-70
£1,500-2,000   DNW

An Empress of India silver medal, complete with neck ribbon, toned.

1877

£600-700 BLO

A pair of Sudan Campaign medals, naming Lieutenant Richard Wolfe, Second Dragoons (Scots Greys), Egypt and Sudan, 1882-89, with two clasps, 'The Nile 1884-85' and 'Abu Klea', undated reverse, and Khedive's Star, 1884-6, both in very good condition.

1882-89

£13,000-15,000 DNW

A British North Borneo Company campaign medal, naming 380 Private Momin, with one clasp 'Tambunan', bronze issue.

Initially seven silver and 116 bronze medals were made. In 1905/06 36 bronze were exchanged for silver.

1898-1900

£800-1,200 DNW

A Tibet medal, naming Cooly Gopal Sing Lama, Science & Technology Corps, with one clasp 'Gyantse', bronze issue, in excellent condition.

1903-4

£280-320 DNW

A rare George V second issue Commonwealth of Australia Meritorious Service Medal, awarded to J. F. Chapple, Gunner, Royal Australian Garrison Artillery, fixed suspension, in excellent condition.

£450-550 DNW

A rare German first class Iron Cross, two-piece screw back and flat plate fixing, pilot's issue, extremely fine.

1939

£150-200 BLO

A group of eight medals awarded to Nurse Estelle Smith, Army Nursing Service (India), comprising Award of Royal Red Cross, GVIR second class dated 1946, with 1939-45, Africa, Pacific, Italy stars, War, Defence and QEII Coronation medals, also British Red Cross Society Merit Award named E. Smith (née Stoddard), mounted as worn, extremely fine.

1939-46

£300-400 BLO

An Albanian Order of Scanderburg Grand Cross set, by Cravanzola of Rome, consisting of a sash badge in silver-gilt, and breast star in silver and enamel, complete with full dress sash, extremely fine and scarce.

This order was issued by the Italian Government occupying Albania during the WWII.

£1,500-2,000 BLO

A Bikaner Commendable Conduct silver medal, in extremely fine condition.

£400-600 BLO

A Kaiser-I-Hind medal, George VI issue, 2nd Class, with silver bar, complete with brooch buckle, in Garrard case of issue, dated, extremely fine.

1946

£500-700 BLO

A very rare Naval general service campaign medal, naming D/JX.146158 W. H. L. Flower, Leading Seaman, Royal Navy, with one clasp 'Bomb & Mine Clearance 1945-53', official correction to 'R.N.', in excellent condition.

1915-1962

£1,200-1,800 DNW

A scarce Bulgarian Order of George Dimitrov 14ct gold medal, decorated in red and white enamel, extremely fine.

Only 4,000 of this order were produced.

£250-300 BLO

ANTIQUITIES

An Attic black-figured belly amphora, attributed to the manner of the Lysippides painter, decorated with Athena flanked by two warriors, Odysseus and Diomedes, the reverse painted with Dionysos flanked by two dancing satyrs, linked lotus buds above each scene, rays above the foot, the details in added red and white.

c520-510BC   *17.5in (44cm) high*

£50,000-70,000   **SOT**

An Apulian red-figured column krater, attributed to the painter of Boston, decorated with a Oscan youth seated on a shield and holding a kantharos and spear.

c350-330BC   *18in (46cm) high*

£12,000-18,000   **SOT**

A large 4thC BC Apulian red figure ware bell krater, obverse showing winged Nike, has been professionally restored from large fragments.

16.5in (42cm) high

£3,500-4,500   **ANA**

A 5th/4thC BC Greek black-glazed pottery dish.

This type of vessel was either used as a bowl or as a stand. They are occasionally called 'salts', although this is a 19thC association.

3.25in (8.5cm) diam

£70-100   **HG**

A Cypriote terracotta juglet, the biconical body with concave neck, trefoil mouth, handle from rim to shoulder, ring base.

7in (18cm) high

£120-180   **ANA**

A fragment from a large architectural tile, Western Asia Minor, Phrygia, Duver, moulded and painted with a figure of a striding griffin.

550-525BC   *7.75in (19cm) high*

£150-250   **HG**

A 4thC BC Greek Gnathian lekythos, of slender ovoid-shaped body, the tubular neck with high flaring mouth of weak bell-shaped form, disc-like rim, convex on top, foot with short stem curving out to a square base-moulding, central band of cross-hatched design framed by single band encircling near base and double band around shoulders, neck with tongues attached to body via lug handle, wash of brownish-red pigment, in excellent condition, with few very minor surface scratches.

29.25in (11.5cm) high

£120-180   **ANA**

A 2nd/3rdC Roman red slipware beaker, floral relief decoration in a frieze with incised hatching below, in good condition, with minor cracks repaired.

4.25in (11cm) high

£400-500   **ANA**

A Roman redware flagon, North Africa, with erotic scene of a couple.

This piece may well have been used as a prize for a victorious gladiator.

5.5in (14cm) high

£700-900   ANA

A 4thC BC late Etruscan amphora, creamy stoneware with red wash decoration.

8.25in (21cm) high

£280-320   ANA

A rare 6th-7thC Byzantine glass flask, green translucent glass of variegated iridescence, with mould-blown Christian symbols in relief.

5in (13cm) high

£1,500-2,000   ANA

A 2nd-3rdC Roman glass unguentarium, with variegated iridescence.

This was used to store perfume.

4.75in (12cm) high

£75-85   ANA

A large 3rdC Roman bronze statuette of Venus.

6in (15cm) high

£1,000-1,300   ANA

A 1st/2ndC Roman bronze draped goddess statuette.

2.25in (6cm) high

£600-800   ANA

A 1stC Roman bronze bust of Mars, of Romano-British style.

3.75in (9.5cm) high

£800-1,200   ANA

A 2nd/3rdC Roman terracotta toy horse, with harness

.

4.25in (11cm) long

£150-200   ANA

A 16thC-11thC BC New Kingdom wooden boatman, wears white kilt, extensive deep red pigment of the torso and face and black pigment of the features and wig remaining.

10in (25.5cm) high

£300-400   ANA

A late Dynastic brilliant blue ushabti, wearing tripartite wig of darker blue glaze and royal beard.

715-332BC   *3.75in (9.5cm) high*

£180-240   ANA

A late Dynastic beaded mask, multi-coloured beaded mask composition, with eyebrow and eye outlined in black with yellow infill and black pupil, yellow nose and red mouth in outline with yellow infill, surmounted by border of green cylindrical-shaped beads laid out in triangular fashion, constitutes face of mummy's shroud.

715-332BC   *5.25in (13.5cm) high*

£200-300   ANA

An English violin, by William H. Luff, the two-piece back of faint medium curl with similar wood to the sides and head, the table of a medium grain and the varnish of a reddish colour on a golden ground, labelled 'William H. Luff, Maker, London, 1986', with case and two silver-mounted violin bows.

14in (35.5cm) high

£3,000-4,000   **GHOU**

A French violin by Charles Adolphe Gand, the one-piece back with almost horizontal narrow curl, the ribs and head of similar curl, the table of fine grain, the varnish of orange/brown colour, with original label 'Gand, Luthier de la Musique du Roi et du Conservatoire de Musique, Rue Croix de Petits Champs, No.24, Paris 1835'.

The back 14.25in (36cm) long

£2,200-2,800   **HT**

An English violin, by Joseph Hill, the two-piece back of medium curl with narrow curl to the sides and head, the table of medium grain and the varnish of a golden-brown colour, with case.

c1700   *14in (35.5cm) high*

£5,000-6,000   **GHOU**

A violin, the two-piece back of faint broad curl with similar wood to the sides and head, the table of a medium grain and the varnish of a light reddish-brown colour on a golden ground, labelled 'Antonius Hieronymus Fr. Amati Cremonen. Andrea fil. F. 1625'.

14in (35.5cm) high

£12,000-15,000   **GHOU**

A rare Italian violin, by Filippo Gragnani, the two-piece back of fine irregular curl with similar wood to the sides and head, the table of a fine grain widening to the flanks and the varnish of a light brown colour, bearing a manuscript label signed 'Filippo Gragnani, Liburni, 18?...', with an Edward Withers' case, with two certificates of authenticity from William E. Hill & Sons stating the instrument has some characteristics of Gragnani.

14in (35.5cm) high

£44,000-50,000   **GHOU**

An English violoncello, by Lockey Hill, London, the two-piece back of plainish wood with faint medium curl to the sides, the later neck and head of plain wood, the table of a fine grain and the varnish of a golden-brown colour, with soft case.

c1790   *29in (73.5cm) high*

£3,500-4,500   **GHOU**

An Italian violoncello, attributed to Antonio Mariani, the two-piece back of plain wood with similar wood to the sides and head, the tale of a medium grain narrowing to the flanks and the varnish of a rich red colour on a golden ground, labelled 'Antonio Mariani fece in Pessaro 1761'.

29.75in (75.5cm) high

£8,000-12,000   **GHOU**

An early 20thC German violoncello, the two-piece back of faint medium curl with similar wood to the sides and head, the varnish of a reddish-brown colour on a golden ground, labelled 'John Werro, importer and maker of musical instruments...', with case and two bows.

29.75in (75.5cm) high

£3,000-4,000   **GHOU**

A Neapolitan mandolin, by Luigi Emberger, the body of 18 plain sycamore ribs, the table and oval soundhole edged with multiple purfling, the scratch plate of tortoiseshell inlaid in ivory with a floral motif, twenty-five brass frets and brass machine heads with ebony pegs, labelled 'Anno 1932, Luigi Emberger, Via Belsiana no. 7, Roma' and stamped 'L. Emberger, Roman' on the face of the head.

23in (58.5cm) high

£1,200-1,800   **GHOU**

A classical Spanish guitar, by Marcelino Lopez Neito, labelled 'Marcelino Lopez, Luthier, Guitarra no. 73, 1955... Madrid', also signed on the label and bearing the maker's stamp to the inner back, with case.

£550-700   **GHOU**

A late 19thC small-bodied lady's guitar, with rosewood back and sides, ebony and boxwood-purled spruce table and open peg box, with home-made case.

£350-450   **GHOU**

A Hofner President model guitar, no. 4622, with original label, with hard case.

£500-600   **GHOU**

A Hofner semi-acoustic arch top guitar, with maple back and sides, signed spruce table, mother-of-pearl slot inlay to the fingerboard and a faux tortoiseshell and mother-of-pearl-veneered solid head.

£160-200   GHOU

A Hofner President model guitar, labelled 'Hofner President Model no. 2299', with maple back and sides, signed spruce table and mother-of-pearl floral-inlaid solid head.

£250-350   GHOU

An early and unusual classical five string banjo, by Alfred Weaver, with 11in (28cm) hoop and mother-of-pearl dot inlay to the fingerboard, stamped 'A. Weaver Maker' on perch rod.

£450-550   GHOU

A concert harp, by J. F. Browne & Co., the fluted column capital moulded in relief with standing angels united by garlands of flowers, the soundboard painted with female figures symbolic of music, stamped 'J.F. Browne & Co Makers, London & 281 Broadway, N. York'.

68in (172.5cm) high

£1,500-2,000   GHOU

An Anglo concertina, possibly by C. Jeffries, with thirty metal buttons on pierced foliate metal ends, six-fold bellows, indistinctly inscribed, with wooden case.

£3,500-4,500   GHOU

A Lachenal & Co. three-row Anglo concertina, no. 102031, with 32 bone buttons on pierced metal ends, six-fold bellows, labelled 'Barnet Samuel & Sons, 32 Worship St, London'.

£1,800-2,200   GHOU

A Steinway concert grand piano, D274, no. 386 241, with black matte finish.
1964

108in (274cm) wide

£25,000-30,000   MIL

A rare mid-19thC stained fruitwood walking stick flute, by Johann Christoffer Selboe of Copenhagen, the four silver-plated keys with slightly domed circular cover, ebony knop with silver-plated mounts, the horn ferrule stamped 'Joh. Selboe' in two places.

20.75in (52.5cm) long

£1,200-1,800   GHOU

Six of a set of 22 hand bells, from C22-G4, including two F sharp hand bells and an A sharp hand bell.

£450-550 SET   GHOU

THE DECORATIVE ARTS MARKET

In the Decorative Arts field, Arts & Crafts is the movement to watch, perhaps because it is a style that suits modern, more minimal interiors. Arts & Crafts pottery is selling well, in particular the big names such as the Martin Brothers and William de Morgan, and although prices for Pilkington's are levelling off they are still selling fairly well. The same can be said for the other stalwarts of the Arts & Crafts movement – the Tudric (pewter) and Cymric (silver) wares designed by Archibald Knox for Liberty & Co.

As far as Art Deco pottery is concerned, the work of Clarice Cliff continues to sell well. Its perennial popularity is perhaps due to the supply of fresh pieces which come onto the market every year and fetch good prices. At the same time there is a thriving collector's club and new books help to maintain interest levels.

Carlton Ware and Shelley have not had the same good fortune. This may be partly due to the perception that they need to be housed en mass in a display cabinet which is not fashionable at the moment. In comparison, pieces by Clarice Cliff, whose designs are more avant garde, can be shown singly to great effect. Prices for Art Deco figures by Lenci and Goldscheider continue to rise steadily and look set to go higher as more and more buyers are won over by their charms. Top prices continue to be paid for Wemyss ware, particularly pieces which are well painted, in bright colours and in perfect condition. For any of these designers, any damage, especially to a relatively common piece, will lower values considerably.

The market for Continental Art Nouveau ceramics continues to be led by Zsolnay, particularly pieces which show fine moulding and exceptionally vibrant lustred glazing.

Furniture from the Arts & Crafts, Art Nouveau and Art Deco movements continues to sell well – especially if it is by a big name such as Émile Gallé or Émile-Jacques Ruhlmann. Pieces in the same style but without the 'hand of the master' are not doing as well, probably because buyers want a name and the cachet that goes with it. This has benefitted prices for pieces by lesser-known names, such as the Scottish Arts & Crafts designer Sir Robert Lorimer, which are performing above expectations.

In glass, the market for Whitefriars has levelled off over the past three or four years. However, rare pieces of Whitefriars – especially designs by Geoffrey Baxter – continue to achieve high prices at auction.

Glass by the Art Deco master – René Lalique – is particularly strong at the moment. The same can be said for the cameo glass of Émile Gallé and Daum Freres as buyers continue to appreciate – and pay good prices for – the skilled craftsmanship of both factories' cameo glass. Perhaps, again, this is because displayed individually and in a good light, this glass can be the centrepiece of any room.

A Boch Frères large ovoid vase, enamel-decorated with floral bands in crackled glazes, stamped 'MADE IN BELGIUM/BOCH Fes./FABRICATION BELGE'.

20in (51cm) high

£2,500-3,000   **SDR**

A large Boch Frères vase, by Charles Catteau, with stylised blossoms, stamped 'Ch. Catteau/Made in Belgium/951 WD962'.

14in (35.5cm) high

£1,800-2,200   **SDR**

A Bough three-handled lustre tyg, decorated by Elizabeth Amour, the cylindrical body painted with garlands of fruit and bearing inscription 'Peep Through Their Stars Tonight I'll Make The Wine', painted marks, dated.

1920   *8in (20cm) high*

£1,000-1,200   **L&T**

A Brannam Pottery twin-handled vase, modelled with reptile handles, the body incised with scaly fish, incised 'WB C H Brannam, Barum 1907', minor glaze nicks.

8.5in (21.5cm) high

£300-350   **WW**

ESSENTIAL REFERENCE: BURMANTOFTS

Burmantofts Pottery was established by William Wilcock and John Lassey in the Burmantofts district of Leeds, Yorkshire in 1845. It was originally a brick and pipe factory.

- In 1879, the pottery passed to James Holroyd who started the production of 'architectural faïence'. The company began producing vases, jardinières, etc in the 1880s.
- In 1888, the company opened its own showroom in London and changed its name to The Burmantofts Company. The following year Burmantofts merged with five other Yorkshire companies to form the Leeds Fireclay Company.
- Early Burmantofts pottery was plain, including bulbous vases, with long slender necks. Later designs are more ornate. More ambitious glazes were used, with sgraffito decoration. The use of applied insects and serpents was popular.
- In 1904, the factory reverted mainly to production of architectural pieces. Production finally ceased in 1957.

A Burmantofts faïence Persian vase, designed by Leonard King, painted with carnations, in shades of blue, aubergine and green on a white ground, impressed and painted marks, 'LK' monogram.

9.5in (24cm) high

£2,500-3,000   **WW**

A Burmantofts faïence Persian vase, designed by Leonard King, design 85, impressed marks, painted monogram, minor glaze loss.

9.75in (25cm) high

£700-800   WW

A rare Burmantofts faïence vase, designed by Leonard King, painted with birds amongst scrolling foliage, in ruby lustre on a white ground, impressed marks, painted 'LK' monogram.

14.5in (36.5cm) high

£1,300-1,600   WW

A Burmantofts faïence Persian vase, designed by Leonard King, design 91, painted with mythical beasts, impressed and painted marks, 'LK' monogram, minor damages.

9in (23cm) high

£700-900   WW

A Burmantofts faïence vase, of waisted form and decorated with a continuous scene of entwined scaly dragons within a woodland setting, impressed 'Burmantofts Faïence England 2197' and black painted 'Col. 118/10'.

8.75in (22cm) high

£300-400   HALL

A Carlton Ware 'Chinaland' ginger jar and cover, printed and painted in gilt and coloured enamels, printed and painted marks, 2948.

5.5in (14cm) high

£360-400   L&T

A Carlton Ware 'Fan' vase, shouldered ovoid form with applied lugs, printed and painted in gilt and coloured enamels, printed and painted marks.

9.75in (25cm) high

£250-300   L&T

A Carlton Ware 'Parkland' vase, printed and painted in gilt and coloured enamels, printed and painted marks, 3523.

6in (15cm) high

£550-750   L&T

A Carlton Ware 'Anemone' Handcraft bowl, printed and painted in gilt and coloured enamels, printed and painted marks, 3694.

9in (23cm) across

£300-400   L&T

A limited edition Clarice Cliff exhibition poster, from an edition of 250, illegibly signed.

£150-200   SK

A Clarice Cliff 'Green Erin' pattern Bizarre Lynton coffee service, comprising a coffee pot, sugar basin, cream jug and four cups and saucers.

£1,500-2,200   GHOU

A Clarice Cliff Bizarre pottery teapot, of conical form, painted in the 'Gayday' design, the domed lid with oblong finial, triangular loop handle, black mark including 'Registration applied for' mark.

9.75in (25cm) wide

£400-600　HT

A Clarice Cliff Bizarre 'Yellow Cowslip' pattern 'Bon Jour' preserve and cover, painted in colours, printed mark, chips.

4.5in (11.5cm) high

£400-500　WW

A Clarice Cliff 'Rhodanthe' wall charger, painted in colours, printed mark.

16.5in (42cm) diam.

£350-450　WW

A Clarice Cliff Fantasque Bizarre 'Summerhouse' cylindrical preserve pot, painted in colours, printed mark, chip to inside rim.

3in (7.5cm) high

£100-150　WW

A Clarice Cliff Bizarre 'Crocus' pattern 'Athens' jug, painted with orange crocuses above green band, printed mark, minor restoration to foot rim.

6in (15cm) high

£120-150　WW

A Clarice Cliff Bizarre 'Newport' pattern shape '200' vase, painted in colours, printed mark.

7.5in (19cm) high

£650-750　WW

A Clarice Cliff Bizarre 'Forest Glen' pattern 'Daffodil' shape flower vase, shape no. 450, painted in colours, and a flower brick, printed marks.

13in (33cm) wide

£500-600　WW

A Clarice Cliff Fantasque Bizarre 'Windbells' part tea set, painted in colours, comprising teapot and cover, one cup, saucer and side plate, printed mark, old restoration to spout.

4.75in (12cm) high

£550-650　WW

A Clarice Cliff Bizarre 'Autumn' pattern 'Stamford' shape tea for two, comprising teapot and cover, milk jug and sugar basin, two cups, saucers and a side plate, printed marks, small chip to spout of teapot and a nick to the rim of one cup.

5in (13cm) high

£1,400-1,800　WW

ESSENTIAL REFERENCE: WILLIAM DE MORGAN

William de Morgan (1839-1917) was a stained glass designer before he became interested in ceramics.

- His work often includes stylised and grotesque flora and fauna inspired by medieval Persian, Moorish and Greek designs. These motifs are usually perfectly related to the shapes on which they are painted. These include decorative plates, vases and, De Morgan's speciality, tiles.
- De Morgan's forms are painted either in lustre, predominantly ruby and copper, or in 'Persian' colours, predominantly green, black and turquoise.
- De Morgan initially painted blanks for other companies. In 1882, he began producing his own ceramics after relocating to William Morris's Merton Abbey Workshops.
- From 1892, he spent the winters in Florence where he worked for Cantagalli.
- He retired in 1907.

A Crown Devon large 'Fairy Castle' vase, painted and printed in gilt and coloured enamels on a jade green ground, printed and painted marks '2406'.

15in (38cm) high

£800-1,200　L&T

A William De Morgan bowl, painted with a frieze of peacocks and serpents amongst apple trees, in ruby and sand lustre, unmarked, hairline to top rim.

13in (33cm) diam.

£2,400-2,800　WW

A William De Morgan charger, painted to the well with a dragon and serpent roundel, the rim with Classical trumpeters in ruby lustre, unmarked, restored.

17.25in (44cm) diam.

£1,300-1,600   **WW**

CLOSER LOOK: WILLIAM DE MORGAN VASE AND COVER

The cover is modelled with stiff leaf foliage and a bud finial

The two handles are modelled as winged grotesques, each with twin scrolled fish tails.

The vase and cover are decorated with a ruby and copper lustre glaze.

The vase is moulded in relief with bands of stylised scaly fish.

The design is similar to the two Livadia vases de Morgan made for the Tsar of Russia – either for his summer palace or his yacht.

A large William De Morgan 'Livadia' vase and cover, by Fred Passenger, 'FP' monogram, finial off, chips.

15in (38cm) high

£11,000-15,000   **WW**

A William De Morgan vase, painted with panels of flowers and scrolling foliate in ruby lustre, unmarked, repaired neck.

11.25in (28.5cm) high

£550-800   **WW**

A William De Morgan ruby and copper lustre vase, painted with birds before stylised foliage, on a white ground, impressed Fulham tulip mark, glazed nick to top rim.

8.25in (21cm) high

£3,000-4,000   **WW**

A William De Morgan solifleur vase, painted with sprays of flowers and foliate, in ruby and copper lustre on a white ground, unsigned.

8.25in (21cm) high

£900-1,100   **WW**

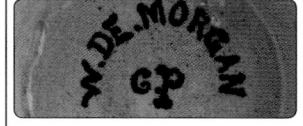

A William De Morgan Persian pedestal bowl, by Charles Passenger, painted with carnations, in shades of blue, aubergine, green and white, painted 'W. DE. MORGAN', 'CP' monogram, light hairline to rim.

4in (10.5cm) diam.

£500-600   **WW**

A William De Morgan twin-handled vase, by Joe Luster, painted with three birds above a crown and two crossed birds, impressed Sand's End roundel, painted 'JJ' mark, professionally restored neck and handles.

10in (25.5cm) high

£2,000-2,500   **WW**

A late Fulham period William de Morgan six tile panel, Mongolian pattern, each painted in the Persian palette with flowerheads and leaves, impressed marks.

Each tile 6in (15.5cm) across

£700-900   **L&T**

A William De Morgan 'Single Rose (Wild Rose)' tile, painted in shades of blue and green on a white ground, impressed 'Merton Abbey' mark, minor frits.

6in (15.5cm) square

£300-350   **WW**

A William De Morgan 'Chicago' tile, painted with two flowerheads in shades of blue, purple, green and brown on a blue ground, impressed tulip mark, minor rim chips.

8in (20.5cm) square

£950-1,100   **WW**

A William De Morgan 'Bedford Park Daisy' tile, painted with alternating panels of daisy and foliage sprays in shades of green, blue and yellow, impressed 'WD Morgan', restored chip to corner.

8.25in (21cm) square

£550-800 WW

A William De Morgan pottery tile, painted with two Chameleons, in shades of blue and green, impressed 'Sand's End' mark.

6in (15cm) wide

£4,000-4,500 WW

A William De Morgan six-tile panel, painted with an owl above a crescent moon amidst carnation flowers, in colours, on a blue ground, impressed Merton Abbey mark, framed.

18in (46cm) wide

£13,000-15,000 WW

A large De Porceleyne Fles tile panel, by Den Hoed, depicting a bird on 25 tiles, mounted on masonite, signed 'CD' with De Porceleyne Fles mark, and 'DELFT'.

28in (71cm) square

£1,000-1,500 SDR

An Auguste Delaherche bulbous four-handled vase, covered in mottled blue-green and brown glossy glaze, with circular stamp and '6860'.

7.25in (18.5cm) high

£650-750 DRA

An Auguste Delaherche large bulbous vase incised with bands of fruiting branches alternating with oxblood and indigo glaze, circular stamp 'AUGUSTE DELAHERCHE 1138'.

13.5in (34cm) high

£3,500-4,000 DRA

A Della Robbia pottery vase and cover, by 'LW', incised and painted with mice running and resting and holding up lanterns with their tails, in shades of green, cream and blue, incised and painted marks, incised 'Shirley', minor professional restoration.

6in (15cm) high

£850-1,000 WW

A Doulton Lambeth pottery vase, by Florence Barlow and Eliza Simmance, depicting a roundel of grouse with a beaded surround within foliate scroll borders in pale green, navy, blue and brown.

12.5in (32cm) high

£500-600 HT

A Doulton Lambeth stoneware Scotch whisky dispenser, decorated in shades of blue, green and ochre.

17in (43cm) high

£750-850 GORL

A Doulton Lambeth stoneware vase, by Hannah Barlow, sgraffito with ponies and cattle within beaded and stiff leaf banding, marks also for Emily Stomer.

11in (28cm) high

£750-850 HT

A pair of Royal Doulton stoneware vases, by Hannah Barlow, incised with a band of resting deer, between foliate borders, in shades of green, brown and white on a buff ground, impressed marks, incised monogram.

13.75in (35cm) high

£3,000-3,500 WW

A large early Doulton Lambeth stoneware vase, by Hannah Barlow, incised with a scene of running deer, the reverse deer at rest, between bands of incised and applied scrolling foliage, incised 'HB' to the body, impressed mark, dated, restored top rim.

1874   *17.25in (44cm) high*

£3,000-3,500   **WW**

A pair of Doulton Lambeth stoneware vases, by Hannah Barlow, incised with resting, grazing and galloping horses, between foliate bands, impressed mark, incised monogram and datemark, minor glaze nicks to base rim.

9.75in (25cm) high

£1,400-1,800   **WW**

A large Doulton Lambeth vase, by Hannah Barlow, with a high flared-collar neck decorated to the body with a deep scrafitto band of sheep in a landscape setting between interlaced scrolled borders, incised and impressed marks.

17in (43cm) high

£1,300-1,600   **FLD**

A large pair of Doulton Lambeth vases, by Edith Lupton, with a flared-collar neck decorated with hand-carved scrolled convolvulus between repeat pattern borders, incised and impressed marks.

12in (30.5cm) high

£1,000-1,300   **FLD**

A pair of tall Doulton Lambeth vases, by Florence Barlow, with high flared-collar necks decorated with pâte-sur-pâte birds in flight over an incised scrolled ground between foliate scrolled borders, incised and impressed marks.

11.5in (29.5cm) high

£1,400-1,800   **FLD**

A large Doulton Lambeth jardinière, of shouldered ovoid form, by Hannah Barlow, with a shallow collar neck decorated with a deep central band of sgraffito decorated cattle in a landscape setting, between banded borders, incised and impressed marks.

13in (34cm) high

£1,100-1,500   **FLD**

A Royal Doulton Chinese jade figure of two cockatoos, designed by Charles Noke, painted in shades of green and white, printed and painted marks.

4.5in (11.5cm) high

£1,000-1,300   **WW**

A pair of late 19th/early 20thC Fulham Pottery stoneware bowls, probably designed by J. P. Seddon, each with brown glaze moulded scroll, stylised floral and foliate decoration, impressed marks.

9in (22.5cm) high

£350-450   **L&T**

A Ludwig Gies 'Moon Sheep' glazed porcelain figure, model number 28809.

1926   *13.25in (33.5cm) high*

£3,000-3,500   **VZ**

A Goldscheider hanging double mask of a woman holding a black mask, with restoration to tight line around hanging hole, and stamped 'Goldscheider/Wien/ Made in Austria'.

13.75in (35cm) high

£400-600   **SDR**

A Goldscheider figure of Diana, designed by Louis Marie Latour, model no. 4310, painted in colours, impressed marks, artist signature, repaired dog's tail, missing bow.

32.25in (59cm) high

£300-500   **WW**

A Goldscheider porcelain figure, 'Austrian Country Girl' by Josef Lorenzl, painted in colours, bears paper label, impressed marks with stamped signature, no. '7228/ 62/ 31'.

8.25in (21cm) high

£200-250   **L&T**

DECORATIVE ARTS

A Goldscheider pottery figural lamp, modelled as a night watchman, wearing a helmet and holding aloft a lantern, on shaped base, signed 'Latour', impressed 'No 3144.152.14'.

34in (86.5cm) high

£950-1,100   **HT**

A large 1930's Goldscheider figure of a female in Spanish style dress, with long flowing lace-effect dress and open fan raised to an oval base, small restoration to hair comb.

17.5in (45cm) high

£1,000-1,200   **FLD**

A large 1930's Dakon-Goldscheider figure of a Dolly Sister, with arms outstretched behind, dressed in a short bat-winged costume with cloche hat, in green and black-painted finish all set to a shaped base, moulded signature with printed marks.

16in (41cm) high

£700-1,000   **FLD**

A Hammersmith stoneware figure, 'The Bull', designed by Harold and Phoebe Stabler, painted in colours, impressed Hammersmith Bridge mark, incised 'Potted by Harold Stabler', reverse signed 'Harold and Phoebe Stabler'.

1914   *13in (33cm) high*

£2,000-2,500   **WW**

A Hammersmith Bridge 'Buster Girl' figure, designed by Phoebe Stabler, painted in colours with bright pink bonnet and ribbon, impressed bridge mark, signature and pencil signature 'Grace Nelson'.

The figure also bears the unusual inscription: 'The Workshop, First Kiln Hammersmith Terr. London 1910'.

1910   *7.25in (18.5cm) high*

£550-650   **WW**

A Hancock & Son Morrisware vase, designed by George Cartlidge, tubeline decorated with red bell flowers, model C18-5, printed mark, painted facsimile signature, cracked.

9.75in (24.5cm) high

£350-400   **WW**

A rare Hancock & Sons Morrisware pot pourri, 'Essence of Past Summers', model C56-1, designed by Georges Cartlidge, tubelined with red roses on a green ground, printed mark, painted green facsimile signature, cover repaired.

8.75in (22cm) high

£700-800   **WW**

A George Jones pâte-sur-pâte plaque, designed by Frederick Schenk, decorated with two young girls by a lily pond, fringed with aquatic plants, on a charcoal ground, impressed factory mark.

c1880   *12in (30.5cm) diam.*

£450-500   **WW**

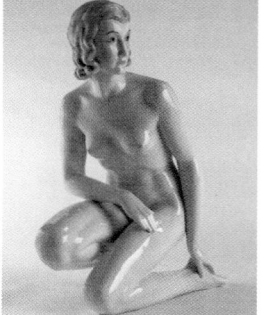

A Keramos figure of crouching lady, decorated in skin tone enamel, with printed marks to foot.

17.75in (45cm) high

£250-300   **L&T**

A Lenci ceramic figure, of a girl with skis, standing with hands on hips, wearing a headscarf and with original wooden ski poles, the whole raised on lozenge base, painted marks.

17.25in (43.5cm) high

£3,000-3,500   **L&T**

A Lenci, 'Ski Figure', painted in coloured enamels and raised on a lozenge-shaped base (crack to base), painted marks 'Lenci/ Made in Italy/ FV/ 697', bears paper label.

17in (43cm) high

£3,500-4,000   **L&T**

A Linthorpe pottery vase, model no.415, designed by Dr Christopher Dresser, with geometric pane under a running olive-green and white glaze, impressed mark, facsimile signature.

8.75in (22cm) high

£550-650   **WW**

CLOSER LOOK: DRESSER VASE

Christopher Dresser (1834-1904) was the first industrial designer. He used design elements from other cultures and from nature to create his designs.

He created hundreds of distinctive designs for the Linthorpe Pottery, many covered in streaky glazes.

This vase is a tube form with central pierced foliate roundel.

Pieces are impressed with his facsimile signature and the initials 'HT' for Henry Tooth, the pottery manager.

A Linthorpe pottery ewer, model no.957, designed by Dr Christopher Dresser, dome form, with angular handle, covered in a running olive, brown and white glaze, impressed marks, facsimile signature 'HT' monogram, professional restoration to rims.

6.25in (16cm) high

£950-1,100   **WW**

A rare Linthorpe pottery vase, designed by Dr Christopher Dresser, impressed marks, facsimile signature.

8.75in (22cm) high

£1,700-2,000   **WW**

A late 19thC Copeland majolica jardinière stand, with a continuous frieze of moulded Classical figures, between bands of moulded floral swags, impressed mark.

24.75in (63cm) high

£1,000-1,200   **L&T**

A late 19thC Goldscheider majolica terracotta figure of a Nubian boy, holding out a wickerwork tray, wearing a straw hat and striped open neck shirt, on an integral canted plinth base.

27.75in (71cm) high

£7,000-8,000   **L&T**

An English majolica oval jardinière, hung with swags upon which putti sit, impressed mark for Joseph Holdcroft, some damages, together with a large majolica stand.

c1880   32in (81cm) high on stand

£550-650   **WW**

A George Jones majolica jardinière stand, in the form of a rustic garden seat, with circular top above three branch-form concave legs decorated with moulded leaves, with central rope-form support on shaped triform base.

17.75in (45cm) high

£700-1,000   **L&T.**

A large 19thC George Jones ovoid majolica jardiniére, with yellow scalloped rim above dark blue body decorated with moulded birds and flowers, the three feet formed from moulded leaf forms, the interior turquoise glazed, impressed monogram.

18.25in (46cm) diam

£4,500-5,500   **L&T**

A George Jones majolica sardine dish and cover, with a blue-glazed basketweave moulded base, the cover moulded with leaves, sardine finial, yellow rims.

c1875   8.25in (21cm) wide

£400-600   **DN**

A Minton majolica chestnut dish, with a metal fitting to the centre, some restoration, impressed marks and date code.

1871 *11.5in (29cm) wide*

£300-500 **WW**

A Minton majolica sardine dish and cover, the turquoise ground body moulded with seaweed, the cover moulded with three fishes, fish finial, brown rims, impressed marks, shape 1383.

8.75in (22cm) diam

£350-450 **DN**

A large Minton majolica stick stand, modelled as a heron standing on one leg and holding a wriggling fish in its beak, before a clump of bullrushes, raised on a circular base, signed by Paul Comolera, impressed marks and date code, damages and old restoration.

Paul Comolera (1818-97) was born in Paris, France. He was a fine sculptor known mainly for his birds in bronze.

1877 *40.5in (103cm) high*

£5,000-6,000 **WW**

A 19thC Sarreguemines majolica jardinière and stand, supported by three high-relief griffons and decorated with leaves and foliage, the circular stand with scalloped edge decorated with lion heads and foliage, impressed marks 'B majolica Sarreguemines 426'

15.75in (40cm) diam

£1,000-1,300 **L&T**

A Wedgwood majolica pie dish, the sides moulded and painted with hanging birds amidst a grape vine, the lid with various game animals and a rabbit finial, some good restoration.

c1870 *10.5in (26.5cm) diam.*

£300-500 **WW**

A Wedgwood majolica game pie dish, moulded with birds, flowers and foliage, some restoration, impressed marks including date code.

1872 *9.5in (24.5cm) high*

£300-400 **WW**

A pair of Royal Worcester majolica wall pockets, each modelled as a nest beneath a branch, with a bird perched on the side, impressed marks, one heavily restored.

c1875 *8.25in (21cm) high*

£300-500 **WW**

A late 19thC majolica model of an elephant, standing four-square with a castle upon its back, unmarked, the base broken across the front foot and reglued.

7.5in (19.5cm) high

£300-400 **WW**

A 19thC majolica teapot in the shape of an apple, a twig forming the handle and spout, the knop moulded as a wren watching a fly, minor damages.

This exceptional price for a majolica teapot is due to the unusual shape and detailing - particularly the knop with the small wren watching a fly. Rarity and a whimsical subject are very appealing to collectors.

6.25in (16cm) high

£5,000-7,000 **WW**

A majolica tazza, moulded with a horse chestnut leaf.

c1870   *9in (23cm) high*

£90-120   **WW**

A majolica sardine dish and cover, decorated with mottled brown and green glazes, unmarked, minor damages.

c1870,   *8.5in (22cm) high*

£200-300   **WW**

A 20thC majolica bear jug, with a pale brown glaze, the nose, ears and eyes painted black, painted registration and US patent mark.

7.75in (20cm) high

£35-55   **WW**

A 19thC majolica cachepot, the sides decorated with stags and hounds, the edges moulded as bamboo, unmarked, damages.

8.5in (22cm) high

£200-300   **WW**

A Martin Brothers stoneware grotesque jar and cover, restoration to head, lid signed 'RW Martin & Brothers, London & Southall, 6-1888', base signed 'RW Martin Southall S. L.'.

1888   *With stand: 8in (20.5cm) high*

£8,000-10,000   **DRA**

A Martin Brothers stoneware vase, incised and painted with thistle on an amber ground, signed '11-1905 Martin Bros London & Southall'.

1905   *10.25in (26cm) high*

£1,500-2,000   **DRA**

A Martin Brothers stoneware vase, decorated with a floral pattern in the Renaissance style, restoration to neck and rim, marked '7-1888 RW Martin Bros London & Southall'.

1888   *7.75in (20cm) high*

£1,800-2,200   **DRA**

A Martin Brothers stoneware vase decorated with dragons, marked '7-1901 Martin Bros London & Southall'.

1901   *11.5in (29cm) high*

£600-900   **DRA**

A Martin Brothers stoneware grotesque spoon warmer, covered in cobalt and teal matte glaze, signed 'Martin London & Southall'.

9in high

£3,300-4,000   **DRA**

A Martin Brothers jardinière, painted with scrolling foliage and seed heads, incised marks to base, 'Martin Bros./ London & Southall/ 1-1896'.

1896   *9.75in (25cm) high*

£500-750   **L&T**

CLOSER LOOK: MARTIN BROTHERS BIRD JAR

The pottery is covered with a tonal blue to salt-glazed decoration. They are often called 'barrister birds'.

The bird is modelled with a sideways glance, a smiling expression, and a quizzical look.

The Martin Brothers produced a series of these birds - each one with its own personality.

Both the jar and cover bear the signature 'R.W. Martin & Bros London and Southall 11-1911'.

A Martin Brothers stoneware bird jar and cover, by Robert Wallace Martin, raised to a turned ebonised base.

1911   *8in (21.5cm) high*

£10,000-14,000   **FLD**

A Martin Brothers stoneware vase, incised and painted with magnolia flowers, in shades of white and ochre, incised marks and '1-1888 Martin Brothers London & Southall', repaired base.

1888   *8in (20cm) high*

£600-800   **WW**

A Martin Brothers stoneware vase, incised and painted with ferocious fighting dragons in shades of brown on a buff ground, incised '8-1894 Martin Bros, London & Southall'.

1894   *8in (20cm) high*

£3,500-4,500   **WW**

A large Martin Brothers sun mask jug, with a narrow-collar neck and lipped spout, decorated with a high relief sun mask below the spout over a patterned ground with tonal blue and ochre glazed finish, incised marks to the base.

1896   *11.5in (29.5cm) high*

£2,500-3,000   **FLD**

A Clement Massier twisted bud vase, with applied silver peapod vine on a lustred ceramic ground, a few very small nicks to top and bottom, signed 'C. M. Golfe Juan'.

6in (15cm) high

£500-750 **DRA**

A Mettlach Art Nouveau charger, by R. Thevenin, with a maiden picking irises in the forest, marked 'METTLACH VB GEGH... NACHBILDUNG GESCHUTZT 2547, R. Thevenin'.

15.75 in (40cm) diam.

£1,700-2,000 **DRA**

A rare Minton Art Pottery moonflask, designed by Dr Christopher Dresser, decorated with a stylised bird with an olive branch in its beak, enamelled in colours on a terracotta ground, impressed marks, date code, with minor rim chips.

1867 *6in (15.5cm) high*

£6,000-7,000 **WW**

A 19thC Mintons stoneware bread plate, designed by AWN Pugin, the border decorated in blue with 'Waste not want not', impressed marks.

14in (35cm) diam

£600-800 **L&T**

A Minton charger, decorated with a kingfisher perched upon water lily leaves with butterflies and insects, within a Persian style border of scrolling flowers and foliage, picked out in tones of blue, turquoise, puce, green and yellow, impressed codes for 'November 1873' and marked 'D/15'.

1873 *15.75in (40cm) diam.*

£250-350 **HALL**

A large Minton Aesthetic Movement moonflask and cover, decorated in gilt with a dragon and pomegranate mon to both sides, on a purple ground, impressed marks, restored collar rim.

13in (33cm) high

£150-200 **WW**

A Minton Pottery charger, printed and painted with Classical figures riding a dolphin, impressed and printed marks.

87.75in (34.5cm) diam.

£120-150 **WW**

A Minton Aesthetic Movement moonflask, painted with panels by William Wise (c.1831-1889), impressed Minton marks, datemark, signed to the panels 'W Wise', hairlines to neck, minor repair to neck at shoulder.

1877 *10.25in (26cm) high*

£500-600 **WW**

A pair of Minton cloisonné jugs, ovoid form with loop handles, painted in colours and gilt on a pale blue ground with stylised flowers and foliage, unmarked, light wear to gilt.

5.75in (14.5cm) high

£350-450 **WW**

A pair of Minton cloisonné vases, designed by Dr Christopher Dresser, on integral stands, enamelled in colours and gilt on a pink ground, impressed marks.

8.5in (21.5cm) high

£1,200-1,500   **WW**

A Minton cloisonné tea caddy and cover, painted with flowers and Chinese characters in colours and gilt on a salmon pink ground, unmarked.

In 1859, the Japanese ports reopened for trade, which caused a craze for all things Japanese in the Western world. Minton & Co. made porcelain copies of cloisonné wares with rich turquoise/pink enamel backgrounds with designs outlined in gold. Many were designed by Christopher Dresser (1834-1904). His designs were angular and modern, inspired by the 19thC Aesthetic Movement.

4.25in (10.5cm) high

£300-400   **WW**

ESSENTIAL REFERENCE: MOORCROFT

William Moorcroft (1872-1945)

- In 1897, James Macintyre & Co. established a design studio within its works headed by William Moorcroft. 'Aurelain' vases were printed patterns, whilst 'Florianware' was decorated in the emerging Art Nouveau style.
- In 1904, Moorcroft won a gold medal at the St. Louis International Exhibition. Afterwards, he insisted on adding his own initials or signature to the pottery that he designed, and overseeing the production of his work.
- Moorcroft resigned to establish his own company in 1912, with financial assistance from Liberty & Co. By this time, Moorcroft's patterns were simpler and bolder, usually with dark grounds and a clear glossy glaze. These included 'Pomegranate', 'Wisteria' and Hazeldine'.
- Queen Mary, a keen collector of Moorcroft's works, granted him a royal appointment in 1929. Shortly before William's death, his eldest son, Walter, took control of the pottery business, which was awarded another Royal Appointment in 1946.
- The pottery is still operating today.

A Moorcroft Florianware bowl with scalloped rim, decorated with anemones and poppies, printed mark, signed in green and with retailer's mark 'Made for J.W. Bridge Ltd, Accrington'.

c1902   *9in (23cm) diam.*

£650-850   **L&T**

A Moorcroft Florianware vase, of waisted form with two loop handles, tube lined with harebells on a white ground, signed to base over printed Florian mark.

c1902-04   *9.75in (25cm) high*

£1,800-2,200   **HT**

A Moorcroft Florianware miniature vase, the flattened ovoid body with tall neck and frilled rim, decorated with anemones and poppies on a white ground, printed factory mark, signed in green, retailers mark.

c1902   *6in (15cm) high*

£900-1,200   **L&T**

A James Macintyre & Co. Florianware vase, by William Moorcroft, with narrow-collar neck decorated in a version of the 'Peacock' pattern in blue, green and yellow over a two-tone blue ground between scale borders, printed marks and full green painted flash signature.

c1900-02   *10.5in (27cm) high*

£2,000-2,500   **FLD**

A James Macintyre 'Alhambra' vase, designed by William Moorcroft, painted in shades of salmon pink, red and blue, highlighted in gilt, printed mark.

c1903   *11.25in (28.5cm) high*

£1,100-1,500   **WW**

DECORATIVE ARTS

A large James Macintyre & Co. twin-handled footed bowl, designed by William Moorcroft, radially decorated in the 'Ochre Tulip and Forget-Me-Not' pattern, full green-painted signature.

This pattern was registered in 1898.
12in (31cm) wide

£1,800-2,200   **FLD**

A pair of Moorcroft Macintyre gourd-shaped vases, decorated with 'Revived Cornflower' or 'Brown Chrysanthemum' design within foliated cartouches, on mottled green and brown ground, green signature.

This is a good pair in a rare shape in excellent condition.
c1912   4.75in (12cm) high

£4,500-5,000   **A&G**

A pair of Moorcroft vases, by William Moorcroft, in the 'Late Florian' pattern, impressed marks and green painted flash signature.

The 'Late Florian' designs were made from c1918 and were popular through the 1920s and 30s. The exquisitely drawn poppies and tulips, with intricate surface patterns, were augmented by the use of strong, rich colours.
15in (38cm) high

£2,400-2,800   **FLD**

CLOSER LOOK: MOORCROFT TEA KETTLE

Unusual, rare shape, particularly collectable in an early pattern.

The kettle has an integral spout and high arched handle.

It is decorated in the 'Claremont' pattern over a tonal green and ochre ground. All Moorcroft's wares were handmade and the naturalistic designs were painted in raised slip.

It bears green painted flash signature, with marks for Shreve & Co, San Francisco.

A James Macintyre & Co. tea kettle, by William Moorcroft, small chip to tip of the spout.
c1905   *6.5in (17cm) high*

£4,500-5,000   **FLD**

A large James Macintyre & Co vase, designed by William Moorcroft, decorated in the 'Revived Cornflower' or 'Brown Chrysanthemum' pattern.

In August 1913 Moorcroft moved to Cobridge, he was still producing many of the MacIntyre patterns. The Moorcroft signature became larger and increasingly significant.
1910-13   10in (26cm) high

£4,000-4,500   **FLD**

A large James Macintyre & Co. jardinière, designed by William Moorcroft, decorated in the 'Celadon Pomegranate' pattern over a pale jade green ground, green painted flash signature.

The 'Pomegranate' design was introduced in 1910.
8in (20cm) high

£2,400-2,800   **FLD**

A William Moorcroft biscuit box and cover, decorated in the 'Claremont' pattern, impressed marks.

This pattern was registered in October 1903. It proved extremely popular and continued in production when Moorcroft opened his factory in Cobridge in 1913. This piece is a rare shape.
c1913-16   6.5in (17cm) high

£3,500-4,000   **FLD**

A William Moorcroft pedestal bowl, with high arched handles, decorated to the whole in the 'Pomegranate' pattern over ochre ground, painted signature, marked 'November 1913'.
5in (13cm) high

£2,200-2,600   **FLD**

A William Moorcroft biscuit box and cover, of rounded cube form, with applied twin loop handles and arched cover handle, decorated in the 'Pomegranate' pattern, over green to ochre colour ground.
6.5in (17cm) high

£1,300-1,600   **FLD**

A William Moorcroft bowl, the exterior bears a band of Latin verse 'Vincit Omnia Veritas' (Truth conquers all) in tonal blue with light flambé glaze, impressed marks and blue painted flash signature.
5in (12.5cm)

£2,000-2,500   **FLD**

A William Moorcroft tea kettle, in the 'Spanish' pattern, full green painted flash signature, high small hairline to the base.

The Spanish design was introduced in 1910 and remained in production until the 1930's.

8in (20.5cm) high

£1,800-2,200   FLD

A pair of large Moorcroft baluster vases, each decorated in the 'Pomegranate' pattern, impressed marks, signed in green.

12.5in (32cm) high

£1,800-2,200   L&T

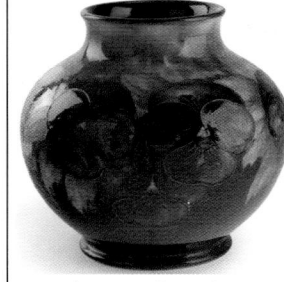

A 1930's Moorcroft ovoid vase, decorated in the 'Pansies' pattern, impressed marks, signed in green.

7 in (18cm) high

£600-800   L&T

A Moorcroft bowl and cover, to commemorate the coronation of Queen Elizabeth and King George VI, on blue and grey ground, impressed marks.

1937   *5.25in (13cm) high*

£300-350   A&G

An American Matt Morgan Art Pottery urn vase, decorated with a painted duck perched on a rock in front of a lake.

The Matt Morgan Art Pottery of Cincinnati, Ohio operated from 1882-1884. Before founding his own company, English-born artist Morgan had worked for a number of years as head of the lithographic department at Strobridge & Co., and worked briefly at the Dayton Porcelain Pottery.

12in (30.5cm) high

£3,000-3,500   ANT

A Bernard Moore vase, with roll collar neck decorated with a Viking long boat to rough seas in tonal lustre glazes, with applied enamel and gilded highlights, painted signature.

7in (18cm) high

£1,000-1,300   FLD

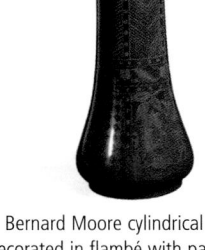

A Bernard Moore cylindrical vase, decorated in flambé with panels of flowers printed marks.

9.5in (24.5cm) high

£300-350   WW

A Bernard Moore bowl, inscribed 'Fond Memory Brings The Light of Other Days', with scrolling carnation flowers, printed mark.

10in (25cm) diam

£600-800   WW

A Nippon urn, painted with farm and lake landscapes on both sides, the body pink and ivory with gilded details and handles, minor wear to gilt, green Nippon stamp.

16.5in (42cm) high

£750-850   CRA

A Pilkington's Lancastrian vase, designed by Richard Joyce, painted with a deer amongst cypress trees, in ruby and copper lustre, impressed mark, painted artist cipher, datemark.

1914   *6.25in (16cm) high*

£1,000-1,500   WW

A Pilkington's Lancastrian solifleur vase, designed by William S. Mycock, painted with Persian motif in shades of blue, ruby and copper lustre, impressed marks, painted artist cipher.

8.75in (22.5cm) high

£1,000-1,200   WW

A Pilkington's Lancastrian solifleur vase, designed by William S. Mycock, painted with a frieze of lions in shades of ruby and copper lustre, impressed marks, painted cipher datemark.

1913   *6.25in (16cm) high*

£850-1,000   WW

A Pilkington's Lancastrian vase, moulded in relief with simple, heart-shaped leaves, covered in an aventurine glaze, impressed marks.

7in (17.5cm) high

£180-240   **WW**

A Pilkington's Royal Lancastrian charger, by William S. Mycock, painted with a galleon at full sail, in blue on a mottled orange ground, impressed mark, painted artist cipher.

14in (35.5cm) diam.

£300-400   **WW**

A Pilkington's Lancastrian ginger jar and cover, by Richard Joyce, painted with hares boxing between stylised flowers in shades of ruby and sand lustre, impressed marks, painted artists cipher, datemark.

1919   *5.25in (13.5cm) high*

£1,200-1,500   **WW**

A Carter Stabler & Adams Poole Pottery 'Persian Deer' pattern vase, shape no. 966, the pattern designed and painted by Ruth Pavely, the base with impressed and painted marks, with hairline crack.

From the collection of Roy Holland, Managing Director of Poole Pottery.

10in (25cm) high

£250-300   **WW**

A Carter, Stabler & Adams Poole Pottery architectural sculpture, 'The Galleon', designed by Harold Stabler, painted in colours, impressed mark, minor chips.

21.25in (54cm) high

£1,500-2,000   **WW**

A Poole Pottery Art Deco vase, signed by Truda Carter, painted by Ruth Pavely, shape no.846, painted with geometric flowers and foliage in shades of green, brown and black on a mushroom ground, impressed, incised and painted marks, minor hairline to top rim.

13in (33cm) high

£1,400-1,800   **WW**

A set of seven original Poole Pottery designs on paper, 'Sugar for the Birds' and 'Female Portraits', painted in colours and annotated, the original design by Olive Bourne.

£450-650 SET   **WW**

A Quimper hand-painted ceramic figure, 'Bigoudene en Priere' by Alexander Goudie for La Musée de la Faïence, limited edition 28/250, painted maker's marks.

17in (43cm) high

£300-500   **L&T**

A Quimper hand-painted ceramic 'Paysan dans un Champ de Ble' figure, by Alexander Goudie for La Musée de la Faïence, limited edition 27/100.

20in (51cm) high

£700-900   **L&T**

A Quimper hand-painted ceramic 'Le Marin' figure, by Alexander Goudie for La Musée de la Faïence, limited edition 9/100, painted maker's marks and inscription by the artist 'Head and re-touching by my hand/ Goudie'.

20in (51cm) high

£1,200-1,400   **L&T**

An Adelaide Robineau porcelain vase, covered with blue crystals on a celadon ground, with artist's 'AR' medallion carved on its side, and marked '526', small bruise on rim.

4.5in (11.5cm) high

£6,500-8,500   DRA

A Rorstrand porcelain vase, carved with white and purple lilies, with green stamp with 'KL/15893/EG', and small nick to foot ring.

7.25in (18.5cm) high

£400-600   DRA

A Rosenthal porcelain figure of a snake charmer, painted in colours, printed mark.

8.25in (21cm) high

£180-220   WW

A Royal Copenhagen figure group, of intertwined male and female figures restrained to a rock, decorated in blue, grey and skin tone enamels, with printed marks to base.

18in (46cm) high

£500-700   L&T

A Royal Dux model of a dog, seated on a cushion, grey painted with highlights, pink seal to base.

10.25in (26cm) high

£350-450   L&T

A Royal Dux porcelain comport, the circular top moulded with foliate swags and tassels, the tapering rocky stem flanked by a shepherdess, her sheep and a boy playing a whistle, raised on a circular base, in pale green and ivory with gilt highlights.

18in (45.5cm) high

£600-800   HT

A Rozenburg twelve-tile panel, painted after David Adolf Constant Artz (Dutch, 1837-1890), with a genre scene of a mother and two children at a kitchen table, framed, signed 'N. ARTZ Rozenburg Den Haag L5', original painting dates from 1884.

Panel: 24in (61cm) high

£1,000-1,300   DRA

A Rozenburg twelve-tile panel, painted after Johannes Christiaan Karel Klinkenberg (Dutch, 19thC), depicting a Dutch cityscape with canal, framed, signed 'N. Klinkenberg' and 'B. Rozenburg', small chip to one tile, 3in (7.5cm) corner line to other.

Panel 24in (61cm) wide

£1,200-1,500   DRA

A Rozenburg twelve-tile panel, painted after Cornelis Springer (Dutch, 1817-1891), depicting a Dutch cityscape with canal, framed, signed 'N. C. Springer B. Rozenburg'.

Panel 24in (61cm) wide

£1,600-1,900   DRA

A Rozenburg eggshell-faceted demitasse and saucer with flowers and a bird, signed Rozenburg Den Haag CH.

Saucer 4in (10cm) diam

£900-1,200   DRA

A Ruskin Pottery Kingfisher lustre stoneware vase, tall cylindrical form, covered in a petrol lustre glaze, impressed 'Ruskin, 1912'.

1912   *11.75in (30cm) high*

£1,000-1,500   WW

A large early high-fired Ruskin Pottery vase, having a footed compressed spherical base rising to a flared trumpet neck, with a deep purple flambé glaze with green-flecked decoration, impressed oval West Smethwick mark.

8.4in (21.5cm) high

£2,000-2,500　　　**FLD**

A high-fired Ruskin Pottery vase, decorated with a flambé tonal purple and red glaze with green flecks, impressed signature and date.

1925　　　*8.5in (22cm) high*

£800-1,200　　　**FLD**

A Johann Von Schwarz Art Nouveau vase, decorated in cuenca with a maiden in profile over multi-coloured poppies, stamped '631 6 71' and illegibly initialled, a couple of minor grinding chips.

9in (23cm) high

£350-450　　　**DRA**

A German Art Nouveau plaque, by Johann Von Schwarz, with maiden and grapevine, stamped 'CH Q 99 VI'.

11in (28cm) wide

£1,400-1,800　　　**DRA**

A Teplitz corseted three-handled vase painted with golden sun, red ink stamp, 'TURN TEPLITZ-BOHEMIA R StK MADE IN AUSTRIA AMPHORA MK 5362'.

16.5in (42cm) high

£900-1,100　　　**DRA**

A Hans Thoma 'Mermaid' faïence relief plate, model no. 106, painted by August Gebhard, signed.

c1903　　　*18.75in (47.5cm) wide*

£2,000-2,500　　　**VZ**

A Troika Pottery vase, modelled in low relief, in shades of green and brown, painted mark, hairline crack.

10in (25.5cm) high

£650-750　　　**WW**

A Troika Pottery wheel lamp base, by Alison Brigden, modelled in low relief, in shades of blue and brown, painted marks.

10.5in (27cm) high

£400-450　　　**WW**

A Watcombe, Torquay, terracotta jug with brass neck and cover, the design attributed to Dr Christopher Dresser, with grotesque dragon handle, impressed birds feet mark, painted '3381'.

10in (25.5cm) high

£500-750　　　**WW**

A pair of Watcombe, Torquay terracotta wall brackets, modelled with a mythical dragon-like beast, glazed turquoise, printed 'Watcombe Torquay'.

6.75in (17cm) high

£300-400　　　**WW**

A Wedgwood fairyland lustre 'Woodland Bridge' and 'Poplar Trees' pattern footed punch bowl, designed by Daisy Makeig Jones, painted and printed in gilt and coloured enamels, printed and painted marks to base 'Z4968'.

11.5in (29cm) diam

£3,000-4,000   **L&T**

A Wedgwood vase and cover, painted with bands of flowers and geometric patterns and a central band of script, in shades of green, blue and yellow on a white ground, impressed and painted marks, painted date, cover cracked and finial re-stuck.

1880   8.75in (22cm) high

£100-140   **WW**

A Wedgwood matt green earthenware vase, designed by Keith Murray, shape no.4197, impressed and printed marks, facsimile signature.

6.25in (16cm) high

£150-250   **WW**

A Wedgwood earthenware vase, designed by Keith Murray, incised cream body covered in champagne, impressed and printed marks, facsimile signature.

6in (15.5cm) high

£200-300   **WW**

A Wedgwood earthenware vase, designed by Keith Murray, covered in a matt blue glaze, impressed marks, printed factory mark.

12.25in (31cm) high

£200-300   **WW**

A rare Wedgwood black basalt beaker vase, designed by Keith Murray, shape no.3884, with three carved chevron bands, printed mark, facsimile signature.

4in (10cm) high

£600-900   **WW**

A Weiner Werkstatte ceramic figure, modelled as a market seller, holding two baskets, his jacket with bold geometric design, painted in pale grey with orange details, impressed marks.

8.75in (22cm) high

£800-1,000   **L&T**

CLOSER LOOK: WEMYSS SLEEPING PIGLET

The sleeping pig is probably the rarest and most desirable of all Wemyss ware. The pigs were designed for children's nurseries and some had a slot in the back so they could be used as a money box. Others were personalised with a child's name and birthdate. Smaller versions were designed to be used as paperweights – these are rarer still.

Collectors are attracted by Wemyss' naive charm. The naturalistic decoration stands out on the clear white background and the more colourful, rare and well-painted the design, the more desirable the piece is likely to be. A sleeping pig decorated with shamrocks sold for over £19,000

Condition is very important: to create the vibrant colours the pottery was fired at a low temperature which means it is susceptible to chips and cracks, and restoration is expensive. As a result, pieces in perfect condition command a premium.

The piglet lies on its side with a contented smile on its face.

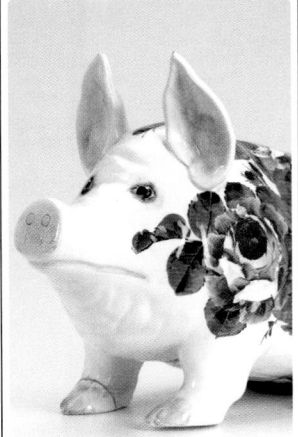

An early 20thC Wemyss Pottery pig, painted with roses, painted 'Wemyss' mark, old repair to front right foot.

16in (40.5cm) long

£800-1,200   **DRA**

An early 20thC Wemyss 'Sleeping Piglet' figure, decorated with cabbage roses, impressed mark 'Wemyss', minor restorations.

6.25in (16cm) long

£12,000-15,000   **L&T**

DECORATIVE ARTS

A Wemyss Pottery 'Cabbage Rose' pig, painted in shades of pink and green on a white ground, impressed and painted 'Wemyss'.

6.25in (16cm) wide

£800-1,200   **WW**

ESSENTIAL REFERENCE: WEMYSS

Wemyss ware was first produced in 1882 at the Fife Pottery. It was the brainchild of Robert Methven Heron, who was assisted by his sister, Jessie, the firm's manager Robert McLaughlan, and master painter, Karel Nekola.

- Wemyss was aimed at owners of country houses, especially those with a large retinue of servants. It exhibited a back-to-nature style, glorying in the fruit, flowers, birds and animals of the British countryside. Every piece is a unique work of art. It was sold exclusively by the London firm, Thomas Goode & Co.
- The range is diverse but it is best known for its pigs, cats and cabbage rose decoration.
- The pottery moved to Bovey Tracey, Devon in 1930, where it was made until 1957.
- Griselda Hill pottery began to make its modern Wemyss ware in 1985, and continues to do so to this day.

A post 1930 large Wemyss pig figure, decorated with cabbage roses, painted marks 'Nekola Pinxt', 'Plichta London' and 'Made in England'.

17.75in (45cm) long

£2,500-3,000   **L&T**

A post 1930 Wemyss cat figure, decorated with cabbage roses, painted mark 'Wemyss Ware/Made in England'.

13in (33cm) high

£2,000-2,500   **L&T**

An early 20thC Wemyss cat figure, decorated with cabbage roses, painted mark 'Wemyss Ware', restorations.

13in (33cm) high

£4,000-6,000   **L&T**

A post-1930 Wemyss cat figure, decorated with cabbage roses, painted mark 'Nekola Pinxt', 'Plichta/London England'.

13in (33cm) high

£2,500-3,000   **L&T**

An early 20thC Wemyss biscuit barrel, decorated with cabbage roses, lid inscribed 'Biscuits', painted mark 'Wemyss', crack to side, restored.

4.75in (12cm) high

£300-500   **L&T**

An early 20thC Wemyss pot-pourri jar and cover, decorated with cabbage roses and inscribed 'Gather Ye Rosebuds While Ye May', impressed mark 'Wemyss', minor restorations.

5in (13cm) high

£800-1,200   **L&T**

An early 20thC Wemyss 'Earlshall' small beaker vase, decorated with a rookery and windmill design, painted mark 'Wemyss'.

4.25in (11cm) high

£300-400   **L&T**

A Wemyss 'Drummond' flower pot, decorated by Karel Nekola, with cabbage roses, impressed mark 'Wemyss Ware/ R. H. & S.'

c1900   *8.5cm (21.5cm) high*

£1,000-1,500   **L&T**

A pair of Wemyss egg cups, one painted with dog roses, the other with sweet peas, each with painted and impressed marks.

2in (5.5cm) high

£1,500-2,000   **L&T**

A Wemyss luggie, decorated with cabbage roses, impressed and painted marks.

4.75in (12cm) high

£500-800 L&T

A small early 20thC Wemyss ewer and basin, decorated with cabbage roses, ewer with impressed mark 'Wemyss', basin with impressed mark 'Wemyss Ware/R. H. & S.'

Ewer 6.25in (16cm) high

£600-900 L&T

A Wemyss heart-shaped tray, decorated with dog roses, impressed mark 'Wemyss Ware/R. H. & S.', minor hairline crack.

c1900 *11.5in (29cm) wide*

£500-800 L&T

Left: A Wemyss loving cup, decorated with tulips, impressed mark 'WEMYSS WARE R. H. & S.'

7.5in (19cm) high

£800-1,200 L&T

Right: A Wemyss three-handled tyg, decorated with apples, impressed marks.

9.25in (23.5cm) high

£1,000-1,500 L&T

A Wemyss twin-handled tray, decorated with cabbage roses, impressed mark.

17.75in (45cm) wide

£1,200-1,500 L&T

An early 20thC Wemyss 'Fife' flower bowl, decorated by James Sharp with tulips, impressed and painted marks 'Wemyss', restored mould crack.

11.25in (28.5cm) wide

£600-900 L&T

An early 20thC Wemyss covered honey box, cover and tray, decorated with beehive and bees, tray and box with painted marks 'Wemyss'.

Box 5.5in (14cm) long

£1,000-1,500 L&T

An early 20thC Wemyss covered honey box, cover and drip tray, decorated by Edwin Sandland with beehive and bees, drip tray with painted mark 'Wemyss', losing colour from knop.

Box 5in (13cm) long

£800-1,200 L&T

A Wemyss low quaich dessert dish, decorated with beehive and bees, impressed mark 'Wemyss Ware/R. H. & S.', restoration to handles, firing crack.

c1900   *7.75in (19.5cm) wide*

£700-1,000   **L&T**

A large Wemyss preserve jar and cover, decorated with bees and beehive, red scalloped rim to pot and cover, impressed mark 'Wemyss Ware/ R. H. & S.', painted 'T. Goode & Co.' retailers mark, restoration to cover.

c1900   *6in (15.5cm) high*

£1,200-1,800   **L&T**

A post-1930 small Wemyss pig figure, decorated with thistles, painted mark 'Nekola Pinxt', 'Plichta/London/England/Made in England'.

4.25in (10.5cm) high

£700-1,000   **L&T**

A post-1930 small Wemyss pig figure, decorated with cornflowers, painted marks 'Nekola Pinxt', and 'Plichta London England', restored ears.

4in (10cm) high

£1,000-1,500   **L&T**

A post 1930 large Wemyss pig figure, decorated with red clover, painted 'Nekola Pinxt', 'J Plichta London' and 'Made in England'.

17.75in (45cm) long

£2,000-3,000   **L&T**

A post 1930 large Wemyss pig figure, decorated by Joe Nekola with thistles, painted marks 'Wemyss/Made in England'.

17.25in (44cm) long

£3,500-4,000   **L&T**

A small Wemyss plate, decorated with a carnation, impressed mark 'Wemyss Ware/R. H. & S.'

c1900   *5.75in (14.5cm) diam*

£250-350   **L&T**

A Wemyss 'Gordon' dessert plate, decorated with yellow irises, with impressed mark 'Wemyss/R.H. & S', and printed 'T. Goode & Co.' retailers mark.

c1900   *8in (20.5cm) diam*

£450-550   **L&T**

A Wemyss 'Gordon' dessert plate, decorated with violet poppies, with impressed mark 'Wemyss/R. H. & S.' and printed 'T. Goode & Co.' retailers mark, restored.

c1900   *8in (20.5cm) diam*

£500-800   **L&T**

An early 20thC Wemyss frilled vase, decorated with carnations, impressed mark 'Wemyss'.

5.25in (13.5cm) high

£500-800   **L&T**

A Wemyss low quaich dessert dish, decorated with raspberries, impressed and painted marks.

7.5in (19cm) diam

£1,000-1,500   **L&T**

A Wemyss low quaich dessert dish, decorated with strawberries, impressed mark 'WEMYSS WARE R. H. & S'.

7.25in (18.5cm) diam

£500-800   **L&T**

An early 20thC Wemyss sponge dish and liner, decorated by Karel Nekola with purple grapes and vine leaves on a black ground, impressed mark 'Wemyss', painted 'T. Goode & Co.' retailer's mark.

7.75in (20cm) diam

£900-1,200   **L&T**

A large Wemyss preserve jar and cover, decorated with purple grapes and vine leaves, impressed mark 'Wemyss Ware/R. H. & S.'

c1900   *6in (15.5cm) high*

£900-1,200   **L&T**

A large early 20thC Wemyss preserve jar and cover, decorated with greengages, impressed mark 'Wemyss', painted 'T. Goode & Co.' retailer's mark.

6.5in (16.5cm) high

£1,000-1,500   **L&T**

An early 20thC Wemyss biscuit barrel and cover, decorated with oranges, the cover inscribed 'Biscuits', impressed mark 'Wemyss' and painted 'T. Goode & Co' retailer's mark, restored lid and rim.

4.5in (11.5cm) high

£300-500   **L&T**

An early 20thC Wemyss 'Japan' vase, decorated with apples, impressed mark 'Wemyss'.

8.5in (21.5cm) high

£600-900   **L&T**

An early 20thC Wemyss miniature sample jug, decorated by Edwin Sandland with black cockerels, impressed and painted marks 'Wemyss', painted initials 'ES', restored handle.

2.25in (5.5cm) high

£1,000-1,500   **L&T**

A Wemyss 'BonJour' cream jug, decorated with two black cockerels and inscribed 'BonJour', impressed mark 'Wemyss Ware/R. H. & S.'

c1900   *2.75in (7cm) high*

£400-600   **L&T**

A large Wemyss tyg, decorated with black cock and hens, impressed marks 'Wemyss Ware/R. H. & S', minor hairline cracks.

c1900   *9.75in (24.5cm) high*

£1,500-2,000   **L&T**

A post-1930 small Wemyss pig figure, decorated with shamrocks, painted marks 'Nekola Pinxt', 'Plichta/London England/Made in England'.

4in (10cm) high

£400-600   **L&T**

A large Wemyss pig figure, decorated in a brown glaze, impressed mark 'Wemyss Ware/R H & S', minor restorations.

c1900   *17.75in (45cm) long*

£3,500-4,000   **L&T**

A large Wemyss pig figure, decorated by Joseph Nekola with black on white, painted marks 'Wemyss/ Made in England', restoration to tail.

19in (48cm) long

£2,500-3,000   **L&T**

A post-1930 large Wemyss pig figure, decorated by Joseph Nekola in black on a white ground, painted marks 'Wemyss/Made in England'.

17.75in (45cm) long

£2,500-3,000   **L&T**

A small Wemyss pig figure, decorated black on white, impressed mark 'Wemyss Ware/R. H. & S.', small chip to tail and one ear, other ear cracked at base.

c1900   *4in (10cm) high*

£1,000-1,500   **L&T**

A Wemyss 'Earlshall' jug, with a rookery design and inscription, and 'Earlshall Faire A.D. 1914', impressed mark 'Wemyss', hairline crack.

5in (12.5cm) high

£500-800   **L&T**

An early 20thC Wemyss jug, decorated by Karel Nekola with stag and deer, impressed mark 'Wemyss' painted 'T. Goode & Co.' retailers mark, minor restoration to rim.

5in (13cm) high

£1,500-2,000   **L&T**

A near pair of Wemyss thistle-shaped vases, painted in colours, both unmarked.

c1900   *Taller 5in (12.5cm) high*

£400-600   **L&T**

An early 20thC Wemyss hat pin holder, decorated with heather and inscribed 'Hat-Pins', impressed mark 'Wemyss', glaze frits to rim.

5.75in (14.5cm) high

£600-900   **L&T**

A small Wemyss plate, decorated with two geese and inscribed 'BonJour', impressed mark 'Wemyss Ware/R. H. & S.', painted mark 'T. Goode & Co.'

c1900   *4.75in (12cm) diam*

£400-600   **L&T**

A late 19thC Wemyss 'Waverley' tray, decorated with forget-me-nots, impressed mark 'Wemyss', minor hairline crack.

17.25in (44cm) long

£1,000-1,500   **L&T**

An early 20thC Wemyss pin tray, decorated by Karel Nekola with a garden bench bearing the inscription 'Soi satisfait des fruits des fleurs, même des feuilles/ Si c'est dans ton jardin à toi que tu les cueilles', impressed and painted mark 'Wemyss', hairline crack to underside, glaze chip.

5.75in (14.5cm) wide

£800-1,200   **L&T**

A Zsolnay tile, with classical scene of satyrs and nude, under lustred glaze, stamped '7893 ZSOLNAY 36'.

11in (28cm) high

£1,000-1,300   **DRA**

A Zsolnay figure, of a maiden with pitcher, covered in lustred glaze, pink five churches medallion, '86?2 36'.

11in (28cm) high

£600-700   **DRA**

A Zsolnay owl figurine, 'Ketupa Ceylonensis,' covered in red glaze, small chips, five churches medallion '8771'.

13.5in (34.5cm) high

£550-750   **DRA**

A Zsolnay jardinière, embossed with weeds and cattails, covered in a lustred glaze, touch-ups to several high points, Y-shaped line on body, five churches red medallion, '4055, 6127B, Korona'.

12in (30.5cm) high

£6,000-7,000   **DRA**

A Zsolnay tapering Art Deco vase, with panels of birds of paradise in relief under lustred glazes, five churches medallion, illegible number.

8.25in (21cm) wide

£3,000-4,000   **DRA**

A Zsolnay boat-shaped centre bowl, topped by two crimson red parrots, covered in marbleised, lustred gold glaze, five churches gold stamp 'MADE IN HUNGARY, 8805E'.

15in (38cm) long

£1,500-2,000   **DRA**

A Zsolnay vase, embossed with geraniums, covered in lustred glazes, hairline and restoration, five churches gold stamp, 'MADE IN HUNGARY, ZSOLNAY PECS, 6166'.

8.75in (22cm) high

£2,500-3,000   **DRA**

ESSENTIAL REFERENCE: ZSOLNAY

Zsolnay was founded by Miklós Zsolnay in 1853 in Pécs, Hungary. It began to expand after his son, Vilmôs, took control in 1865.

- Prior to the 1890s, Zsolnay produced ornate pieces inspired by Islamic pierced wares and traditional Hungarian wares.
- Vilmôs was influenced by the latest design movements across Europe, particularly the Art Nouveau movement. Zsolnay began to specialise in ceramics with crystalline metallic glazes.
- Forms are simple and naturalistic, with low-relief moulded detail. Decorative motifs include tree silhouettes and red skies with lustrous surface.
- The factory still survives as a Hungarian State concern.

A Zsolnay tulip-shaped vase in lustred glazes, restoration to two rim chips, two small glaze bursts on base, green five churches stamp 'ZSOLNAY PECS 5495'

14in (35.5cm) high

£7,000-8,000   **DRA**

An Austrian Art Nouveau tall vase with white and blue blossoms, restoration to one petal and stem, stamped 'R. D. Z. HH 20882'.

19.5in (49.5cm) high

£1,200-1,500   **DRA**

An Arts & Crafts four-tile panel, painted with a figure of Pan below a flowering tree, with exotic birds and animals, painted monogram, framed.

30in (76cm) high

£1,200-1,500   **L&T**

A porcelain plaque, painted with a semi-clad female figure lying by a river reading a book with an urn by her side, in foliated gilt frame, bearing blue crossed swords mark and impressed no. '115'.

10.25in (26cm) high

£2,000-2,500   **A&G**

An Art Nouveau French studio pottery silver-mounted vase, the leaf-moulded tapered oval body in dark green and chartreuse glaze, with sinuous silver mounts to the mouth and foot rims, inscribed signature to base.

c1900   *7in (18cm) high*

£800-1,000   **FRE**

A shouldered vase after Jessie M. King, painted on a porcelain blank with a frieze of girls gathering flowers in a woodland setting, painted initials to base.

8.25in (21cm) high

£350-400   **L&T**

MISS CRANSTON'S TEAROOMS

The temperance movement was becoming increasingly popular in Glasgow in the late 19th/early 20thC. In response, Miss Catherine Cranston, the daughter of a local tea merchant, opened a series of tearooms, the interiors of which were all partially designed by Charles Rennie Mackintosh.

- In 1903, Mackintosh was commissioned to completely re-design the building (including interior design, furniture and exteriors) that later became known as The Willow Tearooms.

A Miss Cranston's part tea set, blue printed in the Willow pattern, comprising a tea cup and saucer, a sugar bowl and a milk jug, printed marks 'Miss Cranston's, Willow, Adderleys Ltd'.

£300-400   **L&T**

An American Arts & Crafts Grandfather clock, with copper numbers, unmarked.

78in (198cm) high

£1,500-2,000   DRA

An American Arts & Crafts oak standing clock, the twin train movement with circular dial enclosed by inset blue glass spandrels.

71.75in (182cm) high

£550-650   L&T

An Arts and Crafts longcase clock, with brass face, hardware and floriform inlay decoration.

78.5in (199cm) high

£4,000-5,000   SDR

A Secessionist style longcase clock, in exotic hardwood veneers with mother-of-pearl inlay, brass banding and German movement.

83in (210.5cm) high

£400-600   SDR

An Aesthetic Movement ebonised mantel clock, for Thomas Russell & Son., 33 Piccadilly and Liverpool, with twin train movement, the case decorated in gilt and coloured enamels with floral panels.

119in (47cm) high

£450-600   L&T

An Arts and Crafts design copper-cased timepiece.

9in (23cm) high

£200-250   A&G

An Aesthetic Movement clock, by Lewis F. Day, Edward & Sons, London and Glasgow, with twin train movement with ebonised case with moulded cornice and flower-carved spandrels and set with two ceramic plaques.

15in (38cm) high

£450-600   L&T

A Liberty & Co. English pewter mantel clock, designed by Archibald Knox, model no. 0761, with blue/green enamelled dial, stamped marks.

8.75in (22cm) high

£3,000-3,500   WW

An early 20thC Tiffany & Co. sterling silver travel clock, the case decorated with foliate sprays enclosing an oval medallion.

2.5in (6.5cm) wide

£1,000-1.300   FRE

A brass-cased wall clock, by Hector Guimard, the case decorated with cast whiplash foliage, hanging chain.

18in (46cm) high

£1,800-2,200   L&T

A Continental silver and enamel desk clock, in the style of Josef Hoffman, indistinctly marked.

3.5in (9cm) high

£900-1,200   FLD

An Art Deco gilt-bronze strut clock, with classic Art Deco hands, with an eight-day French movement with integral key, signed on dial and case 'Finnigans London & Paris', in original case.

c1920   3.5in (9cm) wide

£600-700   RGA

An Austrian Art Deco sub-miniature carriage clock, decorated with silver, sky blue guilloché enamel and black enamel, the back door decorated with silver in a basket weave pattern, eight-day movement with lever escapement, in its original leather case with its original key .

c1920   2.25in (5.5cm) high

£2,500-3,000   RGA

ESSENTIAL REFERENCE: CARTIER

In 1847, Louis-François Cartier took over the workshop of his former-master, Adolphe Picard, in Paris. Management passed to his son, Alfred in 1874, but it was Alfred's sons, Louis, Pierre and Jacques, who were responsible for establishing the worldwide brand name.

- The London branch was established in 1902, after Jacques and Pierre were sent to London to meet the requests prompted by Edward VII's coronation. Whilst still Prince of Wales, Edward had declared Cartier the 'Jeweller of Kings.' Cartier became the official supplier of the English Court from 1904. Pierre opened Cartier New York in 1909. Jacques remained in charge of the London branch
- Cartier is credited with producing the first wristwatch. It was designed in 1904 by Louis Cartier with the help of master watchmaker Edmond Jaeger, for aviator Alberto Santos-Dumont. Louis was also responsible for the 'Mysterious Clocks' and the 'Tutti Frutti' jewellery.
- After the death of Pierre in 1964, the businesses were sold and closed. In 1972, a group of investors led by Joseph Kanoui bought Cartier Paris. They bought Cartier London and Cartier New York back in 1974 and 1976 respectively, combining the Cartier interests in 1979 as 'Cartier Monde'.

A Cartier silver miniature boudoir clock, gilt and guilloché enamel, the white enamel dial signed 'Cartier', the back door in silver with engine turning, with fixed silver gilt handle, fine three-quarter plate eight-day lever movement with integral winding key.

c1920   3.5in (9cm) high

£4,000-4,500   RGA

A rare Cartier miniature strut clock, in the form of a camera, case constructed of gold, silver and leather, decorated with coral winding.

c1920   2.75in (7cm) high

£3,000-3,500   RGA

A German Art Deco sub-miniature carriage clock, decorated with light blue guilloché enamel and silver, eight-day three-quarter plate movement with lever escapement, fully marked on the case and numbered.

c1925   1.5in (4cm) high

£3,000-3,500   RGA

An early 20thC Art Deco gilt-bronze and enamel strut clock, dial marked 'Doxa' and 'Swiss made', with original box.

4in (10cm) wide

£1,300-1,600   RGA

A French Boucheron gold square travel or strut watch, the silvered dial with blue cabochon indicators, a red cabochon 2 and signed 'Boucheron', French eagle head poincons, International Watch Co. movement, cal.132, adjusted 5 positions and 2 temperatures.

c1930

£2,000-2,500   DN

An Art Deco walnut wall clock, with carved stylised floral motifs, Westminster chime, quarter strike pendulum movement.

c1930

£800-1,000   TDG

A pair of Edward Welby Pugin pitch pine 'Granville' chairs, each with carved moulded tablet toprail with six central ebony roundels, on chamfered A-frame.

£2,600-3,000 L&T

A pair of 1860s Gothic Revival oak stools, each with a pierced Gothic apron on chamfered legs.

19in (48.5cm) wide

£2,000-3,000 L&T

A Gothic Revival oak window seat, the seat with chamfered arms raised on curved cross supports, linked by a stretcher.

54in (137cm) wide

£600-800 L&T

A Celtic Revival oak hall settle, attributed to Alexander Ritchie, the rectangular back carved with three panels of elaborately carved Celtic knotwork and mythical beasts, dated.

1899 *50.5in (128cm) wide*

£650-750 L&T

A Gothic Revival oak planter, fitted with a frieze of Minton tiles.

45.75in (116cm) wide

£600-800 L&T

An early 19thC Gothic Revival carved jardinière, possibly a design by A. W. N. Pugin, the top with reversible solid panel above a 'hob nail' carved frieze centred by lancet arches and trefoil spandrels, the plinth base with a broad frieze of pierced tracery enclosing a metal-lined void.

28.75in (73cm) wide

£1,200-1,500 L&T

A mid-19thC French Gothic Revival karelian birch desk and chair, the desk with spire finials over two cupboard doors joined by gothic tracery above a single drawer, raised on carved tapered supports, the chair with a caned high back , raised on round, tapered, beaded legs.

Desk 44in (112cm) wide

£1,500-2,000 FRE

A 19thC Gothic Revival oak court cupboard, the cornice with eight allegorical carved panels, above a single cupboard door above a single drawer raised on straight legs .

34in (86.5cm) wide

£500-600 FRE

A Gothic Revival painted casket, the pitched architectural cover with scalloped mouldings, foliate diaper and a frieze of carved rosettes above sides decorated with foliate-painted sunken roundels.

34.75in (88cm) wide

£800-1,000 L&T

A late 19thC Gothic Revival giltwood archway, attributed to Peter Paul Pugin, the pointed lancet-arched dentil pediment enclosing a quatrefoil and tracery, with lozenges highlighted with punched work.

55in (140cm) wide

£2,200-2,500 L&T

A Scottish Arts & Crafts oak four poster bed, the canopy carved with Gothic tracery and with rosette and flowerhead motifs above a plain headboard with material covering, the front supports spirally moulded and imbricated with flowerheads, shields and acorn motifs, joined by a shaped triple panel foot board corresponding to the canopy.

95in (242cm) high

£4,000-5,000 L&T

ESSENTIAL REFERENCE: CARLO BUGATTI

Carlo Bugatti (1856-1940) was an Italian designer who worked c1880-1910. He designed metalware, textiles, and ceramics, but he is best known for his furniture.

- Bugatti drew inspiration from nature, and Moorish, Egyptian and Japanese art. He was also inspired by the writings of Eugène Viollet-le-Duc, in particular his ideas on the use of decorative elements to draw attention to the structure of a piece, rather than disguise it.
- The particularly strong Moroccan influence can be seen in Bugatti's use of dark woods offset by bold colours and strong, geometric designs, ropework and tassels of silk and wool.
- Some pieces are inlaid with ebony, copper and pewter. Copper may also be wrapped around uprights.
- Carlo was the father of Rembrandt Bugatti, the sculptor, and Ettore Bugatti, the car designer.

An Aesthetic Movement Carlo Bugatti piano stool, of ebonised wood inlaid with white metal kanji, with copper and bone accents, upholstered in camel skin.

20in (51cm) high

£5,000-6,000   SDR

An Aesthetic Movement Carlo Bugatti étagère, of ebonised wood inlaid in metal, bone and mahogany, with a patinated parchment panel, and copper-wrapped details.

c1905   23.25in (59cm) wide

£6,000-7,000   SDR

An oak bench, designed by Carlo Bugatti, with parchment, stencilled parchment, brass and brass nails.

c1902   46.75in (118.5cm) wide

£20,000-25,000   SOT

A partially ebonised oak bench, designed by Carlo Bugatti, with parchment, stencilled parchment, pewter, and copper.

46in (167cm) wide

£9,000-11,000   SOT

An oak corner chair, designed by Carlo Bugatti, with parchment, stencilled parchment, bone, metal cord, pewter, brass and brass nails.

c1902   28in (71cm) high

£7,000-8,000   SOT

A pair of walnut chairs, designed by Carlo Bugatti, with partially ebonised pewter and brass.

c1900   39.5in (100.5cm) high

£9,500-11,000   SOT

An oak pedestal designed by Carlo Bugatti, with parchment copper, pewter, silk cord and brass nails.

c1900   16.5in (42cm) wide

£10,000-12,000   SOT

An important and rare pine and partially ebonised oak Cartonnier, designed by Carlo Bugatti, with parchment, stencilled parchment, pewter, brass and bronze.

c1900   28in (71cm) wide

£45,000-50,000   SOT

A partially ebonised pine table, designed by Carlo Bugatti, with pewter and brass.

c1900   46in (117cm) wide

£8,000-10,000   SOT

An Aesthetic Movement ebonised bench, the moulded back with three upholstered panels above spindle-filled arms and stuff-over seat raised on turned legs.

69.75in (177cm) wide

£1,300-1,600   **L&T**

An E. W. Godwin 'Jacobean' ebonised armchair, probably manufactured by William Watt, with curved open lattice back.

£1,000-1,400   **L&T**

An Aesthetic Movement ebonised and gilt-incised side cabinet, the base with two mirrored doors flanked by panels painted with birds and embellished with kingwood inlay, with mirrored back, bears maker's label 'W. Walker, 119 Bunhill, London E.C.'

45in (114cm) wide

£1,500-2,000   **L&T**

An American Aesthetic Movement carved oak settee, attributed to Allen and Brother, Philadelphia (1870-1875), the crestrail with central figure of an owl within a leafy surround, with incised stiles with squared urn-form finials, the carved and fluted legs joined by palmette and flowerhead-carved seat rail.

85in (216cm) high

£3,000-4,000   **FRE**

An Aesthetic Movement extensive mahogany bedroom suite, comprising a three-door wardrobe, a dressing chest, with tall cheval mirror, a marble-topped washstand with splashback fitted with fourteen tiles by John Moyr Smith, a towel rail, and a pair of bedroom chairs.

Washstand 50in (128cm) wide

£1,400-1,800   **L&T**

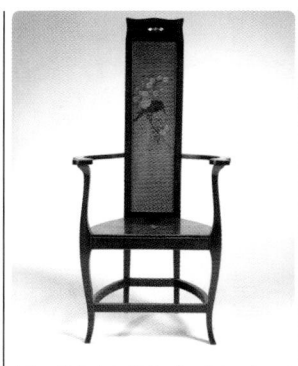

A Scottish Arts & Crafts stained and ebonised beech armchair, inlaid with mother-of-pearl lozenges, the tall panelled back painted with a rook perched on prunus blossom, above curved open arms and solid seat raised on curved legs linked by stretchers.

£2,500-3,000　　　　L&T

A George Walton walnut 'Philippines' side chair, the arched top rail with carved and gilded ribbon edging, centred by a pierced oval aperture above tall caned splat.

£2,500-3,000　　　　L&T

An oak chair with leather upholstery, designed by Frank Lloyd Wright, from the Hillside Home School, Spring Green, Wisconsin.

c1904　　　40in (102cm) high

£17,000-20,000　　　SOT

A mahogany ladder-back chair, designed by Charles Rennie Mackintosh for W. J. Basset-Lowke for the guest bedroom of 78 Derngate, Northampton.

c1917　　34.25in (87cm) high

£15,000-20,000　　　SOTH

A Scottish Arts & Crafts ebonised tub chair, the solid back and arms painted and inlaid with mother-of-pearl with the image of a maiden seated by a window, with two roundels to the arms depicting a windmill and a sailing ship.

£3,500-4,000　　　　L&T

An Arthur W. Simpson, Kendal oak and leather-upholstered armchair and stool.

£1,000-1,500　　　　L&T

An American Odd Fellows oak rocking chair, turned stiles with wide crest rail carved with 'all seeing eye', clasped hands and initials 'I.O.O.F', carved with three linked chains enclosing 'L.F.T.' and the lower 'The Brotherhood'.

c1900

£600-700　　　　　FRE

An armchair and two matching side chairs in the manner of Ernest Archibald, green-stained oak, each with pierced top rails above tapering splats.

£1,000-1,300　　　　L&T

An ebonised wood armchair by George Walton, the back with upholstered panel and spindle panels above curved arms and outswept turned legs.

£1,200-1,500　　　　L&T

A pair of Exhibition mahogany side chairs, by George Logan for Wylie & Lochhead, with tapering backs inlaid with stylised foliate motifs, highlighted with abalone shell.

These chairs were originally designed for the Royal Reception Room at the Wylie & Lochhead Pavilion at the Glasgow International Exhibition, 1901.
1901

£1,600-2,000　　　　L&T

A set of eight Arts & Crafts oak dining chairs, including two carvers, each with slatted backs formed as plant totems with applied embossed metal facings.

£1,000-1,500 SET   L&T

An ebonised oak armchair, attributed to Philip Webb, for Morris & Co., with later loose upholstered cushions, with padded arms, the ladder back on an adjustable ratchet, with bobbin-turned supports.

£4,000-5,000   L&T

A suite of stained oak boardroom furniture, in the manner of James Salmon Jnr., comprising a centre table and eight matching chairs, the table with stylised company initials 'B.L. & Co.', the chairs, including two carver chairs, with broad top rails carved with sinuous plant forms.

Table 40.25in (102cm) wide

£2,300-2,600 SUITE   L&T

A pair of Russian Arts & Crafts birch armchairs, each with incised decorative motifs, each bears metal makers label 'KOHCYACTBO/NO. 25'.

£800-1,000   L&T

An Arts & Crafts oak settle, Edgar Wood, the high panelled back with shaped finials above a plank seat on stem feet.

71.25in (181cm) wide

£2,000-2,500   L&T

ESSENTIAL REFERENCE: MOUSEMAN

Robert Thompson (1876-1955) was an English furniture-maker who signed every piece of furniture with his trademark carved mouse, giving him the name 'Mouseman.'

- Thompson was part of the 1920s crafts revival. He was interested in traditional tools and methods and consequently produced handcrafted oak furniture, inspired by 17thC designs. This furniture is characterised by an uneven, rippled surface created with an adze, a cutting tool with an arched blade.
- His workshop, now known as Robert Thompson's Craftsmen Ltd – The Mouseman of Kilburn, is still open.

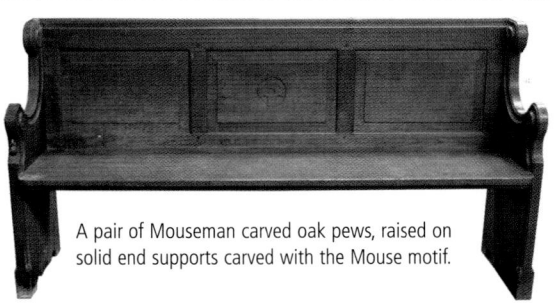

A pair of Mouseman carved oak pews, raised on solid end supports carved with the Mouse motif.

71in (180cm) wide

£2,000-2,500 PAIR   A&G

An oak and elm joint stool, Robert 'Mouseman' Thompson, the dished burr elm seat above four faceted baluster legs.

15.75in (40cm) wide

£800-1,000   L&T

A Robert 'Mouseman' Thompson oak magazine rack.

17in (43.25in) wide

£400-500   GORL

A Morris & Co. mahogany-framed sofa, upholstered in 'Squirrel' pattern wool fabric, raised on spirally fluted turned legs with brass caps and pot casters.

72.75in (185cm) wide

£1,000-1,400   L&T

DECORATIVE ARTS

A Heal & Sons oak 'Letchworth' refectory dining table, bears inset maker's label.

71.25in (181cm) wide

£1,800-2,200   **L&T**

An inlaid mahogany side table, attributed to George Walton, the top with chevron banding above a frieze with chequer panels.

29in (73.5cm) wide

£600-800   **L&T**

An oak table, designed by George Walton, the top raised on hexagonal legs united by stretchers, on trestle feet.

28.75in (73cm) high

£2,000-2,500   **L&T**

A mahogany table, in the manner of George Walton, stamped under apron 'A.S'.

33in (84cm) wide

£500-700   **L&T**

An Arts & Crafts oak gateleg table, the canted top above turned and blocked faceted supports linked by stretchers.

29.25in (74cm) high

£150-250   **L&T**

An Arts & Crafts oak dressing table, by Harris Lebus.

c1905

£1,200-1,500   **TDG**

An 1870s Holland & Son mahogany table, the top above three turned legs with ebonised collars raised on cross stretchers with chamfered curved feet, stamped marks.

41.75in (106cm) diam

£500-600   **L&T**

An oak occasional table, by Sir Robert Lorimer, the hexagonal panelled top with chamfered edging and exposed pegs above carved spirally moulded supports linked by curved stretchers on shaped block feet.

12.25in (31cm) high

£2,700-3,000   **L&T**

An Arts and Crafts linen press, with four shelves and three drawers.

43in (109cm) wide

£1,000-1,300   **DRA**

An oak press, by Sir Robert Lorimer, the cornice carved with flower and berry sprigs, the doors carved with linen-fold panels and enclosing an interior fitted with drawers and hanging spaces.

69.75in (177cm) wide

£9,000-11,000   **L&T**

A 20thC Arts & Crafts walnut standing corner cupboard, in the manner of Stanley Davies, cushion-moulded cornice and faceted frieze, doors with four raised panels and wooden loop handles, interior with hanging space.

40.75in (103.5cm) wide

£1,000-1,300   **HT**

An oak and marquetry-inlaid hall cupboard, by Shapland and Petter, Barnstaple, the single door panelled with elaborate foliate strapwork inlay, flanked by further panels, similarly decorated.

54in (137cm) wide

£800-1,200   **L&T**

An oak hall cupboard, designed by Earnest Archibald Taylor, for Wylie & Lochhead, with door inset with stained and leaded glass panel, above two further doors on stile supports, bears retailers label, stamped serial no '116663'.

c1900   79in (201cm) high

£1,600-2,000   L&T

An Arts & Crafts oak hall stand, by Shapland and Petter, Barnstaple , with embossed copper frieze, centred with an aneroid barometer dial, over central mirror and coat pegs, above marble-top glove drawer, with stick stand below, bearing inscription 'Fair Weather After You'.

52in (132cm) wide

£1,200-1,500   L&T

An Arts & Crafts mahogany with marquetry inlay display cabinet, in the style of Wylie & Lochhead, Glasgow, the three-quarter ledge back with spindle-filled three-quarter gallery central by a panel decorated with angular stemmed foliage, highlighted in harewood, requiring some restoration.

37.25in (120cm) wide

£850-1,100   L&T

An Arts & Crafts oak bureau, with Irish Celtic detail, with carved and stained decoration to fall front, top gallery and sides with mythical creatures and Celtic knots, copper stylised metalware, green-stained interior.

c1900

£800-1,000   TDG

An Arts & Crafts boarded and panelled oak chest, the triple-panel front centred with three dancing maidens in relief, the cut-out ends with carved female musicians.

52.5in (133cm) wide

£130-160   WW

A George Walton mahogany workbox, the shaped and panelled hinged lid with lined interior above two drawers on square tapering legs.

The form of this small workbox conforms to furniture designed by Walton for Elm Bank, York, characterised by its stripped down 18thC references and demonstrating a re-orientation in line from the vertical to the horizontal.

23.5in (59.5cm) wide

£2,000-3,000   L&T

An Arthur W. Simpson, Kendal oak wall cupboard, with open bookshelf with hinged dust protectors carved with rosettes above twin panelled doors similarly carved, bears paper label.

35.75in (91cm) wide

£1,200-1,500   L&T

An oak-framed three-fold draught screen, after C. F. A. Voysey, inset with three stained and leaded glass panels.

74.5in (189cm) high

£2,500-3,000   L&T

A Secessionist three-panel screen, leaded glass, brass, and velvet, unmarked.

Centre panel: 63.5in (161cm) high

£2,500-3,000   DRA

A green-stained sycamore draught screen, George Logan for Wylie & Lochhead, each fold with stained and leaded glass panel depicting a stylised plant form, above linen panels painted with hearts.

72in (183cm) high

£2,000-3,000   L&T

An Arts & Crafts oak fire screen, design characteristic of Charles Voysey, metal tag 'House Furnishers, 36 Donegal St. Belfast, Bell & Mayrs Ltd.'

1907

£250-300   SK

DECORATIVE ARTS

A Scottish Arts & Crafts oak-framed fire surround, with a crewelwork wool panel worked with flowering foliage on a cream ground and surrounding aperture for fireplace.

47in (119cm) wide

£2,000-2,500   **L&T**

An oak overmantel mirror, by Arthur W. Simpson, Kendal, carved with panels of flowering foliage.

45in (114cm) wide

£1,000-1,500   **L&T**

An oak dressing mirror, by Liberty & Co., the mirrored plate with turned uprights having acorn finials and heart-pierced brackets.

32.5in (82.5cm) high

£350-450   **L&T**

An Italian Art Nouveau wood side chair, carved with two ladies' heads, a frog, and flowers, upholstered with pale silk, unmarked.

39in (99cm) high

£2,000-2,500   **DRA**

An Art Nouveau oak and marquetry-inlaid side chair.

£400-450   **L&T**

An early 20thC cast iron and oak seat, by Hector Guimard.

French architect and designer Hector Guimard (1867-1942) is best known for designing the entrances to the Paris Métro.

36in (91.5cm) high

£3,000-5,000   **SOTH**

An Art Nouveau mahogany armchair, in the manner of J.S. Henry, with upholstered panel back above curved arms and slatted gallery pierced with hearts, the upholstered panel seat on square supports linked by a stretcher.

£900-1,200   **L&T**

ESSENTIAL REFERENCE: LOUIS MAJORELLE

French cabinet-maker, Louis Majorelle (1859-1926) trained as a painter before taking over and industrialising his father's cabinet-making business in Nancy in 1879. He later established several workshops to increase his output.

● Majorelle was inspired by nature, the Art Nouveau movement and Emile Gallé.

● His furniture was usually made of dark hardwoods such as mahogany and rosewood, with fluid outlines and large, sculptural gilt-bronze mounts shaped as orchids or water lilies, alongside delicately carved, inlaid or marquetry decoration in fruitwoods, pewter, or mother-of-pearl.

● Majorelle also designed metalware, and he collaborated with the Daum brothers to produce a variety of lamps with glass shades and elegant bronze and iron mounts.

● Majorelle was one of the founding members of the École de Nancy.

A Louis Majorelle mahogany, tamarind wood and gilt-bronze 'Table Aux Nénuphars'.

c1902   *36.5in (92cm) diam*

£350,000+   **SOT**

A Louis Majorelle mahogany two-tiered tea table, with exotic wood marquetry design and gilded bronze handles, signed 'L. Majorelle'.

35in (90cm) wide

£3,000-4,000   **SOTP**

A set of four Emile Gallé Art Nouveau mahogany nesting tables, each with a different inlay, chestnut branch, gladiola stalk, irises, and poppies, unmarked.

Largest: 21.75in (55cm) wide

£3,000-4,000   **DRA**

An Art Nouveau mahogany and inlaid centre table, attributed to Mackay Hugh Baillie Scott.

35.75in (91cm) diam

£3,500-4,000   **L&T**

ESSENTIAL REFERENCE: EMILE GALLÉ

Emile Gallé (1846-1904) was a furniture and glass designer, who founded the École de Nancy in 1901, based on the principles of medieval guilds.

- Gallé was influenced by the history of art, Symbolist poetry and literature, and particularly the natural world, which provided him with inspiration for shapes and well as decoration.
- Gallé's furniture was made from richly coloured or exotic woods, such as rosewood, maple, walnut or fruitwoods.
- His tables and cabinets often stand on carved supports in the shape of dragonfly wings, or featured cornices carved with snails, moths or bats, etc. Other common decorative features include bronze mounts in the form of insects, fruitwood inlays in the shape of natural motifs, engraved verses by Victor Hugo, Paul Verlaine, and Charles Baudelaire.
- Many of Gallé's pieces were unique and were signed.

An Emile Gallé mahogany display cabinet, carved and inlaid with clematis, with a glass door over two fixed shelves, flanked by side shelves, unmarked.

31.5in (80cm) wide

£5,000-5,500   **DRA**

A 19thC Emile Gallé walnut folio stand, with exotic wood flower marquetry design, signed 'Gallé'.

30.25in (77cm) wide

£6,500-7,500   **SOTP**

An Art Nouveau satinwood standing desk, with small glazed door above shelf fronted by baluster-turned supports, inlaid fall front beneath, on square supports with shaped under tier, labelled Howard & Sons, Stamped 11429/5933 .

66in (167.75cm) high

£3,000-3,500   **BWL**

A Scottish Art Nouveau oak sideboard, inlaid with iridescent enamel heart motifs with cupboard doors inset with stained and leaded glass panels.

64.25in (163cm) wide

£2,500-3,000   **L&T**

An oak stickstand, by Shapland and Petter of Barnstaple.
c1905

£1,200-1,400   **TDG**

A mahogany coal purdonium, the hinged base inset with an oxidised plaque with stylised foliage, the sides with copper plate carrying handles the reverse with ivorene label 'Short & Hayes 25 London Road Southampton'.

38.5in (98cm) high

£600-800   **WW**

An Art Nouveau inlaid mahogany display cabinet, fitted with stained and leaded glass panel and flanked by marquetry inlaid doors.

73.75in (187cm) high

£2,000-3,000   **L&T**

An Art Nouveau mahogany-inlaid display cabinet, pierced and inlaid with Art Nouveau whiplash foliage and enclosing an astragal glazed door flanked by corresponding panels.

60.25in (153cm) wide

£2,700-3,000   **L&T**

An Art Nouveau mahogany music cabinet, with twin marquetry inlaid panel doors.

39in (99cm) high

£350-450   **L&T**

An Art Nouveau satinwood and inlaid display cabinet, with open shelf supported by turned columns, enclosing cabinet with single glazed door with inlaid panel.

60in (152cm) wide

£2,000-3,000   **L&T**

An Art Nouveau mahogany bureau bookcase, the lower section with sloping fall embellished with decorative copper hinges and two drawers.

76in (193cm) high

£500-600   **L&T**

An Art Nouveau inlaid mahogany display cabinet, the arched-ledge back with mirror plates on turreted supports, the whole decorated with stylised flowerheads on scrolling tendril stems, highlighted in abalone shell.

55in (140cm) wide

£3,600-4,000   **L&T**

A bentwood desk, designed by Josef Hoffmann, for Jacob et Josef Kohn, the curved ledge panelled back extended to the lower stretcher, with central bevelled mirror plate, above inset writing surface, on curved and bracketed square open supports.

Josef Hoffman (1870-1956) was an Austrian architect and designer who created metalwork, jewellery and furniture. He was a leading member of the Vienna Secession, and one of the founding members of Wiener Werkstätte (est. 1903), for which he designed many tables and chairs in beechwood, mahogany, limed oak, and other ebonised woods. Inspired by the work of Charles Rennie Mackintosh, he favoured linear and geometric designs, though his bentwood designs have gently bent corners. Decoration on his furniture typically consists of open-centred rectangles with a ball motif at intersections,

c1900   *44.5in (113.5cm) wide*

£9,000-10,000   **L&T**

An Art Nouveau mahogany and inlaid bedroom suite, comprising a wardrobe, a dressing table, a pot cupboard and a pair of double bed ends. Wardrobe

82.75in (210cm) wide

£2,800-3,200 SUITE   **L&T**

A rosewood wardrobe, by Louis Majorelle, with wrought metal foliate panels above drawers with conforming handles, the central section with mirrored backplate above wrought iron jardinière base, branded signature mark.

98.5in (250cm) wide

£2,300-2,600   **L&T**

A rosewood display cabinet, Louis Majorelle, each inlaid to the hinges with foliate motifs in brass and mother-of-pearl.

71.25in (181cm) wide

£1,500-2,000   **L&T**

A pair of Art Deco beech and palisander wood armchairs.

£750-850   L&T

A pair of ebonised and parcel-gilt wood chairs, designed by Armand-Albert Rateau, each stamped 'AA RATEAU 1874'.

c1925   *37.25in (94.5cm) high*

£10,000-15,000 PAIR   SOT

A 1930s birch armchair, Gerald Summers, Makers of Simple furniture, single sheet of cut and bent birch plywood.

23.75in (60.5cm) wide

£17,000-20,000   L&T

A pair of Art Deco leather club chairs.

£1,500-2,000   L&T

A set of four Machine Age enamel and chrome metal chairs, unmarked.

29in (73.5cm) high

£500-600   SK

An Art Deco day-bed, in walnut veneers.

c1930

£1,400-1,600   TDG

An Art Deco Belgian thula wood dining table, the top with draw leaves supported by two square end columns in the centre.

c1930   Closed *42.25in (107cm) wide*

£1,600-2,000   SK

An Art Deco birch dining room suite, comprising a sideboard, a side cabinet, and extending dining table, the black laminated top above twin pillars with black plinths, and six matching chairs.

Table 62.25in (158cm) long

£750-1,000 SUITE   L&T

An Art Deco two-tier steel console table, with brass details and marble top.

72in (182.5cm) wide

£2,500-3,000   SDR

An Art Deco forged steel console table, with marble top.

32in (81cm) wide

£1,200-1,500   SDR

ESSENTIAL REFERENCE: GILBERT ROHDE

Gilbert Rohde (1894-1944) founded his New York design studio in 1927, and soon became known for his avant-garde ideas.

- Rohde's furniture was typically made from natural materials like American maple. The sparse hardware was typically metal. Exotic hardwood was used for veneers.
- Rohde had travelled in Germany and many of his pieces were inspired by the Bauhaus. Walter Gropius's influence, in particular, can be seen in Rohde's modular and sectional furniture.
- Much of Rohde's work was designed for corporate manufacturers, such as Herman Miller, Heywood-Wakefield and John Widdicomb. He designed innovative children's furniture for Krohler and a range of tubular steel seating furniture for Troy Sunshade Co. in 1933.
- Rohde's furniture is typically marked. Some custom furniture bears a paper label.

A Herman Miller four-drawer chest, by Gilbert Rohde, in walnut and ash with brass and ebonised wood pulls, Herman Miller label.

48in (122cm) wide

£1,200-1,500   **SDR**

An Art Deco maple chest of drawers, with ebony trim, the drawers with turned rosewood handles, turned tapering legs and brass feet.

39in (99cm) wide

£1,500-2,000   **HT**

A two-door ivory lacquered chest, with black opaline top encircled with gilded bronze, by Jacques Adnet, opens to reveal two compartments with maple shelves.

69.25in (176cm) wide

£20,000-24,000   **SOTP**

An Art Deco burr walnut 'Gentleman's Fitment', two end wardrobes with a central section with cupboards, shelves and drawers including a white vitrolite-lined 'cool' cabinet.

118in (299.5cm) wide

£600-800   **HT**

A 1940s Fontana Arte Italian wall mirror, with shelf, clear and blue-tinted mirrored glass, gilt metal.

89.75in (228cm) high

£10,000-15,000   **L&T**

A white painted jardinière stand, in the manner of Koloman Moser, the oval spindle-filled gallery with black sphere spacers enclosing a liner.

36in (91.5cm) wide

£750-850   **L&T**

A Gabriel Argy-Rousseau pâte-de-verre vase, decorated with four naturalistic thistles on purplish ground, moulded 'G. ARGY-ROUSSEAU' mark.

c1920   6in (15cm) high

£3,000-3,500   DRA

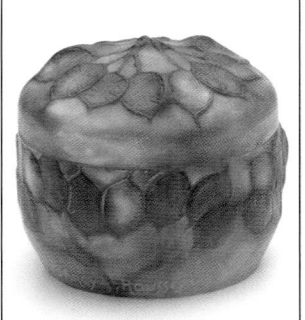

A Gabriel Argy-Rousseau pâte-de-verre box and cover, decorated with formalised honesty leaves, base moulded with 'G-ARGY-ROUSSEAU' mark.

c1920   3.75in (9.5cm) high

£2,000-2,500   DRA

A Gabriel Argy-Rousseau pâte-de-cristal paperweight, patterned with two moths in relief, moulded 'G Argy-Rousseau' signature.

2.75in (7cm) high

£1,200-1,500   DRA

A Gabriel Argy-Rousseau pâte-de-verre veilleuse lamp shade, incised G.ARGY ROUSSEAU, painted FRANCE.

6in (15cm) high

£3,000-3,500   DRA

A Gabriel Argy-Rousseau pâte-de-verre cabinet vase, 'Masques', with two male masks surrounded by ivy leaves, incised G.ARGY ROUSSEAU.

4in (10cm) high

£1,500-2,000   DRA

ESSENTIAL REFERENCE: DAUM FRÈRES

In 1885, Jean-Louis Auguste and Jean-Antonin Daum took over their father's glass factory in Nancy, France, which became known as 'Daum Frères'. Inspired by the Gallé pieces shown at the 1889 Paris Exhibition, they started making art glass in the early 1890s

- Early Daum pieces were inspired by nature and the countryside, and images from the East. Many of their trademark innovative techniques were designed to enhance this naturalistic decoration, such as the cloudy, mottled rich background, coloured enamel detail, the martelé background, patterns at various depths (intercalaire pieces), and applied foil-backed decoration.
- Many new forms were created by the factory, including the 'Berluze' vase, distinguished by its long thin neck.
- Paul and Henri Daum, the sons of Auguste, and Michel Daum, son of Antonin, introduced the Art Deco style during 1920s. The shapes were simpler, and decorated with stylised geometric acid-etched patterns. At this time, electric lamps became an increasingly important area of production, some of which featured bronze or iron mounts designed by Louis Majorelle or Edgar Brandt.
- In 1962, the factory became a public company, and was renamed 'Cristallerie Daum'.

A Daum etched, engraved, applied, and internally decorated glass vase, patterned with sunflowers with applied centres and gilt leaves on streaked red ground, painted and engraved signature 'DAUM NANCY' with Cross of Lorraine mark.

c1900   15.75in (40cm) high

£1,800-2,200   DRA

A Daum Frères glass vase, the mottled brown and blue ground overlaid in tones of green and ochre, applied with a large spider at the centre of its web, flanked by a beetle and a bee against a ground carved with briony leaves and applied with red berries, carved mark 'Daum, Nancy' and cross of Lorraine, underside engraved '54', enamelled collection number '1990,472'.

The spider was a popular motif on Daum cameo glass but the very large and prominent spider on this vase is unusual. Unlike Gallé, Daum did not tend to use poetic quotations but with regard to another vase decorated with spiders and nettles a verse provided inspiration, 'I like the spider and I like the nettle, because they are unloved and because no-one looks on them with sympathy, rather everyone with reproval, at their doleful wishes' (See Noël Daum, Daum, Mastery of Glass, Lausanne 1985, p.56.)

c1905   16.5cm (42in) high

£40,000-45,000   SOTH

A Daum etched and enamelled glass thistle vase, in autumnal palette on frosted opalescent ground, engraved signature 'Daum Nancy'.

16.75in (42.5cm) high

£3,500-4,500   DRA

A rare Daum Nancy freeform cameo and enamel vase, decorated with wild orchids and bumble bee, signed 'Daum Nancy' in gilt on underside.

10in (25.5cm) high

£9,000-11,000   JDJ

A Daum Nancy cameo and applied glass vase, pink and white acid-etched marguerites, each with a foil-backed applied cabochon centre, pale yellow mottled background, acid-etched and gilded signature on underside 'Daum Nancy'.

15in (38cm) high

£12,000-15,000   JDJ

A Daum Nancy wheel-cut vase, autumnal leaf decoration, etched signature to underside of base.

15.5in (39.5cm) high

£1,000-1,500   FRE

A Daum Nancy cameo glass landscape vase, signed in cameo with 'Cross of Lorraine'.

c1910   21in (53.5cm) high

£2,000-4,000   FRE

A Daum internally decorated Art Deco vase, with gilt speckled inclusions, engraved 'DAUM NANCY' with Cross of Lorraine mark.

17in (43cm) high

£1,000-1,500   DRA

A Daum cabinet box and cover, etched, enamelled and gilt with hydrangea and a border of dragonflies on opalescent ground, with applied glass cabochons, gilt signature 'Daum Nancy' with Cross of Lorraine mark.

c1900   3.25in (8cm) diam

£2,500-3,500   DRA

A Daum etched and enamelled scenic vase, with continuous frieze of pond scene with egrets in flight, polychrome and gilt on pale green and mauve ground, gilt signature 'Daum Nancy' with Cross of Lorraine mark.

c1890   8.5in (21.5cm) diam

£3,500-4,500   DRA

A Victor Durand Art Nouveau threaded vase, in gold iridescence with green lappets, some minor losses to threading, polished pontil.

12in (30.5cm) high

£500-700   DRA

A Durand gold-lustred glass vase, with ivory swirls, signed 'Durand 1968-6'.

6in (15cm) high

£550-750   DRA

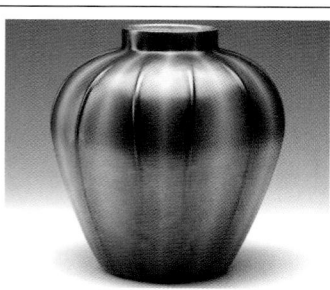

A Durand Glass ginger jar, with heavy ribbing, in deep amber graded to white, yellow interior, unpolished pontil with some roughness, and thumbnail hairline crack, no lid.

9.75in (25cm) high

£500-700   DRA

ESSENTIAL REFERENCE: GALLÉ

Emile Gallé (1846-1904) was a pioneer of the Art Nouveau style in France. He set up his first decorating workshop in Nancy in 1873.

- Gallé used the techniques of historical cameo glass-making, but took the process further by using up to five layers of different coloured glass, which were cut away by hand to create subtle colour graduations. He combined cameo techniques with enamelling, mould casting, marquetry and inlay.
- Gallé's glass is highly naturalistic in form and decoration, incorporating flowers particularly thistles, insects, plants, trees and fossils in the designs.
- Gallé began commercial production of Art Nouveau cameo in c1899. By 1900, the firm was the largest manufacturer of luxury glassware in Europe. Acid-etching was increasingly used on the 'standard' or middle range pieces, though the 'pièces uniques' were still handcrafted by Gallé and his master craftsmen.
- In 1901, Gallé established the École de Nancy, based on the the principles of medieval guilds.
- He died in 1904, leaving his widow to run the factory with Victor Prouvé as art director. A star by Gallé's signature indicates production after his death. The factory closed in 1936.

An Emile Gallé 'Jeanne D'Arc' cameo glass commemorative vase, with panel depicting Joan of Arc on a ground of arabesques, the verso with similar panel featuring a Cross of Lorraine, cameo signature 'Gallé'.
c1895   11in (28cm) high
£8,500-9,500   **DRA**

A glass marqueterie-de-verre vase by Emile Gallé, the delicately striped ground inlaid with four 'Colchium Autumnale', their petals finely carved, the foot applied and carved with leaf forms over foil highlights, engraved mark 'Gallé', enamelled collection number '1990,473'.

Emile Gallé wrote to Victor Champier that he had created 'chalice-form blossoms that seek air and daylight' (see Sigrid Barten and Bernd Hakenjos, Keramik, Glas und Möbel des Art Nouveau, Museum Belerive, Zurich, 1980, p.48.) The designs for this series of vases, now in the Musée D'Orsay, are dated 1897 and the pieces were put into production in 1898. It was in this year that Gallé patented the term, 'marqueterie de verre'.

17.25in (44cm) high
£55,000-60,000   **SOTH**

An Emile Gallé cameo glass 'Pavote' vase, with mauve poppies on martelé frosted ground, signed with cameo snail shell.

7.5in (19cm) high
£5,500-7,500   **DRA**

An Emile Gallé cameo glass vase, with mountainous landscape in mauve, blue, and green, on shaded yellow ground, and 'Gallé' cameo signature.
c1900   12.5in (31.5cm) high
£4,500-5,500   **DRA**

An Emile Gallé cameo glass vase, with wooded lakeland landscape in amber on frosted lemon-yellow ground, and 'Gallé' cameo signature.
c1900   7.75in (19.5cm) high
£1,200-1,600   **DRA**

An Emile Gallé cameo glass vase, patterned with red peony blossoms, vertical Japanese cameo signature.
c1900   18in (45.5cm) high
£1,800-2,200   **DRA**

An Emile Gallé cameo glass vase, in shades of purple, partly fire-polished, cameo signature 'GALLE'.
c1900   12.5in (31.5cm) high
£1,800-2,200   **DRA**

A large Emile Gallé marqueterie-de-verre vase, inlaid and carved glass, the boldly striated ground with two butterflies, the reverse with a third, engraved mark 'Gallé'.
c1900   23.5in (60cm) high
£55,000-60,000   **SOTH**

A Gallé cameo vase, the grey glass body covered in blue and amber glass and acid-etched with flowering convolvulus vines in a landscape, cameo signature to body.
13.75in (35cm) high
£2,000-2,500   **L&T**

An Emille Gallé cameo glass vase, the grey glass body overlaid in yellow and amethyst and acid-etched with the depiction of a lily pond with flowering plants, cameo mark 'Gallé'.
10.5in (26.5cm) high
£850-1,100   **L&T**

An Emile Gallé large cameo glass vase, the graduated peach body cased in deep magenta and cut with a fern pattern, with scroll signature to the lower side.

19in (48cm) high

£1,600-2,000 **FLD**

CLOSER LOOK: GALLÉ CAMEO GLASS LAMP

Up to five layers of glass were fused together before the outer layers were cut back using wheel carving and hand-work to create the design which stands out in relief.

Gallé studied botany and used this knowledge to great effect in his glass designs which feature highly naturalistic decoration.

Lamp design was revolutionised by the advent of electricity which allowed cameo glass shades and bases to be illuminated to make the most of both the light and the glass design.

The carver has cleverly graduated the colour to give a feeling of added perspective.

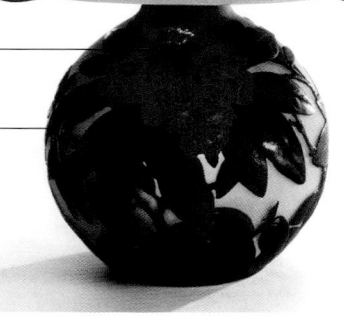

A table lamp designed by Emile Gallé, 'Rhododendron', with mould-blown and wheel-carved cameo glass shade, base signed in cameo 'Gallé'.

c1925 *18in (45.5cm) high*

£100,000-120,000 **SOT**

An Emile Gallé cameo vase, decorated with honeysuckle in mauve against a shaded lemon-yellow ground, cameo signature.

9.5in (24cm) high

£900-1,100 **DRA**

An Emile Gallé electrified exhibition panel of marks and signatures, with a glass negative medallion against an etched brass mat, in gilded frame surrounded with various Gallé signatures.

1904 *16in (40.5cm) high*

£2,500-3,000 **DRA**

A 'Corolla' lamp by Emile Gallé, cameo glass and bronze, the lamp modelled as a lotus flower, the base cast as three leaves and a bud, cameo mark to glass 'Gallé'.

18in (46cm) high

£60,000-70,000 **SOTH**

ESSENTIAL REFERENCE: RENÉ LALIQUE

Previously a master jeweller, René Lalique (1860-1945) began experimenting with glass in his jewellery designs in the 1880s. He developed his interest in glass in the 1890s and opened a shop in Paris in 1902, making perfume bottles and decorative wares for the commercial trade.

- Lalique first produced perfume bottles for François Coty c1907, and then most other leading Parisian perfumeries. Many were made in the Art Deco style.
- Lalique is predominantly associated with pressed glass, but many of his thinner vases were moulded. His pieces were primarily clear, opalescent or frosted, though many were produced in coloured glass, which is now sought after.
- Between 1920 and 1930, Lalique produced designs for over 200 vases and 150 bowls, two of the most popular forms. The crisply moulded details, quality of moulding and virtuosity of the designs gave mass-produced pieces a 'one-off' feel.
- Virtually all pieces produced before Lalique's death in 1945 are marked 'R. Lalique'. Pieces made afterwards are marked 'Lalique'. The company is still operating, now under the name 'Cristallerie Lalique et Cie'.

A Lalique 'Acanthes' vase, cased butterscotch yellow glass with original bronze stand, moulded 'R. LALIQUE' mark, introduced 1921.

Vase 11in (28cm) high

£15,000-18,000 **DRA**

A Lalique 'Acanthes' vase, cased red glass with original bronze stand, moulded 'R.LALIQUE' and engraved 'Lalique' marks, introduced 1921.

Vase 11in (28cm) high

£10,000-12,000 DRA

A Lalique 'Antilopes' vase, clear glass with black enamel decoration, stencilled 'R. LALIQUE FRANCE' mark, introduced 1925.

10.75in (27.5cm) high

£15,000-18,000 DRA

A Lalique 'Aras' opalescent glass vase, moulded with birds amongst thorny branches, etched mark 'R.Lalique, France', introduced 1924.

9in (23cm) high

£2,000-2,500 L&T

A Lalique 'Avallon' vase, deep yellow amber glass with original wood stand, wheel-cut 'R. LALIQUE FRANCE' mark and engraved 'No. 986', introduced 1927.

Vase 5.75in (14.5cm) high

£3,000-4,000 DRA

A Lalique 'Bandes De Roses' vase, clear and frosted glass with sepia patina, moulded 'LALIQUE' with extended 'L' mark, introduced 1919.

9.25in (23.5cm) high

£2,000-2,500 DRA

A Lalique 'Bresse' vase, amber glass with whitish patina, stencilled 'R. LALIQUE FRANCE' mark, introduced 1931.

4in (10cm) high

£1,500-2,000 DRA

A Lalique 'Cariatides' vase and cover, clear and frosted glass with green patina, stencilled 'R. LALIQUE' twice, engraved 'Lalique', introduced 1920.

8in (20cm) high

£4,000-5,000 DRA

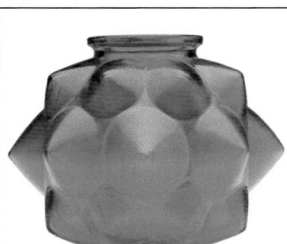

A Lalique 'Champagne' vase, bright green glass, engraved 'R. Lalique France, No. 1004', introduced 1927.

6.5in (16.5cm) high

£2,000-2,500 DRA

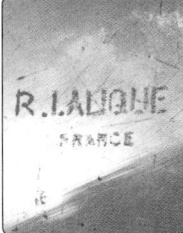

A Lalique 'Chamois' pattern vase, with Sienna patina, the base with acid-etched 'R. LALIQUE FRANCE' mark, introduced 1931.

4.5in (11.5cm) high

£800-1,000 TGM

A Lalique 'Courges' vase, cased opalescent glass with blue patina, moulded 'R. LALIQUE' mark, introduced 1914.

7.25in (18.5cm) high

£1,500-2,000 DRA

MILLER'S COMPARES

A Lalique 'Courlis' vase, deep green glass with whitish patina, stencilled 'R. LALIQUE FRANCE' mark, introduced 1931.

6.5in (16.5cm) high

£3,500-4,000   DRA

A Lalique 'Courlis' vase, red amber glass with whitish patina, stencilled 'R. LALIQUE FRANCE' mark, introduced 1931.

6.5in (16.5cm) high

£5,500-6,500   DRA

Lalique created many variations of the same design even to the point of different pieces having cased interior (pearly white), or patinated colours added to the exterior. However, mostly, the same forms were available only in a limited and specific grouping of colours. Relatively few forms were available in red.

And so the green and red vases above are typical of Lalique, whose red vases tend to be more valuable than other colours in the same design.

Red is rarer than green because it is harder to work with, being prone to 'burning' in the heat and becoming dull in tone.

A Lalique 'Domremy' vase, emerald green glass with whitish patina, engraved 'R. Lalique France No. 979', introduced 1926.

8.25in (21cm) high

£2,500-3,000   DRA

A Lalique red amber glass vase, 'Domremy', designed by René Lalique, No. 979, etched 'R Lalique France No.979', introduced 1926.

8.5in (21.5cm) high

£1,800-2,200   WW

A Lalique 'Escargot' vase, deep red glass, moulded 'R.LALIQUE' mark, introduced 1920.

8.25in (21cm) high

£12,000-15,000   DRA

A Lalique 'Espalion' vase, cased jade green glass, engraved 'R. Lalique France' mark, introduced 1927.

7in (18cm) high

£3,000-3,500   DRA

A Lalique 'Espalion' vase, blue glass, engraved 'R. Lalique France' mark, introduced 1927.

7in (18cm) high

£1,800-2,200   DRA

A Lalique 'Florence' vase, with brown enamel decoration and sepia patina, stencilled 'R. LALIQUE FRANCE', introduced 1937.

7.5in (19cm) high

£3,000-3,500   DRA

A Lalique 'Formose' vase, clear and frosted glass, moulded 'R. LALIQUE' mark, introduced 1924.

6.75in (17cm) high

£1,000-1,400   DRA

A Lalique 'Gobelet Six Figurines' vase, clear and frosted glass with blue patina, engraved 'R. Lalique' mark, introduced 1912.

8in (20.5cm) high

£2,000-2,500   DRA

A Lalique 'Grenade' vase, engraved 'R. Lalique France' mark, introduced 1930.

4.75in (12cm) high

£1,300-1,600   DRA

A Lalique 'Gui' vase, pale pea green glass, moulded 'R. LALIQUE' mark.

c1920   6.5in (16.5cm) high

£1,200-1,500   DRA

CLOSER LOOK: LALIQUE VASE

The cire perdue – or lost wax – technique involves making a plaster cast of the object to be made. This is coated with a layer of wax the desired thickness of the finished object and the central cavity of the mould is filled with clay. The mould is then heated until the wax melts and can be drained off. The space left is filled with molten glass.

This piece is remarkable in the depth of the relief decoration which would have been very difficult to achieve using this technique.

The details of the snakes' bodies have been highlighted with a sepia patina.

A René Lalique 'Huit Serpents' 'cire perdue' cast glass vase, the shoulders modelled with eight entangled serpents, engraved 'R.LALIQUE'.

Reptiles were a source of inspiration to Lalique throughout his life and they appear in some of his most spectacular creations such as the gold and enamel pectoral in the Gulbenkian Museum. The motif also appears in bronze and even on an evening handbag embroidered in silver thread on silk and with silver mounts cast as opposing snakes. In cire perdue, other pieces from this period include several vases, 'Quatre Serpents', 'Quatre Serpents et Grenouilles' and a plafonnier 'Quatre Grouped de Deux Serpents'.

8.25in (21cm) high

£60,000-80,000   SOTH

A Lalique 'Hirondelles' vase, clear and frosted with glass, greyish patina, moulded 'LALIQUE' mark with extended 'L', introduced 1919.

9in (23cm) high

£7,000-8,000   DRA

A Lalique 'Lagamar' vase, clear and frosted glass with black enamel decoration, wheel-cut 'R. LALIQUE' mark, introduced 1926.

7.25in (18.5cm) high

£5,000-7,000   DRA

A Lalique 'Malesherbes' vase, clear and frosted glass with sepia patina, engraved 'R. Lalique France No. 1014', introduced 1927.

9in (23cm) high

£1,500-2,000   DRA

A Lalique 'Moissac' vase, topaz glass, wheel-cut 'R. LALIQUE FRANCE' mark, introduced 1927.

5in (12.5cm) high

£1,000-1,500   DRA

A Lalique 'Monnaie du Pape' vase, stencilled 'R. LALIQUE FRANCE' mark, introduced 1914.

9in (23cm) high

£1,500-2,000   DRA

A Lalique 'Nivernais' vase, bright green glass, engraved 'R. Lalique France, No. 1005', introduced 1927.

6.5in (16.5cm) high

£1,700-2,000   DRA

A Lalique 'Ormeaux' vase, red amber glass, engraved 'R. Lalique France' mark, introduced 1926.

6.5in (16.5cm) high

£1,500-1,800   DRA

A Lalique 'Ormeaux' vase, cased jade green glass, engraved 'R. Lalique France, No. 984'.

c1926   6.5in (16.5cm) high

£6,000-7,000   DRA

A Lalique 'Palissy' frosted glass vase, of ovoid form moulded with shells, moulded mark 'R. Lalique', introduced 1926.

6.75in (17cm) high

£850-950 **L&T**

A Lalique 'Pearls' pattern Agate glass vase, the base moulded 'R. LALIQUE', introduced 1925.

Vases in the pearl pattern are scarce, as the pattern was usually used for perfume bottles or dressing table sets. Furthermore, this example is in Agate glass, which is again scarce.

4.75in (12cm) high

£2,500-3,000 **TGM**

A Lalique 'Perruches' vase, pea green glass, engraved 'R. Lalique France', introduced 1919.

9.75in (24.5cm) high

£6,000-7,000 **DRA**

A Lalique 'Poissons' vase, deep red glass, engraved 'R. Lalique' and moulded 'R. LALIQUE' marks.

c1921 *9.25in (23.5cm) high*

£10,000-12,000 **DRA**

A Lalique 'Rampillon' vase, yellow amber glass, wheel-cut 'R. LALIQUE FRANCE' mark, introduced 1927.

5in (12.5cm) high

£1,200-1,400 **DRA**

A Lalique 'Ronces' vase, red amber glass, moulded 'R. LALIQUE' mark, introduced 1921.

9in (23cm) high

£2,500-3,000 **DRA**

A Lalique 'Sauge' vase, red amber glass with whitish patina, moulded 'R.LALIQUE' mark, introduced 1923.

9.75in (25cm) high

£2,500-3,000 **DRA**

A Lalique 'Sirenes et Cabochons' vase, clear and frosted glass with sepia patina, moulded 'R. LALIQUE' mark, introduced 1914.

7.75in (19.5cm) high

£5,500-6,500 **DRA**

A Lalique 'Sirenes Avec Bouchon Figurine' vase, with stopper, of clear and frosted glass, engraved 'R. Lalique France', flat chip to base of stopper, fleck to inner rim of vase, introduced 1920.

14in (35.5cm) high

£6,500-8,500 **DRA**

A Lalique 'Sylvia' vase, clear and frosted glass with blue patina, wheel-cut 'R. LALIQUE FRANCE' mark, introduced 1929.

8.5in (21.5cm) high

£4,500-5,500 **DRA**

A Rene Lalique vase, 'Tortues', moulded clear glass with sepia patina, of globular form with a flared mouth, the surface covered with tortoises, moulded 'R. Lalique' to underside, introduced 1926.

10.25in (26cm) high

£6,000-8,000 **FRE**

A large limited edition Rene Lalique 'Tourbillons' re-issue vase, with a deep wall relief-moulded with spiral spiked motifs picked out in black enamel over the clear crystal ground, engraved signature and numbered '462 of 999' produced, complete with presentation certificate and box.

8in (21cm) high

£2,500-3,000 **FLD**

A Lalique 'Tournesol' opalescent vase, with remains of light staining, the base inscribed 'R. Lalique France No.1007', introduced 1927.

4.25in (11cm) high

£1,000-1,200 **TGM**

A Lalique 'Fleurons' pattern opalescent glass dish, with moulded 'R.LALIQUE' signature, introduced 1935.

Values depend on the opalescence amongst other factors. This example has an excellent level of opalescence, making it desirable.

10.25in (26cm) diam

£450-500 TGM

A Lalique 'Gazelles' opalescent glass with blue patina dish, moulded 'R. LALIQUE' and wheel-cut 'FRANCE' marks, introduced 1925.

11.5in (29cm) diam

£900-1,200 DRA

A Lalique 'Martigues' opalescent amber glass bowl, moulded 'LALIQUE' mark.

14in (35.5cm) diam

£2,700-3,000 DRA

A 1980's Lalique 'Deux Moineaux' centre bowl, clear and frosted glass, design no. 11000, engraved 'Lalique France'.

15.75in (40cm) long

£350-450 DRA

A Lalique 'Roscoff' opalescent glass bowl, engraved 'R. Lalique France' mark, introduced 1932.

13.75in (35cm) diam

£1,400-1,600 DRA

A Lalique 'Fauvettes' ashtray, amber glass, moulded 'R. LALIQUE' and engraved 'R. Lalique France' marks. c1924.

6.75in (17cm) diam

£500-750 DRA

A Lalique 'Serpent' ashtray, electric blue glass, engraved 'R. Lalique' mark, introduced 1920.

4.5in (11.5cm) diam

£1,500-2,000 DRA

A Lalique glass ashtray, 'Statuette De La Fontaine' No.288, clear and frosted, engraved 'R Lalique', introduced 1925.

4.75in (12cm) high

£850-950 WW

A Lalique 'Nenuphar' inkwell, clear and frosted glass with grey patina, engraved 'Lalique' mark, introduced 1910.

2.75in (7cm) diam

£750-950 DRA

A Lalique 'Serpents' inkwell, in opalescent dark amber, engraved 'R. Lalique', introduced 1920.

6.25in (16cm) diam

£2,000-3,000 DRA

A Lalique 'Trois Sirenes' opalescent glass inkwell, with original cover, moulded 'R. LALIQUE' mark, introduced 1921.

9in (23cm) diam

£7,500-8,500 DRA

A Lalique 'Cleones' opalescent glass box, moulded 'R. LALIQUE' mark, introduced 1921.

10in (25.5cm) diam

£1,500-2,000 DRA

A Lalique 'Panier De Roses' oval box, clear and frosted glass with blue patina, moulded 'R. LALIQUE' mark, introduced 1919.

3.5in (8.5cm) long

£1,200-1,500   DRA

A Lalique 'Quatre Papillons' box, opalescent glass with sepia patina, engraved 'R. Lalique France' mark, introduced 1911.

3in (7.5cm) diam

£1,500-2,000   DRA

A Lalique 'Quatre Scarabees' box, electric blue glass with whitish patina, moulded 'R. LALIQUE' mark, introduced 1911.

3.5in (9cm) diam

£1,500-2,000   DRA

A Lalique 'Tokio' blue glass box, moulded 'LALIQUE' and engraved 'France' marks, introduced 1921.

6.75in (17cm) diam

£4,500-5,500   DRA

A Lalique 'D'Aigle' automobile hood ornament, clear and frosted glass with original chrome collar on black glass bookend base, moulded 'R. LALIQUE' mark, introduced 1928.

7in (17.5cm) high

£2,000-3,000   DRA

A Lalique 'De Coq' automobile hood ornament, clear and frosted glass, moulded 'LALIQUE FRANCE' mark, with Lucite stand, introduced 1928.

7in (17.5cm) high

£1,200-1,500   DRA

A Lalique 'Grenouille' automobile hood ornament, clear and frosted glass, moulded 'LALIQUE', engraved 'R. Lalique France' marks, introduced 1928.

2.5in (6cm) high

£6,500-7,500   DRA

A Lalique 'Hirondelle' car mascot, moulded as a swallow, clear and frosted glass with chromium-plated part mount, moulded mark 'R. Lalique/ France'. No. '1143'.

5.75in (14.5cm) high

£1,800-2,200   L&T

A Lalique 'Libellule' car mascot, clear and frosted glass with amethyst inclusion, mounted on removable turned brass plinth, moulded mark 'R. Lalique', etched script mark 'R. Lalique/ France', no. '1145', chip to foot rim.

8in (20.5cm) high

£2,500-3,000   L&T

A Lalique 'Perche' automobile hood ornament, clear and frosted glass with grey patina, moulded and stencilled 'R. LALIQUE FRANCE' mark.

6.25in (16cm) high

£800-1,000   DRA

A Lalique 'Pintade' automobile hood ornament, clear and frosted glass, wheel-cut 'R. LALIQUE FRANCE' mark, introduced 1929.

6in (15cm) high

£3,500-4,500   DRA

A Lalique 'Coq Nain' automobile hood ornament, clear and frosted glass, moulded 'R. LALIQUE FRANCE' mark, introduced 1928.

8in (20.5cm) high

£750-950   DRA

A Lalique 'Daim' paperweight, clear and frosted glass, moulded 'R. LALIQUE' mark, introduced 1929.

3in (7.5cm) long

£500-700   DRA

A Lalique 'Rhinoceros' paperweight, clear and frosted glass, stencilled 'R. LALIQUE FRANCE' mark, introduced 1931.

4.5in (11.5cm) long

£2,000-3,000   DRA

A Lalique 'Toby' paperweight, clear and frosted glass, stencilled 'R. LALIQUE FRANCE' mark, introduced 1931.

3.5in (9cm) wide

£750-950   DRA

A Lalique clear crystal 'Bellecour Sparrow' paperweight, frosted finish and light grey hue, relief-moulded above blackberries, bears diamond point-engraved signature to the base, introduced 1927.

4.25in (11cm) high

£350-450   FLD

A Lalique 'Deux Figurines' clock, clear and frosted glass, with original decorated metal illuminating base, lower edge of clock polished, mostly inside base, and with internal fracture to one corner, unsigned, introduced 1926.

15.25in (39cm) high

£1,800-2,200   DRA

A Lalique 'Inseparables' frosted and opalescent timepiece, the single train movement with painted circular dial within glass case, moulded with budgerigars, within fitted leather case, moulded mark 'R. Lalique', etched script mark 'France No. 258'.

4.25in (11cm) high

£3,500-4,500   L&T

A Lalique 'Roitelets' clock, clear and frosted glass with black enamel numerals, original movement and hands, small internal bruise behind numeral 3, stencilled 'R. LALIQUE FRANCE' mark, introduced 1931.

7.5in (19cm) high

£1,500-2,500   DRA

A Lalique 'Cerises' rocker blotter, clear and frosted glass with sepia patina, original metal rocker, moulded 'R. LALIQUE' mark, introduced 1920.

6.5in (16.5cm) long

£900-1,200   DRA

A Lalique 'Grupe de Six Moineaux' decorative motif, clear and frosted glass, stencilled 'R. LALIQUE FRANCE' mark, introduced 1933.

11.75in (30cm) long

£1,800-2,200   DRA

A Lalique 'Figurine' clear glass seal, etched in bas relief with a nude, blank seal, etched script mark 'R. Lalique, France'.

3.25in (8.5cm) high

£2,000-2,500   L&T

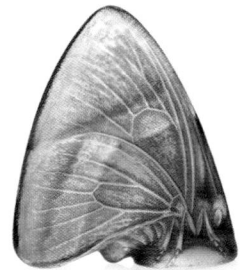

A Lalique 'Papillon ailes ferme' frosted glass seal, with original blue staining, blank seal, etched script mark 'R. Lalique'

2.25in (6cm) high

£1,000-1,300   L&T

A Lalique 'Sorbier' pendant, electric blue glass with blue silk cord, probably original, moulded 'LALIQUE' mark, introduced 1920.

2in (5cm) long

£750-950   **DRA**

A Lalique 'Vase de Fleur' seal, clear and frosted glass moulded as a vase of flowers, with applied gilt seal with monogram, etched mark 'Lalique'.

2.5in (6.5cm) high

£850-1,000   **L&T**

A Lalique 'William' glass, clear and frosted with blue enamel decoration, engraved 'R. Lalique France', introduced 1925.

5.75in (14.5cm) high

£300-400   **DRA**

A Rene Lalique design for a horn hair comb, ink and watercolour on BFK Rives parchment paper, with annotations in Lalique's hand, upper right.

Provenance: Lalique Family collection.

1900   *8.5in (21.5cm)wide*

£2,500-3,000   **DRA**

A Loetz iridescent green vase, with internal trailing tendril decoration and trefoil lip, engraved 'Loetz Austria'.

9.5in (24cm) diam

£1,000-1,400   **DRA**

A Loetz Witwe coupe vase, by Maria Licarz, in oilspot pattern, unmarked.

11.5in (29cm) high

£850-1,100   **DRA**

An early 20thC Loetz iridescent glass vase, of amphora form with twisted handles on a favrile ground, signed 'Loetz, Austria'.

7in (18cm) high

£450-500   **FRE**

An early 20thC Loetz iridescent art glass vase, decorated with a pulled feather design on green favrile ground, unsigned.

5in (12.5cm) high

£1,400-1,800   **FRE**

A Loetz glass vase, designed by Michael Powolny, ribbed amber body with black rim, on three applied black glass ball feet, unmarked.

6.25in (16cm) high

£180-220   **WW**

An early 20thC Loetz Art Nouveau silver overlay vase, the triform dimple body decorated with silver whiplash stemmed flowers over the green Papillion ground.

10.75in (27cm) high

£1,500-2,000   **FLD**

A Monart glass lamp and shade, the turquoise glass with green swirling bands and bubble inclusions, the shade of mushroom form above a squat shouldered base, bears original paper label 'VII.P/29.410'.

12.5in (31.5cm) high

£2,300-2,600   **L&T**

A Monart SA V glass vase, mottled blue and green.

9in (23cm) high

£350-450   **L&T**

A Monart A VII glass vase, mottled pink and purple.

6.75in (17cm) high

£250-350   L&T

A Monart JB VII glass goblet, surface decorated with blue, green, yellow and white.

7in (18cm) high

£1,000-1,300   L&T

A Monart RF IV glass vase, mottled red and orange with aventurine inclusions.

12in (30.5cm) high

£450-550   L&T

A Monart FI V glass vase, mottled pale green with aventurine inclusions.

15.25in (39cm) high

£550-650   L&T

A Monart D glass vase, mottled pale green and pink with aventurine inclusions, bears partial label.

14in (36cm) high

£350-450   L&T

A Monart KC glass vase, mottled green and orange.

7in (18cm) high

£500-600   L&T

A Monart HC VI glass vase, pale blue with bubble inclusions.

7in (18cm) high

£450-550   L&T

A Monart tapering glass vase, with yellow, blue and turquoise craquelure inclusions.

9in (23cm) high

£600-700   L&T

A Monart C VII glass vase, mottled green and blue with surface decoration.

7in (17.5cm) high

£450-550   L&T

A Le Verre Francais Art Deco vase, with stylised Japanese flora in red on mottled orange ground, engraved 'Le Verre Francais'.

19in (48cm) high

£1,700-2,000   DRA

A Charles Schneider mottled glass globular vase, in shades of pink and orange, engraved 'Schneider' mark.

c1925   *10in (25.5cm) high*

£450-500   DRA

A Schneider footed bowl, with bubble inclusions, raised on a turned amethyst glass column and spreading base, stencil-etched mark 'Schneider France'.

14.25in (36.5cm) high

£360-420   L&T

A large Schneider cameo glass vase, in a graduated orange to blue over mottled tan ground and cut in the 'Fig Tree' pattern with a repeat stylised foliate motif, murrine cane to base.

19.4in (49.5cm) high

£2,000-£3,000   FLD

A Barovier 'Crepuscolo' vase, designed by Ercole Barovier, the clear-cased cream and amber glass with aventurine inclusions, the base with remains of factory paper label.

1933-35   *12.75in (32cm) high*

£700-1,000   **QU**

A 1930s Barovier flared glass vase, red cased with clear bubbles and side decoration.

11in (17.9cm) high

£1,800-2,200   **PC**

A Barovier & Toso 'Oriente' vase, designed by Ercole Barovier, honey-coloured glass with silver-foil inlays and wavy bands of blue, purple, red, turquoise, yellow and green.

1940   *7.25in (18cm) high*

£4,500-5,500   **PC**

A Ferro-Toso-Barovier inverted bell-shaped 'Vetro Mosaico' vase, designed by Ercole Barovier, with murrines in opaque yellow and brown.

c1930   *8.5in (21.4cm) high*

£6,000-7,000   **VZ**

A Ferro-Toso-Barovier 'Autunno Gemmato' vase, designed by Ercole Barovier, the 'tortoiseshell' ground with silver inclusions and six large clear glass applications.

Ercole Barovier designed a group of thick-walled pieces in 1935-36 using decorative techniques, including Crepuscolo, Autonno Gemmata, Marina Gemmata and Laguna Gemmata. This piece is typical of the soft shapes used during this period which differ greatly from the lighter, more brightly coloured pieces produced in the years following the Second World War.

1935-36   *11in (28cm) high*

£1,500-2,500   **SOTH**

A Seguso-Ferro 'Pulegoso' pale blue vase, designed by Ercole Barovier.

'Pulegoso', translucent glass that is identified by a countless number of bubbles ('puleghe' in the dialect of Murano) contained in the glass, obtained by chemical reaction during the heating process.

1935-40   *11in (28cm) high*

£4,000-5,000   **SOTH**

An MVM Cappellin footed bowl or tazza, with amber-gold tinted glass, the base with 'MVM Cappellin Murano' acid stamp, designed by Vittorio Zecchin.

1922-25   *4.25in (11cm) high*

£400-550   **QU**

A Seguso Vetri D'Arte beaker vase, designed by Flavio Poli, cased in blue and red, the surface with shallow pulled lobes.

1937   *8in (20cm) high*

£1,200-1,500   **QU**

A Seguso Vetri D'Arte 'Pulegoso' footed vase, the green body with 'foamy' irregular internal air bubbles, diagonal ribbing, the side trails with fine gold foil inclusions terminating in handles.

c1940   *12in (30.5cm) high*

£900-1,200   **QU**

A Seguso Vetri D'Arte 'Sommerso A Bollicine' vase, in red glass with gold inclusions.

c1940   8in (20.5cm) high

£2,500-3,000   SOTH

A Fratelli Toso urn vase, the opaque black baluster body with gold foil inclusions and applied opaque red spiralling trail to neck and double handles.

c1915-20   14.5in (36cm) high

£1,500-2,000   QU

A Venini 'Laguna' bell vase, designed by Tomaso Buzzi, the milky pink body with melted fine gold foil inclusions.

1932   6.25in (15.5cm) high

£2,600-3,000   QU

A Venini 'Sommerso A Bollicine' vase, designed by Carlo Scarpa, the green body with randomly sized internal bubbles and gold foil inclusions arranged in columns, the base with 'Venini Murano' acid stamp.

1934-36   10.5 in (26.5cm) high

£2,500-3,000   QU

A Venini 'A Bolle' vase, of amorphous form, designed by Carlo Scarpa, decorated with a network of controlled internal bubbles, the base with 'Venini Murano ITALIA' acid stamp.

1936   6in (15cm) high

£1,000-1,200   QU

A Venini 'Battuto' vase, designed by Carlo Scarpa, the violet-black double gourd shaped body with hammered effect cut surface, the base with 'Venini Murano' acid stamp.

1940   9.5in (24cm) high

£9,500-11,500   QU

A Venini 'A Bugne' vase, designed by Carlo Scarpa in green glass, later factory signed 'venini italia'.

1940   12in (31cm) high

£22,000-25,000   SOTH

A Venini 'Opalino' vase, designed by Tomaso Buzzi, the blue glass with white lattimo border, circular label 'Venini Murano'.

1932   8.5in (21.5cm) high

£2,000-2,500   SOTH

A 'Cavallino' horse sculpture, the design attributed to Napoleone Martinuzzi for Zecchin-Martinuzzi, the red glass body with moulded ribs and fine gold foil inclusions, with applied legs, tail and mane.

1933.   6.25in (16cm) high

£1,400-1,800   QU

DECORATIVE ARTS

An early 20thC Steuben 'Aurene' glass vase of flattened bottle form, applied with raised handles, signed 'Steuben Aurene' 1914'

13in (33cm) high

£4,000-4,500 **FRE**

A pair of Steuben amber and blue glass candlesticks, waffle mark.

c1920. *12in (30.5cm) high*

£1,000-1,500 **DRA**

A tall Steuben gold Aurene vase, etched 'Aurene 2418', with a few short scratches.

16.75in (42.5cm) high

£550-750 **DRA**

A Steuben Glass Works scent bottle, model no. 3048, decorated aurene glass, engraved 'Aurene' twice.

c1910-1915 *6.5in (16.5cm) high*

£12,000-14,000 **SOT**

A Steuben millefiori flower-form vase, iridescent gold colouring with heart, vine and millefiori decoration with applied gold Aurene foot, marked 'Aurene 578'.

11in (28cm) high

£9,000-11,000 **JDJ**

A Tiffany Studios favrile glass compote, with iridescent green rim on an opalescent base, engraved 'L.C.T. Favrile 1702C'.

6in (15cm) high

£1,000-1,400 **DRA**

A Tiffany Studios carved and internally decorated Favrile glass vase, with leafage in green on gold, engraved 'L.C.Tiffany Favrile 4252J'.

6.25in (16cm) high

£3,000-4,000 **DRA**

A Tiffany Studios leaded-glass window, with trophy centre of crest, ribbons, acorns, oak leaves, and red 'jewels,' surrounded by swirling leaves, unmarked.

28in (71cm) wide

£4,500-5,000 **DRA**

An important Tiffany Studios aquamarine paperweight glass ornament, depicting a single fish swimming against a background of aquatic foliage in an aquamarine sea, engraved 'L.C.Tiffany Inc. Favrile 6508N'.

6.25in (16cm) high

£10,000-12,000 **DRA**

A Tiffany Studios gold Favrile floriform compote, with green tendrils, etched 'L.C.T. Favrile'.

8.5in (21.5cm) diam

£1,000-1,400 **DRA**

A Tiffany Studios gold Favrile pitcher, with green leaf and vine pattern, etched 1257, blacked-out number, 'L C TIFFANY-Favrile'.

8.75in (22cm) high

£1,800-2,200 **DRA**

An early 20thC Tiffany Furnaces Favrile glass and enamel vase, the slender stem and flared faceted rim raised on a blue/turquoise enamelled base, stamped 'Louis C. Tiffany Furnaces, Inc. 151' with monogram.

13in (33cm) high

£500-800 **FRE**

ESSENTIAL REFERENCE: WEBB

In 1855, Thomas Webb (1804-1869) moved his company to Stourbridge, West Midlands, where, by 1859, it became known as Thomas Webb & Sons.

- In the late 19th/early 20thC, Webb produced cameo glass ranges combining clear glass and at least one other colour (red, yellow, blue and white).
- The in-house cameo team was led by two brothers, George and Thomas Woodall. Their specialties were Classical, historical and mythological scenes.
- The factory also produced commercial cameo, generally decorated with floral motifs in white on yellow or white on red ground. Many of the best pieces were the work of Daniel Pearce and his son Lionel, who joined the company in 1884.
- After 1900, the new managing director, Congreve William Jackson, steered the family away from elaborate glass like cameo, as the market was declining rapidly.

A Webb blue cameo glass decorated bowl, the bright cobalt blue sphere layered in shades of blue and white, deeply cut and stippled overall in stylised floral repeating tapestry motif with six medallion elements, carved base stamped with circular 'Webb Gem Cameo' mark.

5in (12.5cm) diam

£5,500-7,500 SK

A Webb Gem cameo glass gilt-enamelled vase, the gilt decoration by Jules Barbe, master decorator, decorated in the Japanese style, the body with red flowers in cameo, gilt branches and leaves on an intricate scroll decorate ground, chevron-decorated base rim, signed 'Thomas Webb & Sons/Gem Cameo'.

1888

£18,000-22,000 SK

A Thomas Webb & Sons cameo-carved glass solifleur vase, milky glass overlaid with peach and white, decorated with a butterfly amongst hibiscus flowers, unmarked.

7.5in (19cm) high

£1,000-1,400 WW

A Webb Gem cameo glass four-layer decorated vase, colourless crystal case in bright red and layered yellow over white cameo-cut and meticulously carved overall in repeating Asian influenced pattern, stamped 'Thomas Webb & Sons Gem Cameo'.

7in (18cm) high

£18,000-22,000 SK

A Webb Gem cameo glass Japonesque decorated bottle vase, in Webb raisin brown overlaid with white, cameo-cut and carved intricately with basketweave motif, above assorted blossoms, with bamboo, grasses and fern, intricate border motifs, stamped 'Thomas Webb & Sons Gem Cameo'.

8.5in (21.5cm) high

£10,000-12,000 SK

A Webb Gem cameo glass decorated vase, citron yellow overlaid in white cameo-cut and carved with a profusion of open-petalled roses. buds, leaves and stems with a moth, butterfly and ivy on the opposite side, marked 'Thomas Webb & Sons Gem Cameo'.

13.75in (35cm) high

£10,000-12,000 SK

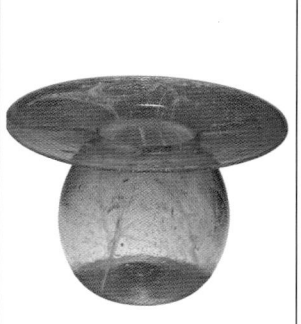

A 'Clutha' green glass vase, by James Couper & Sons, Glasgow, with aventurine and milky inclusions.

6.25in (16cm) high

£900-1,100   **L&T**

An early 20thC pâte-de-verre pedestal bowl, by François Emile Décorchemont, with theatrical face mask handles, bears lozenge mark to the lower side.

c1920   5in (13cm) wide

£1,800-2,200   **FLD**

A D'Argenthal cameo glass cabinet vase, patterned with stylised amber fronds on pale green ground, with cameo signature 'D'Argenthal'.

c1905   4.5in (11.5cm) high

£400-500   **DRA**

A De Vez cameo glass vase, of tapering form, the lemon yellow body overlaid in amethyst and acid-etched with irises, etched cameo mark.

8in (20.5cm) high

£300-400   **L&T**

A pair of 1930's Art Deco Haida region enamelled vases, decorated in the manner of the Wiener Werkstätte with fluted black line cartouches with enamelled birds over a stylised black line leaf-and-flower ground.

5.5in (14cm) high

£300-400   **FLD**

A Haida school glass vase, decorated with a yellow and black grid enclosing carved concave roundels.

13.5in (34cm) high

£600-800   **L&T**

A Bohemian glass Wilhelm Kralik Sohn vase, the blue iridescent body with flashes of gold, green and purple, decorated with a random design of platinum iridescence with flashes of blue and green, housed within an Art Nouveau metal surround.

23in (58.5cm) high

£8,000-10,000   **JDJ**

A Legras enamelled glass vase, decorated with a floral roundel on a mottled orange, yellow and opalescent round, signed 'Legras'.

18in (46cm) high

£2,000-2,500   **FRE**

A Muller Frères etched and enamelled scenic vase, with wooded winter landscape in naturalistic colours on shaded mauve and amber ground, cameo signature.

4.25in (10.5cm) high

£600-800   **DRA**

A Muller Frères large cameo vase, of shouldered ovoid form and cased in deep magenta over cranberry over clear, acid-cut with large peony flowers in bud and full bloom with acid-cut signature to the side.

17.75in (45cm) high

£2,000-2,500   **FLD**

A Muller Frères cameo glass vase, the baluster glass body of clear glass overlaid in blue and acid-etched with a landscape scene, cameo mark.

10.5in (26.5cm) high

£700-1,000   **L&T**

A Quezal eight-light lily lamp, with gold iridescent assembled lily shades on a patinated metal base, shades engraved 'Quezal', base unmarked.

c1920   18in (45.5cm) high

£1,500-2,000   **DRA**

An early 20thC Stevens & Williams cased decanter, with frill-collar neck and hollow blown plume stopper, the body cased in green over clear and flash-cut with Classical inspired foliate scrolls and swags.

10.5in (27cm) high

£600-800   **FLD**

A Wiener Werkstätte gilded and enamelled glass vase, decorated by Reni Schaschl, the body painted in white enamel with figures dancing through trees, with exotic flowering plants below, painted marks.

6.5in (16.5cm) high

£550-750   **L&T**

A Wiener Werkstätte enamelled glass decanter and stopper, clear glass body painted in coloured enamels with lattice design and further decorated in gilt with flower sprigs.

7.25in (18.5cm) high

£550-650   **L&T**

A 1920s German painted glass tazza, by Adolf Beckert, painted in gilt and black enamel with a procession of fauns, the tapered faceted stem on circular spreading base.

13in (33cm) high

£450-550   **L&T**

An Amalric Walter pâte-de-verre crab paperweight, in deep green and blue, incised 'A WALTER NANCY'.

2.5in (6.5cm) wide

£550-750   **DRA**

A Scottish Arts & Crafts stained, leaded and glass panel, depicting Saint Maurice (or Saint Victor) with a donor.

This panel is copied from the original late 15thC painting by Jean Hey, the Master of Moulins. The painting currently hangs in Kelvingrove Art Gallery and Museum, Glasgow. It was bequeathed to the city by Archibald McMillan in 1854 and is thought to be a fragment. A religious scene would originally have appeared to the left of the picture.

19.75in (50cm) high

£1,800-2,200   **L&T**

A pair of Aesthetic Movement stained, painted and leaded glass panels, each of rectangular outline, and painted with female figures within a border of panels painted with flowers, inscribed 'Painting' and 'Music'.

27in (69cm) high

£2,000-2,500 PAIR   **L&T**

A pair of Aesthetic Movement large leaded-glass and painted windows, framed.

c1885.   *33in (84cm) wide*

£5,000-7,000   **DRA**

A pair of Scottish Arts & Crafts stained, leaded and painted glass panels, depicting 'Robert Bruce' and 'Queen Margaret'.

c1890   *38.5in (98cm) high*

£900-1,200 PAIR   **L&T**

An American Philadelphia stained glass window.

PROVENANCE: From the mansion of financier Alexander Van Rensselaer, built in 1898, the corner of 18th and Walnut Street, now the flagship Anthropologie store.

1898   *42.5in (108cm) high*

£7,000-9,000   **FRE**

A Tiffany 'Hearts and Vines' four-panel table screen, each arched patinated bronze and favrile glass panel comprised of three sections, the upper section with twining leafy vines against a yellow ground, above mottled green glass lower sections, unmarked.

c1900   *16.5in (42cm) wide*

£1,000-1,500   **FRE**

An early 20thC leaded glass window, with a mosaic of coloured glass depicting two pillars centring a robed figure holding a child, unsigned.

75in (191cm) high

£3,000-4,000   SK

A pair of stained, leaded and painted glass panels, by Guthrie & Wells Ltd., Glasgow, depicting 'Sir Percival and the Holy Grail', the other depicting the Grail with female attendants, signed and dated 'Guthrie & Wells Ltd.'.

c1930   31.5in (80cm) high

£5,000-6,000 PAIR   L&T

PERFUME BOTTLES

A Lalique 'Dans La Nuit' perfume display bottle, for Worth, sealed, and with original string labels (no contents), moulded 'R. LALIQUE' mark, introduced 1924.

9.75in (24.5cm) high

£1,200-1,500   DRA

A Lalique 'Elegance' perfume bottle, for D'Orsay, frosted glass with brown patina, with frolicking figures, partial label, moulded 'R. LALIQUE' mark, introduced 1914.

3.75in (9.5cm) high

£2,000-2,500   DRA

A Lalique 'Imprudence' factice perfume bottle, for Worth, clear glass with silvered edge detail, moulded 'R. LALIQUE' mark, introduced 1938.

A factice is a large shop-window dummy.

9.5in (24cm) high

£750-950   DRA

A Lalique 'Jaytho' perfume bottle, for Jay Thorpe, clear and frosted glass with sepia patina, moulded 'MADE IN FRANCE' mark, introduced 1928.

6in (15cm) high

£450-500   DRA

A Lalique 'Je Reviens' perfume bottle, for Worth, blue and opaque aqua glass in silver-metal case, introduced 1931.
This is the earliest version of this skyscraper design.

5.5in (14cm) high

£900-1,200   DRA

A Lalique 'La Perle Noire' perfume bottle, for Forvil, clear and topaz glass, moulded 'R. LALIQUE PARIS FRANCE' mark, stopper frozen, introduced 1922.

4.5in (11.5cm) high

£1,500-2,000   DRA

A Lalique 'La Phalene' perfume bottle, for D'Heraud, clear and frosted Amberina glass, designed as a nymph with butterfly wings, moulded 'R. LALIQUE' mark, introduced 1925.

3.5in (9cm) high

£3,500-4,000   DRA

A Lalique 'Le Jade' moulded glass scent bottle and stopper, for Roget et Gallet, Paris, indistinct moulded mark 'R.L. France'.

3.25in (8cm) high

£1,600-2,000   **L&T**

CLOSER LOOK: TRÉSOR DE LA MER PERFUME BOTTLE

This presentation was made for Saks Fifth Avenue, and a corded label in the form of a booklet identifies this example as No. 72 from a limited edition of 100.

The opalescent glass shell-form box contains a clear and frosted glass pearl-form bottle.

The box and bottle are in the original red velvet presentation box lined in gold silk and blue velvet.

The presentation box retains original Saks price tag affixed underneath, indicating a price of $50. Glass box retains partial label on inside lid and both the glass box and bottle are signed by Lalique.

A Lalique 'Trésor de la Mer' perfume presentation, box stencilled 'R. LALIQUE FRANCE', bottle engraved 'R. Lalique France'.

c1936

Glass box 5.75in (14.5cm) long

£100,000+   **DRA**

A Lalique 'Misti' perfume bottle, for Piver, clear and frosted glass with blue patina, butterfly motif, moulded 'R. LALIQUE' mark, introduced 1913.

2in (5cm) high

£1,500-2,000   **DRA**

A Lalique 'Narkiss' perfume bottle, for Roger et Gallet, with company label and Shanghai perfumer's label in Mandarin Chinese, moulded 'R.L.' mark, introduced 1912.

4in (10cm) high

£1,000-1,400   **DRA**

A Lalique 'Orchis' perfume bottle', for Colgate, clear and frosted glass with rose patina, with label, moulded 'R. LALIQUE' mark, introduced 1927.

3.5in (9cm) high

£1,250-1,500   **DRA**

A Lalique 'Rosace Figurines' perfume bottle, clear and frosted glass with sepia patina, figural stopper version, engraved 'Lalique France' mark, introduced 1912.

5in (13cm) high

£1,800-2,200   **DRA**

A Lalique/Viard 'Roses' Baccarat perfume bottle for D'Orsay, crystal bottle with stopper and cover, mounted with R. Lalique figural metalwork designed by Julian Viard, in lavender suede box with gold moiré interior, stamped 'RL' on metal, introduced 1912.

5.5in (14cm) high

£2,000-2,500   **DRA**

A Lalique 'Sans Adieu' perfume bottle, for Worth, green glass with label, in wooden box, moulded 'R. LALIQUE' mark, introduced 1929.

4.25in (10.5cm) high

£500-750   **DRA**

A Lalique perfume atomiser, for D'Heraud, clear glass with black patina, original hardware, hose and ball (hardened), moulded 'R. LALIQUE' mark, introduced 1924.

6.5in (16.5cm) high

£600-800   **DRA**

A 1920s Hoffman shoe-shaped perfume bottle, black crystal with jade 'knot' stopper and enamelled and jewelled metalwork, stencilled 'MADE IN CZECHOSLOVAKIA' mark.

4.5in (11.5cm) high

£9,000-11,000　　　　　　　　**DRA**

A 1920s Hoffman perfume bottle, pink crystal with enamelled and jewelled metalwork on four sides, cupid and Psyche stopper with dauber stub, intaglio 'HOFFMAN' mark.

6.5in (16.5cm) high

£1,000-1,400　　　　　　　　**DRA**

A 1930s Hoffman perfume bottle, blue crystal with stylised jewelled metalwork, highly detailed stopper with dauber, intaglio 'HOFFMAN' mark.

6.6in (16.5cm) high

£1,500-2,000　　　　　　　　**DRA**

A Piver 'Astris' Baccarat perfume bottle, pink crystal with silver star-shaped label, stencilled 'BACCARAT' mark, boxed, introduced 1927.

2.75in (7cm) high

£4,000-4,500　　　　　　　　**DRA**

A Gravier 'Cascade' Baccarat perfume bottle, clear and frosted crystal with pale green patina, stencilled 'BACCARAT' mark, introduced 1926.

4.5in (11.5cm) high

£1,700-2,000　　　　　　　　**DRA**

An Ybry 'Desir du Coeur' Baccarat perfume bottle, pink crystal with stopper and enamelled metal cover, in box with R. Lalique glass pendant and tassel, introduced 1926.

4in (10cm) high

£2,000-2,500　　　　　　　　**DRA**

A Corday 'L'Heure Romantique' Baccarat perfume bottle, crystal with gilded detail, stencilled 'BACCARAT' mark, introduced 1928.

3in (7.5cm) high

£200-300　　　　　　　　**DRA**

A 1920s Ahmed Soliman set of three perfume bottles, Czech crystal with enamelled Egyptian goddesses, with jewelled screw caps, in green leather box.

7.5in (19cm) long

£1,000-1,500　　　　　　　　**DRA**

A 1920s Aristo perfume bottle, purple crystal with enamelled and jewelled filigree metalwork, with dauber, stencilled line 'CZECHOSLOVAKIA', metal tag 'CZECHOSLOVAKIA', 'ARISTO' label.

3.25in (9cm) high

£400-500　　　　　　　　**DRA**

A 1920s Czech perfume bottle, blue and clear crystal with enamelled and jewelled filigree metalwork, on 'lapis' ball feet, dancer stopper with dauber, stencilled oval 'MADE IN CZECHOSLOVAKIA' mark.

6in (15cm) high

£2,000-2,500　　　　　　　　**DRA**

A 1920s Czech perfume bottle, pink crystal with jewelled metalwork, stencilled oval 'MADE IN CZECHOSLOVAKIA' mark.

5in (12.5cm) high

£450-550　　　　　　　　**DRA**

A Langlois 'Shari' perfume bottle, Czech crystal with raised enamelled detail, sealed, with label, stencilled 'BOTTLE MADE IN CZECHOSLOVAKIA' mark.

c1925   4in (10cm) high

£450-550   **DRA**

A 1920s Devilbiss perfume bottle, enamelled and gilded glass with gilded metal and cloisonné enamel stopper, metal and glass ornaments, with dauber, marked 'DEVILBISS'.

4.75in (12cm) high

£2,000-3,000   **DRA**

A Devilbiss perfume atomiser, glass with black and orange decoration, with small acorn top, marked 'DEVILBISS', introduced 1926.

10in (25.5cm) high

£1,200-1,500   **DRA**

A 1920s Devilbiss perfume atomiser, amber glass with gilded finish, with removable atomiser, paper label.

6.25in (cm) high

£250-350   **DRA**

A Devilbiss perfume atomiser, amber glass with wheel engraving, on detailed metal stem and foot, introduced 1926.

5in (12.5cm) high

£500-600   **DRA**

An Arys 'Promenade Matinale' J. Viard perfume bottle, made by Depinoix in clear and frosted glass with sepia patina, with label, boxed.

c1920   4.5in (11.5cm) high

£1,200-1,500   **DRA**

CLOSER LOOK: JULIEN VIARD PERFUME BOTTLE

A Gueldy 'Le Prestige' J. Viard perfume bottle, clear glass with sepia patina, figural stopper, moulded 'J. VIARD' mark, boxed, hinge tear to box, introduced 1922.

6in (15cm) high

£2,500-3,000   **DRA**

The 1920s saw a craze for Egyptian-inspired goods following the discovery of King Tutankhamun's tomb. Many perfume bottles were made in shapes such as Pharoah's heads, sphinxes and pyramids, or decorated with heiroglyphics.

The fitted box was designed to complement the bottle. Having the original box will increase value significantly – particularly if it is in good condition.

The French sculptor Julian Viard was commissioned to design dozens of perfume bottles by a number of manufacturers. Models were sent to glass houses to be made and then finished by Viard's workshop.

There is a wide variation in quality of Viard bottles, as there was a range of producers, but the quality of the surface decoration was usually of the highest standard.

A Lubin 'Enigma' J. Viard perfume bottle, formed as a crystal pyramid with golden sphinx, resting on a bed of lotus in original box with Egyptian scarab graphics, introduced 1921.

3.5in (9cm) high

£14,000-18,000   **DRA**

A Brecher 'Sous la Charmille' J. Viard perfume bottle, made by Depinoix in glass with enamel detail, introduced 1924.

2.75in (7cm) high

£1,300-1,600　　　　　　**DRA**

A Dubarry 'Blue Lagoon' J. Viard perfume bottle, made by Depinoix in clear and frosted glass with multicoloured patina, figural stopper, introduced 1919.

4in (10cm) high

£2,200-2,600　　　　　　**DRA**

A 1930s Coty 'Muguet' perfume bottle, crystal, sealed, with label, boxed, unwrapped for auction.

5in (12.5cm) high

£450-500　　　　　　**DRA**

A deluxe issue Coty Crystal perfume bottle, with enamelled detail, attributed to Marcel Goupy, moulded 'COTY France' mark.

c1925　　　　*4.5in (11.5cm) high*

£500-600　　　　　　**DRA**

A 1920s Coryse 'Rose d'Ispahan' perfume bottle, clear and frosted glass with rose patina, sealed, with label.

6.75in (17cm) high

£500-600　　　　　　**DRA**

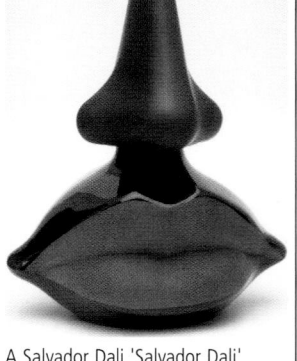

A Salvador Dali 'Salvador Dali' factice perfume bottle, in black (dark blue) glass, after his 1981 painting, 'Apparition du Visage de l'Aphrodite de Cnide dans un Paysage', introduced 1983.

12.5in (31.5cm) high

£600-800　　　　　　**DRA**

A 1920s Dralle 'Ora e Sempre' perfume bottle, crystal with cut stopper, in footed silvered metal holder.

3in (7.5cm) high

£800-1,000　　　　　　**DRA**

A Guerlain 'Sillage' perfume bottle, clear glass with raised enamel drapery and gilded detail, sealed, with label.

c1910　　　　*5.5in (14cm) high*

£450-550　　　　　　**DRA**

A Hermès 'Doblis' perfume bottle, clear and green glass, with label, in paper box replica of Hermès building, Paris.

c1955　　　　*3.5in (9cm) high*

£1,600-2,000　　　　　　**DRA**

A 1950s Kesma 'Larmes de Nuit' perfume bottle, clear and frosted glass, with label, in satin box, label to base reads 'Formule Legrain-Made in Egypt'.

5in (12.5cm) high

£1,000-1,500 DRA

A Lucien Lelong 'Jabot' perfume bottle, clear and frosted glass, sealed, with label, boxed, introduced 1939.

3in (7.5cm) high

£450-500 DRA

A 1920s Marquis 'Niradjah' Depinoix perfume bottle, black crystal with red cased crystal stopper, with label, in deluxe silver and yellow silk presentation box.

3.75in (9.5cm) high

£3,500-4,000 DRA

A 1920s Rochambeau figural perfume bottle, blown glass in shape of a grape cluster with fabric leaves, with labels, in box.

4.5in (11.5cm) long

£300-400 DRA

A 1940s Schiaparelli 'Shocking', 'Sleeping', and 'Zut' mini perfume bottle set, with glass bottles and metal and plastic screw caps, in satin-lined box.

3.5in (9cm) high

£900-1,200 DRA

A 1920s Vantines perfume bottle and face powder gift set, frosted glass bottle with cork tip stopper, resting on a silk powder box trimmed with metallic fabric and Peking glass, with contents, boxed.

Bottle 1.75in (4.5cm) high

£700-800 DRA

A 1900s Yardley & Co 'White Roses' perfume bottle gift set, clear crystal, with labels, in Art Nouveau box.

4in (10cm) high

£450-550 DRA

An Ybry 'Les Fleurs' perfume bottle, crystal with pierced stopper hung with silk cord and enamelled metal tag, boxed, introduced 1928.

3.5in (8.5cm) high

£900-1,200 DRA

A Tiffany Studios tulip lamp, the tulips are vibrant warm orange and yellow and the foliage is medium apple green to deep turquoise, the background is confetti glass, the base is an urn shape supported by five Art Nouveau columns, shade is signed 'Tiffany Studios New York 1905', signed on the burners 'P. Duplex A', base is marked 'Tiffany Studios New York'.

This glass is heavily textured so it sparkles to give the effect of sunset, thus this lamp is commonly referred to as the 'Sunset Tulip'. The base has a single socket and appears to be an original Tiffany conversion which makes this an extremely early Tiffany lamp. This lamp is a rare size.

Shade 14in (35.5cm) diam

£20,000-25,000   JDJ

An early 20thC Tiffany Studios bronze 'Windswept Tulip' lamp, with flowers on a blue confetti glass and string glass ground, the shade and base marked 'Tiffany Studios New York'.

21.5in (65cm) high

£40,000-45,000   FRE

A rare Tiffany mosaic peacock chandelier, peacock feather mosaic pattern in iridescent favrile pink, blue, purple and green glass, and finished with a green swirled peak eye, set against a solid bronze flat conical shade, lit by a very early six-socket cluster with Tiffany chain hooks, unsigned, socket cluster marked 'Benjamin Patents Mar 3 1903'.

38in (96.5cm) high

£35,000-40,000   JDJ

An early 20thC Tiffany Studios bronze 'Tyler Scroll' lamp, the scrolling decoration in dichroic glass on a graduated green ground, raised on a library base with oil font and arms, base and shade marked 'Tiffany Studios New York'.

25in (63.5cm) high

£15,000-20,000   FRE

A Tiffany Studios linenfold table lamp, shade signed on bottom of the apron 'Tiffany Studios New York 1827 Pat. Appl'd For', base is marked 'Tiffany Studios New York 584'.

Shade 19.25in (49cm) diam

£18,000-20,000   JDJ

A Tiffany Studios lamp, the shade is supported by a six-light candelabra base, lamp is finished with rare Linenfold glass top cap, shade is signed 'Tiffany Studios New York 1927 Patent Appl'd For', base is signed 'Tiffany Studios New York.

Shade 19in (cm) diam

£18,000-20,000   JDJ

A Tiffany Studios table lamp, with Woodbine shade on a bronze lamp base with adapted oil-font, a couple of minor breaks, stamped 'TIFFANY STUDIOS NEW YORK'.

17in (43cm) high

£12,000-14,000   DRA

A Tiffany Studios table lamp, with a Four Virtues gilt base with four sockets, a couple of short breaks, stamped 'TIFFANY STUDIOS NEW YORK', shade '1482', base '557'.

25.5in (64.5cm) high

£15,000-20,000   DRA

A Tiffany Studios pomegranate mosaic glass and bronze table lamp, upheld by a three-prong spider, over a three-socket cluster, signed on base 'Tiffany Studios, New York 370' and 'S182'.

16in (41cm) diam

£8,000-10,000   SK

A Tiffany Studios gilded bronze and brown glass lamp, the lampshade imitating pleated silk, signed 'Tiffany Studios New York 590' on the base and 'Tiffany Studios New York 1938, Pat.Appl'd for' on the lampshade.

19.75in (50cm) high

£8,000-10,000   SOTP

A Tiffany Favrile table lamp, the bell-form shade with twelve ribs in gold Favrile, the shade signed 'L.C. Tiffany L167L', the base signed 'L.C. Tiffany-Favrile', enlarged aperture on shade.

16.25in (41cm) high

£1,500-2,000   SK

A Tiffany Studios twelve-light Lily lamp, one shade broken, stamped 'TIFFANY STUDIOS NEW YORK. 382'.

21in (53cm) high

£6,500-7,500 DRA

A Tiffany Studios floor lamp, with a linenfold shade on a bronze harp base covered in verdigris patina, stamped 'TIFFANY STUDIOS NEW YORK', shade '1938 PAT APPL'D FOR', base '423'.

54.75in (139cm) high

£2,000-3,000 DRA

A Handel table lamp, acid-etched shade reverse-painted with pink roses and yellow butterflies, over a classical bronzed base, shade signed 'Handel 6688', and stamped 'HANDEL Lamps' with patent number.

23.25in (59cm) high

£6,000-8,000 DRA

A rare Handel floor lamp, its panelled cattail shade lined with caramel slag glass over a three-socket fluted bronzed base with sphinx, base marked 'HANDEL'.

63in (160cm) high

£18,000-22,000 DRA

A Handel table lamp, acid-etched shade reverse-painted with a Venetian scene, over bronzed base with two-tone patina, shade signed 'HANDEL 5935', and stamped 'HANDEL Lamps' with patent number, base unmarked, 0.5in (1cm) clamshell chip to interior.

25in (63.5cm) high

£5,000-7,000 DRA

A Handel table lamp, acid-etched glass shade obverse-painted with stylised leaves, over a three-socket bronzed base, shade signed 'A. 5940' and Handel patent no., base stamped 'HANDEL', crack around shade.

24.25in (61.5cm) high

£900-1,100 DRA

A Handel glass and bronze table lamp, reverse-painted with textured shade composed of six panelled sides, each panel hand-painted with stylised flowers on interior of shade, rests over three sockets, on ribbed standard raised on circular foot, signed 'Handel 6805' on rim, cloth Handel label on base.

c1920 *22in (56cm) high*

£1,500-2,000 SK

An Oscar Bach table lamp, with original Steuben gold Aurene globe shade, the lamp with pierced and sculpted brass-washed metal base with nude male figures, theatrical masks, and a satyr finial.

25.75in (65.5cm) high

£1,800-2,200 SDR

A pair of brass candlesticks, in the manner of W. A. S. Benson, with counterbalance ball, unmarked.

12.25in (31cm) wide

£250-350 WW

A Bergmann & Loetz cast bronze table lamp, the cast bronze base with figure of a water carrier before a Classical column with ring gallery mounted with a Loetz cameo glass shade, bears cameo signature.

13.5in (34cm) high

£2,500-3,500 FLD

DECORATIVE ARTS

An early 20thC Edgar Brandt marble and patinated metal hanging lamp, with domed marble shade in a metalwork frame suspended by wrought metal linked chain, signed.

14in (36cm) diam

£2,500-3,000   SK

A large gilt bronze and alabaster lamp by Edgar Brandt (1880-1960), the four conformingly pierced lancet supports above a circular fluted collar, on an octagonal Portor marble plinth, bronze base stamped 'E.Brandt'.

37.25in (95cm) high

£40,000-60,000   SOTH

An Edgar Brandt 'Cobra' lamp, gilt-bronze and internally decorated glass shade engraved 'Daum Nancy' with the Croix de Lorraine, base stamped 'E.BRANDT'.

c1925   *19in (48cm) high*

£12,000-15,000   SOT

A Daum 'rain scene' lamp, cameo and enamel glass decorated with rain scene on shade and base, cameo-carved rain drops extend diagonally around the shade and base to give the effect of being blown by the wind, signed 'Daum Nancy'.

13in (33cm) high

£16,000-18,000   JDJ

A pair of Art Nouveau bronze lamps with Loetz glass shades, cast from a model by Gustave Gurschner, cast marks, artist's signature and made in Austria, small chip to the rim of one shade.

19in (48.5cm) high

£7,000-8,000   WW

A wrought iron and glass table lamp by Muller Frerès, the domed shade supported by a stylised scrolling stem, shade with etched mark 'Muller Frès/Luneville', base case with 'Th Béramy.

c1930   *25.25in (64cm) high*

£8,000-12,000   SOTH

A Pairpoint puffy lamp, with hummingbird and chrysanthemum shade.

21.25in (54in) high

£1,500-2,000   POOK

A Pairpoint Puffy pansy lamp, with four large panels reverse-painted in sienna, the exterior with gold enamel highlighting, shade rests on a four-arm base, shade signed 'The Pairpoint Corp'n'.,the base signed 'Pairpoint Mfg.', 'P' within a diamond and 'B3'.

Shade 12in (30.5cm) diam

£10,000-12,000   JDJ

A pair of Prairie School architectural wall lanterns, in bronze and glass, possibly designed by Frank Lloyd Wright, originally fitted for gas.

20in (51cm) high

£9,000-11,000   SK

A pair of Quezel wall lights, with iridescent glass and patinated metal, marked 'Quezel'.

19.5in (50cm) high

£4,500-5,500   SK

A Roycroft hammered copper and mica helmet-shade table lamp, Orb & Cross mark.

14.5in (36cm) high

£2,000-2,500   DRA

A Steuben Millefiori lamp, bright green leaf-and-vine decoration interspersed with millefiori flowers, set against a gold iridescent background with flashes of pink and green, base signed with white enamel mark 'Aurene Haviland & Co.'

8.5in (32.5cm) diam

£8,500-10,500   JDJ

A monumental Steuben moss agate chandelier, inverted bell-shaped shade mounted in metal frame, frame attached to two swirling stylised leaf designs leading to wrought iron arms supporting the shade.

14in (35.5cm) diam

£15,000-18,000   JDJ

A Gustav Stickley chandelier, with five hammered copper drops pierced with hearts and lined in original yellow glass cylinders, no visible mark.

37in (94cm) long

£10,000-14,000   DRA

A wrought iron and moulded glass table lamp by Raymond Subes (1891-1970), the domed mottled orange shade above a tapering stem and circular base, mounted with stylised foliage.

27.5in (70cm) high

£15,000-20,000   SOTH

A Dirk Van Erp hammered copper and mica table lamp, windmill mark with box, original mica.

c1911   16in (40.5cm) high

£5,000-7,000   DRA

A Dirk Van Erp hammered copper and mica table lamp, its shade with spade-shaped riveted straps on a single-socket, pear-shaped base, windmill stamp with 'DIRKVANERP' and remnant of 'D'Arcy Gaw'.

16.5in (42cm) high

£4,200-5,000   DRA

An Art Nouveau Austrian table lamp, with glass, silk and patinated and textured metal, resting on an oak leaf-formed metal support backed by a caramel-coloured silk shade.

25.75in (65cm) high

£1,200-1,500   SK

An Arts & Crafts hammered metal chandelier with Monk's heads, unmarked, brass-wash patina.

£1,000-1,400   DRA

A pair of forged iron tall candelabra, each with three bobeches and twisted shafts.

£1,200-1,500   DRA

A C. R. Ashbee silver hinged condiment jar, with jade cabochons and poppy-patterned spoon, CRA, lion, crest, and 'E' hallmarks.

3in (7.5cm) high

£1,500-2,000　　　**DRA**

A Canadian Birks Arts & Crafts sterling silver heavy gauge tea and coffee set, comprising a teapot, coffee pot, creamer and covered sugar, the bases stamped 'BIRKS STERLING 41/5'.

Coffee pot 10.8in (27.5cm) high

£1,500-2,000　　　**TCF**

A German Bruckmann und Söhne tall silver chalice, with hardstone cabochons and gilt interior, stamped 'B'.

11.25in (27.6cm) high

£1,300-1,600　　　**DRA**

A Cartier enamelled silver pin dish, by Jacques Cartier, initialled 'MMcK' in script, also inscribed 'THE FOUNTAIN OF WISDOM FLOWS THROUGH BOOKS', London.

1929　　*3.5in (9cm) high*

£250-300　　　**L&T**

A pair of James Dixon & Sons silver candlesticks, marks for Sheffield.

1909　　*8.75in (22cm) high*

£2,000-2,500　　　**L&T**

A Christopher Dresser silver toast rack, stamped 'H&H 2556', with registration mark, resoldering at base of one divider.

5in (12.5cm) wide

£200-300　　　**DRA**

A Jugendstil silver photograph frame, designed by Theodor Fahrner, set with chrysoprase cabochons, stamped marks.

2.25in (5.5cm) high

£800-1,200　　　**L&T**

A Gorham sterling silver Art Nouveau footed bowl, the rim decorated with floral baskets.

c1905

£650-850　　　**FRE**

A Guild of Handicrafts hammered sterling silver shaker, with jade cabochons, GH, lion, lion's head, and 'e' hallmarks.

The Guild of the Handicrafts was founded by C. R. Ashbee in Whitechapel, the Cotswolds, in 1888.

2.75in (7cm) high

£700-900　　　**DRA**

A William Hutton & Sons sterling silver milk pitcher, embossed and enamelled with tulips, small flake to one enamelled drop, anchor, lion, shield, 'H' hallmarks.

5.25in (13.3cm) high

£900-1,200　　　**DRA**

A five-piece 'Blossom' tea service, designed by Georg Jensen (1866-1935), comprising teapot, hot water pot, sugar bowl and milk jug, stamped 'Denmark', 'Georg Jensen/ Silversmiths Ltd', 'Sterling' and '2D', sides stamped with maker's hallmark.

22.25in (56.5cm) wide tray

£22,000-25,000　　　**SOTH**

An A. E. Jones hammered silver jar and cover, with applied cruciform decoration with turquoise ceramic cabochons, scratch to body, some minor dents, stamped 'A.E.J', anchor, rampant lion.

4.5in (11.4cm) high

£350-400　　　**DRA**

A Liberty & Co. 'Cymric' hammered sterling silver spoon, marked L&Co, anchor, lion, 'D', CYMRIC, 394.

8in (20.3cm) long

£600-800 DRA

A Liberty & Co. sterling silver shaker, some losses to enamel and a few dents, L&CO, anchor, lion, 'I' hallmarks.

3.5in (8.6cm) high

£350-400 DRA

A Liberty & Co. 'Cymric' silver and enamel tea caddy and matching spoon, designed by Archibald Knox, Birmingham.

1903 *6in (15cm) high*

£6,000-7,000 L&T

A Liberty and Co. silver caddy spoon, designed by Archibald Knox, with shovel-planished bowl below Celtic style intertwined handle.

3.5in (9cm) high

£350-450 FLD

A Liberty & Co. 'Cymric' silver vase, designed by Archibald Knox, stamped marks.

8.75in (22cm) high

£2,000-2,500 L&T

A Canadian Petersen sterling silver small tazza, with stamped maker's marks to base.

3in (7.5cm) high

£400-600 TCF

A Canadian Petersen sterling silver footed bowl, the interior with light gold wash, with stamped maker's marks to base.

3.5in (9cm) high

£500-750 TCF

A pair of Canadian Petersen sterling silver candlesticks, with applied curling leaf supports, with stamped maker's marks to base.

3.25in (8cm) high

£400-600 TCF

A Canadian Petersen sterling silver goblet, the bowl with gold-washed interior, the exterior engraved 'R', with stamped maker's marks to base.

4.5in (11.5cm) high

£750-1,000 TCF

A Canadian Proctor and Ellis Art Nouveau style sterling silver trophy, embossed with horses and carts in a band of panels around the rim, the base stamped 'PROCTOR STERLING 925/1000 FINE' and with the Ellis Brothers mark.

Ellis was the second of a small number of Canadian silver and jewellery companies taken over by Birks. Ryrie Brothers had merged in 1917, with Ellis Brother merging in 1933.

6.25in (16cm) high

£750-1,000 TCF

A silver travelling shaving brush and cover, by Ramsden & Carr, with Tudor rose to the pull-off cover and inner mounted brush, with screw-turned base, London.

1904 *3.25in (8.5cm) long*

£350-450 L&T

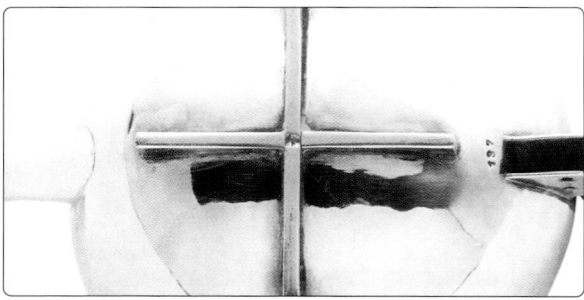

An important and rare silver-plated brass and ebony tea infuser, designed by Marianne Brandt, model no. MT 49, stamped '137' to the underside and to the rim of the lid.

c1927   *6in (15cm) wide*

£150,000-200,000   **SOT**

A silver plate toast rack, designed by Christopher Dresser, for James Dixon & Son, stamped marks, no. 66, stamped facsimile signature.

Designed 1879   *5.5in (14cm) high*

£4,000-5,000   **L&T**

A silver plate cruet stand, designed by Christopher Dresser, for Hukin & Heath, stamped marks 'Designed by Dr. C. Dresser', serial no. '1882'.

Designed 1878   *4.25in (11cm) wide*

£500-700   **L&T**

A silver plate sugar bowl, designed by Christopher Dresser, for Hukin & Heath, in the form of a tureen, stamped marks.

5in (13cm) diam

£900-1,200   **L&T**

PEWTER

A pewter decanter, designed by Joseph Maria Olbrich, manufactured by Eduard Hueck, Lüdenscheid, with raised artist's monogram and 'EDELZINN/1865/E. HUECK'.

31.5in (34cm) high

£5,000-6,000   **SOT**

A pewter punch bowl, with green glass insert, designed by Albin Müller, manufactured by Eduard Hueck, Lüdenscheid, with artist's monogram to both sides.

17in (431cm) wide

£9,000-11,000   **SOT**

A pair of pewter candelabra, designed by Hugo Levan, model no. 4531, manufactured by J. P. Kayser Sohn, Krefeld, with raised mark 'KAYSERZINN/4531'.

10in (24.5cm) high

£5,000-6,000   **SOT**

A Continental pewter grotesque bird inkwell, attributed to Kayserzinn, with ceramic green liner, unmarked.

4in (10cm) high

£350-400 **WW**

A Liberty Tudric pewter biscuit barrel, designed by Archibald Knox, model 0194, stamped marks.

5.5in (14cm) high

£400-600 **GHOU**

A Liberty & Co. 'Tudric' pewter twin-branch table candelabrum, designed by Archibald Knox, stamped marks '0530'.

11.25in (28.5cm) high

£900-1,100 **L&T**

A pair of Art Nouveau Tudric vases, the underside stamped '8/Tudric/029'.

10in (25.5cm) high

£400-500 **HALL**

A polished pewter wall mirror, attributed to Alexander Ritchie, Iona.

16.25in (41cm) wide

£600-800 **L&T**

An Art Nouveau WMF pewter-mounted green glass decanter, the mounts with a maiden and whiplash foliage, with detachable stopper, stamped marks.

15in (38cm) high

£800-1,200 **L&T**

An Art Nouveau WMF pewter and glass épergne, the cut glass central vase and bowl supported by a spreading base cast with whiplash foliage, stamped marks.

19.75in (50cm) high

£600-800 **L&T**

A WMF Art Nouveau polished pewter table centre, with embossed butterflies and curling organic forms and whiplash handles, with replaced green glass liner.

16.5in (42cm) long

£800-1,200 **FLD**

A WMF Art Nouveau polished pewter card tray, embossed with head and shoulder portraits of two ladies within lily leaf-pierced borders, with stamped maker's mark to back.

9.5in (24cm) high

£300-400 **FLD**

An early 20thC WMF polished pewter basket, with the chestnut pattern and a clear glass liner, with stamped marks to base.

13in (33cm) high

£250-300 **FLD**

An Italian early 20thC Art Nouveau polished pewter tray, with high and low relief sculptural form of a maiden lying on a pond with outstretched arms, marked 'Achille Gambo' on the base.

14.25in (36cm) long

£120-180 **FLD**

A pair of American Boston School hammered copper bookends, each with a riveted enamelled insert of a sailboat in polychrome, medium patina, unmarked.

6.25in (16cm) high

£1,000-1,500   **DRA**

An Elizabeth Burton copper jewellery box, with abalone shell inserts to top and to hinged clasp, stamped 'Burton' with hammer, cleaned patina.

6.75in (17cm) wide

£1,600-2,000   **DRA**

A Christofle 'Ecailles' dinanderie copper with silver vase, designed by Luc Lanel, factory stamped and 'B1G'.

c1920   *10in (25.5cm) high*

£1,200-1,600   **FRE**

A copper jardinière, attributed to Margaret Gilmour, with broad rim, repoussé decorated with Celtic knotwork on a hammered ground.

12.75in (32.5cm) wide

£500-700   **L&T**

A Gorham & Co. mixed metal copper and sterling silver small tray, the shaped rectangular tray with applied crabs on a 'cracked ice' surface.

1881   *10in (25.5cm) wide*

£1,700-2,000   **FRE**

A patinated copper and brass 'Teemaschine', designed by Albin Müller, manufactured by Eduard Hueck, Lüdenscheid, stamped with artist's monogram and 'EDUARD HUECK/2029' to underside of kettle.

11.75in (30cm) high

£1,500-2,000   **SOT**

A Newlyn School copper mirror, the frame repoussé decorated with trailing foliage.

15.5in (39.5cm) high

£250-300   **L&T**

A large Newlyn School copper charger, with embossed central Viking style ship within poppy floral border.

22in (57cm) diam

£700-800   **FLD**

An Onondaga Metal Shops hammered copper coal bucket, with embossed floral design, new dark patina, stamped OMS.

16.5in (42cm) high

£1,500-2,000   **DRA**

An Onondaga Metal Shops hammered copper charger, cleaned patina, OMS stamp.

19in (48cm) diam

£500-700 DRA

An exceptional, rare Charles Rohlfs jewellery box, with riveted hammered copper hinges, and wooden key on chain, carved 'R, 1901', interior of lid has green tinted shellac, and lined in original red velvet, original finish, a few minor nicks.

1901 *8.5in (21.5cm) wide*

£12,000-14,000 DRA

A Roycroft brass-washed hammered copper vase, with silver overlay, light wear to patina, Orb & Cross mark.

6in (15cm) high

£500-750 DRA

A Roycroft brass-washed hammered copper bud vase, with full-height buttresses, Orb and Cross mark.

7in (17.5cm) high

£1,500-2,000 DRA

A rare pair of Roycroft hammered copper candlesticks, cleaned patina, Orb & Cross mark.

15in (38cm) high

£2,500-3,000 DRA

A Gertrude Twichell hammered copper and enamel hinged box, decorated in the Pre-Raphaelite style, signed.

Twichell (1899-1937) a graduate of the Rhode Island School of Design, was master craftsman in The Society of Arts & Crafts, Boston. This is an unusual example of her work in that it is enamelled all around, and has figural decoration.

4.75in (12cm) wide

£5,000-6,000 DRA

A Secessionist metal hammered copper jardinière, with brass handles, possibly German or Austrian, embossed with owls and birds of paradise.

12in (30.5cm) high

£600-800 DRA

An Arts & Crafts hammered copper fire screen, embossed with a peacock on a branch, unmarked.

28in (71cm) high

£750-950 DRA

An Arts & Crafts hammered copper vase, with sea life design, artist's cipher 'C?J.', some dents, fine dark patina.

10.5in (26.5cm) high

£300-500 DRA

A Marie Zimmerman Arts & Crafts copper bowl, stamped 'M. ZIMMERMAN MAKER'.

c1920 *14.75in (37.5cm) diam*

£700-1,000 FRE

A Marie Zimmerman Arts & Crafts hand-hammered gilt-copper vase, in the form of an upright flower blossom, stamped 'MAKER-MARIE ZIMMERMAN' and '76'.

c1910 *5.75in (14.5cm) high*

£500-750 FRE

A pair of Gothic Revival brass candelabra, in the manner of Christopher Dresser, probably by Benham & Froud.

19.75in (50cm) high

£400-600   L&T

A brass trivet, by Margaret Gilmour, repoussé decorated with stylised butterfly and plant motifs, bears monogram mark.

10.5in (26.5cm) diam

£550-750   L&T

A brass charger, attributed to Margaret Gilmour, with central turquoise enamel roundel enclosed by repoussé decoration of Celtic knotwork.

23.5in (59.5cm) diam

£800-1,200   L&T

A brass wall sconce, after Margaret Gilmour, the backplate repoussé decorated with a peacock, and a pair of candle sconces below.

30.75in (78cm) high

£500-750   L&T

A Keswick School of Industrial Art brass charger, repoussé decorated with a stylised floral design and Celtic knotwork, stamped mark.

23.25in (59cm) diam

£500-750   L&T

A Keswick School of Industrial Arts brass wall mirror, repoussé decorated with stylised flora and wave pattern with entwined knotwork.

39.5in (100cm) wide

£3,000-3,500   L&T

A cast and wrought brass chamberstick, designed by Richard Riemerschmid, model no. 1459, manufactured by Vereinigte Werkstätten für Kunst im Handwerk, Munich.

7.5in (18.5cm) high

£10,000-12,000   SOT

A Wiener Werkstätte Aufsatz centrepiece coupé, designed by Josef Hoffman, with hammered and chased brass and ribbon handles, stamped 'WIENER WERKSTÄTTE JH MADE IN AUSTRIA'.

1925-131   *7.75in (20cm) high*

£14,000-16,000   SDR

A Scottish Arts & Crafts brass-framed mirror, repoussé decorated with Celtic beasts.

27.5in (70cm) wide

£500-700   L&T

A Scottish Arts & Crafts brass jardinière, the sides repoussé decorated with panels of flowering waterlilies.

12.5in (32cm) wide

£500-700   L&T

An Eric Gill 'St Martin of Tours' patinated bronze relief panel, with cast inscription 'St. Martin/ Pray/ For Us'.

This relief panel was originally commissioned in stone for Campion Hall, Brewer Street, Oxford.

1935   17.75in (45cm) high

£2,200-2,600   **L&T**

A pair of Heintz sterling-on-bronze tall candlesticks, in a pine needle pattern on a dark brown ground, stamped 'PAT.APD FOR 3078'.

14.25in (36cm) high

£800-1,000   **DRA**

A Jarvie bronze candlestick, embossed with spade-shaped leaves, unmarked, original patina.

13.75in (35cm) high

£2,500-3,000   **DRA**

A Lalique gilt-bronze medallion, an unrecorded design depicting a nurse tending a wounded soldier, engraved 'R. LALIQUE'. Provenance, Part of Lalique Family Collection.

c1915   2in (5cm) wide

£400-500   **DRA**

A Tiffany Studios gilded bronze 'Abalone pattern' desk set, comprising a double letter-holder, four blotter corners, an ink blotter, a pen-wipe holder, a perpetual calendar, paper clip, stamp box, cigarette box, and a pen tray, each piece stamped 'TIFFANY STUDIOS NEW YORK'.

£2,500-3,000   **DRA**

An Art Deco bronze plaque, decorated with allegorical figures in relief, mounted on fabric-covered wood board.

30.5in (77.5cm) wide

£750-1,000   **SDR**

A wrought iron and copper coal scuttle, designed by Dr Christopher Dresser, the body detailed with a band of riveted copper below conforming cover and ball finial.

18in (45cm) high

£130-160   **FLD**

A Norman Bel Geddes Ferris wheel-shaped bright chrome cocktail stand, with wire glass accessories and two 'Manhattan' chrome cocktail shakers, missing one rectangular glass insert, two replaced glasses, and one broken glass, unmarked.

24in (60cm) high

£3,000-3,500   **SDR**

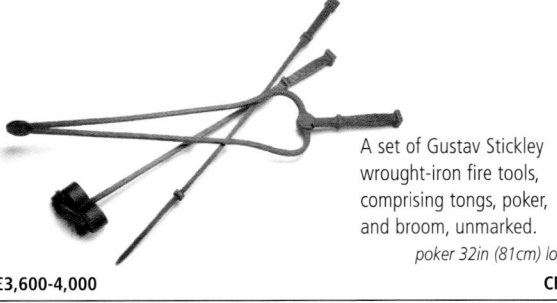

A set of Gustav Stickley wrought-iron fire tools, comprising tongs, poker, and broom, unmarked.

poker 32in (81cm) long

£3,600-4,000   **CRA**

A spelter table lighter, after Lorenzl, modelled as a young girl wearing a floral-detailed trouser suit leaning against the lighter, bears signature.

7.5in (20cm) high

£300-350   **FLD**

A gilt and patinated bronze, 'Joan of Arc', by Louis Ernest Barrias (French, 1841-1905), signed 'E Barrias' and inscribed 'Vous avez pu m'enchainer/ Vous n'enchainerez jamais la Fortune de la France'.

28.5in (72.5cm) high

£2,500-3,500   FRE

A bronze figure, 'GRENADIER, 1st GUARDS 1815', by Sir Joseph Edgar Boehm (1834-1890), signed by the sculptor and with 'Elkington & Co.' foundry stamp.

22.75in (58cm) high

£2,000-3,000   L&T

A poured bronze figure, 'Two relay runners' by Friedrich Büschelberger rectangle base of black-grey marble, base signed 'Büschelberger'.

12in (30.5cm) high

£1,000-1,500   VZ

A gilt-bronze group, 'Mother & Daughter at a Well' by Emile-Joseph-Nestor Carlier, raised on a circular base, signed 'Carlier'.

27.5in (70cm) high

£2,500-3,500   FRE

A bronze figure, 'Nymph', by Albert Ernst Carrier-Belleuse, brown patina, signed 'A. Carrier'.

28.5in (72.5cm) high

£3,500-4,500   FRE

A late 19thC French bronze bust, of Rembrandt, after Albert-Ernest-Carrier-Belleuse, signed on waisted socle and square base.

19.75in (50cm) high

£1,000-1,500   L&T

A bronze bust, of Napoleon Bonaparte, by Renzo Colombo (Italian, d. 1885), inscribed 'R. Colombo' and dated.

1885   *22in (56cm) high*

£1,300-1,600   POOK

A bronze group of 'Charity', by Paul Dubois (1829-1905), with brown patina, signed 'P. DUBOIS' and with foundry seal 'REDUCTION MECANIQUE / A COLLAS'.

24.75in (63cm) high

£4,000-5,000   L&T

A bronze figure, 'La Vitesse', by Fréderic C. Focht, of a man on a rocket hurling an arrow, green-patinated and silvered, on a black marble base, signed 'Fred C. Focht'.

c1925   *34.75in (88cm) high*

£7,500-8,500   SOTP

A bronze figure of a girl, 'Peace', by Edward Onslow Ford, (1852-1901), with green patination, raised on a rectangular green marble base, signed and inscribed 'London' and dated.

The date is significant as it is earlier than the Collie casts.

1889   *21.25in (54cm) high*

£4,000-5,000   L&T

A bronze sculpture 'L'age D'or', by Henri Fugere (French, 1872-1944), medium bronze and gold patinas, modelled as a nude female, her right arm raised and holding a floral spray, signed 'H. Fugere', and inscribed 'Salon des Beaux arts'.

35in (89cm) high

£2,000-3,000   FRE

A polychromed and patinated bronze, 'Femme de Mequinez', by Honore Henri Ple, raised on a waisted socle base, inscribed 'Henri Ple' and dated.

1883   *29.5in (75cm) high*

£15,000-20,000   **FRE**

A pair of gilt-bronze 'Mercury & Venus' figures, after Giambologna, raised on pedestal bases with applied silvered bronze relief panels.

33in (84cm) high

£1,500-2,000   **FRE**

A 19thC bronze figure of a naked male fencer, after Rudolf Kuchler (Austrian), the base incised with guilloché and signature, on a red-and-brown-veined marble plinth, sloping to the front.

16.5in (42cm) high overall

£1,200-1,800   **L&T**

A bronze plaque, by Albert Laliberté, of the profile of Marc Aurèle de Foy Suzor-Coté, moulded 'Paris 1906'.

Marc Aurèle de Foy Suzor-Coté (1869-1937) was a French Canadian painter known for his Impressionist style paintings of Quebec.

8.75in (22cm) high

£2,000-3,000   **TSG**

A bronze group, 'Wrestlers', by Joseph-Maria-Thomas Lambeaux, dark brown patina, signed 'Jef. Lambeaux' and dated.

1895   *29in (73.5cm) high*

£2,000-3,000   **FRE**

A patinated bronze, 'Dancing Figure' by Josef Lorenzl, with silvered patination raised on a stepped green onyx base, signed in the bronze.

13in (33.5cm) high

£1,000-1,500   **L&T**

A silvered bronze figure, 'The Hoop Dancer', by Josef Lorenzl, mounted to a facet-cut onyx base, signed to the lower plinth edge.

11.5in (29.5cm) high

£2,500-£3,000   **FLD**

A bronze statue of the devil, 'Le diablo demeure dans le patrimoine' ('The devil resides in the patrimony') by Albert Laliberte.

17.75in (45.5cm) high

£3,000-4,000   **TSG**

A gilded bronze figure, 'Dancer', by Josef Lorenzl, of a young naked woman in dance position, holding bouquets in both hands, hexagonal agate base, hexagonal condition plate singed 'Lorenzl, UC'.

c1928   *10.5in (26.5 cm) high*

£1,000-1,500   **VZ**

A bronze figure, 'Gladiator', by Ferdinand Lugerth (Austrian 1885-1915), brown/gold patinas, signed and monogrammed, raised on a verde antico marble base.

19.75in (50cm) high

£800-1,200   **L&T**

A gilt-bronze figure, 'Inspiration', by Eugene Marioton, Paris foundry, on a rouge marble base with applied mounts ending in toupie feet, signed 'Eug. Marioton, E. Colin & Cie'.

27in (68.5cm) high

£1,500-2,000   **FRE**

Two late 19th/early 20thC bronze figures of gentlemen, both holding swords, signed 'C. Masse'.

£5,000-6,000   **L&T**

A bronze, with dark brown patina, 'Cupid', after Auguste Moreau, modelled as a standing Cupid, with a marble column, and marble and bronze mounted base.

24in (61cm) high

£1,500-2,000   FRE

A bronze figure, after Charles Raphael Peyre, depicting Cleopatra with the asp, signed in the bronze.

40in (102cm) high

£1,200-1,800   L&T

A 19thC bronze figure of Psyche, after Pieffer, the figure holding an oil lamp in her right hand, and gilt bronze base inscribed 'Pieffer' and stamped 'TIFFANY & Co'.

20in (51cm) high

£1,800-2,200   FRE

A gilt bronze maquette, by Jean-Jacques Pradier, (called James Pradier, Swiss, 1790-1852), modelled as a seated draped beauty, at her feet sit five cherubs engaged in various pursuits, raised on a rectangular base inscribed 'Genius & Thought Enrich Industry & Industry Enriches the Nation', signed 'J. PRADIER' and with foundry mark.

10.75in (27.5cm) high

£800-1,200   L&T

A bronze female nude, by August Puttemans (1866-1927), signed in the bronze.

19in (48cm) high

£700-1,000   L&T

A bronze group, attributed to Charles de Sousy Ricketts, depicting a central naked man flanked by two female companions with another man lying indolently nearby, with dark patination.

5.75in (14.5cm) high

£1,000-2,000   JN

A bronze group, 'Io supported by Nymphs', designed by Charles de Sousy Ricketts, depicting the naked Io flanked and supported by a pair of nymphs, with rich dark patination, signed 'CR'.

Io was the daughter of Inachus, first king of Argos and was seduced by Jupiter who took on the guise of a cloud.

10.5in (26.5cm) high

£6,000-8,000   JN

A French 19thC pair of Etienne Alexandre Stella Classical females, allegorical to the seasons, dark brown patina, signed 'Stella'.

Tallest 38in (96.5cm) high

£10,000-15,000   FRE

A bronze bust, entitled 'La Sibylle', by Emmanuelle Villanis (active 1880-1920), signed 'E. Villanis', and inset with foundry seal for 'Société des Bronzes de Paris', stamped 'J. P. 5235'.

20.5in (52cm) high

£2,000-3,000   L&T

A bronze figure of a dancer, 'La Danseuse Nattova', by Prince Serge Yourievitch (1876-1969), on green marble base, numbered '120'.

8.75in (22cm) high

£1,200-1,800   L&T

An Art Nouveau gilt-bronze bust of a young girl, wearing a headscarf and shoulder length hair, her dress bound with a broad belt and buckle, on a square integral plinth base with canted corners, golden patination, indistinct incised signature to base, [?] 'Aut Nelson'.

17.25in (44cm) high

£1,800-2,200   **L&T**

A late 19thC Italian bronze of the Dancing Faun, after the antique, dark brown patina, raised in an ogee-moulded circular marble base.

23.25in (59cm) high

£2,000-3,000   **L&T**

A 19thC bronze figure of the 'The Dying Gladiator', after the antique, with brown patina.

£2,000-3,000   **L&T**

A pair of late 19thC gilt-bronze figures, depicting Minerva and Mars, standing on stepped pedestals with masks and entwined marlin and foliate-decorated bands, on bun feet.

12.5in (32cm) high

£2,000-3,000   **L&T**

A bronze figure, 'The Borghese Warrior', after the antique, dark brown patina, with 'GLADENBECK BERLIN' foundry mark.

19in (48cm) high

£1,200-1,800   **FRE**

An early 20thC French School standing male nude, bronze dark green and verdigris patina, signed indistinctly with 'Cire A. Valsuani Perdue' foundry seal.

11.5in (29cm) high

£1,000-1,500   **FRE**

A 19thC bronze group,'ANIER DU CAIRE', by Antoine Bofill, (French/Spanish, 1875-1921), modelled as an Arab standing beside a mule, raised on a naturalistic oval base, signed 'A. Bofill' and with impressed monogram.

18in (46cm) high

£4,000-6,000   **L&T**

A late 19thC French bronze group, 'Jockey Up' by Isidore-Jules Bonheur, dark brown patina, signed 'I. Bonheur'.

25in (63.5cm) wide

£5,500-6,500   **L&T**

A bronze figure, 'Bull', by Isadore Jules Bonheur, (French, 1827-1901), dark brown patina, raised on a green marble base.

Bronze 21in (53.5cm) long

£2,000-3,000   **FRE**

A bronze figure, 'Tigress Feeding Her Cubs', by Auguste-Nicholas Cain (French, 1822-1894), modelled as a tigress standing with a boar in her jaws, her three cubs at her feet, signed 'A. Cain', with Susse Freres Edition, Paris, foundry marks and seal.

42in (106.5cm) wide

£5,000-6,000   **FRE**

A bronze figure, 'Figure of a Bulldog', by Charles Curry, signed in the bronze 'C Curry Sc'.

8.75in (22cm) wide

£800-1,200   **L&T**

A bronze figure, 'Cow and Calf', by Paul Eduoard DeLaBriere, (French, 1825-1912), yellow-brown patina, the base inscribed 'Cercle d'agricole de l'arr**met vouziers concours de machault'.

10in (25.5cm) high

£1,000-1,500   **FRE**

A bronze figure, 'Two Hounds', by Alfred Dubucand (French, 1828-1894), medium brown patina, signed 'A. Dubucand'.

6in (15cm) long

£300-500   **FRE**

A bronze figure, 'Lion and Boar', by Christophe Fratin (French, 1800-1864), yellow-brown patina, modelled as a lion holding a boar in its mouth, signed 'Fratin', with Theibaut Freres, Paris, foundry seal.

21.5in (54.5cm) long

£1,500-2,000   **FRE**

A bronze figure, 'Mountain Lion', by Evangelos Frudakis (American, b.1921), bronze, signed, on a black stained wood base.

10.25in (26cm) high

£200-300   **FRE**

A bronze lion group, by Georges Gardet, signed with foundry stamp.

c1900   *23.5in (60cm) long*

£7,500-8,500   **G&H**

A late 19thC German bronze group of a boy on a donkey, the boy seated on the donkey's back and raising a crop, with twin basket panniers either side, the foliate cast base inscribed 'HOCHMUTH'.

6.25in (16cm) wide

£200-300   **DN**

A bronze group, 'Jument Normande et son Poulain' (Normandy Mare and Foal), by Pierre Jules Mene (French, 1810-1879) inscribed on base 'P. J. Mene'.

24in (61cm) wide

£3,500-4,500   **POOK**

A rare bronze group, by Pierre-Jules Mene (French 1810-1879), cast by Coalbrookedale, modelled as a goat and kid, raised on a naturalistic cast oval base, signed 'P. J. MENE'.

9.5in (24cm) high

£1,000-1,500   **L&T**

A silvered bronze figure, 'The Falconer', Pierre Jules Mene (1810-1897), signed 'P. J. Mene'.

31in (79cm) high

£5,000-7,000   **FRE**

A French bronze model of an owl after Jules Moigniez, with outstretched wings, perched on a branch, signed 'J Moigniez', mounted on oval green marble plinth.

32.5in (82cm) high

£2,000-3,000   **L&T**

A French silvered bronze group, by Charles Paillet (1871-1937), modelled as a standing pheasant and two grouse, raised on a naturalistically cast rectangular base and green marble plinth, signed 'ch Paillet, Medaille d'or'.

21.5in (54cm) high

£2,500-3,500   **L&T**

A bronze fish group, 'Carpio Carpio', by Emile Rouff, signed.
c1910 18.5in (47cm) long
£3,000-3,500 G&H

A pair of 18th century bronze female mask sphinxes each with decorative headdresses and tasselled drapes, on underscrolled plinth bases, dark green patination.
15.25in (39cm)
£3,000-4,000 L&T

A bronze sculpture, 'Furietti Centaur', after the antique, dark brown patina, raised on a stepped veined marble rectangular base.
6in (15cm) wide
£600-800 L&T

A pair of 19thC Neoclassical French patinated bronze and gilt ewers, each with acanthus-cast scrolling handles, with griffin terminals raised on a black slate plinth.
15in (38.5cm) high
£3,000-4,000 L&T

A 19thC bronze ewer with foliate and leaf scroll decoration, the top with a triton and a sea nymph holding a conch shell above Classical scenes and foliate garlands, on a fluted spreading foot with plinth base.
22.25in (56cm) high
£300-400 L&T

A bronze figure, 'Leaping Deer', by Gerhard Schliepstein, with dark brown patina, probably executed by H. Noack, Berlin, the rear base edge signed 'G. Schliepstein'.
1924 10in (25cm) high
£2,000-3,000 VZ

A pair of early 18thC Continental, possibly Italian, ormolu figures of horses, each finely cast and chased horse rearing atop an associated black marble base.
31.5in (80cm) wide
£10,000-15,000 FRE

A pair of late 19th/early 20thC French marble and gilt-bronze urns, each with pineapple finial and lotus leaf cover, the swan neck handles with husk and foliate ribbons, the circular fluted and laurel socle on square inset corner base.
£4,500-5,500 L&T

A pair of mid-19thC bronze urns on marble columns of campana form, each with lobed lower section, reeded handles and spreading foot, on stepped cylindrical variegated green marble pedestal with bronze collar.
15.75in (40cm) wide
£1,500-2,000 L&T

A 19thC French bronze vase, cast with frolicking putti and trailing leaves, stamped 'Clodion' below one handle.
15.75in (40cm) high
£3,000-4,000 L&T

A French silvered bronze inkwell, 'Serpent Attacking Two Birds', after Pierre Jules Mene, raised on a green marble base, signed 'Mene'.
9in (23cm) wide
£500-800 FRE

A late 19th/early 20thC French gilt-bronze & ivory figure, 'Victory', raised on a green marble base, signed 'E. Bernoud', lacks spear.

10in (25.5cm) high

£800-1,200   FRE

A gilded bronze and ivory figure, 'La Fileuse', by Albert Carrier-Belleuse, signed.

c1885   2.5in (32cm) high

£6,500-7,500   G&H

A patinated and cold-painted bronze and ivory figure, 'Danseuse', by Demêtre Chiparus, with onyx painted base, engraved 'D. Chiparus'.

c1928   21.5in (54.5cm) high

£25,000-30,000   SOT

A patinated and cold-painted bronze and ivory figure, 'Danseuse de Kapurthala', by Demêtre Chiparus, engraved 'Chiparus' and with embedded foundry disk for 'Les Neveux de J. Lehmann', the figure stamped '54' and 'Made in France' behind one shoe.

22.25in (56.5cm) high

£25,000-30,000   SOT

A patinated and cold-painted bronze and ivory figure, 'Les Amis de Toujours', by Demêtre Chiparus, with a gilt-bronze-mounted onyx swivel pedestal, engraved 'Chiparus', bronze stamped 'MADE IN FRANCE' and '105', pedestal stamped 'MADE IN FRANCE'.

c1928   25in (63.5cm) high

£45,000-50,000   SOT

A bronze and ivory figure, 'Chained Dancer', by Demêtre Chiparus, carved ivory and bronze, gold painted, with brass chain, conical ascending square base of light green onyx, base signed 'Chiparus'.

c1925   12.5in (31.5cm) high

£15,000-20,000   VZ

A bronze and ivory, 'Sculpture Group', by Dambros, cast as two workers seated on a bench, signed in the bronze.

6.25in (16cm) high

£400-600   **L&T**

A bronze and ivory figure, 'Little Pierrot', by Georges Omerth, signed in the bronze, stamped number '5195', raised on a circular onyx base.

7.25in (18.5cm) high

£500-750   **L&T**

A bronze figure, 'Danseuse au Bandeau', by Paul Philippe, cold-painted and parcel-gilt bronze, carved ivory and onyx on wood plinth, cast by Rosenthal und Maedar, signed 'P.Phillipe' and 'RuM'.

c1925   *29.25in (74in) high*

£25,000-30,000   **SOT**

A carved ivory and bronze figure, 'The Source', by Ferdinand Priess, young woman in long, gold-painted garb, which exposes her right breast, leaning on a three-sided parapet wall with applied mythological face, surrounding an arc-shaped protruding base plate with round basin hollow.

c1925   *11.5in (29cm) high*

£10,000-15,000   **VZ**

A cold-painted and patinated bronze figure, 'Charleston Dancer', by Johann Philipp Ferdinand Preiss, carved and painted ivory and marble, base engraved 'F. Preiss'.

c1925   *15in (38cm) high*

£12,000-18,000   **SOT**

A pair of bronze and ivory bookends, Roland, Paris, depicting two seated jesters with eccentric headgear, each with birds perched on their knees, raised on marble plinths, signed on the plinths 'Roland Paris'.

6.25in (16cm) high

£1,800-2,200   **L&T**

A gilt bronze and ivory group, 'Skating Figures', by Louis Sosson, raised on an onyx plinth, signed to the base.

7.5in (19cm) high

£1,500-2,000   **L&T**

A 20thC French bronze and ivory erotic cigarette box, the hinged lid surmounted by a reclining female figure in full-length robe, opening to reveal her 'déshabillé'.

5.5in (14cm) wide

£600-800   **L&T**

An early 20thC Austrian cold-painted bronze figure, 'Running Moor', by Franz Bergman, holding a spear or staff, on a naturalistic base, impressed Bergman amphora, 'GESCHUTZT'.

9.5in (24cm) high

£800-1,200   **FRE**

An Austrian cold-painted bronze group, 'Concubine and Shahib', by Franz Bergman, in bronze, signed 'Nam Greb' with Bergman Amphora mark.

7.5in high (19cm)

£1,200-1,800   **FRE**

A Bergmann cold-painted bronze figure of a carpet seller, the standing figure holding a carpet, bearing Bergmann Amphora stamp.

8in (20.5cm) high

£1,500-2,000   **FRE**

A late 19th/early 20thC Austrian cold-painted bronze figure by Carl Kauba, in the form of a recumbent Native American smoking a pipe, signed 'C. Kauba'.

10in (25.5cm) high

£2,000-3,000   **L&T**

An early 20thC Austrian erotic bronze figure, modelled as a draped young lady, her gown opening to reveal her nude, on a raised marble base.

5.75in (14cm) high

£400-600   **FRE**

A large Austrian cold-painted bronze figure, cast as an Arabic water carrier, the turbanned male figure carrying an animal skin bladder on his back, naturalistic marble plinth.

19in (48cm) high

£1,500-2,000   **L&T**

An Austrian painted bronze group, depicting an Arabian teacher reading from a book to four children seated on a carpet.

5in (13cm) high

£350-450   **A&G**

A large Austrian cold-painted bronze figure, depicting a Native American realistically cast and painted holding a peace pipe in his right hand, stamped 'GESCHUTZT'.

20in (51cm) high

£6,000-8,000   **L&T**

A late 19th/early 20thC Austrian cold-painted bronze figure, in the form of an Arab riding a camel and holding a long rifle.

12in (30cm) high

£1,500-2,000   **L&T**

A late 19th/early 20thC Austrian cold-painted bronze boudoir lamp in the form of an Arab seated beneath a tent.

10in (25cm) high

£1,000-1,500   **L&T**

An early 20thC Austrian cold-painted bronze figure of the slave seller, standing on a tasselled carpet, chain around slave girl's arm is lacking.

8in (20.5cm) high

£1,200-1,800   **FRE**

DECORATIVE ARTS

A late 19th/early 20thC cold-painted bronze falcon, by Bergmann, perched on a rock, bears Bergmann Amphora, stamped 'GESCH'.

6in (15cm) high

£3,000-4,000 **L&T**

A Bergmann cold-painted bronze figure of a bison, stamped '4867' with Bergman Amphora and 'GESCHUTZT'.

11.5in (29cm) wide

£4,500-5,500 **FRE**

A Bergmann cold-painted bronze figure of a cockerel, realistically modelled and painted with inset glass eyes, bearing Bergmann Amphora stamp and 'GESCHUTZT'.

12in (30.5cm) high

£3,500-4,500 **FRE**

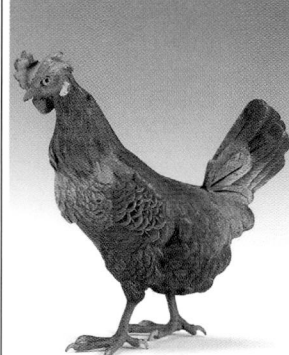

A Bergmann cold-painted bronze figure of a hen, with applied glass eyes, bearing Bergmann Amphora stamp.

8.25in (21cm) high

£500-800 **FRE**

An amusing late 19th/early 20thC Austrian cold-painted bronze figure in the form of a fox carrying a sandwich board.

8.75in (22cm) high

£1,500-2,000 **L&T**

A late 19th/early 20thC Austrian cold-painted bronze picture frame in the form of a cat peering around the frame.

6.5in (16cm) wide

£2,000-3,000 **L&T**

A large late 19th/early 20thC Austrian cold-painted bronze turkey, realistically cast and painted.

10in (25.5cm) high

£1,000-1,500 **L&T**

A late 19th/early 20thC Austrian cold-painted bronze mountain goat, raised on a naturalistic marble base.

14.25in (36cm) high

£3,500-4,500 **L&T**

An early 20thC Austrian cold-painted bronze figure of a bulldog, naturalistically cast and painted.

4in (10cm) high

£250-350 **L&T**

A Victorian painted cast iron model of a fox terrier.

9.25in (23cm) high

£300-500 **L&T**

A late 19th/early 20thC cold-painted bronze group of a jockey and gig, on foliate-decorated rectangular base.

12.25in (31cm) long

£4,000-5,000 **L&T**

A late 19th/early 20thC cast and painted white metal blackamoor, modelled standing holding a lobed oval tray, on rug-draped, stepped plinth, indistinctly signed, damaged.

43.5in (110cm) high

£2,500-3,500 **L&T**

A bronzed white metal figure of a racehorse and jockey taking a jump, by W. Zwick, with shaped wooden base.

22.75in (58cm) long

£400-600 **ROS**

A 19thC Italian marble figure of Lorenzo de Medici, after Michelangelo, with seated figure looking down in contemplation.

32in (81.5cm) high

£3,000-4,000   FRE

A gilt-bronze and ivory fashionable Victorian lady, by Armand Quernard (French, 1865-1925), on a canted white marble base, signed 'Quernard'.

13.5in (34cm) high

£2,500-3,500   L&T

A late 19thC Italian green marble and alabaster figure, modelled as a young woman leaning against a wall, her head turned to the left.

28in (71cm) high

£1,500-2,000   FRE

A late 19thC Italian marble figure of a flower girl, the standing figure with a flower basket in her arms, signed 'H Moreau'.

27.5cm (70cm) high

£1,500-2,000   FRE

A large plaster study, 'Love Triumphant', after N. F. Gillet (1712-1791), depicting Cupid resting against a festooned tree stump, on a plinth base, stamped Musée Du Louvre and inscribed around the top edge: 'Qui que tu sois, voici ton maitre.. il l'est le fut, ou le doit etre' (whoever you are, here is your master.. he is or he should be - i.e. love).

£2,500-3,500   L&T

A white marble bust of W.H. Cassells, by Hiram Powers, inscribed.

Walter Richard Cassells was a poet and critic of theology. He commissioned the bust in 1868.

24in (61cm) high

£5,500-6,500   L&T

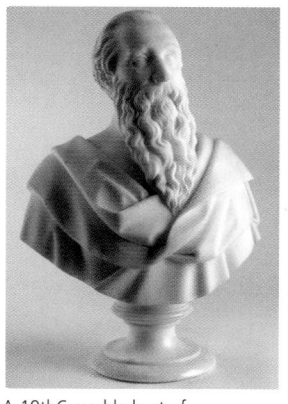

A 19thC marble bust of a gentleman, by Peter Francis Connelly (American 1841-1902), raised on a socle base, signed 'P. F. CONNILLY, FECIT'.

21.25in (54cm) high

£800-1,200   L&T

A white marble bust of a lady, by Alfred Courtens (Belgian, 1889-1967), signed and dated, with a mahogany pedestal.

1921   *31.5in (80cm) high*

£2,000-3,000   L&T

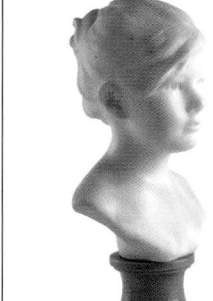

A marble bust of a young girl, by Edouard-Charles-Marie-Houssin (French, 1847-1917), signed 'E. Houssin', on a grey marble socle.

11in (28cm) high

£3,000-5,000   L&T

A pair of early 20thC Italian specimen marble busts of blackamoors, composed of lapis lazuli, sienna, variegated rouge, white carrera and black marbles, on ogee-moulded marble bases.

14.5in (37cm) high

£1,500-2,000   FRE

A pair of late 19thC specimen marble busts, 'Dante' and 'Beatrice', by F. Vichi, raised on canted rectangular marble bases, signed 'F.Vichi, Firenze'.

26.75in (68cm) high

£2,500-3,500   L&T

A 19thC marble stand, the conch shell dish top carved with a central satyr's head flanked by twin serpents and upheld on twin marlin supports on an oval mottled red and black marble pedestal base.

9.5in (24cm) high

£1,000-1,500   L&T

DECORATIVE ARTS

A pair of Blue John and black marble obelisks, the plinths with inset panels on square bases.

17.5in (44cm) high

£5,000-6,000   **L&T**

A 19thC Blue John and marble obelisk with white marble collars and a square plinth base.

14.25in (38cm) high

£4,500-5,500   **L&T**

A 19thC Blue John and marble urn on plinth, the urn with spreading foot on a square black base, the square plinth with white marble collars and outset base.

10in (25cm) high

£3,000-4,000   **L&T**

A 19thC Blue John urn with lobed lower section and separate socle, chips.

7.25in (18cm) high

£2,500-3,500   **L&T**

A Victorian Blue John goblet, the deep-dished bowl on a turned tapered stem, raised on a moulded circular foot.

6in (15cm) high

£2,500-3,500   **L&T**

TERRACOTTA

A late 19th/early 20thC Austrian painted terracotta bust of a Nubian boy, by Goldscheider, model 1365, on plinth base, stamped 'Reproduction R**' and '1365/53'.

21.75in (55cm) high

£2,500-3,500   **L&T**

Left: An early 20thC Goldscheider painted terracotta bust, of a Nubian girl, Model 1102, wearing a turban and a low cut blouse, signed 'J du Perrant and Frederick Goldscheider', stamped 'Reproduction Réservée'.

26in (66cm) high

£2,500-3,000   **L&T**

Right: An early 20thC Goldscheider painted terracotta bust of a Nubian boy, model 1645, wearing a loosely draped robe, with plaque 'F. Goldscheider Vienna', stamped 'Reproduction Réservée'.

23.75in (60cm) high

£4,000-5,000   **L&T**

A late 19th/early 20thC Austrian painted terracotta figure, of a Nubian man, by Goldscheider, Model 895, with a necklace and robed garment, the base with plaque 'F Goldscheider Wien' and stamped 'Reproduction'.

23in (58cm) high

£2,500-3,000   **L&T**

A late 19th/early 20thC Austrian painted terracotta figure, of a seated Nubian youth, by Goldscheider, model 1048, playing a flute, with necklace and loosely draped loin cloth, with plaque stamped 'Goldscheider 1048, Reproduction Réservée'.

41.75in (106cm) high

£4,500-5,500   **L&T**

An early 19thC terracotta figure, depicting 'Diana with a greyhound', by Joseph Gott (1791-1850), signed and dated.

1824   *2.75in (7cm) high*

£3,500-4,500   **L&T**

A late 19th/early 20thC Austrian painted terracotta model of a cat, seated with a ribbon tied around its neck, with inset glass eyes; and another model of standing cat.

8in (20cm) wide and 10 in (25cm) wide

£1,000-1,500   **L&T**

A large Austrian painted terracotta group of two seated cats cradling a young kitten, with inset eyes and on a naturalistic grassy oval base.

18.25in (46cm) wide

£550-650   **L&T**

A 19thC pair of terracotta hounds seated on their haunches, gazing forward attentively, each wearing a collar, on plinth bases, some damages.

28.75in (73cm) high

£2,000-3,000   **L&T**

An area rug, with large leafy pattern, in the style of William Morris, in tones of dark red.

96in (244cm) long

£700-1,000   **DRA**

A room-size rug in an Iznik pattern, in the style of William Morris, on an emerald field.

144in (366cm) long

£700-1,000   **DRA**

An Arts and Crafts 'Hunting' carpet, designed by George Bain, machine woven with huntsmen with dogs, deer, boar and horses, made by Quayle & Tranter Ltd, Kidderminster, label to the reverse.

144in (366cm) long

£2,500-3,000   **L&T**

A 'Donegal' carpet, designed by Gavin Morton and G. K. Robertson, made by Alexander Morton & Co.

187.75in (477cm) wide

£14,000-16,000   **L&T**

A 1930s Nichols Chinese Art Deco room-size wool carpet, depicting an interior vignette surrounded by floral border, on jade ground.

175.5in (445cm) long

£1,500-2,000   **SDR**

A Scottish Art Nouveau silkwork-embroidered panel, a pair of birds perched on a stylised flowering tree reserved on a blue woven cotton ground.

28in (71cm) long

£1,100-1,400   **L&T**

Six panels of Morris & Co. floral-printed cotton fabric, some sewn as curtains, signed on selvage, some fading to one panel.

1880-1900   *56in (142cm) long*

£450-650 SIX   **DRA**

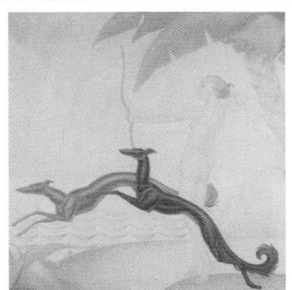

An André David lacquered 'Diane Chasseresse' panel, representing Diana hunting with two greyhounds in a cubist landscape, signed l.r. 'A. David'.

63in (160cm) wide

£25,000-30,000   **SOTP**

A lacquered and gilded 'La Conquète du Cheval' panel by Jean Dunand (1877-1942), featuring two native riders in pursuit of five wild horses, signed 'Jean Dunand' l.l.

24.5in (62cm) high

£30,000-35,000   **SOTP**

THE MODERN MARKET

The appetite for the work of modern designers continues unabated with the work of George Nakashima, Paul Evans, Lucie Rie and Wendell Castle staying at the top of every collector's wanted list. There is increasing interest in the work of contemporary designers such as Ron Arad, and ceramics by European and American potters continue to lure buyers.

As the market grows established collectors are looking for pieces which show individuality while also being typical of a designer's work. So, handmade ceramics such as those by Rie and her contemporaries, and furniture by Nakashima with its natural, free edges, fit this bill.

We may also be seeing buyers starting to move away from production pieces in favour of one-off designs and prototypes which show the hand of the master. Similarly there is increasing demand for examples with provenance, such as a special commission.

And where record prices are concerned there have been some new names on the block in the past twelve months including Gertrude and Otto Natzler, Wharton Esherick and Phillip Lloyd Powell. The Natzlers' hand-thrown ceramics covered with vibrant, volcanic glazes suit current trends. Similarly Esherick and Powell, who were friends with both George Nakashima and Paul Evans (Powell once shared a studio with Evans), made handcrafted organic furniture which is increasingly in demand by collectors. It is interesting to note that Powell is believed to have produced barely a thousand pieces, compared with the 10,000 that are reputed to have been made by Nakashima. This may have a bearing on prices for his work in the future.

Glass from the 20th century's major centres of excellence: the glasshouses of Scandinavia and Murano in Italy continues to find willing buyers, especially for examples which combine vibrant colours with modern forms and for big names such as Barovier, Venini and Seguso or design classics such as the Pezzato range by Fulvio Bianconi for Venini.

An Alvar Aalto laminated birch chair, no. 31.

23in (58cm) wide

£3,000-3,500   **SDR**

A set of four Alvar Aalto stacking leather-topped stools.

18in (45.5cm) wide

£1,500-2,000   **SDR**

An Alvar Aalto tank chair, with birch frame and red wool upholstery.

30.5in (77.5cm) wide

£1,000-2,000   **SDR**

A Finnish moulded fibreglass 'Pastille' chair, designed by Eero Aarnio, for Asko Lahti.

1967-1968

£750-950   **L&T**

A burr ash and fiddled sycamore cabinet-on-stand, designed by Fred Baier.

c1984   *63in (160cm) wide*

£6,000-7,000   **L&T**

A pink and green stained sycamore ply writing desk, designed by Fred Baier, the superstructure with pigeonholes and lidded stationary compartments, raised above a V-shaped support.

42in (106.5cm) wide

£7,500-8,500   **L&T**

A Baumann fils tambour draught screen, with undulating crest and slatted construction, bears makers label.

71.5in (181cm) high

£700-1,000   **L&T**

An early 1990s polished granite and wrought steel centre table, designed by Paul Belvoir, the circular top supported by six scroll legs.

55in (140cm) diam.

£5,500-6,500   **SOTH**

A Fontana Arte coffee table, designed by Dulio Bernabe, with painted and gilded chiselled edge glass top on walnut base, signed 'Dube Fontana Arte'.

1955   50in (127cm) wide
£5,000-6,000   SDR

A lacquered wood desk, storage unit and console, designed by Osvaldo Borsani, for Techno, the desk with an inset writing surface, the storage unit on casters with supply drawer, file drawer and wastepaper compartment, the tripartite console with hinged side sections.

1982   Desk 86.5in (220cm) wide
£4,000-6,000   SOTH

A 1950s oak-veneered cabinet, designed by Osvaldo Borsani, the six cupboard doors each with a carved wood panel depicting an animal within an angled frame.

89.75in (228cm) wide
£6,000-7,000   SOTH

A limited edition 'San Demas' suite, designed by Mark Brazier-Jones, patinated bronze and printed hide upholstery, with winged terminals and claw feet.

The San Dema sofa was produced in a limited edition of 50 in bronze polished/patina and 50 in aluminium. The limited edition chairs were produced in 100 of each metal.

30in (76cm) high
£16,000-18,000   SOTH

A black lacquered wood and black painted steel table 'T102', designed by Osvaldo Borsani and Eugenio Gerli, for Tecno, one leg labelled 'Tecno/Milano'.

c1964   46.5in (118.5cm) wide
£5,000-6,000   SOTH

A Marcel Breuer bentwood chaise-longue, manufactured by Isokon Furniture Co., London, with manufacturer's label.

52in (132cm) long
£7,000-8,000   SOT

A Wendell Castle three-legged corner vanity, in exotic hardwoods and bird's-eye maple veneer, with stool upholstered in tufted leather, both signed 'Castle 92'.

1992   Vanity 54in (137cm) high
£4,000-5,000   SDR

A Wendell Castle miniature bronze 'Angel' chair, with verdigris patina, signed 'Castle 91'.

1991   6.75in (17cm) wide
£750-950   SDR

A 1980s armchair and ottoman, designed by Achille Castiglione, in green suede, the chair with L-shaped armrests, the ottoman formed of two curved sections on a black metal foot.

28.75in (73cm) high
£3,000-5,000   SOTH

A pair of Wendell Castle yellow moulded plastic 'Molar' chairs, moulded 'WC'.

32in (81cm) wide
£1,500-2,000   SDR

A 1970s circular resin and cornelian dining table, designed by Ado Chale, the table top fitted with an internal light, the side of the table top signed 'Chale'.

65.5in (166cm) diam.

£85,000-100,000   **SOTH**

A Kusch & Co 'TV-Relax' chaise-longue, designed by Luigi Colani, formed from shaped polyurethane foam covered in purple stretch fabric.

1969   *28.5in (72cm) high*

£3,500-4,000   **QU**

An Italian 'Tube' chair, designed by Joe Colombo, for Flexform, with vinyl-covered polyurethane foam, plastic cylinders, metal and rubber grips.

1969-1970

£5,000-7,000   **L&T**

An Italian games and dining table, designed by Joe Colombo, for Zanotta, twin top laminated in plastic with height adjusted legs in chrome-plated steel, each corner fitted with pull-out drink/ash trays.

1967   *38.5in (98cm) wide*

£1,800-2,200   **L&T**

A 1960s large four fold painted screen, designed and painted by Robert Crowder.

Crowder, an American, first visited Japan in 1934. The trip began a lifelong love affair with the country and its art. His training with the great painters Shunko Mochizuki and Shimamoto-sensei served him well after his repatriation to the United States in 1943. After a brief stay in Chicago, Crowder moved west, opening a gallery in Los Angeles in the neighbourhood of Greta Garbo and other Hollywood legends. He quickly became famous for his screens and fabulous textiles, which as recently as 2005 were ordered for an international redecoration of the Chanel boutiques.

Each panel 83.5in (212cm) high

£14,000-18,000   **SOTH**

A 1950s rosewood sideboard, designed by Robin Day, for Hille, with veined black marble top and four doors below, satinwood lined.

77in (186cm) wide

£700-900   **A&G**

A Donald Deskey six-drawer D-shaped kneehole desk, of painted and lacquered mahogany.

50in (127cm) wide

£2,500-3,000   **SDR**

A 'Trône' wrought iron chair, designed by André Dubreuil, bent and welded, the shield back rising to an exaggerated scroll, slubbed fabric seat.

c1985   *56.75in (144cm) high*

£17,000-20,000   **SOTH**

A Dunbar walnut cross-legged coffee table, with Murano glass mosaic tile top, green tag and paper label.

54in (137cm) wide

£2,700-3,000   **SDR**

A Dunbar walnut three-legged side table, its top inlaid with sixteen blue and green Natzler tiles, Dunbar metal tag.

15in (38cm) wide

£8,500-9,500   **SDR**

A Dunbar lacquered mahogany credenza, on brass legs with woven-front doors and interior shelves, brass tag.

62in (157.5cm) wide

£2,000-3,000 SDR

A Herman Miller 'ESU 400' storage unit, designed by Charles and Ray Eames, with coloured masonite panels on polished chrome frame.

47in (119cm) wide

£3,000-4,000 SDR

A Zenith Edition 'DAW' chair, designed by Charles and Ray Eames, with fibreglass seat and steel wire and walnut stand, with maker's label to base.

1950 *30in (76cm) high*

£2,000-2,500 QU

A Charles and Ray Eames armchair and ottoman, for Herman Miller, model nos 670 and 671, rosewood ply framed, upholstered in black leather.

£2,000-2,500 L&T

A David Ebner sculpted purple heart console, with zebrawood feet, branded 'D.N.E. 91' and with Asian cipher.

37in (94cm) wide

£3,500-4,000 SDR

A Wharton Esherick walnut armchair, with sculpted back and arms and leather strap seat, signed '1951 W.E.'.

1951 *23.5in (60cm) wide*

£9,500-11,500 SDR

A Wharton Esherick padouk single-arm prismatic bench, the base with small storage compartment and four banks of shallow pivoting drawers illuminated from under the seat.

Provenance: From the estate of Helene Fischer, one of Esherick's most prominent patrons. This piece was featured in the Brooklyn Museum exhibition, 'Masters of Contemporary American Crafts'.

1961 *94in (239cm) wide*

£65,000-85,000 SDR

A Paul Evans welded and etched steel 'Argente' sculpture/room divider, suspended from a patinated metal frame.

This rare piece was part of Evans' 1968 'Sculptures in the Fields' series. He created only three 'Argente' masterpieces and photographed them in a Bucks County field. The Field series is considered to be among the rarest and most important of all Evans' work.

1968 *85in (216cm) wide*

£70,000-80,000 SDR

A Paul Evans copper patchwork swivel cube chair, on castors.

30in (76cm) wide

£14,000-16,000 SDR

A Paul Evans sculpture-front wall-hanging cabinet, with slate top, and interior shelves, signed 'Paul Evans 67 D.C.'
1967   *81in (205.5cm) wide*
£50,000-60,000   SDR

A Paul Evans sculpted and painted steel cocktail table, with plate glass top.
1973   *36in (91.5cm) wide*
£12,000-14,000   SDR

A Paul Evans copper, bronze and pewter console, with smoked glass top, and matching upholstered stool.
54in (137cm) wide
£3,500-4,500   SDR

A 1970s chromium plate and brass patchwork four-poster bed, designed by Paul Evans, entirely covered in panelling, the upper rails fitted for curtains.
120.5in (306cm) long
£8,000-10,000   SOTH

A pair of Danish scimitar chairs, designed by Preben Fabricus and Jorgen Kastholm, upholstered in brown leather on steel frames, branded 'Denmark'.
32in (81cm) wide
£10,000-12,000   SDR

A 1950s white-painted wrought iron bed, designed by Giovanni Ferrabini, the headboard formed as a stylised coronet.

78.75in (200cm) long
£13,000-15,000   SOTH

A 1950s pair of Fontana Arte deep blue glass side tables, each with three curved stands supporting a circular top.
27.5in (70cm) high
£70,000-80,000 PAIR   SOTH

A 1950s pair of Fontana Arte glass and bronze consoles, each with a rectangular top above waisted supports joined by twin cylindrical stretchers.
63in (160cm) long
£13,000-16,000   SOTH

A Piero Fornasetti three-drawer 'Palladian' demi-lune chest, printed in black on white ground, with brass pulls, signed 'Fornasetti/Made in Italy' and with Fornasetti Milano label.
40in (101.5cm) wide
£4,500-5,500   SDR

A Piero Fornasetti metal 'Doberman' umbrella stand.

34.25in (87cm) wide

£500-750 SDR

A Gio Ponti black lacquered four-drawer desk, by Piero Fornasetti, printed with pistol and key motif in silver and gold, on brass feet, signed 'Fornasetti/Milano/made in Italy'.

35.25in (89.5cm) wide

£6,000-7,000 SDR

A Pedro Friedeberg red-enamelled 'Hand and Foot' chair, with left hand seat on right foot base, signed twice 'PEDRO FRIEDEBERG'.

18.25in (46cm) wide

£5,000-6,000 SDR

A pair of bronze stools, designed by Elisabeth Garouste and Mattia Bonetti, each with an embroidered removeable cover depicting a star, both chairs marked 'BG' to one or two legs.

17in (43cm) high

£9,000-11,000 SOTH

Two Frank Gehry wiggle chairs, multiple layers of bonded corrugated cardboard finished at edges with brown hardboard.

c1972 *33.5in (85cm) high*

£750-950 SK

A German fibreglass 'Garden Egg' chair, designed by Peter Ghyczy, for Reuter Products, upholstered interior and articulated top.

1968

£750-950 L&T

A Herman Miller sofa, designed by Alexander Girard, upholstered in its original taupe and blue fabric, on aluminium frame.

72in (183cm) wide

£3,500-4,500 SDR

A pair of Allen Gould string chairs, on tubular black metal frames.

20in (50.5cm) wide

£1,700-2,000 SDR

A mid-20thC concrete and iron bench, designed by Willy Guhl.

76in (193cm) long

£9,500-11,500 SOTH

A Guillerme and Chambon oak sideboard, with two sliding doors inset with tiles and two end cabinets.

90.25in (229cm) wide

£4,500-5,500 SDR

A steel and glass dining table, designed by Philippe Hiquily, the X-form base lacquered and hinged.
c1970   *59in (150cm) wide*
£6,000-8,000   **SOTH**

A 1970s pair of aluminium and injection-moulded occasional chairs, designed by Knut Hesterberg.
28.5in (72cm) high
£5,000-7,000 PAIR   **SOTH**

A Higgins 'Rondelay' screen, of multi-coloured glass discs within original walnut frame.
94.5in (240cm) wide
£5,000-6,000   **SDR**

An Arne Jacobsen Swan chair, manufactured by Fritz Hansen, Denmark, seat in later purple upholstery, four-prong aluminium swivel base with manufacturer's label and control mark.
30in (76cm) high
£650-850   **SK**

A pair of teak and simulated leatherette armchairs, designed by Pierre Jeanneret.
c1955   *35.5in (90cm) high*
£6,500-7,500   **SOTH**

An 'Egg' leather and aluminium chair and ottoman, designed by Arne Jacobsen, model nos 3316 and 3127, manufactured by Fritz Hansen, Denmark, with manufaccturer's label.
c1958   *Chair 41in (104cm) high*
£15,000-18,000   **SOT**

A 1960s green lacquered bureau, designed by Maison Jansen, the fall front enclosing two shelves above an illuminated interior with tooled and gilt-leather surface.
45.5in (116cm) high
£8,000-10,000   **SOTH**

A mid-20thC Finn Juhl red sofa, with wrap-around back, single striped seat cushion in wool upholstery.
75in (191cm) wide
£2,000-2,500   **SK**

A set of four faux alligator vinyl-upholstered side chairs, designed by Finn Juhl, for Baker.
22in (56cm) wide
£1,000-1,500   **SDR**

A Vladimir Kagan cantilevered end table, with brass-trimmed top.
31in (78.5cm) wide
£4,500-5,500   **SDR**

A Dreyfuss walnut contour chair, designed by Vladimir Kagan, upholstered in white leather, 'Kagan-Dreyfuss' branded mark.
28.75in (73cm) wide
£8,000-9,000   **SDR**

A Vladimir Kagan curved floating sofa, on walnut frame, upholstered in indigo chenille.

82.5in (209.5cm) wide

£6,000-8,000 SDR

A steel two-seat leather settee, with tubular wall-mounted headrest, designed by Jorgen Kastholm and Preben Fabricius, for Bo-Ex. *1964*

£4,000-6,000 L&T

An E. Kold Christensen 'PK-80' stainless steel daybed, designed by Poul Kjaerholm, with black leather tufted cushion.

74in (188cm) wide

£6,500-7,500 SDR

A pair of Poul Kjaerholm 'PK22' chairs, covered in brown leather.

25in (63.5cm) wide

£1,800-2,200 SDR

An early Knoll maple credenza, designed by Florence Knoll, on black metal legs.

72in (182.5cm) wide

£1,000-1,500 SDR

A Knoll walnut veneer vitrine cabinet, on iron base, Knoll Associates label, and IBM inventory tag.

48in (122cm) wide

£1,000-1,500 SDR

A parchment and leather occasional 'drum' table, designed by Paul Dupré-Lafon, stamped to upper and lower leather rings 'HERMES-PARIS'.

24.5in (62cm) high

£10,000-12,000 SOTH

A Shiro Kuramata 'How High the Moon' chair, of nickel-plated wire mesh.

27.5in (70cm) wide

£6,000-7,000 SDR

A 1960's pair of Swedish oiled teak and leather chairs, designed by I. Kofod Larsen, for Olof Persons Fatolindustri, marked 'Salen 799'.

30.25in (77cm) wide

£2,000-3,000 PAIR L&T

A pair of Janette Lavèrrière iron rocking chairs, with leather seats.

47in (119cm) high

£2,500-3,000   SDR

A Philip and Kelvin Laverne bronze coffee table, the top depicting an Asian courtyard scene with light polychrome painted details, on bronze 'bundled' legs, signed 'Philip + Kelvin LaVerne'.

60.5in (154cm) wide

£5,000-6,000   SDR

A Philip and Kelvin Laverne bronze coffee table, etched with Creation detail from Michelangelo's 'Capella Sistina', signed 'Philip Kelvin Laverne/After Michaelangelo'.

65in (165cm) wide

£2,500-3,000   SDR

A pair of Christian Liagre corseted carved fir pedestals.

11.5in (29cm) wide

£1,600-2,200   SDR

An early walnut veneer centre table, by David Linley, inlaid with macassar ebony, sycamore and burrwood.

c1985   40in (102cm) wide

£2,500-3,500   SOTH

A pair of Michele de Lucchi prototype 'First' stools, signed 'Michele de Lucchi'.

1992   24.5in (62cm) wide

£350-450   SDR

A white 'Eros' side table, designed by Angelo Mangiarotti, the conical base supporting a detachable kidney-shaped top.

1971   25.5in (65cm) wide

£7,500-8,500   SOTH

A pair of Bruno Mathsson 'Eva' armchairs, with original hemp webbing on bentwood frames.

23in (58.5cm) wide

£2,500-3,500   SDR

A Bruno Mathsson 'Pernilla' lounge chair and ottoman, with original hemp webbing on bentwood frames, branded marks.

25.5in (64.5cm) wide

£1,700-2,300   SDR

A Paul McCobb birch and black laminate men's wardrobe, with shirt drawers and doors, Paul McCobb metal label.

40in (101.5cm) wide

£1,200-1,500   SDR

A pair of 'Barcelona' chairs, designed by Ludwig Mies van der Rohe, model MR-90, bent chromed flat steel joined with chromed screws, original leather strapping.

29in (74cm) wide

£15,000-18,000   SOTP

A set of four 'Brno' chairs, designed by Mies van der Rohe, for Knoll International, these of a later production, manufacturer's marks to the base.
Designed 1930

£1,200-1,500   L&T

A 1970s German Horn moulded Baydur 'Kangaroo' armchair, finished in blue, designed by Ernst Moeckl.

Due to the angled legs, this chair is often known as the 'Kangaroo' chair. Available without arms, it is moulded from a resilient form of structural composite polyurethane produced by Bayer and known as 'Baydur'.

30.5in (76.5cm) high

£100-140   QU

A Borge Mogensen design leather-upholstered three seat settee, with wooden legs, unmarked.

76in (193cm) wide

£1,200-1,600   L&T

A pair of James Mont lounge chairs, upholstered in original orange fabric, embroidered with Asian courtyard scene.

36in (94.5cm) wide

£5,000-6,000   SDR

A James Mont glass top table, with plant stand base.

27.5in (70cm) high

£800-1,000   SDR

A French bent tubular steel 'Djinn' chaise longue, designed by Olivier Mourgue, for Airborne, with foam and stretch wool fabric.
1965   22.5in (57cm) wide

£1,200-1,500   L&T

A Forrest Myers style bent steel console, with pair of matching two-seat benches.

Console 54in (137cm) wide

£1,200-1,500   SDR

ESSENTIAL REFERENCE: GEORGE NAKASHIMA

George Nakashima (1905-1990) was an American of Japanese parentage. He trained as an architect, before turning to furniture design and manufacture.

- His first furniture was made in Seattle 1940-2, before he was interned following Pearl Harbour. In the camps, he met Gentauro Hikogawa, a man trained in traditional Japanese carpentry, who taught him the use of traditional Japanese hand tools and joinery techniques.
- In 1943, American architect, Antonin Raymond, sponsored Nakashima's release from the camp and invited him to his farm in New Hope, Pennyslvania. In 1946, Nakashima set up his 'craft furniture studio' there.
- His furniture is sturdy and made from solid wood, without veneers. Nakashima worked with the texture and organic structure of the wood, choosing pieces with knots and whorls.
- He was influenced by Japanese woodwork, in particular the tea ceremony aesthetic.
- Despite the hand-worked appearance of his work, Nakeshima favoured machine production, which set him apart from the crafts revival movement.

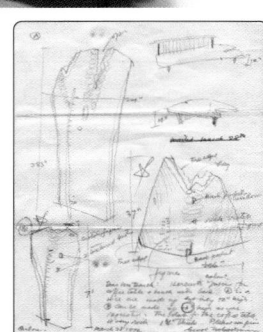

A walnut Conoid bench, designed by George Nakashima, with walnut butterfly joint, free edge seat, with hickory spindles on cylindrical tapering legs.

Accompanied by original paperwork and drawing signed and dated 1972. Inscribed on the underside, 'to the Donches George Nakashima May 1972.'

81in (206cm) long

£17,000-20,000   FRE

A pair of walnut Conoid dining chairs, designed by George Nakashima.

With copy of original bill of sale dated 1968. Irving name to underside of chairs.

35.5in (90cm) high

£8,000-9,000 FRE

A pair of George Nakashima walnut slat-back open armchairs.

30in (76cm) wide

£5,000-6,000 FRE

A George Nakashima walnut lounge chair, with free-edge writing arm.

33in (84cm) wide

£5,000-6,000 SDR

A Conoid walnut coffee table, designed by George Nakashima, the freeform shape top with terminal support and single tapering leg.

With original order receipt and drawing signed and dated 1971.

37in (94cm) wide

£9,000-11,000 FRE

A walnut circular top dining table, designed by George Nakashima, with rectangular tapering legs.

57in (145cm) diam

£3,000-4,000 FRE

A George Nakashima English walnut freeform Conoid coffee table, with single board, the top with one butterfly joint.

1960 *14in (36cm) high*

£12,000-15,000 SK

A George Nakashima 'Minguren I' coffee table, with free-edge buckeye burl top, with natural occlusions and walnut base, with a copy of the original drawing.

1981 *64in (162cm) wide*

£150,000+ SDR

A George Nakashima walnut wall-hanging cabinet, marked with client's name.

72in (183cm) wide

£10,000-14,000 SDR

A credenza, designed by George Nakashima, with free-edge top with dovetails over three vertical sliding grilled doors backed with pandanus cloth, signed and dated 'George Nakashima'.

Accompanied by original drawing signed and dated 1979 and copy of bill of sale dated 1980.

1980 *84in (213.5cm) wide*

£20,000-25,000 FRE

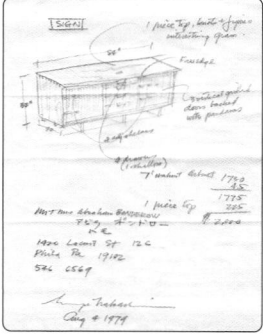

A Herman Miller 'Thin Edge' rosewood chest, designed by George Nelson, with porcelain pulls, Herman Miller foil label.

33.75in (85.5cm) wide

£1,000-1,500   **SDR**

A Herman Miller three-seat sofa and club chair, designed by George Nelson, upholstered in dark olive-green wool.

sofa: 96in (244cm) wide

£2,000-3,000   **SDR**

An 'Embryo' chair, designed by Marc Newson, for Ideé, Japan, in green neoprene, tubular steel and aluminium.

c1988   *30.5in (77.5cm) high*

£3,000-4,000   **SOT**

A Mobilier 'Rio' sculptural lounge chair, designed by Oscar Niemeyer, with bent ash frame and black leather-upholstered cushion.

67in (170cm) wide

£8,000-9,000   **SDR**

A Knoll coffee table, designed by Isamu Noguchi, with plate glass top resting on a birch base.

50.25in (127.5cm) wide

£1,200-1,500   **SDR**

A pair of steel and leather chairs, designed by Arne Norell, each with detachable headrest, the exposed leather webbing elaborately buckled.

c1970   *39in (99cm) deep*

£9,000-11,000 PAIR   **SOTH**

A Kurt Ostervig rosewood partner's desk, with twelve drawers and four pull-out shelves.

67in (170cm) wide

£2,000-2,500   **SDR**

A Vernor Panton four-piece curved modular sofa, its wire framework upholstered in burgundy fabric.

96in (243.5cm) wide

£850-1,100   **SDR**

A pair of Verner Panton wire cone chairs, with upholstered seat pads.

25in (63.5cm) wide

£850-1,100   SDR

An 'Oryx' desk, designed by V. Pargigi and N. Prina, for Molteni and Co., with moulded plastic top, glass, chrome plated steel.

1970   40.5in (103cm) wide

£700-900   L&T

An Italian teak consol table, designed by Ico and Luisa Parisi, for Singer Furniture Company, New York, with brass fittings, bears makers label.

1952   70.75in (180cm) wide

£8,500-10,000   L&T

ESSENTIAL REFERENCE: TOMMI PARZINGER

Tommi Parzinger (1903-1981) was born in Germany and settled in New York City in 1935, where he opened his first showroom, Parzinger Inc. in 1939. The company was renamed Parzinger Originals in 1946.

- Parzinger was trained as a painter and in metalwork, ceramics, glass and furniture design. He melded these talents into refined modern furniture with elegant detailing. His pieces were often covered in shimmering lacquer, leather, or precious wood veneer, with handmade pulls, metal studs and brass outlines. This gave his furniture a sense of luxury, which appealed to clients who found Bauhaus-style design too severe.
- Parzinger was at the height of his popularity in the 1950's, with clients including the Rockefeller, Mellon and Dupont families, as well as Marilyn Monroe.
- He also designed for other furniture manufacturers, including Charak Modern.

A Tommi Parzinger mahogany armoire, with ivory-lacquered doors in a subtle grid pattern, brass hardware and details, covering drawers and shelves, branded 'Parzinger Originals'.

One of only five known, this was the showroom model made exactly to Parzinger's specifications.

51.25in (130cm) wide

£10,000-12,000   SDR

A Tommi Parzinger four-poster queen-size bed, in solid mahogany stained deep brown with high polish finish, no. '185'.

64.5in (164cm) wide

£10,000-12,000   SDR

A Tommi Parzinger unique writing table, with 'Negro Marquina' marble top resting on a gold-stippled wrought iron base, with hand-forged details.

59.75in (151cm) wide

£7,000-9,000   SDR

A Tommi Parzinger six-drawer dresser, in mahogany stained deep brown with high polish, no. '217', and polished brass etched details.

72in (183cm) wide

£10,000-12,000   SDR

A pair of Tommi Parzinger armchairs,
upholstered in pumpkin velvet, on bleached maple bases.

27in (68.5cm) wide

£3,500-4,000   SDR

A Maria Pergay stainless steel bench.

47.5in (120.5cm) wide

£7,500-8,500   SDR

A pair of Charlotte Perriand grey fibreglass doors, with chrome hardware.

76.75in (195cm) high

£1,400-1,600   SDR

An Italian 'I Feltri' chair, designed by Geatano
Pesce, for Cassina, Milan, wool impregnated
with thermosetting resin, stitched edges, early
production.

1987

£2,800-3,200   L&T

A Cassina 'I Feltri' armchair, designed by
Gaetano Pesce, of thick resin-infused wool felt
and tied string laces, with padded, quilted fabric
seat.

1987   *48in (122cm) wide*

£1,800-2,200   SDR

An M. Singer & Sons four-drawer walnut dresser,
designed by Gio Ponti, with Singer labels.

47in (119cm) wide

£7,000-8,000   SDR

An M. Singer & Sons
Italian walnut three-
door sideboard,
designed by Gio
Ponti, enclosing
interior shelves and
drawers.

71in (180cm) wide

£8,500-9,500   SDR

A Gio Ponti oak
coffee table, with
glass top.

41.25in (105cm) wide

£4,000-5,000   SDR

A 1950s satin birch and vellum desk, attributed to Gio Ponti, the rectangular top with three drawers and rounded sides.

50.75in (129cm) wide

£45,000-50,000   SOTH

A David Powell leather-covered fall-front writing desk, its interior with a patterned leather writing surface, satinwood drawers and file compartments, resting on a sculpted maple base.

At first the fall-front desk is a mystery – an ovoid capsule that steps far outside the traditional form to become sculpture. Yet, its interior, once revealed, is a feat of useful details, sinuous dovetailed satinwood drawers and chambers, a flawless desktop created from multi-coloured leather strips, a functional balance to the exterior's sculptural finesse. Its creator was the under-recognised yet influential master furniture maker, David Powell (1926 - 2001). Born and trained in England, he was an apprentice to the foremost British furniture maker Edward Barnsley, then studied at the Royal College of Art. Powell started several design ventures in London, including making furniture for Queen Elizabeth II, before moving to the United States in 1969. He settled in Easthampton, Massachusetts where he practised his craft and started the Leeds Design Workshop with business partner John Tierney, taking on students for almost fifteen years. His influence can still be felt among woodworkers in the area. Powell made relatively few pieces throughout his career, but treated each work as a masterpiece, combining his technical wizardry with a rigorous design sensibility.

1982   *54in (137cm) wide*

£8,000-10,000   SDR

A Philip Lloyd Powell walnut New Hope armchair and ottoman, with fabric-upholstered cushions (not shown).

Chair 29.5in (75cm) wide

£3,000-4,000   SDR

A Harvey Probber extension mahogany and teak dining table, with two 18in (45.5cm) leaves, and six dining chairs, including two arm and four side. table:

78in (198cm) wide

£2,000-3,000   SDR

A Jean Prouvé oak dining table, with iron mounts and angular legs.

78.5in (199cm) wide

£20,000-25,000   SDR

A Jean Prouvé wall-hanging oak cabinet, with single sliding door and black metal shelf.

117.5in (298.5cm) wide

£8,000-9,000   SDR

A pair of Quigley single-door cabinets, designed by Samuel Marx, with silvered metal pulls and stylised 'Greek key' pattern, each with single interior shelf, both marked 'Quigley'.

30.5in (77.5cm) wide

£6,000-8,000   SDR

A unique 'Ring Couch', by Karim Rashid, manufactured by Galerkin, Gardena, California, with wood and steel frame with foam and vinyl upholstery.

2005   *178.5in (453.5cm) diam*

£9,500-11,500   **SOT**

A pair of sycamore nightstands, attributed to Jacques Quinet, with bronze sabots and supports.

27in (68.5cm) high

£2,500-3,000   **SDR**

An Alain Richard rosewood server, with four doors and a single cabinet door, marked with Alain Richard metal tag.

47.25in (120cm) wide

£2,500-3,000   **SDR**

A Willy Rizzo stainless steel coffee table, with integrated ice bucket on swivel base.

49in (124.5cm) diam

£1,700-2,000   **SDR**

A Gerrit Rietfeld pine 'Zig-Zag' chair,

A red and cream-painted child's high chair, designed by Gerrit Thomas Rietveld, and executed by G. A. van de Groenekan, green leather seat and back, the underside stamped 'H.G.M. G.A v.d.Groenekan bilt Nederland'.

An ISA 'Sheriff' sofa, designed by Sergio Rodrigues, in tropical hardwood with black leather cushions, with 'ISA' label.

81in (205cm) wide

c1934 *30.5in (77.5cm) high*	*c1938* *35.5in (89.5cm) high*	
£20,000-25,000 **SOT**	**£14,000-18,000** **SOTH**	**£2,000-3,000** **SDR**

An OCA rosewood coffee table, designed by Sergio Rodrigues, with tray-style top, marked 'OCA'.

59in (150cm) wide

£1,500-2,000   **SDR**

A fruitwood-veneered and wrought iron cabinet, designed by Jean Royère, the cupboard doors with decorative hinges, enclosing an adjustable shelf.

c1953   43.25in (110cm) high

£5,000-6,000   **SOTH**

A 1950s pair of Knoll International '7 Up' chairs, designed by Eero Saarinen, with grey fabric upholstery and tubular chrome metal legs.

1948   33.5in (85cm) high

£200-250   **QU**

An M. Singer & Sons two-piece Italian walnut cabinet, designed by Bertha Schaefer, with angled doors covering speakers and shelves, 'Singer' labels.

1952   40in (101.5cm) wide

£1,200-1,600   **SDR**

An M. Singer & Sons Italian walnut cabinet with angled doors, by Bertha Schaefer, fitted with interior doors, 'Singer' label.

1952   40in (101.5cm) wide

£1,200-1,800   **SDR**

A ribbon coffee table, designed by Silas Seandel, its fibreglass base covered in gold leaf over a Chinese red finish, signed 'SILAS SEANDEL.

This coffee table was one of 15 commissioned by Bloomingdale's, New York.

1978   56.5in (143cm) wide

£3,000-3,500   **SDR**

A stainless steel tub, designed by Silas Seandel, signed 'Silas Seandel'.

2003   15.75in (40cm) wide

£2,500-3,500   **SDR**

A 1960s chromium-plated metal and brushed aluminium-veneered console table, designed by Batistin Spade, with smoked glass top, the drawers with hinged circular concave handles.

48in (122cm) wide

£10,000-12,000   **SOTH**

A 1970s low marble and brushed metal coffee table, designed by Karl Springer, the stone top supported by brass-capped cylinders, one leg with artist's signature.

59in (150cm) long

£4,000-6,000   **SOTH**

A stainless steel rectangular dining table, designed by Karl Springer, with faux shagreen top, top marked with 'Karl Springer' tag.

72in (183cm) wide

£2,000-2,500   **SDR**

A corseted parchment-covered table, designed by Karl Springer.

16in (40.5cm) wide

£1,500-2,000

SDR

A four-door laminated tortoise-pattern parchment cabinet, designed by Karl Springer, flanked by a pair of suede-covered wall units with smoked glass shelves.

128in (325cm) wide

£2,500-3,000

SDR

A polished brass and black leather occasional table, designed by Karl Springer, the oval top on an angled cylindrical support, the underside signed 'Karl Springer 1990' in the leather, provenance Sir Paul Smith.

24in (61cm) wide

£5,000-6,000

SOTH

An XO 'Joe Ship', by Philippe Starck, with four black metal table legs and plate glass top.

Glass not part of the original design, but included here.

1982   50in (127cm) wide

£500-600

SDR

A Disform 'Miss Dorn' black metal chair, designed by Philippe Starck, upholstered in black leather.

1982   21.5in (54.5cm) wide

£400-600

SDR

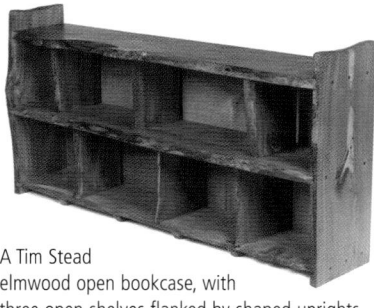

A Tim Stead elmwood open bookcase, with three open shelves flanked by shaped uprights with exposed joints.

68.5in (174cm) wide

£4,500-5,500

L&T

A Directional rocking chair, designed by Kipp Stewart, upholstered in tomato-red brushed fabric on polished steel base.

25in (63.5cm) wide

£1,200-1,500

SDR

A rare Paul Tuttle lounge chair, upholstered in stitched leather, on polished steel frame.

26in (66cm) wide

£2,200-2,600   **SDR**

A carved wood and vellum-covered travertine top console table, designed by Guglielmo Ulrich, with a textured surface, the four frieze drawers flanked by tapering supports.

67.75in (172cm) wide

£10,000-15,000   **SOTH**

A glass fibre reinforced polyester 'chairpiece' prototype, designed by Floris Van Den Broecke, upholstered in polyether foam and stretch Jersey wool.
1969

£4,000-5,000   **L&T**

A moulded plywood 'Queen Anne' chair, designed by Robert Venturi .

24in (61cm) wide

£2,500-3,000   **SDR**

Two mid-20thC tall mahogany-veneered side cabinets, designed by Ole Wanscher, each with different brass handles and four tambour shutters, both with fitted interiors.

51in (130cm) wide

£6,000-8,000   **SOTH**

A Hans Wegner teak daybed, with slatted back and original upholstered drop-in cushion.

78in (198cm) wide

£3,000-3,500   **SDR**

A Hans Wegner teak wall unit, with two sliding doors enclosing shelves, over a six-drawer chest.

71in (180cm) wide

£2,000-2,500   **SDR**

A Hans Wegner 'Model 25' teak armchair, with woven rush seat and back.

28in (71cm) wide

£800-1,000   **SDR**

A banqueting table, designed by Rupert Williamson, of rectangular form with coloured block supports.

1996

236.25in (600cm) long

£5,000-6,000   **L&T**

MODERN DESIGN

A Dunbar walnut long coffee table, designed by Edward Wormley, the top inset with six Tiffany tiles, green Dunbar metal tag.

77in (195.5cm) wide

£5,500-6,500   SDR

A 1940s sap walnut free-standing cabinet, designed by Edward Wormley, for Dunbar Furniture, on X-stretcher base with folding hinged doors enclosing a fitted interior, polished brass sabots to the feet.

51.5in (131cm) wide

£2,500-3,000   L&T

MODERN CERAMICS

A Bernard Leach earthenware bowl, decorated in trailing slip and coloured glazes with fruiting vines, impressed St. Ives and monogram marks.

9.75in (24.5cm) diam

£550-650   L&T

A Bernard Leach, St Ives stoneware vase, covered with a deep grey-green speckled glaze, seal marks.

8in (20.5cm) high

£1,000-1,500   JN

A Bernard Leach 'Medieval' stoneware jug, modelled with a simple repeat pattern under an olive glaze, impressed 'BL' and 'St Ives' seals.

11.5in (29cm) high

£1,000-1,400   WW

A Shoji Hamada stoneware dish, off-white with dark brown foliate spray

19.5cm diam

£1,200-1,500   WW

A 1960s Shoji Hamada faceted bottle, with ladle-pour design.

7.5in (19cm) high

£2,500-3,000   SDR

A Rudy Autio porcelain slab sculpture of a torso, incised and painted with figural decoration, signed 'AUTIO/HKI/81'.

Made at the Arabia Factory in Helsinki, Finland, this piece is accompanied by an original letter from the artist discussing this piece and his great satisfaction with it.

1981   *13.25in (33.5cm) wide*

£3,500-4,000   SDR

A large Claude Conover earthenware vase, entitled 'Kabak', signed and titled.

20in (51cm) high

£3,500-4,000   SDR

A Richard Devore ovoid vase, with asymmetrical rim and 'torn' edges, under crackled light brown glaze.

13.75in (35cm) wide

£4,500-5,000   SDR

A Ken Ferguson hand-built oversized stoneware teapot, with rabbit-form handle covered in verdigris glaze.

23in (58.5cm) high

£3,500-4,000   SDR

A David Gilhooly marbleised ceramic two-piece sculpture, entitled 'Trip to California Stelae', featuring anthropomorphised frogs, signed 'Gilhooly 75'.

1975   *29in (74cm) high*

£2,000-2,500   SDR

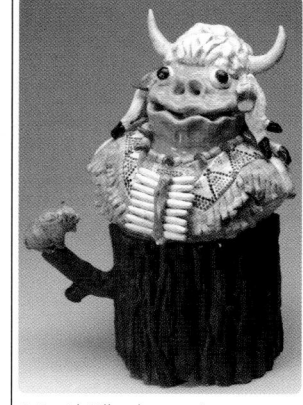

A David Gilhooly two-piece earthenware sculpture, entitled 'Chief Fat Lazy Bullfrog', signed 'Gilhooly/76'.

1976   *21.5in (55cm) high*

£2,000-3,000   SDR

A Natzler tall chalice, covered in mottled sky blue and amber glaze, signed 'NATZLER', paper label 'L712'.

10in (25.5cm) high

£12,000-14,000   SDR

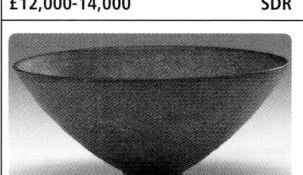

A Natzler small flaring bowl, covered in uranium volcanic glaze, signed 'Natzler'.

5.75in (15cm) diam

£3,500-4,000   SDR

A group of four prototype plates, by Eduardo Paolozzi for Wedgwood, each decorated with abstract designs, each signed by the artist in chinograph verso.

These plates were prototypes to a series produced by Wedgwood in the late 1960s. The designs are derived from one of Paolozzi's screen prints and six production pieces were selected. These plates are one-off prototypes and they are unique as not all of them were in the final series.

10.25in (26cm) diam

£2,000-3,000 GROUP   L&T

A Madoura white clay figural vessel of a peasant woman, designed by Pablo Picasso, with a face painted and incised on her apron, small chips to bottom rim, stamped 'Madoura/plein feu/D'apres Picasso'.

13.75in (35cm)

£2,800-3,200   SDR

A Madoura faïence plate, designed by Pablo Picasso, decorated with leaves, signed 'No. 17/Edition Picasso/67/150/Madoura'.

10in (25.5cm) diam

£1,500-2,000   SDR

A Madoura bird-shaped faïence water pitcher, designed by Pablo Picasso, signed '247/300. EDITION PICASSO 247/300/EDITION PICASSOMADOURA/PLEIN FEU'.

9in (22.5cm) high

£2,500-3,000   SDR

MODERN DESIGN

A Madoura ceramic wall plaque, designed by Pablo Picasso, depicting three figures in white on black matte ground, stamped 'EMPREINTE/ORIGINALE DE/PICASSO/MADOURA/PLEIN FEU'.

7.5in (19cm) wide

£3,000-3,500 SDR

A Polia Pillin square centre bowl, decorated with birds in polychrome glaze.

11.5in (29cm) diam

£1,000-1,500 SDR

CLOSER LOOK: POLIA PILLIN VASE

Polia Pillin (1909-92) is known for her paintings and her painted pots and vases.

They are typically decorated with a young woman's face or dream-like images which were inspired by her experience during the holocaust.

This piece is an unusually large size.

It is fully signed to the base with Pillin's name.

A Polia Pillin tall vase, painted with young ladies and fish, with a dreamlike quality.

22in (56cm) high

£1,800-2,200 SDR

A Polia Pillin studio vase, decorated with a strong red glaze, the base 'W + P Pillin'.
Pieces with plain glazes, particularly such vibrant ones, are scarce. Those covered with textured, 'volcanic' glazes like those produced by the Natzlers are even rarer.

9.5in (24cm) high

£1,000-1,300 ANT

A large Vincenzo Pinto faïence vase, embossed with tribal masks and covered in polychrome volcanic glaze, signed 'PINTO. V./VIETRI/ITALIA.'

24.5in (62cm) high

£1,000-2,000 SDR

A Richard Ginori earthenware dish, 'L'Amazone con Il Corno', designed by Gio Ponti, the red ground painted with a huntress astride a horse, a dog at her feet, black painted mark, 'Richard Ginori, M.229?368E, Gio Ponti'.

14in (35.5cm) diam

£5,500-6,500 SOTH

A Ken Price geometric ceramic vessel.

14.5in (37cm) wide

£3,500-4,000 SDR

A Ken Price tall sculptural vessel, with multiple spouts, covered in mottled brown glaze.

This piece is accompanied by a signed photograph of the piece from the artist along with a letter from Michael Frimkiss, from whom this piece was purchased.

1956 *30.5in (77.5cm) wide*

£7,500-8,500 SDR

An Antonio Prieto footed bulbous stoneware vase, covered in mahogany and amber mottled glaze, signed 'Prieto'.

15.75in (40cm) wide

£1,700-2,000 SDR

A Daniel Rhodes stoneware sculptural torso, marked 'Rhodes'.

50in (127cm) wide

£3,500-4,000   **SDR**

A large stoneware bowl, by Dame Lucie Rie, the mottled pale turqoise ground within a broad bronze-coloured band with 'dribbled' brown decoration, impressed 'LR' seal.

c1975   *64.75in (25.5cm) diam*

£7,000-8,000   **SOTH**

A porcelain bowl, by Dame Lucie Rie, the white ground decorated at the rim with a bronze band and brown 'dribbling', impressed 'LR' seal.

5.75in (14.5cm) diam.

£7,500-8,500   **SOTH**

A Lucie Rie stoneware bottle vase, ovoid with slender neck and flaring rim, glazed with a spiral blue, lavender and brown pitted glaze, impressed 'LR' mark.

Purchased from Lucie Rie at her Albion Mews studio 1982-3.

11.75in (30cm) high

£5,000-6,000   **WW**

A Royal Copenhagen cylindrical vase, designed by Axel Salto, with prunts covered in matte tortoiseshell glaze, incised 'Salto' and with green Royal Copenhagen stamp '/20685'.

6in (15cm) high

£1,500-2,000   **SDR**

A Scheier ceramic sculpture, of a man, woman and child inside a mushroom-shaped pod.

10.5in (26.5cm) high

£1,000-1,400   **SDR**

A Scheier charger, depicting Adam and Eve, outlined in manganese on a celadon ground, signed 'Scheier-45'.

1945   *15in (38cm) diam*

£2,500-3,000   **SDR**

A Toshiko Takaezu ridged stoneware vessel, in mahogany, brown and amber matte glaze, signed '1965/Toshiko TAKAEZU/$65.00'.

1965   *11in (28cm) high*

£3,500-4,000   **SDR**

A Robert Turner ceramic kiln-shape vessel, entitled 'Circle Square #13', with slashes, covered in russet-coloured glaze, signed 'Turner' in black marker, incised mark and title on label.

10in (25.5cm) high

£4,000-5,000   **SDR**

A Peter Voulkos anagama-fired stoneware bowl, in indigo, grey and rust brushed-on volcanic glaze, incised 'Voulkos 96'.

1996   *10.5in (26.5cm) diam*

£1,500-2,000   **SDR**

A Beatrice Wood large fish centre bowl, in blue and white volcanic crackled glaze, signed 'BEATO'.

24in (61cm) wide

£3,000-3,500 SDR

A Peter Voulkos stoneware charger, with gouged and incised surface under buff glaze, signed 'VOULKOS'.

78.5in (199cm) diam

£8,000-10,000 SDR

A Beatrice Wood faïence hen-shaped centre bowl, with applied floral decoration, in pastel glazes, signed 'BEATO'.

16.5in (42cm) wide

£1,600-2,000 SDR

A Betty Woodman slab-built vessel, in sponged folk art amber and green lustre glaze, stamped 'WOODMAN'.

1985   *5in (12.5cm) high*

£2,800-3,200 SDR

A Betty Woodman slab-built 'French Garden' jardinière, stamped 'WOODMAN'.

6.5in (16.5cm) high

£900-1,200 SDR

A Russell Wright long boat-shaped vessel, covered in turquoise and deep plum glaze, stamped script signature.

25in (63.5cm) long

£1,500-2,000 SDR

MODERN GLASS

An AVEM 'Anse Volante' handled vase, designed by Giorgio Ferro, of blue- and clear-cased green glass with an iridescent finish.

1952   *12.5in (31.5cm) high*

£1,800-2,200 QU

An AVEM vase, designed by Anzolo Fuga, of biomorphic near teardrop form with two applied tubular red flowers and a heart.

c1955   *17.5in (44.5cm) high*

£1,700-2,000 QU

A large Barbini 'Scavo' glass vase, with grape and amber pattern, incised 'Barbini Murano' on base.

16.75in (42.5cm) high

£1,200-1,500 SDR

A Barovier & Toso 'Corniola' vase, designed by Ercole Barovier, with seahorse-shaped handle, of marblised opaque red and black glass, with factory paper label numbered '22706'.

1959   *6.25in (16cm) high*

£1,600-1,800 QU

A Barovier & Toso 'Ambrati' mottled red bird sculpture, designed by Ercole Barovier, with opaque white swirl and lightly iridescent surface, the base signed 'Ercole Barovier 1954' and with factory paper label.

1954

£2,500-3,000 QU

A Barovier & Toso 'Crepuscolo' vase, designed by Ercole Barovier, the white opaque inner layer cased in colourless glass with aventurine inclusions, with remains of paper label to base bearing indistinct numbers.

This is a variant of the 1935/36 design by Barovier. For more information see 'Art of the Barovier', by Marina Barovier.

c1950   *13in (33cm) high*

£1,800-2,200 QU

A Barovier & Toso 'Eugeneo' double-handled vase, designed by Ercole Barovier, with fine gold foil inclusions and applied turquoise rim and foot.

1951   *5.75in (14.5cm) high*

£750-850   QU

A Barovier & Toso 'Pezzato' vase, designed by Ercole Barovier, overlaid with alternating striated amber and opaque white and striated turquoise panels.

1956   *9in (23cm) high*

£3,500-4,000   QU

A Barovier & Toso 'A Spina' vase, designed by Ercole Barovier, overlaid with opalescent white and turquoise panels giving a woven effect, the base engraved 'barovier & toso murano' and bearing the factory paper label.

1958   *11.5in (29cm) high*

£3,500-4,000   QU

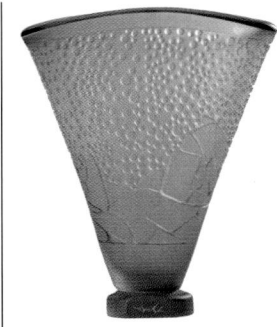

A Dan Dailey cast and blown glass vase, entitled 'Surf Spray Rocks', from the 'Ocean Vase' series, sandblasted and acid-polished, signed on foot, marked 'O-4-79'.

1979   *12.75in (32.5cm) high*

£2,000-2,500   SDR

A Bohumil Elias laminated glass circular sculpture, with abstract design, signed 'Elias'.

7.5in (19cm) high

£600-800   SDR

A Tomas Hlavicka glass egg, laminated, cut and polished, on stand, engraved 'Tomas Hlavicka 2006'.

2006   *7in (17.5cm) high*

£600-800   SDR

A Tomas Hlavicka laminated, cut, and polished glass cube, signed and dated.

2005   *4.25in (10.75cm) wide*

£500-750   SDR

An Orrefors 'Graal' chalice, by Gunnar Cyren, decorated with nudes and animals, engraved 'ORREFORS EXPO Graal V 1149-78 Gunnar Cyren'

9in (22.5cm) high

£900-1,100   SDR

A Gaetano Pesce bowl, entitled 'Sans Titre No. 6', in blue glass with textured interior, signed 'G. Pesce'.

1989-1990   *11.5in (29cm) diam*

£2,500-3,000   SDR

A 1970's Salviati large freeform periwinkle glass vase, by Claire Falkenstein, with three opalescent supports, etched '10/24 Design Claire Falkenstein Salviati', with remnant of Salviati label.

16.25in (41cm) high

£1,500-2,000   SDR

A Steve Tobin figural sculpture, in black glass.

1985   17in (43cm) wide

£750-950   SDR

An Aureliano Toso 'Oriente' vase, designed by Dino Martens, overlaid with a dark violet and white star murrine, and multi-coloured panels of opaque enamels, the neck with fine gold foil inclusions.

Murano glass historian Marc Heiremans shows that photographic archives identify this as model no.5139, one of the earliest model numbers given to the Oriente series. The Oriente range was introduced at the Venice Biennale in 1952, making this one of the earliest designs produced.

c1952   14in (33cm) high

£4,000-5,000   QU

An Aureliano Toso 'Oriente' fish sculpture, designed by Dino Martens, the body overlaid with sections of zanfirico rods, irregular multicoloured panels of opaque enamels and with applied mouth and fins in colourless glass with gold foil inclusions.

1952   12.5in (31.5cm) high

£4,500-5,000   QU

A Fratelli Toso 'Stellato' vase, designed by Pollio Perelda, the colourless cylindrical body overlaid with large stylised star-shaped rectangular murrines comprised of green, blue, orange, red or brown rays, with two factory paper labels to the body.

c1953   13.5in (34cm) high

£6,000-8,000   QU

A Venini 'A Doppio Incalmo' ovoid vase with two adjacent openings, designed by Thomas Stearns, comprised of three sections in red on opaque white, transparent green and black, the surface lightly iridised, the base with 'venini murano ITALIA' acid stamp.

Thomas Stearns (1936-2006) was the first American to design for Venini and worked there from 1959-61 on a Fulbright Travel grant. He had studied at the Cranbrook Academy in the US. He won the Gold Medal at the 1962 Venice Bienalle but the judges rescinded the award when they realised he was American.

Incalmo is a very simple yet difficult technique – each section is separately blown and then joined together when hot. Most pieces are made of two parts, which tend to cool at different rates, so it has to be judged carefully. This one combines three parts, hence doppio incalmo. These pieces could not be mass-produced and only about 30 are known to exist. They are therefore rare and valuable.

1962   4.5in (11cm) high

£12,000-15,000   QU

A Venini glass sculpture with green, clear and amber layers, designed by Thomas Stearns, 'Cappello del Doge', the base etched 'Venini Murano Italia', with circular paster 'Venini S.A. Murano' with vase.

1962   5.25in (13.5cm) wide

£9,000-12,000   SDR

A Venini 'Sirena' figural vase, designed by Fulvio Bianconi, the green body with pulled limbs and neck opening, with 'venini murano ITALIA' acid stamp.

c1950   14.5in (36.5cm) long

£10,000-15,000   QU

A Venini 'A Canne' bottle, designed by Fulvio Bianconi, the colourless body overlaid with vertical alternating green and red stripes, the body marked with the 'venini murano ITALIA' acid stamp,

c1952   16.25in (41cm) high

£1,200-1,500   QU

A Venini 'A Canne' vase, designed by Gio Ponti, the colourless glass body overlaid with alternating blue, red, green violet and yellow canes, the base with 'venini murano ITALIA' acid stamp.

1955   9in (22cm) high

£3,500-4,000   QU

A Venini 'Tronco' cylinder vase, designed by Toni Zuccheri, the clear glass body overlaid with opaque butterscotch coloured veins, giving an almost wood-like effect, the base engraved 'venini italia' and with factory paper label numbered '214/2',

1966   13.5in (34cm) high

£1,600-1,800   QU

A Venini 'La Fiamma' cylindrical vase, designed by Barbara del Vicario, the colourless glass body overlaid with sections of opaque white, turquise, blue and pink canes in a chevron pattern, the base engraved 'venini 86 Del Vicario', and with factory label,

1986   15.75in (40cm) high

£2,300-2,600   QU

A Venini large 'Pezzato' glass globe, designed by Fulvio Bianconi, in cobalt, red and green.

c1950   16in (40.5cm) diam

£500-1,000   SDR

A Venini 'Fazzoletto' glass vase, in turquoise and white incamiciato, etched 'Venini Murano ITALIA'.

10in (25.5cm) high

£400-700   SDR

A Venini 'sommerso' vase, by Laura Diaz de Santillana, with gold leaf on red ground, engraved 'Venini Laura 1987', circular label.

1987   9.5in (24cm) high

£500-700   SDR

A Venini 'Inciso' bottle and stopper, designed by Paoli Venini, in brown glass, acid stamped 'Venini Murano ITALIA'.

1950   11in (28cm) high

£2,500-3,000   SOTH

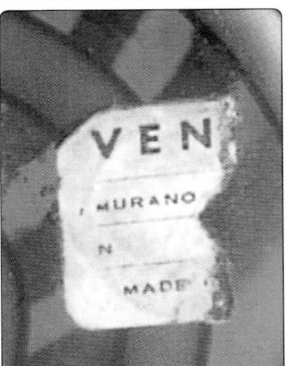

A 1950's Venini 'A Spirale' vase, designed by Fulvio Bianconi, with bulb formation at top, in transparent blue and red striped glass, with partial Venini label.

12.75in (32.5cm) high

£4,000-6,000   SOTH

A Venini screen, designed by Makio Hasuike (b.1938) glass and painted metal, five of the glass panels demonstrate glass techniques, engraved mark 'Venini, Italia, '85'. *Makio Hasuike worked for Seiko and designed 20 clocks for the 1964 Tokyo Olympics. In 1963, he moved permanently to Italy and has collaborated with many international companies.*

Each panel 19.5in (50cm) wide

£7,000-9,000   SOTH

A Vistosi 'Pulcino' bird, designed by Alessandro Pianon, the grey-blue blown body decorated with bands of alternating green and blue circular murrines and impressed murrine eyes, mounted on colourless thighs with applied bent metal legs. *This is a more unusual shape than the more commonly seen spherical orange bird.*

1962   12.5in (31.5cm) high

£2,000-2,400   QU

An Arredoluce floor lamp, in enamelled metal and chrome-plated steel on marble base.

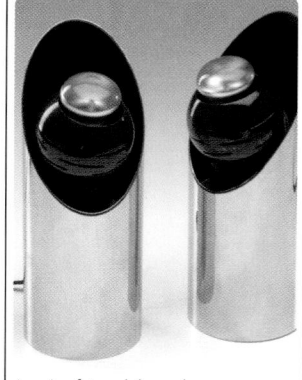

An Arredoluce 'Triennale' brass floor lamp, with enamelled metal shades and handles in primary colours.

69in (175cm) high

£1,700-2,000 SDR

79.5in (202cm) high

A pair of Arredoluce chrome cylindrical lamps, with red enamelled balls, one marked 'Arredoluce/Made in Italy'.

£800-1,000 SDR

9.5in (24cm) high

£500-700 SDR

A pair of rare Arredoluce 'Cobra' table lamps, designed by Angelo Lelii, model number 12919, adjustable magnetic shades with transformers to the base, applied manufacturer's labels.

1962 *24.75in (63cm) high*

£2,000-2,500 L&T

A pair of Azucena 'LTE 8' standard lamps, designed by Ignazio Gardella, glass, marble, each spherical frosted glass shade with three lights and gilt-bronze supports, on a patinated metal cylindrical stem and triform white marble base.

1956 *68.5in (174cm) high*

£14,000-16,000 SOTH

A Mario Bellini 'Chiara' stainless steel floor lamp.

57in (144.5cm) high

£700-900 SDR

A pair of silver-mounted rose quartz candlesticks, by Paul Belvoir, stone column within silver surrounds, fully hallmarked for London.

2007 *12.75in (32.5cm) high*

£10,000-14,000 SOTH

An Italian Achille and Piergiacomo Castiglioni standard lamp, 'Flos', metal with sprayed resin.

1962 *52in (132cm) high*

£700-1,000 L&T

A Maison Desny desk lamp, designed by Jean Desny, with glass plates on chrome base.

4.75in (12cm) high

£2,000-3,000 SDR

A pair of Fontana Arte brass and plate glass double socket table lamps.

base 24in (61cm) high

£6,000-7,000 SDR

A 1950s Fontana Arte brass table lamp, with frosted glass shade, designed by Max Ingrand, waisted base and angular finial with handle, fitted for three lights.

25.5in (65cm) high

£14,000-16,000 SOTH

A Pierre Guariche wall-mounted lamp, with green perforated enamelled metal shade.

46in (117cm) high

£2,000-3,000   SDR

An 'Equilibrium' adjustable standard lamp by Pierre Guariche, gilt-bronze and black-painted metal, the pierced and painted shades on two joint stems balanced on stand, terminating in a ring foot.

1951   *76in (193cm) high*

£14,000-16,000   SOTH

A Missaglia steel and marble gyroscope table lamp, the globular shade composed of polished steel strips, fitted for four bulbs, on a circular marble base with manufacturer's paper label.

26in (66cm) high

£2,200-2,400   SOTH

A pair of James Mont painted wood table lamps, with original parchment shades.

35in (89cm) high

£1,500-2,000 PAIR   SDR

A Tommi Parzinger ceiling light, with frosted plate glass and radiating polished brass arms and finial.

20in (51cm) diam

£2,500-3,000   SDR

A Tommi Parzinger eight-arm floor lamp, in gold-stippled wrought iron with silk shade.

79in (200.5cm) high

£6,000-8,000   SDR

A Seguso Vetri D'Arte glass and brass chandelier, designed by Flavio Poli, with green and yellow pendants hung in two circles, five bulb fittings.

51in (130cm) high

£7,000-9,000   SOTH

An Italian Sirrah chromed steel 'AM-AS' series table lamp, designed by Franco Albini, Franca Helg and Antonio Pira.

33in (84cm) high

£600-800   L&T

A Stilnovo 'Dorane' table lamp, designed by Ettore Sottsass, with light blue Murano glass shade on powder blue coated metal base, clear Murano label.

8in (20cm) high

£500-750   SDR

A 1960s American chromed metal satellite table lamp, the six arms terminating in a spherical shade with a single socket, arms rotate on the baluster-form base.

26.75in (68cm) high

£650-850   SK

A beryllium copper and bronze sculpture, 'Sound Sculpture' by Harry Bertoia (American 1915-1978).

71.75in (182.5cm) wide

£150,000-200,000   **FRE**

A steel sculpture 'Willow Tree' by Harry Bertoia.

12in (30.5cm) wide

£45,000-55,000   **FRE**

A silicon bronze double gong, in three parts, by Harry Bertoia.

108.75in (276cm) high

£150,000-200,000   **SDR**

A bronze and copper sculpture, 'Fan Tree', by Klaus Ihlenfeld (German/American) signed.

1962   *117.5in (298.5cm) wide*

£8,000-10,000   **SDR**

A Philip K. Laverne acid-etched and patinated bronze panel, with still-life of flower vase, in original bronze frame, signed 'Philip K. Laverne'

22.75in (58cm) wide

£1,500-2,500   **SDR**

A rare Philip and Kelvin Laverne sculpted bronze male figural bust, signed 'PHILIP KELVIN LAVERNE'.

22.25in (56.5cm) high

£5,000-6,000   **SDR**

A polished bronze abstract sculpture, 'Sawanna', by Dennis Mitchell, mounted on a slate base and monogramed 'DAM', inscirbed 'No.4' and dated.

1974   *25in high*

£2,500-3,500   **JN**

A Christian Peschke 'Cubist Head' bronze figure, hollow poured, with light brown patina, irregular structured surface.

2002   *38.5in (98cm) high*

£3,500-4,000   **VZ**

A Melvin Lindquist sugar maple flaring vase, signed 'L4 76/Sugar Maple'.

1976   8.75in (22cm) high

£800-1,200   SDR

A Rude Osolnik zebrawood bowl, with uneven rim, signed 'Osolniks Originals/Zebrawood.

6in (15cm) diam

£650-850   SDR

A John A. Sage yellow birch burl-wood bowl, with natural occlusions and free-edge rim, signed 'John A. Sage/1987 Yellow Birch/Burl'.

1987   14in (35.5cm) diam

£900-1,200   SDR

A Marian Kruczek bas relief figural triptych, with rectangular cast concrete inset with an assortment of metal, glass, stone, and plastic found objects, with incised details, inscribed maker's marks and dates, paper, label.

Marian Kruczek is from Krakow, Poland.

1962-63   Centre panel 15in (38cm) high

£500-750   SK

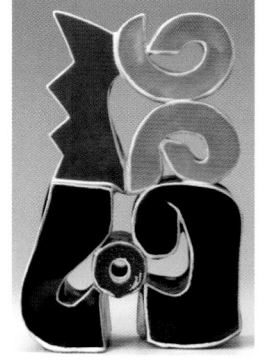

A Hui Ka Kwong faïence sculpture, with black and yellow curls.

20.5in (52cm) high

£1,700-2,000   SDR

An Alexander Calder jute rug, with abstract design in red, blue, orange and black on natural ground.

79in (200.5cm) high

£3,500-4,000   SK

An Edwin and Mary Scheier woven wool tapestry, depicting 'Adam and Eve and the Tree of Knowledge of Good and Evil and the Serpent', entitled 'Adam and Eve', excluding fringe.

85in (216cm) long

£2,500-3,000   SK

A Jack Youngerman tapestry, from an edition of twelve.

103in (261.5cm) long

£1,500-2,000   SDR

An Olivetti 'Synthesis' coatrack/umbrella stand, designed by Ettore Sottsass, in metal and lacquered ABS plastic.

1973   59.5in (151cm) wide

£400-800   SDR

A Tecno model AT16 adjustable coat rack, designed by Osvaldi Borsani, leather, walnut, rosewood and aluminium, the leather-covered revolving stem with eight adjustable coat hooks terminating in spheres, suspended by extendable rods, with Tecno label to pole.

1961   132.5in (337cm) high

£6,000-7,000   SOTH

A Herman Miller 'Watermelon' clock, designed by George Nelson, with gold Howard Miller Chronopak label.

5in (12.5cm) high

£750-1,000   SDR

A National Animated Sign Co. lighted bellhop sign, marked 'National Animated Sign Co./Hot Springs, Arkansas/Phone 6420/America's Sign of Hospitality/SN-4073-A'.

£1,000-1,500   SDR

'Tout Paris A La Revue Des Folies Bergère', designed by Adrien Barrère (1877-1931), printed by Wall & Cie., Paris, restored and repaired.

This ten-sheet poster is the largest and most spectacular poster ever produced for Folies-Bergere. Depicting 'La Belle Otero' at the arm of Arthur Meyer, Louisa Balthy, Henri Rochefort, Brasseur and the Prince of Wales (far right).

1902	152.25in (386.5cm) wide
£11,000-13,000	SWA

'Liquore Strega', designed by Marcello Dudovich (1878-1962), printed by G. Ricordi, Milan, restoration, two sheets.

1906	80.25in (204cm) high
£11,000-13,000	SWA

'Sogno D'Un Valzer', designed by Leopoldo Metlicovitz (1868-1944), printed by G. Ricordi & C., Milan, restoration and restored loss, repaired tears, two sheets.

1910	78.5in (200cm) high
£14,000-16,000	SWA

'Gismonda', by Alphonse Mucha, (1860-1939) Maitre de l'affiche, pl. 27, printed by Chaix, lithograph in colours, in near mint condition, not linen-backed.

1896	15.75in (40cm) high
£1,200-1,500	BLNY

'Waverley Cycles', designed by Alphonse Mucha (1860-1939), printed by F. Champenois, Paris, folds, minor discolouration, wrinkles, creases and bubbling in image, matted and framed.

1898	43in (109cm) wide
£11,000-13,000	SWA

'La Maison Moderne', designed by Manuel Orazi, (1860-1934), printed by J. Minot, Paris.

1900	46in (117cm) wide
£9,000-12,000	SWA

'Clinique Cheron', designed by Théophile-Alexandre Steinlen (1859-1923), printed by Wall & Cie., Paris, depicting an animal lover and protector, restoration, folds.

1905	77.75in (138.5cm) high
£20,000-25,000	SWA

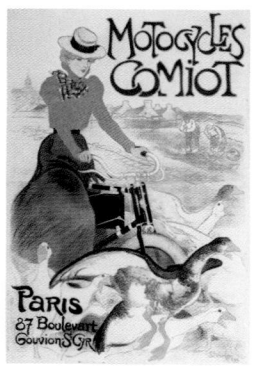

'Motocycles Comiot', designed by Théophile-Alexandre Steinlen (1859-1923), printed by Charle Verneau, Paris.

1899	77in (195.5cm) high
£20,000-24,000	SWA

'Ambassadeurs', designed by Henri de Toulouse-Lautrec (1864-1901), printed by Edward Ancourt, Paris.

1892	56in (142cm) high
£60,000-70,000	SWA

'California/America's Vacation Land', designed by Jon O. Brubaker, (1875-?) printed by Latham Litho. & Printing Co., creases, repaired.

The New York Central Lines began using posters as advertisements in 1925. This poster was the second one they ever issued.

1925   39.75in (101cm) high
£10,000-14,000   **SWA**

'Adirondack Mountains', designed by Walter L. Greene (1870-1956), printed by Latham Litho and Printing Co., New York, repaired tears and creases.

1930   40.25in (102cm) high
£3,500-4,500   **SWA**

'Over Old Indian Trails, The North Shore Line', designed by Oscar Rabe Hanson (1901-1926), printed by Gugler Litho, Milwaukee.

Hanson designed 29 posters from 1923-26. His graphic style and compositional ability made him one of the best US designers of his time.

c1926   42in (106.5cm) high
£4,000-5,000   **SWA**

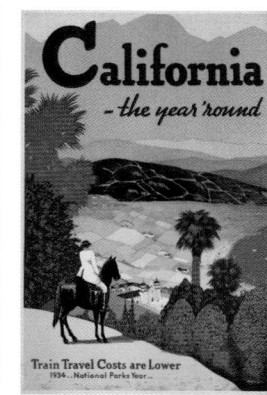

'California - The Year 'Round', designed by Horney (dates Unknown), with a woman on horseback overlooking farmland, a mission and the Pacific Ocean, repaired tears and creases.

1934   41in (104.5cm) high
£5,000-7,000   **SWA**

'San Francisco-Hawaii Overnight!/Via Pan American - To The Orient', designed by Frank Mackintosh (dates unknown), with the Honolulu Clipper disgorging passengers, repaired.

This image celebrates the arrival in Honolulu from San Francisco of Pan American's most advanced, largest and last flying boat, the Boeing 314.

c1938   38.25in (97cm) wide
£5,000-7,000   **SWA**

'Pennsylvania Railroad/Atlantic City', designed by Sascha Maurer (1897-1961), depicting a woman with her back to the ocean facing Atlantic City's boardwalk, reflections of which are visible in the lenses of her sunglasses, restored, creases.

c1940   40.5in (103cm) high
£2,500-3,500   **SWA**

'Rockafeller Center, New York', designed by Leslie Ragan (1897-1972), printed by Latham Litho & PTG. Co. Long Island City, New York, restoration and overpainting.

c1933   41in (104cm) high
£3,500-4,500   **SWA**

'Grand Canyon', by an anonymous designer, silk screen on thick stock, framed.

The Grand Canyon National Park was established through an Act of Congress, signed by President Woodrow Wilson in 1919. Considered one of the Seven Natural Wonders of the World, the canyon stretches over 275 miles and was formed over the millennia by the Colorado River coursing over the rocks of the Plateau.

c1938   19in (48.5cm) high
£4,500-5,500   **SWA**

'Yellowstone National Park', by an anonymous designer, framed.

Yellowstone is America's first National Park. President Ulysses S. Grant signed it into being in 1872. The Park covers areas in three states, primarily Wyoming, but also Montana and Idaho.

c1938   19in (48.5cm) high
£3,000-4,000   **SWA**

'Golf in Northern Ireland', designed by Norman Wilkison (1882-1971), printed by S. C. Allen, London, restoration and repairs.

Wilkinson was a prolific poster artist for the British railway companies in the 1920's and '30's, and a renowned marine painter.

c1925   49in (124.5cm) wide

£10,000-12,000   SWA

'The Forth Bridge', designed by Henry George Gawthorn (1879-1941), printed by David Allen & Sons, London, restoration.

1928   49.75in (126.5cm) wide

£8,500-9,500   SWA

'London Underground, Nightly Carnival', Frederick C. Herrick (1887-1970), printed by The Baynard Press, London, folds and repairs, framed.

Herrick was the only British artist to participate in the 1925 Parisian Exposition Internationales des Arts Decoratifs et Industriels Modernes. In a 'cosmic fresco', he depicts cherubs flitting about constellations which represent Underground stops.

1924   49.25in (125cm) wide

£8,000-9,000   SWA

'A Pigsticking Meet, Visit India', designed by Henry George Gawthorn (1879-1941), printed by Shardlow Ltd., London, restoration and repairs.

In many of his finest posters, Gawthorn employed his signature, stylised graphic ability, to depict the privileged classes engaged in their exclusive and elegant pastimes.

48.75in (124cm) wide

£5,000-6,000   SWA

'Madura', designed by M. V. Dhurandhar (dates unknown), printed by Cooper Litho., Bombay, with a festival parading through the streets before a temple.

c1925   40in (101.5cm) high

£3,000-4,000   SWA

'Australia/Great Barrier Coral Reef', designed by James Northfield (1888-1973), printed by J. E. Hackett, Melbourne.

c1935   40in (102cm) high

£5,000-6,000   SWA

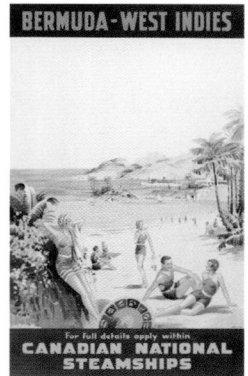

'Bermuda - West Indies, Canadian National Steamships', unknown designer, restored loss and repaired tear.

c1935   37.5in (95cm) high

£2,400-3,000   SWA

'Zermatt', designed by Emile Cardinaux (1877-1936), printed by J. E. Wolfsberger, Zurich.

1908   40.75in (103.5cm) high

£4,500-5,500   SWA

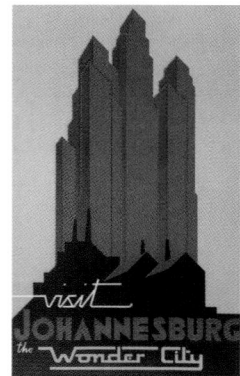

'Visit Johannesburg/The Wonder City', by an anonymous designer, printed by William Brown & Davis, Durban, creases and repaired tears, folds.

40in (101.5cm) high

£700-1,000   SWA

'I Want You', by James Montgomery Flagg (1877-1960), printed for the Leslie-Judge Co., NY, on paper, framed, repaired tears, wrinkles, creases and overpainting.

A prolific illustrator, Flagg was also an extremely patriotic citizen who designed 42 posters during WWI.

1917   39.75in (101cm) high

£1,800-2,200   SWA

'This Is The Enemy!' by Karl Koehler & Victoria Ancona, printed by Grinnell, New York, tears and creases.

This chilling image of a hanging reflected in the monocle of this high ranking member of Germany's military was the winner of the National War Poster Competition of 1942 held under the auspices of the Museum of Modern Art.

1942   34.25in (87cm) high

£2,500-3,000   SWA

'We The People', designed by Howard Chandler Christy (1873-1952), with a Christy girl hovering over a scene of America's founding fathers signing the Constitution, repaired tears and crease.

1937   42.5in (108cm) high

£1,800-2,200   SWA

'Sun Valley', by an anonymous designer, with Gretchen Fraser against a backdrop of mountains, with the village of Sun Valley behind her, restored and repaired.

38in (96.5cm) high

£1,500-2,000   SWA

'Pontresina/KLM', designed by Martin Peikert (1901-75), printed by Klausfelder, Vevey, with a woman lying on a red pillow lifting her legs to reach the sun overlooking a ski resort.

39.5in (100.5cm)

£750-1,000   SWA

'Nunc Est Bibendum/ Le Pneu Michelin Boit L'Obstacle', designed by O'Galop (Marius Rossillon)(1867-1946), printed by Chaix, Paris, restored, repaired tears.

In 1894, at the international exhibition in Lyon, Michelin's staff had arranged a display of a large pile of tyres. Rumour has it that when brothers André and Edouard Michelin saw the arrangement, one of them uttered 'If it had arms it would be like a man'. Shortly after this observation, O'Galop came to the brothers with an idea for a poster, based on a picture he had found of a portly German holding aloft a stein of beer and giving the Latin toast, 'nunc est bibendum' ('now is the time to drink', a line from an ode by Horace). In 1898, with this poster, O'Galop gave birth to Bibendum (the Michelin Man). Depicted at a banquet table, Bibendum is standing with a raised glass filled with everything that could puncture a tyre. On either side of him are two deflated tyres, the one on the left is John Dunlop, the one on the right the director of Continental Tyres. The proud, inflated and healthy-looking Bibendum is not worried about the sharp objects in his glass, because, as the text reads 'the Michelin tyre drinks obstacles'. The rare and historic poster was the first of hundreds of images using Bibendum all over the world, and as a tribute to the beloved icon's effectiveness, he is still appearing in ads over 100 years later.

c1898   61in (155cm) high

£8,000-9,000   SWA

'New Haven R. R.', designed by F. C. Veit, with black and white vignettes of skiers and a speeding train and a colour image of a woman with curly hair below a yellow sky.

40.5in (102.5cm)

£1,500-2,000   SWA

'Olympique Cycles', by Jean A. Mercier (1899-1995), printed by Publicite Vox, Paris, lithograph in colours, linen-backed.

1925   62in (159cm) wide

£1,500-2,000   BLNY

ADVERTISERS

CAMEO
Fine Art and Specialist Auctioneers

24 sales each year specialising in:

- Antiques, furniture and all manner of collectables (monthly);
- Music, Film & Entertainment (quarterly);
- Football & all other sporting memorabilia (quarterly);
- Collectors sales inc. Postcards, Cigarette cards, Coins, Medals etc (quarterly).

Entries now invited for all of the above sales. Single items to collections welcomed. Every lot is photographed & advertised on the internet. Worldwide catalogue distribution. Best prices assured. Competitive commission rates.

Professional valuations for probate & insurance.

CAMEO, Kennet Holme Farm, Bath Road(A4), Midgham, Berks RG7 5UX

Tel 01189 713772

Email office@cameo-auctioneers.co.uk
Website & catalogues:
www.cameo-auctioneers.co.uk

Collection & delivery service available, easy parking available on site

Ibbett Mosely
AUCTIONEERS & VALUERS

A Regular Programme of Sales

of Antique, Victorian and Edwardian Furniture, Works of Art, Silver, Glass, Watches, China, Musical Instruments, Jewellery, etc. etc.

Held in our Saleroom at Otford, Nr. Sevenoaks, Kent

Also valuations carried out for Probate, Insurance and Family Division

Complete house clearances undertaken with personal supervision

Storage facilities available for short periods pending sale

125 High Street, Sevenoaks, Kent TN13 1UT

Telephone: 01732 456731   Fax: 01732 740910

Email: auctions@ibbettmosely.co.uk   Website: www.ibbettmosely.co.uk

Nesbits

CHARTERED SURVEYORS AUCTIONEERS & VALUERS

Monthly sales to include furniture, porcelain, pottery, glassware, silver, jewellery, paintings and collectors' items. Valuations for insurance, probate and family division.

Fine Art and Auction Department, Southsea Salerooms, 7 Clarendon Road, Southsea, Hampshire PO5 2ED

Tel: (023) 9229 5568
Fax: (023) 9273 6503

Email: auctions@nesbits.co.uk
Website: www.nesbits.co.uk

Lambert & Foster — Chartered Surveyors, Estate Agents, Planning Consultants, Auctioneers and Valuers

TENTERDEN AUCTION SALE ROOMS

CONDUCTING
REGULAR MONTHLY SALES HELD AT
THE SALE ROOM
REAR OF 102 HIGH STREET, TENTERDEN,
KENT TN30 6HT

FREE ADVICE FOR SALE BY AUCTION
FREE AUCTION CALENDAR AVAILABLE

FURTHER DETAILS AND ILLUSTRATED CATALOGUES (£2 PLUS P.P.) AVAILABLE FROM THE AUCTION ROOM OR VIA OUR WEBSITE

PROFESSIONAL VALUATIONS FOR PROBATE, INSURANCE AND FAMILY DIVISION, COMPLETE HOUSE CLEARANCES UNDERTAKEN

FOR FURTHER INFORMATION PLEASE CONTACT MRS GLYNIS BRAZIER AUCTION SALE ROOM MANAGER AND VALUER

102 High Street, Tenterden, Kent TN30 6HT
Tel: +44 (0) 1580 762083 Fax: +44 (0) 1580 764317
Email: saleroom@lambertandfoster.co.uk

RICS   www.lambertandfoster.co.uk   Architectural Design PRIMARY FORM

PERIOD CHART

Dates	British Monarch	British Period	French Period	German Period	US Period	Style	Woods
1558–1603	Elizabeth I	Elizabethan	Renaissance	Renaissance	Early Colonial	Gothic	Oak Period (to c1670)
1603–1625	James I	Jacobean					
1625–1649	Charles I	Carolean	Louis XIII (1610–1643)			Baroque (c1620–1700)	
1649–1660	Common-wealth	Cromwellian	Louis XIV (1643–1715)	Renaissance/ Baroque (c1650–1700)			Walnut period (c1670–1735)
1660–1685	Charles II	Restoration			William & Mary	Rococo (c1695–1760)	
1685–1689	James II	Restoration			Dutch Colonial		
1689–1694	William & Mary	William & Mary		Baroque (c1700–1730)	Queen Anne		
1694–1702	William III	William III					
1702–1714	Anne	Queen Anne					
1714–1727	George I	Early Georgian	Régence (1715–1723)	Rococo (c1730–1760)	Chippendale (from 1750)		
1727–1760	George II	Early Georgian	Louis XV (1723–1774)	Neoclassical (c1760–1800)	Early Federal (1790–1810)	Neoclassical (c1755–1805)	Early mahogany period (c1735–1770)
1760–1812	George III	Late Georgian	Louis XVI (1774–1793) Directoire (1793–1799) Empire (1799–1815)	Empire (c1800–1815)	American Directoire (1798–1804) American Empire (1804–1815)	Empire (c1799–1815)	Late mahogany period (c1770–1810)
1812–1820	George III	Regency	Restauration Charles X (1815–1830)	Biedermeier (c1815–1848)	Late Federal (1810–1830)	Regency (c1812–1830)	
1820–1830	George IV	Regency					
1830–1837	William IV	William IV	Louis Philippe (1830–1848)	Revivale (c1830–1880)		Eclectic (c1830–1880)	
1837–1901	Victoria	Victorian	2nd Empire Napoleon III (1848–1870) 3rd Republic (1871–1940)	Jugendstil (c1880–1920)	Victorian	Arts & Crafts (c1880–1900)	
1901–1910	Edward VII	Edwardian			Art Nouveau (c1900–1920)	Art Nouveau (c1900–1920)	

Every antique illustrated in Miller's Antiques Price Guide 2009 has a letter code which identifies the dealer or auction house that sold it. The list below is a key to these codes. In the list, auction houses are shown by the letter A and dealers by the letter D. Some items may have come from a private collection, in which case the code in the list is accompanied by the letter P. Inclusion in this book in no way constitutes or implies a contract or a binding offer on the part of any of our contributors to supply or sell the goods illustrated, or similar items, at the prices stated.

A&G Ⓐ
ANDERSON & GARLAND
Anderson House, Crispin Court, Newbiggin Lane, Westerhope, Newcastle upon Tyne, NE5 1BF
Tel: 0191 430 3000
www.andersonandgarland.com

ALD Ⓐ
ALDERFERS
Alderfer's Auction Gallery
501 Fairgrounds Road
Hatfield, Pennsylvania 19440 USA
Tel: 001 215 393 3000
www.alderferauction.com

ANA Ⓓ
ANCIENT ART
85 The Vale, London N14 6AT
Tel: 020 8882 1509
www.antiquities.co.uk

ANT Ⓓ
ANTIQUE GALLERY,
8523 Germantown Avenue, Philadelphia, PA 19118
Tel: 001 215 248 1700
www.antiquegal.com

BE Ⓐ
BEARNES
St Edmund's Court, Okehampton Street, Exeter, Devon, EX4 1DU
Tel: 01392 207000
www.bearnes.co.uk

BER Ⓐ
BERTOIA AUCTIONS
2141 Demarco Drive, Vineland NJ 08360 USA
Tel: 001 856 692 1881
www.bertoiaauctions.com

BLA Ⓐ
BLANCHET ET ASSOCIÉS
3 rue Geoffroy Marie, 75009 Paris, France
Tel: 00 33 1 53 34 14 44
blanchet.auction@wanadoo.fr

BLNY Ⓐ
BLOOMSBURY AUCTIONS
6 West 48th Street, New York, NY 10036-190
Tel: 001 212-719-1000
http://ny.bloomsburyauctions.com

BLO Ⓐ
BLOOMSBURY AUCTIONS
Bloomsbury House, 24 Maddox Street, London W1 S1PP
Tel: 020 7495 9494
www.bloomsburyauctions.com

BLY Ⓓ
JOHN BLY
Byappointment
Tel: 01442 823030
www.johnbly.com

BRI Ⓐ
BRIGHTWELLS FINE ART
Fine Art Saleroom, Easters Court, Leominster, Herefordshire HR6 0DE
Tel: 01568 611122
www.brightwells.co.uk

BRK Ⓓ
BROOKSIDE ANTIQUES
44 North Water Street, New Bedford, MA 02740 USA
Tel: 001 508 993 4944
www.brooksideartglass.com

BWH Ⓟ
BIG WHITE HOUSE
Private collection

CHT Ⓐ
CHARTERHOUSE
The Long Street Salerooms, Sherborne, Dorset, DT93BS
Tel: 01935 812277
www.charterhouse-auctions.co.uk

CLV Ⓐ
CLEVEDON SALEROOMS
The Auction Centre, Kenn Road, Kenn, Clevedon, Bristol, BS21 6TT
Tel: 01934 830 111
www.clevedon-salerooms.com

CRA Ⓐ
CRAFTSMAN AUCTIONS
333 North Main Street, Lambertville, NJ 08530 USA
Tel: 001 609 397 9374
www.ragoarts.com

DA Ⓓ
DAVIES ANTIQUES
c/o Cadogan Tate, Unit 6, 6-12 Ponton Road, London SW8 5BA
Tel: 020 8947 1902
www.antique-meissen.com

DAH Ⓐ
DEE, ATKINSON & HARRISON
The Exchange Saleroom, Driffield, East Yorkshire
Tel : 01377 253151
www.dee-atkinson-harrison.co.uk

DN Ⓐ
DREWEATTS
Donnington Priory Salerooms, Donnington, Newbury, Berkshire RG14 2JE
Tel: 01635 553553
www.dnfa.com/donnington

DNW Ⓐ
DIX NOONAN WEB
16 Bolton Street, London, W1J 8BQ
Tel: 020 7016 1700
www.dnw.co.uk

DRA Ⓐ
DAVID RAGO AUCTIONS
333 North Main Street, Lambertville, NJ 08530, USA
Tel: 001 609 397 9374

www.ragoarts.com

DUK Ⓐ
HY DUKE AND SON
The Dorchester Fine Art Salerooms, Weymouth Avenue, Dorchester, Dorset DT1 1QS
Tel: 01305 265 080
www.dukes-auctions.com

FLD Ⓐ
FIELDINGS AUCTIONEERS
Mill Race Lane, Stourbridge, DY8 1JN
Tel: 01384 444140
www.fieldingsauctioneers.co.uk

FRE Ⓐ
FREEMAN'S
1808 Chestnut Street, Philadelphia, PA 19103, USA
Tel: 001 215 563 9275
www.freemansauction.com

GBA Ⓐ
GRAHAM BUDD AUCTIONS
PO Box 47519, London N14 6XD
Tel: 020 8366 2525
www.grahambuddauctions.co.uk

GHOU Ⓐ
GARDINER HOULGATE
Bath Auction Rooms, 9 Leafield Way, Corsham, SN13 9SW
Tel: 01225 812 912
auctions@gardiner-houlgate.co.uk

GIL Ⓐ
GILDING'S AUCTIONEERS
64 Roman Way, Market Harborough, LE16 7PQ
Tel: 01858 410414
www.gildings.co.uk

GORL Ⓐ
GORRINGES
15 North Street, Lewes, East Sussex BN7 2PD
Tel: 01273 472503
www.gorringes.co.uk

GUIN Ⓓ
GUINEVERE
578 Kings Road, London SW6 2DY
Tel: 020 7736 2917
www.guinevere.co.uk

GVI Ⓓ
GARTH VINCENT
The Old Manor House, Allington, Nr Grantham, Lincolnshire, NG32 2DH
Tel: 01400 281358
www.guns.uk.com

HALL Ⓐ
HALLS FINE ART
Welsh Bridge, Shrewsbury, SY3 8LA
Tel: 01743 231 212
www.hallsgb.com

HB Ⓓ
VICTORIANA DOLLS
101 Portobello Rd, London, W11 2BQ

Tel: 01737 249 525
heather.bond@totalserve.co.uk

HGS Ⓓ
HARPERS GENERAL STORE
301 Maple Avenue, Mt. Gretna, PA 17064 USA
Tel: 001 717 865 3456
www.harpergeneralstore.com

HT or HTV Ⓓ
HARTLEY'S
Victoria Hall, Little Lane, Ilkley, LS29 8EA
Tel: 01943 816363
www.hartleyauctions.co.uk

JACK Ⓐ
JACKSON'S
2229 Lincoln Street, Cedar Falls, Iowa 5063 USA
Tel: 001 319 277 2256
www.jacksonsauction.com

JDJ Ⓐ
JAMES D JULIA INC
PO Box 830, Fairfield, ME 04937, USA
Tel: 001 207 453 7125
www.juliaauctions.com

JH Ⓓ
JEANETTE HAYHURST FINE GLASS
32A Kensington Church St., London W8 4HA
Tel: 020 7938 1539

JN Ⓐ
JOHN NICHOLSONS
The Auction Rooms, 'Longfield', Midhurst Road, Fernhurst, Haslemere, Surrey GU27 3HA
Tel: 01428 653727
www.johnnicholsons.com

KAU Ⓐ
AUKTIONHAUS KAUP
Schloss Sulzburg, Hauptstrasse 62, 79295 Sulzburg, Germany
Tel: 0049 7634 5038 0
www.kaupp.de

KT Ⓐ
KERRY TAYLOR AUCTIONS
Unit C25 Parkhall Road Trading Estate, 40 Martell Road, Dulwich, London SE21 8EN
Tel: 020 8676 4600
www.kerrytaylorauctions.com

LA Ⓐ
LAYS AUCTIONS
The Penzance Auction House, Alverton, Penzance, TR18 4RE
Tel: 01736 361414
www.davidlay.co.uk

L&T Ⓐ
LYON AND TURNBULL LTD.
33 Broughton Place, Edinburgh, Midlothian EH1 3RR
Tel: 0131 557 8844
www.lyonandturnbull.com

LAW Ⓐ
LAWRENCES' AUCTIONEERS
The Linen Yard, South Street,
Crewkerne, Somerset TA18 8AB
Tel: 01460 73041
www.lawrences.co.uk

LFA Ⓐ
LAW FINE ART LTD.
Ash Cottage, Ashmore Green,
Newbury, Berkshire, RG18 9ER
Tel: 01635 860033
www.lawfineart.co.uk

LOC Ⓐ
LOCKE & ENGLAND
18 Guy Street, Leamington Spa,
CV32 4RT
Tel: 01926 889100
www.leauction.co.uk

MUR Ⓐ
TONY MURLAND AUCTIONS
78 High Street, Needham Market,
Suffolk, IP6 8AW
Tel: 01449 722 992
www.antiquetools.co.uk

NA Ⓐ
NORTHEAST AUCTIONS
93 Pleasant Street, Portsmouth, NH
03801 USA
Tel: 001 603 433 8400
www.northeastauctions.com

NEA Ⓓ
DREWEATTS
The Nottingham Salerooms,
192 Mansfield Road, Nottingham,
NG1 3HU
Tel: 0115 962 4141
www.dnfa.com/neales

PAR or PART Ⓓ
PARTRIDGE FINE ARTS PLC
144-146 New Bond Street, London
W1S 2PF
Tel: 020 7629 0834
www.partridgeplc.com

PC Ⓟ Ⓒ
PRIVATE COLLECTION

PGO Ⓓ
PAMELA GOODWIN
11 The Pantiles, Royal Turnbridge
Wells, Kent, TN2 5TD
Tel: 01435 882200
www.goodwinantiques.co.uk

POOK Ⓐ
POOK & POOK
463 East Lancaster Avenue,
Downington, PA 19335, USA
Tel: 001 610 269 4040/0695
www.pookandpook.com

QU Ⓐ
QUITTENBAUM
Hohenstaufenstraße 1, D-80801,
München, Germany
Tel: 0049 859 33 00 75 6
www.quittenbaum.de

RDER Ⓓ
ROGERS DE RIN
76 Royal Hospital Road, Paradise
Walk, Chelsea, London SW3 4HN
Tel: 020 7352 9007
www.rogersderin.co.uk

RGA Ⓓ
RICHARD GARDNER ANTIQUES
Swan House, Market Square,
Petworth, West Sussex GU28 0AH
Tel: 01798 343 411
www.richardgardenerantiques.co.uk

ROS Ⓐ
ROSEBERY'S
74-76 Knight's Hill, West Norwood,
London SE27 0JD
Tel: 020 8761 2522
www.roseberys.co.uk

ROW Ⓐ
ROWLEY FINE ARTS
8 Downham Road, Ely, Cambridge,
Cambridgeshire CB6 1AH
Tel: 01353 653020
www.rowleyfineart.com

SDR Ⓐ
SOLLO:RAGO MODERN AUCTIONS
333 North Main Street,
Lambertville, NJ 08530 USA
Tel: 001 609 397 9374
www.ragoarts.com

SK Ⓐ
SKINNER INC.
The Heritage on the Garden,
63 Park Plaza Boston MA 02116,
USA
Tel: 001 617 350 5400
www.skinnerinc.com

SOT Ⓐ
SOTHEBY'S (US)
1334 York Avenue, New York, NY
10021, USA
Tel: 001 212 606-7000
www.sothebys.com

SOTA Ⓐ
SOTHEBY'S (AMSTERDAM)
De Boelelaan 30, 1083 HJ
Amsterdam, Netherlands
Tel: 0031 20 550 22 00
www.sothebys.com

SOTH Ⓐ
SOTHEBY'S (LONDON)
34-35 New Bond Street, London,
W1A 2AA
Tel: 020 7293 5000
www.sothebys.com

SOTP Ⓐ
SOTHEBY'S (PARIS)
Galerie Charpentier,
76 rue du Faubourg, Saint Honoré,
75008 Paris, France
Tel: 00 33 1 53 05 53 05
www.sothebys.com

SWA Ⓐ
**SWANN GALLERIES IMAGE
LIBRARY**
104 East 25th Street, New York,
New York 10010
Tel: 001 212 254 4710
www.swanngalleries.com

SWO Ⓐ
SWORDERS
14 Cambridge Road, Stansted
Mountfitchet, Essex CM24 8BZ
Tel: 01279 817 778
www.sworder.co.uk

TAC Ⓓ
TORONTO ANTIQUES CENTER
276 King Street West, Toronto,
Ontario M5V 1J2, Canada

TCF Ⓓ
CYNTHIA FINDLAY
Toronto Antiques Centre,
276 King Street West, Toronto,
Ontario M5V 1J2, Canada
Tel: 001 416 260 9057
www.cynthiafindlay.com

TCT Ⓓ
THE CALICO TEDDY
www.calicoteddy.com

TDG Ⓓ
THE DESIGN GALLERY
5 The Green, Westerham, Kent,
TN16 1AS
Tel: 01959 561 234
www.designgallery.co.uk

TDM Ⓐ
THOMAS DEL MAR LTD
25 Blythe Road, London W14 0PD
Tel: 0207 602 4805
www.thomasdelmar.com

TEN Ⓐ
TENNANTS
The Auction Centre, Leyburn, North
Yorkshire, DL8 5SG
Tel: 01969 623 780
www.tennants.co.uk

TGM Ⓐ
THE GLASS MERCHANT
8 Soxon Close, Caterham, Surrey
CR3 5SY
Tel: 07775 683 961

VEC Ⓐ
VECTIS AUCTIONS
Fleck Way, Thornaby, Stockton on
Tees, County Durham TS17 9JZ
Tel: 01642 750 616
www.vectis.co.uk

VZ Ⓐ
VON ZEZSCHWITZ
Friedrichstrasse 1a, 80801 Munich,
Germany
Tel: 0049 89 38 98 930
www.von-zezschwitz.de

W&W Ⓐ
WALLIS AND WALLIS
West Street Auction Galleries,
Lewes, East Sussex BN7 2NJ
Tel: 01273 480 208
www.wallisandwallis.co.uk

WAD Ⓐ
WADDINGTON'S
111 Bathurst St., Toronto,
Ontario M5V 2R1, Canada
Tel: 001 416 504 9100
www.waddingtons.ca

WDL Ⓐ
MARTIN WENDL
August-Bebel-Straße 4, 07407
Rudolstadt, Germany
Tel: 00 49 3672 4243 50
www.auktionshaus-wendl.de

WW Ⓐ
WOOLLEY & WALLIS
51-61 Castle Street, Salisbury,
Wiltshire SP13SU
Tel: 01722 424 500
www.woolleyandwallis.co.uk

NOTE

For valuations, it is advisable to contact the dealer or auction house in advance to confirm that they will perform this service and whether any charge is involved. Telephone valuations are not possible, so it will be necessary to send details, including a photograph, of the object to the dealer or auction house, along with a stamped addressed envelope for response. While most dealers will be happy to help you, do remember that they are busy people. Please mention Miller's Antiques Price Guide 2009 when making an enquiry.

This is a list of auctioneers that conduct regular sales. Auction houses that would like to be included in the next edition should contact us by 1 February 2009.

LONDON

Angling Auctions
PO Box 2095, W12 8RU
Tel: 020 8749 4175
neil@anglingauctions.demon.co.uk

Auction Atrium
58-60 Kensington Church Street,
W8 4DB
Tel: 020 7937 3259
www.auctionatrium.com

Baldwins
11 Adelphi Terrace, WC2N 6BJ
Tel: 020 7930 9808
www.baldwin.co.uk

Bloomsbury
24 Maddox Street, W1 S1PP
Tel: 020 7495 9494
www.bloomsbury-book-auct.com

Bonhams
101 New Bond Street, W1S 1SR
Tel: 020 7629 6602
www.bonhams.com

Graham Budd Auctions Ltd.
Tel: 020 8366 2525
www.grahambuddauctions.co.uk

Chiswick Auctions
1 Colville Road, Acton, W3 8BL
Tel: 020 8992 4442
www.chiswickauctions.co.uk

Christie's
8 King Street, St. James's, SW1Y 6QT
Tel: 020 7839 9060
www.christies.com

Christie's South Kensington
85 Old Brompton Road, SW7 3LD
Tel: 020 7581 7611
www.christies.com

Criterion Auctioneers
53 Essex Road, N1 2BN
Tel: 020 7359 5707
www.criterionauctions.co.uk

Dix-Noonan-Webb
16 Bolton Street, W1J 8BQ
Tel: 020 7016 1700
www.dnw.co.uk

Lots Road Galleries
71-73 Lots Road, SW10 0RN
Tel: 020 7376 6800
www.lotsroad.com

Rosebery's
74-76 Knights Hill, SE27 0JD
Tel: 020 8761 2522
www.roseberys.co.uk

Sotheby's
34-35 New Bond Street, W1A 2AA
Tel: 020 7293 5000
www.sothebys.com

Spink & Son Ltd.
69 Southampton Road, WC1B 4ET
Tel: 020 7563 4000
www.spink.com

Kerry Taylor Auctions
Unit C25 Parkhall Rd Trading Estate,
40 Martell Rd, Dulwich SE21 8EN
Tel: 020 8676 4600
www.kerrytaylorauctions.com

AVON

Aldridges of Bath
Newark House, 26-45 Cheltenham
Street, Bath BA2 3EX
Tel: 01225 462830

Gardiner Houlgate
9 Leafield Way, Corsham,
Bath SN13 9SW
Tel: 01225 812912
www.gardiner-houlgate.co.uk

BEDFORDSHIRE

W. & H. Peacock
26 Newnham Street,
Bedford MK40 3JR
Tel: 01234 266366
www.peacockauction.co.uk

BERKSHIRE

Cameo Auctions
Kennet Holme Farm, Bath Road,
Midgham, Reading, RG7 5UX
Tel: 01189 713772
www.cameo-auctioneers.co.uk

Dreweatts
Donnington Priory, Donnington,
Nr Newbury RG14 2JE
Tel: 01635 553553
www.dnfa.com

Law Fine Art Ltd.
Ash Cottage, Ashmore Green,
Newbury RG18 9ER
Tel: 01635 860033
www.lawfineart.co.uk

Special Auction Services
Kennetholme, Midgham,
Nr. Reading RG7 5UX
Tel: 0118 971 2949
www.specialauctionservices.com

BUCKINGHAMSHIRE

Amersham Auction Rooms
Station Road, Amersham, HP7 0AH
Tel: 01494 729292
www.amershamauctionrooms.co.uk

Bourne End Auction Rooms
Station Approach,
Bourne End SL8 5QH
Tel: 01628 531500
www.bourneendauctionrooms.com

Dickins Auctioneers
Claydon House Park, Calvert Rd,
Middle Claydon MK18 2EZ
Tel: 01296 714 434
www.dickins-auctioneers.com

CAMBRIDGESHIRE

Cheffins
Clifton House, 1 & 2 Clifton Road,
Cambridge CB1 7EA
Tel: 01223 213 343
www.cheffins.co.uk

Hyperion Auctions Ltd
Station Road, St. Ives PE27 5BH
Tel: 01480 464140
www.hyperionauctions.co.uk

Rowley Fine Art Auctioneers
8 Downham Road, Ely CB6 1AH
Tel: 01353 653020
www.rowleyfineart.com

Willingham Auctions
25 High St, Willingham CB4 5ES
Tel: 01954 261252
www.willinghamauctions.com

CHESHIRE

Frank R. Marshall & Co.
Marshall House, Church Hill, Knutsford
WA16 6DH
Tel: 01565 653284
www.frankmarshall.co.uk

Halls Fine Art Auctions
Booth Mansion, 30 Watergate Street,
Chester CH1 2LA
Tel: 01244 312300
www.hallsestateagents.co.uk

Maxwells of Wilmslow
133A Woodford Road, Woodford,
Cheshire SK7 1QD
Tel: 01614 395182
www.maxwell-auctioneers.co.uk

Peter Wilson Auctioneers
Victoria Gallery, Market Street,
Nantwich CW5 5DG
Tel: 01270 623878
www.peterwilson.co.uk

Wright Manley
Beeston Castle Salerooms, Tarporley
CW6 9NZ
Tel: 01829 262150
www.wrightmanley.co.uk

CORNWALL

W. H. Lane & Son
Jubilee House, Queen Street, Penzance
TR18 4DF
Tel: 01736 361447
www.whlaneauctioneersandvaluers.co.uk

David Lay FRICS
The Penzance Auction House
Alverton, Penzance TR18 4RE
Tel: 01736 361414
www.davidlay.co.uk

CUMBRIA

Mitchells Auction Company
The Furniture Hall, 47 Station Road,
Cockermouth, CA13 9PZ
Tel: 01900 827800
www.mitchellauction.co.uk

Penrith Farmers' & Kidd's
Skirsgill Salerooms,
Penrith CA11 0DN
Tel: 01768 890781
www.pfkauctions.co.uk

Thomson, Roddick & Medcalf
Coleridge House, Shaddongate,
Carlisle CA2 5TU
Tel: 01228 528939
www.thomsonroddick.com

James Thompson
64 Main Street,
Kirkby Lonsdale LA6 2AJ
Tel: 01524 271555
www.jthompson-auctioneers.co.uk

DERBYSHIRE

Bamfords Ltd
The Old Picture Palace, 133 Dale
Road, Matlock, Derbyshire DE4 3LU
Tel: 01629 574460
www.bamfords-auctions.co.uk

DEVON

Bearnes
St Edmund's Court,
Okehampton Street, Exeter EX4 1DU
Tel: 01392 207000
www.bearnes.co.uk

Michael J Bowman
6 Haccombe House, Nr Netherton,
Newton Abbot TQ12 4SL
Tel: 01626 872890
www.invaluable.com/bowman

Hampton & Littlewood
The Auction Rooms, Alphin Brook
Road, Alphington, Exeter EX2 8TH
Tel: 01392 413100
www.hamptonandlittlewood.co.uk

Dreweatts
Honiton Saleroom, 205 High Street,
Honiton EX14 1LQ
Tel: 01404 42404
www.dnfa.com/honiton

Rendells
Stonepark, Ashburton TQ13 7RH
Tel: 01364 653017
www.rendells.co.uk

S. J. Hales Auctioneers
Tracey House, Newton Road, Bovey
Tracey, Newton Abbot TQ13 9AZ
Tel: 01626 836 684
www.sjhales.com

DORSET

Chapman, Moore & Mugford
9 High Street, Shaftesbury SP7 9JB
Tel: 01747 822244

Charterhouse
The Long Street Salerooms,
Sherborne DT9 3BS
Tel: 01935 812277
www.charterhouse-auctions.co.uk

Cottees Auctions Ltd.
The Market, East Street,
Wareham BH20 4NR
Tel: 01929 552826
www.auctionsatcottees.co.uk

Dalkeith Auctions
Dalkeith Hall, Dalkeith Steps,
Rear of 81 Old Christchurch Rd,
Bournemouth BH1 1YL
Tel: 01202 292905
www.dalkeith-auctions.co.uk

Hy. Duke & Son
Fine Art Salerooms, Weymouth
Avenue, Dorchester DT1 1QS
Tel: 01305 265080
www.dukes-auctions.com

Onslows
The Coach House, Manor Road,
Stourpaine DT11 8TQ
Tel: 01258 488 838
www.onslows.co.uk

Riddetts of Bournemouth
177 Holdenhurst Road, Bournemouth
BH8 8DG
Tel: 01202 555686
www.riddetts.co.uk

DURHAM
Vectis Auctions Limited
Fleck Way, Thornaby,
Stockton on Tees TS17 9JZ
Tel: 01642 750 616
www.vectis.co.uk

ESSEX
Ambrose
Ambrose House, Old Station Road,
Loughton IG10 4PE
Tel: 020 8502 3951
www.ambroseauction.co.uk

Brentwood Antique Auctions
45 North Rd, Brentwood CM14 4UZ
Tel: 01277 224599
www.brentwoodantiqueauction.co.uk

Chalkwell Auctions Ltd.
The Arlington Rooms, 905 London
Road, Leigh-on-Sea SS0 89U
Tel: 01702 710383
www.ridgeweb.co.uk

Cooper Hirst Auctions
The Granary Salerooms, Victoria Road,
Chelmsford CM2 6LH
Tel: 01245 260535

Mullucks Wells Inc.
The Old Town Hall,
Great Dunmow CM6 1AU
Tel: 01371 873014
www.mullucks.co.uk

Sworders
14 Cambridge Road,
Stansted Mountfitchet CM24 8BZ
Tel: 01279 817778
www.sworder.co.uk

GLOUCESTERSHIRE
Clevedon Salesrooms
The Auction Centre, Kenn Road, Kenn,
Clevedon, Bristol BS21 6TT
Tel: 01934 830111
www.clevedon-salerooms.com

The Cotswold Auction Co. Ltd.
4-6 Clarence St, Gloucester GL1 1DX
Tel: 01452 521177

Chapel Walk Saleroom,
Cheltenham GL50 3DS
Tel: 01242 256363

The Coach House, Swan Yard,
9-13 West Market Place,
Cirencester, GL7 2NH
Tel: 01285 642420
www.cotswoldauction.co.uk

Dreweatts
St. John's Place, Apsley Road, Clifton
Bristol BS8 2ST
Tel: 0117 973 7201
www.dnfa.com/bristol

Mallams Fine Art Auctioneers
26 Grosvenor Street,
Cheltenham GL52 2SG
Tel: 01242 235712
www.mallams.co.uk/fineart

Moore, Allen & Innocent
The Salerooms, Norcote,
Cirencester GL7 5RH
Tel: 01285 646050
www.mooreallen.com/cat

Smiths, Newent Auction Rooms
16 Broad Street, Newent GL18 1AJ
Tel: 01531 820767
www.smithsnewentauctions.co.uk

Stroud Auctions Ltd
The Old Barn, Bear of Rodborough,
Stroud GL5 5EA
Tel: 01453 873800
www.stroudauctions.com

Tayler & Fletcher
London House, High Street,
Bourton-on-the-Water,
Cheltenham GL54 2AP
Tel: 01451 821666
www.taylerfletcher.com

Dominic Winter Book Auctions
Mallard House, Broadway Lane,
South Cerney GL7 5UQ
Tel: 01285 860006
www.dominicwinter.co.uk

Wotton Auction Rooms Ltd
Tabernacle Road,
Wotton-under-Edge GL12 7EB
Tel: 01453 844733
www.wottonauctionrooms.co.uk

HAMPSHIRE
Andrew Smith & Son
Manor Farm, Itchen Stoke,
Nr. Winchester SO24 0QT
Tel: 01962 735988
auctions@andrewsmithandson.com

George Kidner Auctioneers
The Lymington Saleroom, Emsworth
Road, Lymington SO41 9BL
Tel: 01590 670070
www.georgekidner.co.uk

Jacobs & Hunt Auctioneers
Lavant Street, Petersfield GU32 3EF
Tel: 01730 233933
www.jacobsandhunt.com

May & Son
Delta Works, Salisbury Rd, Shipton
Bellinger, SP9 7UN
Tel: 01980 846000
mayandson@enterprise.net

D.M. Nesbit & Co.
Southsea Salerooms, 7 Clarendon
Road, Southsea PO5 2ED
Tel: 02392295568
www.nesbits.co.uk

**Odiham Auction Sales/
May & Sons,**
Unit 4, Priors Farm, West Green Road,
Mattingley RG27 8JU
Tel: 01189 326824
auction@dircon.co.uk

HEREFORDSHIRE
Brightwells
The Fine Art Saleroom,
Easters Court, Leominster HR6 ODE
Tel: 01568 611122
www.brightwells.com

Morris Bricknell
Stroud House, 30 Gloucester Road,
Ross-on-Wye HR9 5LE
Tel: 01989 768320
www.morrisbricknell.com

Williams & Watkins
Ross Auction Rooms
Ross-on-Wye HR9 7QF
Tel: 01989 762225
www.williamsandwatkins.co.uk

Nigel Ward & Co.
The Border Property Centre,
Pontrilas HR2 0EH
Tel: 01981 240140
www.nigel-ward.co.uk

HERTFORSHIRE
Sworders
42 St Andrew St, Hertford SG14 1JA
Tel: 01992 583508
www.sworder.co.uk

Tring Market Auctions
Brook Street, Tring HP23 5EF
Tel: 01442 826446
www.tringmarketauctions.co.uk

ISLE OF WIGHT
Shanklin Auction Rooms
79 Regent St, Shanklin PO37 7AP
Tel: 01983 863441
www.shanklinauctionrooms.co.uk

KENT
Bentley's Fine Art Auctioneers
The Old Granary, Waterloo Road,
Cranbrook TN17 3JQ
Tel: 01580 715857
www.bentleysfineartauctioneers.co.uk

Canterbury Auction Galleries
40 Station Rd, Canterbury CT2 8AN
Tel: 01227 76337
www.thecanterburyauctiongalleries.com

Dreweatts
The Auction Hall, The Pantiles,
Tunbridge Wells, Kent TN2 5QL
Tel: 01892 544500
www.dnfa.com/tunbridgewells

Gorringes
15 The Pantiles,
Tunbridge Wells TN2 5TD
Tel: 01892 619 670
www.gorringes.co.uk

Ibbett Mosely
125 High Street,
Sevenoaks TN13 1UT
Tel: 01732 456731
www.ibbettmosely.co.uk

Lambert & Foster Auction
Sale Rooms 102 High Street,
Tenterden TN30 6HT
Tel: 01580 762083
77 Commercial Road,
Paddock Wood, TN12 6DR
Tel: 01892 832325
www.lambertandfoster.co.uk

Mervyn Carey
Twysden Cottage, Benenden,
Cranbrook TN17 4LD
Tel: 01580 240283

Parkinson Auctioneers
46 Beaver Road, Ashford TN23 7RP
Tel: 01233 624426
www.parkinson-uk.com

LANCASHIRE
Capes Dunn & Co. Fine Art
The Auction Galleries, 38 Charles
Street, Manchester M1 7DB
Tel: 0161 273 1911

Smythes Fine Art
174 Victoria Road West,
Cleveleys FY5 3NE
Tel: 01253 852184
www.smythes.net

LEICESTERSHIRE
Gilding's Auctioneers & Valuers
Roman Way,
Market Harborough LE16 7PQ
Tel: 01858 410414
www.gildings.co.uk

Tennants Auctioneers
Millhouse, South Street, Oakham,
Rutland LE15 6BG
Tel: 01572 724666
www.tennants.co.uk

LINCOLNSHIRE
Eleys Auctioneers
26 Wide Bargate, Boston PE21 6RX
Tel: 01205 361687
www.jameseley.co.uk

Golding Young
Old Wharf Rd, Grantham NG31 7AA
Tel: 01476 565118
www.goldingyoung.com

Thomas Mawer & Son
Dunston House, Portland Street,
Lincoln LN5 7NN
Tel: 01522 524984
mawer.thos@lineone.net

Ian H. S. Naylor Auctions
20 St Johns St, Wainfleet PE24 4DJ
Tel/Fax: 01754 881210

Marilyn Swain
The Old Barracks, Sandon Road,
Grantham NG31 9AS
Tel: 01476 568861

John Taylors
The Wool Mart, Kidgate,
Louth LN11 9EZ
Tel: 01507 611107
www.invaluable.com/johntaylors

MERSEYSIDE
Cato Crane & Co.
6 Stanhope St, Liverpool L8 5RF
Tel: 0151 709 5559
www.cato-crane.co.uk

Outhwaite & Litherland
Fontenoy Street, Liverpool L3 2BE
Tel: 0151 236 6561
www.lots.uk.com

NORFOLK

Garry M. Emms & Co. Ltd.
Beevor Road,
Great Yarmouth NR30 3PS
Tel: 01493 332668
www.greatyarmouthauctions.com

T.W. Gaze & Son
Roydon Road, Diss IP22 4LN
Tel: 01379 650306
www.twgaze.com

Holt's Auctioneers
Church Farm Barns, Walferton
E31 6HA
Tel: 01485 542822
www.holtandcompany.co.uk

Horners Auctions
North Walsham Sale Rooms,
Midland Road,
North Walsham NR28 9JR
Tel: 01692 500603
www.horners.co.uk

Keys Auctioneers & Valuers
Aylsham Salerooms, Palmers Lane,
Aylsham, NR11 6JA
Tel: 01263 733195
www.keysauctions.co.uk

NOTTINGHAMSHIRE

Arthur Johnson & Sons
The Nottingham Auction Centre,
Meadow Ln, Nottingham NG2 3GY
Tel: 0115 986 9128
antiques@arthurjohnson.co.uk

Mellors & Kirk
Gregory Street, Nottingham,
Nottinghamshire NG7 2NL
Tel: 0115 979 0000
www.mellors-kirk.co.uk

Dreweatts
192 Mansfield Road,
Nottingham NG1 3HU
Tel: 0115 962 4141
www.dnfa.com/nottingham

John Pye & Sons
James Shipstone House,
Radford Rd, Nottingham NG7 7EA
Tel: 0115 970 6060
www.johnpye.co.uk

Northgate Auction Rooms Ltd.
17 Northgate, Newark NG24 1EX
Tel: 01636 605905
www.northgateauctionroomsnewark.co.uk

Peter Young Auctioneers
The Lord Barnby Memorial Hall,
Blyth S81 8HD
Tel: 01777 816 609
www.peteryoungauctioneers.co.uk

T Vennett-Smith Auctioneers
11 Nottingham Rd, Gotham
NG11 0HE
Tel: 0115 9830541
www.vennett-smith.com

OXFORDSHIRE

Holloway's
49 Parsons Street,
Banbury OX16 5NB
Tel: 01295 817777

www.hollowaysauctioneers.co.uk

Jones & Jacob Ltd.
Watcombe Manor Saleroom
Ingham Lane, Watlington OX49 5EJ
Tel 01491 612810
www.jonesandjacob.com

Mallams Fine Art Auctioneers
Bocard House, 24a St. Michael's St,
Oxford OX1 2EB
Tel: 01865 241358

Pevensey House, 27 Sheep Street,
Bicester OX26 7JF
Tel: 01869 252901
www.mallams.co.uk/fineart

Soames Country Auctions
Pinnocks Farm Estate,
Northmoor, Witney OX8 1AY
Tel: 01865 300626
www.soamesauctioneers.co.uk

SHROPSHIRE

Brettells Antiques & Fine Art
58 High Street, Newport
Tel: 01952 815925
www.brettells.com

Halls Fine Art
Welsh Bridge, Shrewsbury SY3 8LA
Tel: 01743 231212
www.hallsgb.com

Walker Barnett & Hill
Cosford Auction Rooms, Long Lane,
Cosford TF11 8PJ
Tel: 01902 375555
www.walker-barnett-hill.co.uk

SOMERSET

Greenslade Taylor Hunt
Magdelene House, Church Square,
Taunton TA1 1SB
Tel: 01823 332525
www.gth.net

Lawrence's Fine Art Auctioneers
South Street, Crewkerne TA18 8AB
Tel: 01460 73041
www.lawrences.co.uk

Dreweatts
66-68 Southover, Wells BA5 1UH
Tel: 01749 678094
www.dnfa.com/bristol

STAFFORDSHIRE

Hall and Lloyd Auctioneers
South Street, Stafford ST16 2DZ
Tel: 01785 258176

Louis Taylor Auctioneers
Britannia House, 10 Town Road,
Hanley, Stoke-on-Trent ST1 2QG
Tel: 01782 214111

Potteries Specialist Auctions
271 Waterloo Road, Cobridge, Stoke-on-Trent ST6 3HR
Tel: 01782 286622
www.potteriesauctions.com

Richard Winterton Auctioneers
School House Auction Rooms,
Hawkins Lane,
Burton-on-Trent DE14 1PT
Tel: 01283 511224
www.richardwinterton.co.uk

Wintertons
Lichfield Auction Centre, Fradley Park,
Lichfield WS13 8NF
Tel: 01543 263256
www.wintertons.co.uk

SUFFOLK

Abbotts Auction Rooms
Campsea Ashe,
Nr. Woodbridge IP13 0PS
Tel: 01728 746323
www.abbottsauctionrooms.co.uk

Durrant's
The Old School House,
Peddars Lane, Beccles NR34 9UE
Tel: 01502 713490
www.durrantsauctionrooms.com

Dyson & Son
The Auction Room, Church Street,
Clare CO10 8PD
Tel: 01787 277 993
www.dyson-auctioneers.co.uk

Lacy Scott and Knight Fine Art
10 Risbygate Street,
Bury St. Edmunds IP33 3AA
Tel: 01284 748600
www.lsk.co.uk

Neal Sons & Fletcher
26 Church Street,
Woodbridge IP12 1DP
Tel: 01394 382263
www.nsf.co.uk

Sworders
The Saleroom, Burkitts Lane,
Sudbury CO10 1HB
Tel: 01787 880305
www.sworder.co.uk

SURREY

Clarke Gammon Wellers
Unit18, Sussex Barn, Loseley Park,
Guildford, Surrey GU3 1HS
Tel: 01483 207570
www.clarkegammon.co.uk

Crows Auction Gallery
Reigate Road, Dorking
RH4 1SG
Tel: 01306 740382

Ewbank Auctioneers
Burnt Common Auction Rooms, London
Rd, Send, Woking GU23 7LN
Tel: 01483 223101
www.ewbankauctions.co.uk

Dreweatts
Baverstock House, 93 High Street,
Godalming GU7 1AL
Tel: 01483 423 567
www.dnfa.com/godalming

John Nicholson
Longfield, Midhurst Road,
Haslemere GU27 3HA
Tel: 01428 653727
www.johnnicholsons.com

Lawrences' Auctioneers Ltd.
Norfolk House, 80 High Street,
Bletchingley RH1 4PA
Tel: 01883 743323
www.lawrencesbletchingley.co.uk

P.F. Windibank Auctioneers
Dorking Halls, Reigate Road, Dorking
RH4 1SG
Tel: 01306 884556/876280
www.windibank.co.uk

Richmond & Surrey Auctions
Richmond Station, Kew Road,
Old Railway Parcels Depot,
Richmond,TW9 2NA
Tel: 020 8948 6677
rsatrading.richmond@virgin.net

EAST SUSSEX

Burstow & Hewett
Lower Lake, Battle,
East Sussex TN33 0AT
Tel: 01424 772374
www.burstowandhewett.co.uk

Dreweatts
46-50 South Street,
Eastbourne BN21 4XB
Tel: 01323 410419
www.dnfa.com/eastbourne

Eastbourne Auction Rooms
Auction House, Finmere Road,
Eastbourne BN22 8QL
Tel: 01323 431444
www.eastbourneauction.com

Gorringes Auction Galleries
Terminus Road,
Bexhill-on-Sea TN39 3LR
Tel: 01424 212994

15 North Street, Lewes BN7 2PD
Tel: 01273 472503
www.gorringes.co.uk

Raymond P. Inman
The Auction Galleries, 98A Coleridge
Street, Hove BN3 5 AA
Tel: 01273 774777
www.invaluable.com/raymondinman

Rye Auction Galleries
Rock Channel, Rye TN31 7HL
Tel: 01797 222124

Scarborough Perry Fine Arts
Hove Street, Hove BN3 2GL
Tel: 01273 735266
www.scarboroughperry.com

Wallis & Wallis
West Street Auction Galleries,
Lewes BN7 2NJ
Tel: 01273 480208
www.wallisandwallis.co.uk

WEST SUSSEX

Henry Adams Fine Art
Baffins Hall, Baffins Lane,
Chichester PO19 1UA
Tel: 01243 532223
www.henryadamsfineart.co.uk

John Bellman Ltd.
New Pound, Wisborough Green,
Billingshurst RH14 0AZ
Tel: 01403 700858
www.bellmans.co.uk

Denham's
The Auction Galleries,
Warnham, Nr Horsham RH12 3RZ
Tel: 01403 255699
www.catalogs.icollector.com/denhams

Sotheby's Sussex
Summers Place,
Billinghursts RH14 9AD
Tel: 01403 833500
www.sothebys.com

Stride & Son Auctions
Southdown House, St John's Street,
Chichester P019 1XQ
Tel: 01243 780207
www.stridesauctions.co.uk

Rupert Toovey & Co.
Spring Gdns, Washington RH20 3BS
Tel: 01903 891955
www.rupert-toovey.com

Worthing Auction Galleries
Fleet House, Teville Gate,
Worthing BN11 1UA
Tel: 01903 205565
www.worthing-auctions.co.uk

TYNE AND WEAR
Anderson & Garland
Anderson House, Crispin Court,
Newbiggin Lane, Westerhope,
Newcastle upon Tyne NE5 1BF
Tel: 0191 430 3000
www.andersonandgarland.com

Boldon Auction Galleries
24a Front St, East Boldon NE36 0SJ
Tel: 0191 537 2630
www.boldonauctions.co.uk

WARWICKSHIRE
Bigwood Auctioneers Ltd
The Old School, Tiddington, Stratford-
upon-Avon CV37 7AW
Tel: 01789 269415
www.bigwoodauctioneers.co.uk

Locke & England
18 Guy Street,
Leamington Spa CV32 4RT
Tel: 01926 889100
www.leauction.co.uk

Warwick & Warwick Ltd
Chalon House, Scar Bank, Millers
Road, Warwick CV34 5DB
Tel: 01926 499031
www.warwickandwarwick.com

WEST MIDLANDS
Biddle & Webb
Ladywood, Middleway,
Birmingham B16 0PP
Tel: 0121 455 8042
www.biddleandwebb.co.uk

Black Country Auctions Ltd.
Baylies' Hall, Tower Street,
Dudley DY1 1NB
Tel: 01384 250220
www.blackcountryauctions.co.uk

Bonhams
The Old House, Station Road, Knowle,
Solihull B93 0HT
Tel: 01564 776151
www.bonhams.com

Fellows & Sons
Augusta House, 19 Augusta Street,
Hockley, Birmingham B18 6JA
Tel: 0121 212 2131
www.fellows.co.uk

WILTSHIRE
Atwell Martin
2 New Road, Chippenham SN15 1EJ
Tel: 01249 449800

Henry Aldridge & Son
Unit 1 Bath Road Business Centre
Bath Road, Devizes SN10 1XA
Tel: 01380 729199
www.henry-aldridge.co.uk

The Hilditch Auction Rooms
Gloucester Road Trading Estate,
Malmesbury SN16 9JT
Tel: 01666 822577
www.hilditchauctions.co.uk

Netherhampton Salerooms
Salisbury Auction Centre,
Netherhampton, Salisbury SP2 8RH
Tel: 01722 340041
www.salisburyauctioncentre.co.uk

Woolley & Wallis
51-61 Castle Street,
Salisbury SP1 3SU
Tel: 01722 424500
www.woolleyandwallis.co.uk

WORCESTERSHIRE
Andrew Grant Auctioneers
St. Marks House, St. Marks Close,
Worcester WR5 3DL
Tel: 01905 357547
www.andrew-grant.co.uk

Griffiths & Charles
57 Foregate St, Worcester WR1 1DZ
Tel: 01906 720160
www.griffiths-charles.co.uk

Philip Laney Fine Art
Malvern Auction Centre,
Portland Road, Malvern WR14 2TA
Tel: 01684 893933
www.invaluable.com/philiplaney

Philip Serrell Auctioneers
Barnards Green Road,
Malvern WR14 3LW
Tel: 01684 892314
www.serrell.com

EAST YORKSHIRE
Gilbert Baitson
The Edwardian Auction Galleries,
Wiltshire Road, Hull HU4 6PG
Tel: 01482 500500
www.gilbert-baitson.co.uk

Dee Atkinson & Harrison
The Exchange Saleroom,
Driffield YO25 7LJ
Tel: 01377 253151
www.dee-atkinson-harrison.co.uk

Hawley's
Albion House, Westgate,
North Cave HU15 2NJ
Tel: 01430 470654
www.hawleys.info

NORTH YORKSHIRE
Boulton & Cooper
St Michael's House, Market Place,
Malton YO17 7LR
Tel: 01653 696151
www.boultoncooper.co.uk

H.C. Chapman & Son
The Auction Mart, North Street,
Scarborough YO11 1DL
Tel: 01723 372424

Cundalls
15 Market Place, Malton YO17 7LP
Tel: 01653 697820
www.cundalls.co.uk

David Duggleby Fine Art
The Vine Street Salerooms,
Scarborough YO11 1XN
Tel: 01723 507111

The Paddock Salerooms
Whitby YO21 3DB
Tel: 01947 820 033
www.davidduggleby.com

Malcolm's No. 1 Auctioneers
The Chestnuts, 16 Park Ave, Sherburn in
Elmet, Nr Leeds LS25 6EF
Tel: 01977 684 971
www.malcolmsno1auctions.co.uk

Christopher Matthews
23 Mount Street,
Harrogate, HG2 8DQ
Tel: 01423 871756

Morphets of Harrogate
6 Albert Street, Harrogate HG1 1JL
Tel: 01423 530030
www.morphets.co.uk

Tennants
The Auction Centre, Leyburn DL8 5SG
Tel: 01969 623780
www.tennants.co.uk

SOUTH YORKSHIRE
BBR Auctions
Elsecar Heritage Centre,
Near Barnsley S74 8AA
Tel: 01226 745156
www.bbrauctions.co.uk

A.E. Dowse & Son
Cornwall Galleries, Scotland Street,
Sheffield S3 7DE
Tel: 0114 272 5858
www.aedowseandson.com

ELR Auctions Ltd.
The Sheffield Saleroom, The Nichols
Building, Shalesmoor, Sheffield S3 8UJ
Tel: 0114 281 6161
www.elrauctions.com

Wilkinson's Auctioneers Ltd.
The Old Salerooms, 28 Netherhall
Road, Doncaster, DN1 2PW
Tel: 01302 814884
www.wilkinsons-auctioneers.co.uk

WEST YORKSHIRE
De Romes
12 New John Street, Westgate,
Bradford BD1 2QY
Tel: 01274 734116

Andrew Hartley Fine Arts
Victoria Hall Salerooms,
Little Lane, Ilkley LS29 8EA
Tel: 01943 816363
www.andrewhartleyfinearts.co.uk

John Walsh & Co. Auctioneers
Ashfield House Auction Rooms,
Illingworth Street, Ossett WF5 8AL
Tel: 01924 264030
www.john-walsh.co.uk

SCOTLAND
Auction Rooms Ltd.
Castle Laurie, Bankside,
Falkirk, Sterlingshire FK2 7XF
Tel: 01324 623000
www.auctionroomsfalkirk.co.uk

Bonhams
65 George St, Edinburgh EH2 2JL
Tel: 0131 225 2266
www.bonhams.com

Loves Auction Rooms
52-54 Canal Street, Perth,
Perthshire PH2 8LF
Tel: 01738 633337

Lyon & Turnbull Ltd.
33 Broughton Place,
Edinburgh EH1 3RR
Tel: 0131 557 8844

4 Woodside Place, Glasgow,
Lanarkshire G3 7QF
Tel: 0141 353 5070
www.lyonandturnbull.com

MDS Auction Co.
15-17 Smeaton Industrial Estate,
Kirkcaldy, Fife KY1 2HE
Tel: 01592 640969
www.scotlandauction.co.uk

D.J. Manning Auctioneers
Carriden, Bo'ness,
West Lothian EH51 9SF
Tel: 01506 827693
www.djmanning.co.uk

McTear's
Clydeway Business Centre,
8 Elliot Place, Glasgow G3 8EP
Tel: 0141 221 4456
www.mctears.co.uk

Sotheby's
112 George St, Edinburgh EH2 3LH
Tel: 0131 226 7201
www.sothebys.com

Taylor's Auction Rooms
11 Panmure Row, Montrose,
Angus DD10 8HH
Tel: 01674 672775
www.scotlandstreasures.co.uk

Thomson, Roddick & Medcalf
44/3 Hardengreen Business Park,
Eskbank, Edinburgh EH22 3NX
Tel: 0131 454 9090

60 Whitesands, Dumfries, DG1 2RS
Tel: 01387 279879
www.thomsonroddick.com

WALES
Anthemion Auctions
15 Norwich Road, Cardiff CF23 9AB
Tel: 029 2047 2444
www.anthemionauctions.com

Bonhams
7-8 Park Place, Cardiff,
Glamorgan CF10 3DP
Tel: 02920 727980

Napier House, Spilman Street,
Carmarthen SA31 1JY
Tel: 01267 238231
www.bonhams.com

Morgan Evans
30 Church Street, Llangefni, Anglesey
LL77 7DU
Tel: 01248 723303/421582
www.morganevans.com

Peter Francis
Curiosity Salerooms, 19 King Street,
Carmarthen, SA31 1BH
Tel: 01267 233456
www.peterfrancis.co.uk

Jones & Llewelyn
Llandeilo Auction Rooms, 21 New
Road, Llandeilo, Dyfed SA19 6DE
Tel: 01558 823430
www.joneslewelyn.freeserve.co.uk

Rogers-Jones & Co.
33 Abergele Road, Colwyn Bay,
Conway LL29 7RU
Tel: 01492 532176
www.rogersjones.ukauctioneers.com

Welsh Country Auctions
2 Carmarthen Road, Cross Hands,
Llanelli, Carmarthenshire SA14 6SP
Tel: 01269 844428
www.welshcountryauctions.com

Wingetts Auction Gallery
29 Holt Street, Wrexham,
Clwyd LL13 8DH
Tel: 01978 353553
www.wingetts.co.uk

AUSTRALIA
Bonhams & Goodman
7 Anderson Street, Double Bay,
New South Wales 2028 Australia
Tel: 0061 2 9327 9913
www.bonhamsandgoodman.com.au

Deutscher-Menzies
1140 Malvern Road, Malvern
Victoria 3144, Australia
Tel: 0061 3 9822 1911
www.deutschermenzies.com

Lawson-Menzies
212 Cumberland Street,
Sydney 2000, Australia
Tel: 0061 2 9241 3411
Fax: 0061 2 9251 5869
www.lawsonmenzies.com.au

Shapiro
162 Queen Street, Woollahra,
New South Wales 2025, Australia
Tel: 0061 2 9326 1588
www.shapiroauctioneers.com.au

NEW ZEALAND
Webb's
18 Manukau Road,
PO Box 99 251, Newmarket, Auckland
1000, New Zealand
Tel: 0064 9 524 6804
www.webbs.co.nz

Specialists who would like to be included in the next edition, or have a change of address or telephone number, should contact us by 1 February 2009.
Readers should contact dealers by telephone before visiting them to avoid a wasted journey.

ANTIQUITIES
Ancient Art
85 The Vale, Southgate,
London N14 6AT
Tel: 020 8882 1509
www.ancientart.co.uk

David Aaron Ancient Arts
22 Berkeley Sq, Mayfair,
London W1J 6EH
Tel: 020 7491 9588

Finch & Co.
Suite No 744, 2 Old Brompton Rd,
London SW7 3DQ
Tel: 020 7413 9937
www.finch-and-co.co.uk

Helios Gallery
292 Westbourne Grove,
London W11 2PS
Tel: 07711 955 997
www.heliosgallery.com

John A. Pearson
Horton Lodge, Horton Rd, Horton,
Near Slough, Berkshire SL3 9NU
Tel: 01753 682136

Rupert Wace Ancient Art Ltd.
14 Old Bond St, London W1X 3DB
Tel: 020 7495 1623
www.rupertwace.co.uk

Ancient & Gothic
PO Box 5390,
Bournemouth, BH7 6XR
Tel: 01202 431721

ARCHITECTURAL
Pattisons
108 London Road, Aston Clinton,
Buckinghamshire HP22 5HS
Tel: 01296 632 300
www.ddd-uk.com

D & R Blissett
c/o Coutts & Co, 440 Strand
London WC2R 0QS

Joanna Booth
247 King's Road, London SW3 5EL
Tel: 020 7352 8998
www.joannabooth.co.uk

Drummonds
The Kirkpatrick Buildings, 25 London
Road, Hindhead,
Surrey GU26 6AB
Tel: 01428 609444
www.drummonds-arch.co.uk

LASSCO
St. Michael's, Mark St (off Paul St),
London EC2A 4ER
Tel: 020 7749 9944
www.lassco.co.uk

Sweerts de Landas
Dunsborough Park, Ripley,
Surrey GU23 6AL
Tel: 01483 225366
www.sweerts.com

Robert Mills Ltd.
Narroways Rd, Eastville, Bristol BS2 9XB
Tel: 0117 955 6542
www.rmills.co.uk

ARMS & MILITARIA
Q&C Militaria
22 Suffolk Road,
Cheltenham, GL50 2AQ
Tel: 01242 519815
www.qcmilitaria.com

Dennis Exall
Tel: 07810 118338

Rod Akeroyd & Son
22 Ribblesdale Pl, Preston, PR1 3NA
Tel: 01772 203845
www.firearmscollector.com

Garth Vincent
The Old Manner Hse, Allington,
Nr Grantham, NG32 2DH
Tel: 01400 281358
www.guns.uk.com

Avrick Antiques
Tel: 01295 738 318
avrick_antiques@tiscali.co.uk

West Street Antiques
63 West Street, Dorking, RH4 1BS
Tel: 01306 883487
www.antiquesarmsandarmour.com

BAROGRAPHS
Richard Twort
Tel: 01934 612439
walls@mirage-interiors.com

CARPETS & RUGS
Atlantic Bay Gallery
5 Sedley Place, London W1R 1HH
Tel: 020 7355 3301
atlanticbaygallery@btinternet.com

C John (Rare Rugs) Ltd.
70 South Audley Street,
London W1K 2RA
Tel: 020 7493 5288
www.cjohn.com

Gallery Yacou
127 Fulham Rd, London SW3 6RT
Tel: 020 7584 2929
galleryyacou@aol.com

Gideon Hatch
1 Port House, Plantation Wharf,
Battersea, London SW11 3TY
Tel: 020 7223 3996
www.gideonhatch.co.uk

John Eskenazi Ltd.
15 Old Bond St, London W1S 4AX
Tel: 020 7409 3001
www.john-eskenazi.com

Karel Weijand
Lion & Lamb Courtyard, Farnham,
Surrey GU9 7LL
Tel: 01252 726215
www.karkweijand.com

Lindfield Galleries
62 High Street, Lindfield,
West Sussex RH16 2HL
Tel: 01444 483817
david@orientalandantiquerugs.com

Richard Purdon Antique Carpets
158 The Hill, Burford,
Oxfordshire OX18 4QY
Tel: 01993 823777
www.purdon.com

Wadsworth's
Marehill, Pulborough,
West Sussex RH20 2DY
Tel: 01798 873 555
www.wadsworthsrugs.com

BOOKS
Biblion
1/7 Davies Mews, London W1K 5AB
Tel: 020 7629 1374
www.biblion.com

Barter Books
Alnwick Station, Alnwick NE66 2NP
Tel: 01665 604888
www.barterbooks.co.uk

George Bayntun
Manvers Street, Bath BA1 1JW
Tel: 01225 466000

David Aldous-Cook
PO Box 413, Sutton SM3 8SZ
Tel: 020 8642 4842
office@davidaldouscook.co.uk

BOXES
Alan & Kathy Stacey
PO Box 2771 Chapel Lane,
Yeovil, Somerset BA22 7DZ
Tel: 02076 444 049
www.antiqueboxes.uk.com

Mostly Boxes
93 High Street, Eton,
Windsor, Berkshire SL4 6AF
Tel: 01753 858 470
CERAMICS
Albert Amor Ltd.
37 Bury Street, St James's,
London SW1Y 6AU
Tel: 020 7930 2444
www.albertamor.co.uk

Andrew Dando
34 Market Street, Bradford-on-Avon,
Wiltshire BA15 1LL
Tel: 01225 422 702
www.andrewdando.co.uk

Brian & Angela Downes
PO Box 431, Chippenham,
Wiltshire SN14 6SZ
Tel/Fax: 01454 238134

Clive & Lynne Jackson
Cheltenham, Gloucestershire
Open by appointment only
Tel: 01242 254 3751
Mob: 07710 239351

Davies Antiques
c/o Cadogan Tate, Unit 6, 6-12 Ponton
Road, London SW8 5BA
Tel: 020 8947 1902
www.antique-meissen.com

E & H Manners
66A Kensington Church Street,
London W8 4BY
Tel: 020 7229 5516
www.europeanporcelain.com

Garry Atkins
Tel: 020 7727 8737
www.englishpottery.com

Gillian Neale Antiques
PO Box 247, Aylesbury,
Buckinghamshire HP20 1JZ
Tel: 01296 423754
www.gilliannealeantiques.co.uk

Hope & Glory
131A Kensington Church Street,
London W8 7LP
Tel: 020 7727 8424

John Howard at Heritage
Heritage, 6 Market Place,
Woodstock, Oxfordshire OX20 1TA
Tel: 0870 444 0678
www.antiquepottery.co.uk

Jonathan Horne Antiques Ltd.
66c Kensington Church Street, London
W8 4BY
Tel: 020 7221 5658
www.jonathanhorne.co.uk

Klaber & Klaber
PO Box 9445, London NW3 1WD
Tel: 020 7435 6537
www.klaber.com

**Mary Wise and Grosvenor
Antiques**
58 Kensington Church Street, London
W8 4DB.
Tel: 020 7937 8649
www.wiseantiques.com

Robyn Robb
43 Napier Avenue, London SW6 3PS
Tel: 020 7731 2878

Roderick Jellicoe
PO. Box No. 50732
London NW6 6XW
Tel: 020 7727 1571
www.englishporcelain.com

Rogers de Rin
76 Royal Hospital Road,
Paradise Walk, Chelsea,
London SW3 4HN
Tel: 020 7352 9007
www.rogersderin.co.uk

Roy W. Bunn Antiques
Tel: 01282 813703
www.roywbunnantiques.co.uk

Steppes Hill Farm Antiques
Steppes Hill Farm, Stockbury,
Sittingbourne, Kent ME9 7RB
Tel: 01795 842205
dwabuck@btinternet.com

Stockspring Antiques
114 Kensington Church Street,
London W8 4BH
Tel: 020 7727 7995
www.antique-porcelain.co.uk

T.C.S. Brooke
The Grange, 57 Norwich Road,
Wroxham, Norfolk NR12 8RX
Tel: 01603 782644

Thrift Cottage Antiques
PO Box 113, Bury St Edmunds, Suffolk
IP33 2RQ
Tel: 01284 702470
www.britishporcelain.com

Valerie Main
PO Box 92, Carlisle,
Cumbria CA5 7GD
Tel: 01228 711342
valerie.main@btinternet.com

W.W. Warner Antiques
The Green, High Street,
Brasted, Kent TN16 1JL
Tel: 01959 563698

Yvonne Adams Antiques
The Coffee House, 3 & 4 Church St,
Stow on the Wold, Glos. GL54 1BB
Tel: 01451 832 015
www.antiquemeissen.com

Julian Eade
Tel: 01865 300349/07973 542971

Barling Porcelain
Tel: 01621 890058
www.barling.uk.com

Tony Horsley
PO Box 3127, Brighton BN1 5SS
Tel: 01273 550770

Greystoke Antiques
4 Swan Yard, Sherborne DT9 3AX
Tel: 01935 812833

Styles of Stow
(see Clocks)

Winson Antiques
Unit 11, Langston Priory Workshops,
Kingham OX7 6UP
Tel: 01608 658856 / 07764 476776
www.clivepayne.co.uk

Judi Bland Antiques
Tel: 01276 857576

CLOCKS, WATCHES & BAROMETERS
P.A. Oxley
The Old Rectory, Cherhill, Calne, SN11
8UX
Tel: 01249 816227
www.britishantiqueclocks.com

Coppelia Antiques
Holford Lodge, Plumley, Moor Rd, Nr
Knutsford, Plumley, WA16 9RS
Tel: 01565 722197
www.coppeliaantiques.co.uk

The Grandfather Clock Shop
The Little House, Sheep St, Stow-on-
the-Wold, GL54 1JS
Tel: 01451 830455
www.stylesofstow.co.uk

Woodward Antique Clocks
21 Suffolk Parade,
Cheltenham GL50 2AE
Tel: 01242 245667
www.woodwardclocks.co.uk

Northern Clocks
Boothsbank Farm, Worsley,
Manchester M28 1LL
Tel: 0161 790 8414
www.northernclocks.co.uk

The Clock-Work-Shop
6A Parchment Street
Winchester SO23 8AT
Tel: 01962 842331
ww.clock-work-shop.co.uk

The Old Clock Shop
63 Hight Street,
West Malling ME19 6NA
Tel: 01732 843246
www.theoldclockshop.co.uk

The Clock Clinic Ltd.
85 Lower Richmond Road,
Putney, SW15 1EU
Tel: 020 8788 1407
www.clockclinic.co.uk

Roderick Antique Clocks
23 Vicarage Gate, London W8 4AA
Tel: 020 79378517
www.roderickantiqueclocks.com

The Clock Shop
The Pitching, Market Place,
Castle Cary BA7 7AL
Tel: 01963 359100
www.castlecaryclockshop.co.uk

Kembery Antique Clocks Ltd.
George Street Antique Centre,
8 Edger Buildings, George Street,
Bath BA1 2EH
Tel: 0117 956 5281
www.kdclocks.co.uk

The Essence of Time
Unit 2, Curborough Antiques & Crafts
Centre, Curborough Hall Farm, Watery
Lane, Eastern Avenue By-Pass,
Lichfield, WS13 8ES
Tel: 01543 418239

The Clock House
75 Pound Street,
Carshalton SM5 3PG
Tel: 020 8773 4833
www.theclockhouse.co.uk

Allan Smith Clocks
Amity Cottage,
162 Beechcroft Rd,
Upper Stratton,
Swindon SN2 7QR
Tel: 01793 822977
www.allansmithantiqueclocks.co.uk

Brian Loomes
Calf Haugh Farm,
Pateley Bridge,
Yorkshire HG3 5HW
Tel: 01423 711163
www.brianloomes.com

Alan Walker
Halfway Manor, Halfway, Nr. Newbury,
Berkshire RG20 8NR
Tel: 01488 657670
www.alanwalker-barometers.com

Baskerville Antiques
Saddlers House, Saddlers Row,
Petworth, West Sussex GU28 0AN
Tel: 01798 342067
brianbaskerville@aol.com

Bobinet Ltd.
PO Box 2730, London NW8 9PL
Tel: 020 7266 0783
Fax: 020 7289 5119

David Gibson
PO Box 301, Axminster,
Devon EX13 7YJ
Tel: 01297 631179
www.davidgibson.co.uk

Derek and Tina Rayment
Orchard House, Barton Rd, Barton,
Nr. Farndon, Cheshire SY14 7HT
Tel: 01829 270429
www.antique-barometers.com

Derek Roberts
25 Shipbourne Road,
Tonbridge, Kent TN10 3DN
Tel: 01732 358986
www.quallityantiqueclocks.com

G.E. Marsh (Antique Clocks)
32a The Square, Winchester,
Hampshire SO23 9EX
Tel: 01962 844443
www.marshclocks.co.uk

Jeffrey Formby Antiques
Orchard Cottage, East St, Moreton-in-
Marsh, Gloucestershire GL56 0LQ
Tel: 01608 650558
www.formby-clocks.co.uk

Jillings Antiques
Croft House, 17 Church Street,
Newent, Gloucestershire GL18 1PU
Tel: 01531 822100
www.jillings.com

John Carlton-Smith
17 Ryder Street, London SW1Y 6PY
Tel: 020 7930 6622
www.fineantiqueclocks.com

Montpellier Clocks
13 Rotunda Terrace, Montpellier
Street, Cheltenham GL50 1SW
Tel: 01242 242178
www.montpellierclocks.com

Patric Capon
PO Box 581, Bromley, Kent BR1 2WX
Tel: 020-8467 5722
patric.capon@saqnet.co.uk

Pendulum of Mayfair
51 Maddox St, London W1S 2PJ
Tel: 020 7629 6606
www.pendulumofmayfair.co.uk

Raffety & Walwyn Ltd.
79 Kensington Church Street,
London W8 4BG
Tel: 020 7938 1100
www.raffetyantiqueclocks.com

Somlo Antiques
7 Piccadilly Arcade, London SW1Y 6NH
Tel: 020 7499 6526   www.somlo.com

Strike One
48A Highbury Hill, London N5 1AP
Tel: 020 7354 2790
www.strikeone.co.uk

The Watch Gallery
129 Fulham Rd, London SW3 6RT
Tel: 020 7581 3239
Fax: 020 7584 6497

Weather House Antiques
Foster Clough, Hebden Bridge,
West Yorkshire HX7 5QZ
Tel: 01422 882808/886961
kymwalker@btinternet.com

Anthony Woodburn Ltd.
PO Box 2669, Lewes,
East Sussex BN7 3JE
Tel: 01273 486666
www.anthonywoodburn.com

Horological Workshops
204 Worplesdon Road, Guildford,
Surrey GU2 6UY
Tel: 01483 576496
www.horologicalworkshops.com

COSTUME JEWELLERY & ACCESSORIES
Cristobal
26 Church St, London NW8 8EP
Tel: 020 7724 7230
www.cristobal.co.uk

Eclectica
www.eclectica.biz

Sara Hughes Vintage Compacts
http://mysite.wanadoo-
members.co.uk/sara_compacts

Linda Bee
Grays Antique Market Mews,
1-7 Davies St, London, W1Y 2LP
Tel: 020 7629 5921
www.graysantiques.com

Lynn & Brian Holmes
By appointment
Tel: 020 7368 6412

Richard Gibbon
neljeweluk@aol.com

Ritzy
7 The Mall Antiques Arcade,
359 Upper St, London N1 0PD
Tel: 020 7704 0127

Sylvie Spectrum
Stand 372, Grays Antique Market, 58
Davies St, London W1K 5LP
Tel: 020 7629 3501
spectrum@grays.clara.net

William Wain at Antiquarius
Stand J6, Antiquarius, 135 Kings
Road, Chelsea, London SW3 4PW
Tel: 020 7351 4905
williamwain@btopenworld.com

DECORATIVE ARTS
Adrian Sassoon
Rutland Gate, London SW7 1BB
Tel: 020 7581 9888
www.adriansassoon.com

Aesthetics
Stand V2, Antiquarius, 131-141 Kings
Road, London SW3 4PW
Tel: 020 7352 0395

Arenski Fine Arts Ltd.
The Coach House, Ledbury Mews
North, London W11 2AF
Tel: 020 7727 8599
www.arenski.com

Art Deco Etc.
73 Upper Gloucester Road, Brighton,
Sussex BN1 3LQ
Tel: 01273 202 937
johnclark@artdecoetc.co.uk

Art Nouveau Originals c.1900
5 Pierrepont Row Arcade, Camden
Passage, Islington, London N1 8EF
Tel: 020 7359 4127

Beth
Stand G043/46, Alfies Antiques
Market, 13-25 Church St,
London NW8 8DT
Tel: 020 7723 5613
Mob: 07776 136 003

Beverley
30 Church Street, Marylebone, London
NW8 8EP
Tel: 020 7262 1576

Circa 1900
Shop 17, Georgian Village, Camden
Passage, London N1 8DU
Mob: 0771 370 9211
www.circa1900.org

Charles Edwards
19a Rumbold Road,
London SW6 2DY
Tel: 020 7736 7172
charles@charlesedwards.com

Fay Lucas Art Metal
Christie's Fine Art Security,
42 Ponton Rd, London SW8 5BA
Tel: 020 7371 4404
www.faylucas.com

**Gallery 1930 - Susie Cooper
Ceramics**
18 Church St, London NW8 8EP
Tel: 020 7723 1555
www.susiecooperceramics.com

H Blairman & Sons Ltd.
119 Mount St, London W1K 3NL
Tel: 020 7493 0444
www.blairman.co.uk

Halcyon Days Ltd.
14 Brook St, London W1Y 1AA
Tel: 020 7629 8811
www.halcyondays.co.uk

Hall-Bakker at Heritage
6 Market Place, Woodstock,
Oxfordshire, OX20 1TA
Tel: 01993 811 332

Harris Lindsay
67 Jermyn St, London SW1Y 6NY
Tel: 020 7839 5767
www.harrislindsay.com

Keshishian
73 Pimlico Rd, London SW1 W 8NE
Tel: 020 7730 8810
Fax: 020 7730 8803

Mike Weedon
7 Camden Passage, Islington,
London N1 8EA
Tel: 020 7226 5319
www.mikeweedonantiques.com

Rainer Zietz Ltd.
1a Prairie St, London SW8 3PX
Tel: 020 7498 2355
Fax: 020 7720 7745

Richard Gardner Antiques
Swan House, Market Square,
Petworth, West Sussex GU28 0AN
Tel: 01798 343 411
www.richardgardenerantiques.co.uk

Robert Bowman Ltd.
8 Duke Street, St James's,
London SW1Y 6BN
Tel: 020 7839 3100
www.robertbowman.com

Rumours
4 The Mall Antiques Arcade,
359 Upper St, London N1 0PD
Tel: 020 7704 6549

Sladmore Sculpture Gallery
32 Bruton Place, Berkeley Square,
London W1X 7AA
Tel: 020 7499 0365
www.sladmore.com

Spencer Swaffer Antiques
30 High Street, Arundel, West Sussex
BN18 9AB
Tel: 01903 882132
www.spencerswaffer.com

Style Gallery
10 Camden Passage,
London N1 8ED
Tel: 020 7359 7867
www.styleantiques.co.uk

Tadema Gallery
10 Charlton Place, Camden Passage,
London N1 8AJ
Tel: 020 7359 1055
www.tademagallery.com

The Coach House London
185 Westbourne Grove,
London W11 2SB
Tel: 020 7229 8311
arenski@netcomuk.co.uk

The Country Seat
Huntercombe Manor Barn, Nr. Henley
on Thames, Oxon RG9 5RY
Tel: 01491 641349
www.thecountryseat.com

The Design Gallery
5 The Green, Westerham,
Kent TN16 1AS
Tel: 01959 561234
www.designgallery.co.uk

The Red House
Duncombe Place, York, North Yorkshire
YO1 7ED
Tel: 01904 637 000
www.redhouseyork.co.uk

Titus Omega
Tel: 020 7688 1295
www.titusomega.com

Van Den Bosch
Shop 1, Georgian Village, Camden
Passage, Islington N1 8DU
Tel: 020 7226 4550
www.vandenbosch.co.uk

A.S. Antique Galleries
26 Broad Street, Pendletonm
Salford M6 5BY
Tel: 0161 737 5938
artnouveau-artdeco.com

Clarion Antiques & Fine Art
Ground Floor, 2 St Georges Sq,
Lytham St Anns, FY8 2NY
Tel: 01253 721903
www.clarionantiquesltd.co.uk

Crafts Noveau
112 Alexandra Park Road,
Muswell Hill, N10 2AE
Tel: 0208 444 3300
www.craftsnoveau.co.uk

Mitofsky Antiques
8 Rathfarnham Road,
Terenure, Dublin 6
Tel: 492 0033
www.mitofskyantiques.com

Garret & Hurst Sculpture
PO Box 658,
East Grinstead, RH19 3GH
Tel: 01342 311729
www.garretandhurst.co.uk

DOLLS AND TOYS
Bébés et Jouets
c/o Lochend Post Office,
165 Restalrig Road, Edinburgh,
Midlothian EH7 6HW
Tel: 0131 332 5650
bebesetjouets@tiscali.co.uk

**Collectors Old Toy Shop
& Antiques**
89 Northgate, Halifax,
West Yorkshire HX1 1XF
Tel: 01422 360434/822148
toysandbanks@aol.com
collectorsoledtoy@aol.com

Sue Pearson
18 Brighton Square, 'The Lanes'
Brighton, East Sussex BN1 1HD
Tel: 01273 774851
www.suepearson.co.uk

Victoriana Dolls
101 Portobello Road,
London W11 2BQ
Tel: 01737 249 525
heather.bond@totalserve.co.uk

Teddy Bears of Whitney
99 High St, Witney, OX28 6HY
Tel: 01993 702616
www.teddybears.co.uk

FISHING
The Old Tackle Box
PO Box 55, High Street,
Cranbrook, TN17 3ZU
Tel: 01580 713979
tackle.box@virgin.net

FURNITURE
Adrian Alan
66/67 South Audley Street,
London W1Y 5FE
Tel: 020 7495 2324
www.adrianalan.com

Alistair Sampson Antiques
120 Mount St, London W1K 3NN
Tel: 020 7409 1799
www.alistairsampson.com

Anthemion
Cartmel, Grange-over-Sands, Cumbria
LA11 6QD
Tel: 015395 36295

Anthony Outred (Antiques)
Blanchard, Froxfield, Nr. Marlborough,
Wiltshire SN8 3LD
Tel: 020 7730 7948
www.outred.co.uk

The Antiques Warehouse
25 Lightwood Road, Buxton,
Derbyshire SK17 7BJ
Tel: 01298 72967

Antoine Cheneviere Fine Arts
27 Bruton St, London W1J 6QN
Tel: 020 7491 1007

Antony Preston Antiques Ltd.
The Square, Stow-on-the-Wold,
Cheltenam, Glos GL54 1AB
Tel: 01451 831586 www.antonypre-ston.com

Apter Fredericks Ltd.
265-267 Fulham Road,
London SW3 6HY
Tel: 020 7352 2188
www.apter-fredericks.com

Avon Antiques
25-27 Market Street, Bradford-on-Avon, Wilts BA15 1LL
Tel: 01225 862052
www.avon-antiques.co.uk

Baggott Church Street Ltd.
Church Street, Stow-on-the-Wold,
Gloucestershire GL54 1BB
Tel: 01451 830 370

Blanchard Ltd.
86/88 Pimlico Road,
London SW1W 8PL
Tel: 020 7823 6310
piers@jwblanchard.com

Brian Rolleston (Antiques)
104a Kensington Church Street,
London W8 4BU
Tel: 020 7229 5892

Charles Lumb & Sons Ltd.
2 Montpellier Gardens, Harrogate,
North Yorkshire HG1 2TF
Tel: 01423 503776
Fax: 01423 530074

Cheverons Antiques Ltd
Unit 8, New Place, Blackboys Road,
Framfield, East Sussex
TN22 5EQ
Tel: 01825 891 223
www.chevertons.com

Christopher Buck Antiques
56-60 Sandgate High St, Sandgate,
Folkestone, Kent CT20 3AP
Tel: 01303 221 229
chrisbuck@throwley.freeserve.co.uk

Christopher Hodsoll Ltd.
89-91 Pimlico Road,
London SW1W 8PH
Tel: 020 7730 3370
www.hodsoll.com

Country Antiques (Wales) Ltd.
Castle Mill, Kidwelly Carmarthenshire,
SA17 4UU
Tel: 01554 890534
www.welshantiques.com

David J Hansord (Antiques)
6/7 Castle Hill, Lincoln,
Lincolnshire LN1 3AA
Tel: 01522 530044

David Love
10 Royal Parade, Harrogate,
North Yorkshire HG1 2SZ
Tel: 01423 565797
david.love@btconnect.com

Denzil Grant
Drinkstone House, Drinkstone, Bury St
Edmunds, Suffolk IP30 9TG
Tel: 01449 736576
www.denzilgrant.com

Didier Aaron (London) Ltd.
21 Ryder St, London SW1Y 6PX
Tel: 020 7839 4716
www.didieraaron.com

Douglas Bryan
By appointment only
Tel: 01580 713103

Elaine Phillips Antiques Ltd.
1 & 2 Royal Parade, Harrogate,
North Yorkshire HG1 2SZ
Tel: 01423 569 745

Freeman & Lloyd
44 Sandgate High St, Sandgate,
Folkestone, Kent CT20 3AP
Tel: 01303 248986
www.freemanandlloyd.com

Georgian Antiques
10 Pattison St, Leith Links, Edinburgh,
EH6 7HF, Scotland
Tel: 0131 553 7286
www.georgianantiques.net

Godson & Coles
92 Fulham Rd, London SW3 6HR
Tel: 020 7584 2200
www.godsonandcoles.co.uk

H.C. Baxter & Sons
40 Drewstead Road,
London SW16 1AB
Tel: 020 8769 5869/5969

H W Keil Ltd.
Tudor House, Broadway,
Worcestershire WR12 7DP
Tel: 01386 852408

Heath Bullocks
8 Meadrow, Godalming,
Surrey GU7 3HN
Tel: 01483 422562
Fax: 01483 426077

Hotspur Ltd.
14 Lowndes Street,
London SW1X 9EX
Tel: 020 7235 1918
enquiries@hotspurantiques.com

Huntington Antiques Ltd
Church Street, Stow-on-the-Wold,
Gloucestershire GL54 1BE
Tel: 01451 830 842
www.huntington-antiques.com

Jacob Stodel
Flat 53, Macready House, 75 Crawford
St, London W1H 1HS
Tel: 020 7723 3732
jacobstodel@aol.com

James Brett Ltd.
42 St Giles Street, Norwich,
Norfolk NR2 1LW
Tel: 01603 628171

Jeremy Ltd.
29 Lowndes St, London SW1X 9HX
Tel: 020 7823 2923
www.jeremy.ltd.uk

John Bly
By appointment:
27 Bury Street, St James's,
London SW1Y 6AL
Tel: 01442 823030
Showroom:
The Courtyard Church Square
Tring, Hertfordshire, HP23 5AE
Tel: 07831 888825/6
www.johnbly.com

John Hobbs Ltd.
107A Pimlico Road,
London SW1W 8PH
Tel: 020 7730 8369
www.johnhobbs.co.uk

John King
74 Pimlico Rd, London SW1W 8LS
Tel: 020 7730 0427
kingj896@aol.com

Lennox Cato Antiques
1 The Square, Church Street,
Edenbridge, Kent TN8 5BD
Tel: 01732 865 988
www.lennoxcato.com

Lucy Johnson
PO Box 84, Carterton, Burford,
Oxfordshire OX18 4AT
Tel: 07071 881232
lucy-johnson@lucy-johnson.com

Mac Humble Antiques
7-9 Woolley Street, Bradford-on-Avon,
Wiltshire BA15 1AD
Tel: 01225 866329
www.machumbleantiques.co.uk

Michael Foster
118 Fulham Rd, London SW3 6HU
Tel: 020 7373 3636
Fax: 020 7373 4042

Michael Norman Antiques
61 Holland Road, Hove,
East Sussex BN3 1JN
Tel: 01273 329 253
Fax: 01273 206 556

Norman Adams
8-10 Hans Rd, London SW3 1RX
Tel: 020 7589 5266
www.normanadams.com

Oswald Simpson
The Chapel Maltings, Long Malford,
Suffolk CO10 9HX
Tel: 01787 379287

Owen Humble Antiques
By appointment only
Tel: 0191 267 7220

Patrick Sandberg Antiques
150-152 Kensington Church Street,
London W8 4BN
Tel: 020 7229 0373
www.antique.net

Paul Hopwell Antiques
30 High Street, West Haddon,
Northamptonshire NN6 7AP
Tel: 01788 510636
www.antiqueoak.co.uk

Peter Bunting
Harthill Hall, Alport, Bakewell,
Derbyshire DE45 1LH
Tel: 01629 636203
www.countryoak.co.uk

Peter Foyle Hunwick
The Old Malthouse,
15 Bridge Street, Hungerford,
Berkshire RG17 0EG
Tel/Fax: 01488 682209

Peter Lipitch Ltd.
120 & 124 Fulham Road,
London SW3 6HU
Tel: 020 7373 3328
www.peterlipitch.com

Phillips of Hitchin (Antiques)
The Manor House, Hitchin,
Hertfordshire SG5 1JW
Tel: 01462 432067
Fax: 01462 441368

R G Cave & Sons Ltd.
Walcote House, 17 Broad Street,
Ludlow, Shropshire SY8 1NG
Tel: 01584 873568
Fax: 01584 875050

R N Myers & Son Ltd.
Endsleigh House, High Street,
Gargrave, Skipton,
North Yorkshire BD23 3LX
Tel: 01756 749587
rnmyersson@aol.com

Reindeer Antiques Ltd.
81 Kensington Church Street, London
W8 4BG
Tel: 020 7937 3754
Fax: 020 7937 7199
43 Watling Street, Potterspury,
Northamptonshire NN12 7QD
Tel: 01908 542407
Fax: 01908 542121
www.reindeerantiques.co.uk

Richard Courtney Ltd.
112-114 Fulham Road, South
Kensington, London SW3 6HU
Tel: 020 7370 4020
Fax: 020 7370 4020

Richard J Kingston
Tel: 01491 574535
Fax: 01491 574535

Robert E Hirschhorn
Tel: 020 7703 7443
hirschhornantiques@macunlimited.net
www.hirschhornantiques.com

Robert Young Antiques
68 Battersea Bridge Road,
London SW11 3AG
Tel: 020 7228 7847
office@robertyoungantiques.com
www.robertyoungantiques.com

Roderick Butler
Marwood House, Honiton,
Devon EX14 1PY
Tel: 01404 42169

Ronald Phillips Ltd.
26 Bruton Street, London W1J 6LQ
Tel: 020 7493 2341
advice@ronaldphillips.co.uk

S J Webster-Speakman
By appointment
Tel: 01502 722252

Stair & Company Ltd.
14 Mount Street, London W1Y 5RA
Tel: 020 7499 1784
stairandcompany@talk21.com

Suffolk House Antiques
High Street, Yoxford, Saxmundham,
Suffolk IP17 3EP
Tel: 01728 668122
Fax: 01728 668122

Oliver Charles Antiques Ltd.
Lombard Street, Petworth,
West Sussex GU28 0AG
Tel: 01798 344443

Thomas Coulborn & Sons
Vesey Manor, 64 Birmingham Road,
Sutton Coldfield,
West Midlands B72 1QP
Tel: 0121 354 3974
jc@coulborn.com

Tobias Jellinek Antiques
20 Park Road, East Twickenham,
Middlesex TW1 2PX
Tel: 020 8892 6892
toby@jellinek.com

Turpin's Antiques
17 Bridge Street, Hungerford,
Berkshire RG17 0EG
Tel: 01488 681886
Tel: 01672 870727

W A Pinn & Sons
124 Swan Street, Sible Hedingham,
Essex CO9 3HP
Tel: 01787 461127

W R Harvey & Co Ltd.
86 Corn Street, Witney,
Oxfordshire OX8 7BU
Tel: 01993 706501
antiques@wrharvey.co.uk
www.wrharvey.co.uk

Wakelin & Linfield
PO Box 48, Billingshurst,
West Sussex RH14 0YZ
Tel: 01403 700004
wakelin_linfield@btinternet.com
www.wakelin-linfield.com

William H Stokes
The Cloisters, 6/8 Dollar Street,
Cirencester, Gloucestershire
GL7 2AJ
Tel: 01285 653907
Fax: 01285 640533

Witney Antiques
96-100 Corn Street, Witney,
Oxfordshire OX28 6BU
Tel: 01993 703902
witneyantiques@community.co.uk
www.witneyantiques.com

Pugh's Antiques
Portley House, Old Ludlow Road,
Leominster, H36 0AA
Tel: 01568 616546
sales@pughsantiques.com
www.pughsantiques.com

Lorraine Spooner Antiques
211 Watling Street West,
Twocester, NN12 6BX
Tel: 01327 358777
lorraine@lsantiques.com
www.lsantiques.com

Destiny Antiques, Art & Design
Nugent Drive, Perth Airport,
Scone, Perthshire, PH2 6PL
Tel: 01738 553273

Jeremy Gow Antique Restoration
Pitscandly Farm,
Forfar, Angus, DD8 3NZ
Tel: 01307 465342
Jeremy@knowyourantiques.com
www.knowyourantiques.com

British Antique Replicas
45 School Close,
Queen Elizabeth Avenue,
Burgess Hill, RH15 9RX
Tel: 01444 245577
www.1760.com

Cross Hayes Antiques
Unit 21, White Walls,
Easton Grey, Malmesbury,
SN16 ORD
Tel: 01666 822877
david@crosshayes.co.uk
www.crosshayes.co.uk

S.W. Antiques
Abbey Showrooms,
Newlands Road, Pershore,
WR10 1BP
Tel: 01386 555580
sales@sw-antiques.co.uk
www.sw-antiques.co.uk

SCIENTIFIC INSTRUMENTS
Early Technology
Monkton House, Old
Craighall,Musselburgh,
Midlothian EH21 8SF
Tel: 0131 665 5753
michael.bennett-levy@virgin.net
www.earlytech.com

Charles Tomlinson
Chester
Tel: 01244 318395
charlestomlinson@tiscali.co.uk

GENERAL
Alfies Antique Market
13-25 Church Street, Marylebone,
London NW8 8DT
Tel: 020 7723 6066
www.alfiesantiques.com

Antiquarius
131-141 Kings Road
London SW3 4PW
Tel: 020 7351 5353
www.antiquarius.co.uk

Christopher Sykes
The Old Parsonage
Woburn, Milton Keynes,
Buckinghamshire MK17 9QL
Tel: 01525 290259

Grays Antiques Markets
58 Davies St,
London W1K 5LP
Tel: 020 7629 7034
www.graysantiques.com

Heritage
6 Market Place, Woodstock,
Oxfordshire OX20 1TA
Tel: 01993 811332

Manfred Schotten Antiques
109 High Street, Burford, Oxfordshire
OX18 4RU
Tel: 01993 822302
www.schotten.com

**Otford Antiques and Collectors
Centre**
26-28 High Street, Otford, Sevenoaks,
Kent TN14 5PQ
Tel: 01959 522025
www.otfordantiques.co.uk

Pantiles Spa Antiques
4-6 Union House,
The Pantiles, Tunbridge Wells,
Kent TN4 8HE
Tel: 01892 541377
www.pantiles-spa-antiques.co.uk

The Ginnel Antiques Centre
Off Parliament Street,
Harrogate, North Yorkshire HG1 2RB
Tel: 01423 508 857

GLASS
Andrew Lineham Fine Glass
PO Box 465, Chichester, West Sussex
PO18 8WZ.
Tel: 01243 576 241
www.antiquecolouredglass.info

**Antique Glass at Frank Dux
Antiques**
33 Belvedere, Lansdown Road
Bath BA1 5HR
Tel: 01225 312367
www.antique-glass.co.uk

Christine Bridge Antiques
Tel: 0208 741 5501
www.bridge-antiques.com

Delomosne & Son Ltd.
Court Close, North Wraxall,
Chippenham, Wiltshire SN14 7AD
Tel: 01225 891505
www.delomosne.co.uk

Jeanette Hayhurst Fine Glass
32A Kensington Church St,
London W8 4HA
Tel: 020 7938 1539
www.antiqueglasslondon.com

Grimes House Antiques
High Street, Moreton-in Marsh,
GL56 0AT
Tel: 01608 651029
www.grimeshouse.co.uk

JEWELLERY
N. Bloom & Son (1912) Ltd.
Tel: 020 7629 5060
www.nbloom.com

J H Bonnar
72 Thistle Street, Edinburgh,
Midlothian EH2 1EN
Tel: 0131 226 2811

T. Robert
PO Box 9, Cromer,
NR27 OHE
Tel: 01263 511865
www.t-robert.com

MODERN
Fragile Design
8 Lakeside, The Custard Factory,
Digbeth, Birmingham, West Midlands
B9 4AA
Tel: 0121 693 1001
www.fragiledesign.com

Francesca Martire
F131-137, Alfies Antique Market, 13
Church Street, Marylebone,
London NW8 8DT
Tel: 020 7724 4802

Rennies Seaside Modern
47 The Old High St
Folkestone, Kent CT20 2RN
Tel: 01303 242427
www.rennart.co.uk

Twentieth Century Marks
Whitegates, Rectory Rd, Little
Burstead, Nr Billericay,
Essex CM12 9TR
Tel: 01268 411 000
www.20thcenturymarks.co.uk

MUSIC
Stephen T. P. Kember Ltd,
3 The Corn Exchange, The Pantiles,
Royal Tunbridge Wells,
Kent, TN2 5TE
Tel: 01959 574067/07850 358067
www.antique-musicboxes.co.uk

Turner Violins
1-5 Lily Grove, Beeston, NG9 1QL
Tel: 0115 943 0333
info@turnerviolins.co.uk

ORIENTAL AND ASIAN
Millner Manolatos
2 Campden Street, Off Kensington
Church Street, London W8 7EP
Tel: 020 7229 3268
Mob: 07900 248 390
www.millnermanolatos.com

Guest & Gray
1-7 Davies Mews,
London W1K 5AB
Tel: 020 7408 1252
www.chinese-porcelain-art.com

Ormonde Gallery
156 Portobello Road,
London W11 2EB
Tel: 020 7229 9800

Roger Bradbury
Church Street,
Coltishall, Norwich,
Norfolk NR12 7DJ
Tel: 01603 737 444

R & G McPherson Antiques
40 Kensington Church Street,
London W8 4BX
Tel: 020 7937 0812
www.orientalceramics.com

PAPERWEIGHTS
Sweetbriar Gallery Ltd
29 Beechview Road,
Kingsley, WA6 8DF
Tel: 01928 788225
www.sweetbriar.co.uk

DIRECTORY OF SPECIALISTS

SILVER

B. Silverman
4 Campden Street,
Off Kensington Church Street,
London W8 7EP
Tel: 020 7985 0555
www.silverman-london.com

C. & L. Burman
5 Vigo Steet, London W1S 3HF
Tel: 020 7439 6604

Didier Antiques
58-60 Kensington Church Street,
London W8 4DB
Tel: 020 7938 2537
www.didierantiques.com

Fay Lucas Artmetal
Christies Fine Art Securities
42 Ponton Road,
London SW8 5BA
Tel: 020 7371 4404
www.faylucas.com

Gerald Sattin
PO Box 20627,
London NW6 7GA
Tel: 020 8451 3295
gsattin@compuserve.com

Goodwins Antiques Ltd
15 & 16 Queensferry Street,
Edinburgh EH2 4QW
Tel: 0131 225 4717

Hannah Antiques
Tel: 01844 351 935

John Bull (Antiques) Ltd.
JB Silverware, 139A New Bond Street,
London W1S 2TN
Tel: 020 7629 1251
www.jbsilverware.co.uk

J. H. Bourdon Smith Ltd
24 Mason's Yard, Duke Street,
St James's, London SW1Y 6BU
Tel: 020 7839 4714

Marks
49 Curzon Street,
London W1J 7UN
Tel: 020 7499 1788
www.marksantiques.com

Mary Cooke Antiques
12 The Old Power Station,
121 Mortlake High Street,
London SW14 8SN
Tel: 020 8876 5777
www.marycooke.co.uk

Nicholas Shaw Antiques
Virginia Cottage, Lombard Street,
Petworth, West Sussex GU28 0AG
Tel: 01798 345 146
www.nicholas-shaw.com

Paul Bennett
48a George Street,
London W1U 7DY
Tel: 020 7935 1555
www.paulbennett.ukgateway.net

Payne & Son (Goldsmiths) Ltd
131 High Street
Oxford, Oxfordshire OX1 4DH
Tel: 01865 243 787
www.payneandson.co.uk

Peter Cameron Antique Silver
PO Box LB739
London W1A 9LB
petercameron@idnet.co.uk

Peter Szuhay
325 Grays Antiques Markets,
58 Davies Street, London W1Y 2LB
Tel: 020 7408 0154
pgszuhay@aol.com

Sanda Lipton
28a Devonshire Street,
London W1G 6PS
Tel: 020 7431 2688
www.antique-silver.com

S & J Stodel
Vault 24, London Silver Vaults,
Chancery Lane, London WC2A 1QS
Tel: 020 7405 7009
www.chinesesilver.com

Shapiro & Company
380 Grays Antiques Markets,
58 Davies Street, London W1K 5LP
Tel: 020 7491 2710

Smith & Robinson
Tel: 020 8994 3783
cwsmith@ukonline.co.uk

Steppes Hill Farm Antiques
Steppes Hill Farm, Stockbury,
Sittingbourne, Kent ME9 7RB
Tel: 01795 842205
dwabuck@btinternet.com

The Silver Fund
1 Duke of York Street,
London SW1Y 6JP
Tel: 020 7839 8935
www.thesilverfund.com

Van Den Bosch
1 Georgian Village,
Camden Passage,
Islington, London N1 8DU
Tel: 020 7226 4550
www.vandenbosch.co.uk

William Walter Antiques Ltd
Vault 3, London Silver Vaults,
Chancery House, Chancery Lane,
London, WC2A 1QS
Tel:020 7242 3248
www.williamwalter.co.uk

Daniel Bexfield Antiques
26 Burlington Arcade,
W1J 0PU
Tel: 020 7491 1720
www.bexfield.co.uk

TEXTILES
Antique Textiles and Lighting
34 Belvedere, Lansdowne Road, Bath,
Avon BA1 5HR
Tel: 01225 310 795/443884
www.antiquetextilesandlighting.co.uk

Esther Fitzgerald Rare Textiles
28 Church Row, London NW3 6UP
Tel: 020 7431 3076
www.estherfitzgerald.co.uk

Fantiques
Tel: 020 8840 4761
paulajraven@aol.com

Junnaa & Thomi Wroblewski
78 Marylebone High Street,
Box 39, London W1U 5AP
Tel: 020 7499 7793
junnaa@wroblewski.eu.com
thomi@wroblewski.eu.com

Rellick
8 Golborne Road,
London W10 5NW
Tel: 020 8962 0089

Vintage to Vogue
28 Milsom Street, Bath,
Avon BA1 1DG
Tel: 01225 337 323
www.vintagetovogue.com

Erna Hiscock & John Shepherd
Chelsea Galleries,
69 Portobello Road, W11
Tel: 01233 661407
www.ernahiscockantiques.com

TRIBAL ART
Jean-Baptiste Bacquart
www.AfricanAndOceanicArt.com

Michael Graham Stewart
173 New Bond Street
London W1S 4RF
Tel: 020 7495 4001
www.graham-stewart.com

**Owen Hargreaves &
Jasmine Dahl**
9 Corsham Street
London N1 6DP
Tel: 020 7253 2669
www.owenhargreaves.com

INDEX TO ADVERTISERS